Reading Difficulties

Instruction and Assessment

Reading Difficulties

Instruction and Assessment

SECOND EDITION

Barbara Taylor

Larry A. Harris

P. David Pearson

Georgia García

McGraw-Hill, Inc.

New York   St. Louis   San Francisco   Auckland   Bogotá   Caracas
Lisbon   London   Madrid   Mexico City   Milan   Montreal   New Delhi
San Juan   Singapore   Sydney   Tokyo   Toronto

This book was developed by Lane Akers, Inc.

This book was set in Palatino by Publication Services, Inc.
The editor was Lane Akers;
the production supervisor was Paula Keller.
The cover was designed by Joseph Gillians.
Project supervision was done by Publication Services, Inc.
R. R. Donnelley & Sons Company was printer and binder.

READING DIFFICULTIES
Instruction and Assessment

 This book is printed on recycled, acid-free paper containing 10% postconsumer waste.

1 2 3 4 5 6 7 8 9 0 DOH DOH 9 0 9 8 7 6 5 4

ISBN 0-07-063182-4

Library of Congress Catalog Card Number: 94-77545

About the Authors

BARBARA TAYLOR is a professor of education and Chair of the Department of Curriculum and Instruction at the University of Minnesota, where she has taught since 1978. A former elementary and high school teacher, she received her Ed.D. from Virginia Tech. She works extensively with teachers on helping children with reading problems.

LARRY A. HARRIS is Associate Dean of the College of Education at Virginia Tech, where he has taught since 1974. After receiving his Ph.D. from the University of Minnesota, he taught at the University of North Dakota and at Indiana University. His current work is in teacher leadership, at the graduate level.

P. DAVID PEARSON is a professor of education and Dean of the College of Education at the University of Illinois. He received his Ph.D. from the University of Minnesota, where he taught for several years before moving to Illinois. His publications include the highly respected *Handbook of Research on Reading,* vols. I and II. His research focuses on reading instruction and reading assessment policies and practices.

GEORGIA GARCÍA is an assistant professor in the College of Education at the University of Illinois where she received her Ph.D. in 1988. Her research focuses on literacy acquisition and instruction of students from diverse linguistic, cultural, and economic backgrounds.

Contents in Brief

Part Three
TRADITIONAL APPROACHES TO ASSESSMENT
OF READING DIFFICULTIES

Part Four
PROVIDING SUPPLEMENTAL READING INSTRUCTION

APPENDICES

Contents

Part Two
INSTRUCTION AND ASSESSMENT
FOR LOW-ACHIEVING READERS

Part Three
TRADITIONAL APPROACHES TO ASSESSMENT
OF READING DIFFICULTIES

Part Four
PROVIDING SUPPLEMENTAL READING INSTRUCTION

APPENDICES

Preface

This book is intended for classroom teachers who want to provide sound instruction and assessment for their low-achieving readers. It was written in response to the perceived need for a reading difficulties textbook that focuses on classroom instruction and assessment in word recognition, comprehension, and vocabulary that is based on students' reading of regular text in normal classroom environments. This seemed a sensible approach since students typically receive most of their reading instruction under these conditions rather than in isolated situations where specialists perform diagnostic skill assessment.

This edition continues to place a heavy emphasis on instruction. Assessment is necessary but only insofar as it helps teachers make decisions about initial and ongoing remedial instruction in reading. For this reason, we have placed the chapters on word recognition, comprehension, vocabulary instruction (Chapters, 8, 10, and 12) before the chapters on assessment of those topics. We provide detailed descriptions of instructional techniques that have been found to be effective in these three areas. In most cases, we follow a model of explicit instruction in which we explain *what* a particular skill or strategy consists of, *why* the skill or strategy is important, and *when* students would use the skill or strategy as they are reading on their own. We also discuss ways in which a teacher can model *how* to perform a particular skill or strategy and provide suggestions for guided and independent practice. An abundance of concrete examples are used to illustrate the recommended strategies.

As described above, the book emphasizes *informal* assessment of students' word recognition, comprehension, and vocabulary skills while they are reading instructional level classroom material. The discussion includes ways in which the classroom instructor can frequently collect, record, and analyze data to determine students' relative strengths and weaknesses in these three areas. We believe that the suggestions provided for both instruction and assessment will prove useful to reading specialists and special educators as well as regular classroom teachers.

This edition continues to use the latest schema-theoretic model of cognitive processing. Likewise, it continues to emphasize motivation (Chapters 4 and 5) because we believe that this topic is of utmost importance when working with low-achieving readers. We provide specific suggestions for assessing motivation and we provide a conceptual understanding of how motivation can be rekindled in students who have experienced difficulty in learning to read.

Major changes in this edition include the following. In Part 1 we have added a discussion of the social aspects of reading to Chapter 1 and have included a new chapter on students who are in at-risk situations (Chapter 3). In Part 2, new discussions of curriculum-based measurement and portfolio assessment appear in Chapter 6. Also, a new chapter on early reading interventions (Chapter 7) shows that most children can now learn to read in first grade. Throughout the book, both research and practical strategies have been updated.

ACKNOWLEDGMENTS

The authors thank the following professors who, after using the first edition of this book, so graciously shared their thoughts and ideas with us: Mercedes Ballou, University of Minnesota; Sandra Berkowitz, Westfield State College, Massachusetts; Carole L. Bond, Memphis State University; John Borsa, University of Missouri; Naomi Feldman, Baldwin-Wallace College, Berea, Ohio; Mary S. Kelly, Teachers College, New York; Grover Mathewson, Florida International University; Jeanne Schumm, University of Miami, and Gerry Shiel, Western Illinois University.

Barbara Taylor

Larry A. Harris

P. David Pearson

Georgia García

Reading Difficulties

Instruction and Assessment

The Fundamentals of Reading Difficulties

The first part of this book sets the stage for what is to follow. In this part we make a statement about our views on the nature of the reading process and how children normally come to be literate. Against this backdrop we examine a number of factors that can interfere with learning to read. Various explanations concerning the causes of reading difficulty are discussed and some of the evidence believed to support these explanations are examined. The at-risk situation also is described, as is the literacy development and instruction of students from diverse linguistic, cultural, and economic backgrounds. Regardless of the causes for reading difficulties, classroom teachers are confronted with the task of addressing and overcoming the symptoms of the problem. Because a child's willingness to continue trying to learn to read in the face of repeated failures is often the initial problem to be tackled by the teacher, we first devote our attention to the topic of motivation—what it is, how it is related to reading, how it can be rekindled, and how it can be assessed—before we turn to the issues of instruction and assessment for low-achieving readers in Part Two.

CHAPTER 1

The Nature of Reading

Overview

As you read this chapter, you may wish to use the following list of themes to guide your understanding and reflection.

- Reading is a language process. It is closely allied to its sibling processes of listening, speaking, and writing. Reading, therefore, is best viewed as an act of communication.
- Reading is a cognitive process. It is closely related to and reliant on other cognitive processes such as attention and memory. Reading, therefore, is best viewed as an attempt to create meaning.
- Reading is a social process. It inevitably requires us to negotiate meaning with the authors we encounter, those with whom we share and discuss the meanings that we take from the printed page, and those with whom we are connected only by sharing a cultural identity.
- Reading is, above all, an interactive process in which the reader, the text (and the author who created it), and the context within which we read come together to determine the nature and quality of our comprehension.
- When reading is viewed from these perspectives, it is possible to develop a framework for understanding the normal course of reading development and the personal and environmental obstacles that hinder development for some students.

To understand the actions and words of our fellow human beings, it helps to know their philosophy of life. To understand our recommendations about teaching and assessing reading, it helps to understand our *philosophy* of reading. Our recommendations are driven by our experience as readers, learners, and teachers and our views of the basic processes involved in reading and learning to read. Our goal in this chapter is to offer you an honest portrayal of our philosophy so that you might better understand and evaluate the recommendations that follow.

When we say that an individual, let's call her Amy Smith, has a reading difficulty, we imply that something has gone awry and that somewhere in her reading development something that ought to have happened did not. Our judgment about the source of Amy's problem is therefore directly affected by our view of what *normally occurs*, how reading *normally develops*. And our recommendations for an instructional program for Amy, or any other student, will be similarly biased. No matter how we couch the language we use to talk about our goals for Amy, we will undoubtedly want to get her back on "the right track." Our conception of the right track is, again, nothing more or less than a view of the normal reading process.

So, as authors of a text on reading difficulties, we are obligated to share our views on the normal course of reading development. In so doing, we hope that what we say later about assessment and instruction will be clearer, and we hope that you will be able to recognize our biases for what they are—the natural consequences of our point of view about how children learn to read.

We regard reading as a language process. It is closely linked to other language processes that children acquire: speaking, writing, and listening. Reading, like the other language processes, is a cognitive process. It is centered in the brain, and it involves all the processes that the brain uses in everyday mental activity: we pay attention, we perceive, we remember, we forget, and so on.

Reading, like all language processes, is also a social process. It is social at several levels. First, it is inherently social in the sense that it always involves communication with an unseen author, whose influence on comprehension and motivation can be monumental. Second, reading is most often learned in the social setting of a classroom or reading group. Even if learned at home, it is learned through interaction with a parent, peer, or sibling. Third, reading enables participation in a whole range of social activities. We read to prepare for a meeting, to belong to a particular social group, or to hold down a particular job.

We believe that reading is, above all, an interactive process, in much the same way as we think of a conversation as an interactive process. As the reader, you are the main player in the interaction, and you bring a great deal to the table—your years of experience as a human being, all of the knowledge that you have accumulated about how the world works, your memory for all of the other texts you have encountered, that special knowledge about how language and print work, and a wealth of purposes and motivations, some positive and some not. But there are other players in this interaction. The authors who have written the texts we are reading bring much to the table, namely, their ideas, codified in print, about some aspect of the world they found important. Often we are not alone in the act of reading; we discuss what we have read with our peers (and sometimes we even change our minds about how we have interpreted a text); in school, the social aspect of reading is as much the rule as the exception, and a new player, the teacher, sits at the table with us. Even the place, the physical location, the context in which we carry out the act of reading is also a kind of player. Context sets constraints (Are we studying or reading for pleasure?), influences our motivation (What is at stake? How much does the content matter to us personally?), and directs our attentional processes (What information do I need to solve what problem?), to name just a few of its more influential functions.

This chapter has been organized to make these points as vividly and as convincingly as possible. First, we will describe the components of the reading process that characterize it as a language process—its bases in the phonology, syntax, and semantics of oral language. Then we will discuss reading as a cognitive process, using the framework of schema theory to describe how reading works. Thirdly, we will introduce reading as a social construct, examining how it influences and is influenced by the social environment. Finally, we will try to convince you that understanding reading activities and reading difficulties becomes easier and more natural when they are examined from these linguistic, cognitive, and social perspectives.

READING AS LANGUAGE

Learning Oral Language

Children learn language. They do it on their own (as long as they can hear others talk), sometimes, it seems, almost in spite of our efforts to perpetuate charming baby talk. When they learn language they develop tacit knowledge about three systems: phonological, syntactic, and semantic.

Phonological Knowledge

The phonological system includes knowledge of the different phonemes (individual sounds) in the language, knowledge of how they are blended together to create words, as well as knowledge of less obvious aspects of the

Language abilities are fundamental to reading. Children can improve their language facility through interactions with people and objects they encounter daily. *(James Silliman)*

sound system—things like stress, juncture, and pitch. *Stress* is exemplified by the difference between "I *found* a red bandana" (I did not buy it) and "I found a *red* bandana" (not a blue one). *Juncture* is characterized by the difference between "*I scream*" and "*ice cream*," in short, word boundaries. *Pitch* enters the picture in terms of the intonation pattern differences between

1. You went downtown.
2. You went downtown!
3. You went downtown?

Since the focus of this book is reading rather than listening, it will not dwell on the phonological system. Phonological knowledge is prerequisite to listening comprehension (if you do not have it, you cannot understand auditory messages), but, once developed, it seems not to play as major a role in listening comprehension as do the syntactic and semantic systems. In other words, a person's ability to discriminate the basic sounds of the language from one another is no guarantee that he will understand what anyone says. On the other hand, factors like juncture, stress, and pitch are important in comprehending written and spoken messages.

Syntactic Knowledge

The syntactic system refers to the orderly arrangement among words in sentences. A child's knowledge of syntax is remarkably sophisticated by the time he enters school. A 6-year-old has probably spoken or understood some 80 to 90 percent of the basic sentence patterns he will encounter or use as an adult.[1]

Syntactic knowledge is at work when we recognize that (4) and (5) but not (6) and (7) are grammatically acceptable English sentences. It is also syntax that accounts for our ability to recognize that (4) and (5) are equivalent in meaning.

4. The boy thanked the girl.
5. The girl was thanked by the boy.
6. Girl was the by thanked boy the.
7. Thanked girl boy was by the the.

It is syntax that is at work when we are able to read (8) and answer questions (9), (10), and (11).

8. The argle zoolked the bordiddy in the ershent because the bordiddy larped the argle.
9. Who zoolked the bordiddy?
10. Why did the argle zoolk the bordiddy in the ershent?
11. What did the bordiddy do to the argle?

Of course, there is no real meaning in (8). Yet we are able to answer (9), (10), and (11) because of our syntactic knowledge and our ability to recognize the syntactic similarities between (8) and the questions (9), (10), and (11). Our ability to answer questions (9), (10), and (11) is evidence that we have actually understood (8); or is it?

Think about what you did when you answered (9), (10), and (11). Then compare it to what you did when you were a student and you were asked that infamous question in your geography classes: What are the major products of X (where X is the name of some country)? If you were clever, you probably searched the text for a sentence beginning with "The major products of X are . . . ." But did you really understand what you read? Did the fact that you could answer the question prove anything except that you could visually match a question with a similar segment of text? For example, close your eyes and try to paraphrase (8). Chances are that you cannot do it. The reason you cannot paraphrase (8) is that there is no way you can integrate those meaningless nonsense words with anything that you already know about—anything that is already *in your head*.

Semantic Knowledge

Your inability to paraphrase (8) underscores the importance of the semantic system. Semantic knowledge includes our knowledge of word meanings (the concepts that underlie the labels we call words). But it is more than that. It also includes our knowledge of the relationships among words. Dogs *are* mammals; dogs *have* ears; dogs *do* bark; dogs *are* loyal; dogs and cats are *both* pets.

It is semantic knowledge that accounts for our surprise when we encounter the words *whale* in the same context as the words *horse, farm,* and *plow,* as well as our smugness when we encounter it in the same context as *shark, dolphin,* or *harpoon.* Semantic knowledge accounts for the fact that most of you will order the random array of words in (12) as they are ordered in (13). You cannot order (12) like (13) by using syntactic knowledge alone.

12. Cows dog barn into the the the chased.
13. The dog chased the cows into the barn.
14. The cows chased the dog into the barn.
15. The barn chased the cows into the dog.

If you use just syntactic knowledge, both (14) and (15) would be acceptable. But knowledge about the world tells you that (13) is the most probable order. The whole process can be pictured schematically as in Figure 1.1.

FIGURE 1.1.   Sources of Information Used in Listening

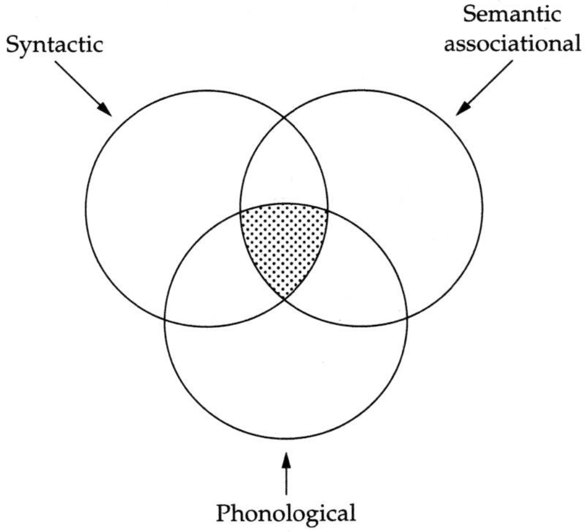

Comprehension of spoken language occurs when all three systems—phonological, syntactic, and semantic—operate interactively. That is, Matthew Jones understands your spoken message, "Come over to my desk because I want to speak with you," when he is able to match the phonological, syntactic, and semantic elements of your utterance with similar elements that are part of his linguistic knowledge—elements he literally carries around in his head. Later we will deal with the issue of how we, as human information processors, organize those elements in memory. For now, however, let us see how all of what we have said about oral language is related to written language comprehension, or reading, if you will.

What Children Learn When They Learn Written Language

About the only thing that changes when one moves from spoken to written language comprehension is the phonological component. While we would not want to argue that spoken and written language are the same, we believe that our general knowledge of semantic and syntactic relations applies equally to comprehension of spoken and written messages.[2] What differs in the case of comprehending written language is that a new code is introduced—the conventions of our writing system. We *see letters* instead of *hearing sounds*. We *see punctuation* instead of *hearing intonation contours*. We *see underlining* or *italics* or *special print* instead of *hearing* the *stress* a speaker gives to various words in a sentence (or more often, we are forced to use the context of the passage, paragraph, or sentence to infer stress). We *see* the *white spaces* between words instead of *hearing* the *juncture breaks* between words. Table 1.1 compares the phonological features of spoken language with graphemic counterparts in written language. In all cases, except for juncture, the advantage is clearly in favor of listening to a message over reading it, especially for stress and pitch.

We believe in the primacy of speech over writing as the more natural mode of language communication. First, speech was a much earlier development in the natural history of humankind.[3] Second, speech is universal but writing is not; all human societies have a spoken language but not all have a written language. Third, with the exception of deaf children, all children learn their spoken language earlier than their written language. Fourth, spoken language is

TABLE 1.1. Written and Spoken Language Counterparts

Spoken	Written
Organized in auditory patterns in temporal sequence	Organized by graphic marks in a two-dimensional directional sequence
Phonemic Units	*Graphemic Units*
1. Significant sounds	1. Letters
2. Stress	2. Italics, boldface, quotes, other special emphasis features
3. Pitch (intonation contours)	3. Punctuation
4. Juncture	4. White space between words

Source: From R. Schreiner (1970), Useful linguistic principles in teaching reading. Paper presented at the annual meeting of the International Reading Association, Anaheim, CA. Used with permission.

learned naturally and seemingly with little conscious effort whereas written language, for better or worse, is usually *taught*, often with torturous effort and great frustration on the part of both teacher and learner.[4] Fifth, if a child has a speech or hearing problem, we immediately look for a neurological, medical, or intellectual cause; on the other hand, even the most avid neurological advocates admit that such organic causes account for but a small portion of the reading failures in our schools. Social and emotional causes are more commonly cited for reading difficulties.[5]

The reading process, in the model in Figure 1.2, is similar to that for listening (Figure 1.1). Figure 1.2 depicts the sources of information used by readers in understanding written messages. The only difference between Figures 1.1 and 1.2 is that graphemic information (the right-hand column of Table 1.1) has replaced phonological information (the left-hand column of Table 1.1) as the third source of information in the model. We contend that, in comparing listening and reading, there is no difference in the role played by syntactic and semantic information. What is added to the reading model is a new *code,* in which graphic symbols represent certain phonological (sound) features of the spoken language: letters represent sounds (more accurately, graphemes represent phonemes), punctuation represents intonation contours, and spaces represent juncture breaks. It is tempting to oversimplify the model by suggesting that this new code, especially letters that represent sounds, be called *phonic* information. Phonic information is defined as a set of rules that tell a reader how to translate (or recode) printed squiggles into sounds. It includes most of what novice readers learn in the phonics component of their early reading programs. It includes the knowledge that the letter *b* translates as the sound /buh/ or the first sound in the word, /b rd/(*bird*). It also includes knowledge, be it implicit or explicit to the reader, about phonics generalizations (when two vowels go walking, the first one does the talking: *ai* → /a/), silent letters (*kn* → /n/ or *gh* → /g/) and certain predictable word patterns (*oll* usually →/ol/ as in *toll*).

FIGURE 1.2. Sources of Information Used in Reading

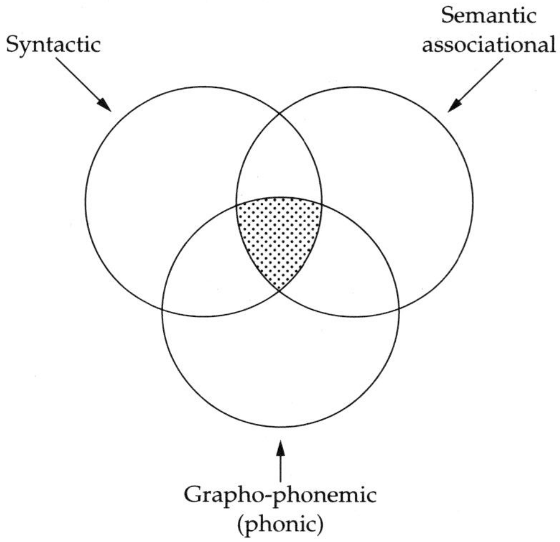

Syntactic

Semantic associational

Grapho-phonemic (phonic)

This model of reading suggests that real reading occurs when all three kinds of information are used in concert (see Figure 1.2). Some theorists, such as Ken Goodman and Frank Smith, argue that efficient readers maximize their reliance on syntactic and semantic information in order to minimize the amount of *print to speech* processing (call this decoding, recoding, phonic, or graphemic analysis) they have to do. They literally predict what is coming and get enough graphemic information to verify their predictions. A single letter of a single syllable may be enough information to verify their predictions. For example, it does not take much graphemic information to confirm the hypothesis that *telescope* fits into the sentence, "The astronomer looked through the _____."

Other theorists, most notably Keith Stanovich, argue that efficient readers rarely use contextual information to "short circuit" the word identification process. Since these readers are so good at word identification processes, including recoding print symbols into speech sounds, they simply do it. Then, argues Stanovich, they reserve their contextual (semantic and syntactic) processing for the more difficult and important process of comprehending the written message.

The final word is not in on this debate, so we have taken the position that good word identification instruction is permissible, even advisable, as long as it is not done in an isolated fashion with little resemblance to the kind of word identification processes that real readers engage in when they are reading.

Regardless of which side of this debate one favors, the basic model in Figure 1.2 still applies to *the whole of the reading process*. And almost all theorists would agree on a few principles. For example, readers must vary the amount of attention they pay to the textual information according to their familiarity with the content: One can read *Time* magazine much more rapidly than a philosophical treatise. In terms of the model, *familiarity* with text can be translated into the degree of congruence between the syntactic and semantic information in the text and the syntactic and semantic relations stored in readers' heads. In simpler terms, familiarity implies *knowing* more about what is in text; hence, processing is simpler and more efficient. Another principle that both groups would agree on is that novice readers allocate more attention to *recoding* print symbols into a speech code than do more expert readers (although the first group would argue that they have not yet realized just how helpful context can be while the second would argue that their decoding skills are not yet adequately developed).

In all these examples of the model at work, a common thread appears: the highly active interactive nature of processing during reading. By *interactive*, we mean that the reader *varies* the relative amount of emphasis on the various sources of information in the head or in the text, depending on the situation. Such a model is to be contrasted with views of reading which, even in the case of efficient readers, assign an invariant set of steps to processing during reading (for example, that all decoding must be completed before the reader can attend to comprehension processes). The present model will allow for situations in which decoding processes become the primary target of the reader's attention. But whenever possible the model demands that the reader's attention focus on semantic/syntactic (meaning) processes.

A Schema Theoretic Perspective on the Reading Process

To illustrate reading as a cognitive process, imagine a reader, Dan, thinking out loud about his understanding of a text right after he reads each segment. In the example, the text is presented in boldface, and Dan's think-alouds are presented in quotation marks.[6]

Business had been slow since the oil crisis.
"Oil crisis, hmm, must be some business related to oil. Let's see—service stations? (no, they boom in crises) cars? (could be cars) could be anything affected by inflation! I'll wait and see."

Nobody seemed to want anything elegant anymore.
"Aha! Expensive cars! . . . or recreational vehicles . . . probably Cadillacs, though."

Suddenly the door flew open and a well-dressed man burst onto the showroom floor.
"This must be a salesman. But, it could be the potential buyer . . . I'll wait and see."

John Stevens looked up from the want-ad section of the morning paper, adjusted his now loose-fitting coat to hide the frayed sleeves of his shirt and rose to meet the man . . .
"Now this is the salesman, right? Times are hard; therefore the want ads, frayed shirt, and weight loss. So the other guy must be the customer, the well-dressed one, I mean."

. . . whose hand-painted tie and rhinestone stickpin seemed incongruous amidst the array of steel-gray and black . . .
"That guy is the customer. And he's one of those got-rich-quick kind of guys. And I bet he's going to buy either a Mercedes or a Rolls Royce, probably a Mercedes. He'll probably pay cash too."

. . . Mercedes sedans. "I'll take it, cash on the line," the man asserted, pointing to the most expensive model on the floor.
"I knew it. He is *nouveau-riche*."

Later, as he completed the paperwork, John muttered to himself, "I'm glad I didn't blow that one." Then he added, "What does he know about elegance, anyway? What does anyone know about elegance anymore?" With that, he smiled and returned to his newfound pastime.
"Aha! We have an existential cynic. He probably remembers better times and, definitely, better customers. He seems resigned to his new fate in life, though."

Each of our protocols for this text would be different from Dan's, but we would all experience certain similarities. For example, although a second reader may not have hypothesized after the first segment that the business was cars, she would have chosen *some* other plausible candidate for the type of business. But after the second or third segment, it is likely that almost any reader would think of expensive cars. Readers will sometimes jump to a conclusion, and sometimes they will decide to wait and see, letting the text dictate the flow of hypotheses. Sometimes readers will make correct predictions; sometimes they will be wrong. When they realize they are wrong, they will probably correct their predictions.

This journey through a hypothetical reader's mind illustrates, at an intuitive level, a number of the processes and hypothesized mental structures that cognitive psychologists and reading researchers use to explain how people process, store, and retrieve information during the act of reading. Although several of the different theories that have arisen, such as Roger Schank's *scripts*, Marvin Minsky's *frames*, and several researchers' *schemata*, share the goal of describing how information is stored in human memory, they do not claim to be theories of reading. Many reading researchers, however, have adopted these theories of cognition to explain how people read.[7]

By analyzing several of the subject's reactions to the "Oil Crisis" text, we can show how each illustrates a facet of schema theory.

To begin with, Dan could never have understood the text without prior knowledge about business, oil crises, automobiles, sales transactions, hard times, and resigned cynicism. In the language of schema theory, the subject had to select a number of already existing *schemata*, or knowledge frameworks, as repositories for the information contained in this specific text.[8] Schema selection, then, is a critical step in comprehension. Two questions about selection must be answered: (1) What is the nature of schemata that readers select? (2) How do readers select them?

What Is the Nature of Schemata?

A basic premise of schema theory is that human memory is organized semantically (as opposed, say, to phonologically or alphabetically). In other words, memory is organized like a thesaurus rather than a dictionary. Presumably, one can possess schemata for all manner of things, ranging from simple objects (chair, boat) to abstract entities (love, hope, fear), to actions (buy, dive, run), to complex events (attending a conference or a football game), to very complex entities (story, novel, world affairs).

A schema for *chair* might be organized as Figure 1.3. This schema, referred to as a semantic network[9], gives a picture of the semantic interrelationships among different schemata; that is, *chair* is a schema, but it also belongs to other classes (for example, *functional furniture*) that are themselves schemata and members of other classes of schemata (*furniture*). Chairs also have certain other attributes, or *slots*, that must be present, or filled, in order to be recognized as chairs. That is, a chair must have some sort of seat, will likely have a back, and will probably have a set of legs of some sort. In addition to the upward organization (*chair* to *functional furniture*), the system also has a downward organization that requires examples (*dining room chair, easy chair*). Schemata are *abstract* by definition and hence correspond not to any particular chair but to some idealized chair that may not even exist.[10]

Schemata for objects and for abstract entities such as *love, hate,* or *fear* appear to be very much like concepts. But schemata for actions and events have a dimension that is not typically associated with concepts—an episodic or sequential dimension. Figure 1.4 depicts a schema that is more like a play than a concept.[11] *Slots,* or *variable slots* (since they can be filled by a variety of specific

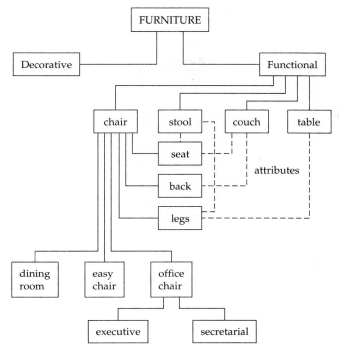

FIGURE 1.3.   Partial Semantic Network for "*Chair*"

Source: From P. D. Pearson (1982), A primer for schema theory, *Volta Review 84,* p. 27.

elements), are akin to the roles in a play. The particular characters who are selected to fill these slots are akin to the actors one might call on to play the roles. The particular entity that fills a variable slot is called a *value*.

In addition to the cast of characters, the *buy* schema has a set of episodes (more slots) that typically take place when a buying activity occurs, as represented in the dotted box in Figure 1.4. They correspond to the scenes in a play.

Along with hierarchical organization there is a great deal of cross-referencing among schemata.[12] For example, if a *buy* schema is selected and the buyer is a criminal, then the separate schema for *criminal* is called up and added to the *buy* schema. The values (actors) that fill variable slots (roles) in one schema are themselves schemata in other parts of a person's semantically organized memory.

How Are Schemata Selected?

How does a reader decide what schema or schemata to select in order to comprehend and remember a particular text? The author may be informative, as in: "This is a story about a man who wanted to buy a car." Usually, however, a reader has to rely on more subtle clues and form hypotheses.

One of the most common ways for a reader to select a schema is to recognize a specific value (for example, a character) as the kind that usually fills a particular variable slot in a schema. He then guesses that that schema is appropriate. In other words, inferential leaps on the part of the reader are often necessary just to decide what the text is about.

Readers draw on their prior knowledge as they attempt to construct meaning for the written text they encounter in books.
(Peter Vadnai)

FIGURE 1.4. Partial Representation of What Might Exist in a Person's *Buy* Schema
Source: From P. D. Pearson (1982), A primer for schema theory, *Volta Review 84*, p. 28.

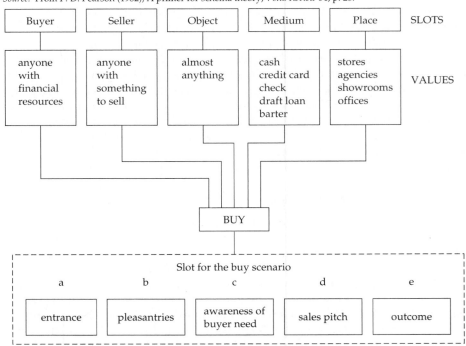

How Do Slots Get Filled?

The process of filling slots is usually called *instantiation*, from the word *instance* (that is, a specific instance is bound to a variable slot). Once a schema is selected, filling slots is usually simple. Having decided that the story was about buying, it was fairly easy for Dan to decide who or what should fill the *buyer*, *seller*, *object*, *medium*, and *place* slots. But again, slots are sometimes filled before schemata are selected; in fact, slot-filling can lead to schema selection.

Slots can also be filled (at least temporarily) before a reader actually finds a likely candidate (value) to fill a slot. Dan suspected that the buyer would pay cash before he came across the information in the text; he also thought that Cadillacs were a likely object early on in his interpretation of the story.

Much slot-filling takes place through inference. In fact, readers are constantly filling slots for which authors specify no values. The reader's best guess, or most likely candidate, to fill a slot not specified by the author is termed a *default value*.

Inferences are also necessary even where the text provides a likely candidate to fill a variable slot. When our hypothetical reader Dan said, "This must be the customer," there was nothing in the text that compelled him to this conclusion. Indeed, inferences are very often necessary just to decide who or what fills what slots in a working schema. This stems from the fact that authors do not provide explicit information when they believe that readers can easily infer values for themselves. And, in fact, as readers we would be upset and bored to death with authors who told us everything. In taking out some of the guesswork they would be taking much of the fun out of reading.

A Word About Inference

Schema theory has shown that reading is only incidentally literal. *Product* measures can tap recognition or recall of explicitly stated information; however, in the *process* of working one's way through a text, tens, hundreds, or even thousands of inferences are necessary. Inference is an essential part of schema selection and instantiation (in deciding who or what in the text fills what slot *and* in filling slots with default values).

Inference arises in another way: The value that fills one slot will affect the choice of a default value for a second slot. When the subject of the sample predicted that the buyer would pay cash for his Mercedes, he assigned cash as a default value for the medium slot because the buyer slot had been filled by a *nouveau-riche* character. In fact, a bank loan would have been his default value for almost any other type of character. Similarly, in a story of a woman who takes eighteen friends to dinner and picks up the tab, the default value for *medium* would be credit card, not cash or check. Slot-filling is an interactive process: How one slot gets filled influences how other slots get filled.

How Do People Change Their Schemata?

Unfortunately, schema theory has been more helpful in explaining comprehension than it has in explaining learning. However, schema theory does include mechanisms for learning.[13] The most common kind of learning within schema theory is what Rumelhart calls *accretion*. The notion of accretion is similar to Piaget's notion of assimilation and Smith's notion of comprehension. Accretion occurs each time an individual experiences an example of a schema and records in long-term memory its particular instantiation. Accretion is what allows a person to recall the specific circumstances involved, for example, in a particular trip to a restaurant. Unlike other forms of learning, accretion does not alter the structure of the schema.

A second kind of learning is *fine tuning*. Although fine tuning has no exact counterparts in Piaget's or Smith's views of information processing, it would be included in what Piaget calls *accommodation* and what Smith calls *learning*. Through fine tuning, the components of schemata are modified in important ways. New variable slots are added, variable slots are changed, or default values are altered. For example, a person who has encountered male automobile salespersons only might have a variable constraint that such salespersons must be male. When a female salesperson is encountered, this variable slot must be modified accordingly.

The third kind of learning, *restructuring*, occurs when old schemata must be discarded in favor of new schemata necessary to accommodate existing and incoming data. Old theories or paradigms are replaced by new ones. The Copernican revolution, the advent of Newtonian physics, and Einstein's notions of relativity are extreme examples of restructuring.[14] Restructuring occurs continually at a more modest level in daily life: a 4-year-old child learns that not all four-legged creatures are cats and is forced to develop specialized schemata for horses, cats, cows, and goats; a teacher learns to shift styles according to student needs; or a student discovers that the laws of commutativity generalize from addition to multiplication but not to subtraction or division.

There are two aspects of restructuring. Schema *specialization* occurs when several new schemata are needed to replace a single one: four subcategories of dogs where one sufficed before. Schema *generalization* occurs when several subschemata are seen to share some common variable slots, and the learner realizes that they can be seen as variations on the same theme: fables and myths are both stories.

How Are Schemata Controlled During Reading?

Sometimes readers engage in what has been variously called top-down processing, schema-based processing, inside-out processing, reader-based processing, or conceptually-driven processing. This is a very active mode of processing in which the reader generates hypotheses, using her store of schemata, about the text to be read. These hypotheses guide the processing of the upcoming text, and hypotheses are either confirmed or negated, in which case they need to be modified. Dan, the subject in the example, revealed several instances in which he engaged in this sort of processing.

Other times, readers are more passive. They engage in what has been variously called bottom-up processing, outside-in processing, text-based processing, or data-driven processing. In this particular mode, the reader decides to suspend judgment, waiting instead for more information from the text before drawing any conclusions. This kind of processing often occurs when a reader initially encounters a text, when a hypothesis has been negated, or when the reader simply cannot understand the sequence of events. Dan gave several such examples.

An interesting way to think about these two control modes is that in top-down processing, a reader is operating within her own schema, but in bottom-up processing, she is trying to operate within the author's schema. And, of course, any competent reader will shift back and forth constantly between the modes in the process of negotiating an interpretation of the text with the author.

Of What Conceivable Benefit Is Schema Theory?

The critical question is: How can teachers and clinicians use schema theory to help them make better diagnostic and instructional decisions about students? Pearson and Spiro (1980) found that five kinds of problems that students exhibit can be explained in a schema-theory framework, with some implications for assessment and instruction. These can be thought of as five reasons for students' failure to comprehend what they read.

Schema Availability

Put simply, if students do not have well-developed schemata for a topic, they will not understand selections about that topic. This phenomenon has been amply demonstrated in the research about prior knowledge. Indeed, Johnston and Pearson (1982) and Johnston (1981) have found that prior knowledge explains individual differences in comprehension better than measured reading ability does.

Regarding assessment of prior knowledge, Langer (1980) and Pearson and Johnson (1978; Johnson & Pearson, 1984) have found that simple free-association techniques with key concepts in a passage provide a quick diagnostic picture of where a student stands with respect to these concepts. Instructively, Hagen (1979) and Thomas (1982) have found that approaches that follow Pearson and Johnson's (1978) semantic mapping paradigm help students acquire wide ranging conceptual knowledge.

Schema Selection

Some students have the prior knowledge but neglect to call it into focus at the appropriate time. These students quite often rely too much on bottom-up processing, failing to realize which of their schemata can be used to comprehend and intercept the text at hand. In this case, remediation is relatively straightforward: Any prereading teaching strategy that brings appropriate schemata into focus will help.[15]

Schema Maintenance

Just because a reader has available and selects a schema for comprehending a passage does not mean that he will maintain that schema throughout the reading. Readers can literally forget what they are reading about. This is a schema maintenance problem. One reason for this problem is that readers may rely too heavily on bottom-up processing, directing all their attention to processing low-level text units (letters, syllables, words), thus leaving no cognitive capacity for the integrative thinking that is necessary for comprehension. Another reason is what some researchers have come to call *inconsiderate* text—text that does not make clear how different ideas in the text should be tied together—which has been found to be more of a problem for poor than good readers. Good readers seem more able to create ties where none are offered by the author.[16]

None of the instructional advice about this problem has been tested. However, clinical experience and a few experimental studies suggest the importance of helping students develop schemata for the ways in which stories and expository texts are organized. This can be accomplished either through systematic questioning techniques or the use of visual representations of the way texts are organized.[17]

Overreliance on Bottom-Up Processing

Overreliance on bottom-up processing is a case of failing to see the forest for the trees. Such readers will make oral reading errors because of attention to graphic features rather than to semantic concerns. In addition, they give verbatim answers from the text when inferences to prior knowledge are called for.

Helping students who have acquired this habit is not easy. Basically, they need to learn two things: that reading should make as much sense as listening, and that comprehension sometimes requires going beyond the text. To help them learn the first principle, some teachers have found that anomaly detection techniques focus attention on reading for meaning. Students are given texts that contain anomalous words, phrases, or sentences, and asked to delete things that do not fit the passages. Obviously, they cannot perform this task unless they have a good idea of what the text is about, that is, unless they operate top-down. For the second principle, discussions in which various students offer different answers for a single question increase the likelihood that a range of questions, some derived from the text and others derived from students' background knowledge, will be elicited. Some teachers have given students questions followed by several answers, asking them to determine which came from the text and which did not. Finally, they are asked to judge which answers are appropriate, in an attempt to demonstrate that sometimes nontextual answers are as good as textual answers.

Overreliance on Top-Down Processing

It is possible for students to rely too much on schema-based (or top-down) processing. Such students make semantically appropriate oral reading errors. Their answers to questions, while sensible, often reveal a cursory or careless reading, or no reading of the text. Although getting the *gist* may serve a student well in most situations, it is a serious disadvantage when careful reading is required (such as in experiments, following directions, poetry, evaluative reading). Sometimes it is essential to work within the author's schema!

Several approaches can be used to counter these tendencies. To help with question-answering behavior, students can complete precisely the same task as bottom-up overreliers (finding good answers within and outside the text), but the goal is different: These students need to understand that it is all right to give answers from the text. For the careful reading problem, students can be given complex directions that must be followed to the letter in order to achieve some outcome. Or they can complete and fill-in-the-blank exercises in which all answers *denote* a semantically appropriate response (for example, *walked, skipped, trudged*), but only one carries the appropriate connotation (for example, Susan felt so happy that she _____ through the park.).

READING AS A SOCIAL PROCESS

The mandate for us to view reading as a fundamentally social process comes from many quarters. Literary theorists remind us that the negotiation of meaning between an author and a reader is a fundamentally social and cultural act. And reading is social at another level within the text, as our hypothetical reader Dan reminds us, when he is struggling with not only the author, but with the characters in the text as well. All of us, as readers, have experienced that same sort of identification with or alienation from characters encountered in texts. And, as we hinted earlier, reading often involves an explicitly social negotiation among members within a classroom community, as, for example, when students get together to hold a conversation about a book they have read. Finally, reading can be viewed as a sociocultural phenomenon. When viewed through such a lens, many thorny issues arise, such as how it gets defined, the context in which it is acquired, whether it is viewed as primarily a tool of social control or emancipation.

Readers reveal a fundamentally social perspective whenever they allow the unseen author of a text to enter their thoughts. Louise Rosenblatt, a champion of this perspective, views reading as a transaction between a reader and a writer to produce a unique interpretation that transcends the original intentions and understandings of the two parties, the reader and the writer, who entered into the interaction in the first place.[18] Readers always have writers in the back of their minds just as writers have an implicit audience in mind when they set pen to paper.

While the act of reading a story silently may be only implicitly social, the way in which reading is acquired and facilitated, both in our schools and at home, is more overtly social. The social context in which reading is encountered, for example, plays a major role in the attitudes that children develop about reading. Children who are introduced to reading in a context that is friendly, warm, and pleasurable are likely to regard reading as a friendly, warm, and pleasurable activity. The social context is also important in the scaffolding provided by a parent who is cooperatively *reading* a storybook with a child. In classrooms, virtually every aspect of reading instruction reveals its social bases: (1) the role of the participants in discussions, including matters of how turns are negotiated, (2) the differential authority ceded to different participants for providing *valid* interpretations, (3) the selection of texts (whether texts are selected by the teacher or by individual students, the process involves social relations), and (4) even the type of assistance provided by teachers and peers.

Moving out from individual classrooms and homes to a broader cultural context reveals yet another aspect of the fundamentally social nature of reading. Historically, access to literacy has been used as a political tool. Throughout history, the sheer denial of access to literacy has been used to keep certain groups in their social and political place. Even when literacy has been granted by those in power to less powerful groups, control over what is available to read has served as the primary means of social control. The fact that literacy has been used as a tool of oppression and social control implies that it can also be used as a tool for emancipation and critical thought. What is true of societies and cultures is also true of classrooms: Reading can be used to control what students know and think or it can be used in more positive ways: to open new vistas, provide a wide array of choices, and to help students learn to take a critical perspective on what they read.

A LOOK AHEAD

As suggested earlier, we have taken you on this journey through the mind, eye, and printed page out into the contexts in which reading is done in order to establish a context for the remainder of our book. The remainder of Part One will embellish the context. Chapter 2 introduces the concept of reading difficulties and explains it in terms of the framework established in Chapter 1. Chapter 3 focuses on students who typically have not been well served by our educational system. Chapters 4 and 5 turn to a very crucial and often underrepresented topic, motivation. If you are or have been a classroom teacher, you do not have to be convinced of the importance of this topic. It permeates the daily life and decisionmaking of classrooms everywhere.

Part Two turns to our main course. It begins with an introduction to the broad issues of instruction and assessment for low-achieving readers (Chapter 6), followed by a chapter on early reading interventions (Chapter 7) and paired chapters on instruction and assessment for three crucial facets of reading and reading instruction: word recognition (Chapters 8 and 9), comprehension (Chapters 10 and 11), and vocabulary (Chapters 12 and 13).

We have adopted what some might regard as an unconventional approach in Part Two. Paired chapters begin with a chapter on instruction and follow with a chapter on assessment. The more traditional approach is first to diagnose, then to remediate. We have violated convention intentionally for three reasons. We begin with instruction because we think that, in the final analysis, it is far more important than assessment. Second, the order implies that instruction should drive assessment and not vice versa; we think that a major problem in American schools is that all too often assessment does, indeed, drive instruction. Third, we hope that staging instruction up front will begin to blur the distinction between instruction and assessment. If we could accomplish that goal, we will have made a contribution to the field.

Part Three turns to issues of convention and implementation. Chapter 14 introduces principles of assessment as they apply to students with reading difficulties. Then two chapters follow on conventional aspects of assessment and instruction; Chapter 15 reviews many of the still popular diagnostic reading tests. Finally, in Chapter 16, we present our *pièce de résistance*—advice about how to organize instruction to help students in both classroom and clinic settings.

Those who are familiar with a more traditional and popular clinical view of reading difficulties may, at first blush, find this approach discomforting. We hope you will stay with us, however, until the "last act," for we hope to convince you that the distinction between classroom and clinic treatment of students who have problems should, like the distinction between assessment and instruction, *go away*.

SUMMARY

Reading is at once a linguistic, cognitive, and social process. As a linguistic process, it is closely allied to the other language processes—listening, speaking, and writing. With those processes, it shares a concern for and reliance upon the phonological (sound), graphemic (written representations of oral language), semantic (word meanings and interrelationships among word meanings), and syntactic (the arrangement of words into meaningful strings) subsystems of language. Of particular interest in this day and age is a changing view of the active (no longer passive) role played by a reader in comprehending written messages.

As a cognitive process, reading relies on those mental operations that comprise most kinds of thinking—attention, perception, encoding, memory, and retrieval. Modern versions of schema theory provide the most convincing and useful account of reading as a cognitive process. Of special interest to one who wishes to understand reading difficulties are the processing problems that schema theory helps to explain. Specifically, schema theory explains problems due to schema availability (no appropriate prior knowledge), schema selection (failure to call up appropriate available schemata), schema maintenance (calling up but then losing the appropriate schema), overreliance on bottom-up processing (paying too close attention to text), and overreliance on top-down processing (paying too much attention to what is already in prior knowledge and not enough to the text).

As a social process, reading is acquired and played out in social contexts, both explicit and implicit, that influence both reader attitude and competence. We read texts written by authors, we learn to read with parents, peers, and teachers, and the interpretations we take from texts are as shaped by our discussions of them as they are by our initial impressions.

As suggested in the preview of upcoming chapters, when dealing with reading and reading difficulties in more detail, we will encounter these problems in different disguises again and again.

Notes

1. Space does not permit a complete treatment of the complexities of the syntactic systems of language. They are far more complex and intricate than we pretend in this chapter.
2. We are indebted to our late colleague, Robert Schreiner, for this idea of contrasts between oral and written linguistic representations.
3. See Gelb (1966).
4. We are not claiming that reading *must be* or *should be* taught in this tortuous fashion, only that it often *is* taught in this way.
5. Others might take issue with us on this distinction in the attribution of cause of oral versus written language problems. There are, unfortunately, few data to evaluate the veracity of claims by either side.

6. We are indebted to David Rumelhart (1980) for the germ of the idea for this extended passage. An initial version of this view of schema theory previously appeared in *The Volta Review 84* (5) (September 1982), pp. 25–34.

7. The following references, consulted in chronological order, would provide a good overview of the development of schema theory in the last 20 years: Collins and Quillian (1969), Lindsay and Normal (1972), Anderson (1977), Rumelhart and Ortony (1977), Collins, Brown, and Larkin (1980), Pearson and Spiro (1980), Rumelhart (1980), and Anderson and Pearson (1984).

8. See Anderson, Reynolds, Schallert, and Goetz (1977), Pearson, Hansen, and Gordon (1979), Pearson and Spiro (1980).

9. See Collins and Quillian (1969).

10. See Shoben (1980).

11. For a fuller treatment, see Rumelhart (1980), or Pearson and Spiro (1980).

12. See Pearson and Spiro (1980).

13. See Piaget (1952), Rumelhart (1979), and Smith (1975) for their respective discussions of comprehension and learning mechanisms.

14. See Kuhn (1962).

15. Specifically, the experimental work of Hansen (1981) and Hansen and Pearson (1983) as well as the advice of Stauffer (1969), Pearson and Johnson (1978), Herber (1970), or Hanf (1971) all contain techniques that will help such students become more active processors of text.

16. The considerate text issue, to our knowledge, was first raised and coined by Anderson, Armbruster, and Kantor (1980). Marshall and Glock (1978–1979) and Irwin (1980) have both examined the effect of considerateness on the comprehension of readers of different abilities.

17. For some examples of techniques to sensitize students to the structure of different types of text, see Gordon (1980), Singer and Donlan (1982), or Bartlett (1978).

18. See Rosenblatt (1978; 1983).

CHAPTER 2

Explaining Reading Difficulties
Overview

As you read this chapter, you may wish to use these themes to guide your understanding and reflection.

- The search for causes of reading difficulty may be somewhat useful, but not nearly so useful as the search for solutions to whatever problems exist.
- There are many types of purported causes of reading disability: neurological, psycho-emotional, and environmental (home and school).
- Of the three, the greatest emphasis is placed on the last since it is the one area that teachers stand the best chance of changing for the better.

In Chapter 1, we devoted considerable explanation to the processes of normal reading development, only twice hinting at issues related to reading difficulties. We did so as a way of introducing our disposition toward discussing reading difficulties; that is, so that you would better understand our explanation of, as well as plans for, instruction and assessment of reading difficulties. In this chapter we turn to a discussion of the explanations that are typically offered for the reading difficulties that so many children seem to exhibit in today's schools. Although it is difficult to develop clear-cut categories, it is convenient to divide the explanations into three categories: neurological, emotional, and environmental (both home and school factors). The logic of this order is that it presents explanations that come *increasingly under your influence* as a teacher; that is, you can do little about the way a child comes *wired* into the world, but you can do more to influence his emotional state through motivational techniques, and you can do even more to influence the environment in which he learns.

THE SEARCH FOR CAUSES:
A DOUBLE-EDGED SWORD

We approach the task cautiously. In all aspects of human discourse, unambiguous *causes* are hard to come by and even harder to validate. When it comes to reading difficulties it is difficult to fix the precise cause for a given student. Dealing with *some* explanatory factors is a more attainable goal, and one that we are more comfortable with.

Furthermore, it is not certain that effective instruction for students who exhibit reading difficulty hinges on precise determination of causes. Like a medical doctor who treats the symptoms of a cold or influenza without great concern for what caused the ailment, educators often focus on treating the symptoms of reading difficulty exhibited by students rather than trying to eradicate its causes.

We advocate this more modest approach on both practical and ethical grounds. First, it is rare that there is a single causal factor for a student who has difficulty learning to read. Second, even if a teacher were able to discover definitive causes for a particular student, chances are that the teacher would not be able to eradicate them. Causes that stem from the home environment are often beyond the control of a teacher. Or they may stem from a psychological trauma so deeply rooted in the student's psyche as to be visible only to a psychiatrist. Third, and most important, a teacher who can make the reading experience successful for a student—irrespective of the sources of difficulty—does a great deal to counter the effect of other negative experiences.

Some may argue that this position discourages teachers from examining a child's educational, medical, or family history. Although it is important for a teacher to be aware of a child's history at a certain point in time, sometimes a little knowledge can be as damaging as it is helpful. Sometimes a teacher may become unduly biased toward a new student because of a remark casually recorded in a student's cumulative folder or noted on a diagnostic workup. And the net result may be unnecessarily low expectations for that student. The dreadful Pygmalion effect, documented by Rosenthal and Jacobson (1968) in the 1960s, suggests that we need to keep an open mind about students.

Our advice regarding a child's educational history is to postpone that look through the folder (especially value-laden comments) until a month or so has passed at the beginning of the year. Let your relationship with each student develop naturally. This advice is based on a belief that all human interactions are, to a certain degree, unique to the individuals involved. You may possess exactly the type of personality that a particular student feels comfortable with, you may be just the teacher the student needs, just the one to succeed where the others have failed. So let time and nature take their course, at least for a while, and then check the records. You may be surprised—even shocked—when you do.

The search for explanation (and hence the checking of educational records) is a double-edged sword, and we encourage restraint in your search; but it would be unprofessional to suggest that teachers postpone obtaining certain kinds of information. For example, if a child has a visual, auditory, physical, or medical problem, a teacher needs to be aware of it in order to properly adapt the instructional environment. A child who has a troubled relationship with a parent or sibling may need extra emotional support.

The potential value (or potential damage) of prior knowledge hinges on what a teacher makes of it, both cognitively and affectively. Damage is done when existing knowledge is used to label a child: "Oh, he can't learn to read; he's retarded (or dyslexic, or a troublemaker, or Jeff's little brother)." The labeling can be used as a rationalization for a teacher's inability to help the student. There is an analogue in medicine. Some doctors discuss a professional malady called *diagnosis by labeling.* Apparently some patients, and some doctors, feel better when they can attach a label to a set of symptoms, even though the labeling will not help one iota with treatment.

Prior knowledge is valuable when it helps to do two things: to obtain a clearer grasp of what to do with a particular student and to bolster a teacher's conviction that he can help that student.

The following anecdote serves to illustrate the point. The faculty of all the elementary schools in a district had been invited to hear a child neurologist discuss the neurological bases of dyslexia. After hearing the presentation, one of the first-grade teachers was overheard to say, "I've been teaching first grade for 15 years. Each year I helped most of the children learn to read, but I always failed with some. And it used to bother me so when I failed. Now I know what was wrong: They all had dyslexia." This is a clear example of the danger of diagnosis by labeling. Her previous conviction that she could and should do everything possible to ensure literacy for her students had been compromised; she now had a convenient excuse to explain away a frustration, and it may have caused her to lessen her efforts with her next group of first-grade students.

Much space has been devoted to this disclaimer about the value of searching for causes and attending too much to prior information about students. We have done so not in the hope that teachers will avoid the search for causes or prior information, but rather that they will approach the task cautiously, with a proper perspective and a healthy dose of common sense.

NEUROLOGICAL EXPLANATIONS

Neurological explanations of reading difficulties tend to focus on *how kids are wired.* That is, within the central (or sometimes, peripheral) nervous system, are there inherited or acquired malfunctions that explain why a student is failing to learn to read? Neurological explanations have a long, varied, and controversial history. In general, the rather obvious problems, such as poor vision and poor hearing, have widespread acceptance in the field among physicians, psychologists, and educators. The less obvious problems, dealing with theories of nervous system organization, have been emphasized by medical doctors and others concerned with neurological development, but they have been deemphasized by educators and psychologists. First, the less controversial issues of vision and hearing are discussed. Then the issues of neurological organization are presented; these explanations tend to fall into two categories: laterality and minimal brain damage.

Visual Problems

Although the relationship of visual problems to reading ability has been studied extensively, the degree to which reading problems are caused by visual problems remains unclear.[1] Myopia (nearsightedness) and astigmatism have not been found to occur more frequently in low-achieving readers than in better readers. On the other hand, hyperopia (farsightedness) has been found to occur more frequently in low-achieving readers. In any case, hyperopia, myopia, and astigmatism are correctable with lenses. Visual problems may be a contributing factor but are probably not a major cause of reading disability in most instances.[2] However, if a teacher suspects a student has a visual problem, it is prudent to recommend that she be screened and referred to a vision specialist if necessary. A bibliography by Weintraub and Cowan (1982) offers more information on the relationship between vision and reading.

Auditory Problems

As with visual problems, mild auditory problems may be a contributing factor but not a major cause of reading disability in most instances.[3] Students with severe auditory problems (for example, deafness, severe hearing loss), on the other hand, do have difficulties with reading.[4] Students with suspected hearing loss should be referred to the school nurse for auditory screening and to a hearing specialist if necessary. A bibliography by Weintraub (1972) contains more information on the relationship between hearing problems and reading.

Lateral Dominance

Human beings tend toward physical symmetry: two each of feet, legs, arms, hands, eyes, ears, and even cerebral hemispheres in the brain. But the physical symmetry does not extend into functional symmetry. People tend to have a dominant hand, leg, eye, and cerebral hemisphere. They prefer to use one side of their bodies, and that side usually functions in a superior manner.

It is interesting to note how long this perception of sidedness has been with us. The word *dextrous,* with its positive connotation, stems from the latin root for *right,* whereas the word *sinister* originally meant *left.* You probably have heard stories from your parents or grandparents about teachers who tried to change a naturally left-handed person into a right-handed writer or eater. Sports such as baseball and tennis with their numerous south paws have done wonders to enhance the image of left-handed people.

Eye dominance is almost as common as hand dominance. Most people have a preferred eye, the one they use to zero in on something or look through a telescope. However, the dominant hand and eye are not always on the same side of the body. People whose dominant eye is on the opposite side of the body from their dominant hand have *crossed dominance.* People who show no particular hand preference (ambidextrous persons, for example) exhibit *mixed handedness,* while people who have no particular eye preference have *mixed eyedness.*[5]

Some time ago, theorists[6] thought that the dominant side of the cerebral hemisphere, the side controlling most language and other cognitive functions, was opposite the dominant side of the body (that is, the left cerebral hemisphere for right-sided persons and the right hemisphere for left-sided persons). When one side of the brain failed to achieve its appropriate dominance over the other, they reasoned, the hemispheres competed in processing visual information, for example. Hence alternative and competing interpretations of the printed message were being processed, resulting in cognitive confusion. The outward symptom of such confusion, they reasoned, was what is commonly called *reversals,* such as *p* for *b, was* for *saw,* or *Rover fed John* for *John fed Rover.* Orton even coined the term *strephosymbolia* (meaning, literally, twisted symbols) to describe the symptoms.

Historically, there have been enough reading disability cases exhibiting both ambiguity in handedness or eyedness and strephosymbolic symptoms to tempt concerned professionals into inferring that the one was the cause of the other. The logic is appealing: Lack of body sidedness yields lack of hemispheric dominance, which in turn yields perceptual confusion in reading.

Research Evidence

Mysterious labyrinth that it is, the brain is still the object of formative research by neurologists and allied scientists. In fact, there has been a renaissance of hemispheric research in the last 20 years. The point is that the final verdict on the relationship between lateral dominance of body or brain and reading disorders is a long way from settled. However, a great deal more is known now than when Orton expounded his theory in 1937.

For example, the relationship between body sidedness and hemispheric dominance is not what Orton reasoned it to be. Several studies[7] indicate that (1) about 80 percent of the population is right-handed, of which about 38 percent are left-eye dominant (indicating widespread crossed dominance), (2) all but a small percentage of the right-handed population is left-hemisphere dominant with respect to language functions, (3) the remaining 20 percent are split among left-handed (about 12 percent) and ambidextrous (about 8 percent) persons, and (4) hemispheric dominance for language among that 20 percent is widely distributed with some right, some left, and some both hemisphere dominant persons (eye dominance is equally as heterogeneous). Hence, the convenient and intuitively appealing notion of a crossover from dominant body (hand plus eye) side to the other hemisphere for language functions is not supported.

Moreover, as Kershner (1983) points out, the hemisphere not associated with language functions plays a major role in reading: spatial relations, form discrimination, and right-left orientation usually have locus of control in the right hemisphere. According to Kershner, the issue is not so much hemispheric dominance as it is hemispheric specialization (hemispheric asymmetry).

Research completed on populations of allegedly disabled readers[8] has tended to find a relationship between laterality confusions (particularly mixed-handedness) and reading, with some notable exceptions.[9]

Research completed on normally distributed populations, including reading disability cases,[10] tends to find no relationship between reading ability and laterality confusions; that is, the incidence of poor readers is just as great among appropriately lateralized students as it is among students exhibiting crossed dominance, mixed- handedness or mixed-eyedness. We subscribe to a point of view similar to the vulnerability argument often given to explain the relationship between low birth weight and subsequent medical or psychological problems. Low birth weight is thought to make infants more vulnerable to their environment. Hence babies of low birth weight born into medically and psychologically nurturing environments stand a good chance of becoming normal toddlers, while the incidence of abnormality is great for low birth weight babies born to a less nurturing environment. By analogy, children who fail to achieve appropriate hemispheric specialization are more vulnerable to their academic environment. If it is supportive and academically nurturing, normal reading growth can be expected. If not, reading difficulties are likely to occur. Such an explanation could conceivably account for the fact that vastly different relationships between laterality and reading are found among normal versus reading disabled populations.

Treatment

Among those who have subscribed to the laterality argument, there has been wide disparity in recommendations for treatment. Orton (1937), for example, advocated hard-core remedial reading instruction. In fact, the Orton-Gillingham[11] approach was developed by June Orton and Anna Gillingham specifically to help strephosymbolic students. By concentrating on synthetic blending of letters in a left-right fashion (*c* + *a* + *t* says /cuh/ + /ah/ + /tuh/ says /kat/), they hoped to avoid possible reversals. That is, you can reverse *was* for *saw* only if you examine the whole word. Letter reversals, such as *d* for *b* or *p* for *g*, were handled by using tactile and kinesthetic reinforcement (sand trays for finger tracing or sandpaper letters) along with symbol-sound instruction. Above all, the instruction was (and is) characterized by a great deal of systematicness and order, with heavy cuing to minimize the likelihood of letter (*b* for *d*) or word (*was* for *saw*) reversals.

By contrast, Delacato (1966) recommended perceptual-motor treatment as a first step in eradicating the reading disorder. Believing, as Orton did, that incomplete hemispheric dominance was the source of the problem, Delacato was convinced that a student must achieve complete subcortical (before the spinal cord hits the cortex at the base of the brain) integration before hemispheric dominance could occur. Hence, students attending a Delacato clinic went through a set of creeping, crawling, walking, and sleeping exercises to establish subcortical integration (complete right-side or left-side dominance). In addition, special glasses were used to help the would-be dominant eye play its role.

If problems persisted after sidedness was firmly established, Delacato recommended other procedures to help achieve hemispheric dominance. For example, since music perception usually has its locus in the hemisphere opposite the language locus, music was eliminated from the lives of students receiving the Delacato treatment.

The profession has not been kind to the Delacato point of view, either in its opinion or its research. Robbins (1966) and O'Donnell (1970) tried the Delacato procedure on large groups of normal and retarded subjects, respectively. In neither experiment was there any advantage for the Delacato procedure over normal—and sometimes diametrically opposite—teaching procedures. Glass and Robbins (1967) took Delacato to task for what can euphemistically be called sloppy statistics in reporting successful cases.

Laterality in Perspective

Where do we stand on this controversial issue? First, we look forward to further research by both neurologists and educators in sorting out the complex relationship between laterality and reading. Second, we agree with Orton's advice to treat students exhibiting laterality confusions with the best available instructional techniques. When all is said and done, once the labeling has occurred, you still have a student who cannot read. And your job as a teacher is to do as much as you possibly can to help. What should be added here is that you should use, as much as possible, materials and techniques that minimize potential reversal problems. Do not conclude, therefore, that we advocate a strict synthetic blending approach. As Smith, Goodman, and Meredith (1970) point out, context can be used to minimize reversals. For example, contrast sentences (1) and (2). The *saw/was* reversal makes sense in (1) but not in (2).

1. Mary saw a girl.
2. Mary was a boy.

In fact, unlike Orton, we recommend that all reading instruction, including instruction for unlocking unknown words, occur in settings where real texts are read for real purposes.

Minimal Brain Damage

Perhaps even more controversial than laterality is the minimal brain damage explanation of reading disability. It has a variety of synonyms that go back more than a century: congenital word blindness, alexia, dyslexia, subclinical insult. The basic symptom of the malady is that earnest teachers have done their very best to teach students to read with little or no success. It is an explanation by default: If teachers have tried so hard for so long with so little success, there must have been some neurological malfunction all along. Balow (1971) summarized the issue succinctly:

> The common acceptance of skill deficiency itself as *prima facie* evidence of neurological disorder can be interpreted as reflecting wishful thinking. If the problem can be defined out of education into the realm of medicine, educators can then remain relatively complacent about their efforts to correct the problem. With such a medical excuse, it is possible to ignore the educational limbo to which most such children are consigned. (pp. 514–515)

Implicit in this argument is the assumption that if we had better devices for measuring neurological defect, we would find insult in these students, hence, the genesis of the terms *subclinical* (below our capacity to diagnose) insult or *minimal* (not enough to really measure) brain damage.

The Evidence

As was the case for laterality, the evidence supporting the minimal brain damage explanation of reading disability is, on the whole, more negative than positive. In fact, what research exists even brings into question the relationship between frank (obvious) brain damage and reading disability.[12]

For example, Ackerly and Benton (1947) reported a case study in which a boy with average intelligence and good reading skills was diagnosed as emotionally disturbed with associated behavior problems. Subsequent medical diagnosis and surgery revealed that a large part of his brain was missing (in spite of the fact that his EEG tracings were normal). Somehow he had overcome massive brain damage and was able to read well.

Byers and Lord (1943) traced the development of fifteen cases of lead-poisoned children (frank brain damage can develop from lead poisoning). The students were not doing well in school, exhibiting symptoms such as visual perception and visual-motor skill problems, fatigue, poor attention, and poor reasoning. However, over half of these children were reading in the normal range for their age.

Yacorzynsky and Tucker (1960) followed the progress of thirty anoxic (low blood and cellular oxygen supply) infants who had been hospitalized up to 150 days after birth. They were compared with the same sex sibling nearest to them in age. The anoxic group had six children with IQ scores below 70, but the control group of siblings had only one. On the other hand, the anoxic group had several students with extremely high IQ scores but the control group had only one such child. In short, the anoxia (a malady commonly associated with frank brain damage) resulted in more deviant, not just lower, IQ scores.

The data from these studies make it difficult for us to accept the argument offered by Clements (1966), for example, that certain behavioral patterns of children in school lead one toward a diagnosis of minimal brain dysfunctions.

Special Treatments for Minimal Brain Damage

Special treatments for allegedly brain-damaged children are not common. However, if so-called dyslexic children as well as those diagnosed as having perceptual or perceptual-motor deficits are considered as a group, there are many programs that purport to serve such students. Rather than attack reading problems directly, these programs tend to focus on treating what their advocates describe as prerequisites to reading. These prerequisites tend to be perceptual or perceptual-motor skills: visual discrimination, hand-eye coordination, left-right scanning, awareness of directionality and laterality, and fine motor control. Remedial activities often include shape discrimination, shape tracing and drawing, games involving finger dexterity, and careful vision scanning (for example, following the line of descent of a ball in a vertical maze).

Although such programs often come with the endorsement of highly qualified specialists,[13] there is little evidence to support their positive contribution to the education of reading disabled students. In fact, those experimental studies that have evaluated the effectiveness of various perceptual-motor training programs[14] consistently show no advantage over control programs with no perceptual motor emphasis.[15]

Brain Damage in Perspective

Like laterality, brain damage explanations of reading disability are both popular and controversial. There is no doubt that a small proportion of reading disability cases exist in which the etiology (causal explanation) can be traced to major or minor brain damage, yet we remain doubting Thomases when confronted with admonitions to treat reading disability with perceptual motor programs or claims that most children who have difficulty learning to read must, therefore, have neurological deficits. What evidence exists just does not support such beliefs. As Balow (1971) points out, the demography (geographic distribution) of reading disability flies in the face of such an argument. The problem is that the preponderance of reading disability cases come from geographic areas in which all aspects of the environment (home, school, and community) are not conducive to academic learning; hence, it is difficult to believe that reading disability is primarily a medical problem. It is likely that the culprit is the educational environment.

Neurological Explanations:
How Should We Regard Them?

It should come as no surprise that we are skeptical of the widespread application of neurological etiologies for reading disabled children. Previous discussion in this chapter has built a strong case to diminish neurological factors as both explanatory factors and treatment variables.

That skepticism is not total, however. We agree with Harris (1970a) that a small proportion of all reading disability cases (perhaps 5 percent to 10 percent) will be the result of some neurological problem. And in *some* of those cases, the student will need to be referred to a neurologist or a residential treatment center. The emphasis is on *some,* as it is not certain to what degree differences in instruction are dictated by a diagnosis of neurological difficulty; that is, what will a classroom, or reading teacher, or for that matter, a special treatment center, do differently for a child classified as neurologically handicapped than a child classified as educationally handicapped? The answer is not clear, as the previous review of special treatment programs indicates. When all is said and done, the task of teaching the child to read remains. Again, we echo the sentiments of Balow (1971):

> Despite evidence that standard frontal assaults on the academic deficiencies of learning disabled pupils are successful (Balow, 1965; Fernald, 1939), such a "stodgy and unglamorous" prescription has seldom ever been followed, quickly giving way in favor of the more seductive dosages of the ever present patent medicine peddler. Some of those patent medicines may well be useful; the problem is that a careful review of the literature on such "cures" as those focusing on motor learning leaves the reader confused at best. This reader is dismayed over the amount of faith necessary and the egregious absence of evidence supporting motor activities for the development of reading, arithmetic, or spelling skills. (pp. 518–519)

PSYCHO-EMOTIONAL EXPLANATIONS
OF READING DIFFICULTY

It is hard to imagine a child with reading difficulties who has no emotional scars. Human beings seem to regard failure in any endeavor with great disdain. All of us avoid some type of physical or mental activities because at some point we experienced failure when attempting them. How many people have given up a complex motor activity such as golf, tennis, or skiing because early endeavors were simply too frustrating? "It's not worth the hassle," is an expression many people use to rationalize their withdrawal from such situations.

School children rarely have any prerogatives, however, when it comes to school subjects that have proven to be frustrating to them. They cannot adopt the total avoidance strategy typical of adults who find themselves in a frustrating situation. They must remain within the instructional setting, like it or not. Hence, they often resort to strategies that allow them to either escape or avoid as much anxiety or frustration as possible.

In short, children with reading difficulties are likely to have emotional scars because they are forced to face the reality of their failures whether they want to or not. And, once failure occurs, it begins its own self-perpetuating course.

The key to dealing with psycho-emotional problems is motivation. When motivation is low, for whatever reasons, students have little enthusiasm for efforts to help them help themselves. Conversely, nothing will help a teacher get off to a better start with an individual child than finding a high level of motivation and enthusiasm. Chapters 3 and 4 offer an extensive discussion of motivational explanations of reading difficulty.

ENVIRONMENTAL EXPLANATIONS OF READING DIFFICULTY

The explanations of reading difficulty discussed so far, although related to the environment in which students find themselves, have focused primarily on characteristics of students themselves; that is, what occurs in their minds and in their hearts. The focus in this section is on external factors. First, factors arising from the home environment are presented and then those related to the school environment are discussed. It is not possible to neatly separate explanations of reading disability that exist within students from those that arise outside; the relationship is interactive, with internal and external factors shaping one another. So the distinction between this section and previous sections is a matter of emphasis and focus only. Further, environmental factors, especially those arising from the school environment, are probably the most important for educators to consider. After all, these are the factors over which teachers exercise some control. Although they have less influence on the home environment, teachers talk to parents, parents talk to teachers, and it is possible that together they can change a situation that is preventing a student from learning in school.

Factors Related to the Home Environment

Nearly everything that occurs in a child's home environment has an effect on everything that happens to the child at school. However, in terms of the child's progress in reading, certain factors are more salient than others. The most important home environmental factors influencing a child's progress in reading are the language environment of the home and the types of values that a child extracts from his home environment. We will introduce these topics in this chapter and expand on them in Chapter 3.

Language Environment

Because we are committed to a view of the reading process as a language process, it should not be surprising that we place much importance on a student's language environment: Reading involves decoding and comprehending concepts that appear in the form of words strung together in sentences, and the child's acquisition of language occurs at home. Specifically, the focus is on two populations for whom the whole language of environment is of special concern; namely, bilingual and bidialectical students.

It has been less than two decades since reading educators have devoted much attention to the linguistically unique child, the child who comes to school speaking a language or a dialect different from the language or dialect spoken in school and used in reading materials. Previously there was an implicit assumption in our instruction that a language difference was the child's problem and not the school's problem. Hence, if a child spoke a language or a dialect that was different, it was his responsibility to acquire the dialect of the school. At the urging of linguists and educators alike, the emphasis began to shift toward a more responsible view in the early 1960s. There exists a rich literature[16] dealing with possible accommodations that teachers can make to aid the linguistically unique child. Each of these accommodations is related to and derived from *assumptions* about the nature of the discrepancy between a child's language and the school's language.

Some have viewed the discrepancy as a deficit. A child who speaks a different dialect speaks a deficient dialect, one that is inferior to the standard dialect. Hence, if this child is to make progress in reading standard dialect then the teacher must first teach the child to speak the standard dialect. If this is not done, the child will continually be disadvantaged compared to the child who speaks standard English. From a deficit viewpoint, then, the teacher's first task is to teach the child to speak standard English, after which reading instruction may ensue.

Others view the discrepancy as a difference, making no value judgments regarding whether dialect—standard or nonstandard—is superior. If a teacher views a language or a dialect discrepancy as a difference rather than a deficiency he or she will take different actions to accommodate the student's needs. Historically, for example, some educators[17] wrote special books for readers who speak Black English. In those books words were spelled the way a speaker of Black English would pronounce them (*post* might be spelled *pos*), special vocabulary terms were used (*bad* meaning really *good*), and accommodations were made in syntax (*he be goin'* instead of *he is going*). Popular in the 1960s and early 1970s, these dialect readers are seldom found in today's schools.

A second accommodation consistent with a difference assumption allows speakers of a special dialect to read materials written in standard English and to pronounce the words in their dialect without penalty. For example, when a child who speaks Black English says *pos* for *post*, the teacher simply accepts that pronunciation as consistent with the child's dialect, making no attempt to remediate the pronunciation as though it were a reading error. In other words, the teacher recognizes the fact that the child sees the *t* in *post* but simply does not say it because in his dialect the appropriate pronunciation for *post* is /pos/ (see Chapter 3).

A third accommodation consistent with a difference assumption is the presence of bilingual reading programs. For example, throughout the United States, there is a growing number of bilingual reading programs in which children are taught to read in both their first language (which, due to demographic realities, is frequently Spanish) and English (the acquired language). By allowing children to read in both languages, their equal status is maintained (see Chapter 3 for a fuller treatment of these issues).

The degree to which these language and dialect differences interfere with learning to read standard English is not clear; interference may depend on instruction. For example, Melmed (1973) found that 9-year-old speakers of Black English have difficulty distinguishing between pairs like *past* and *pass* when they hear these word pairs and when they try to pronounce them in isolation, but they have no difficulty recognizing the difference in meaning between those words when they are used in sentences. In a sense, a child who speaks Black English as a first dialect differs from other readers by possessing a larger set of homophones (words that sound alike but have different meanings and are spelled differently). But when the child is reading, the extra orthographic cues provided by letters like *t* and *s* in *past* and *pass* help the child determine the meaning of the words.

Simons and Johnson (1974) found that second-grade students who spoke Black English as the first dialect made many translations of standard English into Black English when they read orally. Conversely, they also found that these same children made many translations of Black English spellings into standard English (for example, reading *past* and *pass*). What seems to happen to children who are learning a second language or dialect is that they transfer features of each language to the other, at least until they reach a high level of proficiency.[18]

On the issue of dialect and reading, we offer three recommendations. First, we believe that the most sensible position on materials is to allow the students to read materials written in standard English (hopefully, they are culturally interesting) but use your knowledge of predictable dialect differences to help distinguish between a reading miscue and a child who is performing the remarkable feat of translating from one dialect to another.

Second, make certain that you treat all children's dialects with respect. After all, they have devoted many years to learning to speak the way they do. The last thing they need is a teacher who continually tells them, directly or indirectly, that they talk funny.

Third, go ahead and teach standard English but do so in a way that lets children know that they are learning a second dialect and not a superior dialect. Some educators[19] have recommended that a good time to teach standard English is in the secondary years when children recognize the importance of being able to get a job in "the white man's society." There is probably no conclusive evidence regarding the optimal time to teach standard English to a dialect speaker. When it is undertaken, however, it should be with respect. Do not fall into the trap of generating low expectations for a child simply because she speaks a different dialect. The negative effects of unduly low teacher expectations are frightening.

Home, Mainstream Values, and Reading Achievement

Success in a school environment is facilitated when there is a match between the values a child learns at home and the values that prevail in the school environment. Failure, on the other hand, is more likely when these two sets of values conflict. Such a point of view hardly seems controversial. Sociologists and anthropologists have studied value conflict for decades and have confirmed these views. Yet, how well schools are able to accommodate to differences in value orientation among students is not clear. What seems more likely among students who face a value conflict is that those students succeed who are able to change their values in order to accept the school's values, at least *within the context of the school environment.*

We make no judgment regarding the appropriateness or inappropriateness of the school's values. We simply recognize their existence. Similarly, we make no judgment about the validity of values students bring to school but simply point out that value conflict is likely to create problems for students. It is hoped that schools can find ways to accommodate the conflicts that will inevitably arise.

What are the values that underlie the school experience? Any answer to that question is risky and likely to be inaccurate. First, the values may differ slightly from one district or region to another, from one school to another, even from one classroom to another. Second, within a given region, district, school, or classroom, values can change, or there may be some values that conflict with others. Nonetheless, a surprising commonality is found across American classrooms, schools, districts, and regions, especially when it comes to teacher expectations about student performance. Among them are the following:

1. *Individual achievement.* Doing well on assignments, scoring high on tests, and reading accurately all bring the *official* praise of the school and all the benefits that go with that praise.
2. *A competitive spirit.* It is not too difficult to deduce this value from the instructional environment. All one has to do is to observe the fervor of students playing a word identification game, correcting one another's oral reading in the reading circle, or playing in the school yard to realize that schools both promote and capitalize on the competitive spirit.
3. *A balance of aggressive and passive behavior.* This is a subtle combination. Students in school are encouraged to be aggressive in academic pursuits but passive in their behavior. Students should be quiet and keep to themselves when doing assignments or when others are the center of attention. However, when called upon to perform an academic task, they should attack it with a passion. Such a philosophy is an extension of the aphorism "Don't speak unless spoken to (but when spoken to, speak loudly)."
4. *Literacy as central to the school experience.* Clearly, language and reading activities dominate the early curriculum of schools. Also, reading and writing are important prerequisites (sometimes stumbling blocks) to content area learning. Implicitly as well as explicitly, literacy skills are valued in our schools.

By implication, any child whose personal and community values conflict with those in this list of values common to the American school experience is likely to experience difficulty in school (see Chapter 3 for methods of accommodating cultural differences).

Academic achievement is clearly not valued by some students. That is not to say that *achievement* is unimportant; most often such students substitute one kind of achievement (often athletic, sometimes delinquent) for another (academic). Whether they come to school with this disdain for academic achievement or acquire it because of failure is difficult to determine. And when such children are in your classroom, the source of the problem does not seem to matter. But the symptoms are clear; they will not be motivated by and will not work for the traditional incentives of good grades, high marks, or teacher praise.

Clearly, also, the peer group has an important role in helping to shape students' values. A conversation was overheard among some American Indian students returning to their reservation from the "white man's" high school in a nearby town. One young man climbed aboard the bus with two textbooks under one arm. Before he could find a seat he was besieged with catcalls from his peers: "Hey man, you playin' the white man's game?" "You wanna become one of them?" Value conflict can assume a stark reality in the lives of individual students.

Horatio Alger and the dream of American capitalism notwithstanding, competition is not universally valued by all subcultures in our society. It is said that there exist Indian cultures in the Southwest in which the goal in a foot race is that all the entrants cross the finish line at precisely the same time, emphasizing the solidarity of the tribe and equality of its members. Imagine a child from that culture placed in a predominately Anglo classroom playing an allegedly motivating game of phonics rummy in which the goal is to collect the greatest number of cards with similar vowel sounds, and thereby beat the rest of the players. And there is substantial evidence that some minority cultures do not respond well to competitive incentives.[20]

EDUCATIONAL EXPLANATIONS OF READING DIFFICULTY

Fortunately, there are factors operating in the school environment that promote reading failure. We say fortunately because if these factors can account for failure, then their removal or opposition can account for success. Maybe every cloud does have a silver lining. Purposely, this set of explanations was saved for last because this is the one area of causal explanations, the one set of factors, under the control of teachers.

Student Time on Task

Some children fail to learn a given strategy, acquire key concepts, or construct a model of meaning for a passage simply because they have not been provided with sufficient opportunities to participate in the activities that will help them acquire these competencies.

Rosenshine and Stevens (1984), after reviewing several studies on teaching effectiveness, concluded that student *engaged* time on task was one of the single most powerful instructional variables affecting student achievement. The key word in their conclusions is *engaged*. For them it means time when the student is actively working on a reading task (e.g., reading orally or silently, completing an assignment, writing an answer to a question). Just sitting in the classroom does not count. Furthermore, engagement rates are highest when students are working in small groups, next highest in whole class configurations, and lowest when students are working independently on worksheets.[21]

The key issue for the time on task factor is what it is students will spend their time doing. After reviewing substantial literature on the topic Anderson and his colleagues[22] concluded that time spent engaged in oral and silent reading activities was substantially more rewarding, in terms of growth on reading tests, than completing worksheets. What this means is that although we know that additional time on task doing anything will probably generate improvement, the question for teachers is, What do we want students to become more skilled at? Completing workbook pages? Reading text? Copying sentences off the chalkboard? Writing their own books?

Teacher Time on Task

One of the great contradictions of the classroom is that the best readers seem to be able to engage a teacher in a thoughtful discussion of a story for what seems a painlessly endless period of time whereas the lowest performing readers get, in place of a teacher, a well-structured phonics workbook. The irony is, of course, that the best readers probably need the teacher least, and the lowest performing readers need the teacher most (and the workbook least).

Teachers should be on guard about how they spend their instructional time. It is easy to be seduced by the better readers. The time teachers spend with them seems so productive, when in fact they might have done just as well—learned just as much—without as much of the teacher's direct guidance. On the other hand, teachers cannot forsake the better students simply because other students need their attention.

Why is it that low-achieving readers demand more of a teacher's time? First, they are not likely to be familiar with success and they feel less sure about their performance. Hence, they need frequent reinforcement concerning the quality of their work. Because they are not sure, they need to be reassured that they are on the right track. Second, they are more likely to get derailed while reading because they lack well developed comprehension monitoring strategies and fix-up strategies. So they need teacher guidance and scaffolding in the form of modeling (so they can see successful strategies in operation), substantive feedback (so they know they are on the right track or how to correct in midcourse), and encouragement (so they will come to associate successful strategic behavior with a sense of self-efficacy).

Trying Something New

Students who have experienced a steady diet of failure often associate the failure with the instructional approach used by the teacher. So trying a fresh approach is an important part of any plan to help students reverse the cycle of failure. Why are we so reluctant to change? Sometimes our reluctance is bred by lack of knowledge, experience, or confidence; we know only one way to teach a sound-symbol correspondence, for example. Sometimes it is bred by the unwarranted fear that a change in method will only confuse students who can barely learn anything in the current method (usually a traditional approach). If we encourage new approaches with students who are not succeeding with the current approach, who knows what might happen? A modification (big or small) in method may be just the key to reach a particular student or class.

Adopting a Systemic Model of Instruction

As we have worked with teachers and students, and as we have examined the variety of approaches to instruction found in our schools, we have discovered that there is a common core of principles, or features, to high quality instruction. García and Pearson (1991) point out that these features are found in approaches that are as different from one another as whole language and direct instruction. Granted, they get applied differently in different approaches, but the principles stay the same. We describe the García and Pearson consensus model in some detail because it is the basis of our systemic model and supports many of the teaching sections in later chapters.

Teacher modeling

Teachers can and should show students how they perform the tasks they ask students to perform. One reason that modeling or demonstration is so important to good instruction is that processes such as comprehension and word identification are so hard to talk about in the abstract (in the sense of rules or steps) that one almost has to see them to believe them. What is especially helpful are reflective demonstrations—demonstrations in which the modeler talks the students through the processes involved in his performance (what Paris, Cross & Lipson, 1984, call "making thinking public"). The first principle in our model reads as follows:

- **Because reading is an ill-structured knowledge domain, it is more appropriate to provide students with demonstrations of how strategies are applied in real reading situations than it is to offer them either abstract sets of rules or multiple opportunities to practice the strategies in decontextualized contexts. At the very least, rules or practice opportunities ought to be accompanied by reflective demonstrations.**

Coping with complexity

The second feature in our model focuses on the issue of *reducing complexity* during the acquisition of reading competence. It is based upon the assumption that one of the teacher's most important roles is to help students cope with the inherent complexity of learning to read. In an analysis of various instructional approaches, Monda-Amaya and Pearson (in press) found four approaches to coping with complexity: skill decomposition, skill decontextualization, scaffolding, and authenticity.

This skill decomposition controversy underlies many of our current curricular tensions: (a) in early literacy, the tension between emergent literacy and traditional reading readiness, and (b) whether phonics, comprehension strategies, and grammar need to be taught directly. In a sense, the controversy is captured in the question, "Must we teach what must be learned?" On the one side are those who argue that children may not learn what they are not taught directly, explicitly, and intentionally (Gersten & Carnine, 1986; Rosenshine & Stevens, 1984). On the other side of the argument are those who suggest that while it is appropriate, perhaps essential, that students acquire specific skills, those skills are best acquired incidentally while students are engaged in the process of reading and writing (Mills, O'Keefe, & Stephens, 1992). The danger of decomposition is that the breakdown of the curriculum often does not foster knowledge of literacy as a *process* (*whole*), but encourages the view of literacy as a set of specific actions, within which the acquisition of some may be completely dependent upon mastery of others.

The notion of decontextualization further complicates the issue. In order to strip away potential confusing and irrelevant features of the instructional context, specific subskill instruction is often provided out of the context of real reading, writing, and thinking situations. The logic behind decontextualization is similar to the logic underlying decomposition: In both cases, the motivation is to make a complex phenomenon appear simpler. The dark side of decontextualization is its potential to obscure the relationship between the skill as it is taught in school and the skill as it is used in everyday literacy events.

Scaffolding provides an alternative to decomposition and decontextualization as a way of coping with complexity. The scaffolding metaphor, introduced to us by Wood, Bruner, and Ross (1976) and endemic to socially-based views of literacy,[23] is appealing for those who want to carve out a helpful, but not necessarily a controlling, role for teachers. Just like the scaffolding used in building, instructional scaffolds provide *support* and are both *temporary* and *adjustable*. So, instead of breaking a process like reading down into subcomponents, a teacher can provide the social and instructional support needed to allow a student to engage in a complex task that she might not otherwise manage on her own.

A vivid demonstration of scaffolding can be found in Reading Recovery as it has been implemented in the United States.[24] Reading Recovery is the early intervention program for at-risk first graders that was imported from New Zealand in the mid-1980s. While the student is reading, the tutor scaffolds the reading (which is, of course, a real rather than a contrived reading task) by modeling, hinting, cuing, and cajoling the student into a successful reading venture.

At one point in the lesson, students are asked to compose a text-related story (often a sentence or two) and, in the process, to rely on their own knowledge of symbol-sound correspondences to invent spellings for a word. When students encounter difficulty, the tutor often scaffolds the task by providing hints. For example, if the target word is *bumpy,* she might give the student a frame with as many boxes as there are letters and ask the student to fill in as many letters as she thinks she hears. At another point in the typical lesson, when it is time to introduce a new book, the teacher *walks and talks* the student through the book before asking her to read it on her own. These previews provide a conceptual scaffolding that enables the student to perform a complex task that she might not be able to handle independently.

In comprehension instruction, scaffolding might involve a combination of modeling, pointed questions, and elaborative feedback. For example, suppose

| b | u | m | p | y |

a teacher is guiding students in the discussion of a text and asks a question that requires an inference about the motives underlying a character's actions. Some students might be able to piece together the evidence from the various parts of the text on their own. Others, however, would require scaffolding to answer the question. They may need a reminder about the genre and its characteristics ("Remember, this is a mystery story, and what do we know about how mystery writers leave clues for the reader? What clues can you find?"), a quick modeling by the teacher of how to find clues ("I think I'll be able to find something in the first part of the story where the author is setting the scene for the crime."), or a demonstration of how to evaluate a clue's relevance.

Scaffolding allows teachers to get students to work in what Vygotsky labeled the "zone of proximal development," that instructional region just beyond their grasp.[25] With analogies, explicit cues, metaphors, elaborations, and modeling, teachers can create a form of assistance that allows students to complete a task before they cognitively understand how to do it and when to apply it on their own. Scaffolding promotes learning and self-control as long as it is gradually removed as students gain control of the task or process. A useful way to think about the teacher's role in scaffolding is represented in Figure 2.1.

Notice that instruction changes as one moves across the model. At the very left, in the Modeling stage, scaffolding and teacher responsibility are high and student responsibility is minimal. Just the opposite is true on the right side of the model. Responsibility, Figure 2.1 suggests, is released gradually from teacher to student.

Instruction for skills and strategies should begin and end in authentic learning contexts—contexts in which the skill or strategy helps the reader achieve personal goals, such as understanding the story at hand or figuring out

FIGURE 2.1 Gradual Release of Responsibility Model of Instruction.
Source: From P.O. Pearson and M.C. Gallagher (1983), The instruction of reading comprehension, *Contemporary Educational Psychology, 8*, pp. 317–344. Used with permission.

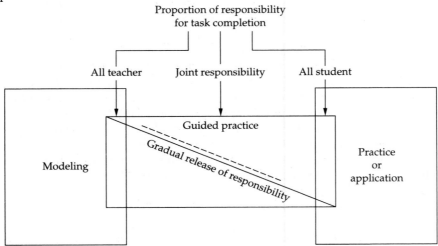

the pronunciation of the word she is currently puzzling over. Decontextualized instruction, if offered at all, should be limited to instances in which the teacher wishes to temporarily highlight some important feature of the skill or strategy and should be followed immediately by a recontextualized application. In summary, here is the principle:

- **To help novices cope with the intrinsic complexity of reading tasks, it is better to provide extensive scaffolding for authentic tasks than it is to decompose and decontextualize those same tasks.**

Authenticity

A third feature is *authenticity.* Students need the opportunity to engage in genuine, everyday literacy tasks. If all of their tasks are specially tailored for a particular instructional context, as they commonly are in workbooks and other instructional materials, they may never learn how to put it all together to comprehend a real text on their own. For purposes of demonstrating or highlighting a particular feature of the strategy, it may be permissible to remove a text segment from its surrounding context, but both the strategy and the text segment should be immediately recontextualized so that students will realize its potential application to real reading.

- **Strategy instruction should occur within the context of trying to comprehend a particular text written by an author for the purpose of communicating a message (informational, entertaining) of some sort to an audience.**

Student Control

The fourth feature of the model is an intrinsic bias toward *student control* of the instructional situation. We do not take quite the radical position advocated by whole language devotees, who would claim that students should always be in charge of their own learning (selecting texts to read and topics for writing), but we do think control by others is too dominant in our current situation. Currently someone else—be it a teacher, an administrator, or a basal author—decides what gets taught when, what gets practiced when, and what the criteria for success and failure are; students have to rely on feedback from others to let them know whether they are becoming literate individuals. Everything we know about the importance of metacognitive control of cognitive processes and everything we know about intrinsic motivation demand that we let students participate in the planning and evaluation of the curriculum to which we subject them. The ultimate goal of teacher assessment should be student self-assessment; the ultimate goal of teacher planning should be to help students learn how to plan their own learning. These goals can only be accomplished in an atmosphere of shared responsibility for curricular decision making. The concept of gradual release of responsibility should be expanded to both the planning and assessment aspects of literacy curricula. The principle reads like this:

- **From the earliest stages of the school literacy curriculum, students of all achievement levels should be involved in planning reading and writing activities and in evaluating their own performance. With additional** experience and expertise, students should take additional responsibility for planning and evaluating their own learning.

Community

The fifth principle is a new principle on community that we want to add to the García and Pearson consensus model. When students, especially students not currently well-served by our educational systems, are members of communities in which reading and writing are viewed and used as tools for learning, enjoyment, and personal insight, then literacy takes on an authentic meaning and purpose that can never be achieved in programs that isolate children for literacy learning or ask them to read and write for reasons that have little or nothing to do with human communication and interaction. In addition to grounding literacy in communicative purposes, a community is a place in which students learn to appreciate and help one another, to read and write together, and accomplish collectively what they cannot accomplish alone. Here is our last principle:

- **All children should be active participants in a community of readers-writers-learners, in which they read and write for, to, and with one another.**

These are the five features of our instructional model—teacher modeling (to let students in on the secrets), scaffolding (to cope with complexity), task and text authenticity (to ensure purposefulness), shared decisionmaking responsibility (to develop self-assessment skill), and community (to guarantee a genuine communicative context for learning). As you read the chapters in Part Two of this book, you will encounter variations of the principles outlined in the model. We systematically address matters of modeling, scaffolding, and student control, and we often address the other components of the model. The framework that we have used for embedding these principles into the instruction suggested in Part Two is to focus consistently on helping students understand the *what, how, why,* and *when* of each strategy. But it is by attending to issues of modeling, scaffolding, authenticity, student control, and community that teachers can help students develop an appreciation for

What is involved in a particular strategy

How you go about using it to solve a genuine reading problem

Why you would ever want to try to use it in the first place

When you would use it.

We believe that the best hope for any teacher is to concentrate on the area of educational explanations of reading difficulty. In those educational explanations come the resources for helping children overcome the problems they have developed.

SUMMARY

This chapter took you on a journey of the etiology of reading difficulties, stopping to visit the neurological, emotional, and environmental factors that have been used to explain reading difficulties. Of all of these, educational factors are most important to teachers because they can be altered to improve student learning and success. In presenting a model that outlines key instructional principles, we hope that we have set the stage for the remainder of this book by convincing you that changes in instruction represent the key to helping students achieve their greatest aspirations for literacy.

Notes

1. See Harris and Sipay (1985), Hartlage (1976), Suchoff (1981).
2. See Harris and Sipay (1985).
3. See Ekwall and Shanker (1983).
4. See Bond, Tinker, and Wasson (1984).
5. The term *mixed dominance,* according to Harris (1970a), is no longer in vogue since it fails to distinguish between eyedness and handedness. Harris offers evidence to support a relationship between mixed handedness and reading disability but no relationship between mixed eyedness or crossed dominance and reading disability.
6. See Orton (1937), for example.
7. See Annett (1972), Groden (1969), and O'Donnell (1970).
8. See Harris (1970a, 1970b) and Harris and Sipay (1985).
9. See Belmont and Birch (1965), Capobianco (1966), and Capobianco (1967).
10. See Balow (1963), Balow and Balow (1964), and Robbins (1966).
11. See Orton (1966).
12. See Balow (1971) for a readable critique of this evidence.
13. See Cruickshank (1966), for example.
14. See Frostig and Home (1964) and Kephart (1960), for example.
15. See Cohen (1966), Jacobs (1968), McBeath (1966), and Rosen (1965).
16. See Simons (1979) or Natalicio (1979).
17. See Baratz and Shuy (1969).
18. See Lambert (1978) and Lambert and Tucker (1972).
19. See Sledd (1969), for example.
20. See Au and Mason (1981), Erickson and Mohatt (1982), Philips (1972), and Tharp (1982).
21. See Fisher, Filby, Marliave, Cohen, Dishaw, Moore, and Berliner (1978).
22. See Anderson, Hiebert, Scott, and Wilkinson (1985).
23. See Vygotsky (1962, 1978) and Moll (1990).
24. See Clay (1987) and Gaffney and Anderson (1991).
25. See Vygotsky (1962, 1978).

CHAPTER 3

The At-Risk Situation

Overview

As you read this chapter you may want to use these themes to guide your understanding and reflection.

- *At-risk* generally refers to those students who are likely to drop out of school or leave school without the literacy skills necessary to obtain self-supporting employment. The majority of these students are poor or they attend schools with severely limited resources.
- Educators need to know more about the interplay among language, culture, and literacy if they are to meet the instructional needs of children from diverse linguistic, cultural, or economic backgrounds.
- Differential instruction frequently has meant that particular groups of students are denied access to the comprehension strategies they need to become active literacy participants.
- Few of the schoolwide, community-based, or federally funded programs developed to serve the needs of low-performing students have included reading programs that are consistent with current reading theory.

If you listen to the radio, read the newspaper, or watch the news on television, you cannot avoid learning about the at-risk situation. You are told about the high percentage of children who live below the poverty level; the increased number of limited-English-proficient children who are entering our schools; the small number of Native-American, Latino, and African-American students who graduate from college; and, the imbalance in school funding that occurs in some states or districts. All of these are characteristics of what many call the *at-risk situation*.

As the demographics of our school-age population change, more teachers are confronted with the dilemma that Albert Cullen depicts in a cartoon in his book. The caption in the cartoon reads

Many Marías,
a Jorge, a Ramón, an Eduardo,
Jesus (two of them),
Cammillo and his sister Consuelo,
Diego, Pedro, Luisa . . .
What can I, Nancy Smith from Maple Road, teach them?
What can they learn from me?[1]

In this chapter, we attempt to address some of Nancy Smith's concerns.

We begin the chapter with a brief excursion into various definitions and uses of the term at risk. Then we describe the at-risk situation vis-à-vis literacy. Next, we turn to some key instructional issues that seem to have affected the literacy development of children from diverse cultural, linguistic, or economic backgrounds. We also discuss the effects of differential instruction at the school, grade, and classroom levels. Throughout our discussion we point out possible instructional changes that educators and teachers could make to better serve these children. Then, we end the chapter by evaluating the reading components of some of the more popular schoolwide, community-based, and federally funded programs that have been designed to improve the academic achievement of low-performing students from low-income backgrounds.

Definition of the Term

If you ask yourself what at risk *really* means, then you are not alone. A myriad of definitions have been proposed, many of which only serve to confuse the situation. Early childhood educators frequently refer to vulnerable preschoolers as high-risk children. Educators in special education sometimes refer to children less enabled physically and mentally as at-risk students. Others consider gifted students to be at risk when their talents are not recognized and nurtured.[2]

At the national level, the term at risk is almost always used to refer to those students who drop out of school early. In terms of reading or literacy, a wider definition would include those students who leave school without the literacy skills needed to pursue further education or to obtain self-supporting employment. While the majority of these students are high school dropouts, some of them graduate from high school but with low literacy skills.

Although the term at-risk students is popular in the educational press, some researchers and educators dislike it. The term is intended to emphasize the fact that these students are at risk in the sense that they are not likely to succeed in our schools given current practices and curricular goals. The objection to the use of the term is that its very use implies that the students and their families or community are to blame for the situation instead of schools or society.[3] We agree with this objection and prefer to focus our attention on the at-risk *situation*; in this way, we can emphasize the impact of instructional and societal issues while, at the same time, describe the students who are affected. In a sense, our approach is inherently more hopeful than approaches that assume that the source of the problem lies in the children. After all, we can change instruction and we can change school structures, but it is more difficult to change the socioeconomic status of children. Furthermore, we wouldn't want to change the cultural heritage that students bring to school. Rather, we want to find ways to take advantage of children's cultural diversity.

Description of the Situation

It is difficult to determine how many students leave school without attaining serviceable literacy skills. Estimates of literacy among high school graduates and dropouts are controversial and inconsistent. Also, the dropout statistics that school districts report generally reflect the number of students who dropped out of school during a particular school year. They do not include those students who moved at the end of the year and who failed to enroll in another school. They also do not account for those students who dropped out of school but who, at a later date, returned to school or obtained a high school diploma through the General Equivalency Degree Program.

Despite these shortcomings, in 1986 one fourth of the nation's 18- and 19-year-olds left school without graduating. Also, larger percentages of Latino (45%) and African-American (35%) students left school early than did Anglo (non-Latino white) students (23%). High dropout rates also are common for Native-American students and for students with limited English proficiency. Most of the individuals who drop out of school are poor, or they attend schools with large numbers of poor students. In fact, poor students are three times as likely to drop out of school as other children.[4]

Current demographic projections do not bode well for the dropout situation. If the current birth rate and dropout rate for various ethnic and social class groups continue at their current levels, then in two or three decades the proportion of poor, non-Anglo students in our schools will increase dramatically. Without changes in our schools, the number of school drop outs will sky-rocket.[5]

How literate are these students? In an attempt to address this question, we consulted the reports of the National Assessment Educational Program (NAEP), a biennial project mandated by Congress to sample and assess the academic achievement of 9-, 13-, and 17-year-olds.[6] Virtually all of the students who participated in the 1984 and 1988 assessments demonstrated that they could perform simple reading tasks, such as following simple written directions or matching simple statements to pictures. The majority of them could read and comprehend shopping lists, menus, brief news articles, and short stories. However, over half of the young adults could not read and understand the type of material found in high-school texts, and very few of them could synthesize and learn from specialized reading materials, such as scientific texts, historical documents, or literary essays. We suspect, then, that when we discuss students leaving school without serviceable literacy skills, we are describing students who are not able to read and learn from high-school texts, not students who cannot decode or compose simple messages. This suspicion is borne out by the NAEP reading results for fourth-grade Latino, African-American, and Anglo students; the three groups of students all demonstrated that they were capable of comprehending short, uncomplicated passages. On the other hand, the overall NAEP reading performance of the Latino and African-American students was considerably lower than that of the Anglo students at all three grade levels (fourth, eighth, and eleventh).

Several characteristics differentiate low-performing readers from their more expert readers. Many of these characteristics are discussed in other chapters in this book (see Chapter 1). Although much of the discussion of low-performing readers focuses on beginning reading strategies, students who drop out of school may, in fact, demonstrate varying levels of literacy development and sophistication. While some of them may not have developed the decoding and cognitive skills necessary for reading, others may not know how to use reading to learn or are not aware of the varied purposes of reading. Some of them can read but simply choose not to read.[7] Such a wide range in reading expertise means that teachers must carefully assess their students' interests and literacy development if they are to successfully address the literacy needs of this particular student population.

Instructional Issues

Many of the students who leave school without serviceable literacy skills are from backgrounds that differ dramatically from those of children who do succeed. While some researchers prefer to focus on the range of attributes that differentiate the children (e.g., socioeconomic status, ethnicity or race, single-parent home, mother's education, non-English language background),[8] others prefer to investigate why our schools have not served all of our students equally as well.[9] In a review of the at-risk literature, García, Pearson, and Jiménez (1990) point out that our schools tend to serve those children who come from an Anglo, middle- or upper-class background much better than they do other children. Along with other researchers, they call for a change in the way we accept, teach, and value children from different linguistic, cultural, or economic backgrounds.[10]

Language, Culture, and Literacy

What then can we say about the instruction of students from diverse linguistic, cultural, or economic backgrounds? García, Pearson, and Jiménez et al. (1990) conclude that in addition to becoming informed about the reading process, educators need to learn more about language and cultural differences and how these factors influence instructional decisions. They specifically need to understand what a multicultural emphasis would mean in terms of materials, instruction, and assessment. We have organized our discussion of language, culture, and literacy around four key issues: print awareness, sociolinguistic styles, language differences, and assessment.

Print awareness

Children who come from backgrounds where they are read to frequently and where they are engaged in parent-child conversations about books seem to do better in kindergarten and first grade than do other children. These children seem to acquire a type of print awareness that gives them a sense of what literacy is all about and allows them to contextualize the types of literacy activities that they generally encounter in first grade. They have heard the repeated patterns of language, become aware of the relationship between oral language and written language, gained a familiarity with the conventions of printed language, and learned that print conveys meaning.[11]

Children who do not come from backgrounds where this type of book reading tradition between parents and children is common, do not always understand the purposes of literacy, at least not in the school-based literacy tradition. Heath's (1983) comparative study of school-community literacy traditions in the Carolina Piedmonts revealed that storybook reading was a common event in the Anglo middle-class community but not in the African-American working-class community. While storybook reading did occur in the Anglo working-class community, the types of parent-child conversations that revolved around it were quite different from what the teachers did with their own preschool children or what they expected from the children in their classrooms.

This mismatch between children's home literacy traditions and school literacy customs has prompted educators to introduce three different but interrelated accommodations. Several educators have developed programs that attempt to provide low-income children and their parents with the types of literacy experiences that many first-grade teachers expect.[12] Edwards (1989), for example, has developed the Parents as Partners program, which helps low-income parents develop the skills needed to read to their children. Critics of parent-child literacy programs charge that the programs aim to change the children and their families and not the schools.[13] However, Edwards found that the teachers she worked with had difficulty specifying the bookreading strategies needed to help children develop the type of print awareness that was expected in school. So, while the parents in the program learned how to better prepare their children for school, the teachers learned what needed to be done to help children outside the school-based literacy tradition develop print awareness. A side benefit of this particular program was that the collaborative effort between the schools and the parents resulted in mutual understanding: The parents became more knowledgeable about and comfortable with the schools, and the teachers learned more about the children and their families.[14]

Providing students with a rich literacy environment in preschool, kindergarten, and the early elementary grades is another option that all schools could pursue. The creation of a rich literacy classroom environment may seem as if it were a rather obvious solution. However, Durkin's (1987) observational study of kindergarten classrooms indicated that many teachers still were emphasizing phonics instruction and related reading-readiness activities. Rarely did the activities focus on literary response, comprehension, or thinking. Children may do well on these decontextualized word and letter tasks but fail to develop the type of print awareness necessary to understand that the goal of reading is to construct meaning.

Some of the print awareness activities that should be a part of early literacy classrooms are discussed in Chapter 7. Among other activities children should be encouraged to

- Repeatedly read predictable books
- Write their own stories and messages through invented spelling, conventional spelling, or student-to-teacher dictation
- Listen to taped readings of books they are reading silently
- Dramatize books
- Read wordless picturebooks
- Discuss what they read with their peers and teachers.

In the process of helping children learn that reading is a meaning-making process, Hiebert (1991) cautions that teachers also need to help students develop independent decoding strategies (making sure students see and discuss the words and letter combinations in the stories). Otherwise, students may not develop the phonemic awareness or word-recognition skills they need to become independent readers. The Reading Recovery Program (discussed in Chapter 7) is an example of a pullout program that has been successful in getting first-grade children, who arrive at school without the prerequisite print awareness we have discussed, acquire the type of reading strategies that they need to read at grade level.

Educators and researchers who have studied the literacy environments of children who do not come from the storybook tradition point out that there are activities *other* than storybook reading that teachers could incorporate into their classroom instruction. For example, teachers could make sure that children's comprehension of environmental print is acknowledged and rewarded. By incorporating activities characteristic of children's home literacy environment into their classroom instruction (such as letter reading and writing, following and creating recipes, playing games, following instructions for home improvement, reading newspapers and magazines), teachers would be sending a message to these children that literacy events common to their families and communities are important and valued in the schools.[15] In a relatively recent development, Moll and his colleagues (1990) have attempted to bridge differences in literacy use in the Latino community and school by inviting Latino children's relatives to share their literacy experiences with the teachers and children and by incorporating these experiences into the school curriculum.

Sociolinguistic styles

Differences in sociolinguistic styles (verbal and nonverbal communication patterns learned through home and community interactions) also may affect children's participation in school. Questioning behavior, small group participation, nonverbal gestures, and ways of talking can all reflect varied interaction patterns. Hymes (1972) points out that

> it is not that a child cannot answer questions but that questions and answers are defined in terms of one set of community norms rather than another, as to what counts as questions and answers, and as to what it means to be asked or to answer (p. xxxi).

Teachers need to understand that, in many ways, the questioning techniques with which they are familiar, and that they use to assess and provide instruction, are techniques that they learned from their parents or teachers as children. Not all children are familiar with the type of discourse pattern that prevails in many classrooms: the adult initiates, the child responds, the adult evaluates. Not all children are comfortable answering nonauthentic questions, in which both the questioner and answerer know that the questioner already knows the answer (such as, "Bobby, what color is this car?").

Differences in sociolinguistic styles have been documented for Hawaiian-dialect speaking children, African-American children in the Carolina Piedmonts, and Native-American children. For example, Philips (1983) observed that Native-American children on the Warm Springs Indian Reservation in Oregon were reluctant to participate when teachers asked for volunteers or called on individual students in a group setting. However, they would respond when the teacher spoke with them individually. They also seemed to become more actively involved in classroom activities when working in small groups directed by fellow students. Interestingly, the small group interaction was characteristic of the students' environment on the reservation. In other words, they were quite accustomed to working in peer collaboration without an adult. Similarly, Au (1981b) reported that Hawaiian dialect-speaking children responded more to the reading program developed by the Kamehameha Early Education Program (KEEP) when they were allowed to use talk story, a type of communal overlapping speech event common to their culture.

Gestures and speaking mannerisms also characterize differences in sociolinguistic styles. In a case study focusing on nonverbal contact between preschool children and their teacher, Byers and Byers (1972) found that the Anglo teacher and African-American children both looked at each other as frequently as did the Anglo teacher and Anglo children, but that their gazes were not synchronized, resulting in less eye contact. Byers and Byers suggest that differences in cultural communication patterns can affect the way in which children learn how to learn. When children and teachers differ in the ways they maintain contact or show interest, then it is difficult for them to interpret each other's behavior and to feel comfortable within the educational context.

Different ways of talking also may affect the teacher's attempt to shape children's thinking and discourse. In a comparative study analyzing the teacher-child interactions that arise during group sharing time, Michaels (1981) discovered an interesting contrast between the Anglo teacher's interactions with Anglo children and African-American children. The Anglo children used a topic-centered approach that the teacher was able to build on by using questions to help shape the structure of the students' presentations so that they paralleled the type of structure found in written narratives. However, she could not follow the episodic logic that united the African-American children's style of presentation; she mistimed her questions and eventually dismissed their presentation style as incoherent and rambling. The end result was that she did not call on these children as often, confused the children as to why she did not let them complete their presentations, and failed to shape the structure of their presentations toward the desired goal of approximating written language, particularly the type of written language that she was interested in.

Teachers should not assume that all linguistically and culturally diverse students will fit certain behavior patterns; to accept diversity is to acknowledge that there is great individual, family, ethnic, class, and community variation, even within groups that are alike in some way. However, they do need to realize that their own communicative interaction patterns in the classroom are influenced by what they learned as children in their interactions with family, teachers, and community members. If a child does not respond in the expected manner, the teacher should reassess the appropriateness of the communicative event for that particular child, instead of assuming that the child is limited in language proficiency or ability. If the activity is required for classroom instruction, then the teacher needs to try to bridge the cultural differences, adapting her instruction while, at the same time, helping the children to acquire different sociolinguistic styles.

If teachers are to bridge differences between cultures, they must become more knowledgeable about the children in their classrooms and the communities in which the particular children are socialized. Heath (1983) found that African-American children in her working-class community were accustomed to analogy type questions, e.g., "What's that like?," and to questions that required them to describe a scene or event. However, they were not used to *why* questions, nor were they used to the contrived questions such as "What happened to Paul in this story?" that teachers frequently use to monitor comprehension. When they were asked an accusative question (usually after engaging in some behavior that was socially unacceptable in the classroom environment), such as "Who told you to do that?," they would either not answer or reply with a clever rejoinder that would draw attention away from their behavior. Heath found that once she shared her findings with the children's teachers they were able to bridge some of the differences by altering their questions, while, at the same time, helping the African-American children gain practice in hearing and using the types of questions that the teachers generally asked. Thus, some mutual adaptation was achieved.

Language differences

We tend to forget that children's acquisition of language is influenced by the language used around them. We also tend to minimize the fact that almost all children acquire the rudiments of their language by the time they are 5 years old. Children raised in a community and household in which a form of Black English is spoken will learn this dialect; similarly, children raised in a community and household in which a form of standard English prevails will learn that dialect.

Young children acquire language by trying to make sense out of the world that surrounds them. In the process they employ language by creating new structures and sayings that they have never heard before (e.g., "broomed the floor," "it's good-morning time"). Through their interactions with adults and the language community that surrounds them they learn what is or is not appropriate or conventional in different situations. It is not surprising then that children from English-speaking backgrounds may enter school accustomed to different accents, vocabularies, and sociolinguistic styles depending on the type of regional (geographic) and social (class) dialects that are used in their environments. In fact, we all speak a dialect of English, although some dialects are closer than others to the standard English found in written texts and broadcast over the airwaves.

Linguists have dispelled the once popular deficit view of dialect. Regarding African-American dialect, they have traced its historical roots and demonstrated that it is as rich and fully formed as any other English dialect. Therefore, its speakers cannot be considered verbally deficient.[16] Although students may accrue considerable economic, social, and political advantage by speaking and writing standard English, they do not need standard English for communication purposes.

Teachers need to separate the goal of standard English acquisition from their reading instruction. For example, many teachers continue to overcorrect the oral reading of children who speak a social dialect or English as a second language. We hypercorrect because we do not understand that when students' pronounce words oddly or substitute one word for another (frequently termed *miscue*) they may not have a decoding or comprehension problem.[17] In order to know whether to correct an error or suggest special help, teachers need to know something about the child's dialect or second language. They also need to understand that there are differences in receptive (reading and listening comprehension) and productive (speaking and writing) competencies, and that children who speak a dialect or English as a second language may possess higher levels of receptive rather than productive competency in standard English.[18] For example, if children who speak an African-American dialect are reading orally and comprehending the text, it is not unusual for them to substitute equivalent words from their dialect for words in standard English, such as *ain't* for *is not* or *he be* for *he is*. Some Asian children who are learning English as a second language may mix-up *he* and *she* because gender is not represented in this fashion in their native language. Before correcting students' oral reading, teachers need to find out if the miscues cause serious problems in reading comprehension. The simplest approach is to ask students clarifying questions to see if they have understood what they have read.

Unfortunately, the overcorrection of dialect and second-language speakers' oral reading has prompted teachers to overemphasize decoding skills in the belief that these children are not ready to understand text. In a middle school familiar to us, second-language children of Indochinese descent were typically placed in the lowest reading class. When asked, the teachers explained that while the students could comprehend text just fine, they could not pronounce all of the words correctly.

Negative reactions to dialect or second-language differences seem to affect reading performance and development more than language differences themselves. Smitherman (1986) recounts an anecdote where a young African-American child attempts to tell the class a story but ceases to participate due to the teacher's constant interruptions and language corrections. Teachers need to be sensitive to the fact that, in an effort to communicate, many children will automatically use the language that they have learned at home because it is part of their personal and social identity. Some dialects are less accepted within the dominant culture than others, not because they are less well developed, but because they reflect social class distinctions. Teachers need to be aware of the cost of preventing children from using their personal language or dialects in school: To prevent children from using the language that they know best is to inhibit their participation.

On the other hand, we need to figure out ways to help dialect-speaking children acquire written and spoken command of standard English, what Delpit (1988) refers to as the *power code,* at the same time that we convey a genuine sense of respect for the dialect that they have mastered. Teachers face a real dilemma here: To withhold such instruction is to deny them access to power; to offer it is to risk denial of their dialect.[19]

Teachers also need to be aware of some of the unique factors that may influence how second-language children develop English reading skills.[20] For example, children who are literate in their native language (i.e., can read and write it) generally will make more rapid growth in English reading than those children who are not. These children already have developed an awareness of what reading is all about, and, depending on their native-language reading experience and instruction, have developed comprehension strategies that can transfer to reading in English. On the other hand, bilingual students may need more time than monolingual students to complete reading tasks in either of their languages. Due to differences in receptive and productive competencies, they may comprehend English text, but not be able to retell it in English as completely as they understood it. Reading in two languages also means that the bilingual reader will have to deal with orthographic, phonological, semantic, and syntactic differences that the monolingual reader does not face. None of these differences are insurmountable, and many of them can be dealt with through English as a second language (ESL) instruction.

Not all second-language students are completely bilingual. Students' oral and literate command of their native language and English may vary considerably. Some students will be very fluent or literate in both languages, others will be fluent or partially fluent or literate in only one of the languages, while others may be semifluent or semiliterate in both languages. Different educational, cultural, and language experiences will result in varied background and vocabulary knowledge. In most cases, second-language students' background and English vocabulary knowledge will differ from that of their monolingual English-speaking peers.

While teachers need to be aware of these unique factors, they should not be deceived by the students' nonnative pronunciation or lack of familiarity with English reading vocabulary or knowledge domains and skills, particularly those covered in basal reading lessons. While these students may not speak fluent English, or may not know all of the English vocabulary words, topics, or skills that the monolingual children know, they may have developed sophisticated comprehension strategies that they can use while reading in their native language or English. Teachers need to communicate with students, their former teachers (especially bilingual education or ESL teachers), and parents in order to determine the comprehension strategies that these children possess and use. They also need to make sure they know how their students are interpreting a given text by providing them with the opportunity to raise questions, identify unknown vocabulary, and ask for points of clarification. Teachers need to understand that bilingual children frequently demonstrate increased comprehension of English text when they are allowed to use their native language to help discuss and make sense of what they are reading in English.[21]

Assessment

Much of the discussion in this chapter, and in other chapters in this book, address assessment issues. We have chosen to review only a few points that, while pertinent to the literacy-assessment of all children, are especially salient to the literacy assessment of students from diverse backgrounds.[22]

Educators need to remember that formal (normed- and criterion-referenced) tests reflect the values and knowledge domains of the test writers who create them and of the educators and government officials who commission them. When the values and knowledge of students differ from those of the test writers and educators, their academic potential may be seriously underestimated. For example, in a study with fifth- and sixth-grade Latino and Anglo students, García (1991) found that the English reading test performance of the Latino students was adversely affected by the range of test topics on the test and by the test writers' convention of paraphrasing the language of the text in the question and answer choices. The overall test performance of the Latino students was lower than that of the Anglo students; however, it did not differ on those passages for which both groups of students had the same levels of prior knowledge. Furthermore, when García asked the Latino students open-ended questions about the passages orally (not in writing) or when she translated key words in the paraphrased test questions or test items into Spanish, the Latino students displayed greatly improved reading comprehension of the passages. She concluded that using English reading test scores of Latino students for placement purposes would seriously underestimate their reading comprehension potential.

Because assessment is used to help plan children's reading instruction, it can impact the type of instruction that children receive. Readiness and early reading tests used at the preschool, kindergarten, and first-grade levels frequently ask children to identify pictures or vocabulary items, many of which are unfamiliar to low-income children or children from diverse linguistic and cultural backgrounds. Some of these tests ask children to repeat phrases or sentences in standard English. Given what we have discussed about differences in children's literacy traditions, sociolinguistic styles, and language or dialect use, it should not be too surprising to discover that children from diverse backgrounds generally score low on such tests. Yet, due to their low test performance, they frequently receive labels such as language delayed and are given additional help in speech or placed in transitional classrooms.[23]

To overrely on a test score for placement decisions is to place children's literacy development at risk. First, this practice does not encourage us to find out what these children do know; instead, we focus on what they do *not* know. Second, it places children in a learning context in which they are forced to master the isolated skills and decontextualized knowledge measured on the tests. Third, children who are labeled tend to lower their estimations of themselves and their consequent achievement aspirations.

We also need to remember that a given test provides us with only a partial picture of an individual's performance. Many times the performance, as evaluated, is far removed from actual literacy tasks. A low score on a standardized reading test does not tell us if the child had the appropriate background knowledge to perform well on the test, if the child did not know how to utilize the appropriate reading strategies, or if the child was not able to determine the best answer and had a problem with reasoning strategies. Perhaps, most importantly, the low score does not provide us with the diagnostic information needed to help the child improve her literacy performance.

Teachers need to give children the opportunity to show what they can and cannot do, with and without help, on both familiar and unfamiliar tasks and materials. This type of situated/dynamic assessment can help teachers make better decisions at the same time that it allows students to become involved in their own self-evaluation. Informal assessment measures (sometimes called authentic assessment) —anecdotal records, story retellings, student-teacher conferences, samples of student work or portfolios, and oral miscue analyses—

can be extremely useful in helping teachers learn about the strengths and weaknesses of students. However, informal measures, like formal measures, can be misused and misinterpreted.

When teachers rely on these measures, they need to pay attention to cultural issues. Children interpret classroom events through the perspective of their cultural background; their behavior can, therefore, be easily misinterpreted. For example, a teacher may interpret a child's reticence to participate as a sign of inability when the child is simply unaccustomed to the activity or unsure about the teacher's expectations.

If the assessment of students from diverse backgrounds is to improve, then educators need to learn more about the cultures and languages of these students. Educators need to improve their communication with the children, the children's parents, and members of the children's community. Parents have to feel comfortable with schools, and know that they can ask a teacher about the child's performance or question why the child is viewed as unresponsive in school when the child constantly talks at home. Teachers, on the other hand, have to be willing to listen to parents and to seek out alternative explanations for students' behavior.

Differential Instruction

Educators frequently talk about meeting the individual needs of children, and, in fact, we emphasize this point in this book. However, dispositions to individualize and accommodate can become prejudicial when they lead to serious differences in teacher expectations, curricular coverage, and instruction. For students who have been marginalized by our system of education, these dispositions can, quite unintentionally, block access to the reading opportunities and strategies that they need to become successful readers. This type of prejudicial instruction can occur at the school, grade, or classroom level.

Converging evidence suggests that students in low-income schools receive less opportunity to engage in authentic literacy tasks than do children in middle- or high-income schools. In a comparison of fifth-grade classrooms across socioeconomic levels, Anyon (1980) revealed that teachers in the low-income schools held low expectations for their students' academic achievement and provided them with instruction that emphasized rote learning and limited student decisionmaking. On the other hand, teachers in the high-income schools held high expectations for their students and emphasized process-oriented learning and student decisionmaking. Similar findings were reported by Dorr-Bremme and Herman (1986) in a study that investigated the influence of normed- and criterion-referenced tests on instruction. They discovered that teachers at low-income schools reported spending more time preparing their students for formal tests than did teachers at the other schools. Clearly, some of this was due to the fact that many of these students were participating in state and federal programs that required such testing. However, the teachers also reported that they spent time preparing for such tests because they were very concerned about their students' performance on basic skills and thought that commercial tests were the best way to evaluate this type of performance. Content analyses of these measures suggest that the students have been taught not to read and comprehend, but to master decontextualized tasks[24]. Unfortunately, increased performance on decontextualized tasks does not necessarily translate into increased knowledge about, interest in, or performance on authentic literacy tasks.

Similar findings have been found within schools. For example, a study that focused on literacy achievement at the middle-school level found that students tracked in the low reading classes received less opportunity to do silent reading, were not assigned reading outside of class because the teachers did not think that they would do it and were given very little decisionmaking responsibility as compared to students in the middle or high reading classes. Teachers thought that they could better serve the needs of the students by ability grouping them in homogeneous classes, although classroom observations of the reading instruction provided in the lower classes revealed that the students were not shown how to improve their reading comprehension.[25]

Within a given classroom children labeled as poor readers tend to receive instruction that is qualitatively different from that offered to better readers. While grouping, in and of itself, is not necessarily negative (for positive aspects see Chapter 16), the way in which teachers organize their groups and the type of instruction that they present to the students in the lower groups can adversely affect reading development. For example, when working with children in low reading groups, teachers seldom require silent reading, often ask literal recall questions instead of inference questions, monitor oral reading meticulously, and interrupt oral reading frequently. The net result is that students in low groups read fewer minutes and fewer words than do students in the average or high reading groups.[26] If the students are in a classroom where the teacher uses a basal reading series, the teacher may not allow them to proceed to the comprehension strategies and lengthier text until they have first mastered the decontextualized basic skills frequently listed at the beginning of the scope and sequence charts. As a result, the low-performing reader receives a heavy dose of phonics instruction with little opportunity to engage in authentic literacy tasks.

Low expectations and a reluctance to involve low-performing readers in higher-order tasks that focus on *real* reading have been characterized as the *basic skills conspiracy*: First, you have to get the words right and the facts straight before you can get to the *what ifs* or *I wonders*.[27] A consequence of this conspiracy has been that many students are not given the opportunity to achieve in reading. In a large-scale study looking at first-grade achievement, Dreeben and Gamoran (1986) reported that instructional time and curricular coverage were better predictors of academic achievement than were race, socioeconomic status, aptitude, or ability group placement. In fact, they determined that the first-grade reading achievement levels of African-American and Anglo students were not differentiated by socioeconomic status or race when the children received the same type of instruction.

What then can educators do to safeguard against the basic skills conspiracy? One thing that we can do is make sure that all students, regardless of their reading level, dialect, or first language, receive reading instruction that facilitates the development of reading comprehension strategies. Chapter 10 in this book addresses this issue. García and Pearson (1991) recommend that all children should learn how to determine what is important in what they are reading, how to synthesize or summarize information, how to draw inferences, how to answer and ask inferential questions, and how to monitor and repair their comprehension (Dole, Duffy, Roehler, & Pearson, 1991).

Of course, important to the development of comprehension strategies is the activation of children's prior knowledge or schemata. If we want students to learn how to integrate new knowledge with old knowledge, they need to read both familiar and unfamiliar material. Content analyses of basal reading series and tradebooks suggest that the amount of multicultural literature available is limited.[28] Nevertheless, teachers interested in the reading development of students from diverse backgrounds need to know what is available and how to use it (see Appendix A for a list of multicultural materials).

Instructional Programs

A variety of programs have been developed to deal with the reading or academic performance of low-achieving students (Reading Recovery, reciprocal teaching, DISTAR, Success for ALL, Chapter 1). Whether a program is useful for students from diverse linguistic, cultural, or economic backgrounds probably depends on the extent to which its philosophy and underlying framework are consistent with current reading theory and with what we know about language and cultural differences. So far, very few programs have been developed with both of these factors in mind. In this section, we briefly evaluate some of the newer schoolwide and community-based programs as well as some of the wide-scale federal programs that have been funded to deal with the academic and literacy achievement of low-performing students.

Schoolwide or community-based programs

One of the few programs that has combined both knowledge about the children's culture with that of current reading theory is the KEEP program in Hawaii.[29] The original aim of this program was to develop an instructional delivery method consistent with current reading theory that would improve the reading performance of Hawaiian dialect-speaking children of Polynesian ancestry. The reading instruction is organized so that children first discuss what they know about a topic they will be reading, then they silently read sections of the text (a page or two), with the teacher asking them clarification questions at the end of each section to make sure that they have comprehended what they have read. After they have finished the silent reading, the students and teacher discuss what they read and how it relates to their own experiences or prior knowledge about the topic. Au (1979) points out that the last part of the lesson is critical for students from diverse backgrounds because it gives them an opportunity to link their reading to their own experiences, making the reading more relevant. In the process of developing the program, the educators discovered that the children's participation increased when they were allowed to use talk story, a type of overlapping discourse pattern that was characteristic of their Hawaiian culture. In the talk story tradition, an individual child might initiate a partial answer to a question posed by the teacher. Then other children, without raising their hands or waiting to be called on, add to the previous child's answer. This informed turn-taking process continues until the group as a whole completes the story or response.

Teachers interested in the cultural adaptation employed in KEEP need to understand that talk story is unique to this culture. When a teacher trained in the KEEP program was transferred to work on a Navajo reservation, many of the culturally adaptive techniques that she had learned to use in the KEEP program proved inappropriate. What was appropriate, however, was the knowledge that different cultures may have different norms and regulations for talk and interaction. This insight allowed the KEEP teacher to adapt the instructional part of the program to reflect the norms and values of the Navajo children with whom she was working.[30]

Not all of the schoolwide and community-based programs recently developed include reading programs that are consistent with current reading theory. Teachers interested in these programs need to evaluate the reading components of these programs carefully. For example, the Accelerated Schools program conceptualized by Levin (1987) lengthens the school day in an attempt to give low-achieving students the additional time they need to catch up with their peers. An underlying premise of the program is that low-achieving students can become average-achieving students or better by presenting them with a challenging curriculum that is faster paced than typical classroom instruction and that involves high-level cognitive functioning. Although this program eschews the type of slowed-down remedial instruction that many low-achieving students currently receive, the type of reading instruction implemented is determined by site-based management teams. As a result, some of the programs used or cited as being appropriate for accelerated schools, such as Mastery Learning or DISTAR, are at odds with current reading theory.

The Yale Child Center Study developed by Comer (1988) and his associates is another example of an interesting and successful program designed to improve the achievement of low-income, innercity children. Like the Accelerated Schools Program, no systematic effort has been devoted to developing a reading component consistent with current reading theory. This program is based on collaborative work at two African-American schools in New Haven, Connecticut, with the primary goal being to change the participation levels of the staff and parents in order to change the school climate. Although the schools have a social skills curriculum that helps to integrate the students' community and potential work experiences with what they learn in the classroom, the reading programs originally adopted (e.g., a sight-word oriented basal reading program and a code-emphasis linguistic reading program) by site-based management teams were somewhat outdated and not consistent with current reading theory.

A major strength of the Comer program, however, is parent participation and the collaboration it sparks among parents, teachers, and community leaders. These schools have overcome the general lack of communication that frequently occurs between low-income parents and schools. Comer attributes the reduced level of student misbehavior to the participation of parents in the schools. After being involved in the program for three years, the majority of the parents (92%) reported that they thought they were knowledgeable enough about mathematics and reading instruction at the schools to teach the subjects themselves. Over three fourths of the parents said that they expected their children to attend college.

Wide-scale federal programs

While federal guidelines almost always dictate eligibility for federally funded programs (such as Head Start, Chapter 1, Learning Disabilities and Special Education, Bilingual Education) and program evaluation guidelines, they do not specify the type of reading instruction that the children are supposed to receive. Not surprisingly, reading instruction provided in the programs varies widely in type, scope, and quality. The only federally funded program that specifically addresses cultural and linguistic diversity is Title VII/Bilingual Education.

The most well-known federally funded reading program is Title I/Chapter 1 of the Education Consolidation and Improvement Act (also discussed in Chapters 3 and 16). This program aims to increase the funding and support services provided to states and districts with major concentrations of low-income students. Students are eligible for the services if the school they attend has the prescribed number of low-income students in attendance and if the student's academic performance is below grade level. Over three fourths of the children enrolled in Chapter 1 receive reading services.

Although Chapter 1 services can be provided in a variety of ways, they typically are provided in a pullout setting. A trained reading specialist generally works with small groups of students outside of the regular classroom for 30–40 minutes four to five times a week. Despite the increased reading performance of some students enrolled in the program, the program has come under attack. Critics charge that there frequently is little coordination between the program and the classroom, that time is lost as children move between the classroom and the program, that instruction at the upper-grade levels tends to overemphasize lower-order skills, and that a good bit of the students' time is spent on worksheets and not on the reading of connected text. They also claim that few of the students actually complete the program able to read on grade level. A serious problem with the program is that students frequently are assessed on a wide range of tests in order to determine their specific reading difficulties. Instruction then tends to be geared toward mastering the decontextualized tasks on the tests. This emphasis on testing results in lost instructional time and limited opportunities to pursue authentic literacy tasks.[31]

Special education (including learning disabilities and behavior disorders) is another federal program that frequently includes low-achieving readers. Special education services are funded by PL 94–142, Education of All Handicapped Children's Act. This federal initiative targets children who for physiological or neurological reasons need additional help. The law guarantees that all handicapped children—even those mildly handicapped (i.e., learning disabled)—receive appropriate educational services. McGill-Franzen (1987) argues that a serious consequence of this legislation has been that as funding for Chapter 1 has been cut, districts have classified children who normally would be served by Chapter 1 as learning disabled.

Almost all of the children served by PL 94–142 are placed in self-contained classrooms for at least part of the day. Observational research has documented that children in special education classrooms do not receive reading instruction that is qualitatively superior to what they would receive in the regular classroom.

In many cases, the children actually do less oral or silent reading and receive less literacy instruction than they would in the regular classroom.[32]

Researchers who have studied Chapter 1 reading instruction and PL 92–142 reading instruction complain about what García et al. (1990) have termed the *extra help conspiracy.* Allington and McGill-Franzen (1989) point out that instead of changing the type of reading instruction that low-performing readers receive in the regular classroom, we have "sent them down the hall" where they receive a more intense, and frequently inferior, version of the classroom instruction that has already failed them. Many critics of these two programs support the Regular Education Initiative, which would eliminate the use of pullout or self-contained classrooms to provide services for low-performing readers. Instead, funds currently used to pay for Chapter 1 or PL 94–142 would be used to provide students with additional support and instruction in the regular classroom.

A third federal initiative, Title VII/Bilingual Education, affects those children who have been identified as limited-English-speaking or limited-English academic proficient, irrespective of their family's income. The general guideline that has underscored federal funding has been that limited-English-speaking children should receive ESL instruction, academic instruction in English, and academic instruction in the native language "to the extent necessary to allow a child to progress effectively through the educational system".[33] Limited funding at both the state and federal levels, however, has meant that only 15 percent of all eligible children are actually receiving some type of second-language service (instruction in a bilingual program or ESL instruction by itself).[34]

Although the federal government currently funds three types of programs (transitional bilingual education, special alternative instructional programs—predominantly ESL programs, and developmental bilingual education), almost all of the children served by Title VII/Bilingual Education funding are enrolled in transitional bilingual education programs. Children in this program typically receive ESL instruction as they continue to learn academic subjects, including reading and writing, in their native language. As the children become more proficient in English, their instruction in the academic subjects, including reading and writing, shifts into English. By third or fourth grade the majority of the children have been exited out of the program and are working in the all-English medium classroom where they no longer receive instructional services related to their second-language status. If children are enrolled in a transitional bilingual education program or an ESL-type program for longer than three years, federal regulation now requires school districts to submit written justification demonstrating that the children's lack of English proficiency is impeding their academic progress.

Those bilingual educators who are critical of the transitional bilingual education model and of the ESL models funded under the special alternative instructional programs contend that none of these models provide second-language children with the time or the opportunity to develop conceptual knowledge at a high cognitive level in their native language so that they can rely on this knowledge to help master academic content in English when they are immersed in the all-English setting.[35] Granted, the transitional bilingual education model includes a native-language component. However, there is not enough time in the standard 3-year period for the bilingual teacher to cover the appropriate grade-level elementary curriculum in mathematics, science, and social studies and teach the children to read and write in two languages—their native language and English.

Many bilingual educators prefer the developmental bilingual education model or a late-exit transitional bilingual education model (where students stay in the transitional program for 5–6 years, continuing to receive instruction in their native language as they receive instruction in English). In the developmental model, second-language children are enrolled in the same classroom as native-English speaking children. The two groups of children learn each other's language as they learn academic material in both languages. Students in the developmental program, as in the late-exit transitional program, usually stay in the program for 5–6 years, giving them time to develop two languages and a high level of conceptual knowledge in both languages. Proponents argue that the second-language children's self-concepts are heightened and that parental participation tends to be higher than in the transitional bilingual education program or in one of the ESL-special alternative instructional programs. Recent studies also have demonstrated that students in the developmental and late-exit transitional programs make higher gains in English reading and English language skills than do comparable students enrolled in one of the other program models.[36]

Teachers involved in Chapter 1, Special Education, or Bilingual/ESL programs can try to offset some of the criticisms that we have reported. For instance, they can make sure that the instruction provided in these programs facilitates the development of reading comprehension strategies (see Chapter 10). In addition, they can improve the level of coordination and communication that occurs between themselves and the classroom teachers. By providing their students with the opportunity to develop comprehension strategies appropriate to their ages and by maintaining contact with the classroom teacher, Chapter 1, Special Education, and Bilingual/ESL teachers can make sure that their students are receiving the type of instruction necessary to make a successful transition to the regular classroom.

Better communication across the settings also means that there are more opportunities for teachers to share ideas and information. Working together, the classroom teacher and the Chapter 1, Special Education, and Bilingual/ESL teacher can create a more detailed profile of the individual student's progress and achievement. This cooperation should not end once the children have left the program. For example, the bilingual teacher can help the classroom teacher identify and address some of the unique language and cultural factors that may continue to influence the academic performance of bilingual students in the regular classroom once they have been exited from the bilingual program (see the discussion under language differences).

SUMMARY

This chapter has focused on the at-risk situation. At the national level, this term predominantly has been used to focus on those students who drop out of school early. Most of these students are poor, and a disproportionate percentage of them are non-Anglo. Although we do not know the level at which dropouts can read and write, we suspect that most of them are able to decode simple material.

Conflict between home and school, in literacy traditions and sociolinguistic styles, and the inability of our schools to accommodate these differences, may have adversely influenced the literacy development of these students. It is not so much language differences, in and of themselves, but our attitudes toward language differences that drive us to instructional practices that adversely affect students' progress. Low expectations coupled with a reluctance to involve low-performing readers in higher-order tasks that focus on *real* reading have trapped us in a basic skills conspiracy, and the net result is that students don't get the opportunities they need to develop reading comprehension expertise.

There is a broad range of instructional programs focused on helping students—KEEP, Accelerated Schools, Yale Child Center Study, Chapter 1, Special Education, and Bilingual/ESL Education. We need to evaluate these programs according to their consistency with current reading theory and with language and cultural knowledge.

Teachers can bridge language and cultural differences by becoming more informed about children and their communities. They must make sure that all students, regardless of their level of reading achievement, dialect, or first language, receive reading instruction that helps them create meanings for the texts they encounter.

Suggested Activities

1. Conduct an interview with a parent from a cultural or linguistic orientation other than your own. Ask the parent about her schooling experiences and those of her children. How do the experiences differ from your own?
2. Observe the type of instruction that is provided to students in low- and high-tracked reading classes or reading groups. Pay attention to the types of comprehension strategies that are fostered in the two settings. To what extent are all of the students engaged? To what extent do you see evidence of differential instruction?

Suggested Reading

GARCIA, G. E. and PEARSON, P. D. (1991). The role of assessment in a diverse society. In E. Hiebert (Ed.), *Literacy for a diverse society: Perspectives, practices, and policies* (pp. 253–278). New York: Teachers College, Columbia University.
This chapter reviews both formal and informal literacy assessment measures, noting the extent to which the measures reflect or distort the literacy performance of students from diverse backgrounds. Specific recommendations are delineated for changes in assessment practices and policies at the district, school, and classroom level.
GARCIA, G. E. and PEARSON, P. D. (1991). Modifying reading instruction to maximize its effectiveness for *all* children. In M. S. Knapp & P. M. Shields (Eds.), *Better schooling for the children of poverty: Alternatives to conventional wisdom* (pp. 31–59). Berkeley, CA: McCutchan.

The authors review the current instructional situation from the perspective of the low-performing student. They define a comprehension-based curriculum and provide suggestions for teacher implementation.

LINDFORS, J. (1987). *Children's language and learning* (2nd ed.). Englewood Cliffs, NJ: Prentice-Hall.

This text reviews language acquisition theory and presents the reader with useful information about children's language acquisition. Specific attention is given to children who speak a nonstandard dialect of English or who speak English as a second language. Classroom suggestions for language arts instruction are provided.

SMITHERMAN, GENEVA (1986). *Talkin and testifyin: The language of Black America.* Detroit: Wayne State University.

This book introduces the reader to the features and use of Black English.

WILLIAMS, JAMES D., and SNIPPER, GRACE CAPIZZI (1990). *Literacy and bilingualism.* New York: Longman.

The authors review the theories and research related to bilingual education and bilingual literacy. They also present strategies and methods that teachers can employ in the classroom to help facilitate the literacy development of bilingual children.

Notes

1. Cullen (1978).
2. Much of the discussion in this chapter is based on García, Pearson, and Jiménez, (1990).
3. Davis and McCaul (1990), Moll (1991).
4. National Center for Educational Statistics (1988), Committee for Economic Development, 1987.
5. Pallas, Natriello, and McDill (1989).
6. See Mullis and Jenkins (1990) and Applebee, Langer, and Mullis (1987).
7. Vacca and Padak (1990).
8. See Levin (1988), Pallas, Natriello, and McDill (1988).
9. See Davis and McCaul (1990), Moll (1991).
10. See Davis and McCaul (1990), Wehlage & Rutter (1986).
11. Among others, see Adams (1990), Clay (1987), McCormick and Mason (1989), Teale and Sulzby (1986).
12. *FIRST TEACHERS: A family literacy handbook for parents, policy-makers, and literacy providers* (1989).
13. Auerbach (1989).
14. See Edwards and García (1991).
15. Edwards and García (in press).
16. Labov (1982).
17. See Burke, Pflaum, and Krafle (1982), Goodman, K. and Buck (1982), Goodman, Y., Watson, and Burke (1987).
18. See Savignon (1983), Troike (1969).
19. We suggest that the teacher allow the children to use their own dialect while she speaks standard English. However, the teacher can provide opportunities for group work where she solicits ideas from the students, but translates these ideas into standard English on a flip chart or blackboard. The teacher can then point out the different syntactic and semantic features of standard English as she writes the children's story. For example, she can say, "I put apostrophes because it's possessive." Whether she would tell the children that she used the word "cannot"

because it means the same as "ain't" probably would depend on the age of the children, their confidence in their own writing, and her rapport with them. Once the children are confident in their ability to engage in literacy activities, understand that the purpose of these activities is to communicate, and are willing to take the risks needed to give quality written and oral presentations, then the teacher can provide the students with legitimate opportunities to use standard English (such as a school newspaper, a formal presentation to the principal, a newsletter to the PTA).

20. For further information on second-language children's reading see Barnitz (1985), García, Jiménez, and Pearson (1989).
21. García (1991), Saville-Troike (1984).
22. Much of the discussion on assessment is based on García and Pearson (1991).
23. Karweit (1989).
24. Edelsky and Harman (1988), Stallman and Pearson (1990), Valencia and Pearson (1987).
25. García, Stephens, Koenke, Pearson, Harris, and Jiménez (1989).
26. See the various studies by Allington (1980a, 1980b, 1983) as well as Collins (1982) and McDermott (1977).
27. García, Pearson, and Jiménez (1990).
28. Logan and García (1983), Rollock (1984), Bishop (1987).
29. Au (1981b), Au and Mason (1981).
30. Jordan, Tharp, and Vogt (1985).
31. See Allington and McGill-Franzen (1989), Johnston and Allington (1991), Madden and Slavin (1987), Rowan and Guthrie (1989).
32. Allington and McGill-Franzen (1989), Leinhardt, Zigmond, and Cooley (1981).
33. August and García, E. E. (1988), p. 8. Also, see "Legislative Update—Changes in the law" (1988).
34. National Education Association (1990).
35. Cummins (1979), Cziko (1992); Troike (1984).
36. Cziko (1992).

CHAPTER 4

MOTIVATION AND READING

OVERVIEW

As you read this chapter use the following list of themes to guide your understanding and reflection.

- In literate societies children are motivated to learn to read because it is an important part of mastering their environment.
- Learner-oriented views of motivation hold that a child's natural curiosity and desire to succeed with important tasks provide the teacher with the necessary base for motivation, whereas other views emphasize external rewards that the teacher manipulates to shape behavior.
- Human behavior is typically motivated in complex ways often involving intrinsic as well as extrinsic factors.
- Children who encounter difficulty in learning to read often develop low self-concepts and feelings of helplessness leading to counterproductive behaviors that interfere with subsequent attempts to provide remediation.
- Some readers fall into a self-defeating pattern called *passive failure.*
- Good readers seem to attribute any difficulties they encounter in learning to read to factors they can control (such as effort), whereas low-achieving readers are more likely to believe they are powerless to prevent their own failures.
- Teachers can help children who have developed feelings of helplessness by redirecting their attention to factors over which the children have some control.
- Informal assessment devices and techniques such as questionnaires and interviews can be helpful to the teacher in identifying factors that contribute to insufficient motivation.

In 1976 the film *Rocky* set box office records throughout the United States and abroad. Since then *Rocky II–V* have elevated the main character to a folk hero of sorts. In the first film the reigning heavyweight boxing champion of the world, Apollo Creed, decided to give an unknown boxer the chance to fight for his title in Philadelphia to mark the nation's bicentennial. Rocky Balboa, a local club fighter who, during the day, collected payments from dock workers for a loan shark and spent most evenings bumming around his neighborhood, was chosen. Rocky went into training for the fight under the most difficult of circumstances. After weeks of hard work and sacrifice, he nearly upset Creed in a hard-fought match. Rocky lost the fight but gained great status among his neighbors, a good amount of money, and a lovely girl friend. His life was transformed, virtually overnight, from poverty and anonymity to fame and fortune. Although not written by Horatio Alger, the story fits into a popular theme in literature exemplified by the Alger stories: Through hard work and strength of character even the lowliest person can leave behind his miserable existence and rise to the top.

Motivation propelled Rocky to success. Rocky wanted to be somebody. He wanted to improve his situation and his prospects for the future. Opportunity knocked and Rocky was motivated to put enormous physical and emotional energy into getting ready for the fight.

Each of us can remember times when we have been just as motivated as Rocky. We can also remember times when we let something slide that we knew should be done because of a lack of motivation. Motivation plays a critical role in human behavior.

This chapter looks first at motivation as a psychological construct in order to understand its origins, how it operates, and what teachers can do to develop and nurture it. It also looks at how motivation influences reading and how teachers can assess the level of motivation of students in order to develop a plan for improving it. Chapter 5 will then offer several case studies involving low motivation and a number of specific activities for motivating low-achieving readers.

WHAT IS MOTIVATION?

In order for humans to survive, certain needs have to be met. Obviously food and water satisfy the basic needs of hunger and thirst. Without these necessities a person would die. The satisfaction of these needs gives rise to *primary drives.* These drives are unlearned in the sense that no one teaches an infant to become hungry or thirsty or to engage in sucking as a means of satisfying these drives. Other primary needs that seem to be fundamental to human survival include sleep, shelter, and procreation.

With respect to motivation, needs activate or energize the individual. This inner push that stems from the need to satisfy a drive is probably the most fundamental form of motivation. Is it fair to say that Rocky was motivated to train for the heavyweight title fight by the need for food? Rocky had to eat. He earned his money by fighting. In order to fight he had to train. Thus, through a series of links, he was training to eat. But Rocky was not starving when the opportunity to fight for the title came up. He earned a subsistence living by collecting debts for a loan shark. He also earned an occasional dollar or two by boxing in a local club. He was not fighting to satisfy a basic need as much as he was fighting for recognition and a feeling of importance. Are these needs the same as hunger or thirst?

Here it is helpful to introduce the notion of *secondary* needs. Primary needs are unlearned, that is, they occur instinctively, but secondary needs are learned. For example, infants growing up in one culture learn to eat at particular times and to eat particular types of food. Over time their basic need for food develops certain habits. In our own culture it is fairly predictable that they will eat three times a day and that hamburgers or hot dogs will form part of their diet. As much as our acculturation tempts us to deny it, there is no instinctive basis for either of these patterns of behavior. Other cultures eat only twice a day and favor insects, for example. Who is to say which set of behaviors is most basic?

The point is that even though secondary needs are learned or acquired, they have the same capacity as basic needs to energize or activate behavior. Exactly what needs children acquire as they mature reflects the culture they live in as well as their own values and tastes.

To return to Rocky Balboa for a moment: If we agree that Rocky was not fighting to satisfy a basic need (for example, he was not starving), was he fighting to satisfy an acquired need? If we conclude that the cash he would receive for the fight was the primary source of motivation for Rocky, this is clearly an acquired need. Money has no inherent value, but it can be used to satisfy various primary and secondary needs, including hunger.

Evidently, Rocky was fighting to satisfy an acquired need. However, if we stopped at this point in our consideration of why Rocky was motivated, our explanation would be only partially complete. Recent research on motivation (Ames & Ames, 1984, Maehr, 1989, Weiner, 1985) indicates that individuals seem to approach tasks with a set of thoughts and perceptions that guide their behavior. Accordingly, we might assume that Rocky's decision to fight was determined by his belief that the fight was valuable for him because it would enable him to attain a personal goal, that he understood what was required of him, and that he thought that he had the ability to accomplish this task. This suggests that the source of motivation can be a complex matter.

Sources of Motivation

In a literate society, schools have the responsibility for teaching children how to read. Clearly this is not a primary need such as eating or sleeping. If it were, teachers would have a relatively easy task. All children would learn to read in order to survive. Although reading does not qualify as a primary (survival) need, children have other needs that can serve as the basis for teaching them to read. Whether these needs are primary or acquired, unlearned or learned, is an interesting philosophical question that bears directly on the matter of motivation.

According to one school of thought,[1] human beings have a basic need to achieve competence or to become self-actualized. Despite some differences in the detail of their theories, White and Maslow both posit an energizing force within humans that causes them to strive for mastery of their environment. Weiner (1974) might logically be grouped with these theorists on the basis of his research on need achievement as a motivating force in human behavior. Piaget's notions about cognitive development are also quite consistent with this school of thought. In essence, these experts would agree that children are constantly striving to make sense of their world and to structure their interactions with the world so that they can be in charge of their own destiny.

This learner-oriented view of motivation has immediate and far-reaching implications for the way in which teachers approach reading instruction. A central premise of this view is that external rewards are less effective motivators than a child's own feelings of satisfaction when a goal has been achieved. Also basic to this view is the notion that personal interest in a topic or task is a critical part of establishing sustained motivation. The teacher's role is to create an environment that stimulates the child's natural curiosity and desire to succeed. In short, meaningfulness of what is learned is vitally important to the learner.

A second school of thought, represented by Skinner (1953) or Hull (1952), emphasizes the importance of external rewards as motivating devices. Teachers are placed in the role of selecting which goals to pursue and establishing a reward system that will motivate learners toward those goals. Personal interest is a factor only to the extent that the rewards offered must be attractive to the child. It is the teacher who motivates and the child who responds. Meaningfulness of what is to be learned is less important than the appropriateness of the rewards offered.

Extrinsic and Intrinsic Motivation

One's beliefs about the nature of motivation influence how they view the relative importance of internal and external sources of reward. Motivation occurring for reasons that lie within a task and within the person, such as feelings of satisfaction or competence, is usually called *intrinsic* motivation. For example, Rocky Balboa proved to himself that he was nearly the equal of the heavyweight champion of the world. Rocky also gained status in the eyes of the sports world and enhanced his reputation with his friends by fighting. These social rewards appear to have an extrinsic basis—that is, they lie outside the person. This leads us to external motivation, which is discussed next.

Motivation that occurs for reasons that lie outside the individual or the task (for instance, for an external reward) is called *extrinsic* motivation. In Rocky's case the money he could earn for fighting is a clearcut example of an extrinsic reward that could generate extrinsic motivation. Other possible extrinsic motivators for Rocky were the chance to have a personal manager-trainer, the chance to get back his locker at the local gym (something he had recently lost because he seemed to be going nowhere as a boxer), and his increased status.

Even though intrinsic-extrinsic distinctions have been highly controversial among researchers (Lepper & Hodell, 1989), they are still useful concepts. However, they should not be taken as mutually exclusive because some motivators have both internal and external elements. For example, winning the fight would have earned Rocky a belt that accompanies the title. Although valuable in its own right, at a hock shop for example, the belt is symbolic of high achievement. How did Rocky view the belt? Was he interested in this tangible reward worth several hundred dollars? Probably not, at least not when he was doing well financially. Later, had he won the belt but become destitute, the extrinsic value of the belt might have outweighed its intrinsic value and been sold for cash to buy a sack of groceries. It is important to realize that individuals will often pursue a given task for both internal and external rewards.

In a classroom setting the value of extrinsic rewards is often hard to calculate. Where does symbolism begin and end for the student? When does a good grade give him a sense of satisfaction or feeling of competence and when does it literally earn him a ticket to the circus or save him a swat on the posterior at home? Motivators that may look straightforward and simple to the teacher may become distorted and complex from a child's perspective.

From the standpoint of learning, the most powerful motivation seems to occur when students perceive themselves to be engaged in a task for their own reasons (intrinsic) rather than engaged in a task to please others, obtain a reward, escape punishment, or avoid some other extrinsic pressure (Deci & Ryan, 1985, Lepper, 1983). Brophy (1987a, 1987b) distinguishes between motivation to perform a task and motivation to learn from a task. Humans seek to master what they believe to be important. They want to control their own destiny. Such motivation is internal. Teachers can and must seek to build, nurture, and capitalize on this intrinsic need to improve one's self.

At the same time, extrinsic rewards are often effective, and sometimes the only recourse with children who have learned to dislike reading. By rewarding a student for his achievement the teacher attempts to encourage (or motivate) subsequent attempts. Extrinsic rewards can take the form of symbols (grades, gold stars), treats (candy), substitutes for treats (tokens, money), and praise. The success of praise, as with any other extrinsic reward, depends on the student's interpretation of the teacher's behavior (Stipek, 1988). For example, Brophy (1981) points out that teachers do not always use praise well. He provides guidelines for effective uses of praise that are summarized in Table 4.1. The teacher's goal should be to employ extrinsic motivation until sufficient success has been achieved by the student for his own intrinsic motivation to replace the need for external rewards. In providing tangible incentives for particular behaviors such as reading a page without errors, answering ten questions correctly, or reading a novel from cover to cover, teachers attempt to associate the tangible reward with a sense of accomplishment and self-worth. When that bond becomes strong enough, the tangible incentive can be removed because the child's internal sense of self-worth that accompanies achievement will have become strong enough to motivate further attempts to achieve.

Human Behavior Is Motivated in Complex Ways

The case of Rocky Balboa has been used to examine the principle of motivation. The primary question has been: What motivated Rocky to fight Apollo Creed? We have considered a variety of possible motives, ranging from pride to hunger. In actuality it is easy to see that Rocky, like most people, is seldom motivated by a single factor. Rocky probably had five or six competing, perhaps even conflicting, motivations.

To help a student learn to read, we need to recognize the complexity of what motivates that student and adjust our approach accordingly. We need to know something about his general disposition toward reading, his areas of personal interest, and his concept of himself as a person and as a reader. If he dislikes reading and has a backlog of negative experiences associated with learning to read, motivation will be much more difficult. We will not be able to approach him from the standpoint of mastering his environment. For reasons we will explore later, he has probably abandoned trying to learn to read and may even deny that reading is important. With effort, intrinsic motivation can be rekindled, but probably will not provide the most effective starting point. Extrinsic motivation will have a better chance of succeeding at the outset. Which rewards he will value must be discovered as well as how they should be provided. Only by starting to know the student better as an individual will we gain a sense of what motivates him.

TABLE 4.1 Guidelines for Effective Praise

Effective Praise	Ineffective Praise
1. Is delivered contingently	1. Is delivered randomly or unsystematically
2. Specifies the particulars of the accomplishment	2. Is restricted to global positive reactions
3. Shows spontaneity, variety, and other signs of credibility; suggests clear attention to the student's accomplishment	3. Shows a bland uniformity, which suggests a conditioned response made with minimal attention
4. Rewards attainment of specified performance criteria (which can include effort criteria, however)	4. Rewards mere participation, without consideration of performance processes or outcomes
5. Provides information to students about their competence or the value of their accomplishments	5. Provides no information at all or gives students information about their status
6. Orients students toward better appreciation of their own task-related behavior and thinking about problem solving	6. Orients students toward comparing themselves with others and thinking about competing
7. Uses students' own prior accomplishments as the context for describing present accomplishments	7. Uses the accomplishments of peers as the context for describing students' present accomplishments
8. Is given in recognition of noteworthy effort or success at difficult (for *this* student) tasks	8. Is given without regard to the effort expended or the meaning of the accomplishment (for *this* student)
9. Attributes success to effort and ability, implying that similar successes can be expected in the future	9. Attributes success to ability alone or to external factors such as luck or easy task
10. Fosters endogenous attributions (students believe that they expend effort on the task because they enjoy the task and/or want to develop task-relevant skills)	10. Fosters exogenous attributions (students believe that they expend effort on the task for external reasons—to please the teacher, win a competition or reward, etc.)
11. Focuses students' attention on their own task-relevant behavior	11. Focuses students' attention on the teacher as an external authority figure who is manipulating them
12. Fosters appreciation of and desirable attributions about task-relevant behavior after the process is completed	12. Intrudes into the ongoing process, distracting attention from task-relevant behavior

Source: Brophy, J. (1981). Teacher praise: A functional analysis. *Review of Educational Research, 51,* 5–32.

Motivation and the Affective Domain

Thus far we have looked closely at the internal and external sources of motivation. Several other factors must also be examined to fully understand motivation. First, we will look at the phenomenon of *passive failure* in reading. Then, we will look at attitudes and how *attitudes* about reading affect motivation. Next, we will consider how *interests* are related to motivation. Finally, the topic of *self-concept* will be examined with respect to its impact on motivation.

Passive Failure in Reading

A fairly extensive body of literature has developed in recent years in which children who have experienced repeated failures with reading or some other task are portrayed as *passive failures.* Such children are easily discouraged and do not persist with tasks as do children who have developed positive self-concepts. In an integrative review of research, Johnston and Winograd (1985) state that a variety of domains have contributed to understanding the characteristics of passive failure and why passive failure might occur in reading. An explanation of how beliefs of students about themselves as readers affect their reading performance will be examined first within the domain of metacognition, and next within the domains of achievement motivation, attribution theory, and learned helplessness.

Metacognition

While there are numerous definitions of metacognition, it is often referred to as *thinking about thinking* (Baker & Brown, 1984, Jacobs & Paris, 1987). The research on metacognition has focused on the ability of students to assume an active role in their learning: "that is, their ability to consciously organize and use their knowledge, to know when they do not know, and to know how and where to seek assistance for learning and problem solving in future situations" (Wang & Palincsar, 1989, p. 71). Several studies have shown that poor readers have less metacognitive knowledge and fewer metacognitive experiences. More specifically, Johnston (1985) and Paris and Jacobs (1984) report that poor readers lack knowledge about reading strategies, that there is a difference between good and poor readers' awareness of the purposeful and flexible use of strategies, and that poor readers lack adequate knowledge about the reading process. Likewise, Palincsar and Ransom (1988) state that poor readers are generally unaware of their own strategy use and do not engage deliberately in strategic operations that require planning, flexibility, and monitoring their own performance. Further, even when poor readers are aware of their comprehension problems, they often don't know what to do to repair those problems. To use the popular language, they lack fix-up strategies.

What is important to note is that these poor readers fail not because they lack the ability to do the tasks, but rather because they do not employ goal-oriented strategies, flexibly, efficiently, or perhaps not even at all (Johnston & Winograd, 1985). As Paris, Lipson, and Wixson (1983) point out, "strategies combine components of both skill and will" (p. 305). In other words, it is not just the reader's skill that is crucial to efficient reading behavior, but their motivation or willingness to respond to reading as well.

Achievement Motivation, Attribution Theory, and Learned Helplessness

Research on achievement motivation has focused on the role of the individual's unobservable thoughts and feelings such as one's expectancy about reaching a goal and the value one places on attaining it (Covington, 1983, Dweck & Elliott, 1983, Wigfield & Asher, 1984). For example, it is known that individuals are the most successful when they set goals of moderate difficulty level, are committed to pursuing these goals, believe they have the competence needed to successfully complete the task, and approach the goal concentrating on success as opposed to avoiding failure. Furthermore, it is known that individuals are more successful when they develop a strong internal locus of control (Rotter, 1966) and believe they have some personal control over their own learning.

Building on the work of Rotter, Weiner (1979, 1984, 1985) has theorized that, in the process of trying to accomplish a task, people typically develop explanations for their successes or failures. According to Weiner, individuals naturally search for understanding of why events occur, especially when the outcome is important or unexpected. For example, an individual's reaction to the question "Why did I fail this test?" will have an impact on the likelihood of undertaking future activities, the intensity of work at those activities, and the degree of persistence in the face of failure.

Specifically, Weiner posits that individuals attribute success or failure to factors that are internal or external, stable or unstable, and controllable or uncontrollable. Internal factors include the amount of effort expended and one's ability to perform a particular task. External factors include the difficulty of a task and luck. If individuals are internally oriented, they attribute the success or failure on a particular task to factors over which they can assume some personal responsibility. On the other hand, if individuals are externally oriented, they attribute their performance to factors over which they have no responsibility and, in turn, over which they have no control. Further, individuals can attribute success or failure to stable or unstable factors. Ability is generally viewed as stable over time, whereas effort, luck, or mood are viewed as unstable because they can change from task to task.

To illustrate, suppose you wanted to hit a golf ball from the tee to a green that is 150 yards away. What determines how well you succeed in accomplishing that feat? Different people give different explanations. One person may do poorly and attribute the outcome to the difficulty of the task saying, "Even a pro finds it hard to land the ball on the green." Another person might attribute the outcome to ability, saying, "I'm not a very good golfer." A third person might say, "I didn't concentrate on that shot," thereby implying, "I could do better if I tried harder."

Likewise, it is argued that students attribute their reading performance to a variety of factors. Specifically, there is evidence to suggest that low-achieving readers often attribute their reading failure to factors beyond their control. Low-achieving readers usually believe it is lack of ability that accounts for their reading failure whereas good readers attribute their occasional failures to lack of effort.

Similarly, low-achieving readers who attribute their failure to lack of ability naturally feel helpless and passive about reading. The phenomenon of *learned helplessness* refers to the perception by individuals, from a series of trials, that they have no control over the outcome of events. When they continue to fail even though extra effort is expended, it convinces them that success is unrelated to effort. In contrast, better readers seem to believe their failures are due to lack of effort.

Dweck (1986) and Diener and Dweck (1980) suggest that students approach tasks from either a mastery orientation or a learned helplessness orientation. Mastery-oriented students tend to have more self-confidence, focus their thinking on the task at hand rather than on themselves, and focus on problem-solving strategies when they encounter obstacles (Anderson, 1989). On the other hand, Anderson (1989) states that when learned-helplessness students encounter obstacles they tend to focus on their own inability and helplessness, something that results in less attention to the task and its solution. These characteristics are consistent with the findings of a recent study of motivation problems among poor readers (Butkowsky & Willows, 1980).

Bristow (1985) suggests that despite having good intentions, teachers often unwittingly reinforce the beliefs of low-achieving children concerning the cause of their difficulty (lack of ability) by expressing sympathy for their failure. In contrast, these same teachers often become angry when better readers fail, thus conveying the impression that their failure is due to lack of effort, not lack of ability. Additionally, Johnston and Winograd (1985) emphasize that less successful readers are treated differently than more successful readers in a variety of ways that reinforce less successful children to attribute their failure to low ability. For example, the research based on classroom observations indicates that teachers

1. Give less successful children the answer or shift the question to another child (a comparison) rather than refocus or adjust the question.
2. Reward inappropriate answers or behavior of less successful students.
3. Criticize less successful children more often for failure.
4. Praise less successful children less frequently for success.
5. Pay less attention to and interact less with less successful students.
6. Wait less time for less able children to answer.
7. Demand less from less successful students.
8. Provide briefer and less informative feedback to less successful students' questions.
9. Use less effective but more time-consuming methods of instruction when time is limited (Johnston & Winograd, 1985, p. 285).

Later we will explore various means for helping low-achieving readers overcome the passive behavior that seems to accompany their learned helplessness. But first, let's look at how attitudes, interests, and self-concept are important to motivation.

Attitudes

The term *attitude* is often used to refer to a person's predisposition toward a topic.[2] People having a positive or favorable attitude toward nuclear power, for example, would generally favor the generation of power by nuclear reactors and probably support the construction of additional reactors. Positive feelings about a topic usually emanate from previous pleasant experiences with that topic. Thus, we would not expect residents of Chernobyl to have positive

This woman's attitude toward running causes her to jog for conditioning purposes just as her attitude toward reading for information might encourage her to read the daily newspaper. *(Peter Vadnai)*

feelings about nuclear power because of the personally disruptive and life-threatening experiences they went through in 1986.

Attitudes are often a matter of degree rather than kind; that is, we are less likely to be totally negative or positive than we are to be partially positive or negative. Thus, in an opinion poll (which basically measures attitudes), respondents are often given an opportunity to strongly agree or disagree with a statement, mildly agree or disagree, or to indicate neutral feelings. Some opponents of nuclear power feel strongly enough to attend hearings, stage protests, and even go to jail to express their resistance. Others write letters and contribute money to the cause but keep their resistance at a lower level. Some talk about their opposition at cocktail parties. All have negative attitudes about nuclear power, but the degree or intensity of their negative feelings varies considerably.

These illustrations suggest that at least three factors are critical with respect to attitudes. First, an attitude has a focus; that is, we do not speak of attitudes in general but about attitudes on specific topics or issues. Second, attitudes develop from experience with a topic, either direct or indirect. And third, attitudes typically fall somewhere on a continuum ranging from absolutely favorable on one extreme to absolutely unfavorable on the other extreme. Furthermore, these attitudes can change. Let's consider the implications of these principles for attitudes toward reading.

Attitudes Toward Reading

One's attitude toward reading centers around what one believes reading entails and how one feels about that belief. In a recent survey, Heathington and

Alexander (1984) found that while teachers see positive attitudes toward reading as important, they spend very little time specifically fostering good attitudes. A poor attitude toward reading is usually the result of either misconceptions or negative feelings (or both) about reading (Duffy & Roehler, 1986). For example, if students equate reading with the completion of worksheets, then a major misconception exists. If students have always felt they were poor readers, they will probably have a negative attitude about reading. Misconceptions and negative attitudes about reading can be changed if students are engaged in real and meaningful tasks that are challenging enough to remain interesting, yet easy enough to accomplish with reasonable effort. Because reading ability is affected by student attitudes toward reading, teachers should assess and plan instruction that promotes positive feelings (Fredericks, 1982).

Interests

How is attitude toward reading, even in an applied sense, related to motivation? Mathewson (1976) addressed this question by indicating that motivation is the energizing force that actually causes reading to occur when a favorable attitude toward reading exists. He uses the term *interest* to describe the action orientation that occurs when a positive attitude and motivation are both present. Mathewson believes that a favorable attitude toward reading by itself does not cause an individual to read. Interest becomes the main factor that triggers actual reading.

Oritz (1983) states that interest is a quality generated by the individual, but that students are often unaware of their own ability to generate interest. For example, if a student responds "That book is boring" it implies that he believes interest is a quality of the material rather than a state of mind. When this is the case, it becomes difficult for the student to see a reason for engaging in a task related to this book. The challenge for the teacher is inducing students to generate their own purposeful and meaningful tasks related to the boring book, tasks that they consider interesting and relevant to their own learning. However, before a teacher can assist students in generating appropriate tasks, it is first necessary to determine what things interest the students. Accordingly, interest is another element that should be included in an assessment of motivation.

It is important to note, however, that high motivation can work in the absence of a positive attitude toward reading. This can occur in two ways. First, the topic may be of such personal importance to readers that they will read something related to that interest even though reading is not a favored activity (for example, when adolescents need to read the state vehicle code in order to pass a driver's license test). In this situation internal motivation is at work. On the other hand, rewards can be offered that provide external motivation for readers who would not normally read a selection. These observations about motivating reading in the absence of positive attitudes will be especially important in a later section on instruction.

Self-Concept

A person's self-concept is defined by Quandt and Selznick (1984) as "all the perceptions that an individual has of himself; especially emphasized are the individual's perceptions of his value and his ability" (p. 1). Restated, we might say that self-concept relates to what a person thinks of himself or herself.

Realistically speaking, people rarely think of themselves in totally positive terms because it is human nature to recognize one's own faults and weaknesses. Bandura (1977) uses the term *self-efficacy* to refer to an individual's beliefs about his competence or capabilities on a particular type of task. The research has shown that individuals who feel more competent typically engage in a greater number of activities, expend greater effort, persist in the face of difficulties, and attain a higher level of performance (Bandura & Schunk, 1981; Schunk, 1989). Therefore, a good or positive self-concept usually accompanies feelings of competence and importance. One aspect of self-perception relates to one's success with reading (learning to read and using reading in real life settings). A person could have a good self-concept and not be able to read, of course, but in a literate, print-oriented society, reading difficulty is likely to have a strong negative impact on self-concept.

Stipek (1988) suggests that in such situations, students who maintain low perceptions of competence will often exhibit feelings of anxiety, which has a debilitating effect on motivation and learning. Recently there has been an upsurge of research on the relationship between anxiety and achievement. Current views postulate that anxiety can be a result of the individual's perception of the task that makes them fearful and stressful. For example, when a student feels incompetent regarding the completion of a task, she will focus on self-criticism and expectations of failure, which in turn leads to anxiety and a threat to the student's self-esteem. For a current review of the literature on anxiety see Sarason, 1980.

Self-concept develops largely in response to interactions with others. A *self-perception* develops as we compare ourselves with others. School curriculum often unwittingly underscores negative self-comparisons by using a graded measuring device (i.e., the basal series) and arranging a race of sorts through the various levels of the series.

Self-concept also has a *self-other* dimension involving children's views of how others view them. Constantly told, directly or indirectly, that they are doing poorly with reading, children can soon accept their fate and begin performing down to these expectations. A self-fulfilling prophecy begins to operate as such children become problem readers because of their feelings of inadequacy. The real tragedy is that too often the well-meaning teacher has contributed to this demise through efforts to motivate with comments such as, "You're falling behind. You're not doing well. You aren't trying hard enough." Though we do not wish to advocate a simplistic, Pollyanna approach to reading instruction, it is clear that the *self-other* perceptions of children can be critical in their development of a reading self-concept that may affect their future reading performance.

Another dimension of self-concept is the *self-ideal*. This relates to what individuals wish they could do. As with self-perceptions and self-other perceptions, the development of self-ideals is heavily dependent upon interactions with people who are important to children (significant others). This normally includes teachers, peers, and of course, parents. If the people who are important to children regard reading as important and give evidence of this belief, children will develop a positive disposition toward reading. Furthermore, if these significant individuals help children monitor their own progress rather than compare them with other children, reading self-concept will be enhanced. With a healthy self-concept, children are better able to withstand the temporary setbacks and frustrations that invariably accompany the acquisition of any new ability.[3]

Children with poor reading self-concepts, whether justified by their progress or not, will gravitate toward what Quandt and Selznick call *counteractions*. Counteractions are defense mechanisms that anyone employs in the face of repeated failure with an important task. One counteraction is to deny the importance of the activity—in this case, reading. Does the child really believe reading is unimportant? Probably not at first, but over time the child may actually begin to accept this defense as true. The solution may or may not be to attack the defense mechanism and *prove* to the child that their perception is wrong. A better solution is probably to tackle the negative self-concept by giving the child success experiences, by praising and documenting progress, and by indicating that you think the child is worthy and capable. If this can be done in reading situations, all the better, but instruction may have to begin with something else, such as puzzles or games, and gradually lead into reading.

A second counteraction unsuccessful readers often employ is to hide or disguise their lack of ability.[4] Illiterate adults, and older children in particular, become very adept at hiding their reading disability. A skilled teacher will make allowances for the individual's fragile ego by not publicly displaying the disability and will privately support them with an understanding attitude. Trust and rapport must be established before instruction can proceed and, again, improvement of the individual's self-concept is the best starting point. Several specific strategies for approaching this problem are offered in the following chapter.

Another counteraction is simply to make it clear that we really did not try to succeed at an activity. Covington (1984) posits that individuals naturally strive to protect their sense of self-worth when it is threatened, particularly by maintaining a belief that one is able. Therefore, an individual may often approach a task by focusing on how to avoid failure rather than on how to achieve success. This works fine if the activity is an optional one such as riding a bicycle or playing softball. We may suffer temporarily for lacking a skill of this type, but life rolls on. This is not so true with a skill as important as reading. Children may attempt to protect their egos by not trying, but the problem of illiteracy will not go away.

ASSESSING MOTIVATION TO READ

It would be convenient if there were a single test instrument that collected all the needed information about reading motivation, but unfortunately none exists. Some useful data can be collected by commercially produced instruments; other information can be gathered informally by teachers. However, no formula exists for putting all the pieces together to arrive at an accurate assessment of a student's motivation for reading. Ultimately, as with all assessments, it will be the task of the teacher to weigh and interpret all the information available, to seek additional information where needed, and to develop a working hypothesis that guides instructional efforts. A teacher's conceptualization of motivation determines what information should be gathered and how it should be interpreted. It makes sense that information in the following areas is useful:

Attitudes toward reading

Areas of personal interest

Records of reading undertaken—what was and was not liked

Self-concept

We now examine how each of these topics can be assessed.

Assessing Attitudes toward Reading

Educational measurement is not an exact science. Any assessment is subject to some error and this is particularly true concerning affective topics such as the motivation to read. Later, once a variety of devices and procedures for gathering such information have been described, certain cautions will be discussed in using and interpreting the results of such measures.

It is sufficient to say, as an introduction to this topic, that people's feelings are elusive and ever-changing. This probably explains why very few formal measures of reading attitude are available. Alexander and Filler (1976) identify eighteen attitude assessment instruments or procedures reported in the published literature but properly refrain from calling them formal tests. Rather, they suggest that these instruments may be useful in helping classroom teachers devise their own instruments. We agree that few such devices can be used without adaptation to the local setting. Attitudes toward reading can be assessed through a variety of informal techniques, including questionnaires, incomplete sentences, teacher observation, interviews and conferences, and reading attitude scales, which will be examined.

Questionnaires

Nearly every adult has had experience with a questionnaire. Given a particular topic, questions are asked that reveal the respondent's position on that topic. With respect to attitudes about reading, the questions seek to ascertain *if* you read, *when* you read, *what* you read, and perhaps *why* you read. Typically, questionnaires present a forced choice between *yes* and *no* as a response, though some may provide for a response of *undecided* or *I don't know.*

Questionnaires are relatively easy to construct and may readily be adjusted to fit the reading level of the group and even the local situation. A sample questionnaire developed for upper-grade children is presented in Figure 4.1. Notice that the questions are constructed so that a response of yes suggests a positive disposition toward reading. By totaling the number of yes responses for each child and ranking the scores from high to low, a teacher can quickly see which children are least likely to spend time reading. It requires a leap of faith to conclude that either the score or the rank of a child is an accurate index of the child's attitude toward reading, however, and such a leap is not advisable.

Name   Age   Date

DIRECTIONS: Read each of the statements given below. Respond by circling *Yes* or *No* to indicate if the statement applies to you.

Yes   No   1. Reading is my favorite subject in school.

Yes   No   2. I would rather read a good book than watch TV.

Yes   No   3. I usually understand what I read in books.

Yes   No   4. I have gotten to know some interesting people in books.

Yes   No   5. Sharing books in school is fun.

Yes   No   6. Reading out loud to a parent or friend is fun.

Yes   No   7. I would like to hear my teacher read a story out loud every day.

Yes   No   8. I like to receive books as gifts.

Yes   No   9. Members of my family borrow books from the library.

FIGURE 4.1. Reading Attitude Questionnaire

What is justified, however, is a search for further information about each child using the other devices described here. Patterns of behavior gathered over time give rise to a working hypothesis that "Alice avoids reading whenever possible perhaps because of a negative attitude." Causes for this tentative conclusion and possible solutions can then be explored.

Questionnaires Using More Sensitive Scales

As stated earlier, an assessment device will be more useful if it allows for a range of responses, other than yes or no, and if it specifies reading of a particular type or topic rather than reading in general. Instead of asking children to answer yes or no to a question such as "Do you like to read?" a range of responses (Likert-type scale), such as *Always—Usually—Sometimes—Seldom—Never,* can be provided. It is also possible to offer children an opportunity to indicate the quality and intensity of their feelings regarding a concept. Thus, the following scale (Alexander & Filler, 1976) is employed to measure quality:

Where on the following scale would you rate reading?

Good   _____   _____   _____   _____   Bad
Happy   _____   _____   _____   _____   Sad

Intensity is measured with a scale using adjectives such as *strong-weak, big-little,* and so forth.

The sample question above may also be framed differently so that it is more direct. For example, the question might ask "Do you like to read before going to bed at night?" Or the question may give several alternatives: "Before going to bed at night I like to: (a) read, (b) listen to the radio, (c) watch TV, (d) play with a game or toy." Alexander and Filler (1976) call devices of this sort *paired choices.* Pairings may be presented with two or more choices. With older children a yes or no questionnaire can be modified with a scale that asks students to rate their level of agreement with each statement: "I like to read before going to bed: strongly agree—agree—disagree—strongly disagree."

Any questionnaire, regardless of the scale used or type of response made, should sample enough behaviors (that is, have enough questions) to provide a reliable assessment. At least twenty items are needed to yield a useful picture of the child's disposition toward reading. Even then, we must recognize that questionnaires, as well as other paper-and-pencil devices to be described later, ask students to report what they believe or prefer. Inaccuracy can creep in if they really do not know their own mind on a question.

Incomplete Sentences

Another relatively simple-to-make device that can provide useful insights about children's attitudes toward reading consists of short phrases or stems that elicit a response (a word or phrase) that completes the sentence. For example, a stem could state "I would rather read than _____." The respondents reveal something about their disposition toward reading in their responses. As with a questionnaire, incomplete sentences can be developed to reflect local concerns and conditions. A sample of assessment using incomplete sentences is presented in Figure 4.2.

The value of incomplete sentences depends on the teacher's ability to combine this information with other information about attitude toward books and reading. No simple scoring scheme is available for summarizing or interpreting the responses. Some teachers gain further insight into children's feelings about reading by discussing some of their more revealing responses in a one-to-one conference. For example, it would be important to discuss the response to the following stem: "I think reading *a book is a waste of time.*" A pattern of negative responses such as this signals a serious problem that needs immediate and individual attention. An isolated response of this sort may mean the student is merely having a bad day or is struggling with a difficult book right now. Here the problem is much less serious but still worth a few minutes of conversation between teacher and pupil.

Teacher Observation

Teachers have countless opportunities during the course of a day to gain a sense of their pupils' attitudes toward reading. Some clues are obvious while others are more subtle. The teacher who makes it a point to watch for the quick frown or the eager volunteer when a reading activity first begins can gain valuable information that confirms or belies a working hypothesis about a student's attitude toward reading. Simple anecdotal records provide a way to document fleeting incidents that may eventually add up to a significant insight. Some teachers use 3 x 5 index cards to quickly jot down notations such as "Pete became so engrossed in a Hardy Boys Mystery that he was last in line for lunch

Name   Age   Date

DIRECTIONS: Complete each sentence in whatever way describes you best.

1. Reading books at home is _____

_____.

2. The best book I ever read was _____

_____.

3. Reading is hard when _____.

4. Most books are _____.

5. When I see a library I _____

_____.

6. Reading class is _____.

7. I think reading_____.

8. When my teacher reads a book to us I _____

_____.

9. I think the newspaper is _____.

10. My favorite magazine is _____.

FIGURE 4.2. Sentence Completion

today." Other teachers use a notebook with a page for comments on each child; some have checklists that help them focus on behaviors they find revealing.

Figure 4.3 presents a sample checklist that could be used to record a student's behavior over an entire day. Although it would not be practical to complete such a checklist every day, a teacher could pay attention to the types of behavior noted on the checklist several times a semester. One strategy is to watch one or two children each day noting their behavior on the checklist. Another strategy is to watch for a particular type of behavior among all the pupils in a class one day, then focus on another type another day. In either case, systematic observation is taking place. Over time this builds a useful database that enables a teacher to go beyond general impressions in drawing conclusions or planning instruction.

Teacher observation should also note the incidental happenings that occur in a classroom every day. Some events are visible to everyone (for example, Mary cries out of frustration with the difficulty of the science textbook), while others are seen only by the alert teacher (Scott participates actively in a discussion

Name _____ Date _____ Teacher's Name _____

Class _____ Period _____

DIRECTIONS: Indicate which behaviors are observed during the period of observation by making a check in the margin.

The student was observed

_____ 1. Carrying a library or paperback book not assigned by the teacher.

_____ 2. Reading for recreation.

_____ 3. Discussing a book he had read independently.

_____ 4. Participating in a discussion about a topic of personal interest.

_____ 5. Describing an article she read in the daily newspaper.

_____ 6. Browsing in the classroom library.

During reading class the student

_____ 7. Volunteered to read a passage aloud.

_____ 8. Participated in a discussion of the assigned reading.

_____ 9. Looked up the meaning of an unknown word in the dictionary or glossary.

_____ 10. Expressed an interest in reading further about the topic.

_____ 11. Identified an application of an idea from the assigned reading to his own life.

_____ 12. Appeared confused or unsure about the assigned reading.

During an oral reading activity the student

_____ 13. Listened attentively.

_____ 14. Answered or asked questions about the material shared.

_____ 15. Volunteered to take a turn reading aloud.

FIGURE 4.3. Teacher's Observation Checklist

about rodeos). Such observations belong in an anecdotal record to be used later when planning a science lesson or locating books for the classroom library.

Interviews and Conferences

Of the various approaches suggested here for assessing attitudes toward reading, perhaps the most difficult to arrange is the personal interview. It is a very time-consuming activity to meet periodically with each child in a classroom. In addition, the problem of keeping the other children in a classroom productive while a teacher sits with one child may seem overwhelming.

Even though there is no magical solution to these issues, a one-to-one session has the greatest potential from an assessment standpoint. Surrounded by the information gathered from questionnaires, incomplete sentences, or observations, a teacher can explore what all the indirect information means. Straightforward questions can be asked: "Do you enjoy reading, Henry? What kind of books do you prefer? Do you read at home? Does anyone ever read to you?" Reasons for a negative attitude can be sought: "What do you dislike most about reading? What causes you trouble when you read? What do you think would make reading class more enjoyable? Why?"

Questions such as these can be asked on a written questionnaire, of course, but children may be hampered by their inability to express themselves in writing. The personal attention they receive in a conference or interview should encourage the child to speak freely. The sensitive teacher is able to read nonverbal cues in a face-to-face meeting that may provide insight not possible otherwise.

Some may believe that all this is well and good but irrelevant, because interviews are virtually impossible to arrange. Several suggestions should make it clear that interviews can be managed. First, not everyone has to be interviewed. Although it is desirable to organize an instructional program around conferences, a teacher may choose to interview only children whose attitudes are a cause for concern. This plan should reduce a teacher's interview load by half or even two thirds.

A second suggestion is described in greater detail by Harris and Smith (1986). They suggest that conferences be made a part of the weekly schedule with time set aside for perhaps two or three short conferences per week. Other children are given time to read a book of their choice silently for the twenty or thirty minutes this involves.

Other possibilities exist of course (such as using aides to free the teacher for conference time, holding conferences before or after school or during library period), if the idea of meeting with children one-to-one is a priority.

Alexander and Filler (1976) suggest that interviews be structured to some extent. This can be accomplished by completing a questionnaire or a complete-sentence device orally with the child or by using a set of prepared questions.

Published Reading Attitude Scales

An advantage can sometimes be gained by using assessment instruments that have been developed by specialists and subjected to reliability and validity studies. Alexander and Filler (1976) summarize a number of published attitude assessment instruments. Among the better known questionnaires they describe is a twenty-five-item inventory designed for use in first grade through sixth grade developed by the Department of Education, San Diego County, San

Diego, California. Known as the *San Diego County Inventory of Reading Attitude* (no date), the instrument has been examined for validity through item analysis procedures and has an established .79 split-half reliability. The inventory is not unlike the questionnaire presented in Figure 4.1. The child is asked to answer yes or no to questions such as "Do you think that reading is the best part of the school day?" and "Do you like to read catalogues?"

Another well-known instrument designed for third grade through twelfth grade and having a five-point scale (strongly agree to strongly disagree) was developed by Thomas H. Estes (1971). The *Estes Reading Attitude Scale* is a twenty-item instrument consisting of statements such as "Most books are too long and dull." The scale was developed through tryout and selection of items having demonstrated validity. Reliability estimates on a split-half basis were reported to be satisfactory.

A more extensive inventory having seventy items was developed by Kennedy and Halinski (1975). Although designed for secondary grades only, the extraordinarily high reliability reported for this survey (.94) makes it a good model for teachers at all levels by suggesting a broad range of item types. Kennedy and Halinski use a four-point Likert-type scale.

Alexander and Filler (1976) presented two attitude scales by Betty S. Heathington that are designed for use with elementary-age children. The Heathington Primary Scale uses a unique answer format that appears to have special value with young children. As the teacher reads a question (for example, "How do you feel when you go to the library?"), children select a face that represents their response.

The Heathington Intermediate Scale uses a strongly agree—strongly disagree type scale with five points. The Primary Scale includes twenty items and the Intermediate Scale twenty-four items.

Another published inventory by Askov (1973) designed for primary-age children does not require reading or writing ability and reports high validity and reliability.[5] We believe published instruments of the type described here can be of value but prefer to see teachers develop their own instruments whenever possible. With experience, teachers will probably feel more comfortable using devices they have made.

Assessing Children's Interests

Reader interest is of primary importance in considering motivation to read. With respect to intrinsic factors, probably no other variable energizes a person to act in so strong a way as interest does. High personal interest in seeing a rock concert will cause people to stand in line for hours or even days to get a ticket. Interest in seeing one's offspring perform explains the unusually large crowds at those PTA/PTO meetings that feature children performing, as in a music festival. Personal interest accounts for the popularity among 10-, 11-, and 12-year-old girls for Judy Blume's books dealing with the approach and onset of puberty.

If further support is needed, consider how you spent your leisure time last weekend. There is a very good chance that personal interest accounted for a fair share of that time. If you are an avid skier, you probably skied a lot. If you enjoy gardening, hiking, jogging, sewing, playing backgammon, or strumming guitar, one of these activities may have occupied your time.

Children behave very much as adults when it comes to what they like to read. The girl scout who is working on a merit badge for woodworking will be attracted to a magazine article on how to select the correct sandpaper (if she faced that dilemma). Another child with different interests would lack the motivation to read the same article and, if forced to do so, would probably find it irrelevant and maybe even meaningless.

To motivate the second child to read the article on sandpaper, an external motivation would be required. Personal interest becomes important even in this case, however. Offer a child a chance to earn tokens that can be exchanged for free time building a model race car as a reward for reading the article on sandpaper and it may elicit a positive response—motivation. Make the reward a chance to earn a gold star or even a good grade in reading for the day and motivation may go by the boards (on the assumption that these are not meaningful rewards). Personal interest—or personal payoff—is a major factor in motivation at all levels. The classroom teacher needs to know how to identify topics that interest each child and how to capitalize on those interests in planning instructional activities.

An Interest Inventory

Teachers often use interest inventories to collect valuable information that can be used to locate reading material geared to individual student interests. The incomplete sentence approach described in the previous section is readily adaptable to surveying interest. Items can be constructed that probe many aspects of the child's life for possible interests. Use of leisure time is often an index of personal interests, for example. A sample interest inventory based on incomplete sentences is presented in Figure 4.4.

Interest can also be surveyed through the use of a questionnaire. We recommend the use of a five-point scale on an interest questionnaire to provide students with an opportunity to express the strength of their interests. A sample interest inventory using a questionnaire format is presented in Figure 4.5.

Records of Recreational Reading Habits

One particularly good source of information about student reading preference is a record of books they have read previously. Such information can be gathered in a number of ways, the simplest being a log or journal kept by students showing the title, author, and date on which a book was started and completed. A record of this sort can easily be passed from teacher to teacher as students progress through school. Sometimes children can be enticed into writing a brief reaction to the book by each bibliographic entry. These reactions serve to focus on a child's level of interest in the topic and provide an indication of his willingness to

Name _____   Age _____   Date _____

DIRECTIONS: Complete each sentence in whichever way describes you best.

1. My favorite television show is _____.

2. My favorite kind of music is   _____.

3. If I could get one person's autograph, I would most prefer _____

_____.

4. On the weekend I like to   _____

_____.

5. My favorite sport is   _____.

6. I like to read about _____.

7. My favorite magazine is   _____.

8. The part of the newspaper I read first is _____

_____.

9. The best book I ever read was _____.

10. I like to collect _____.

11. I enjoy movies about _____.

12. Most evenings I   _____

_____.

13. If I had three wishes they would be

a. _____.

b. _____.

c. _____.

FIGURE 4.4. Interest Inventory Using Incomplete Sentences

read more along the same line. For example, a teacher can see at a glance that Cheryl preferred romantic novels and historical fiction set in pre-Civil War days. Science fiction, on the other hand, received a less than enthusiastic reception.

Another approach to tracking reading habits is to first develop a list of topics and then record titles of books read by a student under the appropriate category. As titles accumulate in one area, a teacher gains a sense of the student's reading preferences. Possible categories might include sports, humor, adventure, romance, travel, biography, nonfiction, hobbies, and so forth.

A unique record-keeping form might show a floor plan of the school library. Students could indicate where in the library they found each book they have read by pasting a gold star on the form in the appropriate spot. Stars clustering in the reference section would indicate a student is interested in books of world records, perhaps, or how-to books.

These examples only suggest the types of record-keeping devices a teacher can employ to identify what a child is reading. Although the focus here has been on records of books read, personal interests may be reflected even more directly by the types of magazines, brochures, and other nonbook materials that students read. Here, too, a log of what has been read recently would be useful to the teacher in understanding a child's interests.

FIGURE 4.5. Interest Inventory

Name _____   Age _____   Date _____

DIRECTIONS: Place a check in the column that indicates how the statement applies to you.

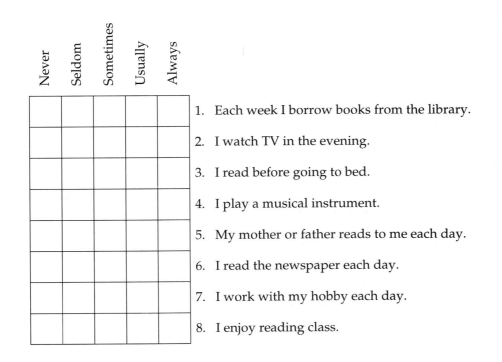

Never	Seldom	Sometimes	Usually	Always	
					1. Each week I borrow books from the library.
					2. I watch TV in the evening.
					3. I read before going to bed.
					4. I play a musical instrument.
					5. My mother or father reads to me each day.
					6. I read the newspaper each day.
					7. I work with my hobby each day.
					8. I enjoy reading class.

Teacher Interviews and Observations

Whether structured as an interview or left more open to general observation, a teacher's interactions with students offer many opportunities to gain a feel for their personal interests. In an interview a teacher may get an idea of students' interests by asking a general question about what hobbies they enjoy or what television shows they have watched lately. Even a friendly invitation to "Tell me about yourself, Ann. What are some of your interests?" will be sufficient to gain insights about an individual's interests not ordinarily available in a group instructional setting.

Teachers can also identify topics that interest students by watching their reaction during a lesson (that is, their reaction to a book or story that is being discussed or their level of involvement in a discussion of upcoming school and community events, such as an athletic event, an election, a circus, or a band concert). Before and after class, teachers can often detect interests by merely observing students interacting informally with their peers. Teachers who themselves participate in such conversations and reveal some of their own interests and activities to students often find a greater willingness by class members to share information about their out-of-school lives.

Assessing Self-Concept

Self-concept can be assessed in exactly the same way as attitudes and interests. Incomplete sentences are especially useful and can be constructed to focus primarily on reading self-concept or on self-concept in general. Some sample stems are given below:

1. People usually think I'm _____
2. When I read out loud my classmates _____
3. I'm good at _____
4. I'm not good at _____
5. Learning to read is _____
6. When I fail at something I _____
7. When I try something new I _____
8. My teachers think I'm _____
9. My parents get upset when _____
10. The thing I do best is _____

Teacher observation is probably the best assessment strategy with respect to self-concept. Quandt and Selznick (1984) suggest that teachers pay particular attention to comments children make about themselves and watch for children's reactions to daily interactions. Apparent lack of interest and concern must be viewed as possible indications of poor self-concept. Children's reactions to a disappointment or failure can be a particularly revealing event for the watchful teacher as can the willingness to volunteer answers. Obviously, level of confidence is directly related to self-concept. Reluctant risk takers who seem unsure of themselves often have poor self-concepts as do children who ask excessive questions about an assignment.

CAUTIONS ABOUT ASSESSMENT IN THE AFFECTIVE DOMAIN

Any kind of assessment is subject to a certain amount of error. Assessment conducted with human subjects is particularly difficult. Some important principles of assessing reading are offered in Chapter 14, Assessment Principles Applied to Remedial Reading. In the present chapter there is an even greater concern with respect to errors in assessment. That is to say, the attempt to assess human feelings is even more difficult than the assessment of human cognition. The fact that it is difficult makes it no less important, however.

Teachers must resist the temptation to ignore the affective domain on the grounds that error can creep into the assessment. Rather, the possible sources of errors must be recognized and special effort taken to keep them to a minimum. Teachers must also interpret affective assessments with special caution in recognition of the limitations described here.

Possible Sources of Assessment Error

To be helpful, information that will be used in planning classroom activities must be reliable. As will be discussed in Chapter 14, reliability is concerned with consistency. In addition to the usual factors that affect the reliability of test results, the affective domain presents another consideration: Human feelings change or can vacillate over relatively short periods of time. This means that information gathered from a well-designed questionnaire on personal interests may be out-of-date soon after it is collected. The very act of responding to the questionnaire may cause introspection that triggers a resolution by respondents to broaden their interests. It is also likely that they are unsure what they think about some matters. One day they might cite several interests; the next day, in a different frame of mind, they might respond more selectively. Attitudes and self-concept are probably more stable than interests but are nevertheless subject to the same fluctuations.

One way to deal with reliability is to use recent information only, thereby acknowledging the likelihood of change over time. Another solution is to use information from several sources so the teacher is not depending on a single questionnaire or interview to give an accurate picture. Finally, the length of any data collection device should be sufficient to gather an adequate sample of responses. For example, Alexander and Filler (1976) recommend no fewer than twenty items on a questionnaire.

Reliability is one of several important considerations with respect to accuracy in assessment. A second factor of equal importance is the concern for validity—whether an instrument measures what it claims to measure and, from an application standpoint, whether that measure is of practical value. Because of the scarcity of well-developed instruments of established validity, there is no simple way of studying the validity of new instruments. Statistical validity established by correlating the results of a teacher-made device with some widely accepted measure is not possible, for example.

In assessing affective factors, care should be taken to avoid getting socially acceptable responses from students. What may be called a measure of student attitude toward reading, for example, may actually measure students' ability to figure out what the teacher wants to hear ("I like books"; "I enjoy reading"; "I read a lot"). Validity is highest when students understand that the results will be used in their own best interests and when trust between student and teacher is high.

Another consideration when paper-and-pencil instruments are used is the students' ability to read and write. Inability to read the items on a questionnaire obviously prevents children from giving valid responses, as does the inability to express honest thoughts in writing when confronted with an incomplete-sentence task. Obviously, shyness or suspicion can affect what children share even in an interview. Again, student trust is critical. Validity can also be increased if provisions are made to help students respond to the task without prejudice. The questions can be read aloud by the teacher, for example, and responses can be dictated to an aide or volunteer parent.

Validity will be improved if the teacher has a clear notion of what an attitude is and how it is reflected in children's actions, verbal and nonverbal. The same is true of interests and self-concept. Beyond that, the best assurance of validity is the corroboration gained by comparing results across a variety of sources and the emergence of patterns over time. Teachers should be diagnosticians seeking to put information together for the purpose of formulating a hypothesis.

SUMMARY

This chapter looked briefly at theories concerned with how motivation occurs. It distinguished between external and internal motivation, and it suggested that success is the key to internal motivation. When constant failure is experienced, children become passive, feeling helpless about their ability to control the factors that cause their failure. In such cases internal motivation dwindles and the teacher is faced with manipulating external rewards to encourage a child to respond.

The assessment of motivation is best pursued on many fronts, using both published and teacher-made devices. Although difficulties exist in measuring elusive often-changing factors related to motivation, the teacher can gather information on attitudes, interests, and self-concept that is useful in determining how to approach the child who seems unmotivated.

Suggested Activities

1. Select a character such as Rocky Balboa from a popular book or movie. Analyze the character from the standpoint of motivation. Identify what goal or goals the character seems to be pursuing in the story. Make a list of internal or intrinsic and external or extrinsic rewards that you believe motivate the character.

2. Develop a questionnaire that asks respondents to reveal their attitudes about some topic of current interest, such as types of music, political preference, career opportunities, physical fitness activities, or other topics where opinion can vary. Ask several acquaintances to complete the questionnaire. Ask for feedback on how the questionnaire could be more comprehensive, less obtrusive, longer or shorter, and so forth. Revise in accordance with these suggestions and ask several more people to complete the

revised version. Summarize what this experiment has taught you about the development of attitude surveys.

3. Arrange to interview a colleague concerning his recollections of learning to read. Focus your questions on the extent to which success or failure with classroom reading instruction affected his self-concept as a child. Relate those feelings to the person's current attitude toward reading for enjoyment.

Suggested Reading

AMES, R., and AMES, C. (Eds.) (1984). *Research on Motivation in Education* (Vol. 1): Student motivation. New York: Academic Press.

AMES, R., and AMES, C. (Eds.) (1989). *Research on Motivation in Education* (Vol. 3): Goals and Motivation. New York: Academic Press.

Includes a collection of articles that focus on a cognitive view of motivation. Examines a wide range of motivational issues in the classroom.

JOHNSTON, PETER H., and WINOGRAD, PETER N. (1985). Passive failure in reading. *Journal of Reading Behavior, 17,* 279–301.

This article presents a conceptual framework for understanding how children who have difficulty with reading react to repeated failure. The authors draw on the notion of learned helplessness as a way of explaining the self-defeating behaviors such children exhibit. Suggestions are given for preventing and overcoming what the authors refer to as passive failure in reading.

QUANDT, IVAN, and SELZNICK, RICHARD (1984). *Self-concept and Reading.* Newark, DE: International Reading Association.

Discusses the relationships between reading and self-concept. Techniques and strategies that an elementary school teacher can employ to improve self-concepts while teaching children to read are described. Tests and informal observation procedures that can be used to diagnose self-concepts are presented.

STIPEK, D. J. (1988). *Motivation to Learn: From Theory to Practice.* Englewood Cliffs, NJ: Prentice-Hall.

A practical guide that offers readers an understanding of theories of achievement motivation and the application of these theories to educational settings. Special emphasis is placed on strategies that can be used to motivate students in school.

WIGFIELD, ALLEN, and ASHER, STEVEN R. (1984). Social and motivational influences on reading. In P. David Pearson (Ed.), *Handbook of Reading Research* (pp. 423–452). New York: Longman.

Summarizes and synthesizes research concerning how motivation and socialization are related to learning to read. Reviews achievement motivation theory as it relates to reading and discusses the influence of home and school on motivating performance in school. Examines the effects of repeated failure on children's willingness to strive and offers suggestions for the classroom teacher in coping with learned helplessness.

Notes

1. See Maslow (1970) and White (1959).
2. See Klausmeier and Ripple (1971).
3. See Bristow (1985).
4. See Johnston (1985).
5. Other published instruments of note include those by Sartain (1970) and Gallian (Cooper, Cooper, Roser, Harris, & Smith, 1972).

CHAPTER 5

INCREASING MOTIVATION

Overview

As you read this chapter use the following list of main ideas to guide your study and reflection.

- Most children are motivated in learning to read by the success they experience with the school reading program. Brian Bussell is a typical example.
- The motivation that normally accompanies success can go astray when repeated failure is encountered, as in the case of Debbie Howard.
- Some children who have experienced success with reading may still need special attention in the area of motivation, as in the case of Sam Brady.
- Behavior modification is an approach to motivation that uses external rewards in a systematic fashion to shape desired behaviors.
- Specific ideas worth trying as motivational devices are described in this chapter, such as the teacher reading aloud, peer tutoring, cooperative learning, using games in the classroom, and using the daily newspaper.
- Letter grades have very limited value in motivating children, especially unsuccessful readers.
- Parents and teachers working together can help students reach their full potential.

This chapter considers how a teacher of reading can approach the challenge of motivation. The previous chapter made the point that many children are largely self-motivated; that is, they approach learning to read with confidence and a desire to achieve competence. An approach to reading instruction that recognizes and capitalizes on that predisposition seems advisable in those cases. The teacher will want to help self-motivated students see how their personal needs and interests can be realized through reading (for example, recreation, problem solving, gathering information). The teacher will also want to nurture the positive feelings self-motivated students have about themselves as competent readers through praise and the maintenance of record-keeping devices that document growth and progress. In this way the self-satisfaction that motivates such students continues. Their history of successful experiences with reading will enable them to persist in the face of occasional disappointment and difficulty.

BRIAN BUSSELL: A SELF-MOTIVATED READER

Brian Bussell represents a case of self-motivation. As a 10-year-old, Brian entered fourth grade having had a series of successful experiences with reading. He learned to read without trauma beginning in first grade, but even prior to entering school he had happy, reinforcing experiences with books in the company of a parent or grandparent who enjoyed holding Brian and sharing a story with him. He took naturally to the daily reading and writing activities given by his teacher to help him acquire and practice certain skills. He found such tasks relatively easy, in fact, and almost always completed them on time and with accuracy.

Brian also enjoyed reading aloud and received praise consistently for having good expression. He joined in discussions about the stories his reading group completed every day, giving evidence through his comments that he readily understood the characters and events. During free time in school and in the evenings at home it was not unusual for Brian to read a book for recreation. In fact, he had a collection of paperback books he had purchased over the years with money given to him by his mother for that purpose.

When Brian first experienced difficulty reading the fourth-grade science textbook used in his school, it was surprising and somewhat frustrating to him. He found the vocabulary to be difficult and the concepts rather abstract. The science book also had diagrams and charts unlike anything he had seen in books before. He was tempted to give up at first and wanted to avoid science. But with the teacher's help he discovered that he was not alone in his difficulty; several other good readers were also struggling. Brian's teacher seemed supportive and understanding concerning the problem he was having and offered help in the form of study guides that gave Brian direction in reading the book. With the teacher's guidance he gradually grew more confident. A breakthrough of sorts occurred when the class began studying fossils and Brian remembered a rock he had found during a hike on vacation the previous summer. He brought the rock to school and learned that it was truly a fossil. Science took on a new meaning and the information found in books took on new importance for Brian.

This anecdote illustrates several important points. First, it suggests that many children succeed with a rather routine, conventional approach to beginning reading instruction. It is, in fact, the exception that a child does not succeed. A second implication is that motivation is not a special problem for many children. Their readiness for reading and the importance attached to learning to read will prompt most children to attend to assigned tasks so long as they continue to be successful. (This is not to suggest that a teacher may not have to spend time occasionally explaining the nature and importance of a task to get a student to put forth effort, nor to deny the value of the teacher providing feedback on daily work as an incentive for students to complete it. We are not in any way suggesting that teachers can ignore or take for granted the motivation of children like Brian. We *are* suggesting that external rewards such as gold stars, tokens, and treats are not essential.)

Third, the anecdote suggests that even successful readers have occasions when they experience difficulty. On such occasions their history of successes encourages them to persist in the face of failure.

Finally, the teacher's attitude and skill at providing the necessary assistance are critical in helping even the self-motivated. Here Brian's teacher was patiently supportive and evidenced confidence that the problem would be surmounted. It can be inferred that Brian's teacher reminded him that he had solved such problems before and that with time and effort he would again succeed. If this response is one of acting as a cheerleader of sorts, it is also significant that Brian's teacher did more than cheer. The teacher also developed study guides and related the topic under study to something Brian had experienced firsthand (fossils). In other words, Brian's teacher did not manipulate the student but respected his need to master a task. The teacher concentrated on what could be done to support Brian's efforts from both an attitudinal and instructional standpoint.

When Self-Motivation Is Lost

Some children have lost the self-motivation to read that characterizes children like Brian. A number of explanations for this loss were examined earlier. An approach to reading that depends on self-motivation will be unlikely to succeed in these cases. Rather, the teacher will need to play a much more dominant role by consciously establishing specific goals to be achieved and identifying rewards to be earned for reaching those goals. Extrinsic motivation becomes the *modus operandi* until the child begins to see intrinsic value in reading and reading-related matters.

Two types of children can be identified among those who lack self-motivation: those who *cannot* read and do not, and those who *can* read and do not. Though the reasons for their behavior are probably very similar, in both cases the challenge is to make reading relevant to the daily lives of the students. When reading becomes a tool that helps the student solve personal problems and needs or pursue personal interests, motivation to read becomes intrinsic.

DEBBIE HOWARD: AN UNSUCCESSFUL READER

Unlike her older brother who had difficulty with reading from the beginning, Debbie was moderately successful with reading in first grade until late in the school year. Then she began to experience repeated failures; by the end of second grade, she was a remedial reader who claimed to hate reading. And the claim was legitimate. The frustration, anger, and shame she felt during attempts to read were real. Actual physical manifestations of her dislike were evident in her appearance and manner. She frowned constantly, clenched her fists, gritted her teeth, and fidgeted in her seat. A physician examining Debbie would have found a racing pulse, increased blood pressure, and shortness of breath during reading. Debbie was clearly not a candidate for motivation techniques that appealed to her missing desire to master the important task of reading.

The best avenue open to Debbie's teacher is to identify specific tasks that can be achieved quickly and successfully for the attainment of a specific reward. As much as possible, the tasks should not obviously be connected to reading, at least not to reading as she has come to know it. And, most important of all, the teacher should identify topics and activities that reflect Debbie's personal interests as a means of gaining her attention and participation. It is important to remember that Debbie is not without motivation. Although she has failed at reading, she likes to engage in other activities such as roller skating or bird watching, for example. It is through these areas of interest that the teacher can approach Debbie, gain her trust, establish rapport, and rebuild what is bound to be an unstable self-concept. Gradually the planned activities can be brought around to recording events and ideas in writing, listening to information the teacher shares from a book, and finding ideas in magazines relevant to Debbie's interests.

The teacher still has one additional problem even after she has gained Debbie's trust and nurtured her self-concept: Debbie does not read successfully. For some reason, toward the end of first grade, Debbie experienced repeated failures with reading. Until Debbie learns to construct meaning from the printed page, the activities described above will only work on the symptoms of the deeper problem. In reality, motivation and instruction cannot be separated as is commonly done in texts like this one. Restoring Debbie's intrinsic motivation to read necessarily involves dealing with the problem that caused her to stop trying in the first place.

In Debbie's case, she was doing reasonably well in first grade reading until late in the year. Was something introduced to her group at that time that explains her difficulty? Was there a new skill or set of skills she could not learn? Or was there a change at home that distracted Debbie and caused her to fail? Could the problem be related to a vision or hearing defect that flared up in March? These questions probe for a possible cause of Debbie's failure. In most cases there are a number of causes that interact. Taken singly, each factor is probably insufficient to cause a major breakdown but combined, they exacerbate the problem and cause defeat for the child. That is exactly what happened in Debbie's case.

An analysis of the situation reveals that late in the school year Debbie's reading group had reached the heavy word identification phase of the first grade skills program. What had been a whole word approach shifted to synthetic word analysis with emphasis on identifying isolated sounds. Debbie found this to be a difficult task that confused and frustrated her.

At the same time Debbie's parents began a difficult marital breakup. Her father moved out of the house and visited with Debbie and her brother only on weekends. The trauma associated with this separation and divorce worked directly on Debbie's feelings of security, distracting her with thoughts of home.

Unfortunately, Debbie also experienced a low-grade ear infection late in the school year that went undetected altogether. The immediate result was difficulty hearing and a feeling of listlessness. A mild hearing loss in one ear was the long-term result of the infection.

A special reading teacher began working with Debbie early in third grade. By piecing together the available evidence, the teacher developed a general picture of what led to Debbie's difficulties with reading. What she was confronted with was a child who read well below her peers, disliked reading intensely, and resisted putting forth any effort related to learning to read.

At first, the teacher concentrated on getting to know Debbie better, learning about her personal interests, her attitudes toward school and reading, and her self-concept. Debbie's interest in roller skating became the key to establishing a point of contact. The teacher arranged to take Debbie roller skating at a local rink one Saturday afternoon. There she learned that Debbie wanted very much to have her own pair of skates. The teacher suggested that they gather some information on the cost of various brands and types of skates from sales brochures and catalogs available at the rink and at a local sporting goods store. They developed a chart that displayed information about each skate according to categories such as cost, color, and features (type of eyelets for lacing, height of boot, etc.). The teacher suggested that Debbie dictate a letter to her parents explaining why she wanted a pair of skates, which ones she preferred, and why. The letter was written, read, and revised, and reread a number of times. Certain words were taken from the letter and written on index cards in short phrases, such as *white roller skates* and *steel ball bearings*. The teacher helped Debbie appreciate how many words she could recognize by developing a chart that recorded how many cards Debbie had learned.

The letter was shared with Debbie's parents and a suggestion made that Debbie be permitted to earn the skates by earning points for completing certain reading tasks. Reading an entire (easy) book, for example, earned ten points, completing a daily assignment two points, and so forth. Debbie's parents agreed to support the idea, and over a 2-month period Debbie earned enough points to get the skates. She also made significant progress on a number of reading and reading-related tasks that improved her ability to read independently. By documenting her progress with charts and checklists, Debbie's teacher helped her see that she could be successful with reading. By finding reading materials that related to Debbie's interest in roller skating, the teacher also sought to cultivate an intrinsic source of motivation to read. Once the cycle of failure was turned around, Debbie began to think of reading and of herself as a reader in more positive terms.

In contrast to Brian Bussell's teacher, Debbie's teacher found it necessary to manage the student using the reward system. Although she respected Debbie as an individual and sought to work through personal interests, she played a much more overt role in deciding what should be done and motivating Debbie toward those ends. She did this in a humane way, to be sure, but still made the instruction teacher-directed.

SAM BRADY: A RELUCTANT READER

"You won't get away with that when you're in school next year," was a threat Sam Brady heard from his mother dozens of times before starting first grade. As a result, he entered school full of resentment and apprehension concerning what he would encounter there. As fate would have it, Sam's first teacher was a no-nonsense type who assumed all children were guilty until proven innocent. She approached reading instruction strictly from a standpoint of drill and memorization.

Over the years she had developed a fairly intricate system of rewards and punishments that enabled her to gain and hold a pupil's attention. The child who could accommodate her approach would learn to associate spoken words and their printed counterparts, to mark long and short vowels, to divide words into syllables, to find main ideas, and so forth.

Sam learned to read partly from sheer repetition and partly from working to receive good grades. The good grades kept his parents and his teacher off his back. He understood the system of doing Job A to earn Reward X because he faced it at school and at home. "Do this homework page correctly and earn a chance to play outside at recess." "Dry the dinner dishes every night and earn a week's allowance that could buy candy and a ticket to a movie." It was not very long before Sam approached nearly every situation with a "What's the payoff for me?" attitude.

In second grade Sam's teacher quickly saw that he had become dependent upon extrinsic rewards. She set up a contract system involving various treats and privileges that could be earned by Sam for completing certain work. He thrived in that environment, reading many stories and completing many modules of work to receive his payoff.

All of this seemed quite innocent and functional because Sam was learning to read nicely, if recognizing words and gaining an author's message were all that one considered. What Sam was not gaining was any intrinsic appreciation of reading. Reading was simply a means to an end for Sam; unfortunately the end was not self-satisfaction or self-improvement but some concrete rewards.

All of this began to come apart when Sam entered third grade. His teacher was in her second year of teaching and full of fresh concern for individualizing reading instruction. The teacher implemented a free-choice reading program involving self-selection, self-pacing, and teacher-pupil conferencing, as described by Ryder, Graves and Graves (1989), Roser and Frith (1983), and Spiegel (1981).

For many of Sam's classmates this approach proved to be optimal. Free to pick books on topics they enjoyed, previously unmotivated pupils began to read more regularly and with greater understanding. But for Sam the method was a disaster. With no extrinsic payoff for reading, Sam saw no reason to participate. His teacher exhibited patience based on her belief that some children took longer to find themselves with this approach than others. By the end of the first semester Sam still had not finished reading a single book in its entirety. Concerned that perhaps he was unable to read, the teacher asked a special reading teacher to test Sam. The results indicated that Sam could read, of course, but that he saw no need to since there was no reward to be gained by doing so.

Satisfied that Sam could read, the teacher then established a system of incentives to motivate him to read. For reading a short book Sam could earn two points. Reading a magazine article or a short story was worth one point. Points were accumulated and could be used to buy time at one of the interest centers the teacher had created in several classroom locations. One center housed games such as Monopoly, Clue, chess, checkers, and so forth. Another center contained art supplies to make a special project. Other centers were designed to appeal to a variety of interests: handicrafts, model buildings, and even an animal center with gerbils and an aquarium, for example.

Sam began to read again for the chance to earn one of these rewards. But the teacher realized this short-term solution failed to address the problem of getting Sam to read for his own satisfaction. So along with the program designed to award points, the teacher instituted two additional ideas. First, she created interest groups that periodically brought together pupils who were reading about similar topics for the purpose of book sharing. Here the aim was to promote discussion about books read that would cause others in the group to become interested in something someone else had enjoyed.

The teacher also used interest inventories and pupil-teacher conferences to discover how Sam spent his out-of-school time. This, in turn, suggested school activities that would capitalize on Sam's established interests. Those activities initially focused on exploring the topic through various means, such as viewing films and videotapes, and later turned to reading and reading-related activities.

You will recognize this strategy as the one used in the previous case by Debbie Howard's teacher with the topic of roller skating. Finding a way to connect schoolwork with the child's world is basic to cultivating intrinsic motivation. In Sam's case, short-term goals could be reached by providing extrinsic rewards. He was willing to read a book to earn a reward, just as Debbie was willing to do written assignments to earn points that could be exchanged for a pair of roller skates. But Sam and Debbie both needed to value reading personally, for their own ends, not because their teachers thought reading was important.

Teachers are sometimes fooled by some pupils' apparent lack of involvement in school activities. "Sam isn't interested in anything" is sometimes heard. What teachers mean by that statement is "anything I try to get him to do in school." All children have personal interests. The unresponsive child in the classroom is often an active participant in playground conversations and out-of-school activities such as 4H, scouts, or sports. It is a mistake to conclude that disinterest in reading, math, social studies, science, health, and so forth, *in school* indicates a lazy or uninquisitive mind, however. If those subjects can be made relevant to the child's daily life and leisure time pursuits, interest can be created.

Returning to Sam Brady, his teacher discovered that Sam enjoyed sketching and painting in his free time. This insight gave the teacher the idea to make a mural that could be displayed with poems the class had written during the winter. She specifically asked Sam to include birds and animals in the mural. When he expressed concern about his ability to do this, she suggested they go to the library to find a book about how to draw animals. A useful reference was found and perhaps for the first time in his life Sam's own interests and needs provided the impetus for reading. The teacher seized this opportunity to introduce Sam to other books related to his interest in art. She suggested that Sam's parents take him to an art museum where brochures, pamphlets, and even a printed program of activities and exhibits could be obtained. These items provided information about different types of art, the lives of various artists, and so forth. This, in turn, opened up a variety of topics that Sam was willing to read about in books ranging from biographies to encyclopedias. Sam's personal interests had been used to create the motivation to read.

The approach taken with both Sam and Debbie illustrates a favorite method for dealing with reluctant readers—temporary use of extrinsic rewards for the purpose of gaining positive experiences with reading. Those positive experiences gradually cultivate the intrinsic motivation that normally grows from personal interests and the self-satisfaction gained from learning to read.

USING BEHAVIOR MODIFICATION

The use of extrinsic rewards can be an effective way to encourage students to engage in particular behaviors. Certain cautions have been expressed about the effectiveness of extrinsic rewards in reshaping long-term behavioral patterns. Evidently behavior changes that are motivated by intrinsic factors are more long lasting. Children who read a book to earn a treat, for example, will acquire a commitment to reading only if the prospect of the external reward causes behavior that comes to be valued for its own sake. Otherwise, once the treat is no longer offered, they will stop reading.

When using the behavior modification approach, the rewards offered must be ones that have value to the child. Tokens awarded for meeting goals might be used to "buy" time on a woodworking project, for example. (James Silliman)

Extrinsic rewards can be offered under any number of circumstances, some of which seem to have a better chance than others of causing the individual to internalize the motivation and effect lasting change. One approach to the use of external rewards that has proven effective in making the important transition to internal motivation has been labeled *behavior modification.*

Behavior modification is a strategy designed to eliminate undesired behaviors and reinforce desired behaviors. Reinforcement is provided on a systematic basis to shape an individual's behavior. A typical program involves the following:

1. The behavior to be modified is identified. Inappropriate behavior is targeted for elimination and desirable behavior is targeted for development.
2. The nature of the goal toward which the teacher is working is described in terms of the child's behavior.
3. The level of behavior is observed and recorded for frequency to provide a baseline against which progress can be assessed.
4. The conditions under which the target behavior occurs are identified and recorded.
5. The consequences of the target behavior are identified and recorded.
6. An intervention program designed to increase or decrease the target behavior is developed. The contingencies, that is, the reinforcers (rewards) and the conditions for receiving reinforcers are specified.
7. The program is implemented and records are kept of the target behavior.[1]

This approach takes various forms but has several basic principles that are described below.

The first principle is critical to the subsequent internalization of motivation: The individual whose behavior is to be modified must help establish the need for change. Ideally the individual initiates this step himself (for example, the student says, "I'd like to stop wasting time during reading class."), but in actuality the teacher often identifies the problem and raises it for the student's consideration ("You don't seem to be getting your daily assignments done. I've observed that you spend a lot of your work time doing other things such as straightening your desk, sharpening your pencil, and so forth. I think you need to stop activities that are not related to your assignment. What do you think?"). Unless the student recognizes a need for change, helps develop a plan to alter his behavior, and agrees to the conditions of that plan, there is very little chance that long-term changes in their behavior will be effected. Once the program is over, an unwilling participant can easily slip back into old behavioral patterns. (Even *willing* participants in a program to change behavior often find it difficult to resist backsliding once the program is completed.)

A second principle underlying behavior modification programs is that changes in behavior are sought on a gradual schedule. Typically, a final behavior is approached in stages. For example, a boy who needlessly gets out of his seat twenty times a day is first asked to reduce that behavior to fifteen times a day. Next, the goal is reduced to ten times a day, and so on. Rewards are earned for meeting each intermediate goal, and steady progress is made toward the final goal (only getting out of his seat when necessary).

A third principle basic to behavior modification is establishing or selecting meaningful rewards. The child who dislikes and, therefore, avoids reading will probably not be willing to work for the reward of a book. What rewards will work vary from case to case, of course, and are limited to some extent by philosophical as well as cost and nutrition factors. Candy treats may motivate behavior, for example, but their use may be unacceptable due to health and expense considerations. Some programs with older students have gone as far as to use trading stamps and portable radios for rewards. What motivates one child may not work with another. What one teacher uses may offend another teacher. The advice to teachers in this respect is that extrinsic rewards must be attractive to the learners involved.

MOTIVATION STRATEGIES

In the folklore of teaching there are probably as many ways to motivate children to read as there are ways to cure hiccups. Popular teaching magazines such as *Grade Teacher, Instructor, Mailbox Magazine,* and *Learning* often feature articles in which practicing teachers share a variety of ideas that have been successful for them. Reading conferences invariably include sessions on motivating students who are experiencing difficulty. Publishers of instructional materials often stress the high motivational value of their products. Needless to say, this widespread concern for and attention to motivation is well-deserved. Despite the emphasis given in this chapter on intrinsic motivation, there is much to be said for using techniques and materials that make reading attractive, enjoyable, and stimulating.

What follows is a sample of various strategies a teacher can use to encourage students to read. The teacher must keep in mind, however, that ultimately motivation has to come from the learners themselves if they are to become habitual readers outside of a school setting. The activities presented here can help students develop positive dispositions toward reading by providing successful experiences in reading, by making reading personally meaningful and useful, and by enabling students to become active learners.

Reading Aloud

A simple activity that has the effect of arousing student interest in a particular book or author is oral reading by the teacher (or by students who have rehearsed ahead of time what they will read). Primary grade teachers seem to be most prone to engage in this activity, but teachers at intermediate, middle, and secondary levels have employed this approach effectively. Students of all ages seem to enjoy listening to a skillful presentation of good literature. By choosing carefully what to share, a teacher can expose children of various reading abilities to literature they might not select on their own. Through discussion and explanation, student attention can be focused on the subtleties of characterization, plot development, use of language, and so forth.

Teachers who regularly read aloud attest to the power of this activity for creating interest in a book. Even students who do not read much on their own

Teachers who read regularly to their students often arouse interest in a topic and demonstrate that reading can be enjoyable. *(James Silliman)*

often ask if they can have a book when the teacher is finished sharing it with the class. Other books by the same author or on the same topic can also be introduced to a class while the teacher is sharing a particular book.

Some schools have parent volunteers share a favorite book over the span of several weeks or a month. This approach introduces variety into the read-aloud program, demonstrates that nonteachers enjoy reading too, and creates the opportunity for the parent of a reluctant reader to demonstrate the value he places on reading. If the teacher still wants to read aloud during this period, children can be given a choice as to which group they will join, the teacher's or the parent's (see Trelease, 1989 for suggestions).

See the Movie: Read the Book

Most of us have had the experience of seeing a film at a local theater or on television and then are spurred on to read the book on which the film was based. Just why this happens probably varies among people, but the responses may spring from curiosity about how the book and film compare, interest created by an actor's portrayal of a character, or the desire to relive an entertaining experience at our own pace. In any event, motivation to read occurs.

Children and adolescents often react in much the same way. Whether the film is a full-length Disney cartoon feature such as *Dumbo,* or an adventure such as *Stand by Me,* students seem to be interested in reading the book on which a film was based (or a book that is related in some way to the story and characters introduced in the film). Marketing experts have long known about this fact and have reaped the commercial benefits of products based on films. Many years ago it was *Davy Crockett*, then it was *Star Wars*, and more recently it was *Teenage Mutant Ninja Turtles* that fit this pattern.

Whereas films used to grow from books, nowadays books often grow from films or more commonly, from television programs. While teachers may have legitimate concerns about the literary quality of many books that develop from film or television scripts, children are highly motivated to read them and this provides an opportunity to cultivate the reading habit. Critical reading skills and personal standards of taste can also be developed through skillful analysis and discussion of books that capitalize on the popularity of some films and television programs. The teacher can also encourage children to see an upcoming film or television program as an interest builder in high-quality literature. Stevenson's *Treasure Island* or Wilder's *Little House on the Prairie* could be promoted in this fashion, for example.

One way of promoting greater interest in a book is to have several students who have seen a film such as Disney's *Beauty and the Beast* and have also read the book by the same title participate in a panel discussion. The teacher or student can serve as a moderator who asks questions and moves the discussion forward. This activity also promotes careful analysis and review of a book by students who are members of the panel.

Displaying Evidence of Book Reading

In an extremely useful brochure titled *50 Ways to Raise Bookworms*, Hillerich (no date) describes a multitude of ways to encourage children to read. The title of the brochure refers to one type of activity that provides visible evidence of the reading going on in a classroom. A bookworm, cut out of sections of colored paper, is formed on the classroom walls and on each section the title of a book and the name of the child who read it is written. The bookworm grows as books are completed and recorded on new sections that are added to the bookworm's body by members of the class. The body of the bookworm curves over and around bulletin boards, windows, doors, and chalkboards.

Variations of the bookworm idea can range from paper footprints on the walls that carry out a Bigfoot theme to paper leaves on branches of a tree or decorations on the silhouette of a bulletin board Christmas tree. Inventive teachers create numerous ways to highlight the fact that one student read *Madeline*, another student read *A Snowy Day*, and another student read *Peter Rabbit*. Basic to all these ideas is the fact that every child can contribute to the class project. Charts showing number of books read are not used because they make someone a winner and everyone else a loser. Competition should be deemphasized as a motivational device because it discourages the very children who are most in need of recognition for the reading they complete. We seriously doubt that contests of any sort have long-term beneficial effects insofar as encouraging the reading habit. Each child can be encouraged to do better than she has done in the past (read more books, read on a greater variety of topics), but reading to outdo a classmate has no redeeming value.

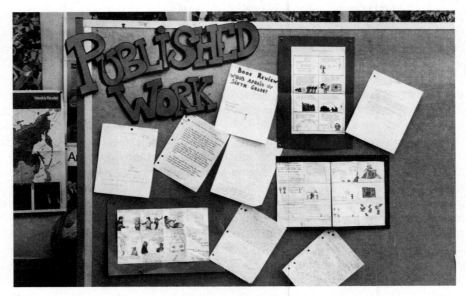

Classroom displays that show children as reading often encourage others to read as well. *(Peter Vadnai)*

Develop an Advertising Campaign

One of the most important values of book sharing is that students develop an interest in reading a selection recommended by one of their peers. Students can share their reactions to a book in a number of ways—dramatization, artwork, oral or written reports, and so forth. One means that students seem to enjoy is developing an advertising campaign designed to entice others to read a particular book. A broadly based campaign can include designing and creating an attractive dust cover for the book, writing and producing 30- or 60-second mock commercials for television and radio, writing a book review that highlights the good features of the book, dressing in the costume of a character in the book, creating a billboard display, posing as the author on a mock television talk show, and so forth. If videotape equipment is available, students might produce their own commercial. This activity can be even more fruitful if several students who read the same book cooperate on the development of the advertising campaign.

Of course, time and space should be set aside for the students to present the advertising they develop to their classmates. This gives the students a goal to work toward and exposes other members of the class to the book. The result will often be an eagerness to get and read a copy of the featured book.

Using Comic Books

At first blush it might seem odd, even self-defeating, to encourage the use of comic books in school. Comic books often compete directly with trade books for the child's time. Why, then, include a discussion on using comic books and comic strips in a chapter on motivating children to read?

First, comic books are included because they are so prevalent. To ignore comic books or to write them off as unworthy is to deny their existence. Students will continue to read them despite the contempt teachers may hold for them. Wright (1979) reported that millions of comic books are distributed and purchased annually. Primary, intermediate, and middle school students all read comic books, with peak interest existing among 12- to 14-year-olds. Consequently, it seems better to recognize the popularity of comic books and take advantage of the interest they engender.

A second reason for using comic books in school is that many of them are extremely easy to read and, consequently, can be used to help some unsuccessful and reluctant readers develop a sense of personal accomplishment. Using several readability estimates, Wright (1979) calculated that just over 50 percent of the comic books included in his sample fell below a third grade level; a number were below a second grade level. This does not mean all comic books are easy to read, of course, but suggests that children who have difficulty reading a textbook may be able to succeed with materials the teacher helps them select. Arlin and Roth (1978) caution that low-achieving readers spend most of their time looking at the illustrations in comic books so a strategy that leads to text processing must be adopted (students could act out a story reading the text as a script, for example).

Wright (1979) also reports that publishers are making use of the appeal of comic books. Holt, Rinehart and Winston, for example, has published a dictionary for beginners (*The Super Dictionary*) that includes heroes such as Superman, Batman, and Wonder Woman. The Macmillan Series r basal program including several stories published by Harr Wagner uses a comic book format to present stories of high interest that are accompanied by audiotapes with narration and sound effects. Many similar items are available from other publishers as well.

Comic strips in the daily newspaper also have high appeal to students. Some comic strips form a continuous story (*Dick Tracy, Gasoline Alley*), but others are primarily self-contained (*Peanuts, Hi and Lois*). Students can be asked to collect installments over a period of time, turning them into a book of sorts. Collections of comic strips are available in book form, of course, and these too, can be useful tools in getting students to read. Comic strips for more sophisticated ,audiences (*Doonesberry, Gil Thorp*) can stimulate discussions of current events and problem solving of a true-to-life nature.

The transition from comic book to trade book reading is not as abrupt as it may first appear. Students who have been reading comic books can read short, high-interest, low-vocabulary books such as those published by the Field Enterprise Company, for example. Topics of personal interest preferred in comic book reading (for example, humor, romance) can be reflected in the types of books offered as an alternative to comics. Words learned in comic books can be used to create a pool of known words for vocabulary study. Students can even try their hand at rewriting a comic book as a piece of nonillustrated prose. Details of setting, characterization, and plot would be added by the student as an exercise in creative writing. The books produced in this manner would be a transition reader of sorts, having greater meaning to a student who has previously read the comic book version. Reed (1988) offers suggestions for parents and teachers that can help draw students into reading as well as locating appropriate books.

Group Process Strategies That Motivate Students

Two group process strategies gaining popularity among classroom teachers are cooperative learning and peer tutoring. These strategies have been proven effective with many students and especially with low-achieving students (Wircenski, Sarkees, & West, 1990). While similarities exist between these two approaches, they are also quite different in some important ways. In cooperative learning, for example, all students work together to achieve a group goal. In contrast, with a peer tutoring arrangement, one student, the tutor, is teaching the other student. However, in both approaches, students help other students learn in a noncompetitive environment. Both approaches also have the advantage of shielding students from failure, something that is especially important to students.

The literature indicates that working in small groups may be motivating for several reasons. Glasser (1986) points out that students have strong desires to affiliate and, accordingly, often come to school to be with their friends. Thus, cooperative learning and peer tutoring provide the means for students to share and take risks without feeling that they are cheating when they help someone else learn—a fear that can occur in more traditional approaches where students work independently.

Davidson and O'Leary (1990) specify that cooperative groups are useful in a variety of ways for motivating students. Groups provide

1. *Intrinsic motives*—interest, curiosity, and desire for understanding often arise in group explorations.
2. *Social motives*—evidenced or demonstrated by statements such as "We're all in this together" and "I want to do my part well and not let the group down."
3. *Ego-integrative motives*—as when group members acknowledge, recognize, or praise each other's contributions.
4. *Sense of competence*—students in groups often develop a confidence in their own abilities to reason and to solve problems.
5. *Mutual respect*—group members learn to nurture and support one another, including those from other ethnic, racial, and social groups.
6. *Active participation*—cooperative groups foster active participation, which in itself is motivating to many students (Davidson & O'Leary 1990, p. 32).

General consensus can be found in the literature regarding the positive effect of cooperative learning and peer tutoring on achievement, intergroup relations, social acceptance of mainstreamed students, gains in self-esteem, peer support for achievement, and positive attitude toward school and the subject being studied (Slavin, 1990). Each strategy will now be discussed in greater detail.

Peer Tutoring

Peer tutoring involves placing students in one-on-one teams with one student assuming the role of the teacher and the other student assuming the role of the learner. Students of the same grade level may work together, or older students in a higher grade level may work with younger students. The pairing of older students with younger students is known as *cross-age tutoring.* Students who are involved in a peer tutoring program often show improved reading skills, gains in self-confidence, improved interpersonal skills, and gains in positive attitudes toward school and learning. Furthermore, both students in the tutoring pair show gains (Cohen, Kulik, & Kulik, 1982).

One effective means for encouraging some students to read is having them read aloud to younger children. For example, a 10-year-old reader who is reluctant to sit down with a book for his own recreation or improvement may find attractive the idea of reading to a first-grade child. The opportunity to be the person in charge, so to speak, motivates some children. Others may simply enjoy working with and helping younger children. Still others may see this as a way to break away from the normal routine of the classroom. For whatever reason, students of all ages are usually willing to spend a considerable amount of time selecting a book to be shared, rehearsing their oral reading to achieve fluency, and reading aloud to younger students. Each of these activities has potential value as a learning experience for the student, particularly if a teacher supervises each step, offers suggestions, and gives feedback on strengths and weaknesses of the student's performance.

Labbo and Teale (1990) described a study in which fifth-grade low-achieving readers were paired with kindergarten students. The fifth graders selected a book, practiced reading the book aloud for several days, generated discussion questions, and then shared the book with a number of kindergarten children. Not only did the fifth-grade students' reading improve but their self-confidence as readers grew as well.

The advantages of a program that features youth reading to youth are manifold. First, the older students often spend more time reading under these circumstances than they would otherwise. Second, the success they experience and the recognition they receive gives them confidence for reading. Third, the practice students get in reading silently and orally contributes to the improvement of their own reading even if the material is quite easy for them. They are still meeting words and phrases in various contexts and trying to convey an author's meaning through good oral interpretation. If the older students are low-achieving readers, the easy material they read may even be at or close to their own recreational reading level (this is especially good for their growth). Fourth, the younger children receive individual attention in a small group situation and are exposed to a higher level of language than they would be otherwise. Finally, the teacher of the younger children has more time to work with individual or small groups who are not participating in the read-aloud activity at the time. More detailed suggestions on how to establish and maintain a peer tutoring program are offered by McAllister (1990).

Cooperative Learning

Johnson and Johnson (1990) caution that simply putting students into groups and expecting them to work together will not necessarily achieve the intended outcomes. Instead, they believe that cooperative learning will be effective only when teachers keep the following principles in mind:

1. *Clearly perceived positive interdependence.* Each group member must feel positive about the role they played for the benefit of the group goal. They contend that the following elements are necessary to achieve positive interdependence:

   - Establishing mutual goals (goal interdependence)
   - Dividing labor (task interdependence)
   - Dividing materials, resources, or information among group members (resource interdependence)
   - Assigning individual student roles (role interdependence)
   - Giving joint rewards (reward interdependence)

2. *Considerable face-to-face interaction.* The verbal and nonverbal interactions among four to five member groups are equally important.
3. *Individual accountability.* Students must take personal responsibility for mastering the material, in addition to contributing to the group.
4. *Frequent use of relevant interpersonal and small group skills.* Students must be taught how to work together successfully—for example, listening, taking turns, and participating actively within the group.
5. *Periodic and regular group processing.* Students need to reflect on how well their groups are working to achieve their goals and analyze how they might improve their effectiveness.

The Teacher's Role in Cooperative Learning

In order to successfully implement cooperative learning in the classroom, the teacher must purposefully structure the group experience. Madden (1988) recommends that when teachers are first getting started with cooperative learning they progress through a series of steps.

The first step is to take time to build a positive human environment in the classroom. This can be accomplished by providing opportunities for students to develop positive perceptions about themselves by means such as identifying a student of the week who is featured on a bulletin board. Another activity of the same nature involves children in writing and producing their own "All About Me" book.

As a second step, students should be given the opportunity to become more aware of their classmates and to help them feel good about themselves. Units would focus on topics such as friendship, awareness, trust, tolerance, and problem solving. For example, students could interview one another for the purpose of writing biographical sketches that would be published as a classroom anthology having entries for each member of the class.

The third step involves introducing activities that have the potential to get students talking to one another on topics about which they may not share common views. Examples might include planning a class field trip or spending money earned through the PTA carnival.

As the final step, students undertake tasks in which they are asked to share the responsibility of completing a task as part of a learning team. For example, students could develop an exhibit about family leisure time activities or write a creative story. Often such activities will yield a tangible product that reinforces the positive aspects of cooperative and group effort.

Madden (1988) points out that special considerations may be necessary when low-achieving readers are placed in cooperative teams to complete a reading task. If low-achieving readers are asked to function in two areas simultaneously (i.e., completing a reading task and interacting in a cooperative group), the task should be limited to those reading skills that the low-achieving readers have already mastered until they have learned to operate comfortably in cooperative teams. Madden (1988) also recommends that initially teachers create fewer numbers of cooperative groups until children gain skill and confidence with this approach. For example, while as many as one third to one half of the students are working in groups, the remainder of the class could be involved in independent reading activities.

Similarly, Johnson and Johnson (1984) advise teachers to be conscious of what they are trying to accomplish with cooperative groups. These authors outline the following specific teacher strategies as appropriate for ensuring that cooperative learning has the desired results:

1. *Clearly identify the lesson's objectives.* The teacher must identify not only academic objectives but objectives that focus on group skills as well.
2. *Groups are constructed with specific features in mind.* The following factors should be considered in group construction:

   Group size. Generally groups should consist of three to five students. Initially, group size should only be two or three members until members are experienced in cooperative group work.

   Group ability. As much as possible, the groups should be heterogeneous in terms of academic ability, gender, and racial mix.

   Length of time group members will work together. Determine if long-term groups or new groups formed each day would be most appropriate for the lesson.

   Room arrangement. Desks or tables should be arranged so group members are able to face each other and talk.

   Instructional materials. Determine if each member requires instructional materials or whether one copy per group is sufficient.

   Group member roles. One way to ensure that everyone participates is to assign roles to each member; for example, have a member who summarizes the goals, a member who checks to make sure all other members can answer questions about the goal, a member who checks for mistakes, and a member who can ensure that group members can relate the new goals to previously learned goals.

3. *Explain the task and cooperative goal structure.* The teacher must communicate to the students the task to be accomplished, that a group goal must be

achieved, that each group member is accountable for a specified portion of the group's goal, and which evaluation criteria will be used.

4. *Monitor group effectiveness and intervene to provide academic or group process assistance.* Teachers need to monitor carefully to ensure the students are performing the tasks necessary to reach the desired goal while working cooperatively.

5. *Evaluate group achievement and assess how well members collaborated together.* The group product should be evaluated. Students need to determine if their collaboration was productive.

Programs That Use Collaborative Learning in Reading Instruction

Cooperative learning comes in a variety of forms. Many of these can be applied to reading instruction. Several programs that have produced successful results are described below.

Cooperative Integrated Reading and Composition (CIRC)

CIRC was developed and designed at Johns Hopkins University by Robert Slavin and his colleagues (Slavin, 1991). This program was designed to apply cooperative learning principles to reading, writing, and language arts instruction in Grades 2 through 6. In this program, while teachers work in traditional reading groups using basals and literature-based readers, the remaining students work in teams comprised of two pairs from two different reading groups. (For example, two readers from the top-level reading group may pair with two readers from the low-level groups.) In place of workbook assignments, these paired teams work on activities such as retelling a story, reading to one another, making predictions about the outcome of a story, writing responses to a story and practicing spelling, decoding, and vocabulary. During the language arts component, students help each other in writing drafts, revising, editing, and publishing their final paper. Instruction on language mechanics is integrated within writing assignments. For assessment, students take a quiz only after their teammates have determined they are ready. Certificates are given to students based on the average performance of all team members.

In two field experiments, Slavin (1987) and his colleagues reported that the CIRC program contributed significantly to reading and language achievement in students. These results indicated that students performed better on standardized measures of reading vocabulary, reading comprehension, language mechanics, language expression, and spelling.

Cooperative Reading Teams

In Cooperative Reading Teams (Madden, 1988, Duffy & Roehler, 1986) three or four children of varying abilities and needs work together on a particular project. Accordingly, poor readers are grouped with more able students. It appears that the attitudes, motivation, and achievement of low-achieving readers improves when they meet in cooperative reading teams.

Assignments are varied within the teams to be compatible with student's abilities. However, the task undertaken by each student is crucial to the successful completion of the group project. While Madden (1988) emphasizes the use of heterogeneous groups during reading instruction, he also stresses that content area classes provide opportunities for students to work in cooperative reading teams as well.

Reciprocal Teaching

Palincsar and Brown (1986, 1989) embody cooperative learning and expert scaffolding in a procedure known as reciprocal teaching. In this strategy, the students and teacher engage in a dialogue to comprehend text. Reciprocal teaching takes place in a cooperative learning group and includes four strategic activities: questioning, clarifying, summarizing, and predicting. In this approach, the teacher first asks a question on the main content of a section of text that the teacher and students are jointly attempting to understand. This is followed by the teacher summarizing the main idea of that passage. If disagreements about meaning occur, the group rereads and discusses until a consensus is reached. Finally, the students predict what will happen in the next section of text. As the next cycle begins, students take turns assuming the dialogue leader role. Throughout this process, the teacher's role is to be sensitive to instances where insufficient scaffolding is causing comprehension problems and then provide guidance and feedback to the discussion leader and respondents.

Palincsar and Brown (1986) report that reciprocal teaching has been proven successful in large and small group settings, in a peer tutoring situation, in content area instruction, and listening comprehension instruction. Furthermore, since small segments of reading are used in this strategy, the low-achieving reader is less likely to be overwhelmed by too much reading (Richardson & Morgan, 1990). Reciprocal teaching is discussed in greater detail in Chapter 10.

Motivating with Letter Grades and Teachers' Comments

The use of letter grades and teacher's comments as motivational devices is a highly complex matter. There is no denying the fact that some students do put forth greater effort when they know a grade will be given on an assignment. The American system of schooling makes heavy use of letter grades and most parents and teachers regard them as a means for motivating students. Indeed, college admission and real-life employment often depend to some extent on the grades a student has earned in school. It seems reasonable to assume, then, that those who recognize the importance of grades in their lives will be motivated by them. Grades become the academic equivalent of the monetary reward system used in the job market.

Space does not permit a thorough analysis of the many issues surrounding the topic of grading.[2] For our purposes several conclusions from Kirschenbaum, Simon, and Napier (1971) are relevant. Generally speaking, the students who earn good grades would probably do well in school even if there were no grades. However, low-achieving students are rarely motivated by the threat of grades. The word *threat* is used advisedly because unsuccessful students hold very little hope for achieving the good grades that some students see as an extrinsic reward for a job well done. Even when they do try hard in school, low-achieving students generally expect to receive low grades because the quality of the work they produce is usually poorer than that of the better students. Low grades, consequently, become a type of punishment.

The question of low-achieving students then becomes: Is learning enhanced by the threat of punishment? For students who fail in school more often than they succeed, the answer is probably *no*. The threat of poor grades often embitters these students and causes them to put forth less effort because even their best will not be A work.

Teachers who work with low-achieving readers are in a problem situation when it comes to grading. The low-achieving student who works especially hard and makes extraordinary gains deserves an A by all reasonable standards. Yet the unreasonable standard that requires grades to be assigned on a comparative basis is typically invoked. Put in the form of a question the community might ask, the issue becomes, "How can a fifth grader (or an eighth grader, or a twelfth grader) get an A in reading when he is struggling to complete a second-grade book?"

The teacher who responds to this question by citing the progress students have made is reminded that employers, other teachers, and parents will interpret the A as a measure of their ability. "That's unfair to the students who really earned an A," the teacher hears. Following is an observation about what is at fault in this situation and several suggestions concerning how to maximize the motivational effects of grades for all students. Also described is how teachers' comments can be employed to have special motivational value.

Grading becomes a shorthand method of communicating information about a student's progress and level of achievement. The problem is that the communication is incomplete. What should be described in considerable detail gets reduced to a single letter grade. Instead of describing what the student has learned to do, what she is working on now, and what she has not yet learned in reading, science, math, and so forth, the student's performance is reduced to a simple code that has come to have a simplistic meaning in American society. The grade C designates average, B means good, and A means excellent. If the student gets an A in math, everyone is elated and the school mill grinds onward. But what does that grade *really* represent? Is the student performing well given her ability in math? What progress has she made on fractions, and has she learned the material that she did not know last grading period when she got a B in math? How was the grade determined? Does it represent the quality of daily work (including the insightfulness of her comments and questions in discussions), or is it based strictly on written work? Does neatness affect the grade received on daily written work? Should it in math? Or is the grade based solely on test performance? If so, what type of test was used? Were math concepts tested or just calculation ability? Were problem-solving abilities tested?

This line of questioning could go on, but the questions raised serve to illustrate the point: Grades obscure more than they reveal. Too many students are satisfied if they get a good grade on an assignment whether they learned anything or challenged themselves or not. Too many teachers are satisfied with just grading the papers and making an entry for each student in the grade book. The problem with grading in general and with grading as a motivational device in particular is that form is victorious over substance. Students can earn good grades by figuring out what the teacher expects. Teachers can award good grades on the basis of who parrots back the expected facts. Standards can be fixed arbitrarily and those who fall short are labeled slow or lazy. Grades can be used as leverage to motivate students. Some students respond and that seems to give the system validity; others do not and the blame is theirs.

Why have schools settled for a letter grade system as a means for communicating information about a student's progress? For a variety of reasons to be sure, but primarily because it is efficient and it makes educators think they understand its meaning. By using a system that reduces all the details down to one generalization (A, B, C, D) the teacher need not bother looking carefully at each response and deciding what it tells about the student's growth. The parent need not bother with the details either so long as good grades are received (this is relative of course—an A is good in some homes, a C in others). When poor grades are received the focus is often on improving those grades, not on getting at the cause of the learning failure. In effect, the grades become an end in themselves.

A proposed solution is to do away with grades altogether in the interest of forcing all parties involved to talk about the student's progress as an individual learner. The concerned parties include the student, her parents, and her teacher. The means for communicating include face-to-face conferences, the telephone, and the postal service. What greater motivational device is there than for the student to realize that the people she cares about are interested in her progress?

Is this proposal realistic? Not altogether. Unfortunately, society is not willing to pay the price that such a personalized educational system would cost. Teachers who face dozens of students each day simply cannot invest hours communicating with each student and parent. Nevertheless, direct contact should be valued and sought whenever possible. Descriptions of progress can be employed in place of, or to supplement, report cards and letter grades. This can certainly be the case with students having difficulty in a subject. It is these students who are most vulnerable to the damage an impersonal grading system can inflict.

Another proposal for making grades a more useful motivational device for all students is to give grades on several bases. A teacher may grade students against a fixed standard and against each other, but also against themselves. In other words, if a sixth grader is reading at first-grade level, he may receive a D or F in reading on a comparative scale, but if he is making strides and trying hard, he should receive an A on a second, personalized scale. It is preferable that no child get less than a C if he is making satisfactory progress regardless of his level of performance. In those situations in which school policy requires a low grade, a teacher can furnish additional information to help both student and parents get a more complete picture.

Some teachers supplement letter grades on report cards with checklists and written comments giving greater detail with respect to gains being made and areas needing improvement. This approach is preferred, which leads into the upcoming discussion.

Can you as a student recall the last time a professor made written comments in the margin and at the end of your paper? How did you react? Even if the comments were not entirely positive and your letter grade disappointing, you probably appreciated the fact that written comments were provided. That is how students typically react and it is amazing to learn how seldom professors give that type of feedback.

Children are no different in this respect. A teacher should write comments throughout when reading and correcting written work. It is better to read every other assignment carefully and make comments than to read every assignment and make no comments. The tone of the comments should be supportive, emphasizing things the student did well, with criticisms held to a manageable number. This approach gives students something to work on for improvement without overwhelming them. A study by Page (1958) reported that students who received written comments from teachers that were "relevant and helpful" performed better on a subsequent task than students who got no comment, or a standard comment such as "A—excellent paper." In a more recent study, Butler and Nisan (1986) also found support for the value of written comments by the teacher.

Finally, teachers' comments should focus on how the student is doing as an individual. It is more encouraging to a student to be told, "This paper shows real progress since last month. But you still need to check your spelling carefully," than the starker version, "Your spelling is terrible." Comments on written work should instruct and encourage the child on a daily basis. They should be used generously and regularly as motivational devices. They communicate far more to students concerning their progress than do letter grades.

Using Games to Motivate Reading

Children of all ages are attracted to games. Evidence of this is plentiful at Christmas and Hanukkah time when games of various types are given. Electronic games have been especially popular in recent years. Teachers have long appreciated the high interest games have for children. Authors such as Daniels (1971), Cleary (1978), Wagner and Hosier (1970), and Spache (1976) have described ways in which games can be incorporated into the reading curriculum in a substantial, not superfluous, way.

Games can contribute to the development of reading ability in several ways. First, many games call for some limited amount of reading, such as reading the directions for the game (this is usually an exacting kind of reading requiring careful attention to detail), reading labels on a playing board, reading cards that the player draws during his turn, and so forth. Games that fall into this category are *Monopoly, Password, Junior Scrabble,* and *Trivial Pursuit,* for example.

One might reason that the amount of time spent playing a game could better be spent reading a book if practice with reading is the goal. But children enjoy variety and a well-rounded reading program ought to have room in it for various types of activities. The kind of reading students engage in while playing a game does illustrate directly the value of reading in a way they should find personally meaningful. The importance this insight may have for students and their attitude toward reading should not be discounted.

A second way games can contribute to the development of reading ability is through games that are designed specifically for reading practice. Word identification is sometimes practiced through a rummy-type card game that involves drawing word cards and matching pairs of words, for example. Or a dominoes-type game can be played with tiles that display high-frequency words that are matched. Many other examples could be given. In all cases such games focus directly on reading (usually phonics and word identification). Companies such as Milton Bradley and Ideal develop and distribute hundreds of reading games. However, it is easy to develop homemade reading games of this type. From the standpoint of motivation, students are often willing to apply themselves in a game situation while practice on the same skill through a written assignment would be met with apathy.

To the teacher who protests that school cannot always be fun (and games), the response is in the affirmative. Neither should school always be a drag. Games have their place in the overall program as a way of adding variety, but constant use of games lessens their novelty and thereby their motivational value. Games provide practice but they are ill-suited to the task of introducing or teaching a skill. That would be akin to learning through trial and error. When using reading games teachers should make sure that students practice skills correctly. For example, it makes little sense in a rummy game described earlier to have students match cards incorrectly but get credit because none of the players knows the difference. One of the players, or an observer who is fully competent at the skill being practiced, should monitor the progress of the game. Otherwise the game provides practice in performing a skill incorrectly.

A third way games can contribute to a reading program is by allowing students to associate enjoyment with school and with reading class in particular. This encourages a more positive disposition toward reading. Interviews with children reveal that doing workbooks and reading aloud often describes their strongest perceptions of what constitutes reading. If all we can add to this perception is that reading includes playing games, we have accomplished little. If the *application* of reading to uses such as playing games, following directions, and so forth can be added to other healthy perceptions of reading, the results will be worthwhile.

One other matter related to the topic of games concerns how best to use them to gain optimum motivation. Stated as a question, a teacher might ask, "Should games be a reward for students who get their work done, or should all students get to participate?" The answer is *yes* to both questions. Sometimes the opportunity to play games is effectively used to promote completion of assigned work. Daniels (1971) gives a detailed description of how a program can be established in which points are earned during the week that can be used to *buy* free time on Friday. Free time can be spent playing games. Some students will respond positively to a system of this sort.

We caution, however, that under such a plan students may never get to play games. These may be the very students who most need a change of pace and a chance to enjoy school and reading. For this reason it may be wise to have some occasions on which everyone gets to play games (particularly games that involve planned rather than incidental reading). This can be accomplished by purchasing, making, or borrowing games that relate to the instructional needs of the students. Those who need practice on phonics can play "consonant rummy" or "fish for vowels." Those who need help with affixes can play "prefix concentration." After playing a reading game or two for a set period of time, a brief free-choice period can follow, one that allows students to play any of the games (reading games or games involving reading only incidentally).

Cleary (1978) describes a variety of game and gamelike activities that could be employed in classrooms where variety is sought. The activities she describes are obviously appropriate for all learners, but some could be used to reward students who complete assigned work. No conflict is seen in using both approaches at the same time.

The Language Experience Approach

Most people have probably had the experience of coming across an old term paper, letter, or report they wrote, which they reread with much interest. That same type of interest seems to be generated by the use of the language experience approach to reading.

The language experience approach has been described in considerable detail in a variety of sources.[3] It is an approach to reading and writing instruction that involves story dictation, chart development, and group oral reading (see Chapters 8 and 10). The fact that students write (or dictate) their own stories makes this approach highly motivating.

The Newspaper as a Motivational Device

In these days of tight school budgets, it is increasingly difficult to find the funds to purchase books, games, and many other attractive materials that publishers have developed for reluctant readers. This is unfortunate because in recent years a nice array of items has become available on topics that interest children (such as motocross racing, hang gliding, deep sea diving, and so forth).

Though not as colorful, the daily newspaper is used by many creative teachers to capitalize on students' awareness of trends and fads in contemporary society. No textbook begins to approach the range of topics covered in the daily newspaper. Furthermore, the newspaper is relatively inexpensive (even free if a day-old copy is brought from home by students or if unsold copies are donated by a distributor), and constantly changing. Studies have shown that the overall reading level of daily newspapers is relatively low (often averaging about sixth-grade level) with a range of levels being represented within the same issue. This means nearly any student in a classroom can find an article, feature, or even a section that he can read. Given a high level of interest in a specific topic, students may even manage articles that would normally be difficult for them.

From a motivational standpoint, the appeal of using the newspaper is that each student's personal interest can be served. Whether it be sports, the horoscope, TV schedules, or advice to the lovelorn, the newspaper contains such a broad range of features that personally meaningful material can be found for nearly everyone.

It is beyond the scope of this discussion to explore in detail the various ways a newspaper can be used to teach reading. Cheyney (1984), Criscuolo (1981), Rupley (1979), and Gitelman (1983) are examples of resources available to help teachers use the newspaper as an instructional device. Many newspapers sponsor local programs that provide specific suggestions for using the newspaper as part of the curriculum. The American Newspaper Publishers Association Foundation, The Newspaper Center, Box 17407, Dulles International Airport, Washington, D.C. 10041, publishes a regular newsletter "Teaching with Newspapers." Also check your local newspaper—many of them have programs you can employ in your classroom.

Using Contracting to Motivate

Contracting is not a new teaching idea and seems to have a positive motivational affect on some students. As the name suggests, the teacher and student jointly develop an agreement concerning what work will be accomplished over a set period of time. The agreement is summarized in writing and signed by both parties. Typically the contract states that an agreed-upon grade will be awarded for completing the work specified in the contract. Students who contract for an "A" normally complete more work of a more difficult or complex nature than do students who contract for a lesser grade.

The rationale for contracting is based on a belief that students will be more willing to engage in activities that they help select and design. It is fundamental that contracts be truly negotiated with provision being made for the preferences and special abilities of the student. Thus, in a social studies setting the student with an artistic flair might arrange to complete a particular unit of study such as Lincoln's presidency with a mural, a collection of sketches, or a collage. The significance of these materials could be explained in a written paper or audiotape. Students sometimes work together to complete a contract, each one contributing according to their special talents.

The most obvious application to a reading situation is for student and teacher to contract for the completion of certain books and practice exercises. With a little imagination, this meager beginning can be broadened to include more active and potentially rewarding experiences. The student could agree to read aloud to a parent, sibling, or younger child for a specified number of minutes per week. The contract could include making several trips to the library, developing a bibliography of books on a particular topic, reading at least two of those books, and sharing one of them with peers in some creative manner. It is evident that contracting creates an opportunity for the student to personalize and expand the normal classroom routine. This often proves stimulating to students and has the advantage of making them responsible for their own learning within a framework approved by the teacher. A successful beginning contract can provide a foundation from which longer and more involved contracts may be built. This is particularly good for older low-achieving readers who need to feel that they are making progress and controlling their own destinies.

Parents and the Home Environment as Sources of Motivation

The strategies presented thus far have the common feature of helping to make reading important to the child. While the teacher has control over these strategies in the classroom, students still spend the majority of their time outside the school. As Henderson (1988) has pointed out: "The family, not the school, provides the primary educational environment for children." She goes on to say: "Students' attitudes about themselves and their control over the environment are critical to achievement; these attitudes are formed primarily at home, though they can be profoundly influenced by experience at school" (Henderson, 1988, p. 53). Thus, parents and teachers must work together in helping students reach their full potential.

Recently we have seen a growing public awareness of the connection between parents, teachers, and students. This is evidenced at the local, state, and federal levels (Epstein, 1991, Nardine & Morris, 1991). Additionally, we are seeing professional organizations devote columns and even entire issues of journals to inform educators of current research findings and practical ideas on the theme of parent participation (*Phi Delta Kappan*, 1991, *Educational Horizons*, 1988, *Language Arts*, 1989, *The Reading Teacher,* monthly column).

Most importantly, research findings consistently support this movement. When parents are involved in schools, there are significant advantages: improved student achievement scores, improved student attendance, improved community support for schools, and improved student motivation, self-esteem and behavior.

Moreover, research concerning parent participation has documented positive effects for low-achieving students (Henderson, 1988). Likewise, many authorities have agreed that parent involvement facilitates children's reading development (Ervin, 1982, Fredericks & Taylor, 1985, Grinnell, 1989, Roser, 1989). For example, in her landmark study, Durkin concluded that parents have a marked impact on young children learning to read. (Durkin, 1966). She concluded that parents who engage in supportive activities at home such as reading, talking, and sharing experiences can have a powerful effect on their child's reading achievement.

Fredericks and Rasinski (1990, p. 692) indicate that the current emphasis on whole language throughout the reading curriculum naturally lends itself to establishing and strengthening the bond between home and school. "Because of the whole language emphasis on the meaningfulness and functionality of reading and its goal of making lifelong readers, a strong home connection is a natural, necessary element." Fredericks and Rasinski offer the following list of projects and possibilities that have been used successfully in many schools:

1. *Journals*—Each family member contributes to a daily or weekly journal of family activities.
2. *Tape Recording*—Parents can tape record favorite stories they read to their children, and the child can later select and listen to the story again.
3. *Wordless Picture Books*—Family members can create original stories, write them down, or record them on a tape recorder to accompany wordless picture books.
4. *Calendar of Activities*—Teachers can develop individual language arts activities for several different children's books shown on the individual days of a calendar for each month of the year that families can share at home.
5. *Holiday Packets*—In connection with holiday periods, a teacher can place books, games, drawing and writing activities, and other relevant projects in a large reclosable freezer bag to be carried home by each student.

6. *Book Talks*—Invite parents to visit the classroom to share and talk about children's books they enjoyed when growing up.
7. *Videotapes*—Students can develop their own series of whole language activities for selected books and record them on videotapes that become available for students to check out to view at home.

The number and types of opportunities for engaging parents in their child's learning are numerous. Many references exist that help the teacher with her own classroom (Fredericks & Taylor, 1985, Ervin, 1982) and in assisting parents who are seeking guidance (Monson & McClenathan, 1979, Boehnlein & Hagar, 1985, Stoll, 1989, Parent Booklet Series, 1989).

SUMMARY

This chapter provided several case studies to illustrate how motivation operates in different situations. Brian Bussell's case was described as typical of the normal motivation that grows from success in learning to read. Two cases in which self-motivation had been lost were also presented: Debbie Howard, a child who experienced difficulty with learning to read in second grade, and Sam Brady, a capable, but unwilling reader. The approach used by each of these children's teachers to motivate them was described. A special approach to motivation known as behavior modification was described as were a number of other strategies, such as cooperative learning, making connections between movies and books, and using comic books in the reading program (to name a few). Letter grades were discussed with respect to their capacity to motivate, especially low-achieving readers. The importance of parent participation was presented as a means for improving student motivation, self-esteem, and behavior.

Suggested Activities

1. Take five minutes to write down some problems you anticipate having when students work together in small groups. Next, take five minutes to jot down your ideas about how you could eliminate these problems. Then, depending on your present situation, form small groups with other students, other teachers, or other interested professionals to exchange these ideas.
2. Experiment with the behavior modification strategy described in this chapter to see whether you can reduce or even eliminate a behavior you would like to avoid or increase a behavior you would like to build up. Remember to gather baseline data as a first step and then set an intermediate target that can be reached within a reasonable period of time. See how long it takes you to achieve the final objective. You may want to maintain a chart that shows progress toward your goal. If no other behavior occurs to you, consider using this strategy to increase the amount of time you devote to recreational reading.
3. Suppose that Sam Brady, the third case study reported in this chapter, had not been interested in sketching and painting but preferred to spend his leisure time fishing. How might you approach the challenge of motivating

Sam to read using the principles suggested in this and the previous chapter? Compare your approach to the approach one of your colleagues suggests. Identify the advantages and disadvantages of each approach.

Suggested Reading

BRISTOW, P. S. (1985). Are poor readers passive readers? Some evidence, possible explanations, and potential solutions. *The Reading Teacher* 39:318–325.

Presents evidence that suggests low-achieving readers are passive because of repeated failures. Offers specific suggestions the classroom teacher can follow to help such children develop active reading behaviors, thereby enhancing comprehension.

CIANI, A. J. (Ed.). (1981). *Motivating reluctant readers.* Newark, DE: International Reading Association.

Included in this booklet are ten essays written by participants in an institute on motivating reluctant readers. Specific strategies are described to help classroom teachers, reading clinicians, and parents with the task of motivation. Special attention is given to finding and developing materials that arouse and maintain interest and in using methods that cause student involvement.

JOHNSON, D. W., JOHNSON, R. T., HOLUBEC, E. J., and ROY, P. (1984). Circles of Learning: Cooperation in the Classroom. Alexandria, VA: Association for Supervision and Curriculum Development.

Features a general overview of cooperative learning. Major components included are the teacher's role, methods for teaching cooperative skills and myths about cooperative learning.

MCALLISTER, E. (1990). Peer teaching and Collaborative Learning in the Language Arts. Bloomington, IN: ERIC Clearinghouse.

Provides specific ideas of how to use peer teaching and collaborative learning in classrooms. Explains not only how to do things but the principles behind the practices.

SLAVIN, R. E. (1990). Cooperative Learning: Theory, Research, and Practice. Englewood Cliffs, NJ: Prentice Hall.

Summarizes the theory, research, and practice of a variety of cooperative learning methods. Provides detailed guidelines to apply these methods in elementary and secondary classrooms.

SPIEGEL, D. L. (1981). *Reading for Pleasure: Guidelines.* Newark, DE: International Reading Association.

Discusses the importance of a recreational reading program as a way of enhancing the regular instructional program. Emphasizes the motivational aspects of reading for pleasure and describes ways to expand reading interests through recreational reading. Provides specific suggestions for initiating a recreational reading program and for managing time and materials.

Notes

1. See MacMillan (1973) and Ringness (1975).
2. For those who are interested, an excellent book by Kirschenbaum, Simon, and Napier (1971), titled *Wad-Ja-Get?: The Grading Game in American Education,* presents a penetrating look at grading as a whole, the advantages and disadvantages of various grading systems, and a review of the relevant professional literature on the topic.
3. See Hall (1981), Van Allen (1976), Stauffer (1970), Veatch, Sawicki, Elliott, Flake, and Blakey (1979), and Harris and Smith (1986).

Instruction and Assessment for Low-Achieving Readers

Part Two expounds the main theme of this book: The classroom teacher is in the best position to identify where difficulties are being experienced by low-achieving readers. Daily instructional activities provide an ongoing opportunity to assess needs, adjust instruction to those needs, and evaluate the effectiveness of those adjustments. Instruction is most effective when it is provided in an explicit fashion that emphasizes *what* a particular skill or strategy entails, *why* the skill or strategy is important, and *when* readers would use the skill or strategy as they are reading on their own. The teacher must also demonstrate *how* a particular skill or strategy can be performed, then provide opportunities for learners to practice in guided and independent activities.

By collecting and recording information on a regular basis, the classroom teacher is in a position to determine the relative strengths and weaknesses of each child. Part Two discusses in detail how these themes are carried out in the fundamental areas of word recognition, comprehension, and vocabulary.

Overview of Reading Instruction and Assessment

Overview

As you read this chapter these key ideas may be used to guide your understanding and reflection.

- Classroom teachers can effectively assess low-achieving readers based on classroom reading tasks.
- Instruction should include demonstration and careful scaffolding for strategies that help students make sense of text. All instructional strategies are directed toward comprehension, but occasionally they focus on strategies that enable comprehension such as word recognition or vocabulary.
- To stimulate optimal reading growth, independent reading is an important part of every child's reading program.
- Students need to read material at an appropriate level of challenge.

Rosie is a fifth-grade student who is comfortable reading material that is intended for third graders. She also scores at about a 3.5 level on standardized tests. She knows her phonics and can decode fairly well. For the most part she is fluent, but she occasionally stumbles over multisyllabic words. Her biggest problem seems to be in the area of comprehension. Rosie cannot answer comprehension questions very well after reading materials in her independent reading program (mostly trade books, but an occasional basal used as an anthology). She does not seem to know when she is not understanding something; she may tell her teacher that she understands what she has read but it is clear to the teacher, from retellings, group participation, and one-on-one book talks, that she misses a lot. Not surprisingly, Rosie does very poorly when it comes to answering questions from her content textbooks.

Rosie may seem like a typical low-achieving reader to many observers. And she may be easily overlooked because she decodes fairly well. A teacher who attributed her meager comprehension to limited background experiences might be even more likely to neglect her on the grounds that schools cannot fill in all the gaps left by experience. Besides, some would argue, there just is not enough time in the regular classroom to help someone like Rosie; remedial reading, most likely down the hall in a special class, is her only hope.

We disagree. Even from our brief description we see grounds for believing that several of Rosie's reading problems can and should be addressed in the regular classroom. Even Rosie's minor problem in word recognition can be resolved by a classroom teacher. To help her gain confidence in tackling multi-syllabic words, she could become a member of a short-term "big words" group with other students in the class having similar difficulties. Working with the teacher, they can search their tradebooks, basal, and content texts for big words to bring to the group for cooperative analysis.

Rosie's greatest problem is in the area of comprehension, where she does not appear to be monitoring for meaning very well (noticing when she is and is not comprehending) and is not using fix-up strategies when her comprehension has failed. Rosie would benefit from instruction in comprehension monitoring and comprehension-building strategies, which would help her do a better job answering questions. Careful assessment of her comprehension performance on classroom reading tasks would be needed before a teacher could determine which comprehension strategies Rosie needs to add to her repertoire. Students with similar needs in comprehension might be temporarily assembled for special instruction.

Classroom teachers can assess the strengths and weaknesses of readers like Rosie on the basis of their performance on everyday classroom reading tasks. Teachers can provide effective instruction in word recognition, comprehension, and vocabulary when students with similar needs are grouped together. The term *low-achieving readers* refers to students who are reading below grade level and whose reading difficulties are interfering with their school achievement. Part Two of this book provides suggestions for assessment and instruction for low-achieving readers in word recognition, comprehension, and vocabulary. Although many of the strategies discussed are learned by better readers with minimal instruction, low-achieving readers will often need much more extensive guidance, including explicit strategy instruction and substantial scaffolding of daily activities.

The strategies outlined in this text are also fair game for reading specialists, reading tutors, and special education teachers. Instruction for these strategies could be appropriate for all readers without regard to their level of performance or the label (e.g., remedial or special education) that a system may have placed on them. It may be the case that some so-called average and above average students will also benefit from such instruction.

THE IDEAL RELATIONSHIP BETWEEN READING PROCESSES, READING INSTRUCTION, AND READING ASSESSMENT

If teachers worked in an ideal educational world with unlimited resources, they would have no need to differentiate among these activities: asking students to engage in a reading comprehension activity, instructing students on how to perform a comprehension strategy, and assessing students' ability to use such a strategy. A skilled teacher with a strong background in learning and literacy development and a range of texts varying in topic and difficulty can do all three tasks—engagement, instruction, and assessment—more or less simultaneously with a student. It would only be necessary to sit down with a student reading a passage and ask him to engage in some comprehension task, such as summarizing the passage.

Then, depending upon the student's initial success at the task, the teacher can decide how much extra instructional support (what we have called scaffolding in Chapter 2) the student will need in order to complete the task successfully. Imagine that a teacher has asked a fifth-grade student to summarize a passage from her social studies text about the first year of the Pilgrims' life in America. This scaffolding can take the form of extra clues, as in (1).

1. My guess is that a good summary would have to say something about how the Pilgrims got to this country and about how they survived their first winter.

Or a teacher could model the strategy even more explicitly, as in (2).

2. When I read this passage, I look at the first sentence and the last sentence to see if they tell me what the whole passage is about. Then I develop a working summary, such as "It is about the Pilgrims in their first year in America." Then I check the rest of the passage to see if it fits. I add to my summary or I change it depending on the new ideas I run into. So in this passage, I stayed with the first year in America idea but I added the idea of dual hardships of the tough voyage and the difficult winter.

Or it can take the form of turning an open-ended task into a multiple-choice task, as in (3).

3. Well, let me give you two possible summaries and you tell me which one you think is the best.

   - It is about the Pilgrims' voyage across the ocean to this country, their first winter in America, and their joy when Spring came.
   - It is about what the Pilgrims learned from the dual hardship they experienced—a difficult voyage and a tough winter.

Or, it could take the form of directing the students to another resource (for example, the text or their own prior knowledge), to help them with the task, as in (4) and (5).

4. I bet if you look at the first sentence in each paragraph on pages 63 and 64, it would help you to come up with a good summary.
5. Hey, wait a minute, all you have to do is to think about this for a minute and you will realize that you already know a lot about the Pilgrims and what they learned that first year. And if you can say that in a sentence or two, it might be a good summary for this passage.

Or it might take the form of offering the student some advice about whom to consult, as in (6).

6. I bet if you got together with George, and the two of you put your heads together on this (you know, you both know quite a bit about the Pilgrims), you could work out a real helpful summary.

Or it might offer a different task perspective as in (7).

7. Think of it this way. Suppose your friend George walked into class right before you were going to take a test on this passage and announced that he had not read it. What could you say to him in just a few sentences that at least would give him a clue about what was important in the passage?

In what sense can such interactions permit engagement, instruction, and assessment simultaneously? The engagement is transparent; the student is asked to perform the comprehension task. The scaffolding illustrated in each example can be thought of as instruction, or, at the very least, instructive teacher actions. Assessment enters the picture in at least two senses. First, the teacher has to judge whether or not the student's initial attempt is successful or unsuccessful (notice that on-line assessment of success results in an immediate instructional decision). Second, the amount and degree of teacher support that the student needs in order to complete the task becomes an index of the degree of independence the student has developed for this comprehension task. Such a judgment is likely to be extremely useful in planning future instructional activities.

This ideal world is all too remote from the reality that teachers face in schools. Few teachers have the time to work extensively in the kind of one-on-one situation implied in our examples. Furthermore, not all teachers have had the opportunity to study and reflect upon the learning and literacy acquisition processes for them to do such on-line diagnosis and instruction (some call this approach dynamic assessment). Realities demand adaptation of this integrated and dynamic model of engagement-instruction-assessment. Wherever possible, however, techniques that permit or even encourage such integration (for example, the instructional technique of reciprocal teaching in Chapter 10) are presented. Although such integration is always an ultimate goal, we have, for purposes of clarity, chosen to discuss instruction and assessment as separate, but interrelated, endeavors.

APPLYING EXPLICIT INSTRUCTION

Chapters 8, 10, and 12 emphasize explicit instruction in reading strategies. By explicit instruction we mean the following steps: (1) teacher explanation of *what* a strategy consists of, (2) teacher explanation of *why* this strategy is important, (3) teacher modeling of *how* to perform the strategy, (4) teacher explanation of *when* to use the strategy in actual reading, (5) guided practice, in which the teacher and students work through several examples of the strategy together using authentic text, and (6) independent practice, in which students continue to use the strategy on their own. Too often, instruction in reading consists of steps (1) and (6), with the key activities in (2) through (5) omitted. Consequently, students may not fully understand specific strategies and may not learn how to apply them when actually reading.

Teacher demonstration of reading strategies is important because many students need to see a clear demonstration of how to perform a specific strategy before it means anything to them. By demonstrating, we mean the teacher talking aloud as she performs the strategy for a group of students. Demonstrating is not easy. It is difficult for skilled readers to be explicit about mental processes that they perform automatically. However, demonstration has been found to be effective in improving students' reading performance. Chapters 8, 10, and 12 provide numerous examples of teachers demonstrating specific strategies. Although this modeling will vary from teacher to teacher, it is important that the teacher always try to be explicit about how to perform a particular reading strategy.

Guided practice is the logical follow-up to demonstrating. In guided practice the teacher and students attempt to talk aloud as they perform the just-modeled strategy with *actual text*, or what we like to call the "everyday" texts of the classroom. Actual text is stressed here because worksheets are of little use in promoting or evaluating real acquisition of important strategies. There is no guarantee that students will learn to transfer strategies practiced on worksheets to everyday texts.

Responsive elaboration (Duffy & Roehler, 1987) is an important component of the guided practice phase of instruction. As a student is practicing a strategy, the teacher asks questions as needed about the students' mental processing associated with the strategy. For example, if a child were unable to decode a word when reading aloud, the teacher might say, "Okay, you're stuck on a word. What things have you learned to do to figure out the word?" Responsive elaboration helps students understand and monitor their own processing strategies and may help them reconstruct this processing when it is not progressing as needed to accomplish a particular task (e.g., when trying to figure out an unknown word).

In addition to demonstration and guided practice, it is important for teachers to be explicit about *why* a particular strategy is important to learn and about *when* students should consciously use the strategy during actual reading. We do not propose that students consciously use specific word recognition, comprehension, and vocabulary strategies whenever they read. It is only when decoding and comprehension are not progressing smoothly (common problems of low-achieving readers) that students should think about specific strategies they can apply to facilitate their reading. Teachers should help students by being explicit about *when* specific strategies might be used.

In Chapters 8, 10, and 12 suggestions for instruction in word recognition, comprehension, and vocabulary will focus on strategies which students can apply to actual reading instead of on skills which they practice in isolation on worksheets. As mentioned above, the classroom teacher or special reading teacher can effectively provide instruction in specific strategies to groups of low-achieving readers based on diagnosed needs. Suggestions for actually implementing reading programs in the classroom and clinic are presented in Chapter 16.

INFORMAL ASSESSMENT

Chapter 8, 10, and 12 discuss teaching and learning strategies that students must acquire if they are to become fluent, thoughtful readers. In order to provide beneficial instruction, teachers need to know which strategies students already possess and which ones they need to develop. Teachers also need to evaluate student progress after instruction in order to decide whether instruction has been effective and whether it should continue or be changed.

Chapters 9, 11, and 13 discuss approaches to assessment that are informal, direct, and frequent. Teachers can use these assessment techniques to identify difficulties for the purpose of planning appropriate instruction and to evaluate students' progress in using these strategies. Informal, direct, and frequent reading-based assessment means weekly or biweekly assessment of students' performance on specific strategies while they are actually reading connected text. These informal assessment techniques provide the most valid data possible pertaining to the specific instructional strategies identified in Chapters 8, 10, and 12.

Formal reading measures typically do not provide the kind of information teachers need in order to determine the instructional needs of individual students. For example, group achievement tests provide little diagnostic information and are of questionable content validity, thus limiting their usefulness for instructional planning. Individual diagnostic reading tests (such as those reviewed in Chapter 15) and criterion-referenced reading tests (the type commonly built into basal reader programs) generally assess reading skills in isolation or in short, unnatural passages. These tests provide only a small number of items and are often based on a small sample of reading material. Consequently, these tests do not directly or adequately assess students' performance on the specific strategies contained in this text. For example, because commercially prepared diagnostic and criterion-referenced tests assess word recognition skills in isolated lists rather than in everyday texts, they are not useful for directly assessing students' ability to *apply* phonics knowledge to reading.

Informal, frequent reading-based assessment of students' reading performance has a number of important features. First, it has high content validity and is instructionally relevant. Students' performance on strategies they are learning to use with actual text can be measured directly and interpreted easily for purposes of instruction. Second, it can be very reliable. When students' performance on specific strategies is measured repeatedly with real materials, stable patterns of errors and persistent problems can be identified. Third, frequent reading-based assessment can be relatively easy for teachers to develop and use if it is based on data taken from regular classroom reading tasks. Fourth, frequent reading-based assessment is useful for monitoring students' progress and for making instructional changes on a regular basis.

Stanley Deno at the University of Minnesota and his colleagues have done extensive work with curriculum-based measurement (CBM) in schools in Minnesota. Using the everyday texts of the classroom, teachers take weekly one-minute timings on students to determine the number of words read correctly per minute. This information is used to monitor reading ability and growth and to determine instructional effectiveness. A measure like words read correctly per minute will provide a barometer of success or progress. And as long as teachers recognize that guide measures serve as a monitoring function rather than a curriculum-directing function, they can be a useful part of a complete assessment system. In several studies, this approach to evaluation and instructional change has been found to facilitate student achievement.

In Chapters 9, 11, and 13 we will focus on informal, direct, frequent, and situated measures of students' performance on word recognition, comprehension, and vocabulary strategies used when reading everyday texts. All four adjectives are important. These measures are *informal* in that they are teacher-developed rather than commercially available; nonetheless teacher assessment can be systematic, relevant, and reliable. The measures are *direct* in that they are designed to assess precisely what students need to learn or have been learning to use when reading. The measures are *frequent* in that they are collected at least several times for initial assessment and at least once per week as soon as instruction begins. The measures are *situated* in that they are based on students' performance when reading everyday text.

In some instances, such as assessment of basic sight word knowledge or knowledge of symbol-sound correspondences, we violate our own basic principles by presenting informal assessment procedures for tasks in isolation, such as reading lists of basic sight words or giving sounds for symbols in isolation. In these instances, we see the isolated tasks as quick, straightforward ways to obtain initial information about students' basic sight word and phonics knowledge. In all such cases, additional suggestions are provided for assessing this knowledge when students are reading everyday text. For example, in addition to assessing students' knowledge of symbol-sound correspondences in isolation on an informal phonics inventory, we discuss looking for patterns of errors in weekly samples of students' oral reading; this contextualized approach provides useful information about which symbol-sound correspondences are not easily applied.

The interpretation of the informal assessments must be left up to the teacher. Acceptable levels of performance cannot be recommended because such levels would be arbitrary. Even the conventional mastery levels (80 percent correct) on criterion-referenced skills tests, such as those *still* found in basal programs, are arbitrary. To interpret informal assessment data teachers must form reasonable expectations for individuals on various decoding, comprehension, and vocabulary tasks, and then use the assessment data to determine if a student's performance and overall progress are acceptable given those expectations.

Completing a Reading Difficulties Record Sheet

Chapters 9, 11, and 13 discuss many aspects of word recognition, comprehension, and vocabulary knowledge that may be important to assess for low-achieving readers. For word recognition the majority of the recommended assessment can be completed through oral reading analysis (discussed in Chapter 9) based upon everyday reading assignments. For comprehension, students' retellings or their responses to oral or written questions following everyday reading assignments can form the basis of a diagnostic profile. In vocabulary, students' ability to use contextual and structural analysis and the dictionary can often be assessed through commercially available material or by observing their use of analysis during everyday reading assignments. Students' knowledge of specific words taught for specific reading assignments can also frequently be assessed through teacher assignments or discussion.

In short, classroom teachers can gather most of the assessment needed by using regular classroom activities and materials. The only modification to the regular teaching routine involves taking notes during oral reading, categorizing questions asked, recording or taking notes about retellings, keeping additional records on various aspects of students' reading performance (as explained in Chapters 9, 11, and 13), and then analyzing these data to plan for special instruction. Figure 6.1 provides a reading difficulties record sheet that teachers may find useful in their assessment of low-achieving readers. Various aspects of this summary sheet are explained in Chapters 9, 11, and 13.

FIGURE 6.1. Reading Difficulties Record Sheet

Student's Name _____

Age _____   Grade _____

I. Instructional Level

   A. IRI

      Comments:

   B. Ongoing assessment of instructional level (from oral reading analysis sheet and comprehension questions)

      Comments:

II. Word Recognition

   A. Basic sight words not known/frequently missed (from informal test and/or oral reading analysis)

      Comments:

(*Cont.*)

FIGURE 6.1. Reading Difficulties Record Sheet (*Cont.*)

131

CHAPTER 6
*Overview of Reading
Instruction
and Assessment*

B. General word recognition strategy

    1. Student's comments:

    2. Degree to which unfamiliar words deliberately and successfully decoded
       (from oral reading analysis sheets)

Comments:

C. Phonic analysis

    1. Informal phonics inventory   Date _____

Results:

    2. Consistent errors in symbol-sound correspondence knowledge and/or ability
       to analyze 1 and 2+ syllable words (from oral reading analysis sheets)

Comments:

(*Cont.*)

FIGURE 6.1. Reading Difficulties Record Sheet (*Cont.*)

D. Structural analysis—inflectional endings and/or knowledge of affixes

    1. Informal testing

      <u>Date</u>   <u>% Correct/Comments</u>

    2. Consistent errors (from oral reading analysis sheets)

    Comments:

E. Contextual analysis

    1. Self-correction of nonsemantic substitutions (from oral reading analysis sheets)

    Comments:

    2. Automaticity/phrasing

    Comments:

(*Cont.*)

FIGURE 6.1. Reading Difficulties Record Sheet (*Cont.*)

133

CHAPTER 6
Overview of Reading
Instruction
and Assessment

III. Comprehension

    A. Comprehension monitoring

        1. Knowing when do/don't understand

        Comments:

        2. Locating sources of comprehension difficulty

        Comments:

        3. Using fix-up strategies

            a. Student's comments:

            b. Comments:

        4. General comments

    B. General Comprehension

        Comments:

(Cont.)

FIGURE 6.1. Reading Difficulties Record Sheet (*Cont.*)

C. Drawing inferences

Comments:

D. Reading for important ideas

Comments:

IV. Vocabulary

A. General knowledge (from formal test)

B. Using Context

Comments:

C. Using the dictionary

Comments:

(*Cont.*)

FIGURE 6.1. Reading Difficulties Record Sheet (*Cont.*)

135

CHAPTER 6
*Overview of Reading
Instruction
and Assessment*

D. Structural analysis

Comments:

E. Secondary meanings/homographs

Comments:

F. Learning of specific words

Comments:

G. Interest in unfamiliar words

Comments:

V. Recommendations for Special Instruction

A reading specialist provides word recognition instruction to two low-achieving readers with similar needs. (*James Silliman*)

Since these additional activities will be time-consuming, we recommend that no classroom teacher have responsibility for more than six to eight students who require special attention and that a building reading specialist assist the classroom teacher with assessment and instruction. If a teacher has more than six or eight such students, our recommendations for assessment and instruction are still viable. Record keeping, however, will be more difficult and probably less complete. Chapter 16 will address the issue of meeting students' needs in the regular classroom.

Portfolio Assessment

Another valuable part of a complete assessment system is a student portfolio. This informal assessment technique involves building a portfolio of a child's work to demonstrate progress over time. A variety of materials can be placed in a child's portfolio:

1. A chart showing a child's word recognition accuracy rate on passages of increasing difficulty
2. A chart showing a child's accuracy on comprehension questions
3. Samples of a child's writing about books read, a reading log, a record of books read in class or independently
4. Samples of daily reading assignments, special projects, personal responses to books or stories

5. Observational notes written by the teacher about the child's reading performance, and
6. A checklist of reading performance, completed by the teacher, by the student, or collaboratively (see Figure 6.2).

Portfolio assessment is useful because the tasks completed in order to create the artifacts placed in the portfolio are authentic, ongoing, and multifaceted (Valencia, 1990). Because it emerges from daily work, the preparation of a portfolio does not have to become an overwhelming task.

INDEPENDENT READING

Most teachers and reading experts would probably agree that time spent reading is important for children's reading growth. A number of research studies have documented that time spent reading at school and at home does, in fact, lead to gains in reading achievement.

Unfortunately, children do not spend a lot of time reading at school or at home. Kurth and Kurth (1987) found that students in grades one, three, and five engaged in silent reading for about 10 minutes during a 60 minute reading period. Taylor, Frye, and Maruyama (1990) found that fifth- and sixth- grade students averaged about 15 minutes of reading per day at home. Anderson, Wilson, and Fielding (1988) found that fifth-grade students averaged about 10 minutes per day reading books at home.

Independent reading should be an important component of any elementary reading program. Children need time to read at school and should be encour-

FIGURE 6.2. A Reading Abilities Checklist

	Low	Moderate	High
1. Degree to which student reads for pleasure.			
2. Success in using phonics and meaning clues to decode unknown words.			
3. Ability to decode grade-appropriate material fluently.			
4. Ability to understand what is read.			
5. Ability to express ideas orally and in writing about material read.			
6. Metacognitive abilities in reading.			

Comments:

aged to read at home. Above all, we learn to read by reading; especially low-achieving readers need to spend as much time as possible reading. A substantial amount of independent reading should be directed toward self-selected reading. Finally, we need to recognize that in moving toward independent reading, we will be increasing motivation. Students report that pleasure reading in school is particularly appealing.

Techniques to motivate students to read were presented in Chapter 5. Chapter 16 presents plans that schedule time for all students, including low-achieving readers, to engage in independent reading in the classroom. Additionally, there are booklists in Appendix A (one focuses on books for low-achievers, and the other presents a list of books from a diverse array of cultures). We hope these lists, while certainly not exhaustive, will help teachers assist readers in locating books that are interesting, appealing, challenging, and manageable.

INSTRUCTIONAL READING LEVEL

In determining materials that students can read, educators have distinguished three levels of reading: independent, instructional, and frustration. The independent level is conceptually defined as material students can handle on their own; instructional level, as material they can handle with a teacher's support; and frustration level, as just that—material so difficult that trying to read it frustrates readers.

For optimal reading growth, it is important that all reading material be at an appropriate level of difficulty; that is, challenging but not frustrating. It must be neither too difficult for students to decode and understand nor so easy that it does not provide challenging practice that will lead to growth. If readers have to struggle too much with decoding and err on too many words, their comprehension will suffer. To struggle excessively with comprehension is frustrating for any reader, but it is extremely frustrating for readers who have not experienced much success.

The term *instructional reading level* is used by reading educators to refer to the most difficult level of material that a student can handle given assistance from a teacher. Ideally, it is material that is just beyond a student's grasp, material that if scaffolded properly will lead to growth. Word recognition errors are few at this level (about 90–95 percent accuracy) and comprehension is reasonably high (they get most of the ideas in the selection). In general, reading instruction for students should be based on instructional reading level material.

It is important to point out that identifying instructional reading level is an inexact procedure. Students' ability to read material at a particular level will vary depending on their interest and background knowledge for particular reading selections. For example, a student who is generally reading on fourth-grade level may be able to read a story written on sixth-grade level if she is very interested in or knowledgeable about the topic. Consequently, using readability formulas to determine reading levels of materials will yield gross estimates at best.

Instructional reading level is an inexact yet important term. But the best way to determine instructional level is to determine how students respond to the materials used in the classroom. Initial placement can be approximated by using the popular informal reading inventory procedure (see Chapter 15 for these techniques). To check the reliability of initial placements, teachers need to apply the logic and procedures of the informal reading inventory to samples of the students' weekly reading. These samples should be taken and analyzed at least weekly. In short, students' ability to decode and comprehend their reading material should be closely monitored. If material is too easy or too difficult, appropriate changes in terms of reading level/reading group should be made.

Grade-equivalent reading scores from standardized achievement tests are often readily available and they might present a quick, easy way to determine instructional reading level. However, the score does not really reflect reading level but compares students to peers in terms of reading achievement. If Amy, for example, gets a grade norm score of 6.1, it does not necessarily mean that she can handle sixth-grade material; all it means is that she got the same number of items correct as was the mean for all those students who were in the first month of sixth grade when they took the test. Because of widespread misuse, the International Reading Association passed a resolution requesting publishers of norm-referenced tests to discontinue the use of grade-equivalent scores (see *Journal of Reading*, 1981). Grade-equivalent scores are further discussed in Chapter 14. They are of limited and questionable value in determining instructional level.

Administering and Interpreting an Informal Reading Inventory

Informal Reading Inventories (IRIs) are collections of short reading passages written at different reading levels. Usually, there are at least two passages at each reading level, pre-primer through sixth grade, one of which is to be read orally by a student and one to be read silently. A student reads passages of increasing difficulty until a frustration level is reached. Frustration level is that level at which a student has to struggle considerably with word recognition or comprehension. Based on the student's word recognition accuracy and comprehension accuracy at various reading levels, an instructional reading level is determined. (IRIs are discussed fully in Chapter 15.)

In addition to assessing word recognition accuracy and performance on questions, a new informal reading inventory by Leslie and Caldwell (1990), *Qualitative Reading Inventory* (reviewed in Chapter 15), incorporates several important ideas from recent research on reading assessment. This inventory assesses a student's background knowledge for a particular topic. Comprehension is assessed through an analysis of students' retellings of passages read as well as through answers to explicit and implicit questions.

Directions for administering and interpreting IRIs vary from one inventory to another (Jongsma & Jongsma, 1981). We recommend following whatever directions accompany the IRI for a particular basal series. However, the following set of general guidelines could be followed to administer an IRI and to interpret students' performance on it.

Instead of using a graded word list (words in isolation) to determine beginning reading passages, a procedure that has not been found to be particularly accurate or informative, teachers can simply have students begin reading at a level that is two years below their actual grade placement. Passages at this level should be relatively easy for most students to read. If this is not the case, students should read passages at an easier level.

The conventional procedure for an IRI involves having a student first orally read one of the two passages at a given level as the teacher records word recognition errors. The student then answers the comprehension questions, which the teacher asks aloud, without looking back at the passage. Next, the student silently reads the other passage at that level and answers the questions. If the student is not at the frustration level in either word recognition or comprehension, the same procedure is continued with the passages at the next level.

There is some disagreement among reading experts and across IRIs as to what should be counted as a word recognition error. The following should be counted (see Figure 6.3 for definitions): substitutions, omissions, insertions, and unknown words pronounced by the teacher (the student just could not say anything). The following should *not* be counted as word recognition errors: repetitions, self-corrections, hesitations, "mispronunciations" due to dialect, missed punctuation marks. Repetitions and self-corrections, in particular, are often counted as errors on IRIs. However, both repetitions and self-corrections are usually positive signs, indicating that a student is attempting to read for meaning and can self-correct a word that does not make sense. For this reason, repetitions and self-corrections should not be counted as errors. Of course, dialect-motivated "mispronunciations" are not mispronunciations at all; they are simply the appropriate application of a different set of pronunciation rules.

There is also some disagreement as to what criterion levels should be used to determine instructional and frustration levels. Although there are problems

FIGURE 6.3. Definitions of Word Recognition Errors and Nonerrors

Counted as Errors

Substitutions   Any word (exiting for exciting, was for saw, dog for dogs) or nonsense word (relatisting for relaxing) that is substituted for an actual word in the text.
Omission   Any complete word that is omitted by the reader.
Insertion   Any word or string of words that do not occur in the text but are inserted by the reader. An inserted string of words should be counted as one error.
Teacher pronunciation   Any word that the teacher pronounces for a student after waiting at least 5 seconds. Only difficult, important words should be pronounced for students to encourage them to try words on their own.

Not Counted as Errors

Hesitation   Any word on which a student hesitates before pronouncing, mispronouncing, or receiving teacher assistance.
Self-correction   Any word that is originally mispronounced but is spontaneously self-corrected by the reader.
Repetition   Any word or words that are repeated entirely or partially by the reader.
"Mispronunciation" due to dialect   Any word that is "mispronounced" due to dialect
Omission of punctuation mark   Any punctuation mark that is omitted by the reader.

with IRIs, they are our best current alternative for instructional placement. Students, particularly low-achieving readers, cannot grow optimally in reading if they are frequently confronted with material that is difficult to decode or comprehend. Therefore, for better or worse, the existing convention is acceptable: that instructional reading level be defined as the level at which a student can read with approximately 95 percent accuracy in word recognition and approximately 75 percent accuracy in comprehension, averaged across silent and oral passages. It is also recommended, with reservation, that frustration level be defined as the level at which a student is reading with less than 90 percent accuracy in word recognition and less than 70 percent accuracy in comprehension.

Because these criteria cannot be specified with pinpoint precision, the teacher should regard them as guidelines needing generous interpretation. If a real discrepancy occurs between word recognition and comprehension accuracy, it is recommended that more faith be put in the word recognition scores. This is because comprehension accuracy scores are generally based on a small number of questions, typically between four and ten questions per passage. If a teacher is unsure about a student's placement level, the lower level should be used because it will prove less frustrating; besides, it will be more encouraging to move up to a higher level than to move down to a lower one.

Since informal reading inventories are administered on a one-to-one basis, teachers will not be able to use the procedures very often due to time constraints. Teachers should administer IRIs at the beginning of the school year to their students in order to determine the level of challenge they can accommodate in the materials they read on a daily basis. As an added benefit, they can obtain initial information on their students' strengths and weaknesses as readers. During the remainder of the year, teachers should continue to assess students based on their oral reading performance on daily reading tasks and, when justified, should adjust their group membership and the difficulty of their daily reading materials.

The techniques used with an informal reading inventory to assess word recognition ability are valuable. However, the techniques, when applied to daily reading tasks in what is called oral reading analysis (discussed in Chapter 9), actually provide *better* data about a student's instructional reading level and word recognition difficulties than when used with a single administration of an informal reading inventory.

SUMMARY

This chapter provided an overview of our approach to engagement, instruction, and assessment. Specific instructional techniques will be explained in Chapters 8, 10, and 12. Our approach to assessment, based on frequent measures of daily performance in reading, will be elaborated in Chapters 9, 11, and 13. The reading difficulties summary, presented in this chapter as a way to systematically record assessment data, will also be elaborated in Chapters 9, 11, and 13. Finally, the concept of instructional reading level is key in reading instruction; it can be determined through the use of an informal reading inventory and ongoing assessment of students' daily reading experiences.

Suggested Activities

1. Administer either a commercial IRI or an IRI in a basal reader to several children. Determine their instructional reading level.
2. On three different occasions listen to several children read (50–200 words) aloud from material in which they have been placed for instruction. Take notes on their oral readings. Have them finish reading the story. Ask them to answer (orally or in writing) approximately ten questions about the story. Based on the three samples determine whether or not the students are reading at their instructional level. If students are not available, your instructor may be able to provide you with an audio tape on which one or more children are reading orally and answering questions.

Suggested Reading

ANDERSON, R. C., WILSON, P. T., and FIELDING, L. G. (1988). Growth in reading and how children spend their time outside of school. *Reading Research Quarterly, 23,* 285–303.
The importance of independent reading is stressed.

BAUMANN, J. F., and SCHMITT, M. B. (1986). The what, why, how, and when of comprehension instruction. *The Reading Teacher, 39,* 640–647.
The authors explain how to provide direct instruction in the area of reading comprehension.

DUFFY, G., and ROEHLER, L. (1987). Improving reading instruction through the use of responsive elaboration. *The Reading Teacher, 40,* 514–521.
Responsive elaboration is explained and examples are provided.

DUFFY, G., ROEHLER, L., and HERRMAN, B. (1988). Modeling mental processes helps poor readers become strategic readers. *The Reading Teacher, 41,* 762–767.
Mental modeling is explained and examples are presented.

McKENNA, M. C. (1983). Informal inventories: A review of the issues. *The Reading Teacher, 36,* 670–679.
The author reviews the issues related to use of informal reading inventories.

POTTER, M., and WAMRE, H. (1990). Curriculum-based measurement and developmental reading models: Opportunities for cross-validation. *Exceptional Children, 57,* 16–25.
The value of curriculum-based measurement is presented.

VALENCIA, S. (1990). A portfolio approach to classroom reading assessment: The whys, whats, and hows. *The Reading Teacher, 43,* 338–340.
An excellent description of portfolio assessment in reading is presented.

VALENCIA, S., and PEARSON, P. D. (1987). Reading assessment: Time for a change. *The Reading Teacher, 40,* 726–732.
The authors convincingly argue that the ways in which we assess reading performance must be changed to foster effective instruction.

ZIGMOND, W., and SILVERMAN, R. (1984). Informal assessment for program planning and evaluation in special education. *Educational Psychology, 19,* 163–171.
The advantages of informal assessment in schools are discussed.

CHAPTER 7

Early Intervention for Beginning Readers

Overview

As you read this chapter, these themes may help to guide your understanding and reflection:

- We have experienced a revolution in how we think about early reading.
- Students who are potentially at risk for failure to learn to read should be identified as early as possible in Grade 1 so that they may receive accelerated instruction that allows them to catch up with their peers before the end of the year.
- Irrespective of the type of reading instruction that children receive, the development of phonemic awareness is important for all children, especially those at risk for failure.
- Early and continued success is important for all children, but especially those who are at risk for failure.
- An intensive but balanced literacy program, one that includes lots of opportunity for successful experiences in writing and reading a variety of types of materials, helps children develop phonemic awareness, phonics knowledge, improved reading skill, and a positive self-image of themselves as readers and writers.

There is no skill more essential to success in school than reading. It has, in our society, assumed the status of a developmental task, along with learning to walk, talk, throw a ball, dress a doll, and share the attention of an adult. So the school careers of kids who do not learn to read early in Grade 1 are in jeopardy. Unfortunately, variability in reading skill emerges quite early in Grade 1. Even more telling, the probability is very high (about .80) that a child who does not make it out of the low group in Grade 1 will still be in the low group in Grade 4.[1] Juel (1988) is convinced that the development of good decoding skill is the key to early success. Her thesis is that students who are good decoders are exposed to roughly two or three times as many running words as poor decoders. Since the effect of "just reading" has been demonstrated to affect both vocabulary (word meaning) development (Anderson & Nagy, 1991, Beck

& McKeown, 1991) and comprehension (Pearson & Fielding, 1991), the effect of early word identification skill is all the more crucial to early success, at least according to Juel.

The best way to break the cycle of failure that so many low-achieving students experience is to identify, as early as possible, those who are at risk for failure to learn to read and to shape a new set of literacy experiences for them, a set of literacy experiences that will put them on a par with their classmates as quickly as possible.[2] Children at risk for failure need accelerated not remedial experiences. In this chapter, we will discuss several programs and processes that are designed to do just that.

The Development of Early Reading
Emergent Literacy

In the domain of early reading, that period beginning with literacy development at home and continuing into the first few years of schooling, the dominant change in the last decade has been a major shift in both name and substance. What we have traditionally labeled "reading readiness" is now called "emergent literacy." We used to think of this period as a time in which students acquired the readiness skills (such as visual discrimination, auditory discrimination, left-right progression of print) that would get them ready for reading instruction once they reached first grade. Within the new emergent literacy tradition, this period is seen not as a set of stages or a time when skills are acquired sequentially (see Sulzby & Teale, 1991), but as a continuous period of print exploration by children. Unlike the reading readiness tradition, the emergent literacy tradition does not distinguish between pre-reading (a stage in which the child is not yet a reader) and reading. Instead, it suggests that all attempts at all ages to create meaning, to interpret the broad range of texts that even the young children encounter, constitute attempts to read. Furthermore, it does not matter whether those texts are print, picture, icon, or experience in origin. Similarly, all attempts to send a message (regardless of whether the text is print, scribble, picture, or gesture) constitute attempts at writing. Consequently, there is no pre-writing stage of development. Since they are naturally predisposed to make sense of the worlds they encounter, all children are, by their very nature, readers and writers. This does not mean that novices are no different from experts. Indeed, expertise involves the development of several kinds of knowledge—world knowledge, linguistic knowledge, print knowledge, text knowledge, and functional knowledge about how literacy is used in everyday life. Conventionality in reading and writing (i.e., knowledge of the conventions of print) is seen as the development of just one more special kind of knowledge.

Phonemic Awareness

In the last decade we have learned much about the critical role played by phonemic awareness in the development of early reading, apparently for both the ability to decode and to read for meaning (Adams, 1990; Juel, 1991). Phonemic awareness consists of two components: (1) the ability to segment the speech stream of a spoken word, e.g., /cat/, into component phonemes /cuh + ah + tuh/ and (2) the ability to blend separately heard sounds, e.g., /cuh + ah + tuh/, into a normally spoken word /cat/.

The findings on the relationship between phonemic awareness and early success in reading are provocative. First, children who possess high degrees of phonemic awareness in kindergarten or early in first grade are very likely to be good readers throughout their elementary school careers (Juel, 1991). Second, very few children who are successful readers at the end of Grade 1 exhibit a low level of phonemic awareness. Third, children who have low phonemic awareness early in Grade 1 are very likely to be poor readers at the end of the year unless their phonemic awareness has been developed either directly or indirectly during the school year. Fourth, phonemic awareness by itself does not necessarily lead to success; there are some children who develop average or better levels of phonemic awareness throughout the school year but are still unsuccessful as readers. Taken together, and apparently irrespective of mode of instruction, these findings suggest that phonemic awareness is a necessary but not a sufficient condition for the development of decoding and reading.[3]

While we can be confident of the critical role of phonemic awareness in learning to read, we are not nearly so sure about the optimal way to enhance its development. While both Juel (1991) and Adams (1990) have documented the efficacy of teaching it directly, they also admit that it is highly likely to develop as a consequence of learning phonics, learning to read, or even learning to write, especially when teachers encourage students to use invented spellings. Recent work (Windsor & Pearson, 1992) suggests that in whole language classrooms in particular, invented spellings (encouraging students to spell words the way that they sound) may be the medium through which both phonemic awareness (because students have to segment the speech stream of spoken words in order to focus on a phoneme) and phonics knowledge (because there is substantial transfer value from the focus on sound-symbol information in spelling to symbol-sound knowledge in reading) develop.

We are persuaded that some early attention to phonemic awareness in the first grade instructional program benefits all readers, but most directly those who are at risk for failure in Grade 1. And most of the intervention programs that we describe in the next section attend to phonemic awareness either directly or indirectly. In one of the programs, Early Intervention in Reading, phonemic awareness is an explicit instructional goal.

EARLY INTERVENTION PROGRAMS

A Tutorial Approach

Over the past 25 years, Marie Clay has developed an early intervention program designed to accelerate the reading development of children who, left to partake in the normal diet of classroom instructional activities, would end up far behind their classmates by the end of Grade 1. Dubbed *Reading Recovery*, the program has developed a foothold in the United States and many other English-speaking countries between 1985 and the present.[4]

The program begins with the assumption that in a normal, heterogeneously constituted classroom of first graders, the lowest 20 percent are likely to be at risk for failure to learn to read in Grade 1. Over a period that usually ranges from 12 to 16 weeks, these students receive 30 minutes of tutoring per day from a highly qualified, specially trained *Reading Recovery* teacher. The evaluative data collected so far, both in New Zealand and the United States, are very encouraging. After the period of accelerated training, over 80 percent of the children are returned to regular classroom instruction where they are able to benefit from the normal instruction provided to the average readers. Because *Reading Recovery* uses highly experienced, extensively trained tutors, it has been criticized for being cost ineffective. Of course, the crucial long-term test of its cost-effectiveness is whether the children who are returned to regular instruction are able to make normal progress in the regular classroom over the next 5 to 6 years of school. If, on the other hand, *Reading Recovery* children show up on the rolls of other special, and expensive, remedial programs, such as Chapter 1 and Learning Disabilities, then neither the children (in terms of savings to the psychological damage that failure causes) nor the schools (in terms of real dollar savings) will have benefited from the program. So far, the results have been good. Some of the studies in Ohio, for example, indicate that fewer than 20 percent of the *Reading Recovery* students have entered other special programs through Grade 5.

In the course of a 30 minute *Reading Recovery* lesson, the student and the teacher traverse many literacy landscapes, engaging in a host of strategies in search of bringing meaning to the printed page.[5] One of the most striking characteristics of a *Reading Recovery* lesson is the materials that the children read. All are storybooks written especially for beginning readers. The pictures are colorful, but also highly related to the story conveyed in the text. The texts are always predictable, although by a variety of criteria of predictability standards. For example, some of the texts are predictable because they contain a repetitive syntactic pattern or a consistent "refrain" or "chorus," as in example (1).

Pages 2–3: Brown Bear, Brown Bear, What do you see?

Page 4: I see a yellow bird looking at me.

Page 5: Yellow Bird, Yellow Bird, What do you see?

Page 6: I see a red dog looking at me.

Page 7: Red Dog, Red Dog, What do you see? Anon, anon

Some of the texts are predictable on the basis of sound—because of the use of rhyming patterns or alliteration, as in examples (2) and (3).

Who can tell the time?

Who can flip a dime?

Who can solve a crime? Anon, anon

The Lumpets live on Lavender Lane. They live in a liner with lavender locks. Anon, anon

While the books are predictable and simple, they are very different from the "basalese" that we are accustomed to seeing in early readers, particularly the preprimers, of commercial reading programs. One of the basic differences is authorial intent. Typically, the storybooks used in *Reading Recovery* were written to entertain children rather than to comply with some criterion of word frequency, alliteration, or repetition. The fact that they are also predictable on the basis of a syntactic pattern or a sound pattern is accidental and serendipitous;

the authors used repetition or alliteration or rhyming because they wanted the stories to appeal to children *not* because they wanted them to be predictable. Nonetheless, *Reading Recovery* students learn something about phonemic awareness and symbol-sound correspondences because of their exposure to these kinds of books.

As striking as the materials are the techniques used by the teachers with the students. A typical lesson, at least after the program is in full swing, begins with the student rereading 1–3 books that have been introduced and studied in earlier lessons. As the students read the books, the teacher takes a running record, which is Clay's version of an oral reading error analysis. These running records of words that the child (a) can read correctly, (b) cannot read at all, and (c) struggles to decode form the basis of the teacher's judgment about the child's growth in reading and word identification skill as well as future instructional activities for the student.

As the student is reading these familiar storybooks, the teacher engages in a great deal of situated instruction; that is, he provides the student with a variety of short mini-lessons dealing with phonics (he might point out the predictability of particular letter-sound correspondence), contextual analysis (he might point out the usefulness of reading to the end of the sentence or consulting the pictures in order to develop or corroborate an hypothesis about a word's pronunciation or meaning), or comprehension monitoring (he might encourage the child to reread a sentence, a paragraph, or a page while listening carefully to the oral reading to see if it really makes sense). Some who have witnessed the letter-sound instruction in *Reading Recovery* have dubbed it "phonics on the fly" in order to emphasize that the phonics instruction is always contextualized; that is, the instruction has an immediate short-term goal within the current reading situation: If you learn the sound that "t" makes, it will help you unlock this word that is stumping you right this minute.

In the middle of a *Reading Recovery* lesson comes a mini-writing lesson. Using words and their constituent phonics elements from the previous story, the teacher assists the child in composing a text (ranging from a short sentence initially to a paragraph or so in later lessons). As the student tries to write the story, the teacher invites her to figure out the spellings for herself, thus encouraging what some have come to call "invented spellings." If a student is experiencing difficulty the teacher scaffolds the activity by providing extra hints and clues. For example, the teacher might draw a frame for the word, with boxes for each letter, and encourage the student to fill in as many boxes as she knew for sure. If the student is unsure about the spelling of a particular sound, the teacher might ask her to narrow it down to two choices and then tell her which is correct, or she might narrow the sound to two letter options and ask the student to select from that pair. Or she might remind the student of the spelling of a rhyming word that she feels the student already knows. Many observers of *Reading Recovery* believe that this mini-lesson in writing is the key to the phonics instruction within the program. We agree for two reasons. First, while geared toward SOUND-letter rather than LETTER-sound relationships, there is nonetheless bound to be substantial transfer from this spelling activity to reading phonics knowledge. Second, during this invented spelling activity, the student is constantly forced to deal with phonemic awareness. As she gropes for letters to map onto the sounds in the spoken words, she has to be able to segment the stream of speech for a given word into constituent phonemes. We have come to the conclusion that spelling activities are the likely source of growth in phonemic awareness in *Reading Recovery*, in other early intervention programs, and in literature-based and whole language programs that do not contain an explicit phonics program.

A Restructured Pullout Program

Hiebert, Colt, Catto, and Gury (1992) have developed a very successful reading intervention program in which Chapter 1 teachers and aides work with Chapter 1 students in Grade 1 in small groups of three or four. Under this model, the Chapter 1 teacher works with the highest three or four children out of a group of six to eight for 30 minutes a day for the first 15 weeks of school, and the aide works with the lowest three or four. Halfway through the school year the teacher and aide switch students.

Activities focus on reading and rereading predictable books, writing rhyming words, and writing in journals. Students also receive instruction in patterns of words. Each day children reread one review book and read one new book several times. Next, children write selected rhyming words from the books with pre-formed letters on magnetic boards or with felt-tip markers on acetate sheets. Two or three times a week children also write about topics of choice in personal notebooks. After writing, children again reread predictable books.

Children take books home to read, with a parent signing a form indicating that this is done. When children read at home ten times, they receive a trade book they can keep.

By the end of the school year 77 percent of the children were able to read at a primer level on an informal reading inventory, and 55 percent were reading on an end-of-first-grade level or higher. Only 18 percent of Chapter 1 comparison children (not receiving this restructured instruction) were reading on a primer level or higher by the end of the year.

This program is exciting because it has the potential to reach many first-grade children. Children who receive special reading help through Chapter 1 can potentially become adequate or better readers by the end of first grade through a systematic, intensive small group instructional program such as the one just described.

A Classroom-Based Intervention

One limitation of the *Reading Recovery* program is that it is expensive because of the one-on-one tutoring and, therefore, may be difficult for many schools to provide. A second limitation is that *Reading Recovery* is a pullout program; children leave their classrooms to be tutored. This often causes disruptions for all students. Also, it may be difficult for students who are tutored to make the transition to small or large group reading instruction.

A classroom program, simply called *Early Intervention in Reading,* is a program similar to *Reading Recovery* in intent. However, the program is used by first-grade classroom teachers with a group of low-achieving students (i.e., the bottom 20 percent) within the regular classroom. In this program classroom teachers begin working with at-risk first-grade children in October before they have a chance to actually fail in reading and continue working with them throughout most of first grade so they will not fall considerably behind their peers (Taylor, Frye, Short, & Shearer, 1992).

For 15 to 20 minutes a day for 21 to 24 weeks a group (five to seven in number) of at-risk students works with the classroom teacher. Generally, students work on one story for 3 days. Reading material for the first 12 weeks or so consists of summaries of picture books. Very short picture books (40-60 words at level A, 60-90 words at level B) can be used as well. (The original books are first read aloud.) Later, the actual picture books are used as the reading material. The shortened books or very short books are used at first so that the children can feel successful with stories that interest them but that are short enough so they can read them successfully. (Books used in the program are listed in Figure 7.1. An example of a story summary is shown in Figure 7.2.)

With the teacher the children read the shortened or very short story on a chart. Using the chart, the teacher works with the children on the sounding and blending of phonemes within words to develop children's phonemic awareness. At first words with short vowel sounds are stressed. The teacher also teaches children about the sounds of letters and the importance of using context clues and meaning to decode words as the chart is read.

On Day 1 of a story children in the group write five words from the story, phoneme by phoneme. Words are printed in a series of boxes with one phoneme per box. (See Figure 7.3.) The teacher provides help as needed. On Days 2 and 3 the children write a sentence about the story. The group decides on a common sentence. The teacher asks the children to give her the letters for as many sounds in the words they are trying to spell as she thinks they can successfully provide. She quickly tells them the rest of the letters. For example, if the children were writing "The chick couldn't swim," the teacher may ask the children what letters spell /ch/ and /ĭ/ and tell them that the two letters "ck" come at the end of *chick*.

Each day the children reread old stories or the new story with a partner or an aide. The partner may be from the group or may be another student in the class.

The shortened stories are reproduced in booklet form on half-page sheets of paper. The children illustrate their booklets in their free time.

On the third day the teacher listens to each child individually reread the story they are working on. Notes are kept about the child's word recognition accuracy and progress. As the child is reading, the teacher is careful to help the child with difficult words but also encourages the child to sound and blend easier words and to think of what word would make sense in the story. Throughout the instruction an emphasis is placed on teaching the children strategies they can use to decode unknown words when they are reading on their own. The 3-day cycle of activities is listed in Figure 7.4.

At the end of the third day children should be reading their stories with at least 92 percent accuracy. If not, easier stories are needed. The story is sent home at the end of the third day so the child can read it to a parent. The books are returned to school so the child can continue to practice rereading them in the classroom.

Like *Reading Recovery*, teacher training is an important part of the *Early Intervention in Reading* program. Twice a week a teacher trainer observes each

Group A – 40–60 word summaries (October–November)

Five Little Monkeys Jumping on the Bed
Ask Mr. Bear   Marjorie Flack
Rosie's Walk   Pat Hutchins (actual book read by students)
You'll Soon Grow into Them, Titch   Pat Hutchins
Herman the Helper   Robert Kraus
Milton the Early Riser   Robert Kraus
I Wish I Could Fly   Ron Maris
All By Myself   Mercer Mayer
Just for You   Mercer Mayer
Imogene's Antlers   David Small

Group B – 60–90 word summaries (November–January)

Charlie Needs a Clock   Tomie dePaloa
Across the Stream   Mirra Ginsburg
Three Kittens   Mirra Ginsburg
Good Night, Owl   Pat Hutchins
Geraldine's Blanket   Holly Keller
Round Robin   Jack Kent
Owliver   Robert Kraus
Stone Soup
If You Give a Mouse a Cookie   Laura Numeroff
The Farmer and the Noisy Hut

Group C – 90–150 word summaries, 50–150 word books (January–March)

A Dark, Dark Tale   Ruth Brown (actual book read by students)
Freight Train   Donald Crews (actual book read by students)
School Bus   Donald Crews (actual book read by students)
Hattie and the Fox   Mem Fox
The Monkey and the Crocodile
The Three Billy Goats Gruff
The Chick and the Duckling   Mirra Ginsburg (actual book read by students)
The Doorbell Rang   Pat Hutchins
The Very Worst Monster   Pat Hutchins

Group D – 100–200 word books, actual books read by students (March–April)

You'll Soon Grow into Them, Titch   Pat Hutchins
Herman the Helper   Robert Kraus
All By Myself   Mercer Mayer
Just for You   Mercer Mayer
The Bear's Toothache   David McPhail
There's a Nightmare in My Closet   Mercer Mayer
Planes   Anne Rockwell
If you Look Around You   Fulvio Testa
If you Take a Paintbrush   Fulvio Testa

FIGURE 7.1. Some of the Stories Used in the Early Intervention in Reading Program

The Farmer and the Noisy Hut

A man lived in a hut with his mother, his wife, and six children.

It was very crowded and noisy.

The man went to see the wiseman. The wiseman told him to put the chickens, goat, and cow in the hut.

Now it was *very, very* crowded and noisy.

The wiseman told the man to take the animals out of the hut.

It did not seem crowded and noisy any more.

FIGURE 7.2. An Example of a Story Summary, from Level B of the Early Intervention in Reading Program

classroom teacher who is learning to use the procedures. The teacher trainer provides feedback on the effectiveness of the teacher's techniques as well as suggestions for improvement.

The *Early Intervention in Reading* program has been systematically studied in four school districts over the past 3 years, and results are promising. For example, in District A 67 percent of the children in the program (from the lowest 20 percent of their class in terms of emerging reading ability in October) were reading by the end of first grade. Approximately 50 percent were reading on an end-of-first-grade level or better in May. As a group their mean percentile score on a standardized reading test increased from 29 to 37 between October and late April.

In comparison, only 36 percent of comparable low-achieving students in District A (not in the program) were reading by May. Approximately 20 percent were reading on an end-of-first-grade level or better. As a group, the mean percentile score of these students on a standardized reading test was 34 in September and 27 in late April. District A is a suburban district that uses a literature-based reading program.

th	a	t

i	t

n	e	s	t

d	u	ck

n	o	t

FIGURE 7.3. Sounding, Blending, and Writing Phonetically Regular Words Phoneme by Phoneme

DAY 1

20 MINUTES WITH AIDE OR PARTNER

- The students reread two "old" books with aide.
- The students work in partners each taking turns rereading "old" books.

20 MINUTES WITH TEACHER (AIDE MONITORING OTHER CHILDREN IN CLASS)

- The teacher reads actual book.
- The teacher models the sounding out and blending of four or five selected words as chart is read.
- The teacher guides the students in sounding out and blending selected words in isolation while students match, trace, and point to individual phonemes (of the selected words) on their own papers. (Levels A and B)

DAY 2

20 MINUTES WITH AIDE OR PARTNER

- The students receive their personal copy of the shortened version of the story or the very short story. With the guidance of the aide, they read the story together.
- The students reread one or two "old" stories with the aide or a partner if time permits.

20 MINUTES WITH TEACHER (AIDE MONITORING OTHER STUDENTS IN CLASS)

- The students reread the shortened version of the story or the very short story with the teacher. or the students reread the chart with teacher (track with teacher and read chorally).
- The teacher aids the students in sounding out and blending selected words. The students write up to five of these words on paper as the teacher guides them.
- The students write one sentence together as a group about the book (perhaps in journals). The teacher spells some of the words and guides the students in the spelling of others.

DAY 3

20 MINUTES WITH AIDE OR PARTNER

- The aide hands out the scrambled version of the shortened story. Students will work individually or with partners to put the strips in the correct order. They will then take turns reading them in the correct order. (Only Group A Books, optional).
- Children may illustrate their books if time permits.
- Aide listens to children read independently as others are working on above activities.

20 MINUTES WITH TEACHER (AIDE MONITORING OTHER STUDENTS IN CLASS)

- While reading the chart, the teacher models phonemic segmentation and blending (optional).
- The students read small books in a group with the teacher (optional).
- The students write one or more sentences about the story. Again, the teacher spells some of the words and guides the students in the spelling of others. (Teacher models correct form at all times.)

FIGURE 7.4. Three-day Cycle of Activities in the *Early Intervention in Reading* Program

- The students illustrate their personal copy of the shortened version while the teacher listens to individuals read from their little books.

    (The teacher and aide should alternate students so they are listening to different children on different days.)

HOME

- The students are asked to take the little book home to read with someone.
  They are asked to bring the book back signed by the person they read it to.

DAY 4 (ONLY IF NEEDED)

In most cases, we would expect that the students will be fluently reading the shortened versions or very short stories by the end of Day 3. The following activities are optional and should be used as the teacher sees fit. They may be activities that students work on individually, with a partner, or with the teacher or aide.

- Text Scramble – the words of the shortened text are scrambled
- Creative Dramatics
- Reread little book with partner
- Reread little book with teacher (individually)
- Individuals reread "old" books
- Partners reread "old" books

It is hoped that students will begin work on a new book on the fourth day in most cases and continuously work on a 3-day cycle. These children need intense work on a daily

FIGURE 7.4. Three-day Cycle of Activities in the *Early Intervention in Reading* Program (*cont.*)

The *Early Intervention in Reading* program also has been used in a suburban and urban district using a systematic phonics program for the first 6 months of first grade, followed by the use of a basal reader program, and a rural district using a basal reader program throughout first grade. Results similar to those reported above have been found in these other districts as well. One particularly appealing feature of this program is that it is classroom teachers who are providing 20 minutes a day of systematic, quality, supplemental reading instruction and who are making an important difference in the end-of-first-grade reading attainment of their lowest emergent readers.

A Whole-Class Approach

Cunningham, Hall, and Defee (1991), a professor, curriculum coordinator, and first-grade teacher, respectively, worked collaboratively to develop a multifaceted, nonability grouped approach to first-grade reading instruction in the regular classroom. All children in the class participated in the program. The program has been very successful in eliminating reading failure for most children within the first-grade classrooms in which the approach has been implemented.

The 2-hour reading/language arts time is divided into four 30-minute blocks. In the writing block the teacher guides the children in writing about topics of choice and in revising and editing one piece out of every three to be published. Writing conventions and invented spelling are modeled daily.

In the basal block the children receive instruction from a basal reader series. The teacher begins by working with the whole class, following suggestions in the manual. Then children work in pairs, taking turns reading pages of the story or taking turns as "teacher" and "student" as workbook pages are completed. Instruction is paced to complete the entire first-grade program by the end of first grade.

In the real books block children engage in self-selected reading, and the teacher reads aloud to the class. Children read by themselves or with a partner and are encouraged to talk about what they have read.

In the working with words block the students are involved with the "Word Wall." This is a bulletin board to which five common words from the basal are added each week. Each day the teacher or children call out five words from the wall, the class chants and claps the letters in each word, writes the word, and chants and claps it again. During this block children also are involved with "Making Words" in which they are given a limited number of letters. After the teacher calls out a word, the children manipulate the letters at their desk to make the word. One child makes the word with large letters on the chalkboard ledge. As part of this process, word patterns are emphasized (i.e., *red, rid, rip, dip, sip*).

In addition to the above activities, some additional individual and small group instruction is provided. In particular, children receive additional help rereading the current basal preprimer or reading preprimer from other basal programs. Membership in the small group, which meets for 15 minutes a day, changes daily with everyone in the class reading in the group at least once a week, and children who need the extra reading help reading in the group on most days.

By May all of the children in the class were reading on at least a preprimer level on an informal reading inventory, and 83 percent were reading on an end of Grade 1 level or better. Similar results were found the following year at the same school. At another school in the district with the most at-risk students (79 percent receiving free or reduced lunch), all of the first graders in the school were reading on at least a preprimer level by the end of the year, and 57 percent were reading on an end-of-first-grade level or better.

The results of this whole-class program are very impressive. A particularly interesting point worth noting is that a variety of approaches, basal instruction, process writing, self-selected reading of literature, and systematic working with words are used. Most importantly, all children within the regular classroom learn to read in first grade.

Reflections

Four successful early reading intervention programs have been described. The programs have obvious differences but also some similarities which are worth noting. All of the approaches involve repetitive reading of simple stories, working with words to heighten children's awareness of the letters and sounds within words, and writing. Perhaps more importantly, all of the programs are based on the premise that most children in first grade can learn to read by the end of the school year.

There is not, and does not need to be, one best method for working with low-achieving readers in first grade. What is important is that a sound, systematic, consistent early reading intervention program be implemented in first grade, because such a program will benefit many children and significantly reduce the incidence of reading failure in first grade.

OTHER TECHNIQUES

The Use of Big Books to Teach Decoding

In recent years many wonderful big books, large versions of popular picture books, have become readily available. The big books greatly appeal to children and can be an excellent tool for the teacher to use to teach decoding. Children can follow the teacher's hand as he reads from left to right, as he stops to segment and blend together the sounds of a particular word, or as he stops to ask, "What word beginning with the letter 'd' would make sense in this sentence?"

Decoding taught in this manner is directly related to the way in which a child should decode when reading a book independently. By contrast, decoding taught through words listed in isolation on the chalkboard or through worksheet drills is only indirectly related to the decoding children will need to be able to do when reading stories on their own.

If big books are not available or in short supply, a part of a story or story summary can be printed on a chart. Trachtenburg and Ferruggia (1989) discuss a successful program in which at-risk first graders helped the teacher create a story summary that was printed on a chart. Children also may want to help illustrate pages of a story or story summary written on a chart.

Using Predictable Materials

Bridge, Winograd, and Haley (1983) have developed a program for teaching basic sight words to beginning readers that makes use of predictable books and group language experience stories. Predictable books are stories with repetitive and/or predictable structures. A list of predictable books is presented in Figure 7.5. The pattern in this type of book provides good opportunities for students to practice reading high-frequency words. Students reading at a beginning primer level have been found to learn more basic sight words through this program than students using only regular basal primer material. An example of instruction using predictable books follows.

First, the teacher reads a predictable book aloud to the students, then rereads it, encouraging them to join in as much as possible. The students take turns chorally reading the book with the teacher. The next day they again read the story that has been reproduced on a chart. The purpose of this is to practice reading the story without the aid of pictures. The students are given sentence strips to place under the appropriate lines of the story on the chart. They are also given, in order, individual word cards that they place under the matching words on the chart. On the third day, the students read the

Asch, Frank. *Just Like Daddy.* Prentice-Hall, 1981.

Barrett, Jude. *Animals Should Definitely Not Wear Clothing.* Atheneum, 1970.

Brown, Margaret Wise. *Good Night Moon.* Harper and Row, 1947.

Burningham, John. *Mr. Gumpy's Outing.* Scholastic, 1970.

Carle, Eric. *The Very Hungry Caterpillar.* Hamion Hamilton, 1970.

Carlstrom, Nancy. *Jesse Bear What Will You Wear?* MacMillan, 1986.

Christelow, Eileen. *Five Little Monkeys Jumping on the Bed.* Clarion, 1989.

Crews, Donald. *Freight Train.* Greenwillow, 1978.

Crews, Donald. *School Bus.* Greenwillow, 1978.

dePaolo, Tomi. *The Comic Adventures of Old Mother Hubbard.* Harcourt Brace Jovanovich, 1981.

Emberly, Barbara. *Drummer Hoff.* Prentice Hall, 1987.

Fox, Mem. *Hattie and the Fox.* Bradbury, 1986.

Ginsburg, Mirra. *The Chick and the Duckling.* Macmillan, 1972.

Ginsburg, Mirra. *Three Kittens.* Crown, 1973.

Hutchins, Pat. *Rosie's Walk.* Macmillan, 1968.

Hutchins, Pat. *You'll Soon Grow into Them, Titch.* Greenwillow, 1983.

Kraus, Robert. *Herman the Helper.* Windmill, 1974.

Krauss, Ruth. *The Carrot Seed.* Harper and Row, 1945.

Langstaff, John. *Over in the Meadow.* Harcourt Brace Jovanovich, 1967.

Martin, Bill, Jr. *Brown Bear, Brown Bear, What Do You See?* Holt, Rinehart, & Winston, 1967.

Mayer, Mercer. *Just For You.* Western, 1975.

Nodset, Joan. *Who Took the Farmer's Hat?* Scholastic, 1963.

Pearson, Tracey Campbell. *Old MacDonald Had a Farm.* Dial Books for Young Readers, 1986.

Peppe, Rodney. *The House that Jack Built.* Delacorte, 1970.

Raffi. *Five Little Ducks.* Crown, 1989.

Raffi. *Tingalayo.* Crown, 1989.

Shaw, Charles. *It Looked Like Spilt Milk.* Harper and Row, 1947.

Tolstoy, Alexei. *The Great Big Enormous Turnip.* Franklin Watts, 1968.

Zemach, Margot. *The Teeny Tiny Woman.* Scholastic, 1965.

FIGURE 7.5. Predictable Books

story chorally from the chart. Word cards are placed in random order at the bottom of the chart, and students match the word cards with the words on the chart.

Group language experience stories can be used in the same manner except that on the first day the teacher begins with a discussion of a particular topic. Next, the students dictate a group language experience story on the topic, and the teacher and the students then reread the story. A more detailed discussion of the language experience approach is presented later in this section.

Shared Poetry and Songs

Familiar poems, Mother Goose rhymes, and songs can be printed on charts and used to teach initial decoding skills. Also, because the rhymes or songs are familiar, the children will be successful rereading the material. Consequently, they will experience early success in reading.

Children may read a familiar poem or song from a chart without actually looking closely at the words; however, if a particular child is interested in learning to read, he typically will want to look at the words printed on the chart to see if he can make any sense out of decoding the words on the page.

Mother Goose rhymes work well because they are well-known and loved by children. Raffi has recently published some of his popular songs, like *Tingalayo* (1989) and *Five Little Ducks* (1989) as picture books. Other books containing popular songs like *Old MacDonald* and *The Farmer in the Dell* are also available. These illustrated versions of rhymes and songs might first be read aloud and enjoyed before turning to versions of the rhymes and songs printed on charts.

Using Key Words and Pictures to Learn Symbol-Sound Correspondences for Consonants and Vowels

For children just learning to read, short vowel sounds are particularly difficult for them to remember. It is useful to highlight the short vowel sounds for children by placing the vowels and corresponding pictures of key words beginning with the short vowel sound on a chart. As can be seen in Figure 7.6, the key words and corresponding pictures that were selected for the vowels begin with the short vowel sound for each particular vowel.

The chart can be referred to frequently when the teacher is helping children decode words in simple stories containing short vowel sounds. For example, if children were reading a story summary of *Herman the Helper* (Kraus, 1974) on a chart and had difficulty decoding *help*, the teacher might provide assistance by referring to the short vowel chart. "What sound does this word begin with? Yes, the sound /h/ for the letter 'h.' Now, if you can't remember one sound to try for 'e,' the short vowel sound, you can look at the short vowel chart. The short sound for 'e' is /e/ as in 'elephant.' We know the sound for 'l' is /l/ and for 'p' is /p/. If you blend the sound together, /h/-/e/-/l/-/p/, you get *help*."

Using Writing and Spelling to Teach Children about Symbol-Sound Correspondences and to Develop Their Phonemic Awareness

Having beginning readers write simple sentences about stories they have read will improve their phonemic awareness, knowledge of symbol-sound correspondences, and consequently their ability to decode. This writing should be done with considerable teacher modeling and assistance that can be provided in a small group situation.

One approach, described above in the section on the *Early Intervention in Reading* program, involves the teacher asking a small group of students to agree on a sentence to write about a story just read. Or, the children could write a sentence about a book read aloud by the teacher. Perhaps the teacher has just read *The Three Billy Goats Gruff* to the class. An exchange with a group of low-achieving students involving writing might include the following:

TEACHER: Okay, we've come up with the sentence, "The three billy goats gruff went across the bridge." Who remembers how to spell *the*? Great, John, "t" "h" "e." Write this on your paper. Remember to use a capital "t" because

a	apple	
b	ball and bat	
c	caterpillar	
d	duck	
e	elephant	
f	flower	
g	glasses	
h	house	
i	igloo	
j	jam	
k	kite	
l	lamp	
m	monkey	
n	nest	
o	octopus	
p	puppy	
q	queen	
r	rose	
s	snake	
t	tree	
u	umbrella	
v	vase	
w	wings	

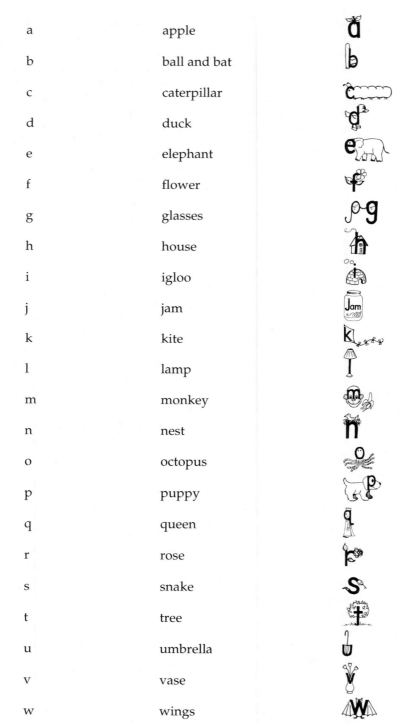

FIGURE 7.6. Picture Mnemonics for the Letters of the Alphabet

x	"exit" sign	eXit
y	yellow (colored in yellow)	Y
z	zzz (a person snoring)	Z

long and short vowel sounds and the most common vowel pair sounds are presented in Figure 8.6.

FIGURE 7.6. Picture Mnemonics for the Letters of the Alphabet *(cont.)*

we're starting a sentence. Now, let's work on the next word. What two letters make the sound at the beginning of *three*?

KRIS: "th"

TEACHER: That's right. Now what sound do you hear next?

DAN: /e/

TEACHER: /e/ is at the end of the word, but there is a letter before this. Listen. *Three.*

DAN: "r"

TEACHER: That's right. Write down "r" next to "th" and put "ee" at the end. *Three* has two "e"s at the end. Now what letter do you hear at the beginning of *billy*?

SUSAN: "b"

TEACHER: Great. What letter comes next?

KRIS: "e"

TEACHER: No, let's look at the short vowel chart. The sound /i/ is what you hear at the beginning of *igloo* so it's spelled by the letter "i." What letter do you think comes next in *billy*?

JOHN: "l"

TEACHER: That's right. You can't hear it, but *billy* has two "l"s. So, write down two "l"s and put a "y" at the end. How do we start *goats*?

SUSAN: "g"

TEACHER: Correct. Now the sound /o/ in *goats* is spelled with "oa." So if you are trying to figure out a word with "oa" in it when you are reading, a good sound to try would be /o/. What should we write down next on our papers for *goats*?

KRIS: "t"

TEACHER: Yes, and at the very end of the word you can hear "s." The "s" makes the word plural and shows that there is more than one goat.

As can be seen in the above example, the teacher is developing children's phonemic awareness and ability to sound and blend the phonemes in words. She is teaching them about symbol-sound correspondences. She is also mentioning important components of writing mechanics (i.e., "The" begins with a capital because it is the first word in the sentence.) and spelling (i.e., "Goats" is plural and consequently ends with "s.") as opportunities arise.

SUMMARY

This chapter has stressed the importance of early intervention for low-achieving emergent readers. Effective programs have used children's literature, included repeated reading, stressed phonemic awareness, and made use of writing about stories read. It is encouraging that early intervention programs have helped many low-achieving emergent readers to start reading in first grade.

Suggested Reading

CUNNINGHAM, P., HALL, D., and DEFEE, M. (1991). Non-ability grouped, multi-level instruction: A year in a first-grade classroom. *The Reading Teacher, 44,* 566–571.

HIEBERT, E., COLT, J., CATTO, S., and GURY, E. (1992). Reading and writing of first-grade students in a restructured Chapter 1 program. *American Educational Research Journal, 29,* 545–572.

JUEL, C. (1988). Learning to read and write: A longitudinal study of fifty-four children from first through fourth grade. *Journal of Educational Psychology, 80:* 437-447. Children who were poor readers in first grade were still poor readers in fourth grade. Problems of poor readers are discussed.

PINNELL, G., FRIED, M., and ESTICE, R. (1990). Reading recovery: Learning how to make a difference. *The Reading Teacher, 43:* 282-295. The successful one-on-one tutoring program for at-risk first-graders is discussed.

STANOVICH, K., (1986). Matthew effects in reading: Some consequences of individual differences in the acquisition of literacy. *Reading Research Quarterly, 21:* 360-406. A convincing case is made for the fact that children who become poor readers enter first grade with low phonemic awareness. The need for early intervention that stresses phonemic awareness training is stressed.

TAYLOR, B., SHORT, R., FRYE, B., and SHEARER, B. (1992). Classroom teachers prevent reading failure among low-achieving first-grade students. *The Reading Teacher, 45,* 592–597.

Notes

1. See Stanovich (1986).
2. See Juel (1988), Pinnell, Fried, and Estice (1990), Stanovich (1986), Taylor, Frye, Short, and Shearer (1992).
3. See Adams (1990), Juel (1988), Stanovich (1986).
4. See Pinnell, DeFord, and Lyons (1988).
5. See Pinnell, Fried, and Estice (1990) for a more detailed description.

CHAPTER 8

WORD RECOGNITION INSTRUCTION

Overview

As you read this chapter you may want to use these themes to guide your understanding and reflection.

- Decoding is an important part of the reading process, but it is only a means to enable students to achieve the ultimate goal of reading comprehension.
- Word recognition instruction should focus as much as possible on words found in everyday texts.
- Explicit instruction in a word recognition strategy will explain to students *what* the strategy is, *why* the strategy is important, *how* to perform the strategy, and *when* to use the strategy in the reading of connected text.
- Students experiencing difficulty with word recognition typically need help in learning how to use phonic and contextual analysis to unlock unfamiliar words when reading everyday texts.
- In addition to developing word recognition accuracy, emerging readers need to develop word recognition fluency.

All readers, especially low-achieving readers, must realize that learning to read well involves more than learning to decode well. Decoding is necessary, but not sufficient, for good comprehension. Decoding instruction should emphasize and lead to meaning identification, not just correct pronunciation. This approach to decoding instruction will help low-achieving readers to develop the ability to read for meaning. Reading instruction that focuses exclusively on decoding may be detrimental to students' reading comprehension.

Nevertheless, decoding is a necessary part of the reading process, and poor decoding skills are characteristically one of the factors that differentiate unsuccessful readers from successful ones.[1] This chapter examines those aspects of word recognition accuracy and fluency that may cause problems for low-achieving readers.

GENERAL MODEL OF WORD RECOGNITION INSTRUCTION

Instruction in word recognition should not focus on decoding to the exclusion of comprehension. Decoding is necessary, but not sufficient, for reading comprehension to occur. Conversely, comprehension aids word recognition and decoding: The better that students understand what they are reading, the greater the bank of resources (i.e., stored meanings) they bring to the task of unlocking difficult words. To emphasize this comprehension-decoding link, we discourage isolated word recognition instruction and practice. Occasionally, to make a particular point about a symbol-sound correspondence or a process, an excursion into isolated instruction can be justified if the task is immediately recontextualized (that is, put back into everyday reading). We are all too familiar with low-achieving readers who can perform word recognition strategies in isolation but cannot use them during everyday reading. In fact, students who receive special reading instruction can easily fall victim to the "basic strategies" conspiracy detailed in Chapter 3. If you recall, students who spend all of their time practicing basic strategies in isolated instructional activities never get a chance to engage in higher-order activities, nor do they get an opportunity to see how phonics strategies get integrated into everyday reading. As a result, phonics stands out there by itself, completely divorced from reading.

Unfortunately, text-related reading instruction occurs too infrequently in our classrooms.[2] Teachers tend to be givers and helpers with written assignments in both word recognition and comprehension; that is, teachers spend too much time helping students complete written assignments.[3] Direct, explicit instruction in word recognition strategies is frequently lacking.[4] Explicit instruction in word recognition strategies includes the following steps:

1. An explanation of *what* the strategy is
2. An explanation of *why* the strategy is important
3. A demonstration of *how* to perform the strategy
4. An explanation of *when* to use the strategy in the reading of connected text
5. Guided practice, independent practice, and application of the strategy while reading everyday text

Most of the word recognition strategies in this chapter will be covered using the above steps.

We take as a given that word recognition instruction is useful only to the degree that it enables comprehension. It should neither be conceived of nor taught as an end unto itself. Yet, in order to help some students achieve adequate comprehension, it may be necessary for brief periods of time to focus instructional attention directly on their word recognition skills. When we do so, we may find that either *accuracy* or *fluency* underlies their comprehension difficulty.

Accuracy is a critical attribute of skilled reading. Even though readers can tolerate some inaccuracies in word recognition and still maintain their comprehension, there are practical limits to the number of inaccuracies that can be tolerated before comprehension breaks down. Furthermore, even if it does not break down, inaccuracies can render the comprehension process slow and tedious when a reader constantly has to return to words to reread them.

One important strategy that readers use to figure out unfamiliar words is phonic analysis. Low-achieving readers often have less knowledge than successful readers about symbol-sound correspondences, particularly as they pertain to vowels, and they are not skilled at using this knowledge flexibly while reading.[5] They may have difficulty with segmenting (decomposing words into phonemes or syllables) and blending phonemes or syllables.[6] They may also have difficulty applying whatever word recognition skills they do possess while reading connected text.[7]

Another important aspect of decoding is contextual analysis. Readers, especially successful readers, appear to use context only when they have to, as in the case of mediated, or noninstantaneous, word recognition.[8] Successful readers, for the most part, have reached a more or less automatic stage in word recognition whereas low-achieving readers have to depend more on contextual analysis.[9] Interestingly, successful readers appear to devote their contextual analysis energies not to decoding but to comprehension. Hence, when successful readers make an oral reading substitution, they are more likely than low-achieving readers to make one that is congruent with the overall meaning of the text. This is because they are constantly monitoring their reading for meaning. Ironically, low-achieving readers, who appear to devote their contextual analysis energies to identifying unknown words rather than to comprehension, tend to make more oral reading substitutions that are not congruent with the meaning of the text. Moreover, regardless of how they attempt to allocate their energies, low-achieving readers do not use context as effectively as they should, even in mediated word recognition.[10]

In addition to word recognition accuracy, *fluency* (an index of the degree to which a reader's oral reading resembles everyday spoken language) is an important aspect of skilled reading.[11] Since skilled readers' word recognition is both automatic and quick, they can use their freed-up cognitive capacity for comprehension processes. In short, readers who are automatic in word recognition can think more about what they are reading. In addition to being less automatic in word recognition than successful readers, low-achieving readers generally have been found to be slower at decoding.[12]

In the sections that follow, you will find instructional strategies that teachers can use to help students develop word recognition accuracy and fluency. You will find strategies to develop (1) basic sight word knowledge, (2) knowledge of symbol-sound correspondences, along with the ability to use this knowledge flexibly (for example, variant vowel sounds), (3) ability to break words into parts, sound out parts, and blend parts back together, (4) use of context clues, (5) use of structural analysis, and (6) ability to apply word recognition skills to actual reading. To facilitate fluency you will encounter strategies that nurture automatic word recognition and lead to smooth, speechlike oral reading.

DEVELOPING A BASIC SIGHT VOCABULARY

Skilled readers automatically identify most words as sight words. That is, they use immediate, as opposed to mediated, word identification. They are able to do this because they have seen most words they come across in print many times before. However, we do not recommend that emerging readers be drilled on new words over and over again until they have memorized them as sight words. This "whole word" approach to identifying new words is too slow and inefficient, especially for learning how to identify unfamiliar words on one's own. The simultaneous use of contextual and phonic analysis to decode unfamiliar words is a much more efficient and realistic approach to word recognition for an emerging reader.

Nevertheless, there are some instances in which the whole word approach should be used, in which students should receive repeated, meaningful exposures to words until they learn them as sight words. For example, students reading at a preprimer or primer level essentially have no word recognition skills, and if they are taught some sight words, they can begin to read simple text as they are developing their word recognition skills. Examples of words that might be learned this way are *Jan, Ken, play, ball,* and *good* (that is, high-interest, emotional, and high-frequency words).

Also, primary grade readers who lack sufficient basic sight words will benefit from meaningful drills on certain high-frequency words until they know them instantaneously as sight words. These words (for example, *is, an, the, said, was, there, they*) occur so frequently in primary level reading materials that students should learn to recognize them instantly as sight words in order to maximize their reading fluency.[13]

Many basic sight vocabulary lists have been developed.[14] One list developed by Mason and Au (1990) is presented in Figure 8.1. Mason and Au report that these are the 200 most frequently occurring words in children's reading material, and that the first 100 words make up about half of the words in a typical school reading text.

In general, students learn to recognize instantly these basic sight words without receiving special instruction, simply through repeated contact when reading. However, some of these words are difficult to learn for low-achieving readers. Many of the words in Figure 8.1 are verbs and function words (prepositions, conjunctions, auxiliary and past tense verbs, and relative pronouns) that do not carry a great deal of meaning by themselves. Many are very low-imagery words. Low-achieving readers may need extra help in learning some of these high-frequency words as sight words.

General Method for Teaching Basic Sight Words

There has been a fair amount of controversy about whether it is best for beginning readers to learn sight words in context or isolation.[15] Ehri and Wilce (1980) concluded that there are benefits to both approaches. Students evidently learn more about the semantic features of words when they are exposed to them in context but learn more about their orthographic features when they are exposed to them in isolation. Consequently, Ehri and Wilce recommend that instruction in sight words include work with words in isolation and in meaningful contexts.

McNinch (1981) has developed a method for instructing low-achieving readers in sight words that involves teaching the word in both context and isolation. Teachers using this approach have reported it to be effective. This approach is particularly useful for low-achieving readers who have had difficulty learning high-frequency sight words, such as those on the Mason and Au list. Explicit instruction using McNinch's approach might look something like this.

How. First, the teacher presents the word to be learned in context in an *oral* sentence. Then, the teacher reads the word to the students as they *see* it (on the chalkboard, overhead, or sentence strip) in the *written* context of one or more sentences or phrases. If possible, the other words in the sentences or phrases should also be in the students' sight reading vocabulary. (Initially, the other words might come from group language experience stories. See the section on language experience, later in this chapter.) The basic sight word being taught in each sentence or phrase should be highlighted by the teacher, such as by underlining or other methods.

Second, the word is written by the teacher in isolation on the board, the overhead, or the back of the sentence strip. The teacher then asks the students questions about it to focus their attention. For example

FIGURE 8.1. 200 Most Frequently Occurring Words

1. the	31. but	61. into	91. long	121. also	151. great	181. sound
2. of	32. what	62. has	92. little	122. around	152. tell	182. below
3. and	33. all	63. more	93. very	123. another	153. men	183. saw
4. a	34. were	64. her	94. after	124. came	154. say	184. something
5. to	35. when	65. two	95. words	125. come	155. small	185. thought
6. in	36. we	66. like	96. called	126. work	156. every	186. both
7. is	37. there	67. him	97. just	127. three	157. found	187. few
8. you	38. can	68. see	98. where	128. word	158. still	188. those
9. that	39. an	69. time	99. most	129. must	159. between	189. always
10. it	40. your	70. could	100. know	130. because	160. name	190. looked
11. he	41. which	71. no	101. get	131. does	161. should	191. show
12. for	42. their	72. make	102. through	132. part	162. Mr.	192. large
13. was	43. said	73. than	103. back	133. even	163. home	193. often
14. on	44. if	74. first	104. much	134. place	164. big	194. together
15. are	45. do	75. been	105. before	135. well	165. give	195. asked
16. as	46. will	76. its	106. go	136. such	166. air	196. house
17. with	47. each	77. who	107. good	137. here	167. line	197. don't
18. his	48. about	78. now	108. new	138. take	168. set	198. world
19. they	49. how	79. people	109. write	139. why	169. own	199. going
20. at	50. up	80. my	110. our	140. things	170. under	200. want
21. be	51. out	81. made	111. used	141. help	171. read	
22. this	52. them	82. over	112. me	142. put	172. last	
23. from	53. then	83. did	113. man	143. years	173. never	
24. I	54. she	84. down	114. too	144. different	174. us	
25. have	55. many	85. only	115. any	145. away	175. left	
26. or	56. some	86. way	116. day	146. again	176. end	
27. by	57. so	87. find	117. same	147. off	177. along	
28. one	58. these	88. use	118. right	148. went	178. while	
29. had	59. would	89. may	119. look	149. old	179. might	
30. not	60. other	90. water	120. think	150. number	180. next	

What is the first letter?

What is the last letter?

How many letters are in the word?

Please spell the word.

Please trace the word.

Third, students practice reading the word in sentences or phrases. Again, as much as possible, all other words should already be a part of the students' reading vocabulary.

Fourth, students practice reading the word in actual text, such as in a book or a language experience chart or story. The teacher asks questions that require students to use the word in order to answer the questions. The teacher may also ask students to reread a sentence in the text containing the word.

Fifth, students engage in independent practice involving the word under study. Independent practice activities may include trying to find the word in other books or language experience stories or playing games using the word. Examples of activities that may be used for independent practice are provided below.

What, *Why*, and *When*.   In addition to following the steps of the McNinch procedure, it is important for the teacher to explain to students *what* they will be learning: They will be learning how to read a word that they will often come across in text. The teacher should also explain *why* this is important: It is important to learn this word because it shows up a lot in books. Finally, the teacher should explain *when* this will be helpful: They will remember this word and read it as they come across it again in their reading.

Activities to Provide Practice in Sight Words

Once instruction has occurred using the approach just outlined, a teacher can engage students in practice activities such as these:

1. Ask the students to find additional examples of the word in books or language experience stories and try to read the sentence in which the word occurs. Students may also want to look in magazines and newspapers. If the material is consumable, let the students underline the word with multi-colored pens or make a collage of the word. Students can even make charts indicating the number of times they find particular words.

2. Encourage the students to tape themselves as they read a number of basic sight words they have been working on. The words should be written in isolation and in sentences on cards. While looking at the cards, students can listen to their recordings and evaluate their own accuracy and fluency with the words and sentences.

3. Encourage the students to use these basic sight words in their own writing or as they create word games. Give the students a number of these sight words plus a number of other high-imagery words. Let them write individual, partner, or small-group language experience stories using these words. Then they can share their stories with one another to provide added practice in reading these words in natural contexts.

4. Have the students play games using a number of the basic sight words they have been working on. Games such as concentration, checkers, and bingo can be developed in ways that incorporate word recognition practice. These can be games that the students themselves have created in Activity 3. Also, board games can be used in which a player goes x number of steps forward on a track if the player knows a basic sight word he has been practicing. With games, however, it is important that students be directed to actually read aloud the words they are trying to learn as they come across them. In this way they actually are receiving practice in reading the words. Otherwise, a student may be able to make a match in a concentration game, for example, by turning up "there" and "there" without being able to read the word. As games are created, try to make them so that the specific words and sentences can be changed as the students make progress in gaining personal control over a large corpus of sight words.

Using Language Experience Stories to Develop Students' Basic Sight Vocabulary

The language experience approach to teaching reading involves an individual student or group of students' dictating stories about topics of interest and then rereading the stories many times as practice reading material.[16] The language experience approach is a particularly effective way of helping low-achieving readers to develop a basic sight vocabulary for a number of reasons. First, the reading material is interesting to the students and they will read with a high level of engagement because they have created the stories themselves. Second, the stories provide material that low-achieving readers who are older can and will read because, unlike much of the basal primer material, it is not too immature for them. Third, students feel good about using this material because they are generally proud of their stories and usually can reread them fairly successfully. Fourth, the use of language experience stories is often perceived as something different by older low-achieving readers and therefore novel enough to motivate them.

Language experience stories may be dictated by a group of students or by an individual. We have found that individual dictations are particularly motivating to students because they are extremely proud of and interested in their own stories.

In using the language experience approach, the teacher first engages the student or group in a brief discussion about a topic for a story, such as "How I spend my free time" or "My favorite TV show" or "What I think of the classroom hamster." Second, the teacher records the story. It is important to record the story exactly as it is dictated. If the teacher alters or corrects a story too dramatically, students may not experience the exhilaration and success of creating their very own piece. It is also important to keep the dictated story short at first. If the story gets very long, the children may not be able to reread the story and consequently may not feel successful. Third, the teacher rereads the story orally, tracking or running her hand under the words as they are read. Fourth, the teacher helps the individual or group reread the story orally several times. Finally, each story is put into a collection of language experience stories that students continue to reread both orally and silently as practice reading material. This last step is an important part of the approach that is often neglected. Beginning readers need to practice rereading familiar, manageable material, and their language experience stories provide an enjoyable and satisfying source of such material.

An individual's collection of language experience stories can be used to reinforce basic sight words upon which the teacher has been focusing. For example, if the teacher has been helping students learn the basic sight word *there*, students can read through their language experience stories to see how many times they can find examples of this word. The word can be underlined each time it is found and the number of times a word is found can be noted on a chart.

It is inevitable that language experience stories will include many of the basic sight words precisely because these words are such an important part of any communication act, be it oral or written. To demonstrate how many basic sight words can be found in just a few short language experience stories, Figure 8.2 shows three stories created by a third-grade student reading on a first-grade level. Out of a total of 103 words, these three stories contain 31 different basic sight words and 62 basic sight words in all from the 200 words on the Mason and Au list.

Avoiding Automatic Errors

A common problem for low-achieving readers (typically it begins toward the end of first grade) is that they automate certain errors. For example, a child sees *this* but says /*that*/. The incorrect response is overlearned to the extent that it becomes the model response for the child. In another example (in Figure 9.5 but based on Figure 8.7), *every* was automatically misread as *very*. Automatic errors

FIGURE 8.2. Language Experience
Stories by a Third-Grade Student

My Summer Vacation

I went for a ride. I rode my new bike.
I went to church. I played a game.
Me and my mom went to the beach.
I played ball. I got hot.

Yellow

Yellow makes me feel like I am by the
sun. Yellow smells like trees blowing
in the wind. Yellow smells like a field
of flowers.

Air Pollution

Some days it is a nice fresh day or it
can be one of the pollution days. It
can get in your lungs and make you sick.
It can sting your eyes. Pollution is a
very bad thing for people.

are often made when reading basic sight words; that is, a child may automatically misread quite a few basic sight words. When asked to reexamine the word, the child often can read the word correctly, thus corroborating the force of habit view of those automatic errors.

Unless a particular word is misread a few times over a few readings, drill on specific basic sight words is not what readers need to reverse their disposition to misread common words. One way to point out the problem to the child is to share findings from the oral reading analysis sheets (explained in Chapter 9) with the child. The child and teacher can discuss why it is important to read these words accurately (for example, if you don't, you can misunderstand things).

A second strategy begins with the child reading into a tape recorder. When replaying the tape and following along with the book, the child can be on the look-out for words misread automatically. This activity has the side benefit of encouraging comprehension monitoring (attending to the sense of the reading) and word recognition accuracy simultaneously.

USING PHONIC ANALYSIS

Phonic analysis is an essential decoding tool. Segmenting a word into parts, attaching appropriate sounds to these parts, and blending the parts together is one of the primary strategies a reader should use to decode a word not instantly known at sight. Furthermore, research has demonstrated consistently that systematic, intensive phonics instruction provides children with a distinct advantage in word analysis skills and a modest advantage on comprehension tests.[17]

Although phonic analysis is extremely useful, it also can be confusing to a beginning reader for a number of reasons. The English language has fifty-two symbols, approximately forty-four sounds, and several hundred symbol-sound relationships (Mazurkiewicz, 1976). These numbers point out a major problem with phonic analysis, that there is considerable irregularity or unpredictability in symbol-sound correspondences. For example, the symbol *a* has a different sound in each of these words: *bad, aloud, take, want, ball, park.* Students may become overwhelmed and confused if they are taught too many symbol-sound correspondences. They simply cannot remember several hundred of them. There is a list of symbol-sound correspondences that are most beneficial to teach because they are both common and useful later in this section.

Another problem with phonic analysis is that there are very few phonics rules that occur with enough regularity to warrant teaching as rules. Clymer (1963) carried out a study on the utility of phonic rules in primary grade reading material. Bailey (1967), Burmeister (1968), and Emans (1967) performed similar studies. These studies all suggest that some phonics rules that are frequently taught to students are misleading if taught as hard-and-fast rules because there are so many exceptions. For example, Clymer found that the double vowel rule (when two vowels are together, the first one is long and the second is silent) held only 45 percent of the time. He found that the silent *e* rule (when there are two vowels, one of which is a final *e*, the first vowel is long and the *e* is silent) held only 63 percent of the time.

Therefore, symbol-sound correspondences involving vowels should not be taught as infallible rules. Instead, children should be taught to be flexible when trying to come up with the appropriate sound for a vowel or vowel pair. For example, students may be taught that a good sound to try first when decoding a word with the CVCe (consonant, vowel, consonant, silent *e*) pattern is the long sound of the vowel. However, if students do not come up with a word that makes sense, they should be flexible and try another sound for the vowel, such as the short sound (for example, *live*).

There are two basic approaches to teaching phonics, an explicit approach[18] and an implicit approach, sometimes called synthetic and analytic approaches. In an explicit approach, the sounds of individual letters in words are identified and blended together (/c/, /a/, /t/, *cat*). In an implicit approach, sounds of letters are never pronounced in isolation and consequently blending is not stressed (for example, *c* makes the sound that is heard at the beginning of *cut*, *a* makes the sound that is heard at the beginning of *at*, and *t* makes the sound that is heard at the beginning of *toy*). Research suggests that an explicit approach to phonics instruction may be superior to an implicit approach.[19] As pointed out in Chapter 7, skill in phonemic segmentation and blending has been found to differentiate successful and unsuccessful readers. Also, students receiving extra instruction in blending have been found to make superior gains on beginning reading achievement tests.[20]

Based on this research, we cautiously support a flexible approach to phonics instruction that begins with a focus on segmenting and sounding word parts and then blending the parts together. It is important that sounds of individual letters not be distorted, such as /cuh/ /ah/ /tah/ for *cat*. One way to minimize this problem is to say individual sounds as quickly as possible as opposed to drawing them out. Another approach in blending instruction and practice is to include only that subset of consonants whose sounds can be continued as they are pronounced. For example, the sounds of *s, z, sh, f, v, m, n,* and *r* can be continued indefinitely. By contrast, the consonant stops in our language can only be pronounced if some vowel sound is added to them. Common stops are *b, p, d, g, t, k,* and *c*. After sounding and blending instruction with the continuants occurring in initial consonant positions, as in CVC patterns, students should be able to transfer their sounding and blending strategy to stops without specific instruction and practice.

In spite of the problems with sounding out word parts and blending the sounds together, instruction in sounding and blending is useful if applied to the decoding of words that are causing problems in actual text. Many low-achieving readers may have learned the basic symbol-sound correspondences in isolation but may need help in applying this knowledge to the reading of connected text. In other words, they need to learn how to break a word into parts, sound out the parts, and blend the parts together to come up with a word that makes sense in context. But there is one thing a teacher always needs to remember about intensive decoding instruction, especially blending: Once you get the children into it, you have got to get them out of it! Children need to develop rapid, automatic decoding. Blending, like other decoding skills and strategies, is only a means to an end, not an end in itself. The real end to decoding instruction is comprehension. In the remainder of this section, strategies are discussed that help students learn symbol-sound correspondences and help them apply this knowledge to the decoding of unfamiliar words in text.

A problem with many of the teaching suggestions and materials currently available for teaching symbol-sound correspondences is that they direct students to move from sound to symbol instead of from symbol to sound. For example, students are often presented with a set of pictures and instructed to write down the letter representing the beginning sound of each picture. Skill in activities such as this provides no assurance that students are also skilled in coming up with the appropriate sound when they see a particular symbol. Therefore, instruction and practice in phonics should proceed as much as possible from symbol to sound instead of from sound to symbol. Examples of this type of instruction and practice will be provided in this section.

As mentioned earlier, it is important to limit the number of symbol-sound correspondences that are emphasized in instruction to avoid overwhelming and frustrating students. Some correspondences are so confusing and complex that they are best avoided altogether. For example, attempting to teach students all of the different sounds for the symbol *ou* will not be fruitful (for example, those in *ounce, cousin, ought, soup, would, though*); readers are not going to take the time to recall all of these different sounds when trying to decode an unfamiliar word containing *ou*. Other correspondences may be highly predictable, but they apply to so few words that instruction in them seems pointless. There simply are not enough examples to which they apply (for example, *o* followed by *ld* has the long sound). Time and effort should be directed to a relatively small number of symbol-sound correspondences that are most common. A recommended list is presented in Figure 8.3.

FIGURE 8.3. Common Symbol-Sound Correspondences

Consonants   b, d, f, h, j, k, l, m, n, p, qu, r, s, t, v, w, x, y, z
  c as in can, come, cut
  c as in cent, city, cycle
  g as in game, gone, gum
  g as in gem, ginger, gym

Blends   bl, br, cl, cr, dr, dw, fl, fr, gl, gr, ld, mp, nd, ng, nk, nt, pl, pr, rk, sc, sk, sl, sm, sn, sp, st, sw, tr, tw, wr, sch, shr, spl, spr, squ, str, thr

Digraphs   ch, ph, sh, th (think, then), wh (which, who)

Vowels
  Short sounds: a (hat), e (bed), i (sit), o (not), u (run)

  Long sounds: a (caked), e (here), i (bite), o (hope), u (cute)

  R-controlled: ar (far), er (her), ir (fir), or (for), ur (fur)

  L-controlled: al (ball)

  Vowel pairs: ai (rain), ay (day), au (author), aw (law), ea (meat), ea (head), ee (feet), ei (weight), ei (receive), ew (few), oa (boat), oi (boil), oo (book), oo (food), ou (cloud), ow (slow), ow (now), oy (toy)

Applying Our General Model to Symbol-Sound Instruction

Teaching Consonants

To teach the symbol-sound correspondence for a consonant, blend, or digraph, you may wish to try these steps:

1. *What.* Explain what the students will be learning. They will be learning what sound to try when they come across a difficult word, or word not known instantly, containing a particular consonant, blend, or digraph.

2. *Why.* Explain why this is important. This is important because if students have to figure out an unknown word that contains this letter or letters, knowing what sound to try out for the letter will help them a great deal.

3. *How.* Provide instruction in the symbol-sound correspondence. Write two or three examples of words containing the consonant, blend, or digraph on the board (for example, *sun, sing, sad*). If possible, these initial examples should come from words that the students already know or have been exposed to through familiar reading material, such as language experience stories. Ask the students to tell you what letter or letters the words have in common, then read the words or ask the students to read them. Ask the students if the letter under study (*s*) has the same sound in all of the words. Identify the letter sound (/s/) and explain that this is the usual sound for this letter or cluster of letters. Have the students write the two or three examples on a piece of paper. Do not worry about their spelling of other parts of the word; monitor to see if the target correspondence is spelled correctly.

4. *Provide guided practice.* Ask the students if they can think of any more words beginning with the same sound as the letter under study (*s*) to add to the list (*Susan, summer*). Write these words on the board and have the students add them to their list. Also, accept words that have the same sound but are not spelled with that letter. For example, when teaching the sound of *s*, students might suggest words such as *cent* and *cider*. When this occurs, congratulate the student for getting the right sound, show the students how to spell the word, and tell them that you will study that sound later. To give the students practice going from symbol to sound, write a few more words on the board (*silly, song, soap*). Pronounce all but the initial letter for them (*illy, ong, oap*), and ask them to blend the initial sound and the rest of the word together to come up with each whole word. Have students add these new words to their list. To provide students with practice in reading all of the words on their list, make up oral sentences in which a word is missing. Ask the students to point to the correct word from their list that would fit in the blank in the sentence ("The _____ is shining." "I will _____ a _____." "That is a _____ thing to do." "The boy felt _____.").

5. *When.* Encourage students to think about how they could use this new knowledge when they are reading everyday texts. If they are trying to decode a word that contains this letter (*s*), they should remember the sound of the letter (/s/) and use this sound when trying to sound out the word. Illustrate this by finding several words beginning with *s* in everyday texts

and applying knowledge of the *s* symbol-sound correspondence in order to discover their pronunciation. The text might be a language experience story, a story recently read by the students, or a short paragraph containing a number of *s* words.

6. *Provide for independent practice.* Students should try to apply their new symbol-sound correspondence knowledge as they read everyday texts or engage in word games. Suggestions for independent practice are presented later in this section.

Teaching Vowels

The steps for teaching the symbol-sound correspondences for vowels or vowel pairs are similar to the steps described above. However, a few modifications should be made. To teach the symbol-sound correspondences for vowels or vowel pairs, try this sequence of activities:

1. *What.* Explain what the students will be learning. They will be learning what sound or sounds to try when they come across a difficult word containing a particular vowel or vowel pair.
2. *Why.* Explain why this is important: This is important because if students have to figure out a difficult word that contains this vowel or vowel pair, they will need to know what sound or sounds to try out.
3. *How.* Provide instruction in the symbol-sound correspondence. Write two or three examples of words containing the vowel or vowel pair (*fat, sad, band*) on the board. Read the words to the students or ask them to read the words. Have them copy the words on a piece of paper. Ask students to tell you what letter or letters the words have in common and ask them if the letter being studied (*a*) has the same sound in all of the words. Identify the sound of the vowel or vowel pair (/a/). Explain that this is one common sound they might try to use when they have to decode a difficult word containing the letter being studied (*a*), particularly when the word contains a particular spelling pattern (for example, a CVC or CVCC pattern).
4. *Provide guided practice.* Write several more examples on the board (*tap, black, fast*). Ask students to decode these and then add them to their list. It is best to give students the examples instead of asking them to supply words because a particular vowel sound can be spelled in different ways (*laugh* has the short *a* sound). Provide the students with oral sentences in which a word is missing and ask them to point to the correct word from their list that would fit in the blank.

   The teacher may want to work with phonograms to generate more words with the vowel sound under study. A phonogram is a common spelling pattern consisting of a vowel followed by one or more consonants (*-at, -ike, -and, -ight*). After discussing one symbol-sound correspondence for the letter *a*, the teacher might work with the *-at* phonogram. He might show students the word *cat*, write *fat* below it, and ask the students the word. This procedure could be followed with the examples *bat, sat,* and *pat.* Next, the teacher and students could try to generate as many words as possible from the *-ad* phonogram. A list of common phonograms is provided in Figure 8.4.

ack	ay	id	ite
ad	eat	ide	ock
ade	ed	ight	old
ake	eed	ike	ook
all	eel	ill	op
ame	eep	im	ot
an	eet	in	uck
and	ell	ine	ud
ang	en	ing	un
ar	eat	ink	ung
at	et	ip	up
ate	ick	it	ut

FIGURE 8.4. List of Common Phonograms

5. *When.* Explain when students should use what they have learned as they are reading on their own. If they are trying to decode a word that contains this vowel (*a*), they should remember that one good sound to try, particularly when the word has a particular pattern (CVC), would be the sound they have just worked on (short *a*). Illustrate this by decoding several short *a* words in actual text (language experience story, basal story, paragraph containing short *a* words).

6. *Provide independent practice in the vowel or vowel pair under study.* (See page 21 for examples.)

Special issues in teaching about vowels. Once two sounds for one vowel or vowel pair have been introduced (short *a*, long *a*), it is important to compare words containing the same vowel or vowel pair but different vowel sounds. For example, after receiving instruction in the short sound of *a* (as is usually found in words following the CVC pattern), and the long sound of *a* (as is often found in words following the CVCe pattern), a student needs practice in distinguishing between these two sounds for the symbol *a*. To do this, the teacher and students might start with a list of ten words containing the letter *a*. The students would decode the words, with the teacher's help if necessary, and write them under the appropriate category, short *a* or long *a*. Then, to reinforce this comparison in the context of sentences, students might use these words to fill in blanks in oral sentences or written sentences. An example is provided in Figure 8.5.

It is also useful for the teacher to direct students' attention to minimal pair contrasts; in this case, words that differ only in terms of the presence or absence of the final silent *e* (*man, mane; cap, cape*). The teacher might work with the students on fill-in-the-blank activities such as "The _____ (man, mane) put his _____ (cap, cape) on his head." In this situation students have to attend to the presence or absence of the feature *e*, which distinguishes *man* from *mane*, in order to fill in the blank correctly.

When comparing words with the same vowel symbol but different vowel sounds, it is important for the teacher to help the students understand the notions of diversity and flexibility in applying decoding knowledge. They must realize that each vowel letter will map onto many vowel sounds (diversity); hence they must be willing to try more than one vowel sound (flexibility) until they find something that makes sense in the context. For example, when trying to decode an unfamiliar word containing the letter *a*, the students should

First _____ is ground into flour. Then it is sold to a bakery. The flour is mixed with other things until it is _____ for baking. The _____ is baked and then sold to a food store.

Every winter Indians trapped _____ . They sold the thick, brown furs to men from France. In the 1600s and 1700s people in France wanted _____ coats to keep them warm and _____ hats for their _____ . This was a sign of _____
_____ .

bread	*heads*	*wheat*	*beaver*	*ready*	*wealth*	*real*
meat	*beavers*	*seal*	*seals*			

FIGURE 8.5. Example of Short Modified Cloze Passages to be Used as a Practice Phonics Activity for the Symbol-Sound Correspondence for *ea*

remember that the word might have the short *a* sound or the long *a* sound. If the word follows the CVC pattern, a good sound to try first would be the short *a* sound; if it follows the CVCe pattern, they might try the long *a* sound first. In multisyllabic words, students might try a second sound for *a* if the first sound does not work. What is important for students to remember is that if first attempts at decoding produce a word that does not make sense, they should be flexible and try to decode the word again using another *a* sound.

To help students apply this notion of flexibility, the teacher should be consistent when helping students with decoding during oral or silent reading. For example, after a student has finished reading aloud a page in which she read *luke* for *look,* the teacher could point out the sensibleness of this error, and ask the student if she could think of another sound to use for *oo* when decoding *look.* If that does not help, the teacher should offer the student a meaning clue such as, "It means to see." Or, if a student has asked for help with the word *bread,* the teacher should ask the student if he could think of two common sounds for *ea* or, if necessary, provide words already known to the student such as *head* and *meat.* The teacher should remind the student to try each sound, short *e* and long *e,* when attempting to decode *bread.*

One common type of phonics lesson encourages the comparison of words with the same vowel sound but different vowel symbols. This type of comparison might conceivably be useful for spelling but not for reading. When trying to spell *plate,* it is argued, students should generate as many long *a* spellings as they can; they might spell it using the CVCe pattern (*plate*), or with *ay* (*playt*), or with *ai* (*plait*). We can see how one might develop an argument, based upon flexibility, to justify this technique for spelling (and we can also see how one might develop an equally strong argument, based on sheer confusion, to condemn the approach). However, it makes little sense as a reading tool. When students are trying to decode *display,* it is not very helpful to know that the long *a* sound is represented by *ay* and *ai* as well as the CVCe pattern. In other words, flexibility in reading requires students to map many vowel sounds onto a single symbol; just the reverse is true for spelling. The point of this example is to avoid mixing instruction in a way that confuses students on this important concept of flexibility.

Learning vowel sounds is difficult for some low-achieving readers or beginning readers.[21] It is not surprising that symbol-sound correspondences for vowels or vowel pairs are more difficult to learn than for consonants; single vowels and many vowel pairs map onto more than one sound, which generally is not the case for consonants. Therefore, it may be useful for students, especially those who are reading on at least an end-of-first-grade level but experiencing difficulty remembering vowel sounds, to have a set of pictures and key words for the vowel sounds causing them difficulty. For example, the short *a* sound might be represented by the word *bat* and a picture of a bat. These vowels, key words, and pictures can be listed on individual charts to which students can refer when attempting to decode difficult words while reading. Examples of key words and pictures for the long and short vowel sounds and the most common vowel pairs are presented in Figure 8.6.

FIGURE 8.6. Key Words and Pictures for Vowels and Vowel Pairs

a	ă	(bat	)	or	ā	(cake	)
e	ĕ	(bell	)	or	ē	(me	)
i	ĭ	(six	**6**)	or	ī	(five	**5**)
o	ŏ	(sock	)	or	ō	(Coke	)
u	ŭ	(sun	)	or	ū	(cube	)
ea	ea	(head	)	or	ea	(meat	)
oa	oa	(boat	)				
oo	oo	(school	)	or	oo	(foot	)
ow	ow	(cow	)	or	ow	(snow	)
oi	oi	(oil	)				
oy	oy	(boy	)				
ee	ee	(feet	)				
ai	ai	(rain	)				
ou	ou	(house	)				

Independent Practice for Symbol-Sound Correspondences

Independent activities that might be used to provide students with necessary practice in using symbol-sound correspondences include the following:

1. Direct the students to teach the newly learned symbol-sound correspondence to someone else. Even if these "students" already know the correct sound for the symbol under consideration, it will be useful for them to go through the steps of teaching the symbol-sound correspondence.
2. Have the students complete a modified cloze passage in which several words containing one or more recently learned symbol-sound correspondences are provided after each blank. Or, a list of words containing the symbol-sound correspondences could be provided at the bottom of the page. An example of the type of activity described was presented in Figure 8.5. In any fill-in-the-blank type activity it is important that students be given some incorrect and potentially confusing distractions in which they will have to come up with the correct sound for the symbol in order to fill in the blank correctly, such as "I _____ (hat, hate) to wash dishes, most of all the frying _____ (pan, pain)."
3. Let the students play a game such as bingo, concentration, rummy, or a track game. The words to be read aloud in order to advance in the game should be words containing the symbol-sound correspondence to be practiced. The cautions about games that were made in the section about basic sight words also apply to symbol-sound correspondence activities.
4. Let students look through old magazines to find pictures representing words containing the symbol-sound correspondence under consideration. Students can make a collage of these pictures. The teacher can help the students label their pictures with letters and/or words in order to emphasize the symbol-sound correspondence.
5. Direct the students to find examples of the symbol-sound correspondence in old language experience stories or in stories they have recently read. Students may want to make a chart to keep a record of the number of examples (or the actual words) that they found on a particular day.

Good examples of phonics games and other activities for practicing with symbol-sound correspondences are provided in a vocabulary book by Johnson and Pearson (1984).

Specialized Phonics Techniques

Learning to Segment, Sound, and Blend Phonemes

The ability to break a word into individual phonemes, or sounds, and blend the sounds together into a word are important reading skills. In a number of studies, high correlations between phonemic analysis and synthesis skills and beginning reading achievement have been found.[22] Furthermore, Williams (1980) has demonstrated that training in phonemic analysis and syntheses contributes to success in beginning reading.

Williams (1980) has developed a supplemental decoding program called the ABD's of reading (for analysis, blending, and decoding) that has been used successfully to improve the decoding skills of learning disabled readers ranging in age from seven to twelve. It includes these steps and features:

How. First, the students are taught how to aurally (no print is used in this step) analyze words at the syllable level. The students are shown how to tell what syllable occurs in the initial, middle, and final positions in a three-syllable word. Syllables are represented by individual wooden (or cardboard) squares, something that becomes important later in the program when individual sounds of specific letters are represented by squares. Then, students are shown how to aurally analyze two- and three-letter syllabic units into constituent phonemes. At this point, individual phonemes are represented by individual squares. Students are shown how to break CV and CVC units into individual phonemes. Next, students are shown how to blend two- and three-phoneme CVC units together. CV-C units are blended first, followed by C-VC units, and finally C-V-C units.

After the above auditory analysis and synthesis work, symbol-sound correspondences for a small number of consonants (seven) and vowels (two) are taught. Then, students are shown how to combine the analysis and synthesis skills with this symbol-sound correspondence knowledge to decode CVC units. Letters are now written on the individual squares and students manipulate and decode all the possible CVC combinations from the seven consonants and two vowels.

After the initial analysis, blending, and decoding instruction, five new consonants and one new vowel are introduced. By manipulating the squares, students practice decoding as many CVC units as possible from the fifteen letters. They then practice decoding CCVC, CVCC, and CCVCC units. Finally, they practice decoding two-syllable patterns (for example, CVCCVC).

The content of the ABD program is taught in twelve units. For each unit the teacher demonstrates the task to be learned, then has students perform the task with other examples. To help students focus on context, words are used in sentences or are identified as nonsense words by the teacher and students. The real words are also used in simple comprehension activities and games. A more detailed description of this extensive program can be found in Williams (1979).

What, Why, and When. It is important for the teacher to explain to students the purpose of such a decoding program. Repeatedly, the teacher should explain *what* students are doing this for: They are learning how to sound and blend syllables to build simple words and nonsense words by manipulating squares. The teacher should explain *why* this is important: It will teach them how to sound and blend real words they come across in everyday reading. In everyday reading, meaningfulness will help them decide whether or not the words they sound out are correct. The teacher should explain *when* they would use this as they are reading on their own: When they are stumped by a difficult word, they can break it into individual sounds and blend the sounds back together, just as they have learned to do with the letters on the squares.

Because this program deals to a great extent with words in isolation, it should be used as a supplemental decoding program (as intended) for students who struggle with reading on a primer, first-, or second-grade level. The program is useful because it teaches students more than symbol-sound correspondences; it teaches them how to apply this knowledge, through phonemic analysis and blending, to come up with candidate pronunciations that they can then match against their repertoire of auditory vocabulary to evaluate the viability of the pronunciation.

Learning to Segment, Sound, and Blend Word Parts in Multisyllabic Words

In a study of third-, fourth-, and sixth-grade students' decoding ability, Durkin (1984c) found that the students lacked any organized strategy for attacking difficult words and that their syllabication and blending skills were inadequate. She concluded that intermediate grade readers need more instruction in syllabication and blending to provide them with a set of organized skills for attacking difficult multisyllabic words.

Providing students with instruction and practice in formal syllabication is not recommended. Intensive drill in segmenting large quantities of words in isolation (as the dictionary would segment them), or memorizing and following formal syllabication rules does not seem very useful. However, students do need to develop a disposition to analyze big words, challenging words, into smaller, more manageable units. Syllables are natural candidates for these more manageable parts. Having done an analysis, students can sound out these units and blend them together. Doing this will not be very useful, however, if applied to words that are not in a reader's listening vocabulary. After all, achieving a match with a word already within one's listening vocabulary is really the only means available to a reader to evaluate the viability of a candidate pronunciation. In the case of low-achieving readers, listening vocabularies usually exceed reading vocabularies and decoding ability. Hence they represent an "ideal" population of students for whom a complete syllable strategy—segment, pronounce, blend, evaluate viability—should be beneficial.

How. The teacher should explain to students that a longer word is made up of syllables, usually with one vowel or vowel pair in each syllable. To get a start on an approximate pronunciation, students can start by breaking the word between the vowel and following consonant or between two consonants if there are two consonants together. If the syllable ends in a consonant, a good sound to try first when sounding it out is the short vowel sound. If the syllable ends in a vowel, a good sound to try first when sounding out the syllable is the long vowel sound, but there is a chance that the vowel might have a short sound. Following these guidelines, students should try to segment and sound out the syllables in difficult words they come across in everyday reading material. After saying a word slowly at first, they should try to say it again more quickly and see if the attempted pronunciation helps them think of a word that they already know *and* that makes sense in the passage. If students cannot think of a word, they should, in the spirit of flexible disposition, go back to the word and try some different sound in search of a candidate pronunciation.

What, Why, and *When.* The teacher should explain *what* the students will be learning to do and *why* this is important: They will be learning a long word strategy, a strategy to use when they have to figure out a difficult, longer word. Such a strategy will enable them to pronounce big words on their own without any help. The teacher should model the above procedure with several multisyllabic words in material that the students are currently reading. For guided practice the teacher and students should work through several other examples from the students' current reading assignment. The teacher can also encourage students to write down troublesome words and their page numbers during silent reading. The students can bring these stumpers back to their groups. Working with their peers and/or the teacher, students attempt to use the long word strategy to generate viable pronunciations.

Another simple technique found to be effective is for the teacher to put dots between syllables in difficult longer words taken from actual text (for example, *con•si•der•a•tion*). This helps students decode the specific words under consideration and at the same time encourages the application of the long word strategy during everyday reading.

USING CONTEXTUAL ANALYSIS

The research on context use reveals a troublesome irony: Although low-achieving readers rely on context more than successful readers for help with mediated word recognition, they use context less effectively than successful readers. Low-achieving readers have been found to produce more meaning-changing substitutions in word recognition than successful readers and to self-correct fewer of these erroneous substitutions.[23] They have also been found to make less use of semantic information on cloze passages than successful readers.[24] These results suggest that low-achieving readers may not use context as effectively as they should to help them decode unfamiliar words and to help them self-correct substitutions that interfere with the meaning of the text.

Later in this chapter we introduce a general word recognition strategy that encourages students to use context clues in connection with their phonics knowledge to decode difficult words during everyday reading. But first, we present two strategies that are designed to help low-achieving readers monitor and repair their reading output—they monitor for what makes sense and they repair by learning to self-correct contextually inappropriate pronunciations.

Using Context to Self-Correct

Pflaum and Pascarella (1980) have developed a program to help students learn to use context to determine whether pronunciations make sense and to correct pronunciations in order to maintain meaning. The program has proven effective in improving the reading level of all but beginning readers. Apparently novice readers are still struggling to acquire the conventions of printed language to such an extent that monitoring for meaning is difficult.

The instructional program consists of twenty-four lessons, twelve focusing on substitutions that change sentence meaning and twelve focusing on self-correction of erroneous substitution. For each lesson, students are told *what* they will be learning, *why* it is important, *how* it is related to previous lessons, and *when* they can use it in their own reading. The teacher first models the activities to be learned in a particular lesson and then helps students perform these activities. The monitoring lessons, which focus on detecting word recognition substitutions that do not make sense, include these activities:

1. Students underline the substitutions made by a recorded reader (on a tape) in each of ten sentences.
2. Students underline the substitutions (two in each of five paragraphs) made by a recorded reader and discuss the seriousness of each substitution (based on whether or not it interferes with meaning).
3. Students record their own reading of a short selection, listen to the tape, and underline their own substitutions.
4. While listening to a tape of a reader, students underline twice the substitutions (one in each of five paragraphs) that interfere with the meaning of the paragraph and underline once the substitutions (one in each of five paragraphs) that do not interfere with meaning.
5. Students record their own reading and underline serious substitutions twice (ones that interfere with meaning) and less serious substitutions once (ones that do not interfere with meaning).

The twelve repair lessons, which focus on self-correcting substitutions that do not make sense, include these activities:

1. Students indicate corrections made by a recorded reader by marking them on a copy of the reading material. In some instances the recorded reader might talk aloud about substitutions that do not make sense. For example, if reading, "The horse stumbled and fell off the clith," the recorded reader could say, "Clith? That doesn't make any sense. I'd better look at that word again."
2. Students discuss the purpose of the recorded reader's corrected substitutions.
3. Students discuss words appropriate for blanks in fifteen sentences, given initial letter cues.
4. Students learn to use context first, then initial letter cues, and then final letter cues to help them come up with possible words for blanks in sentences. To do this they list a number of possible words for the blank in a sentence. Then, they eliminate those that do not fit because of initial letter and those that do not fit because of final letter.
5. Students correct the substitutions made by a recorded reader by using context and the initial and final sounds of the missing words.
6. Students record their own reading and analyze their own corrections. They can correct the substitutions they made while reading by stopping the tape when they hear a substitution and correcting it.

Many of the foregoing activities lend themselves to learning pairs or even triads. Two students could work together to mark substitutions of a recorded reader. Or they could record substitutions, independently compare their records, and perhaps even listen to the tape a second time. They could take turns reading into a tape recorder and then work together to detect one another's substitutions and self-corrections.

These two children are listening to what they have read into the tape recorder to locate miscues. (*James Silliman*)

Oral Reading for Meaning

The oral reading for meaning technique (Taylor & Nosbush, 1983) is another procedure that teachers can use to encourage students to correct anomalous substitutions at the same time as they help students learn how to use context to unlock challenging words. In addition, the procedure can be used to provide on-the-spot instruction for word recognition skills that appear weak, based on the student's oral reading. The oral reading for meaning procedure includes several steps:

How. In a one-to-one situation the student orally reads a 250- to 300-word excerpt from a book that is on her instructional level. The teacher may help with difficult words, but in general lets the student read without interruptions. While the student is reading, the teacher records oral reading errors.

After reading, the teacher immediately provides feedback on some positive feature of the student's oral reading. If possible, teachers should note and commend the students' voluntary self-corrections, emphasizing that self-correction is the natural thing for readers to do during everyday reading.

Next, the teacher picks out some examples of senseless substitutions made by the student. Assuming that these are in sentences containing good context clues, the teacher can show the student the substitutions one at a time and invite rereading of each sentence to see if she can come up with a word that makes sense. Then the student can use phonics cues (like beginning and ending letter sounds) to verify the appropriateness of the new pronunciation. Just as in early activities where we encouraged the use of context to evaluate the appropriateness of pronunciations generated from a decoding strategy, here we encourage turning the tables so that decoding is used to monitor a contextual strategy. By emphasizing both sequences, students eventually develop the set for diversity and flexibility that is so crucial to successful reading.

As a final step, the teacher can search for a word recognition skill with which the student had difficulty during the oral reading and provide immediate instruction. Suppose for example a student had trouble with -*ow* words, reading *know* for *now* and *hoe* for *how,* the teacher can focus on these words, introduce several examples of other -*ow* words from the *now* family, contrasting them with several from the *know* family. In this way, the teacher can draw the student's attention to the fact that the symbol -*ow* has two different sounds. This on-the-spot instruction should be particularly meaningful and memorable to the student because of its immediate proximity to the -*ow* problem experienced by the student. This approach is in the same spirit as phonics on-the-fly within the *Reading Recovery* program discussed in Chapter 7.

Another variation on the same theme: Instead of basing on-the-spot instruction on substitutions that were just made, the teacher can review the oral reading material for examples that fit earlier instruction. If, for example, the student received instruction the previous day in different sounds for the symbol -*ea*-, the teacher could find -*ea*- words in the selection the student just read aloud and bring the words to the student's attention. The student could write the words containing -*ea*- under the example *head* or the example *meat*. An example of an oral reading for meaning session is presented in Figure 8.7.

What, Why, and *When.* The teacher should be sure to explain to the students *what* they are trying to accomplish through the oral reading for meaning procedure and *why* this is important: The teacher is helping the student learn to monitor for meaning when reading and to self-correct substitutions that do not make sense in the context of the material being read. When the student recognizes a substitution that does not make sense, he should attempt to self-correct. To do this the student should think of a word beginning with a particular sound that would make sense in the material he has just read.

An important aspect of the oral reading for meaning procedure is that it be carried out on a regular basis. For the desired reading behaviors to develop, this procedure should be undertaken at least twice a week. Obviously time constraints limit a classroom teacher's use of this procedure on an individual basis to a few students at a time. But after 6 weeks or so, the teacher can phase the procedure out with one set of students and begin using it with a second set.

With modifications, this procedure can be used with a group of students. As students are taking turns reading aloud and a nonsemantic substitution is made, the teacher and students can stop to talk about the substitution and the fact that it does not make sense. The group can also try to correct the substitution error by using contextual and phonic analysis.

To Your Good Health*

however^sc

Long ago there lived a king who was such a mighty ruler that whenever he sneezed

everyone in the whole country had to say, "To your good health!" Everyone said it

sheep

except the shepherd with the bright blue eyes, and he would not say it.

The king heard of this and was very angry. He sent for the shepherd to appear

before him.

thorn   every

The shepherd came and stood before the throne, where the king sat looking very

grand and powerful. But however grand or powerful he might be, the shepherd did

after^sc

not feel a bit afraid of him.

"Say at once, 'To my good health!' " cried the king.

"To my good health!" replied the shepherd.

my^sc   my^sc   your

"To mine—to mine, you rascal!" stormed the king.

mission

"To mine, to mine, your Majesty," was the answer.

"But to mine—to my own," roared the king and beat his chest in rage.

"Well, yes; to mine, of course, to my own," cried the shepherd and gently tapped his

breast.

A fifth grade student made mistakes when reading as indicated in the preceding.
The teacher gave the student the following feedback:

1. First, she praised the student for self-correcting after reading "however" for
   "whenever," "after" for "afraid," and "my" for "mine." She pointed out that the
   student should always self-correct when she read a word that didn't make sense.

2. Second, the teacher pointed out to the student two substitutions that didn't make
   sense. She showed her that she said "thorn" for "throne" and "mission" for "majesty."
   She helped the student decode these two words using the cues of context plus the
   first and last letter sound. She again reminded the student that she should stop and
   try to correct errors like this that didn't make sense.

FIGURE 8.7. Example of an Oral Reading for Meaning Session

3. Third, the teacher helped focus the students attention on the symbol-sound correspondence for "thr." On a sheet of paper she listed a few examples of words beginning with "thr" and then asked the student if she could think of any other words beginning with "thr." The teacher added these words to the list and then made up a few sentences, leaving a blank where one of the "thr" words on the list belonged. She had the student point to and say correct words for the blanks from the list of "thr" words. Since the student had confused "every" with "very," the teacher could have elected to provide her with some on-the-spot instruction in distinguishing between these two words instead of providing her with help in "thr" words.

* The passage in Figure 8.7 from To Your Good Health in *A Lizard to Start With* of the READING 720 series by Theodore Clymer and others, © Copyright, 1976, by Ginn and Company. Used with permission.

FIGURE 8.7. Example of an Oral Reading for Meaning Session (*cont.*)

STRUCTURAL ANALYSIS

Structural analysis deals with units of meaning instead of units of sound or units of print. Typically, when teachers focus on structural analysis they engage students in the process of breaking words into morphemes, or meaning-bearing units, as a means of identifying their pronunciation or meaning. Morphemes, the basic units of meaning, can be free or bound. Free morphemes are units that can stand by themselves, such as simple words such as *book, judge,* and *farm.* Bound morphemes are meaning-bearing units that cannot stand by themselves as independent words. They include combining forms of basic word families, such as the *pos* family (meaning put, as in *position, depose, repose, propose*). The class of bound morphemes also includes inflectional endings, such as plurals (*e, es*), verb tense markers (*ed, ing, s*), comparative endings (*er, est*), and possessives (*'s, s'*). Next to subclass of word families, the largest subclass of bound morphemes in English is affixes (prefixes and suffixes), such as *pre* (a prefix) and *ment* (a suffix) in the word *prejudgment.* All affixes alter or augment the meaning of the forms to which they are added. An important distinction between suffixes and inflectional endings is that suffixes almost always change the part of speech of the form to which it is applied; for example, *judge* (a verb) becomes *judgment* (a noun) becomes *judgmental* (an adjective) becomes *judgmentally* (an adverb).

Structural analysis can become a useful word recognition strategy and is a natural complement to syllabication. Since the vast majority of affixes are monosyllables, their recognition affords students a double whammy—they get a unit that has both a predictable pronunciation and a predictable meaning. For example, the reader may be able to figure out a word such as *unhappiness* after breaking off the syllables *un* and *ness.*

The use of structural analysis to determine the meanings of unfamiliar words can be a valuable skill. For example, a reader may not know the meaning of the word *nonprofit* but may recognize that the word is made up of *non* and *profit.* The reader may then be able to come up with an approximate meaning for the word because she knows that *non* means *not* and *profit* means *to make money.* A good discussion of structural analysis in identifying words and in determining word meanings can be found in Durkin (1981b). In this chapter the discussion will be limited to structural analysis skills used in word recognition. Specifically, strategies for helping students become familiar with inflected endings and affixes will be discussed. The use of structural analysis to develop word meanings will be discussed in Chapter 12, the chapter on vocabulary instruction.

Inflectional Endings

The dilemma for the teacher with regard to inflections is that inflection switching due to unattentive oral reading seldom changes meaning very dramatically. Also students do not usually need much instruction in inflectional endings because their skill with oral language almost automatically predisposes them to read words with the proper inflections. For example, in "The two boys played ball," *two* prepares the reader for *boys* rather than *boy.* In "The boy was running," *was* signals *running* rather than *run* or *ran.* Even the ambiguous phonemic mapping of the plural inflection, *s,* as /s/ in *cats,* /z/ in *dogs,* and /ez/ is *bushes* causes few, if any, problems for readers at any skill level. This is because the phonemic realization is completely determined by the phonemic environment of a given word. So plural form *s* is always voiced /z/ following a vowel or a voiced consonant (*d* or *b,* as in *beds* and *cabs*), unvoiced /s/ following an unvoiced consonant (*t* or *p,* as in *cats* or *caps*), and extra voiced syllable /z/ following a consonant in the sibilant family (*s, z, sh, ch, age*). These same contextual constraints apply to the past tense marker, *ed.*

The most common source of inflection substitution or omission is dialect or the influence of first language speech conventions. For example, in a Reading Recovery class at the University of Illinois, a Cambodian child never pronounced the past tense marker, *ed,* or the plural inflection, *s.* This is clearly due to a combination of a different tradition for tense and plural markers in his first language and his emerging proficiency in English. In Black English, the tradition of final consonant cluster reduction will produce /nab/ rather than /nabd/ for *nabbed* in the sentence, "He nabbed the robbers." In instances like these two, teachers need to find out whether the variation from conventional pronunciations influenced comprehension before initiating any instructional intervention.

However, when students who speak standard English persist in mispronouncing familiar words because they have inflections added to them (for example, a student does not recognize *ing* in *running*) or frequently do not self-correct errors involving inflections (for example, a student reads /gurl/ instead of /gurlz/ in "the girls were walking"), they may need some instruction in understanding how inflections work in the English language and why it is important to pay attention to them. Whenever instruction about inflectional endings is provided, it can include the following steps and features.

What, Why, and *When.* As a first step, the teacher should explain to the student *what* they will be working on. (They will be looking at word endings.) The teacher should explain *why* this is important and *when* to focus attention on word endings. (It is important to recognize word endings when consciously decoding words because they help you understand the ideas more precisely.)

How. The teacher can point out a student's substitutions involving endings from the oral reading analysis notes. Also, the teacher can find appropriate examples from the students' language experience stories or from familiar reading material. For example, the teacher might find verbs ending in *ed,* write these words for the students, ask them what the words have in common, and ask them what the ending has done to the meaning of the verb. The teacher would ask the students to read the words with and without the *ed* ending. Then, the teacher would ask the students to think of a few more verbs ending in *ed* and write them down. To apply this instruction to words in the context of sentences, the teacher could present students with oral or written sentences in which words are missing. The students' task would be to read the correct words from the list that fit in the blanks.

For a practice activity the students might complete a modified cloze passage in which blanks in the passage were followed by a word without the inflectional ending as well as the same word with the inflectional ending. Students would have to use context and be able to read both words to select the appropriate word for the blank (for example, Tom *want, wanted* to go to the park. We *want, wanted* to go to the zoo next week.). Also, for practice, students might make a collage of words with the inflectional ending that have been cut out of newspapers or magazines.

Perhaps nothing works better for this type of problem than taking a few minutes to walk through several examples in the students' current text reading assignments to illustrate how inflections influence meaning and how the failure to pay close attention to them can misguide comprehension.

Affixes

Familiarizing students with common prefixes and suffixes enables them to recognize these word parts when attempting to decode unfamiliar words. For example, when confronted with the long word *unbelievable,* students might have a better chance of identifying the word if they first recognize *un* as a prefix and *able* as a suffix, thus leaving the more easily recognized base word *believe.* Therefore, when coming across multisyllabic words, students should check to see if the words contain any prefixes or suffixes. If so, the reader should first look for and read the root word and then reread it, adding the prefixes and suffixes. A list of common prefixes and suffixes is presented in Figure 8.8. Explicit instruction in recognizing affixes is described below.

What, Why, and *When.* The teacher should focus on a particular affix that has appeared a number of times in the students' reading material and explain that they will be learning to recognize words containing that particular affix. This will help them recognize the affix in less familiar words, words in which affix knowledge will help students attain both an approximate pronunciation and a likely meaning.

How. After looking at a particular root word and affix, the teacher and students should discuss how the word changed in meaning when the affix was added. Then the teacher and students should try to generate a list of other words containing the affix under consideration. The students should read this list and then fill in the blanks of oral or written sentences with appropriate

Prefixes

anti	mons
bi	non
circum	over
co (con, com, col, car)	pre
counter	re
de	semi
dis	sub
fore	super
in (im, il, ir)	trans
inter	un
intra	under
mal	
mid	

Suffixes

able	less
ance (ancy, ence, ency)	like
ation	ly
ative	ment
dom	most
er (or)	ness
fold	ous
ful	ship
hood	tion (sion, ion)
ible	ty
ic	ward
ish	y
ism	

FIGURE 8.8. Common Prefixes and Suffixes

words from the list. This type of practice activity is commonly found in commercial reading programs.

For an additional practice activity, students can play a concentration game that involves pairing root words and affixes after receiving instruction in a number of affixes. Or, students can see how many words they could generate from a word wheel containing affixes and root words.

To help students apply knowledge of affixes to reading, the teacher and students should locate words containing prefixes and suffixes when reading and practice decoding these words by breaking off the prefixes and suffixes from the remainder of the word. For independent practice, students can locate and keep a list of additional words containing affixes when reading independently.

A GENERAL, ALL-PURPOSE WORD RECOGNITION STRATEGY FOR EVERYDAY READING

Students may know the most common symbol-sound correspondences but may not know how to apply this knowledge in decoding unfamiliar words during everyday reading. Consequently, it is important that students learn a general word recognition strategy to use when reading on their own. Also, it is important to devote enough time to guided practice in using this general strategy. To provide students with a strategy for decoding a challenging word, we recommend the following all-purpose strategy.

I. *Use context clues.* Read to the end of the sentence and remember to be thinking of a word that would make sense in the sentence as you engage in step IIa or IIb.

IIa. *Find a family for a one-syllable word.*
1. _____ C + V _____. If the word is one syllable, see if the word fits into a *family* that you recognize. If so, blend the beginning sound with the family to come up with the word (for example, *s-ight*, *sight*).
2. If you still do not recognize the word, try the short or long vowel sound first as you sound out each letter in the word. Blend the sounds together. Try the other vowel sound (long or short) if necessary. Use your vowel key word chart (Figure 8.6) if you have forgotten sounds of a particular vowel.
3. *CVVC.* If the word has a CVVC pattern, try one common sound that comes to mind for the vowel pair as you sound out each letter in the word. Blend the sounds together. If necessary, try another common sound for the vowel pair. Use your vowel key word chart if you cannot remember sounds to try for the vowel pair.

IIb. *Apply the long word strategy for a 2+ syllable word.* If the word is a multisyllabic word, break the word into parts with one vowel or vowel pair per part. Sound out each part, trying either a short vowel or a long vowel sound first and then trying the other if necessary. Blend the sounds of the word parts together. Remember that you should be trying to think of a word you know that would make sense in the sentence. Because this strategy will only help you approximate a word, remember to be flexible and try different vowel sounds for different parts.

III. *Ask for help or skip the word.* If you still do not recognize the word, ask for help or skip the word and read on.

How. To initially teach this general word recognition strategy, the teacher should write the steps on a chart, using as few words as possible to keep it simple, and go over the steps with the students. A chart for students reading on a first- or second-grade level might contain the following:

I. Use context
II. Sound it out (try one vowel sound, try another if necessary)
III. Ask for help or skip it

Then, the teacher should model the strategy for the students. The teacher reads from a text and lets the students follow along. The teacher locates a potentially challenging word and pretends that she does not know it. Then she talks aloud as she goes through the steps in figuring out the word. This discussion should include various examples, such as coming up with a word after recognizing a common phonogram and blending it with the initial sound. Alternately, the teacher should provide examples of looking at the spelling pattern in a one-syllable word (CVC, CVCe, or CVVC), sounding out the word, blending the sounds together, and checking to make sure that the word makes sense. Also, the teacher should provide examples of skipping the word and going on with the reading. An example of a lesson in which the teacher models the general word recognition strategy is provided in Figure 8.9.

After modeling the strategy for the students, the teacher asks them to restate the steps they should follow when coming to an unfamiliar word. The teacher rereads the chart with the students and then lets them take turns orally reading actual text. The group should stop at difficult words to go through the steps of the general word recognition strategy.

The procedure described above will have to be repeated with the students, at least in some modified form, a number of different times. Also, it is important to be consistent when students read aloud or ask for help with an unfamiliar word. Instead of simply telling students words or telling them to sound the word out, the teacher should remind them of the general word recognition strategy and help them go through its steps in an attempt to decode the word.

To provide students with practice in learning this general word recognition strategy, the teacher can let students listen to a tape in which an expert reader is modeling this overall word recognition strategy. The reader should demonstrate or model how to use the general word recognition strategy by coming to unknown words and talking through the use of the different steps in the procedure. Students can follow along by reading from the same book. They can write down the words not known by the reader and indicate whether or not the reader used the general word recognition strategy effectively. For example, if the reader came up with the word *heap* after she read to the end of the sentence, looked for a common phonogram but did not recognize *eap,* and then sounded out the word, trying two different sounds for *ea,* students would write *yes* by the word *heap* on a sheet of paper. If the reader did not read to the end of the sentence, sounded out the word as *hep* and continued, students would write *no* by the word *heap.* At the end of the reading, the reader on the tape (or the teacher) could discuss with the students what they wrote down on their papers.

To practice applying the general word recognition strategy to everyday reading, students can read aloud into a tape recorder. Then, working in pairs, they can play the tape back, list the unfamiliar words they had to decode, and indicate if they used the general word recognition strategy effectively. Or, working in pairs, students can simply take turns reading aloud and monitor one another in terms of whether or not they were following the general word recognition strategy they had learned.

DEVELOPING WORD RECOGNITION FLUENCY

So far discussion has focused on techniques for helping low-achieving readers learn to decode words accurately as they read. In addition to identifying words correctly, emerging readers must learn how to identify words automatically and rapidly, just as skilled readers do. The benefit of rapid, context-free, automatic word identification is that it frees attentional capacity and short-term memory space for use in comprehension.

Generally, automaticity in word recognition develops through repeated exposure to words through reading. Therefore, wide reading experience is rec-

TEACHER: Today we are going to work some more on the steps to follow when you come to a word you don't know as you are reading. The steps of the general word recognition strategy are: (1) use context clues, (2) sound the word out, (3) ask for help or skip the word. I'm going to show you how to follow these steps. It is important to know how to do this, because there will be times you won't know a word and you will need to try to figure the word out to better understand what you are reading.

Let's imagine I am reading along and come to a word I don't know, *r-a-k-e* in the sentence, "In the fall we *r-a-k-e* . . . ." First, I use context clues. To do this, I read to the end of the sentence, "In the fall we _____ leaves." The word has something to do with leaves in the fall. Second, I see if I can sound out the word, remembering the content. To do this, I see if I can figure the word out by looking at the first letter plus the rest of the word. *R* plus "ake." Well, I recognize *ake*. *R* plus *ake* is *rake*. That makes sense. "In the fall we rake leaves."

Now, let's imagine I come to another word I don't know. "One tree was a beautiful *s-h-a-d-e* . . . ." I read to the end of the sentence, "One tree was a beautiful _____ of red." It has something to do with a red tree. Let's see, *sh* plus *a-d-e*, I don't really recognize *a-d-e*. Let's see, the word ends in an *e* so the *a* must be long. /sh/ + /ā/ + /d/. Oh, *shade*. That makes sense. "One tree was a beautiful shade of red."

Now let's turn to the story "The Messy Room" on page 12 in our reading book. We'll take turns reading aloud. When one person comes to a word he/she doesn't know, the rest should not shout out the word. Together we'll go through the steps of the general word recognition strategy to figure out the word. Okay, Sara, why don't you start reading.

SARA: "One day Kate's mother said Kate had to clean her room. It was very messy. Her clothes were in a . . . ." I don't know that word.

TEACHER: Okay. What should Sara do first? Roger?

ROGER: Read to the end of the sentence.

TEACHER: Good. Sara, can you read to the end of the sentence?

SARA: Her clothes were in a _____ by her bed."

TEACHER: Okay, the word has something to do with clothes by the bed. What should Sara do next to figure out this word *h-e-a-p*, Mike?

MIKE: See if she can sound it out by looking at the first letter plus the rest of the word.

TEACHER: Great! Sara, can you do this?

SARA: No. I don't know *e-a-p*.

TEACHER: That's okay. Can you think of what to do next?

SARA: No.

TEACHER: Who knows? Mike?

MIKE: She should try to sound it out letter by letter.

TEACHER: How should she do this?

MIKE: Well, one sound to try for *ea* would be /ē/; /h/ + /ē/ + /p/, /hep/. That makes sense. "Her clothes were in a heap by her bed."

TEACHER: Very good. Good try Sara. Roger, will you please read next.

FIGURE 8.9. Lesson on the General Word Recognition Strategy

ommended to help develop students' word recognition automaticity (as well as beginning readers' word recognition accuracy and all readers' comprehension abilities). In addition, there exist several specific strategies to develop students' automaticity.

Repeated Reading

Repeated reading involves reading a passage a number of times to increase reading fluency and comprehension. Repeated reading may be unassisted or assisted (i.e., an audiotaped oral reading of the passages is followed).

Repeated reading increases reading rate and accuracy.[25] Gradual transfer has been found to new, unpracticed passages. Repeated reading also leads to greater comprehension of the passage read repeatedly as well as to new, unpracticed passages.[26]

Samuels (1979) has developed a particular method of using the repeated reading strategy to develop students' automaticity and reading rate. It consists of rereading short passages a number of times until certain levels of word recognition and reading rate are reached. Explicit instruction in this procedure might be as follows.

What and *Why*. The teacher explains to students that they will be rereading short interesting passages several times until they can read them accurately and at a faster rate than when they started. This will help them learn to read faster and with better comprehension.

How. The teacher helps students select short, interesting passages (50–300 words) that are relatively easy for them to read. They read one passage aloud into a tape recorder, to an aide, or to a partner and record their reading rate and number of word recognition errors. Students practice rereading the passage (silently or orally) several times and then they read it aloud again and, using a stopwatch, record their reading rate. They also document their word recognition errors. They do this until they are able to read the passage with less than two errors and at a criterion rate that is 50 words per minute better than their first attempt (unless the initial rate was very fast, say over 150 words per minute). After each timed reading, a comprehension question can be asked to focus students' attention on comprehension as well as on word recognition accuracy and rate. Students then go on to a new passage that they continue to reread until they again reach their criterion reading rate (as determined from the first passage) and their same low error rate.

Samuels has found that on subsequent passages, students' initial reading rate increases. Also, it requires fewer repeated readings for students to reach their criterion reading rate. In addition to increasing reading rate, the procedure enables students to increase their word recognition automaticity and comprehension for individual passages.

Implementation Issues

Dowhower (1989) provides a number of useful guidelines for implementing repeated reading in the classroom. She recommends that passages be short, 50 to 300 words long. She also finds that children reading less than 45 words per minute will benefit from the assisted repeated reading approach. Once these children are reading at 60 words per minute on the initial reading of an unpracticed passage, the unassisted repeated reading approach should be used. Samuels (1979) has recommended that a student read a passage repeatedly until a predetermined mastery level of 50 words per minute faster than a baseline rate is reached. Dowhower (1987) has found that a predetermined reading rate works well for low-achieving readers. Others have recommended that a passage be read no more than three to five times because diminishing returns set in after five timings.[27]

Group Repeated Reading

Lauritzen (1982) has modified the repeated reading technique for use with groups of students. Reading selections consist of poems, song lyrics, folktales, and other stories that have one or more of the following qualities: (1) strong rhyme, (2) definite rhythm, (3) obvious sequence, (4) strong oral literature patterns. Students are motivated to reread these selections because of their appealing nature.

The teacher first reads the story or poem aloud. The students follow along either with a copy of the book or from a copy on a chart or on the chalkboard. Next, the students echo-read a line, sentence, or paragraph of the selection. Finally, the teacher and students chorally read the selection. For independent practice the students continue to reread the story or poem individually or in pairs.

Koskinen and Blum (1986) have developed a procedure called Paired Repeated Reading in which students work with a partner. A student reads a passage three times as a partner listens. The reader evaluates his performance

The teacher is using the group repeated reading technique with this picture book to develop students' fluency. (*James Silliman*)

after each reading. The partner tells the reader how his reading has improved after the second and third readings. After the third reading the roles are reversed.

Book Memorization

Chomsky (1978) has developed a listening-while-reading technique that involves repeated reading of a single selection until it is memorized. In the process of learning to read a particular selection, students become automatic in terms of word recognition for the particular selection and are able to read the selection fluently.

Students select a story or selection from an appealing book. The selection should be on a second- to fifth-grade reading level and should take about fifteen minutes of listening time. It does not matter if the students are not reading at the book's level. The teacher has the individual selections put on tape and the students then listen to their reading selections over and over (perhaps ten to twenty times for first- or second-grade-level readers) until they can read them without the use of the tape. Every two to three days, as students are in the process of learning their selections, the teacher listens to them read the pages they know without the tape. After one story or selection is learned, the process is repeated with a second selection.

In addition to developing automaticity, this technique offers older students who are reading on a first- or second-grade level a choice of more interesting and more complex material to read. Chomsky found that low-achieving third-grade students reading on a first- or second-grade level were very motivated to learn to read their selected books and extremely pleased with themselves when they were finally able to read them to others.

Chunking

A number of studies have found that students' comprehension of specific texts is enhanced when the material is segmented into meaningful phrases for students. The procedure may be beneficial because it enables readers to focus less attention on individual words and helps them process text in phrase or idea units, just as skilled readers allegedly do. In contrast to word-by-word reading, chunking is designed to promote automaticity. Not only do fluent readers decode individual words automatically, they read automatically in phrase units. Consequently, attention to chunking can be useful for helping low-achieving readers read in meaningful phrases instead of word by word.

What and *Why.* Explicit instruction in chunking might look something like this. The teacher should explain to students that they will be learning how to divide text into meaningful phrase units because this will improve their reading fluency and consequently their reading comprehension.

How. First, the teacher should present a model of how expert readers chunk texts when they read orally. The teacher might point out that while there are no definite places where the text *must* be divided, we can learn a lot by listening to expert readers as they read orally. If we can determine where they generally pause to catch their breath, we might be able to develop some chunking strategies for ourselves.

One technique involves presenting texts on an overhead projector while students listen to recordings of expert readers reading it. Both the students and the teacher (at the overhead) can mark the points in the text at which the readers have paused. Later the class can discuss the strategies that the experts appear to have used to decide upon pausal points. Generally what the students will find is that expert readers always pause at the end of sentences. Within sentences, fluent readers generally pause slightly before and after prepositional phrases, before or after dependent clauses, and between independent clauses; they may pause slightly between subjects and predicates or between verbs in compound predicates. An example of a sentence segmented into meaningful phrase units would be as follows: In the morning/John got up/and got dressed/before he went downstairs/for breakfast.

Next, the teacher and students chorally read the chunked text. An unsegmented section of text and another section that has been segmented in inappropriate places are also read and compared to the meaningfully segmented text. Students then reread the meaningfully segmented text one or two times and attempt to segment a second passage with teacher guidance. This second passage is read several times.

For individual practice students can read a new teacher-segmented passage several times. They then can segment a passage on their own and practice reading it in meaningful phrase units.

When. The teacher should explain to students that instead of reading in a word-by-word manner, they should attempt to mentally segment text into meaningful phrases whenever they read.

Enhancing Reading Rate

Fluent adult readers read silently at a rate of about 250 to 300 words per minute. Normally developing readers have reached the lower end of this range (250 words per minute) by ninth grade. As with word recognition automaticity, wide reading is the best means of developing reading rate. Generally, as students gain experience with reading, they begin to read automatically at an adequate reading rate. But some readers, especially low achievers, make progress in automatic decoding without becoming fast enough to be regarded as fluent. They can benefit from specific instruction and practice in increasing their reading rate. To provide teachers with some normative standards, slow silent reading rates for various reading levels are presented in Table 8.1. In addition to repeated readings and phrase reading, timed readings can also help students enhance their reading rate.

Timed Reading

The teacher explains to students that they will be timing their reading and keeping a chart of their reading rate in an attempt to increase it. If they learn how to read a little bit faster, their reading fluency will improve and there is a good chance that their reading comprehension will improve as well. Also, because they have a considerable amount of reading to do in school, it will be beneficial to learn how to read a little bit more quickly.

TABLE 8.1. Average and Slow Reading Rates

Grade Level	Range or Rates (wpm)	Slow Rate (wpm)
2	70–100	
3	95–130	
4	120–170	120
5	160–210	160
6	180–230	180
7	180–240	180
8	195–240	198
9	215–260	215
12	225–260	225

Source: Adapted by Richek, List, and Learner (1983), Reading problems: Diagnosis and remediation, from Harris and Sipay, *How to increase reading ability,* 7th ed., Longman Inc., 1980.

To do timed readings, students simply read short (100–300 word), interesting passages and answer several comprehension questions on the material. They record their reading rate in words per minute and their percent of comprehension accuracy on a graph. It is important that students select passages that are not above their instructional level so they will not have to struggle with decoding.

We do not recommend the use of reading machines to increase reading rate if students have to read in an unnatural manner, such as line by line. However, intact short passages that are shown on the computer for a certain amount of time would be another tool for students to use to increase their reading rate.

SUMMARY

This chapter examined strategies for developing low-achieving readers' word recognition accuracy and fluency. It stressed the importance of explicit instruction in word recognition, in which the teacher explains *what* a particular skill is and models *how* to perform it, discusses with students *why* the skill is important, and explains *when* they can use it as they are reading on their own.

Word recognition instruction is an important component of the reading comprehension process. In many cases, word recognition enhances comprehension; in other cases, it is enhanced by understanding the text, as in the case of using context clues. However, word recognition should not be regarded as an end in itself. For this reason, instruction and practice in word recognition should focus on and be realized in everyday reading. Work with words in isolation should be kept to a minimum. Instructional strategies that will help students learn how to apply word recognition skill to everyday reading should be the goal of an effective word recognition curriculum.

Suggested Activities

1. Use the individual language experience approach on at least three occasions with one child who is reading on a first-grade level or lower. Make a

booklet of stories for the child and be certain that the student repeatedly rereads the stories in his booklet.

2. Teach the symbol-sound correspondence for a vowel or vowel pair to a child or small group of children who do not know the correspondence, following the steps outlined in the chapter. Be sure to help the student attack words in actual text containing the symbol-sound correspondence being taught. If children are not available, teach the symbol-sound correspondence to a group of peers in your class.

3. Use the oral reading for meaning procedure, preferably once or twice a week, with a student who frequently makes nonsemantic substitutions and does not tend to correct these miscues.

4. Teach a student to use the general word recognition strategy outlined in the chapter. After modeling the strategy, be sure to use the strategy with the student while reading everyday text. If a child is not available, teach the general word recognition strategy to a peer in your class.

5. Use the repeated reading procedure with a student who is not a very fluent reader.

Suggested Reading

ADAMS, M. J. (1990). Beginning to read: Thinking and learning about print. Cambridge, MA: MIT Press.

An important extensive book reviewing research on emergent reading and beginning reading instruction.

DOWHOWER, S. L. (1989). Repeated reading: Research into practice. *The Reading Teacher, 42*:502–507.

Reviews research on repeated reading and provides suggestions for classroom practice.

PFLAUM, S. W. and PASCARELLA, E. T. (1980). Interactive effects of prior reading achievement and training on the reading achievement of learning disabled children. *Reading Research Quarterly, 16*: 138–158.

The authors describe the program they used to improve learning disabled students' contextual analysis skills.

RASINSKI, T. W. (1989). Fluency for everyone: Incorporating fluency instruction in the classroom. *The Reading Teacher, 42*: 690–693.

Provides some useful suggestions for building fluency instruction into the reading curriculum.

Notes

1. See Ehri and Wilce (1983), Juel (1983), and Stanovich, Cunningham, and Feeman (1984a).
2. See Mason (1983).
3. See Durkin (1978–1979, 1984b), and Mason (1983).
4. See Williams (1985).
5. See DiBennedetto, Richardson, and Kochnower (1983), Ehri and Wilce (1983), Juel and Roper-Schneider (1985), Manis (1985), Mason (1976), Perfetti (1985), Rosso and Emans (1981), and Venezky and Johnson (1973).
6. See Durkin (1984c), Lewkowicz (1980), Stanovich , Cunningham, an d Feeman (1984a), an d Williams (1980).

7. See Durkin (1984c).
8. See Juel (1980, 1983), Stanovich (1980), and Stanovich, Cunningham, and Feeman (1984a).
9. See Juel (1980, 1983), and Stanovich (1980).
10. See Beebe (1980), D'Angelo (1982), Leslie (1980), Pflaum and Pascarella (1980), and Willows and Ryan (1981).
11. See Ehri and Wilce (1980), LaBerge and Samuels (1974), Manis (1985), Stanovich (1980), and Stanovich, Cunningham an d Feeman (1984a and 1984b).
12. See Ehri and Wilce (1983), Manis (1985), Stanovich (1980), and Stanovich, Cunningham, and Feeman (1984a).
13. The reader is referred to Johnson and Pearson (1984) for a more detailed discussion on developing a basic sight vocabulary.
14. See Dolch (1942), Moe (1973), and Otto and Chester (1972).
15. See Arlin, Scott, and Webster (1978–1979), Ehri and Roberts (1979), Ehri and Wilce (1980), Nemko (1984), Rash, Johnson, and Gleadow (1984), and Singer, Samuels, and Spiroff (1974).
16. The reader is referred to Hall (1981) for an in depth discussion of the language experience approach.
17. See Anderson, Hiebert, Scott, and Wilkinson (1985), Bond and Dykstra (1967), Chall (1983), and Pflaum, Walberg, Karegianes, and Rasher (1980).
18. See Anderson, Hiebert, Scott, and Wilkinson (1985).
19. See Anderson, Hiebert, Scott, and Wilkinson (1985) and Chall (1983).
20. See Haddock (1976).
21. See DiBennedetto, Richardson, and Kochnower (1983) and Mason (1976).
22. See Calfee, Lindamood, and Lindamood (1973), Chall, Roswell, and Blumenthal (1963), Fox and Routh (1975), Helfgott (1976), and Liberman (1970).
23. See Leslie (1980), Pflaum and Bryan (1980), and Willows and Ryan (1981).
24. See Willows and Ryan (1981).
25. See Samuels (1979), Carver and Hoffman (1981), Dowhower (1987).
26. See Dowhower (1987), O'Shea, Sindelar, and O'Shea (1985).
27. See O'Shea, Sindelar, and O'Shea (1985), Spring, Blunden, and Gatheral (1981).

CHAPTER 9

WORD RECOGNITION ASSESSMENT

Overview

As you read this chapter you may want to use these key concepts to guide your understanding and reflection.

- Oral reading analysis is an effective technique for assessing a student's word recognition abilities when actually reading.
- Oral reading analysis should be conducted once or twice a week with students experiencing difficulty in word recognition.
- Written records of students' oral reading can illuminate patterns of difficulty and patterns of progress over time.
- Based on a student's relative strengths and weaknesses in word recognition, as assessed through oral reading analysis, a teacher can determine the most appropriate types of instruction.

Our general approach to assessing students' word recognition strategies is to study how they apply those strategies while they are reading text orally. Our approach is based upon the assumption that indirect (and typically decontextualized) measures—such as multiple-choice tests of letter-sound knowledge, sight-word knowledge, morphemic analysis, or even context clues—may provide an inaccurate picture of how students really use these strategies while reading. Oral reading analysis, a highly flexible assessment technique, which serves as the basis of our entire approach to word recognition assessment, is presented in detail as a prelude to more specific assessment strategies for each of the areas of word recognition introduced in Chapter 8: general word recognition, basic sight vocabulary, phonic analysis, contextual analysis, and structural analysis.

ORAL READING ANALYSIS

Oral reading analysis is one of the oldest and most widely used techniques for determining students' reading strategies. Different variations appear under a variety of labels. Before World War II, Donald Durrell and Marianne Monroe referred to oral reading error analysis. In the 1960s, Ken Goodman coined the term miscue analysis to emphasize the meaning-seeking character of the alleged errors students made while reading orally. Marie Clay, founder of Reading Recovery (see Chapter 7), used the term running record to capture the sense of oral reading analysis as an ongoing method of monitoring both word recognition and getting meaning while reading.[1]

In oral reading analysis the teacher listens to an individual student read aloud, records the miscues, and notes on an oral reading analysis sheet challenging words successfully decoded by the student. By challenging, we mean words not readily known by a student and words for which the student had to consciously and deliberately discover the pronunciation. Over time, the teacher collects the data from a number of oral reading samples to determine general strengths and weaknesses in word recognition as revealed by patterns of behavior. Also, if the teacher has provided instruction in a skill, she can use these data to evaluate the student's progress in applying that skill. Oral reading analysis can reveal valuable information about a reader's habitual approach to decoding as well as the reader's basic sight word and symbol-sound correspondence knowledge. The reader's ability to use word-level fix-up strategies, to apply phonics knowledge to reading, and to use context clues to attack difficult words can also be detected. Ideally, oral reading analysis should be conducted once or twice a week with low-achieving readers who are reading below grade level or who reach frustration level, at least in part, because of difficulties in word recognition.

Oral reading analysis has the advantage of focusing on students' word recognition skills in everyday situations.[2] Furthermore, if carried out regularly, oral reading analysis can become a nonthreatening, nontestlike assessment procedure.

Many teachers are hesitant to use oral reading analysis. Some teachers believe that oral reading, because of its public and performative features, can be threatening to children, especially if it bears any resemblance to a test or an evaluation. Others mention the fact that it is difficult and time consuming to collect and analyze the data. Some critics point out the informal and interpretive nature of oral reading analysis and opt for data gathered from published tests to assess low-achieving readers. Finally, some educators believe that if they can place their students appropriately, i.e., at their instructional level in a basal program, diagnosis will be unnecessary.

With regard to students feeling threatened, teachers who use oral reading regularly do not find it threatening to students. Children come to view the teacher's notetaking during oral reading as a natural part of the activity. Moreover, when teachers can demonstrate that the notetaking helps students improve their reading, students are even more receptive to the activity.

With regard to time involved, it is relatively easy to take notes during oral reading if an appropriate form is available (such as the one presented in Figure 9.1 and explained later in the chapter). What is important is that the teacher get into the *habit* of taking notes when students read aloud. Since it is time consuming to analyze data collected from oral reading analysis, dated analysis can be reserved for readers who have clear word recognition difficulties. Teachers should also collect data on an oral reading analysis sheet to facilitate data interpretation and do one or more of the following to analyze the data: (1) take time to fill in as much of the oral reading analysis sheet as possible immediately after a student has read (while completing the sheet have students reread the material to partners), (2) build time into their schedule, such as an hour once or twice a month, to analyze data from several (e.g., four or more) oral reading sessions per low-achieving reader, and (3) get assistance with data analysis from the reading resource teacher.

We have already revealed our conviction that commercially published diagnostic tests are of questionable content validity at least in part because they are based on unnatural reading tasks (see the discussion of informal assessment in Chapters 6 and 14). On the other hand, data collected by teachers during everyday oral reading and analyzed using the techniques discussed in this chapter provide, if collected over time, reliable evidence about student progress and problems. What is important is that a teacher know how to recognize significant recurring word recognition problems. The remainder of this chapter will be devoted to aspects of word recognition performance that are important for the teacher to consider when analyzing oral reading notes in search of significant word recognition problems and progress.

With regard to the view that oral reading analysis is unnecessary once students are placed at the appropriate level in the basal, we believe that diagnosis is essential for all students, especially students experiencing difficulty in word recognition. Further, based upon years of experience, ours as well as many practicing teachers, we believe that oral reading analysis is an excellent (perhaps the best) method for gathering relevant data.

Conducting Oral Reading Analysis

To conduct oral reading analysis, a teacher begins by listening to a student orally read a 50–200 word segment from his everyday reading material (basal, textbook, or trade book). The amount to be read depends on the reading level of the student (younger children read shorter passages). The teacher records on an oral reading analysis sheet the student's oral reading errors and the correct words, along with any challenging words that were deliberately and successfully decoded. The book and page numbers are also recorded. An example of the type of sheet that might be used is presented in Figure 9.1.

It is important that the material read aloud be on the student's instructional level. Students make different kinds of errors when they are reading material at different levels of difficulty, e.g., instructional versus frustration levels.[3] In general, readers make more nonresponse and graphophonic errors (errors that are phonetically similar) and rely less on meaning and context clues when at their frustration level than at their instructional level.[4] Presumably, this is because readers devote so much attention to decoding when reading at their frustration level that they attend less to context and meaning. Instructional plans should be built around error patterns revealed during instructional level reading.

While listening to a student read aloud, the teacher should record notes on the elements listed below on an oral reading analysis sheet. A suggested recording system is also listed.

We recommend an oral reading analysis sheet for recording notes about oral reading (see Figure 9.2) because teachers we work with have found it so

KEY		ORAL READING ANALYSIS SHEET
1. Substitution is written above actual word tp = teacher pronunciation, sc = self-corrected		Story:
2. + = successfully used, – = unsuccessfully used, 0 = didn't try, blank = automatic		
3. + = self-corrected, – = not self-corrected, 0 = semantic substitution		Child:
4. Substitution did not involve correct analysis — one syllable		
5. Substitution did not involve correct analysis — multisyllabic		Date:
6. Apparent difficulty, i.e. sound-symbol correspondence, basic sight words, inflectional endings, affixes		
7. Unfamiliar words deliberately and successfully decoded (sd)		Teacher:

	1 Error	2 General Word Recognition Strategy	3 Non- semantic substitutions	4 1 Syllable Word	5 2+ Syllable Word	6 Apparent Difficulty	7 Successfully Decoded

Number of words _____ Number of errors _____ Word recognition accuracy _____
Number of times nonsemantic substitutions self-corrected/total number of nonsemantic substitutions _____
Number of semantic substitutions
Number of "didn't try" errors
Number of errors involving analysis (columns 4 and 5) _____
Number of times words deliberately and successfully decoded (columns 2 and 7) _____
Number of times words deliberately but unsuccessfully decoded (column 2) _____
Number of times words automatic but wrong (column 2) _____

FIGURE 9.1.   Oral Reading Analysis Sheet

useful. When using our system (or your own specially developed system), there are several features of any student's oral reading that you will want to take note of.

Type of Element	Recording System
Substitution	Write the word substituted above the actual word. If an ending or part of a word has been omitted, circle what was omitted.
Repetition	Draw a wavy line under the repeated words.
Insertion	Insert the word or words with a caret.
Omission	Circle the omitted word or words.
Teacher Pronunciation	Put "TP" above the unknown word to indicate that the teacher pronounced the word for the student after waiting at least 5 seconds.
Self-Correction	Put "SC" after a substitution to indicate that the word was corrected spontaneously by the student. The original substitution should also be recorded.
Successfully Decoded Word	A word that obviously was not known instantly but was successfully decoded by a student should be listed. Marked as ``SD''

An example of a teacher's notes based on a student's oral reading is provided in Figure 9.2. (Ignore columns 2 through 5 of this chart for now. They will be explained later in the chapter.)

FIGURE 9.2.   Teacher's Notes on Student's Oral Reading

A Swim

Toad and Frog went down to the river. [river]

"What a day for a swim," said Frog.

"Yes," said Toad, "I will go behind these rocks and put on my bathing suit." [this, rock(s) omitted, TP TP]

"I don't wear a bathing suit," said Frog.

"Well, I do," said Toad. "After I put on my bathing suit, you must not look at me until I get in the water." [SD]

"Why not?" ask Frog. [not circled]

"Because I look funny in my bathing suit. That is why," said Toad. [like^sc SD new]

Frog closed his eyes when Toad came out from behind the rocks. Toad was wearing [weering] his new bathing suit.

"Don't peek," he said. [Do not]

Error	General Word Recognition Strategy	Nonsemantic Substitution	1 Syllable Word	2+ Syllable Word	Apparent Difficulty	Successfully Decoded
P. 40 rīver						
river	–	–			ĭ	
this						
these	0					
rock(s)	0				(s)	
bathing TP	0					
suit TP	0					
P. 42 (not)						water
like SC						
look	+	+				funny
new						
^bathing suit						
weering						
wearing	–	–			ea	
Do not						
Don't		0			n't	

9 errors in 100 words = 91% accuracy in word recognition

Number of times nonsemantic substitutions self-corrected out of total number of nonsemantic substitutions 1/3

Column 1 Substitution is written above actual word from text.

Column 2 Indicates whether or not general word recognition strategy was used: + = used successfully; – = not used successfully; 0 = student didn't try (word consciously omitted or pronounced by the teacher); blank = not applicable (student decoded word automatically even though he or she did not read the correct word)

Column 3 Indicates whether or not a nonsemantic substitution self-corrected; + = nonsemantic substitution corrected; – = nonsemantic substitution not corrected; 0 = semantic substitution.

Column 4 Notes about apparent difficulty with a particular word.

Column 5 Indicates unfamiliar words that were successfully decoded.

Note: An expanded version of this oral reading analysis sheet is presented in Figure 9.3.

Source: The passage in Figure 9.2 is from *Frog and Toad Are Friends*, pp. 40–42, by Arnold Lobel. Copyright © 1970 by Arnold Lobel. Reprinted by permission of Harper & Row, Publishers, Inc.

FIGURE 9.2. Teacher's Notes on Student's Oral Reading (*cont.*)

Oral reading analysis can be conducted with students on an individual basis or in a reading group. The advantage of working with a student individually is that, in addition to collecting diagnostic information, the teacher can respond immediately to instructional needs. If students read orally in a group, the teacher should be sure to take notes on the performance of each individual and insist that other students restrain the (sometimes irresistible) instinct to call out words that may challenge a particular reader. Otherwise, you will not get an opportunity to witness that student's problem-solving approach, that is, what she does when she encounters some difficulty.

Thus far we have limited our discussion to *how* to conduct oral reading analysis but have said very little about how to use the collected information for diagnostic and evaluative purposes, an issue we will turn to as specific aspects of word recognition are examined.

BASIC SIGHT VOCABULARY

As discussed in Chapter 8, basic sight words are high-frequency words that students should be able to recognize instantly. It is important to assess the basic sight word knowledge when students are reading at or below a third-grade level. Students reading above this level probably know most of the words on a basic sight word list, such as Mason and Au's list presented in Chapter 8. Any frequently missed basic sight words for students reading above grade level will become apparent through oral reading analysis and other daily reading activities.

The conventional way to evaluate a student's ability to identify basic sight words is to use word cards in an individual assessment. To do this, the teacher prints all of the words from a basic sight word list on one side of a card. The teacher also writes the word in a simple sentence on the back of the card, using surrounding words that he thinks early readers will know. Then, the teacher simply shows, or flashes, the words to the student, beginning with the first-grade words. If a word is not known, the teacher flips the card over to see if the student can read the word in the context of a sentence. Those not known by a student either in isolation or in the context of a sentence comprise the body of words with which to begin that student's instruction.

Following instruction and practice in learning specific sight words, this approach can be used to assess knowledge of instructed words. The number of words known can be recorded on a progress chart, or specific words known can be checked off on a progress chart.

Another useful method for screening students on their knowledge of sight words has been described by Johnson and Pearson (1978). This procedure is a paper-and-pencil task that involves the teacher's reading a basic sight word and the student's circling the correct word from among four choices that are visually similar. A portion of the test might look like this:

Words Read by Teacher	Student's Paper
1. where	1. were, where, when, went
2. then	2. then, they, there, the
3. our	3. are, out, our, oar

Johnson (1976) found correlations ranging from .86 to .91 between scores based on this format and scores from the flashcard approach described earlier. An advantage of the circle-the-word test is that it can be administered to a group of students. A disadvantage is that it assesses students' ability to *recognize* basic sight words but not their ability to *read* them. There is no guarantee that because students circle a word correctly on the test they will be able to identify the word when coming across it in text. Nevertheless, the paper-and-pencil assessment of basic sight word knowledge may be useful as an initial screening device. If a student does poorly on the circle-the-word test (missing even a few words from a word list that is below his instructional reading level), further assessment is probably needed.

However, the most useful assessment of a student's basic sight word knowledge comes from observation of the student's performance during everyday oral reading. From records of a student's oral reading, the teacher can determine if any basic vocabulary words have been repeatedly missed. These words then become a point of focus during instruction. These same records reveal which basic sight words have been read correctly by the student during actual reading. A student who misreads *the* seven of ten times has different instructional needs than a student who misreads *the* one of ten times.

Some practitioners, recognizing full well that most reading involves the reading of connected text with rich contexts, prefer to assess sight word knowledge both in and out of natural contexts in order to gain insights into students' ability to benefit from context in recognizing familiar words. We concur in this practice.

GENERAL WORD RECOGNITION STRATEGY

A general word recognition strategy involves following a set of steps to decode a challenging word. Students' knowledge and use of a general word recognition strategy should be assessed if word recognition difficulties contribute to their reading below grade level. One way to assess a student's knowledge of what to do with an unknown word is to ask the student directly during an interview opportunity. The teacher asks the student to list the steps to follow when coming to an unknown word and also to explain what he actually does in such situations. In both cases it would be useful to record the student's responses to see if his knowledge of correct decoding procedures matched his actual decoding behavior during real reading.

This leads directly to the second suggestion for assessing a student's use of a general word recognition strategy: *observe* strategy use during an oral reading session. When taking notes on a student's oral reading the teacher can record information on what the student does when the student encounters challenging words. For example, the student (1) might try to decode a challenging word and achieve a correct pronunciation, (2) try to decode the word but produce a miscue, (3) not even try to decode the word but look at the teacher for help, or (4) omit the word and continue reading. Words deliberately but incorrectly decoded are listed under the substitution column of the oral reading analysis sheet. (These substitutions are marked with a minus [-], for unsuccessfully decoded, in column 2 of Figures 9.2 and 9.3.) Words not attempted and either pronounced by the teacher or omitted are also recorded in the substitution column. (These substitutions are marked with a "0," for not attempted, in column 2 of Figures 9.2 and 9.3.). Words incorrectly decoded and subsequently self-corrected are recorded in the substitution column. (These substitutions are marked with a plus [+], for correctly decoded, in column 2 of Figures 9.2 and 9.3.) Words not known instantly but subsequently decoded correctly are also listed on the oral reading analysis sheet (see Figure 9.2, column 5 and Figure 9.3, column 7) because they provide data on the frequency of successful strategy application.

Column 1   Substitution is written above the actual word from the text; SC= self-correction, TP=teacher pronunciation.

Column 2   Indicates whether or not the general word recognition strategy was used: + = used successfully; − = not used successfully; 0 = student didn't try (word consciously omitted or pronounced by the teacher); blank = not applicable (student decoded word automatically even though she did not read the correct word).

Column 3   Indicates whether or not a nonsemantic substitution was self-corrected: + = nonsemantic substitution self-corrected; − = nonsemantic substitution not self-corrected; 0 = semantic substitution.

Column 4   Indicates whether or not substitution involved incorrect analysis of a 1 syllable word.

Column 5   Indicates whether or not substitution involved incorrect analysis of a 2+ syllable word.

Column 6   Indicates apparent difficulty in terms of symbol-sound correspondence knowledge. Other notes can be made here as well, such as difficulty with basic sight words, inflectional endings, affixes.

10/2		1 Error	2 General Word Recognition Strategy	3 Nonsemantic Substitution	4 1 Syllable Word	5 2+ Syllable Word	6 Apparent Difficulty	7 Successfully Decoded
P. 78	1	striked struck		0	X		ŭ ed	whiz
	2	began begin		0			ĭ	swish
	3	scared screamed	−	−	X		scr ea	
		cheeks SC knees	+	+				
P. 79	4	game came		−			ca	crack
	5	plat plate	−	−			ā (CVCe)	
		no SC now	+	+				
Totals		5	2− 2+	2/5	2	0		3+

Number of words __118__   Number of errors __5__   Word recognition accuracy __96__ %

Number of times words deliberately and successfully decoded ("pluses" in columns 2 & 7) __5__

Number of times words deliberately but unsuccessfully decoded ("minuses" in column 2) __2__

Number of times word automatic but wrong ("blanks" in column 2) __3__

Number of times nonsemantic substitution (substitution that doesn't make sense) is self-corrected/total number of nonsemantic substitutions   __2/5__ = __40__ %

Number of semantic substitutions (Os in column 3) __2__

Number of "didn't try" errors (Os in column 2) __0__

Number of errors involving analysis (Xs in columns 5 and 5) __2__

FIGURE 9.3. Oral Reading Analysis Sheets Based on Four Sessions

10/5		Error	General Word Recognition Strategy	Nonsemantic Substitution	1 Syllable Word	2+ Syllable Word	Apparent Difficulty	Successfully Decoded
P. 85	1	ĕliss easily	−	−		X	ea	mouth
	2	father farther		−			ar	fearful
	3	expeller explore	−	−		X		candle
	4	suched touched	−	−				
P. 86		take SC look	+	+				
	5	family flame	−	−	X		ā (CVCe)	relight
	6	frice fierce	−	−	X		ler/ri	finally
	7	growling glowing	−	−		X		
		shout SC shouted	+	0				
	8	recozicle recognize	−	−		X		
Totals	8		7− 2+	1/9	2	4		5+

Number of words __143__   Number of errors __8__   Word recognition accuracy __94__ %
Number of times words deliberately and successfully decoded ("pluses" in columns 2 & 7) __7__
Number of times words deliberately but unsuccessfully decoded ("minuses" in column 2) __7__
Number of times word automatic but wrong ("blanks" in column 2) __1__
Number of times nonsemantic substitution (substitution that doesn't make sense)
is self-corrected/total number of nonsemantic substitutions   __1/9__ = __11__ %
Number of semantic substitutions (Os in column 3) __1__
Number of ``didn't try'' errors (Os in column 2) __0__
Number of errors involving analysis (Xs in columns 4 and 5) __6__

10/12		Error	General Word Recognition Strategy	Nonsemantic Substitution	1 Syllable Word	2+ Syllable Word	Apparent Difficulty	Successfully Decoded
P. 99	1	cran canyon	−	−		X		decided
	2	nature national	−	0		X	tion	
	3	grōg gorge	−	−	X		gor/gro	

FIGURE 9.3. Oral Reading Analysis Sheets Based on Four Sessions (*cont.*)

10/12	Error	General Word Recognition Strategy	Nonsemantic Substitution	1 Syllable Word	2+ Syllable Word	Apparent Difficulty	Successfully Decoded
P. 100	4 where were	–	–			were	squirrel
	5 winding winding	–	–			ī	lizards
	6 cross chose	–	–	X		ō (CVCe)	weather
Totals	6	6–	0/5	2	2		4+

Number of words __118__   Number of errors __6__   Word recognition accuracy __96__ %
Number of times words deliberately and successfully decoded ("pluses" in columns 2 & 7)   __4__
Number of times words deliberately but unsuccessfully decoded ("minuses" in column 2)   __6__
Number of times word automatic but wrong ("blanks" in column 2)   __0__
Number of times nonsemantic substitution (substitution that doesn't make sense)
is self-corrected/total number of nonsemantic substitutions   __0/5__ = __0__ %
Number of semantic substitutions (Os in column 3)   __1__
Number of ``didn't try'' errors (Os in column 2)   __0__
Number of errors involving analysis (Xs in columns 4 and 5)   __4__

10/16	Error	General Word Recognition Strategy	Nonsemantic Substitution	1 Syllable Word	2+ Syllable Word	Apparent Difficulty	Successfully Decoded
P. 103	1 neighborhood neighbor's	–	–			's	clever
	neighborhood SC neighbor		+				
	2 was is		0			is	
P. 104	3 bouncing TP basket	0			X		lemonade
	4 breakfast	–	–		X	ea	honey
	5 silling sliding by	–	–		X	ī sli/sli	
	6 around^by my car						
	7 quiet quite	–	–	X		ite/iet	
Totals	7	4– 1+	1/5	1	3		3+

Number of words __113__   Number of errors __7__   Word recognition accuracy __94__ %
Number of times words deliberately and successfully decoded ("pluses" in columns 2 & 7)   __4__
Number of times words deliberately but unsuccessfully decoded ("minuses" in column 2)   __4__
Number of times word automatic but wrong ("blanks" in column 2)   __1__
Number of times nonsemantic substitution (substitution that doesn't make sense)
is self-corrected/total number of nonsemantic substitutions   __1/5__ = __20__ %
Number of semantic subsitutions (Os in column 3)   __1__
Number of ``didn't try'' errors (Os in column 2)   __1__
Number of errors involving analysis (Xs in columns 4 and 5)   __4__

FIGURE 9.3. Oral Reading Analysis Sheets Based on Four Sessions (*cont.*)

Frequently a student may identify a word automatically but incorrectly (for example, *this* for *the*). The miscue may or may not be self-corrected by the student. In either case the student has not deliberately attempted to decode an unknown word and, consequently, there would be no notes about the student's use of a general word recognition strategy. It is nothing more than a straight-forward substitution. (This type of miscue is indicated by a blank in column 2 of Figures 9.2 and 9.3.)

Teachers should study several samples of a student's word analysis attempts gathered over time in an effort to understand how the student deals with challenging words. It may become apparent, for example, that the student habitually waits for the teacher to pronounce the words or omits the words altogether and continues reading. Or, the student may try to attack most unknown words but with little success. After instruction in the general word recognition strategy presented in Chapter 8, the incidence of unknown words deliberately and successfully decoded, as recorded on oral reading analysis sheets, should increase if instruction has been effective.

PHONIC ANALYSIS

Two aspects of phonic analysis, symbol-sound correspondence knowledge and the ability to analyze, or segment, monosyllable and multisyllabic words correctly, are important elements of a reader's repertoire. Assessing students' symbol-sound correspondence knowledge should be done in a manner that moves from symbol to sound as opposed to sound to symbol and, as often as possible, should be based on everyday reading. Even more important, students' ability to generate pronunciations for challenging words (during which students need to apply phonics knowledge) should be assessed during everyday reading.

Problematic Aspects of Phonics Assessment

Before discussing specific strategies for assessing phonics knowledge, several problems seen with many phonics tests should be addressed. One common problem is that students are often given sounds and asked to provide or recognize symbols instead of being given symbols and asked to provide sounds. Furthermore, some paper-and-pencil tests provide three or four words that have the same beginning sound or vowel sound as a picture that is shown or a stimulus word pronounced by the teacher and then the student is asked to circle the correct word. The choices are not read to the students, so they have to know the letter that represents the sound in the picture or stimulus word and be able to find the correct word. For example, the teacher asks the students to circle the word that begins with the same sound as *sun* from among the following choices: *ship, sat, chin, zoo*. Or, the teacher asks them to write the letter that they hear at the beginning of the word *sun*. When assessing vowels, the teacher may read a word and ask the students to circle the correct word from among three or four choices. For example, the teacher reads the word *pin* and has students circle the correct word from among the choices *pine, pan, pin, pain*.

The problem with sound-to-symbol assessment is that it does not tell us about the phonics skills a reader must use when decoding challenging words. The fact that a reader can provide the correct symbol for a sound is no guarantee that he can give the correct sound for the same symbol. In other words, a student may be able to tell you that *sat* begins with the same sound as *sun*, given the choices *ship, sat, chin*, and *zoo*, but you still do not know if the student will provide the *s* sound when trying to decode the word *sunny*. Phonics knowledge is often tested in a recognition mode (for example, What word from among the four choices begins with the same sound as a stimulus word or picture?) because of the perceived efficiency in administering a group paper-and-pencil test instead of individual assessments. However, such assessments do not necessarily indicate what a particular student does when she sees a symbol and has to produce a sound, which is, of course, precisely what must be done in decoding an unfamiliar word.

Some phonics tests attempt to assess from symbol to sound skills by asking students to read lists of words. While these tests avoid the recognition mode problem, they overlook the fact that students may be reading at least some of the words as sight words. If so, there is no guarantee that the student really knows the symbol-sound correspondence being tested. For example, if a student reads *seat* as a sight word, the teacher really does not know whether the student knows that the "long a" sound is one of the sounds that the symbol *ea* may have.

Another common approach to phonics testing is to ask a student to pronounce letters in isolation. The problem with this approach is that it is difficult to isolate some sounds. For example, the sound for the letter *b* often comes out a /buh/; a vowel sound has been attached. Similarly, even though some students may be able to sound out unknown words, they may not be able to sound out the individual letters in words. Conversely, some students may be able to give a sound in isolation for a consonant, blend, vowel, or vowel combination but be unable to apply this phonics knowledge when attempting to decode a word.

In short, we find little to commend in any of the common approaches to assessing phonics knowledge, be they group or individual strategies. As with other aspects of word recognition, we favor inferences about phonics knowledge based upon oral reading.

Phonics Assessment Through Oral Reading Analysis

To assess a student's weaknesses in symbol-sound correspondence knowledge based on her ability to analyze words correctly when reading, it is important to keep careful records and analyses of a number of oral reading samples. The following three types of symbol-sound substitutions are worth recording and analyzing:

1. A student gives an incorrect sound for a particular symbol. For example the substitution of *began* for *begin* fits this category whereas *cran* for *canyon* would be recorded as a more complex substitution involving a multisyllabic word—as illustrated in number 3 below.

2. A student incorrectly segments a monosyllabic word into phonemes. Sometimes the student will add or subtract phonemes (*family* for *fame* or *flame* for *fame*). Sometimes the student may reverse their order (*quiet* or *quite* or *on* for *no*). At other times, the student may combine a phoneme subtraction or addition with a symbol-sound mismatch (*striked* for *struck*).

3. A student incorrectly segments syllables (*eliss* ["short e"] for *easily*) or incorrectly analyzes the phonemes in multisyllabic words (*expeller* for *explore*). In the first case, a three-syllable word came out as a two-syllable word. In the second, a two-syllable word came out as a three-syllable word. In many instances, this type of substitution also involves one or more symbol-sound correspondence mismatches that are readily apparent ("short e" for *ea* in the case of *eliss* or *easily*).

An example of record keeping based upon these categories is presented in columns 4, 5, and 6 of Figure 9.3. Additional examples are presented in Appendix C. (Column 3 of the chart will be explained later in the chapter in the section on contextual analysis.) In addition to indicating whether or not word recognition substitutions involved incorrect analysis of one-syllable words or words with two or more syllables (see columns 4 and 5 in Figure 9.3), the teacher should list apparent symbol-sound correspondence mismatches ("short e" for *ea* in *easily*, see column 6 in Figure 9.3).

Based on such data, the teacher should look for recurring problems such as frequent substitutions involving a particular symbol-sound correspondence (for example, *ea*) or a high incidence of substitutions involving incorrect analysis of one-syllable or multisyllabic words.

Consider, for example, a teacher's notebook entries based on one student's oral reading in Figure 9.3. Billy Stone, a fifth-grade student, can comfortably read material judged to be at a third grade level of difficulty. Over four samples Billy made fifteen word recognition substitutions involving symbol-sound correspondence knowledge; three of these involved the CVCe pattern, three involved *i*, and three involved *ea*. Billy made seven substitutions involving the analysis of one-syllable words and nine substitutions involving words with two or more syllables. This would suggest that Billy may benefit from instruction in the CVCe pattern, in sounds for *i*, and in sounds for *ea* as well as instruction in applying this knowledge to actual reading. Billy may also benefit from instruction in how to segment, sound, and blend one-syllable words and words with two or more syllables.

Actually, if a teacher were listening to a student read on a regular basis, such as twice a week, she would have more than four samples on which to base decisions about areas in need of instruction. In other words, four oral reading samples are not sufficient for assessment but are included here only for the purpose of illustration.

Another technique used to investigate a student's weaknesses in the area of phonics involves a self-report procedure. The student is asked to write down all words encountered during independent reading that he has difficulty decoding. The teacher discusses with the student why he had difficulty with a particular word. For example, a student might say that he had trouble with *screamed* because he did not know the sound for *scr*. From discussions with the student and from an analysis of the words identified by the student as trouble-some, the teacher may be able to discern several patterns of errors. Armed with this information and the information gathered during oral reading, an appropriate instructional program can be planned.

We feel that considerable valuable information can be collected and summarized on the oral reading analysis sheet; however, in response to teacher demand, we have developed a simplified version. This simpler version was requested by busy classroom teachers who did not feel that they could find the time to complete our more detailed oral reading analysis sheet. The basic difference between the full version (Figure 9.3) and the simpler version (Figure 9.4) lies in the number of categorizations that need to be recorded for a given error and in the numerical summaries that are created. Suppose, for example, that a teacher does not have time to count the different types of errors (as shown at the bottom of each day's reading in Figure 9.3). The teacher instead can look at where the most "x"s occur over several oral reading analysis sessions to determine an appropriate instructional focus. For example, in Figure 9.4, the most frequent type of error is the automatic error (marked with an "x" in column 3).

Since the same type of automatic error appears consistently across *several* sessions, it becomes a likely candidate as an area of focus for this particular child.

STRUCTURAL ANALYSIS

Structural analysis brings the element of meaning to assessment because almost all structural units (inflections, affixes, and root words) convey meaning as well as sound.

Inflectional Endings

Substitutions involving inflectional endings (see Chapter 8), like all substitutions and other oral reading errors, can be a problem if the errors interfere with meaning. However, as we noted in Chapter 8, inflections are tricky, and teachers must be careful to determine whether a lack of attention to inflections is a reading problem or simply the systematic application of a reader's dialect or second language. A teacher who infers that a Black dialect speaker's pronunciation of /pas/ for *passed* indicates a lack of attention to inflections makes a grievous instructional error if he drills the student on inflections.

When students appear to be having genuine difficulty with inflectional endings, there are several assessment strategies that may be used to determine the initial performance level and to evaluate progress following instruction.

One technique for assessing a student's skill in reading inflections correctly involves a paper-and-pencil task similar to many workbook activities. A sentence containing a blank is present along with several words. For example

1. Tina _____ to go to the game. (wanted, wanting)
2. Last night my dad _____ me with my homework. (helps, helped)

Key:

1. Substitution is written above actual word, SC = self-corrected, SD = successfully decoded.

2. "X" indicates that error involved analysis difficulty.

3. "X" indicates that error was automatic but wrong.

4. "X" indicates that error impaired the meaning of the text. "SC" indicates that error (which impaired meaning) was self-corrected.

5. Notes are listed about difficulties related to phonic element, basic sight word, etc.

1 Error	2 Analysis Difficulty	3 Automatic Error	4 Impaired Meaning	5 Notes
however SC whenever				
sneez(ed)		X		-ed
country SD				
sheep shepherd	X		X	
thorn throne	X		X	thr
look(ing)		X		-ing
every very		X		BSW-very
powe(ful)		X		-ful
after SC afraid			SC	
my SC mine				
your you		X		BSW-you
storm(ed)		X		-ed
mission majesty	X		X	

*The analysis is based on the text and oral reading errors shown in Figure 8.7.

FIGURE 9.4. A Short Form of the Oral Reading Analysis Sheet*

The student is asked to select the correct word for the blank. Choices comprise the same word with different endings. If the student does not know all of the words in a particular sentence, the teacher should read the sentence to the student. Even the base word of the answer can be read aloud if necessary, but the two choices should be read by the student. A progress chart can be kept indicating percentage of blanks filled in correctly on a series of assessments taken over time. One advantage of this type of task is that it can be administered to a group. A disadvantage is that it does not really tell the teacher what a reader is doing during everyday reading.

A second procedure for assessing a student's skill in reading inflectional endings is to keep a record of the word recognition substitutions and omissions involving inflectional endings made during oral reading. A high incidence of substitutions or omissions means that a closer evaluation, and perhaps some instruction, is called for. And, above all, remember that reading miscues must be evaluated in terms of the students' oral language patterns involving inflectional endings.

Regardless of the method of reading assessment used, a teacher has an obligation to determine whether the inflection substitutions or omissions are interfering with comprehension. A simple way to do this is to ask a question that requires students to have understood the intent of the inflection even if they omit it or mispronounce it. For example, a student who consistently omits the past tense marker, *ed*, could be asked when a particular action in the story occurred to determine whether the student understood the meaning conveyed by the inflection.

Affixes

Recognizing affixes (see Chapter 8) aids students in the syllabication and decoding of unknown words. A group-administered paper-and-pencil task could be used to assess students' skill in recognizing affixes in text. Such an assessment might involve asking students to circle all of the prefixes and suffixes they could find in a given text segment. Even a short story or a newspaper article on which the students can make notes might serve as the reading material for this task. Alternatively, if the material is not consumable, a piece of acetate can be placed over a page of everyday reading material, and the students can locate affixes with a grease pencil or overhead transparency pen.

As has been true of all of our paper-and-pencil measures discussed in this chapter, this approach can be administered to a group, and the cost of the group advantage is the failure to assess affix recognition during everyday reading. Again, oral reading presents an informal and unobtrusive opportunity to observe how students handle inflections when they are reading. A high incidence of substitutions involving affixes indicates that the student does not attend to them carefully while reading and probably could use instruction emphasizing their crucial role in comprehension.

CONTEXTUAL ANALYSIS

The best method for determining students' disposition toward using context to aid the word recognition process is through oral reading analysis. Of particular interest is the incidence of nonsemantic substitutions that are self-corrected by a student during oral reading (see substitutions marked with a plus [+] in column 3 of Figures 9.2 and 9.3). A nonsemantic substitution is a miscue that does not make sense in the context of its passage (see substitutions marked with a minus [–] in column 3 of Figures 9.2 and 9.3). A semantic substitution, by contrast, is a miscue that does make sense in the context of its passage (see substitutions marked with a "0" in column 3 of Figures 9.2 and 9.3). As pointed out in Chapter 8, low-achieving readers tend to make more and correct fewer nonsemantic substitutions than do good readers. A relatively low incidence of self-corrections on nonsemantic substitutions indicates a failure to monitor for meaning and a failure to capitalize on the advantage that context offers in helping to decode difficult words.

A record can be kept of the ratio of nonsemantic substitutions that were self-corrected during a number of oral reading activities. Looking once again at Figure 9.3, we see that two of Billy's five nonsemantic substitutions on Day 1 were self-corrected, one out of nine on Day 2, zero out of five on Day 3, and one out of five on Day 4. These data indicate that Billy did not self-correct most word recognition substitutions that interfered with meaning. Clearly this is an area in which Billy needs some assistance.

FLUENCY

Fluent readers read as if they were speaking, not reading. To assess the ability to read automatically and effortlessly teachers should pay particular attention to fluency during oral reading. A student who has to consciously or deliberately decode many words is neither automatic nor fluent. Comments on a student's automaticity or lack thereof should be recorded on the reading difficulties record sheet (see Figure 9.5). After instruction in automaticity and chunking (see Chapter 8), progress in these areas should show up during oral reading. Audio tapes kept over time provide a powerful demonstration to students of their progress in fluency.

Once students are decoding fairly automatically, teachers can assess their silent reading rate (when reading instructional level materials) and compare it to the normative rates in Table 8.1. Several samples should be used initially to determine a student's reading rate. Also, several comprehension questions and a retelling of the story should be used to determine if the student has comprehended the material. A progress chart, indicating the reading rate in words read correctly per minute and the comprehension score for each passage read, can be kept.

Curriculum-Based Measurement: Words Read Correctly in 1 Minute

Stan Deno at the University of Minnesota and his colleagues have pioneered the use of curriculum-based measurement (CBM) in the form of frequent, 1 minute timings from students' everyday reading material to assess students' reading ability.[5] The number of words read orally in a fixed amount of time has been found to correlate highly (.78 and .80) with reading comprehension scores (e.g., literal and inferential subtests of the Stanford Achievement Test).[6]

Student's Name <u>Billy Stone</u>

Age _____ Grade __5__

I. Instructional Level

A.	IRI	Level	Word Recognition Accuracy	Average Comprehension	Oral Comprehension	Silent Comprehension
Date	9/16	2^2	96	85	90	80
Instr. level	3'	3^1	95	75	75	75
		3^2	89	70	75	65
		4	85	60	70	50

Comments:

B. Ongoing assessment of instructional level (from oral reading analysis sheets and comprehension questions)

Date	Pages/Book	Word Recognition Accuracy	Comprehension
10/2	78–84, lvl 3'	96 (p. 78)	85
10/5	85–90, 3'	94 (p. 85)	75
10/12	99–102, 3'	96 (p. 99)	70
10/16	103–108, 3'	94 (p. 103)	65

Comments:

10/19   WR Acc. and Comp. Okay at level 3'.

II. Word Recognition

A. Basic sight words not known frequently missed (from informal test and/or oral reading analysis)

Comments:
10/19   None from 10/2–10/16

B. General word recognition strategy

1. Student's comments:
10/5   He says he tries to sound out a word he doesn't know.

2. Degree to which unfamiliar words deliberately and successfully decoded (from oral reading analysis sheets)

Comments:
10/19   On 10/2, 5 SD*/2 NSD; on 10/5 7 SD/7 NSD; on 10/12, 4 SD/6 NSD; on 10/16, 4 SD/6 NSD. Could use help with general word recognition strategy.
*SD = successfully decoded; NSD = not successfully decoded

FIGURE 9.5.   Reading Difficulties Record Sheet Instructional Level and Word Recognition

C. Phonic analysis

1. Informal phonics inventory date _____

Results:

2. Consistent errors in symbol-sound correspondence knowledge and/or ability to analyze 1 and 2+ syllable words (from oral reading analysis sheets)

Comments:
10/19   From 10/2–10/16, 3 errors with CVCe, 3 errors with *i*, 3 errors with *ea*. Review of each of these needed. From 10/2–10/16, 7 errors with 1 syllable words, 9 errors with 2+ syllable words. Needs help analyzing 1 and 2+ syllable words.

D. Structural analysis—inflectional endings and/or knowledge of affixes

1. Informal testing
      Date   % Correct/Comments

2. Consistent errors (from oral reading analysis sheets)
      10/19   From 10/2–10/16, none.

E. Contextual analysis

Self-correction of nonsemantic substitutions (from oral reading analysis sheets)

Comments:
10/19   From 10/2–10/16: 2/5, 1/9, 0/9, 1/5 nonsemantic substitutions corrected. Seems to need help with this. Try oral reading for meaning.

F. Fluency

1. Rate
      Date   Pages/Book   Words per Min.   Comp.

Comments:

2. Automaticity/phrasing
      Comments:

FIGURE 9.5.   Reading Difficulties Record Sheet (*cont.*)

Teachers using CBM in reading have students read passages taken from their everyday reading material. Students are timed for 1 minute, and the number of words read correctly is counted and graphed. One minute timings are taken at least once a week. This measure is seen as a general measure of reading ability. A teacher hopes to see a low-achieving reader make steady progress toward the grade appropriate average reading rate.

One large urban school system in the midwest has developed grade level reading rate norms (Marston & Magnusson, 1988). Approximately 8000 randomly selected students read from the level of the basal reader typically read by students in Grades 1 through 6. For example, second graders read from the first level of the basal series read in second grade, or the 2.1 book. Fifth graders read from the fifth grade basal. Average number of words read correctly per minute by students in January and June were as follows:

	Jan.	June
Grade 1	52	71
Grade 2	73	82
Grade 3	107	115
Grade 4	115	118
Grade 5	129	134
Grade 6	120	131

It is important to remember that longer, harder words are going to be found in Grade 6 material. Consequently, sixth grade students in the above data would not have read more slowly than fifth graders if they had read the fifth grade material. In fact, when Deno had 360 students in Grades 1 through 6 from six school districts in Minnesota read a Grade 3 passage in June, the number of words read correctly per minute per grade level were as follows:

Grade 1   40

Grade 2   107

Grade 3   124

Grade 4   145

Grade 5   161

Grade 6   182

What all of this means is that the CBM approach validated by Deno and his colleagues can serve as a good barometer of students' rate and fluency. Other things being equal, sophisticated students read faster, and everyone improves over time. So as long as the data are used sensibly and in concert with other measures, CBMs can provide a useful part of a complete classroom-based evaluation of an individual's progress.

USING THE READING DIFFICULTIES RECORD SHEET TO PLAN INSTRUCTION

We have introduced a number of ways to collect and analyze oral reading data in order to locate sources of word recognition difficulty. But the interpretation of these data is the most critical part of the process because it has implications for teaching and learning.

Students who are not recognizing most of the words (approximately 90 to 95 percent accuracy) can be considered to have difficulty with word recognition. Either the material they are reading is too difficult or they need extra instructional assistance or both. When additional assistance is implicated, teachers need to evaluate *relative strengths and weaknesses* in a student's word recognition performance. The record sheets that we have suggested in this chapter provide a first step in making that evaluation. The first few pages of the reading difficulties record sheet, presented in Figure 9.5, can be used to summarize data collected from several oral reading sessions. For example, the data in Figure 9.5 is a summary of the information recorded in Figure 9.3.

Billy Stone is in the fifth grade but has been placed in a 3–1 (first half of third grade) reader for instruction. Ongoing assessment of Billy's instructional level reveals that the 3–1 level appears to be a good instructional level for Billy (see I.B. of Figure 9.5). Because Billy is not decoding with 90 to 95 percent accuracy at his grade level, the teacher should suspect that he has difficulty with word recognition.

Billy's teacher believes the oral reading analysis suggests that Billy would benefit from instruction in the general word recognition strategy. Four samples of oral reading reveal that Billy was unable to decode most of the unfamiliar words he encountered.

Billy has made repeated symbol-sound correspondence mismatches that involve the CVCe pattern (three substitutions), words with *i* (three substitutions), and words with *ea* (three substitutions). It can also be seen that 7/25 (or 28 percent) of Billy's substitutions involved inappropriate analysis of one-syllable words, and 9/25 (or 36 percent) of his errors involved inappropriate analysis of multisyllabic words. These data suggest the need for instruction in vowel sounds for words with the CVCe pattern, sounds for the symbols *i* and *ea* and analysis, or segmentation, sounding, and blending of one-syllable and multisyllabic words.

This teacher is keeping oral reading analysis notes as students are engaged in oral reading. (*Peter Vadnai*)

The data also suggest that Billy is not monitoring for meaning. He self-corrected nonsemantic substitutions only 17 percent of the time (only four non-semantic substitutions out of twenty-eight). This would suggest focusing instruction on the use of context as an aid in decoding.

On the other hand, Billy does not appear to need special instruction in basic sight words or in structural analysis. Very few of his substitutions involved basic sight words and no basic sight words were missed frequently. Also, very few errors involved inflectional endings and affixes.

Again, we want to point out that a student's reading difficulties record sheet should be based on more than four reading samples. Four samples have been included here for the purpose of illustration. In the classroom or clinic, low-achieving readers with difficulties in word recognition should be reading aloud to the teacher at least once or twice a week. This will provide numerous samples that can be analyzed for initial and ongoing assessment and evaluation of pupil progress.

Classroom teachers may be wondering how they would have time to collect the type of data presented in Figures 9.3 and 9.5. It is important to remember that frequent, painstaking records would be kept only for a very specific set of students—those low-achieving readers with clear-cut word recognition difficulties.

When listening to a student read, the teacher needs to record only word recognition substitutions (column 1) and words successfully decoded (column 7) on a chart as shown in Figure 9.3, along with notations indicating whether or not the general word recognition strategy was used successfully in decoding efforts. The rest of the information in Figure 9.3 (columns 3, 4, 5, and 6) can be filled in at a later date. The teacher should devote 20 minutes to oral reading analysis several times a week. The teacher can work with a group of students for a 10-minute period, focusing on students with word recognition difficulties and making notes as individuals read aloud. The students can then reread this material in pairs while the teacher spends the next 10 minutes completing columns 3 through 6. Additional suggestions for scheduling time to help low-achieving readers during the reading period will be discussed in Chapter 16.

To enter data on the reading difficulties record sheet, the teacher should periodically (such as every 4 to 6 weeks) analyze the data from four or more oral reading sessions. Our experience has suggested that a teacher needs 1 to 1.5 hours to complete this task for a group of twelve students. Once the data from a number of oral reading sessions have been collected, a person with expertise in reading difficulties, such as the classroom teacher or the reading resource teacher, can enter the data on the reading difficulties record sheet (Figure 9.5), analyze it, and decide on recommendations for supplemental instruction.

In Chapter 16 all of the instructional recommendations for Billy Stone in the areas of word recognition, comprehension, and vocabulary will be reviewed and a specific program of instruction will be recommended. An additional reading difficulties record sheet on a child, Travis, is in Appendix C.

SUMMARY

Oral reading analysis is the primary assessment tool recommended for use by a classroom teacher or special reading teacher to determine strengths and weaknesses in word recognition. Oral reading analysis can be used to gain information about a student's use of a general word recognition strategy, basic sight vocabulary, skill in phonic, contextual, and structural analysis, and fluency. The use of a reading difficulties record sheet to collect data based on a student's oral reading provides a useful tool for recording information and planning instruction.

Suggested Activities

1. Conduct oral reading analysis on at least three occasions with a student who is not proficient in word recognition. Record necessary information (columns 1, 2, and 7 of Figure 9.3) on an oral reading analysis sheet as the student is reading, and complete the chart after the student has finished reading (columns 3 to 6 of Figure 9.3).
2. Based on the data from three or more oral reading analysis sheets, fill out the word recognition section of a reading difficulties record sheet for a student. If you have not been able to complete oral reading analysis sheets because a child was not available, you may be able to complete a reading difficulties sheet on a student based on oral reading analysis sheets provided by your instructor. Or you may want to use the completed oral reading analysis sheets in Appendix C.

Suggested Reading

CLAY, M. (1985). *The early detection of reading difficulties* (3rd ed.). Portsmouth, NH: Heinemann.

A detailed description is provided of taking a running record while a low-achieving student is engaged in oral reading.

DENO, S. (1985). Curriculum-based measurement: The emerging alternative. *Exceptional Children, 52*: 219–232.

The value of curriculum-based measurement is discussed.

FUCHS, L., DENO, S., and MIRKIN, P. (1984). The effects of frequent curriculum-based measurement and evaluation on pedagogy, student achievement, and student awareness of learning. *American Educational Research Journal, 21*, 449–460.

Research supporting curriculum-based measurement is presented.

MARSTON, D., and MAGNUSSON, D., (1985). Implementing curriculum-based measurement in special and regular education settings. *Exceptional Children, 52*: 266–276.

Authors discuss how to implement curriculum-based measurement in reading within a school district.

Notes

1. See K. Goodman (1967) for one of the earliest analyses of miscues or Y. Goodman, Watson, and Burke (1987) for a more recent treatment. For Clay's running record approach, see Clay (1985).
2. See Wixson (1979).

3. See Pikulski and Shanahan (1982b).
4. See Biemiller (1979), Kibby (1979), Leslie and Osol (1978), and Williamson and Young (1974).
5. See Deno (1985), Fuchs, Fuchs, and Deno (1982), Fuchs, Fuchs, and Maxwell (1988).
6. See Deno, Mirkin, and Chiang (1982), Potter and Wamre (1990).

COMPREHENSION INSTRUCTION

Overview

As you read this chapter use the following list of main ideas to guide your understanding and reflection.

- Metacognition, in which readers are aware of and have control over their comprehension, is an important part of the reading comprehension process.
- Low-achieving readers often need assistance in developing specific comprehension strategies to use when reading on their own.
- Low-achieving readers often need assistance in learning how to monitor and repair comprehension.
- Explicit instruction in a comprehension strategy helps students understand *what* a strategy is, *why* it is important, *how* to perform the strategy, and *when* to use the strategy.

Effective reading comprehension involves more than understanding the message on a printed page. Reading comprehension is also a metacognitive process in which readers are aware of and have control over their comprehension. Successful comprehenders of text generally understand that the purpose of reading is to read for meaning. They know how to use specific strategies to facilitate comprehension, and they monitor their own comprehension as they read, implementing fix-up strategies when comprehension has failed.[1]

Low-achieving readers may have trouble with reading comprehension for a number of reasons. They may not actively read for meaning, focusing more on reading as a decoding process than as a meaning-getting process.[2] Also, they may not know how to use comprehension-fostering strategies and may not be as effective as good readers at monitoring their own comprehension.[3]

Reading instruction designed to improve low-achieving readers' comprehension of text should stress that meaning getting is the purpose of reading. Students should be taught specific comprehension strategies they can use when reading on their own, and they should be taught why these strategies are important. Low-achieving readers should also be taught to monitor their reading comprehension and to stop and apply appropriate fix-up strategies when they do not understand what they are reading.

225

CHAPTER *10*
Comprehension
Instruction

PROBLEMS WITH CONVENTIONAL READING COMPREHENSION INSTRUCTION

Unfortunately, conventional reading comprehension instruction, developmental or corrective, is often inadequate for a number of reasons. First, many teachers do not provide students with explicit instruction in how to perform comprehension strategies. Too often they merely mention skills (for example, "The main idea is the most important idea in a paragraph.") and then help students complete worksheets on these skills. In a study of thirty-nine intermediate grade classrooms, Durkin (1978–1979) found that comprehension instruction in which teachers did or said something to improve students' ability to comprehend actual text occurred less than 1 percent of the time during the reading period.

In addition to the lack of explicit instruction, reading comprehension instruction often fails to provide for adequate transfer to actual reading of connected text. Far too often reading comprehension skills are practiced in isolation on skill sheets, and students are not taught how to transfer these skills to real reading situations.[4] There is no guarantee that skills covered on skill sheets will be used by students when they read actual text on their own.

For example, Taylor, Olson, Prenn, Rybczynski, and Zakaluk (1985) found that sixth-grade students who appeared to be quite skilled at "reading for main ideas" on the basis of their performance on multiple-choice skill sheets (88 percent correct), did significantly less well when asked to answer multiple-choice questions on main ideas in their social studies book (73 percent correct), and did very poorly when asked to generate main ideas for paragraphs in their social studies book (40 percent correct). Similar results were found in a second study.[5]

Low-achieving readers need to be shown explicitly how and when comprehension strategies should be used when engaged in independent reading. Although they cannot possibly use all of the comprehension strategies that have been taught, there are times when the conscious use of a particular strategy will be useful or even essential.

The third concern deals with the overwhelming number of skills that are taught or practiced, many of which will not be useful to students when they are reading connected text on their own. For example, it would be difficult to explain to students how numbering sentences in the sequence in which they appear in the text would enhance their comprehension. Instead, teachers need to focus their comprehension instruction on strategies that students can actually use when reading independently.

The final concern is that students are not taught to be metacognitively aware of their own understanding as they read. That is, they have not learned to be aware of when they do or do not understand what they are reading. They are also not taught how to use specific fix-up strategies when their reading comprehension has failed. Many good readers may have learned to do this on their own, but many unsuccessful readers appear to be in need of instruction in comprehension monitoring.

MODEL FOR READING COMPREHENSION INSTRUCTION

The remainder of this chapter provides suggestions for sound reading comprehension instruction. Strategies are discussed that will help students become better comprehenders when reading on their own. The strategies fall under one or more of the following aspects of comprehension, all of which are essential:

1. Developing metacognitive awareness and monitoring comprehension
2. Fostering general comprehension
3. Drawing inferences
4. Reading for important ideas and studying
5. Using or developing prior knowledge

In most cases the strategy is presented using the following steps:

1. An explanation of *what* the strategy consists of
2. An explanation about *why* the strategy is important
3. An explanation of *how* teachers can model the strategy
4. An explanation of *when* the strategy should be used in independent reading
5. Provisions for guided practice with actual text
6. Provisions for independent practice with actual text

Obviously teachers should do certain things routinely to enhance students' comprehension of specific texts. For example, sound developmental reading instruction includes introducing difficult vocabulary, activating students' prior knowledge, asking thought-provoking questions for stories and books, and encouraging students to reflect on their experiences with text.[6] The focus in this chapter, however, will be on student-directed, as opposed to teacher-directed, comprehension strategies that poor comprehenders can learn to use independently. Not all strategies need to be taught to all low-achieving readers. Chapter 11 provides guidance on which strategies to teach to particular students based on diagnosed needs.

METACOGNITIVE AWARENESS AND COMPREHENSION MONITORING STRATEGIES

Many low-achieving readers are not aware that they can and should control their own reading. They do not realize, for example, that previewing will probably facilitate their comprehension of content textbook material or that strategies such as summarizing or self-questioning will help them remember what they have read.

Unlike good readers, many low-achieving readers do not check their comprehension as they read.[7] That is, they are not aware of whether they do or do not understand what they are reading. Furthermore, they have inadequate fix-up strategies for improving their comprehension when it is faltering.[8] In this section techniques to develop students' metacognitive awareness and their comprehension monitoring and repairing abilities will be discussed.

Metacognitive Checklist

Low-achieving readers may need specific help in order to engage in metacognitive activities when reading. The checklist below might be displayed on a chart in the room or printed on a card that a student could keep as a personal copy.

1. Get ready to read (i.e., read headings, look at pictures, think about what I already know).
2. Monitor my comprehension while reading (i.e., notice when I'm not understanding, use fix-up strategies).
3. Improve my comprehension while reading (i.e., ask myself questions, stop to assess where I am).
4. Check my comprehension and study after reading (i.e., create a summary, ask myself questions, create a story map or graphic organizer).
5. Help myself answer questions (i.e., use lookbacks, question-answer relationships, or self-monitoring checklist).

The checklist was kept simple to avoid overwhelming students. The activities listed in parentheses are only examples, however. These activities, along with others that would be appropriate, are discussed in the remainder of the chapter.

Comprehension Rating

An instructional procedure developed by Davey and Porter (1982) has been found to be effective in improving low-achieving readers' comprehension monitoring skills. The procedure is designed to help students (1) understand the purpose of print, (2) focus their attention on meaning while reading, (3) evaluate their comprehension while reading, and (4) develop fix-up strategies to improve their comprehension.

How. Step 1 of the procedure, helping students to understand the purpose of print, involves teacher demonstration and modeling. Through the use of cloze passages the teacher can show students that even if they do not read every word in a paragraph, they can still understand what they are reading. After discussing the importance of comprehension, some personal fix-up strategies, such as rereading or looking up a difficult word in the dictionary, can be introduced. The teacher can also model comprehension monitoring while reading aloud to the students. ("I understand this paragraph, so I'll go on," "This paragraph doesn't make sense; I'd better reread it").

Step 2, establishing criteria for understanding, involves a three-point comprehension-rating task. First working in groups and then working individually, students rate sentences, paragraphs, and longer texts as (1) "I understand well" (I have a clear, complete picture in my head and could explain it to someone else), (2) "I sort of understand" (I have an incomplete picture in my head and I couldn't explain it to someone else), or (3) "I don't understand." The teacher and students share their ratings for different sentences, paragraphs, and texts and discuss their reasons for particular ratings.

Students are also shown how to locate sources of comprehension difficulty in naturally occurring text. Examples of texts that might be used are presented in Figure 10.1.

Step 3, developing fix-up strategies, is implemented once students show competence with the first steps. Attention is directed to both word level and idea level fix-up strategies.

Word level fix-up strategies include the following:

1. Read around the word (maybe you can skip the word without much loss of comprehension or can figure the word out from context clues)
2. Use context clues for help in decoding or predicting what a word means
3. Look for structural clues within words
4. Sound out words
5. Use a dictionary
6. Ask for help

Idea level fix-up strategies include the following:

1. Read on to make it clearer
2. Reread carefully to make it clearer
3. Look again at the title, pictures, headings
4. Ask yourself questions
5. Put ideas into your own words as you go along
6. Picture the ideas in your head while you read
7. Relate ideas to your personal experience
8. Ask someone to clarify things

Students are given a list of these fix-up strategies. Each strategy is modeled by the teacher (the teacher talks aloud as he performs the strategy) and then practiced by the students. Finally, students practice choosing and using fix-up strategies when they experience comprehension difficulties during actual reading. They are asked to make notes or mark places in the text where they use fix-up strategies and later to explain to the teacher what strategies they used. If they are unable to do this independently, they can read individually with the teacher, receiving guidance about what fix-up strategies to use when they know they are experiencing comprehension difficulties.

What, Why, When. The preceding discussion focused on *how* to model various aspects of the Davey and Porter comprehension-rating procedure and how

FIGURE 10.1. Examples of Passages to Use with the Comprehension-Rating Task

The sources of comprehension difficulty that students should identify are in italics.

London is a beautiful city. There are many famous old buildings like the Houses of Parliament and Westminster Abbey. *Many are buried there.*

The firefighters worked hard all morning. Sam was really hungry. *She* went to lunch at 11:00 A.M.

Dust storms swept across the Great Plains in the 1930s. Farmland was destroyed. *Many people moved.*

This teacher is modeling the technique of comprehension monitoring for a group of intermediate grade students. *(Peter Vadnai)*

Steps 2 and 3 can be used with actual text during guided and independent practice. In addition, it is important for the teacher to do the following:

1. *What*—Explain to students that they will be learning to decide whether what they are reading makes sense.
2. *Why*—Explain to students that this is important because if what you're reading doesn't make sense, it is time to do something about it.
3. *When*—Explain to students that they can monitor their comprehension as they are reading on their own. They should stop every so often (e.g., at the end of every paragraph or page or any time they notice something's unclear). Then they should ask themselves whether or not they understand what they just read. If their answer is *no*, they should decide on the reason they are having difficulty and select an appropriate word level or idea level fix-up strategy.

The comprehension-rating procedure described above was used with fifth- and sixth-grade students who were poor comprehenders. Compared to a control group, students trained in the procedure had better scores on a reading comprehension test, generated better summaries of what they read, and were more successful in identifying idea level comprehension difficulties.[9]

Other Techniques Involving Comprehension Monitoring

Comprehension monitoring is an important part of the reciprocal teaching strategy discussed in the next section. After introducing the concepts of comprehension monitoring and fix-up strategies to students through the comprehension-rating procedure, a teacher may want to continue to develop students' comprehension abilities through the use of reciprocal teaching. One appealing feature of reciprocal teaching is that students work in small groups. The complexity of comprehension monitoring and comprehension repairing may stand a better chance of becoming everyday routines if students can see that they are helpful to their peers.

The purpose of the question-answering checklist, described in the general comprehension strategies discussion below, is to help students decide whether or not they have done the best job possible answering written questions. The self-monitoring checklist, described in the section on inferencing, is designed to help students monitor their answers to inferential questions in particular.

GENERAL COMPREHENSION STRATEGIES

This section discusses a number of strategies that have been found to improve students' general ability to comprehend text when reading on their own.

Imagery

Encouraging children to make pictures in their minds as they read has been found to improve their comprehension and their comprehension-monitoring ability.[10] Gambrell and Bales (1986) worked with low-achieving readers in small groups in Grades 3 and 4 to improve their comprehension-monitoring ability through the use of imagery. Students were instructed to make pictures in their minds to help them remember what they read. After reading sentences such as "The sad little boy watched his ice cream fall out of the cone," children were asked to tell what they could remember about each sentence. Specific information not recalled was probed further. For example, if the students did not mention that the boy was sad, a teacher might ask "How did the little boy feel?" Students might also be asked to describe the mental picture they made about the little boy feeling sad. After working with sentences, children read and made mental pictures of paragraphs and then short texts.

Gambrell and Bales found that 70 percent of the low-achieving readers used imagery when encouraged to do so and that about 65 percent were able to detect inconsistencies in the passages they read (into which explicit and implicit inconsistencies had been inserted). Children who had been instructed in the use of imagery were significantly better at detecting inconsistencies in text than low-achieving readers who did not receive the imagery training.

Student-Generated Questioning

Student-generated questions during or after reading have several virtues. They help students interact with the text, they improve their comprehension, and they help students become more independent as learners.[11] They have also been found to (1) increase involvement in the process of comprehension, (2) help focus attention on important information, (3) improve text processing time, and (4) help readers monitor their own comprehension.[12] Generally, however, students develop better self-questioning strategies when teachers demonstrate how they go about the task themselves. Simply telling students to ask themselves questions while reading will be ineffective.

Self-Questioning While Reading Narrative Text

A self-questioning technique that has proved successful with both elementary[13] and secondary students was developed by Singer and Donlan (1982). It involves students asking themselves story-specific questions about elements such as character, goal, obstacles, outcome, and theme. Only one story element is covered in a particular lesson. Examples of general and specific questions for the story "The Three Little Pigs" are presented in Figure 10.2.

Specific instructional steps to follow in this self-questioning procedure are presented below.

What. Students need to understand that they will be learning how to ask and answer questions about stories they read.

Why. Students should know that this approach will improve their ability to understand the stories they are reading.

How. Teachers can begin by demonstrating the questions that they might ask as they read a story. The teacher begins with a story element, such as a character, and explains that a story can either be about one character or a group of characters working together toward a common goal. The teacher then asks a general question about the main character, shows how to convert it into a story-specific question, and finally answers the question. Several other examples of story-specific questions that could have been asked are then presented. (Is this story about all three pigs or is it mostly about the third pig? Is this story about the wolf or the third pig?) Several questions are also discussed that are inappropriate because they do not pertain to the main character. (Where does this story take place? What other characters are in this story besides the three pigs and the wolf?) On subsequent days the same modeling procedure is repeated with the other story elements.

FIGURE 10.2. General and Specific Questions for "The Three Little Pigs"

Story Element		General and Specific Questions
Character	GQ	Who is the leading character?
	SQ	Is this story more about the wolf or the third pig?
Goal	GQ	What is the leading character trying to accomplish?
	SQ	What does the third pig hope to accomplish in this story?
Obstacles	GQ	What obstacles does the leading character encounter?
	SQ	How does the wolf create problems for the third pig?
Outcome	GQ	Does the leading character reach his or her goal?
	SQ	How does the third pig overcome the wolf?
Theme	GQ	Why did the author write this story?
		What does the author want to show us about life?
	SQ	What did I learn from the story "The Three Little Pigs?"

When. Students can learn that it is useful to ask and answer questions about the major story elements whenever they are reading a story that seems difficult to understand.

For guided practice, the teacher and students work together generating story-specific questions about the main character for other stories in tradebooks or in their basal reader. Good and bad story-specific questions are discussed. For independent practice, students work through several more stories on their own, generating and answering story-specific questions about the main character.

After helping students learn how to generate and answer a story-specific question about the main character, the teacher can extend the discussion to the element of goal. For guided and independent practice, students should generate and answer questions about both the leading character and his goal. By the time that all story elements have been covered, students should be able to generate and answer story related questions about the main character, goal, obstacles, outcomes, and the theme of stories they read.

Group Story Mapping

Idol (1987) has developed a story mapping procedure somewhat similar to the self-questioning technique described above. This procedure has been found to be effective with mixed groups of low-achieving and average-reading third- and fourth-grade students.

After students read a short story, they completed a story map with their teacher's help. Children worked in small groups but also filled in individual copies of the story map by copying the group responses onto their own papers. After completing the story map as a group, the children independently answered written comprehension questions related to the story map elements. An example of a story map sheet is in Figure 10.3.

In the second phase, once the children were comfortable with completing the story map as a group process, they were asked to fill in the story map on their own as or after they read the story. As a group, the students then completed a story map with the teacher writing down responses. Children were allowed to make any corrections they felt were necessary on their individually completed maps. After turning in their books and maps, students independently answered written comprehension questions about story elements.

In the third phase, students were asked to complete story maps independently as they silently read stories and then answered written comprehension questions. A group map was no longer completed.

In the final maintenance phase, students silently read stories and answered written comprehension questions without first completing story maps. Over the four phases students read twenty-one stories.

Idol found that students' performance, in general, on the comprehension questions improved from about 70 percent correct to about 90 percent correct in the maintenance phase. Low-achieving readers' comprehension, specifically, improved from about 40 percent correct to about 80 percent correct. Improvements in low-achieving students' listening comprehension of stories and narrative journal writing were also found, suggesting that the students had acquired a sense of story structure that would transfer across literacy tasks.

Reciprocal Questioning

Helfeldt and Lalik (1976) found that their reciprocal student-teacher questioning strategy, based on the ReQuest procedure[14] had a positive effect on fifth-grade students' reading comprehension. This is a very simple procedure whereby students learn how to ask thought-provoking questions that help

FIGURE 10.3. An Example of a Story Map

Main Character(s):	General Description of
Setting:	
Time(s)	Place(s)
Problem:	
Events Related to the Problem:	
Resolution:	

them interpret or better understand the material they have read. Steps include the following:

What. Students are told they will be learning how to generate questions that ask readers to interpret material they have read. Often these are *why* and *how* questions instead of *what, where,* or *when* questions. They require students to make inferences, or to interpret what is happening in a story.

Why. Students are told that if they ask each other interpretive questions about material they have read in small groups, their understanding of the material improves.

How. The teacher introduces vocabulary and asks several questions to motivate reading. The students read the assigned text and answer the motivating question in a small group discussion. Then, the teacher begins to ask thought-provoking, interpretive questions about the material. Every time a student correctly answers a question, the student then gets to ask the teacher a question. The student question then is followed by another teacher question. By observing and imitating teacher questions, students learn to ask good interpretive questions. Helfeldt and Lalik found that after fourteen 45-minute lessons with the teacher, students' inferential reading comprehension improved. An example of teacher-student questioning for a story is presented in Figure 10.4.

When. Students are told that after completing a reading assignment, they may want to work in groups of three or four and ask each other interpretive questions about the material they have read. Whoever answers a question correctly gets to ask the next question.

Guided practice occurs whenever the teacher and students engage in the reciprocal questioning model. For independent practice, students can work in small groups of three or four and ask each other questions about a story or an informative selection they have read.

Reciprocal Teaching

A reciprocal teaching model that develops skill in monitoring and improving comprehension for low-achieving readers has been developed by Palincsar and Brown (1984). The model involves students taking turns assuming the role of teacher and engaging a small group of readers in the study activities of questioning, summarizing, clarifying, and predicting. Palincsar and Brown found that students who learn to use the reciprocal teaching model make substantial improvements in their ability to answer comprehension questions based on textbook material, gains that are maintained over time. For example, Palincsar and Brown found that seventh-grade students who initially answered comprehension questions with only 40 percent accuracy after independent reading were able to read with 70 to 80 percent accuracy after engaging in the reciprocal teaching model for 15 days. Students have also made significant gains on other reading comprehension measures after learning how to use the model. Recently, Palincsar and Brown have applied the strategy to whole class instructional settings with similar success. It has even been used, albeit in a listening mode, with first graders.

How. The teacher works with a group of five or six poor comprehenders, modeling how to lead a dialogue about a paragraph of textbook material. After

Tico was a bird who had no wings. Luckily, the other birds were his friends and brought him food. Tico wished that he could fly like the other birds. One night he dreamt that he had golden wings. When he woke up, his dream had come true. Tico was happy and flew around all day with his new golden wings. The other birds left Tico alone. They thought Tico felt he was better than the rest of them because he had golden wings. Tico was sad and lonely. One day Tico gave a golden wing to a man who needed money to buy medicine for his sick child. Tico now had a black feather where the golden feather had been. One by one Tico gave away the rest of his golden feathers to people who needed help. His wings turned completely black. Tico flew back to his friends, the other birds. They were glad to see him because now he was just like them. Tico was happy and excited. But even though he looked the same as the others, he felt he was different because of his memories and dreams.

Reciprocal Questioning

TEACHER:	How did Tico feel when he had no wings?
STUDENT A:	He felt sad.
TEACHER:	Good. Now you ask me a question that will really make me think about the story.
STUDENT A:	What did Tico dream?
TEACHER:	He dreamt he had golden wings. That question is okay, but the answer is right in the story. Try to ask another question that doesn't have an answer right in the story but will help me understand the story better. Maybe you can think of a question that starts with "how" or "why."
STUDENT A:	How did Tico's friends feel about him when he had golden wings?
TEACHER:	Good question. They were jealous. They thought he felt better than everybody else, but he didn't really feel this way. Here's another question. Why was Tico happy and excited at the end of the story?
STUDENT B:	He was happy to be back with his friends.
TEACHER:	Good. Any other reasons he may have been happy?
STUDENT B:	Maybe he was happy about the things he had done.
TEACHER:	Great. Now you ask me a question about the story that will make me think.
STUDENT B:	Do you think Tico should have gone back to the other birds at the end of the story?
TEACHER:	Great question. Yes, because I think he was happy they accepted him again. But even though they thought he was just like them, he still felt a little special because of his memories of the good things he had done.

FIGURE 10.4. Example of Reciprocal Teacher-Student Questioning Based on the Story "Tico and the Golden Wings" by Leo Lionni

the group reads one paragraph, the teacher calls on one student to answer an important question regarding the paragraph. Then, the teacher summarizes the paragraph in a sentence or two. Confusing aspects of the paragraph, if any, are discussed and clarified, and a prediction about future content is made if one comes to mind. The procedure is then repeated with the next paragraph.

At first, students tend to be relatively passive observers but become more actively involved in the model as they attempt to assume the role of teacher. As one student attempts to lead the group through the four activities of questioning, summarizing, clarifying, and predicting, the teacher offers a considerable amount of guidance and feedback. The teacher helps students generate important questions and reword unclear questions, and initially may even construct questions for students to mimic. ("What would be a good question about monarch butterflies that starts with *why?" No response.* "How about, Why do monarch butterflies fly south for the winter?") The teacher also provides many clues at first about what would be good summary statements for paragraphs. ("What's this paragraph about? How about, Monarch butterflies fly south for the winter because _____.") In addition, the teacher offers much praise and positive feedback. ("That was a clear, important question. You came up with a good summary statement. I like your prediction.")

Palincsar and Brown have found that after fifteen lessons students learn through practice, guidance, and feedback how to ask important questions and generate good summary statements for paragraphs. An example of a reciprocal dialogue on the 15th day of instruction is presented in Figure 10.5.

What, Why, and When. During each lesson, it is useful to explain to students that they are learning how to ask important questions that help summarize, clarify, and make predictions about paragraphs of informative text.

Through continued application, they should learn these strategies will help them better understand what they are reading. They should also be encouraged to use this technique whenever they are reading on their own.

The teacher provides feedback as a group of students practices the reciprocal teaching technique. (*Peter Vadnai*)

TEXT:	A dolphin is a mammal, not a fish. A baby dolphin gets milk from its mother until it is about a year and a half old. At six months it also begins to eat small squid. Adult dolphins live on fish and squid.
STUDENT A (TEACHER):	What does a baby dolphin eat?
STUDENT B:	Milk and squid.
STUDENT A:	Correct, very good. My summary for this paragraph is that it is about what dolphins eat.
TEACHER:	Very good. Would you please select the next teacher?
TEXT:	The dolphin breathes through a hole on the top of its head. The hole closes every time the dolphin goes under water. The dolphin can stay under water for about six minutes before it has to rise for more air.
STUDENT C (TEACHER):	How does a dolphin breathe?
STUDENT D:	Through its mouth.
STUDENT C:	No.
STUDENT A:	Through a hole on the top of its head.
STUDENT C:	Correct. This paragraph is about how dolphins breathe.
TEACHER:	Great job!
STUDENT B:	I have a prediction to make.
TEACHER:	Good.
STUDENT B:	I think it might tell about how dolphins swim.
TEACHER:	Okay. Can we have another teacher?
TEXT:	A dolphin lives for about 30 years. During that time, it doesn't sleep very much. A dolphin sleeps for just a few minutes at a time and then wakes up. Most of the time a dolphin is awake and ready to go.
STUDENT D (TEACHER):	Does a dolphin sleep very much?
STUDENT B:	No.
STUDENT D:	That's correct. To summarize: A dolphin doesn't sleep very much.
TEACHER:	That is a good start, Billy, but I think there might be something else to say in the summary. There is more important information to include. In addition to learning that a dolphin doesn't sleep very much, what else do we learn that is important and related to this idea?
STUDENT D:	That a dolphin lives for 30 years?
TEACHER:	Okay. But what else do we learn about sleeping?
STUDENT C:	That a dolphin sleeps for just a few minutes at a time.

FIGURE 10.5 Example of a Reciprocal Dialogue After Fifteen Lessons

TEACHER: Great. This paragraph is mostly about how dolphins sleep. Okay. Next teacher.

TEXT: Dolphins swim very fast. They can move through the water at 30 miles an hour. Their bodies bend easily so they can move well as they swim through the waves.

STUDENT B (TEACHER): My question is, How do dolphins swim? I got my prediction right!

TEACHER: Great. Okay, someone; how do dolphins swim?

STUDENT A: Fast.

STUDENT B: Why?

STUDENT A: Because their bodies bend with the waves.

STUDENT C: I don't understand exactly what that means.

TEACHER: Does anyone think he or she can explain it?

STUDENT B: I think it means they bend to go with the waves instead of through them.

TEACHER: Good.

FIGURE 10.5. Example of a Reciprocal Dialogue After Fifteen Lessons *(Cont.)*

Text Lookbacks

Students are often asked to answer questions about what they have read. A seemingly obvious strategy to use when they are uncertain about an answer involves looking back in the text. However, poor comprehenders are not as skilled in using text lookbacks to answer questions.[15]

A simple strategy developed by Garner and colleagues (1984) has been found to improve middle grade students' use of text lookbacks. The teacher uses relatively concise (200–300 words) passages that are printed on two pages. Two text-based questions (the answers can be found in the text) and one reader-based question (the answer comes from students' prior knowledge) are written on a third page. An example is presented in Figure 10.6.

The steps of the procedure include the following:

What. Students will be learning to look back in the text to help them answer questions.

Why. Students learn that looking back can help them find the answers to questions. As simple as this sounds, many students do not use text lookbacks when they need to.

How. The teacher begins by demonstrating the strategy, looking back to the first or second page of the prepared passage to answer the two text-based questions. The teacher then explains that while looking back will give you relevant information, it will not allow you to locate the reader-based question.

When. Students should use this strategy whenever they are having difficulty generating answers to questions about what they read.

PAGE 1   Every fall monarch butterflies fly south. Some fly almost 2,000 miles from
         Canada to Mexico. They fly about 11 miles an hour and may cover about 80
         miles in one day. They fly during the day and stop at night. They find a tree
         like a pine tree to roost in because they can easily cling to pine needles.

PAGE 2   People used to think that the monarch butterfly slept through the winter. But
         monarchs cannot live in a place where it stays below freezing for several days.
         That is why they have to fly south before winter comes.
             No one knows exactly how monarchs find their way south. They cannot see
         very well, so they cannot find their way by landmarks. It remains a puzzle to
         scientists.

PAGE 3   *Text-based question:* How many miles does a monarch butterfly travel in one day?
         Text-based question: Why do monarchs fly south for the winter?
         Reader-based question: How do you think the monarch finds its way south?

FIGURE 10.6. Example of a Passage and Questions to Use with the Text Lookback
Strategy

For guided practice, the teacher and students first work through several
shorter passages. Then, they use the procedure with textbook chapters or informational pieces in anthologies.

A Question-Answering Checklist

Writing answers to questions after reading is a common activity in elementary
classrooms. However, many students appear to have difficulty with this task.

Gaetz (1991) analyzed 223 sets of written answers to basal reader questions
from 118 average and below average fourth-, fifth-, and sixth-grade students.
Using a 2–1–0 scoring system, he found that students' mean score was only 52
percent correct. In an analysis of the incorrect or partially incorrect answers,
Gaetz found that 14 percent were attributable to students not answering all
parts of a question (e.g., when asked to give two reasons for something, the student gave only one). Nine percent of the incorrect responses were attributable
to students reading questions incorrectly (e.g., when asked why something
happened, the student explained when it happened). Another 35 percent of the
incorrect responses were due to the students' responses being too general (e.g.,
when asked to explain a character's problem, the student only said, "He was in
trouble."). An additional 35 percent of the incorrect responses were simply
incorrect (and not attributable to any of the above categories). In a final 6 percent of the instances, no response was given to a question.

To help children do a better job of answering written questions after reading, Gaetz taught children to use a checklist that asked the following questions:

A. Did I answer all parts of the question?
B. Does my answer belong with this question? (Did I read the question cor-
   rectly?)
C. Did I say enough to answer the question so someone else will understand?
D. Did I get ideas from the text and from my memory so the answer makes sense?
E. Did I answer all of the questions? If not, why?

Question D was designed to help children draw on clues in the text as well as from memory to answer inference questions. Children needing help in this area would also benefit from the procedures described in the next section on inferencing.

Students who used the checklist outscored other children who did not use it when answering questions after reading stories (77 percent correct versus 58 percent correct). Even without the checklist present, children who had learned the approach outscored those who had not on written answers to questions about basal stories.

STRATEGIES TO IMPROVE INFERENCING

Inferencing is an inevitable part of the reading process. Readers must make inferences across sentences, such as in connecting anaphoric terms (for example, pronouns) with their antecedents. Readers must make slot-filling inferences, in which they insert unstated information, such as causal relationships, to make text comprehensible (for example, Mary was crying. [because] She fell down.). Readers also make many elaborative inferences as they read, connecting text with prior knowledge.[16]

In addition to inferences that readers make automatically as they read, students are frequently asked to answer inference questions after reading in order to expand their comprehension of what they have read. Inference questions also serve as a window into what is going on in the reader's mind while processing text. Consequently, inference questions are important from both an instructional and an assessment perspective. Low-achieving readers, as compared to good readers, appear to have difficulty making inferences as they read[17] and also in answering inferential questions after reading.[18]

The remainder of this section will present several instructional techniques designed to improve students' general ability to draw inferences as they read or answer questions. Inferencing and inference questions cover many of the traditional comprehension skills commonly found in basal reader programs or district curriculum guides. For example, skills such as cause-effect, sequence, anaphoric relationships, drawing conclusions, and predicting outcomes are all examples of inferences. We will not decompose inferencing into subskills, however, because readers do not do this on a conscious level as they read. That is, readers do not consciously say, "Oh, here is a cause-effect relationship," or "I must connect this anaphoric term to its antecedent," as they are reading. Inferencing is a process that occurs holistically as readers are making sense of text.

Question-Answer Relationships

Raphael[19] has developed a successful instructional program to improve students' ability to answer inferential questions. Students are taught to identify how they come up with an answer to a question that might be primarily "in the book" or "in my head."

There are two types of "in the book" question-answer relationships (QARs). With "right there" QARs the question is literal and the question and answer come from one sentence. For "think and search" QARs, the question is inferential; the answer is in the text but comes from more than one sentence.

There are also two types of "in my head" QARs. Both require inferential reasoning. With an "author and you" QAR the answer is not in the story, but there are clues in the story. The reader must combine information from what he already knows along with information in the text to come up with an answer. For "on my own" QARs the answer is not in the story and can be answered from personal experience. In fact, the question can be answered without reading the story. Raphael has found that instruction and practice in identifying question-answer relationships are particularly effective in terms of improving unsuccessful readers' question-answering ability.

How. Instruction can begin with an explanation of the two general categories, "in the book" and "in my head." Then, the two types of QARs within each category are explained. An example of each of the QARs is presented below with an accompanying passage. It is important to keep in mind that both the question and the answer must be considered in order to come up with the appropriate label.

Billy went to the zoo. He saw a snake in a cage. Billy's mom knew he was scared.

Right There QAR: Where did Billy go? To the zoo.

Think and Search QAR: Why was Billy scared? He saw a snake.

Author and You: How did Billy's mom know he was scared? He probably acted scared when he saw the snake.

On My Own QAR: Are you scared of snakes at the zoo? Only the big ones.

Teachers may want to begin by presenting several brief passages and one question and answer from each of the QAR categories for each passage, as in the example above. They can explain why the QAR label is appropriate for each question and answer given for a passage. Then students can be asked to explain QAR labels for questions and answers related to particular passages. Very soon, however, students can learn to apply the technique to stories and articles they encounter in their school texts. They can also learn to ask the questions, provide the answers, and label the QAR strategies.

What, why, and when. It is important that the teacher help the students understand that they will be learning how to figure out how the text and the "head" can both be used as resources to help them answer questions. This understanding will improve their ability to answer the kinds of questions they get so often in assignments. The teacher should also help students use this skill as they are working on their own.

Using a Self-Monitoring Checklist

Carr, Dewitz, and Patberg (1983, 1989; Dewitz, Carr, & Patberg, 1987) found that teaching sixth-grade students to ask themselves monitoring questions about their answers to inferential questions improved their inferential comprehension. Questions that students asked themselves focused on forward and backward clues (explained below) that could be used to answer inferential questions. They found that the instruction was particularly beneficial for low-achieving readers.

How. Instruction in this strategy begins with the completion of cloze passages. First, the teacher can present several single sentences with one cloze blank per sentence to demonstrate the cloze procedure. For a sentence such as "Most of the houses on the block are painted _____," students are asked to generate a number of possible answers, such as white, yellow, and purple, which are listed on the board. The teacher and students discuss why some answers seem to be more appropriate than others. Also, the teacher points out that students have to rely primarily on background knowledge to fill in the blank in this type of situation.

Second, the teacher presents several short passages in which students use a *forward* clue; they must read past the cloze blank to fill in the blank with an appropriate answer. For a passage such as "Most of the houses on the street are painted _____. When it snows there is almost no color on the street at all," students provide a variety of answers. The teacher and students discuss how *snow* is a forward clue that helps students come up with the answer *white* for the cloze blank.

Third, the teacher presents several passages in which students use a *backward* clue; they must refer to information previous to the cloze blank to fill in the blank with an appropriate answer. For a passage such as "After the rain Rover was rolling on the ground. Susie ran to catch her dog and slipped in the _____," students provide a variety of answers. The teacher and students discuss how *ground, rain,* and *slipped* are backward clues that help students come up with the answer *mud* for the cloze blank.

Fourth, students work on a three-to-five-page passage excerpt from a content textbook in which cloze blanks have been inserted. After filling in the cloze blanks, the teacher and students discuss appropriate answers and whether forward or backward clues were helpful in coming up with these answers.

Fifth, students are asked inferential questions about the completed passage. The questions are similar to the cloze exercises in that they require students to use forward and backward clues to find one-word answers. The teacher and students discuss appropriate answers as well as the forward and backward clues that helped them come up with these answers.

Sixth, students are shown how to use a self-monitoring checklist to help themselves fill in cloze blanks and answer inferential questions. The self-monitoring checklist from Carr, Dewitz, and Patberg (1983) is as follows:

1. Does the answer make sense?
2. Does the answer make sense in the sentence?
3. Is the answer based on a combination of knowledge you had before you read the passage and clues in the passage?
4. Is there a forward clue in the same sentence, paragraph, or passage?
5. Is there a backward clue in the same sentence, paragraph, or passage?
6. Did the clue make you change your answer or is your answer the same?

The teacher demonstrates how to use the checklist. Students are given individual copies of the checklist and encouraged to ask themselves the questions on the checklist when completing cloze blanks or answering questions on content textbook material.

What, Why, and When. Lessons, including Steps 4 through 6 in the preceding list, should be carried out for about 20 days over a 6- to 8-week period. In addition to the procedure explained above, it is important that the teacher explain to the students that they are learning how to ask themselves questions about their answers to questions on content textbook material and how to use forward and backward clues to help them answer the content textbook questions. Students should be told that using forward and backward clues and the self-monitoring checklist will help them do a better job answering inferential questions about material they read in their content textbooks. They should also be told to use the self-monitoring checklist whenever they are asked to answer questions about content textbook material.

Inference Awareness

Gordon (1985) has found an inference awareness strategy that improves students' ability to successfully answer inference questions. It involves the teacher showing students how to use both textual information and personal knowledge to answer inference questions and to provide the reasoning that led to each answer.

What, Why, and How. First, the teacher explains that inference awareness is the skill of using clues from the text and the reader's own background knowledge to guess what the author has implied but not directly stated. The teacher explains that if students do this, they will have better comprehension and will do a better job of answering inference questions. The teacher then models the inference process by reading a paragraph, asking and answering a question, and providing the reasoning involved. A think-aloud procedure is then used to make the reasoning process explicit. An example is presented below:

1. Teacher reads text: "Billy's ball was headed for the window. There was the shattering of glass. Mr. Jones came out of the house. He was yelling in an angry voice."
2. Teacher asks: "Why was Mr. Jones angry?"
3. Teacher answers: "Mr. Jones was probably angry because the ball broke his window."
4. Teacher provides reasoning: "Well, I know from my own experience that if a ball is heading for a window and there is a shattering of glass, the ball probably broke the window. The text says the ball was heading for the window, there was a shattering of glass, and Mr. Jones was angry. I combine my own experience with information from the text to determine that the window broke. I can use that information to answer the question. Mr. Jones was angry because Billy's ball broke his window. That's my reasoning. I put together my own ideas and experiences with what the author has written to get a new idea of my own."

After modeling the process several times, the teacher and students engage in guided practice. The teacher reads a paragraph or two from a basal reader or content textbook, asks a question, and gives an answer. Students write down evidence from the text and their experience that led to the answer. The teacher and students discuss the reasoning and the information that led to the answer.

Next, the teacher reads a paragraph or two of text and asks a question that students answer. The teacher then cites evidence from the text and from background knowledge that led to the answer. This is followed by a teacher-student discussion about the reasoning process that produced the answer. An example is presented below:

1. Teacher reads: "After school, Carl and Tom stopped at the drugstore. Then Carl went to Tom's house for a while. When Carl got home, his mom said dinner was ready. Carl told his mom he wasn't hungry yet."
2. Teacher asks: "Why did Carl tell his mom he wasn't hungry yet?"
3. Students answer: "Maybe he had something to eat before he got home."
4. Teacher cites evidence: "From the text—drug store, Tom's house; from my memory—get candy at drugstore, snack at friend's house, full before dinner."
5. Teacher–student discussion: "On the way home from school Carl and his friend stopped at the drugstore and probably bought some candy. Then Carl went to Tom's house and probably had a snack. So, by the time Carl got home, he was not hungry for dinner."

Finally, the teacher asks an inference question for a paragraph or two of text. Students answer the question, support the answer with evidence, and explain the reasoning involved in coming up with the answer to the question. As is evident from Figure 2.1, the point of this sequence is to gradually release responsibility from the teacher to the student for completing the entire activity.

When. Teachers can help students learn that if they are having difficulty answering a question, they should look for evidence in the text and their own experience and think about how these clues could lead to a reasonable answer. Students should use this skill when reading on their own. If they finish a paragraph that does not make very much sense, they should look for a confusing sentence in the paragraph. Then, they should ask themselves a question, most likely a *why* question, about the confusing sentence. For example, if readers felt confused at the end of the paragraph about Carl, they might ask themselves, "Why wasn't Carl hungry yet?" The only difference, in this case, from the example provided earlier, is that readers are responding to their own question instead of responding to a teacher-generated question.

STRATEGIES TO HELP STUDENTS READ
FOR IMPORTANT IDEAS AND STUDY

Reading for important ideas is essential when dealing with informative text. Although readers cannot possibly remember all the ideas in their textbooks, they can pick out the most important ones. Whereas skilled adult readers mentally summarize important ideas after reading and studying text,[20] students, particularly low-achieving readers, often have difficulty doing so.[21]

Summarizing Textbook Selections

Taylor (1982) has developed a summarizing study procedure that has been found to improve middle grade students' comprehension and memory of the important ideas contained in their content textbooks.[22] The procedure focuses on teaching students how to summarize several important ideas after reading sections of text and how to study the summaries they generate.

What and Why. First, the teacher explains to the students that summarizing means being able to list or explain the most important ideas contained in a section of text. Students are told that they cannot possibly remember all the ideas contained in their content textbooks so it is important to learn how to identify and remember the most important ideas.

How. The teacher demonstrates how to read one section of textbook material at a time (a section goes from one heading to another and is usually two to four paragraphs long) and how to select two or three words from the section heading that reflects its topic. Talking aloud, the teacher then shows how to turn the topic into a complete sentence that reflects the most important idea from the section and writes this main idea on the board. Next, one to three other important ideas from the section are written down. It is important that the teacher state these ideas in her own words. It is important that students learn how to limit the number of important ideas from a section, since they have a tendency to write down too many ideas. Teacher modeling involves explaining why certain ideas would not be good main idea statements because they are either too general or too specific and why others are not important enough to write down after the main idea.

This procedure is repeated for a few more sections until a typical three- to five-page reading assignment from a content textbook has been covered. Finally, the teacher models how to study from the written summary by reading it over and reciting the important ideas it contains. An example of a summary is presented in Figure 10.7.

For guided practice the teacher and students work together through several sections of a reading assignment, summarizing in the manner specified above. The teacher can provide instructional support to the extent necessary.

FIGURE 10.7. Example of a Summary for a Textbook Selection
Egypt is a Developing Nation.

A. *Egypt depends on the Nile.* Most of the people in Egypt live along the Nile because so much of the country is a desert. The Egyptians use the Nile for irrigation and for generating electricity.

B. *Cairo is a mixture of the old and the new.* Cairo, the capital of Egypt, has many modern buildings and people in Western dress. There are also old buildings and people in clothes of the type worn long ago.

C. *Farming in Egypt is old-fashioned but becoming modernized.* Many farmers are poor and use animals instead of machines. Some farmers are starting to use machines and modern methods.

D. *Egypt's leaders are working hard to solve the nation's problems.* Egypt doesn't have enough food for all its people. It also needs to become more industrialized.

For example, as illustrated in Chapter 6, the teacher may give students extra clues as to what topics might be included in a summary, he may direct students to specific parts of the text, or he may provide students with several possible summaries and have them pick the one that is best. Also, a discussion contrasting good and poor main idea statements for sections, as well as other good and poor statements, seems to be useful in helping students choose a few important ideas to remember from a section. For independent practice, the students working alone or with a partner summarize the remaining section or two from a reading assignment and then practice studying their summary.

When. It is important that the teacher explain to students that if they cannot summarize a page or section of text, they need to reread it and use a fix-up strategy, such as identifying main ideas for individual paragraphs, to improve their comprehension. If students are reading particularly difficult material and realize they are going to have difficulty comprehending it, they should consider writing a summary for each section as they go along and then review what they have written down.

Self-Questioning on Main Ideas

A self-questioning study technique developed by Andre and Anderson (1978-1979) has been found to improve comprehension among low verbal ability secondary students. Davey and McBride (1986) found a modification of the procedure to be effective with sixth-grade students. Students are taught to identify the main idea of each paragraph as they are reading and are then shown how to generate and answer a question about that main idea. They repeat this procedure with the next paragraph.

For example, given a passage on monarch butterflies, students might identify main ideas and generate questions such as those in Figure 10.8.

Specific steps to follow in this self-questioning study procedure are as follows:

What. Students learn how to ask and answer questions about the main ideas of paragraphs as they read informative text.

Why. This strategy will improve their comprehension of the material they are studying.

How. First, the teacher demonstrates how to identify main ideas for paragraphs, then decides on one or two words that state the topic of the paragraph. Next, a main idea sentence about the topic of the paragraph is generated. The teacher provides several examples of possible main idea sentences for a particular paragraph as well as several inappropriate main idea sentences. Then the students are shown how to generate and answer a question about the main idea and are provided with several examples of possible questions that could have been generated for a particular paragraph. Several inappropriate questions are also discussed.

When. Students should use the self-questioning procedure whenever they are reading textbook material that seems particularly difficult to understand. They should then start over, identifying main ideas for paragraphs and generating and answering questions on these main ideas.

Every fall monarch butterflies fly south. Some fly almost 2,000 miles from Canada to Mexico. They fly about 11 miles an hour and may cover about 80 miles in one day. They fly during the day and stop at night. They find a tree like a pine tree to roost in because they can easily cling to pine needles.

People used to think that the monarch butterfly slept through the winter. But monarchs cannot live in a place where it stays below freezing for several days. That is why they have to fly south before winter comes.

No one knows exactly how monarchs find their way south. They cannot see very well, so they cannot find their way by landmarks. It remains a puzzle to scientists.

Topic of paragraph 1 Monarchs fly south

Main idea of paragraph 1 Monarch butterflies fly south every winter just like birds.

Possible question What do monarch butterflies do every winter?

Topic of paragraph 2 Why monarchs fly south

Main idea of paragraph 2 Monarchs have to fly south for the winter or they will freeze.

Possible question Why do monarchs fly south for the winter?

Topic of paragraph 3 How monarchs fly south

Main idea of paragraph 3 No one knows exactly how monarchs migrate.

Possible question How do monarchs find their way as they are flying south?

FIGURE 10.8 Example of the Main Idea Self-Questioning Procedure

For guided practice, the teacher and students work through several paragraphs together. Good and bad main idea statements for paragraphs and good and bad questions on the main ideas are discussed. For independent practice, students work through several more paragraphs on their own and discuss their main idea statements and questions with a partner or larger group.

Writing About Content Area Reading Material

Cudd and Roberts (1989) have had success teaching elementary children to use paragraph frames to guide their writing-to-learn about what they have read in informational books. This writing, in turn, enhances their comprehension of the material.

A paragraph frame might be sequential. Children could be given the following structure to guide their writing if the reading material were about a sequence of events: summary statement (i.e., Before a monarch butterfly becomes a butterfly, it goes through several changes.) first, . . . next, . . . , finally, . . . , and concluding statement (i.e., The ugly green caterpillar has turned into something beautiful.).

Other paragraph frames include enumeration, reaction, and compare and contrast. An enumeration frame begins with a main idea and includes other important ideas related to the main idea that do not have to be presented in a particular sequence. For example, an enumeration frame might begin with a summary statement followed by words such as for example, in addition, also, and a concluding statement (i.e., As you can see, . . .).

In a reaction paragraph, a student reacts to what has been read. A reaction paragraph might begin with a summary statement followed by phrases such as

I learned that, another fascinating thing was, besides this I learned that, one thing I would like to learn more about is or the most interesting thing I learned was. To get children to relate things they already knew to what they learned from their reading, they might begin a reaction paragraph with, "Although I already knew that . . . , I learned some new things by reading this story. I learned that . . . ."

In a compare and contrast paragraph, a student tells about ways in which two things are similar or different. Cudd and Roberts recommend introducing these two concepts separately. They provide the example of a contrast frame dealing with insects and spiders. "Insects differ from spiders in several ways. First, . . . second, . . . , and finally, ..." It is helpful to fill out a grid dealing with different categories to be compared or contrasted as a prewriting activity.

Obviously, the different types of paragraph frames will have to be explained, followed by teacher modeling and guided practice in the use of each type of frame. Students will also need guided practice in the selection of an appropriate frame for a particular text. A reaction frame is always a good default option. Posters in the classroom could remind students of the different types of frames to use and steps to follow when writing-to-learn about informational texts.

An appealing aspect of the use of paragraph frames is that it is a technique that students can learn to use on their own when independently reading informational texts. Older students could be instructed to use paragraph frames as an independent study strategy.

Content Area Mapping and Writing

Several researchers have successfully used a mapping technique with either elementary or secondary students to improve their comprehension of content textbook material.[23] Improved performance on a state-mandated basic-skills assessment in reading and writing was also attributed, at least in part, to the use of the mapping technique.

What and How. The teacher would begin by mapping textbook selections with students. At this point the teacher might give a blank map to students and help them fill it in. With a sequential map, a series of boxes would be connected with arrows. With a main topic-major ideas map, a box in the middle of a map would be connected to boxes representing the major ideas discussed about the main topic. Smaller boxes could be added to elaborate on major ideas. An example of a main topic-major ideas map can be seen in Figure 10.9.

Another common type of map would be a classification map. Peresich, Meadows, and Sinatra (1990) provided an example of "Part of the Circulatory System." This general heading would be connected to "Blood Cells" and "Blood Vessels" which would be connected to "Platelets," "Red Blood Cells," "White Blood Cells," and "Arteries," "Veins," and "Capillaries," respectively.

Once a map is filled in, students can write an essay, reflecting the ideas on their map. In the work by Peresich, at least a paragraph was to be written about each major idea on a map.

After students learn how to map text with the teacher, they should create maps on their own or with a partner for sections or chapters of their textbooks. At this point, students should not be limited to a particular type of map, such as

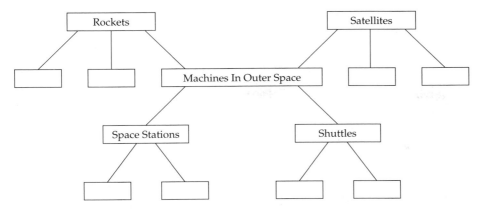

FIGURE 10.9. A Main Topic-Major Ideas Map

a sequential or classification map. They should be expected to map the text in the way they think makes the most sense. Completed maps can be shared in class and possibly modified.

When and why. Clearly students need to learn that these techniques are particularly useful for content textbooks, although stories can be successfully mapped as flowcharts. And they should come to realize that by re-representing text in a quasivisual form, they increase the likelihood that they will learn and remember important concepts.

A Modified SQ3R Study Strategy

Many upper elementary students have not learned how to study textbook material effectively, a skill that they will need as they continue into high school and beyond. Adams, Carnine, and Gersten (1982) have developed a study strategy, adapted from the SQ3R procedure[24] that has been found to improve fifth-grade students' comprehension and memory of social studies material. Students who could effectively decode material in their social studies textbook but did not effectively study the text when instructed to do so received individual instruction in this study strategy. In a related article, Jacobowitz (1988) discusses her modification of the SQ3R procedure for use with high school and college students.

How. The teacher demonstrates each step of the study strategy shown below. The student then uses each step independently with new material. After several lessons, the demonstrations cease, and the student studies silently except for reciting aloud to the teacher (Steps 5 and 6 below). The teacher gives the student feedback on whether she is accurately following the study strategy and is selecting important information to study. The steps of the study strategy are listed below. An example is presented in Figure 10.10.

1. Read the heading and subheadings (title and subheadings for sections A through D)

2a. Recite the first subheading (Egypt and the Nile River)

3a. Ask a question about this section (Why is the Nile River something important to Egypt?)

4a. Read the section to come up with an answer to the question and to remember other important information.

5a. Reread the subheading and recite the important information (Egypt and the Nile River—The Nile River is important to Egypt because Egypt uses the Nile for electricity and irrigation. Most of the people in Egypt live along the Nile.)

2b. Recite the second subheading (A Mixture of the Old and the New)

3b. Ask a question about this section (In what ways is Cairo a mixture of the old and the new?)

4b. Read the section to come up with an answer to the question and to remember other important information.

5b. Reread the subheading and recite the important information (A Mixture of the Old and the New—Cairo is a mixture of the old and the new. Cairo has many modern buildings and people in Western dress. There are also old buildings and people in clothes of the type worn long ago.)

Steps 2 through 5 are repeated for the third and fourth sections. At the end students reread the subheadings and try to recall the important information from each section.

FIGURE 10.10. Example of the Modified SQ3R Study Procedure Used with a Passage on Egypt (outlined in Figure 8.8)

1. Preview the passage (600 to 800 words) by reading the headings and subheadings.
2. Recite one subheading at a time.
3. Ask yourself a question about what would be important to learn from the section, based on the subheading.
4. Read the section (from one subheading to the next) to find important information. Try to find the answer to your question and also identify other important information to remember.
5. Reread the subheadings and recite the important information. State the answer to your question as well as other important information you learned about in the section. Repeat Steps 2 through 5 with the next section.
6. Rehearse. After completing Steps 2 through 5 for each section, reread each subheading, look up from the passage, and try to recall the important information from each section. Repeat Steps 2 through 5 for a section if you cannot recall any information from the section.

What, Why, and When. In addition to teaching students how to use the study strategy, the teacher should explain that they will be learning a procedure that will help them learn textbook material. Throughout school (middle, high school, and so on) students will be expected to read and study textbook material independently in order to pass examinations and to prepare themselves for further schooling.

STRATEGIES TO HELP STUDENTS USE
OR DEVELOP BACKGROUND KNOWLEDGE

251

CHAPTER 10
*Comprehension
Instruction*

A reader's background knowledge plays a crucial part in the reading comprehension process. People comprehend reading material by relating the new information in the text to their background knowledge.[25] Readers use their background knowledge as they read in order to make inferences regarding unstated information and also to make elaborations that enhance their comprehension.[26]

The more background knowledge readers have about the content of a reading selection, the greater their comprehension of the material.[27] Consequently, taking the time to build students' background for unfamiliar reading material is important and beneficial.[28]

Although students are rarely given reading material about which they have little or no background knowledge, it is important that this knowledge be activated and used in the reading process. Helping students activate and use their relevant background knowledge before reading enhances their comprehension of the material.[29]

In the remainder of this chapter, three effective strategies that help students activate and use their background knowledge will be described.[30] Unlike the other strategies described in this chapter, these are teacher-directed; that is, they are not designed to be used by students independently.

Using the Experience-Text-Relationship Method to Discuss Stories

Au (1979, 1981) has developed a questioning strategy (ETR for experience-text-relationship) that has been successfully used as the basic approach to comprehension instruction in the Kamehameha Early Education Program (KEEP) for Polynesian-Hawaiian children who have a potentially high risk for educational failure.[31] In this approach, students at the same reading levels meet in small groups of about five to read and discuss a story with the teacher.

What and How. The lesson begins with an *experience* phase. The teacher activates students' background knowledge and builds their interest by asking a question related to their personal experience. For example, given a story entitled "The Noisy House," the teacher might ask students what the phrase *noisy house* means to them. The teacher then encourages the students to talk about their own experiences related to this topic. Alternatively, the teacher might have them look at a picture from the story and guess what the story will be about or ask about a problem they may have had that is similar to the problem in the story. For example, the teacher might ask, "Did your mother or father ever complain that your neighbors were too noisy?"

One or more *text* phases follow the experience phase. Here the teacher has the students silently read several passages of a story after first setting a purpose for their reading, such as "Read to find out which house was the noisy one." When the students have finished reading, the teacher asks a question related to the purpose-setting statement as well as other questions about the text they have just read. An attempt is made to ask questions from a variety of levels.

Through the text-based questions the students get the opportunity to practice conventional comprehension skills such as cause-effect, sequence, and main idea.

A *relationship* phase follows the text phase. This may occur several times during a story or only at the end of a story. Here the teacher asks questions to help the students make connections between the story and their own experiences. The teacher may ask students to compare their own experiences in dealing with a particular problem with those of the main character. For example, the teacher might ask, "What have you done or would you do if you had noisy neighbors like those in the story?" The teacher may ask the students if their predictions made at the beginning of the story were correct. Often, the teacher tries to develop an important idea in the story by relating it to the students' lives.

Why and When. Au (1981a) reports that students who have been involved with the ETR method on a regular basis often begin to internalize certain aspects of the process and to use it when reading on their own. These students have been found to have better reading comprehension than others who have not received the lessons. A similar procedure, Concept-Text-Application (CTA), has been developed by Wong and Au (1985) for use specifically with expository text in the elementary grades. If students receive both variations of this approach, their comprehension of both narrative and expository text should begin to improve.

Using Background Knowledge to Draw Inferences

Hansen and Pearson (1983) have developed an approach to story discussion that draws heavily on students' background knowledge. The approach was found to be effective in improving elementary grade readers' inferential comprehension.

What and Why. The first step in the procedure is to engage students in a metacognitive discussion prior to reading a story. This discussion encourages them to prepare for the story by thinking about similar experiences they have had. After reading the story the students are asked about the purpose of the preparatory discussion. The students respond that they have been comparing their own real-life experiences to what will happen in the story. The teacher then asks why they have done this and they respond that this will help them understand and remember the story better. The teacher might then ask them to repeat this process with another story, such as one about a circus. After thinking about how this topic may also be related to their own experiences, they may come up with answers such as "I might think about a circus I've been to" or "We could see if the circus in the story is like one we've been to." The purpose of this metacognitive discussion is to remind students that as they are reading it is important to think about their own related experiences.

How. After engaging in a brief metacognitive discussion, the teacher leads the students in a strategy discussion. The teacher asks students to compare something from their own lives to something that might happen in the upcoming story. To do this the teacher selects three important concepts from the story and generates a pair of questions for each concept. For example, for a story about a boy who dislikes coyotes the teacher might ask the following:

1a. This story is about a boy who doesn't like a certain kind of wild animal. Tell us about a wild animal you don't like.

1b. In the story, Antonio doesn't like coyotes. Why do you think he doesn't like coyotes?

2a. Try to recall a time when an adult tried to give you some advice. Tell us how you reacted.

2b. In the story, Antonio's grandfather tries to give him some advice. How do you suppose he will respond to this advice?

3a. Tell us about a time when you changed your mind about a person or animal you didn't like.

3b. In the story, Antonio changes his mind about the coyote. Why do you think he does this?

The point of this discussion is to lead the students through the inferencing process they should use as they read; that is, the relating of new information to old information. It is by relating the new information in the text to the known background knowledge that comprehension of the text occurs.

When. After the metacognitive and strategy discussions, which usually take about 20 minutes, the students read a selection and engage in a postreading discussion. The teacher then asks several inference questions in which the students have to combine information in the text with their own background experience. For example, the teacher might ask, "How do you think Antonio felt at the end of the story?" "Why do you suppose the coyote tried to take care of the lost puppy?" "Why do you think people often change first impressions?" Such questions help students realize the need to use their background knowledge in order to help them interpret what they are reading.

Using the PReP Procedure

Langer (1984) has developed a Pre-Reading Plan (PReP) to assess and activate students' background knowledge for key concepts in a content reading assignment. The procedure is used with a group of about ten students prior to reading the assigned textbook material. PReP is a quick, effective way for the teacher to assess students' level of background knowledge for a particular reading assignment. The procedure has also been found to improve students' comprehension of content textbook material.

When. Langer used 700–800 word content area passages but the technique is quite flexible; it could, for example, easily be applied to informational trade books. Before using the procedure, the teacher selects about three major concepts from a content textbook reading selection. For example, from a passage about farming on the Great Plains the teacher might select dry farming, dust storms, and conservation.

What and Why. The teacher explains to students that they will be drawing upon what they already know about important concepts that will appear in the material they are going to read. The students are told that the prereading discussion will enable the teacher to determine if any background building discussion is necessary before reading the story. They are also told that the discussion will activate their existing background experience which, in turn, will improve their comprehension of the material because people comprehend new information by relating it to what they already know.

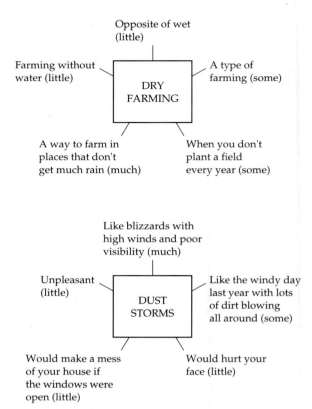

Figure 10.11. PReP Procedure: An Example of
Students' Responses to Key Concepts

How. The first step is to have students make associations with the first important concept. "Tell me anything that comes to mind when you hear the term dry farming." The teacher jots down students' responses on the board. An example is presented in Figure 10.11.

The second step is for the teacher to ask the students to reflect on their initial associations. "What made you think about _____?" This helps students to further develop their associations with the concept under discussion and to listen to the ideas of others.

The third step is to ask students to reformulate their knowledge about the concepts being discussed. "Based on our discussion, do you have any new ideas about _____?" This step allows students to talk about any new or modified associations, based on the discussion. The procedure is then repeated for the next major concept.

Based on the students' responses during Steps 1 and 3 of the procedure, the teacher can determine whether students have much, some, or little background knowledge about the concept being discussed. If students have much background knowledge about the concept being discussed, responses will take the form of superordinate concepts ("Dry farming is one way to farm in a place that gets very little rainfall."), precise definitions, analogies, or the linking of one concept to another ("Dust storms and blizzards both have high winds and make it difficult to see."). If students have some background knowledge about the concept being discussed, responses will take the form of examples ("Dust storms are like what happened last year when it was very dry and the wind blew lots of dirt into the air."), attributes, or defining characteristics ("Dry farming is when you don't plant a field every year."). If students have little background knowledge about the concept being discussed, responses will focus on low-level associations, such as tangential links ("Dry farming is the opposite of wet farming."), morphemes, such as prefixes, suffixes, and root words (*conserve*), words that sound like the stimulus word (*conservation-reservation*); and firsthand experiences that focus on tangential information ("Dust storms must hurt your face.").

Langer (1981) has found that students with *much* or *some* background for the major concepts in the reading material will be able to read the text with adequate comprehension assuming, of course, they have relatively little difficulty in terms of decoding. Students with *little* background knowledge of the major concepts in the reading material usually will benefit from a more extensive background discussion designed to build their background knowledge prior to reading.

In addition to being a useful assessment tool, PReP enhances students' comprehension of a particular text. The procedure helps students activate relevant background knowledge and make links between important text concepts and their past experiences.

Previewing Expository Text

Previewing headings in a textbook chapter or segment prior to reading is a commonly recommended reading strategy and a component of a number of successful studying techniques.[32] Many previewing strategies that have been developed, such as use of an advanced organizer, are teacher-directed. However, a simple, straightforward strategy that students can use when reading on their own is to review and reflect on all headings and subheadings in a textbook selection prior to reading. Over time, students come to learn that authors use headings and subheadings to reveal the organization of their ideas—the major topics and subtopics. Students also come to realize that by previewing this organization they can enhance their comprehension.

SUMMARY

Readers of this chapter may have wondered why particular strategies were organized as they were. In fact, it may be helpful to summarize what is covered in this chapter by organizing the strategies somewhat differently, according to comprehension monitoring and comprehension fostering activities. Basically, all of the strategies discussed in this chapter are useful comprehension monitoring and comprehension fostering activities designed to improve students' reading comprehension.

Several of the strategies discussed are useful as *comprehension-monitoring strategies* and many are useful as fix-up strategies. For example, in addition to the general comprehension-monitoring strategies involved in the comprehension-rating procedure, the summarizing procedure and the self-monitoring checklist procedure are useful comprehension-monitoring activities. Students can use these activities either to check their understanding as they are reading or as they are answering questions.

In addition to general fix-up strategies discussed as part of the comprehension-rating task, the text lookback strategy, the QAR procedure, and the inference awareness procedure are useful fix-up strategies for students to use when answering questions proves difficult. The reading for main idea activities are useful fix-up strategies for students to consider using when comprehension has failed.

Many of the strategies discussed are useful in enhancing comprehension in a general sense, in improving students' inferential comprehension, or in improving students' ability to read for main ideas. In particular, two self-questioning procedures and the reciprocal teaching procedure are considered general *comprehension-fostering strategies.* The procedures dealing with background knowledge are regarded as general comprehension-fostering activities.

The strategies dealing with inferences—the text lookback procedure, the reciprocal questioning procedure, the QAR procedure, the self-monitoring checklist procedure, the inference awareness procedure, and the background knowledge procedure—are regarded as useful in helping students do a better job drawing inferences as they read. Many of these strategies are also designed to help students do a better job answering inferential questions after reading.

The strategies dealing with important information—the main idea self-questioning procedure, the reciprocal teaching procedure, the reading for main idea activities, the summarizing procedure, the study procedure, and the mapping procedure—are seen as useful in helping students read informative text.

All of the strategies covered in this chapter can be taught through small-group, as opposed to individual, instruction. In fact, some strategies, such as the reciprocal questioning procedure and the reciprocal teaching procedure, require cooperative group instruction. Chapter 11 discusses informal assessment strategies that can be used to determine which students in a classroom or clinic may benefit from small-group instruction in comprehension-monitoring activities, fix-up strategies, general comprehension-fostering activities, and comprehension instruction in drawing inferences or reading for main ideas.

Suggested Activities

1. Prepare appropriate materials and teach the comprehension-rating procedure to a student or small group of students. If a child is not available, teach the procedure to a group of peers in your class.
2. Locate appropriate reading material and teach the reciprocal-teaching procedure to a group of two or three students. If children are not available, work with peers in your class. With children, the procedure should be carried out on more than one occasion (children will not learn the technique in one lesson). Keep a chart of the student's performance on comprehension questions answered after reading the material. As you are teaching this procedure, be sure to stress *what, why, how,* and *when* as discussed in the chapter.

3. Prepare appropriate examples and teach the QAR procedure to a student or small group of students. If children are not available, teach the procedure to a group of peers in your class. Be sure to stress the *what, why, how,* and *when* of the procedure, as discussed in the chapter.
4. Locate appropriate reading material and try out the PReP procedure with several students or a group of peers in your class.

Suggested Reading

CARR, E., DEWITZ, P., and PATBERG, J. (1989). Using cloze for inference training with expository text. *The Reading Teacher, 42:* 380–385.

Comprehension monitoring and a successful training program to improve students' comprehension are described.

FLOOD, J., and LAPP, D. (1990). Reading comprehension instruction for at-risk students: Research-based practices that can make a difference. *Journal of Reading, 33:* 490–498. Research is summarized on seven general practices that have been found to improve students' reading comprehension abilities.

IDOL, L. (1987). Group story mapping: A comprehension strategy for both skilled and unskilled readers. *Journal of Learning Disabilities, 20:* 196–205.

The author discusses a story mapping strategy that was used with mixed groups of low-achieving and average reading intermediate grade students to improve their comprehension of stories.

PALINCSAR, A., and BROWN, A. L. (1984). Reciprocal teaching of comprehension-fostering and comprehension-monitoring activities. *Cognition and Instruction, 1:* 117–175.

Palincsar and Brown describe a successful procedure called reciprocal teaching that they developed to improve low-achieving readers' comprehension of expository text.

PERESICH, M. L., MEADOWS, J. D., and SINATRA, R. (1990). Content area mapping for reading and writing proficiency. *Journal of Reading, 33:* 424–432.

A mapping technique to improve reading and writing is discussed.

RAPHAEL, T. E. (1986). Teaching question-answer relationships, revisited. *The Reading Teacher, 39:* 516–522.

A revised version of the successful question-answer relationship technique to improve inferential comprehension is presented.

Notes

1. See Baker and Brown (1984) and Paris and Jacobs (1984).
2. See Baker and Brown (1984) and Ryan (1981).
3. See Baker and Brown (1984), Paris and Myers (1981), and Wagoner (1983).
4. See Durkin (1984a, 1984b).
5. See Taylor (1985b).
6. See Tierney and Cunningham (1984).
7. See Garner (1980) and Owings, Peterson, Bransford, Morris, and Stein (1980).
8. See Davey and Porter (1982), Garner and Reis (1981), and Golinkoff (1975-1976).
9. See Davey and Porter (1982).
10. See Pressley (1976, 1977), Sadoski (1985), Gambrell and Bales (1986).
11. See Anderson and Biddle (1975).
12. See Andre and Anderson (1978-1979), Baker and Brown (1984), and Singer (1978a).
13. See Nolte and Singer (1985) and Singer and Donlan (1982).
14. See Manzo (1969).
15. See Garner and Reis (1981), and Garner, Wagoner, and Smith (1983).

16. See Anderson and Pearson (1984) and Reder (1980).
17. See Bridge and Tierney (1981), Bransford et al., (1982) and Reder (1980).
18. See Holmes (1983), Raphael, Winograd, and Pearson (1980), and Wilson (1979).
19. See Raphael and Pearson (1985) and Raphael and Wonnacutt (1985).
20. See van Dijk and Kintsch (1983).
21. See Brown and Day (1983), Taylor (1985c), and Winograd (1984).
22. See Doctorow, Wittrock, and Marks (1978) and Taylor and Berkowitz (1980).
23. See Taylor and Beach (1984) and Taylor (1985a, 1986).
24. See Robinson (1941).
25. See Anderson and Pearson (1984).
26. See Reder (1980).
27. See Johnston (1984a), Langer (1984), and Pearson, Hansen, and Gordon (1979).
28. See Hayes and Tierney (1982) and Stevens (1982).
29. See Hansen (1981) and Langer (1984).
30. See Au (1979), Hansen (1981), and Langer (1984).
31. See Tharp (1982).
32. See Adams, Carnine, and Gersten (1982) and Taylor (1982).

CHAPTER 11

COMPREHENSION ASSESSMENT

Overview

As you read this chapter you may find the following list of main ideas helpful in guiding your understanding and reflection.

- Initial assessment and ongoing evaluation of students' reading comprehension should be based primarily on regular classroom materials and reading assignments.
- In the area of comprehension monitoring, it is important to determine the extent to which students do and do not understand what they are reading, their ability to locate sources of comprehension difficulty, and their success in using appropriate fix-up strategies to repair comprehension failures.
- To better understand students' comprehension, a teacher can ask students to explain how they have come up with their answers to questions, to generate questions, or to create summaries of what they have read.
- It is essential to keep written records of readers' performance on comprehension tasks in order to identify strengths and weaknesses and plan instruction accordingly.
- As with word recognition, regular classroom materials should be used as much as possible for initial assessment and ongoing evaluation of comprehension. In general, this assessment should be based on frequent samples of students' comprehension performance. The teacher should then use these data to plan appropriate instructional activities.

This chapter begins with a brief description of a metacognitive questionnaire that teachers could use to get an overview of what their students know about reading comprehension strategies and monitoring. Then, the discussion of specific comprehension strategy assessments will parallel the discussion of comprehension instruction presented in Chapter 10. First, assessment of students' comprehension monitoring strategies is discussed. Next, assessment of students' general reading comprehension strategies is presented. How well students infer and read for important ideas is then discussed. The chapter concludes with a discussion of how to use the reading difficulties record sheet in the area of comprehension.

After completing their assigment, the students
will record their progress on the chart behind
them. *(Peter Vadnai)*

METACOGNITIVE AWARENESS
AND COMPREHENSION MONITORING

Determining Metacognitive Awareness

Questionnaires can provide useful information about a student's metacognitive
awareness pertaining to use of comprehension-fostering and comprehension-
monitoring strategies. The questionnaire in Figure 11.1 is designed to be completed collaboratively with a student in a one-on-one situation, even though
group-administered forms could be readily developed; indeed they already
exist (Wixson, Yokum, Alvermann, & Lipson, 1986).

With the metacognitive questionnaire, the student is first asked an open-
ended question (items 1a–6a), followed by a question about the students' use of
specific metacognitive reading activities. The open-ended questions ask about
strategies for getting ready to read, fix-up strategies for dealing with unknown
words and lack of understanding while reading, fix-up strategies for dealing
with hard-to-answer questions, and strategies to facilitate memory of material
read.

As an alternative to asking a student to report on her use of metacognitive
strategies in a formal interview or through a questionnaire, a teacher could simply observe the student while reading, taking care to record evidence about the

1. a. What do you do to get ready to read? (Most relevant for students in Grade 4 and up in reference to content textbook reading.)
   b. How often do you: Read headings, read an introductory or concluding paragraph (if available), look at pictures and read picture captions, think about what you know that is related to what you are going to read?
2. a. When you can't decode a word, what do you do?
   b. How often do you: Skip over the word, sound out the word, use context clues to decode the word, ask for help?
3. a. When you do not know the meaning of a word, what do you do?
   b. How often do you: Use context clues to predict what the word means, use a dictionary, ask for help?
4. a. When you do not understand something you are reading, do you stop? If you stop, what do you do next?
   b. How often do you: Keep reading but try to clear up the confusion; reread carefully; look at the title, pictures, headings (if available); ask yourself important questions; put ideas in your own words; picture ideas in your head as you read; relate ideas to your personal experience; ask someone to clarify things?
5. a. When you have a question you are having trouble with, what do you do?
   b. How often do you: Look back in the text for clues, think about what you know that might help you answer the question, try to combine ideas in text and from your memory to answer the questions.
6. a. What do you do to help you remember what you have read?
   b. How often do you: Try to summarize important ideas as you read, ask yourself and answer important questions as you read, jot down important ideas as you read?

FIGURE 11.1. Metacognitive Awareness Questionnaire

student's *apparent* use (or lack of use) of prereading, fix-up, and postreading strategies. For example, a teacher may observe that a student takes notes when he is uncertain about the meanings of particular words he encounters during reading. Or she may observe that another student vocalizes her uncertainty when she is unsure about the meanings of words. Another alternative for gaining information about metacognitive reflection involves the use of retrospective think-alouds. The think-alouds can be in response to audiotapes of oral reading or videotapes of discussion groups, or they can simply be interviews in which students talk about the thinking that went into a particular written assignment or even the reading of a particular text.

In the metacognitive questionnaire in Figure 11.1, students are asked what they do when they encounter difficulty answering questions. Those responses, subject as they are to students telling us what they think we want to hear, should be complemented by real performance data. What do students actually do when they are encountering difficulty with questions?

Low-achieving readers, in particular, may not realize when their answer to a question does not make sense. To assess this ability, the teacher could ask students to highlight the questions and answers they were unsure about. Students who seldom highlight questions that they answered incorrectly merit further study. Teachers need to find out whether the students genuinely cannot distinguish between on-target and off-target answers or whether they are uncomfortable admitting that they do not know the answers to questions. If students are not sensitive to when they are on- and off-target, then they can benefit from some modeling of uncertainty by the teacher.

Similarly, low-achieving readers also may not know what to do when confronted with a question they cannot answer. Working with students individually or in small groups, the teacher could ask students what they might do to produce reasonable answers to difficult questions. Students who have little to say would appear to be either unaware or unable to use fix-up strategies to answer difficult questions. In the section on drawing inferences we will discuss assessment of students' knowledge of how to go about answering a difficult inference question.

Students unaware of either their own difficulty in answering questions or of what to do about it might benefit from the text-lookback procedure, the question-answer checklist procedure, the QAR procedure, the inference checklist procedure, or the inference awareness procedure, all of which were discussed in Chapter 10 as strategies to help students answer questions.

Assessing Comprehension Monitoring

A critical feature of metacognition is the ability to monitor and control the ongoing comprehension process. Regardless of the tools teachers use in assessment (questionnaires, interviews, observations, or think-alouds), there are three questions that need to be addressed about students' comprehension monitoring.

First, can students discriminate between situations in which comprehension is going well and when it is faltering? Or, as Tom Anderson (1980) has expressed it, can students tell the difference between the *clicks* of comprehension and the *clunks* of comprehension? Second, can students locate sources of comprehension difficulty when they know comprehension is faltering? And third, can students select and use appropriate fix-up strategies to resolve their comprehension failures? Because comprehension monitoring is essential for reading, comprehension-monitoring skills of all readers should be assessed, even when it appears that word recognition, and not comprehension, is the primary area of difficulty.

Do Students Know When They Are Comprehending?

To assess students' comprehension-monitoring skill, they can be asked to rate individual paragraphs and sections of text (such as three- to four-page sections in a content textbook). A three-point rating system, such as the one developed by Davey and Porter (1982) and discussed in Chapter 10, could be used. It allows students to rate paragraphs or longer sections of text as something they understand very well, moderately well, or not very well. Reading material could be copied so that blanks for ratings could be built into the material. An example is provided in Figure 11.2.

These ratings should be compared to the students' scores on the comprehension questions at the end of the material (see Figure 11.2). A positive relationship should be apparent. That is, students' comprehension scores on specific paragraphs or passages should roughly match their comprehension ratings on these same paragraphs and passages. It is apparent that in Figure 11.2 the

DIRECTIONS: In each blank at the end of the paragraph put a 1 if you understood the paragraph well, a 2 if you understood the paragraph somewhat, and a 3 if you did not understand the paragraph. In the box at the end of the page also put a 1, 2, or 3 to indicate your understanding of the entire passage. Then answer the comprehension questions.

Please Pass the Potato Chips!

1. Americans buy more than 600 million bags of potato chips each year. If people had to make potato chips in their own kitchens, they might not eat so many.   _1_

2. From field to factory, potato chips are made by machines. A machine digs the potatoes in the field. A second machine puts them in sacks. A truck takes them to the factory. There, they are fed into a peeling machine. They are tumbled over rough machinery that scrapes away the skins.   _2_

3. The next machine cuts the potatoes into slices, which are washed in cold water. The slices are cooked in hot oil in a frying machine.   _1_

4. The potatoes turn a golden color. They are now thin chips that ride along on a moving steel belt. Salt is sprinkled on them from above. Any chips that are broken or too brown are removed. The finished chips go into a machine that makes bags and puts in the chips. This machine also weighs and seals the bags.   _2_

5. When you put your hand into the bag, you are the first to touch the chips. Machines have done all the work.   _1_

$\boxed{1}$

X 1. The machine that is used in potato fields
      (a.) takes the potatoes to the factory.   c. digs the potatoes.
      b. cuts the potatoes into pieces.   d. peels the potatoes.

X 2. The word in paragraph 2 that means *not smooth* is _____scrapes_____.

X 3. The words "weighs and seals the bags" in paragraph 4 tell about the word _machine_.

4. The story does not say so, but it makes you think that
      a. potato chips are washed just before they go into bags.
      b. potato chips are made by hand.
      (c) potato chips are a favorite American snack.

X 5. The golden potato chips ride along on a belt made of
      (a.) rubber.   c. wood.
      b. paper.   d. steel.

6. Potatoes are sliced in the field.
      Yes   (No)   Does not say

7. On the whole, this story is about
      (a.) making potato chips.
      b. digging potatoes.
      c. how potato chips are sorted.

X 8. Why are potato chips made by machines? (Check the story again.)
      (a.) It is a faster way to make millions of chips.
      b. Workers would break too many of the potato chips.
      c. Workers would eat too many of the chips.

FIGURE 11.2. Example of a Comprehension Rating Task

✗ 9. Which of these sentences do you think is right?
　　　(a.) Potato chips are made from the skins of potatoes.
　　　b. Potato chips are cooked in hot water.
　　　c. Several machines are used in making potato chips.

Number correct _3/9_

The passage and questions in Figure 11.2 are from *Reading for Concepts,* level D, 2/e,
© Copyright, 1970, by Webster Division, McGraw-Hill Book Company. Used with permission.

FIGURE 11.2. Example of a Comprehension Rating Task *(cont.)*

student was not very skilled in rating his comprehension because in almost all cases he rated his comprehension as high despite missing quite a few questions. Students who are repeatedly unable to tell with any degree of accuracy when they do and do not understand what they are reading need instruction in self-monitoring (see the comprehension rating procedure discussed in Chapter 10).

Can Students Locate Sources of Comprehension Difficulty?

To assess students' skill in locating sources of comprehension difficulty, the teacher could interview students individually. The teacher should ask students to look over a comprehension rating assessment activity, such as the one presented in Figure 11.2, and point out or explain what caused them comprehension difficulties in places where they rated their comprehension as poor. Alternatively, the teacher could ask students to reread material on which they had low comprehension scores and try to explain the cause of their difficulty. Using notes taken on students' comprehension monitoring ability, the teacher should decide whether individual students need specific instruction in locating sources of comprehension difficulty. Again, the comprehension rating procedure by Davey and Porter (1982) could be used for instruction.

Can Students Select and Use Appropriate Fix-Up Strategies?

To assess students' skill in using appropriate fix-up strategies, the teacher can use a self-report procedure. The teacher can ask students to list what they usually do when they are having trouble understanding what they read (it does not matter whether the source of confusion is a specific word, idea, sentence, or paragraph). For example, he could ask something such as, "Tell me some things you do when you come across a word you don't know." The teacher could also have students tell or write down what they do to fix up comprehension difficulties in specific instances, such as on the comprehension rating assessment task in Figure 11.2, where they indicated poor comprehension. In addition, the teacher could ask students to keep notes whenever they encounter comprehension difficulties in independent reading and also on their attempts to remedy the problem. These notes could be discussed in a later conference

Directions: In the spaces below write down the page and paragraph number when you notice you are having trouble understanding what you are reading. Write down what you think is causing the problem (a particular word or a sentence) and write down what you did to fix up your comprehension failure.

Page and Paragraph	Cause of Difficulty	Fix-Up Strategy
106, no. 2	tumbled	reread, sounded out
106, no. 4	1st sentence	read on

FIGURE 11.3. Example of a Comprehension Rating Record Sheet (based on passage in Figure 11.2)

setting or they could become part of a metacognitive interview. An example of a record sheet students could use for this activity is presented in Figure 11.3.

The teacher might have students complete a questionnaire on fix-up strategies. Items for both word-level and idea-level fix-up strategies could be included. Examples are provided in Figure 11.3.

Finally, the teacher could work with students individually or in a small group and have them read until they noticed a comprehension difficulty. The teacher could then ask the student to explain what was causing the problem and what should be done in terms of a fix-up strategy. The teacher should keep notes on students' ability to select and successfully use appropriate fix-up strategies to remediate comprehension failure. Assessment activities such as these can serve as the basis for teacher decisionmaking about a student's need for special instruction in the use of word-level and idea-level fix-up strategies.

ASSESSING GENERAL COMPREHENSION

This section will discuss the use of questions and other strategies that can be used to measure general comprehension. It will discuss students' ability to comprehend narrative and expository text as well as their literal and inferential comprehension ability.

Consistent with the general preference for frequent classroom assessment, acceptable performance on a comprehension task should be based on informed teacher judgment rather than some arbitrary levels or standards of acceptable performance. Teachers should collect data frequently on the everyday sorts of tasks that students complete in response to reading selections in their anthologies or trade books. Such data, if gathered systematically over time, can provide a teacher with a valuable and useful profile of students' overall comprehension development.

Comprehension depends on a number of factors such as background knowledge, motivation, and task understanding. Students with little background knowledge about a topic, students who are not motivated, and students who do not understand what they are supposed to do will perform poorly on almost any comprehension task. Teachers need to be sure to assess students' comprehension in response to a wide range of topics, texts, and tasks. If we have learned anything about the nature of reading disability in the past decade, it is that reading disability, like reading ability, is an interactive phenomenon that varies from situation to situation. Disability is a *dynamic* rather than a *static* phenomenon. Thirteen-year-old Carlos Aquirre may appear to be a poor reader when he is asked to respond to the fifteen open-ended questions on a worksheet that he completed after reading Jean George's *Julie of the Wolves*. But ask Carlos to evaluate the usefulness of written directions for assembling a bicycle or engage him in a discussion of the ethics of the characters in *My Brother Sam is Dead*, and you will get a very different picture of Carlos as a reader.

Using Questions to Assess Comprehension

Of all the techniques used to determine comprehension of text, the oldest and still the most popular is to ask students a few questions about what they have read. Questions are the staple of comprehension tests, workbook pages, classroom discussions of stories, and normal everyday conversation. There is nothing inherently wrong with using questions to assess students' comprehension. But some kinds of questions provide more appropriate and useful assessments of comprehension than others.

The ultimate criterion a teacher should use to judge the quality of comprehension questions is simple: Do the questions focus on what is important to understand about the text? In other words, good questions should focus on important ideas, not trivial details.

A few other words of caution about questions are in order. Students who have difficulty understanding what they are reading may have learned to answer questions by writing down any answer as quickly as possible in order to get the task completed. For assessment purposes, teachers should supervise students closely when answering questions to be sure that they are working

Students' performance on daily comprehension tasks provides valuable assessment data. *(Peter Vadnai)*

carefully. A teacher may find that some students actually do quite well on questions when they slow down and work carefully.

In a series of studies, Davey (1989) has found that low-achieving readers, in general, do have more difficulty than better readers on free response questions, in which they are asked to write answers. Low-achieving readers are also less effective than better readers when looking back in the text to answer free response questions. Additionally, Davey has found that low-achieving readers have more difficulty than better readers answering comprehension questions when the assessment is timed. These are all factors that a teacher should keep in mind when using questions to assess low-achieving students' reading comprehension. In general, timed tests should be avoided with students who are experiencing difficulty.

It is also important for teachers to bear in mind that some students do poorly when answering comprehension questions because they have difficulty writing. Consequently, it is a good idea for teachers to keep records of both written and oral question-answering activities so that they can determine if a student's difficulty with writing clouds the teacher's judgment about the student's comprehension.

Narrative and Expository Text

One way to assess students' general ability to comprehend narrative and expository text is to keep records of their success in answering questions based on instructional level text. Alternatively, a teacher might have students generate questions about such text. Students often find this task enjoyable because it is something different. The teacher should stress that questions should be about important information, not unimportant details. Based on teacher judgment, inability to ask important questions about narrative or expository text would be an indication of poor general comprehension of the material.

Students might also be asked to select the best questions among a set of choices. Inability to select the best questions for recently read narrative or expository material would be another indication of poor general comprehension.

Students' ability to select the best summary of a narrative or expository selection from among two or three choices could be used as yet another indication of their general comprehension. Such summaries should be concise statements of the important ideas, or major points, the author was trying to make in expository text or should highlight the important story elements (themes, morals, lessons, basic plot elements) in narrative text. Students generally find it easier to select appropriate summaries for texts than to generate them.

Students in need of instruction in understanding either expository or narrative text would benefit from such comprehension-fostering procedures (discussed in Chapter 10) as self-questioning, reciprocal questioning, and reciprocal teaching.

Literal and Inferential Comprehension

In addition to assessing students' general comprehension of narrative and expository text, the teacher should consider students' literal and inferential comprehension. One way to do this is to keep records of students' performance on literal and inferential questions. Literal questions have both the question and answer in one sentence (see "right there" QARs in Chapter 10). Inference questions, however, require the reader to combine information from two or more sentences to generate an appropriate answer ("think and search" QARs, or text-based inference questions) or to combine information in the text with personal knowledge to generate an appropriate answer ("author and you" and "on my own" QARs, or prior knowledge-based inference questions). When you are using this approach, be sure to incorporate both narrative and expository text that is written at the instructional level of the students.

Students doing poorly on written and oral literal questions may need to learn how to "interrogate" the text, so it may be useful to engage students in activities like the text-lookback procedure and the QAR procedure discussed in Chapter 10. If inference is a problem, a more careful search is necessary to pinpoint the source of difficulty. To better understand why a student is having difficulty with inferential comprehension, the procedures in the next section on drawing inferences should be followed. Students with inferential problems might benefit from the QAR procedure, the self-monitoring checklist procedure, and the inference awareness procedure discussed in Chapter 10.

Recurrent Question-Answer Behaviors

In Chapter 10 we described a study by Gaetz (1991) in which he analyzed elementary students' written responses to basal reader questions. The five categories developed by Gaetz could be used by the classroom teacher to analyze students' routine written answers to postreading questions. This analysis could be done over a number of samples to determine if there are any recurrent problems for particular students. There is no reason to limit this classroom assessment technique to basals; it works equally as well with tradebooks, textbooks, or anthologies.

The categories for written responses receiving partial or no credit were as follows:

A. Response did not answer all parts of the question
B. Response did not answer the question that was asked but answered a different question (as if the student read the question incorrectly)
C. Response was too general to sufficiently answer the question
D. Response was incorrect (and not attributable to category A, B, or C)
E. No response was given

Assume that students have just read a passage about problems of cities and suburbs. Here are examples of different categories of incorrect or partially incorrect responses:

A. What were three problems of cities that you read about?
They are noisy.
B. What is the megalopolis called Bowash?
Because it's so big with lakes to wash in. (It seems as if the student were trying to answer, Why is the megalopolis called Bowash?)

C. What is a suburb?
    It's a place out of a city.
D. Why have many cities not had enough tax money?
    Cities haven't had enough tax money because there's hardly any people in them.

A student with a recurrent problem in writing answers to questions, such as responses that are too general, would benefit from Gaetz's procedure. For example, the teacher might ask a student to locate answers that seemed too general or vague and then help the student produce a more specific, complete response. Also, students having difficulty answering written questions would benefit from the question-answer checklist procedure described in Chapter 10. They also may benefit from one or more of the inferencing strategies discussed in this chapter, particularly if they had numerous incorrect responses in category 4.

Retelling a Story

The story map described in Chapter 10 can be used to guide a teacher's assessment of a students' ability to retell a story. After reading a story, students are asked to retell the story concisely (the length of the retellings will depend upon the age of the students and the complexity of the plot). Whether oral or written, it should contain important information about the main character, setting, problem, key events, resolution, and any theme that might be present or inferred. Teachers should use their knowledge of story structure (perhaps summarized in a story map) to determine if the students have omitted information important to the story's development. If students have difficulty with retellings, they will benefit from several of the instructional activities in Chapter 10; namely, story mapping, reciprocal teaching (applied to narratives), and even self-questioning.

Drawing Inferences

As mentioned in Chapter 10, students' answers to inference questions serve as a convenient window to their inference processing ability when reading. However, a teacher should go beyond students' initial answers to inference questions and ask additional probing questions. A teacher can inquire about and take notes on how students came up with particular answers or about what might be done to answer questions left unanswered. A teacher can help students answer difficult questions and take notes on what kind and how much support has to be provided. A teacher can also provide several answers for an inference question and ask a student to explain why one answer appears to be better than another.

A group discussion is presented in Figure 11.4 to illustrate the approach to inference assessment that is recommended. In this discussion the teacher asks students to explain how they came up with their answers and whether they have used the book or their background knowledge to help them. The teacher also provides students with clues when they cannot answer questions.

A reading group consisting of four low-achieving readers in the third grade has just finished reading a story about a little girl who puts on a magic show. The teacher asks the students inference questions on the story and also asks them how they came up with their answers.

Teacher: Why was Madge special? (*text-based inference*)

Lisa: She was a magician.

Teacher: Good. Tell me how you came up with your answer.

Lisa: Well, it said so.

Teacher: Show me where.

Lisa: It says, "Madge was very special. She was a great magician."

Teacher: Good. How did Jimmy Smith feel about Madge's magic tricks at first? (*text-based inference*)

Pat: He liked them. (*Incorrect answer*)

Teacher: How did you come up with this answer?

Pat: I don't know.

Teacher: Do you see a clue at the bottom of page 127?

Pat: It says, "Everyone clapped. Jimmy Smith didn't."

Teacher: Good. Do you see another clue at the top of page 128?

Pat: No.

Jimmy: It says he said her first trick was not so hard.

Teacher: Good. Now, Pat, based on these two clues how do you think Jimmy Smith felt about Madge's magic tricks?

Pat: He didn't think they were very good.

Teacher: Great! Could Madge have pulled a chicken, fox, and goat out of her hat? (*prior knowledge-based inference*)

Susan: No.

Teacher: How do you know?

Susan: Well, a fox and a goat are too big.

Teacher: That's right. How did you come up with your answer? Did you use the book or your head?

Susan: I guess I used my head.

Teacher: Great. How did Jimmy Smith feel about Madge's last trick of pulling a rabbit out of the hat? (*text-based inference*)

Jimmy: He liked it.

Teacher: Good. How did you come up with your answer?

Jimmy: I don't know. He looks happy in the picture.

Teacher: Okay, but look for a clue at the bottom of page 131.

Jimmy: I don't see anything. I think pulling a rabbit out of a hat was a good trick.

Lisa: It says, "Gee," said Jimmy Smith. "A real rabbit. How did you do it?" That shows he liked it.

Teacher: Good. How do you think Madge learned to be a magician? (*prior knowledge-based inference*)

Lisa: I don't know.

Teacher: Why do you think you can't answer the question?

Lisa: It doesn't say anything about that.

Teacher: How could we answer the question?

Lisa: I don't know.

Susan: You can learn magic tricks from books. Maybe Madge did that.

Teacher: Good. Where did you get your answer, from the book or from your head?

Susan: From my head.

FIGURE 11.4. Example of Probing Questions to Assess Students' Inferencing Ability

It is important that periodically a teacher take notes on such a questioning session for the purpose of collecting assessment data. Notes from the discussion presented in Figure 11.4 might look like the following:

Lisa—Good job explaining text-based inference question (TBIQ or "think and search" QAR). Unable to answer or explain how to answer prior knowledge-based inference question (PKBIQ or "on my own" QAR).

Pat—At first, answered TBIQ incorrectly. Couldn't explain how he came up with answer. Could find one of two clues and could then answer question correctly.

Jimmy—Found clue to a TBIQ. Used picture and prior knowledge to answer second TBIQ. Couldn't locate clue in text.

Susan—Answered and explained two PKBIQs.

Such notes collected over time enable a teacher to understand and evaluate a student's inferencing ability. The teacher can look for patterns in his notes that may reflect one or more of the following problems: difficulty answering text-based inference questions, difficulty answering prior knowledge-based inference questions, difficulty locating clues in text to answer text-based inference questions, and difficulty determining whether answers to questions come from the text or prior knowledge.

Once students have learned the question-answer relationship technique presented in Chapter 10, assessment data on students' inferencing ability can be collected in the form of a paper-and-pencil task. Students can be directed to answer text-based and prior knowledge-based inference questions and to indicate whether answers to questions are literal ("right there"), text-based inferences ("think and search"), or prior knowledge-based inferences ("author and me" or "on my own"). Records can be kept of how well students answer the different types of inferencing questions and the extent to which they are able to identify where their answers have come from.

Reading for Important Ideas

As discussed in Chapter 10, reading for important ideas is an essential, yet often underdeveloped, disposition when reading expository, or informative, text. Because most students have difficulty reading for main ideas of paragraphs (Taylor et al., 1985), instruction in this skill may benefit the entire class. About the time that students reach third grade it becomes important to begin assessing their skill in reading for main ideas in the expository paragraphs that will increasingly confront them. At about the fourth-grade level teachers should begin assessing students' ability to summarize the important ideas contained in the longer passages of their content textbooks.

To document students' progress in reading for main ideas, teachers can keep records of students' success in generating main idea statements. One very simple approach begins by asking students to number the paragraphs in a two- to three-page section of regular textbook material. The students' task is to list a topic and write a main idea sentence for each paragraph without copying directly from the text. Because it is probably a new task for students, it is important for the teacher to demonstrate this task and guide students' practice a few times before starting to keep records on their performance.

To determine if students who are reading below grade level need special instruction in this skill, the teacher needs to make sure that their performance is assessed on passages that are written at their instructional level. If their performance is measured only on grade-level passages, then their ability to identify main ideas may be confounded by the obstacles that they face in reading grade-level text.

As discussed in Chapter 10, summarizing important ideas involves stating a few important ideas to remember from a section of text as opposed to stating a main idea for every paragraph in the section. To assess students' skill in summarizing the important ideas of two to three pages of informative text, records can be kept of students' success in writing summaries of instructional level material. Students' summaries can be scored for a number of important ideas included in any number of sections, a section being designated by a heading. Ideally, a summary should contain approximately one to three important ideas per section of text. The teacher would put a check by the sentences in students' summaries that express important ideas as opposed to those relating relatively unimportant details. An example of this type of scoring is provided in Figure 11.5.

Chapter 10 discussed teacher support in the form of providing summarizing clues and alternative summaries. When providing such instructional support with an individual or a small group, a teacher can collect assessment data by noting how much instructional support has to be provided in order for a student to succeed at the task. For example, the teacher might jot down that Fred, Sara, and Chris were unable to summarize a section of their social studies text when clues were provided as to what topics to include in the summary (for example, "I think the summary should say something about the Nile River, Cairo, farming in Egypt, and Egypt's problems."). However, the teacher might also note that they were able to select the best summary for the section given two choices. Over time such notes should reflect the need to provide less instructional support.

FIGURE 11.5. Example of a Summary Scored for Important Ideas

Section	Type of Idea	
1	+	(+) Israel is an ancient nation fighting to become a modern
1	0	one. (0) In one city there are enough teachers and schools that all the children can get an education.
2, 2	+, +	(+) Israel's biggest problem is its land. (+) Most of it is
2	0	unusable for farmland. (0) Some of it can be used for grazing.
2	+	(+) But new steps are being taken to make more farmland like draining swamps and irrigating fields.
3	+	(+) May 14, 1948, is an important date for Israel because
3	X	that is the day it became a nation. (X) Israel is still fighting today.

SCORING: + = important idea; 0 = unimportant idea; X = idea that does not come from the text

5 important ideas in 3 sections = 1.7 important ideas per section.

Assessing Background Knowledge

When making judgments about a reader's comprehension of specific material, the teacher should consider the extent of the student's background knowledge of the material to be read. Any reader's comprehension will suffer when very little is known about the topic. In some instances a student's poor performance on comprehension questions may be due primarily to this fact.

There are a number of ways a teacher can assess students' background knowledge of material they will read. In Chapter 10 the PReP technique was discussed in which the teacher asks students to relate what they know about several of the major concepts developed in the reading material. Based on the students' knowledge, the teacher judges whether students' background knowledge is high, moderate, or low.

A similar procedure has been described by Zakaluk, Samuels, and Taylor (1986). The teacher has individuals free-associate orally or in writing with several key concepts from material they are about to read. For example, a series of free associations for Egypt might include Nile, desert, Cairo, Sadat, pyramids, and Africa. A series of free associations for Cairo might include Egypt, noisy, and big city. Based on this information the teacher might conclude that an individual knew a moderate amount about Egypt but very little about Cairo.

A teacher might also make a list of terms, some of which were related to material to be read and some of which were unrelated. Students could be asked to put check marks next to all the words on the list related to the topic about which they were going to read. For example, a list for a section in their social studies book on Alaska might include the following: oil, resorts, tundra, permafrost, cattle, mountains, desert, farmland, big cities, hydroplanes, and pipeline. Based on an individual's performance on this task, the teacher could determine whether the student had high, moderate, or low background knowledge of the material to be read.

Records of students' comprehension should reflect the extent of their background knowledge for material they have read. For example, in Figure 11.6 under the section on general comprehension a column on background knowledge has been included and completed.

Completing and Using the Reading Difficulties Record Sheet

This chapter has discussed a number of ways to assess students' comprehension. As with word recognition, assessment has depended heavily on teacher interpretation. In this section the teacher is provided with suggestions for interpreting these data.

Chapter 9 considered Billy Stone's performance on the Reading Difficulties Record Sheet in the area of word recognition. It was determined that Billy, a fifth-grade student reading at a beginning third-grade level, had difficulty with particular aspects of word recognition. We will now investigate Billy's performance in the area of comprehension to determine his need for additional instruction.

The comprehension-monitoring section of Figure 11.6 shows that Billy is not particularly skilled at monitoring his comprehension of text. In four

III. Comprehension
  A. Comprehension monitoring
    1. Knowing when do/don't understand

Date	Pages/Book	Overall Rating	Comprehension (%)
10/2	78–84, level 3′	1	85
10/5	85–90, 3′	1	75
10/12	99–102, 3′	1	70
10/16	103–108, 3′	1	65

   Comments:
   10/19   Always thinks he understands well.

    2. Locating sources of comprehension difficulty

   Comments:
   10/5   Unable to do this, pp. 85–86, 3′ book
   10/6   Unable to do this, pp. 103–104, 3′ book

    3. Using fix-up strategies
      a. Student's comments:
      10/5   For a word—"Ask the teacher," idea/paragraph—"I don't know."
      10/16   For a word—"Ask someone," idea/paragraph—"I don't know."
      b. Comments:
      10/19   Doesn't really understand notion of fix-up strategies.
    4. General Comments
      10/14   Would benefit from comprehension rating procedure.
  B. General comprehension

Date	Pages	Book	% Accuracy Narrative	% Accuracy Expository	% Accuracy Literal	% Accuracy Inferential	Background Knowledge	Other Notes
10/2	78–84	3′	85 (17/20)		90 (9/10)	80 (8/10)	H	
10/5	85–90	3′	75 (15/20)		90 (7/10)	60 (6/10)	M	
10/12	99–102	3′		70 (14/20)	80 (8/10)	60 (6/10)	M	
10/16	103–108	3′		65 (13/20)	80 (8/10)	50 (5/10)	L	poor attention

   Comments:
   10/19   More trouble with expository than narrative text. Okay with literal
           questions. Some trouble with inference questions. Would benefit
           from reciprocal teaching procedure.
  C. Drawing Inferences

Date	Pages	Book	Notes
10/16	85–90	3′	Missed 2 $TBIQ_s$* and 2 $PKBIQ_s$.* Couldn't tell whether answers came from text or head.
10/14	99–102	3′	Missed 2 $TBIQ_s$ and 2 $PKBIQ_s$. Still unable to tell where answers to questions came from.

   *TBIQ = text-based inference question; PKBIQ = prior knowledge-based infer-
     ence question

  Comments
     10/19   Seems to need help with text-based and prior knowledge-based infer-
             ence questions. Try QAR procedure.

FIGURE 11.6. Reading Difficulties Record Sheet: Comprehension

D. Reading for important ideas

Date	Pages	Book	% Correct/ Paragraph M.I.	No. Important Ideas/ No. Sections
10/12	99–100	3'	30 (3/10)	
10/16	103–104	3'	20 (2/10)	
10/18	2 pgs.	library book	30 (3/10)	

Comments:

    10/19   Can give topic sometimes but not main idea. Needs instruction.

FIGURE 11.6. Reading Difficulties Record Sheet: Comprehension *(cont.)*

instances, Billy rated his comprehension of what he was reading as good or 1 = I understand (see the comprehension rating task in Chapter 10), even though his performance on comprehension questions ranged from 65 to 85 percent. Also, on two occasions, Billy was unable to locate sources of comprehension difficulty and had little to say in terms of word-level and idea-level fix-up strategies. Based on this information, the teacher believes that Billy may benefit from instruction in the comprehension-rating procedure, described in Chapter 10.

Section B of Figure 11.6 shows that Billy appears to have more difficulty answering questions after reading expository text and less difficulty with narrative text. The teacher believes that Billy would benefit from the reciprocal teaching procedure, a general comprehension-fostering technique designed for use with expository text.

Section B also reveals that Billy appears to have difficulty with inference questions. Section C reveals that Billy has difficulty explaining where answers to inference questions come from. The teacher believes that the QAR procedure designed to help students answer inference questions would benefit Billy.

Section D of Figure 11.6 reveals that Billy has considerable difficulty generating main ideas for paragraphs. The teacher believes this is an area in which Billy would benefit from special instruction. To facilitate your study of this technique, a reading difficulties record sheet on another child, Tami, is included in Appendix C.

Chapter 9 pointed out that instructional decisions should be based on more than four reading samples. Only three or four samples of comprehension performance have been included for illustration purposes. However, even after four or five samples a teacher may want to summarize findings and begin with instruction in areas of clear need, adding instruction in other areas as weaknesses become apparent and as time allows.

You may be wondering at this point how a teacher would have time to provide Billy and six to eight other low-achieving readers with the additional instruction in both word recognition and comprehension that they need. As noted in Chapter 9, all of the special instruction recommendations for Billy (word identification, comprehension, and vocabulary) will be considered in Chapter 16. Chapter 16 will also discuss how a teacher would plan for and implement additional instruction for six to eight low-achieving readers in the classroom.

SUMMARY

This chapter discussed ways to assess students' level of comprehension-monitoring. The use of a metacognitive questionnaire and questioning techniques as well as less traditional tasks, such as question generation and summary selection, to assess students' general reading comprehension were discussed. The chapter described the use of probe questions to assess students' inferencing. After discussing the assessment of students' ability to find important ideas and presenting techniques for assessing students' background knowledge, the chapter concluded with a discussion of how to complete the Reading Difficulties Record Sheet and plan for additional instruction in comprehension.

Suggested Activities

1. Prepare appropriate materials and have a student rate her understanding of paragraphs within longer passages and answer questions on the passages. Based on the student's ratings and answers to questions, determine whether or not the student has been accurately rating her comprehension. If a student is not available, your instructor may be able to provide you with three or more passages on which a student has rated comprehension and answered comprehension questions.
2. For one or two students, look at their answers to questions for three expository texts and three narrative texts (provided by your instructor). You will also need to look at the texts. Based on the student's performance, complete section III.B. of Figure 11.6. To do this you will need to decide which questions were literal and which were inferential. Or, you may want to look at the questions and answers in Appendix C.
3. Direct a student to summarize the main ideas (important ideas only) of two or three informative passages. Score the summaries, based on the procedures discussed in the chapter. If a student is not available, you can score several summaries written by a peer in class or your instructor may be able to provide you with several summaries written by a student, along with the corresponding texts.

Suggested Reading

DAVEY, B. (1989). Assessing comprehension: Selected interactions of task and reader. *The Reading Teacher, 42:* 694–697.

> Davey discusses research that points out that poor readers have particular difficulty with timed assessment of reading comprehension, text lookbacks, and free response questions.

PARATORE, J. R., and INDRISANO, R. (1987). Intervention assessment of reading comprehension. *The Reading Teacher, 40:* 778–783.

> The authors present an excellent description of the assessment procedures they use at the Center for the Assessment and Design for Learning at Boston University. The procedures are closely tied to intervention and to recent research in reading.

CHAPTER 12

VOCABULARY INSTRUCTION

OVERVIEW

As you read this chapter use the following list of main themes to guide your understanding and reflection.

- Vocabulary knowledge is highly related to reading comprehension.
- Contextual analysis, the use of context to determine approximate meanings for words, is a valuable vocabulary strategy that students can use when they are reading independently.
- Vocabulary strategies in which students relate new words to personal experience, such as semantic mapping, have been found to be particularly effective.

Vocabulary knowledge has been found to be highly related to reading comprehension.[1] Davis (1944, 1968) investigated the reading process by factor analyzing reading comprehension subskills and concluded that reading comprehension was comprised of two primary skills, knowledge of word meanings, or vocabulary, and reasoning ability. In addition, Thorndike (1973) found correlations between vocabulary knowledge and reading comprehension to range from .66 to .75 for 10-, 14-, and 17-year-olds in fifteen countries.

Vocabulary knowledge is important in the reading comprehension process for a number of reasons.[2] One view is that people with larger vocabularies normally have greater verbal ability which, in turn, facilitates their reading comprehension. A second view is that readers with larger vocabularies come across fewer unfamiliar words that interrupt the fluency of their reading, thereby enhancing comprehension. A third view is that readers with larger vocabularies have broader background knowledge and richer conceptual networks that facilitate comprehension.

VOCABULARY DEVELOPMENT: INCIDENTAL LEARNING VERSUS EXPLICIT INSTRUCTION

The three notions just described about the relationship between vocabulary knowledge and reading comprehension lead to different approaches to vocabulary development. The first view suggests that direct instruction makes little difference in terms of vocabulary development whereas the second view suggests that direct instruction in specific words is extremely beneficial. The third view suggests that vocabulary development will be enhanced if students learn to relate new concepts to their existing concepts and background knowledge.

There is considerable debate about the best way to develop students' vocabulary because there is little agreement as to which of the above three views is most accurate. The debate is further fueled by a related question concerning the degree to which readers develop vocabulary through incidental learning as they are exposed to unfamiliar words in context.

Nagy, Herman, and Anderson (1985)[3] have argued that direct instruction in specific words is a slow and inefficient method of vocabulary development. They have shown that readers do use context to learn the meanings of unfamiliar words. In fact, Nagy, Herman, and Anderson (1985) have argued that this is *the primary means* of vocabulary development and that wide reading experience is probably the best means of developing students' reading vocabulary.

In contrast, others have argued that direct instruction in vocabulary is essential for good vocabulary growth.[4] They believe the process of learning new words incidentally through repeated exposures in context is a slow and difficult means of vocabulary development. In their view, many repeated exposures to unfamiliar words in text are required before meanings are learned. Furthermore, adults have been found to frequently skip over unfamiliar words as they read.[5] It has also been demonstrated in several studies that intermediate grade students are not very skilled at using context to determine meanings of unfamiliar words.[6]

Advocates of direct instruction in vocabulary also point out that comprehension of specific reading passages is enhanced through passage-specific vocabulary instruction.[7] Additionally, it has been found that certain unfamiliar words are learned better through direct instruction than through incidental exposures in reading material.[8]

There is some validity to all three views of vocabulary development presented at the beginning of this chapter. While we support the view of Nagy, Herman, and Anderson (1985) that wide reading is probably the best means of vocabulary development, we also believe that there are some general vocabulary strategies that students can be taught to use when reading on their own. Furthermore, direct instruction in passage-specific vocabulary benefits comprehension and certainly is not detrimental to general vocabulary growth. Finally, recent research suggests that future recall of new words will be increased if direct instruction focuses on relating words to students' background knowledge.[9]

PROBLEMS WITH CONVENTIONAL VOCABULARY INSTRUCTION

One problem with current vocabulary instruction is that it is not very instructive; that is, very little instruction, direct or indirect, is provided.[10] At best, the teacher presents target words in isolation or in sentences before a selection is read. Then the students decode the words and infer their meanings from the context of the sentences or look them up in a glossary or dictionary. Sometimes students are asked to use the target words in sentences of their own, and after reading the selection in which the words occur, students may be asked to complete a practice sheet in which they use the words. At worst, teachers do not introduce the target words at all or they simply list them on the board, pronounce them, and discuss their meanings briefly.

A second problem with conventional vocabulary instruction is that it tends to focus on rote drill and memorization as opposed to activities that help students actively relate new words to their existing knowledge and conceptual network.[11] Recent research on effective vocabulary instruction has shown that for optimal learning, students need to be actively involved in learning new words through repeated exposures.[12] These exposures should help students relate new words to existing knowledge and experience so that students can retain the new concepts.[13]

A third problem with conventional vocabulary instruction is the lack of focus on strategies that students can use to determine meanings, or approximate meanings, of unfamiliar words when reading on their own. Students need to become independent learners to maximize vocabulary growth.

GENERAL MODEL OF VOCABULARY INSTRUCTION

This chapter looks at vocabulary development in two different ways. First, it discusses strategies that students can learn to use when reading on their own, such as the use of contextual analysis, structural analysis, and the dictionary. As with word recognition and comprehension strategies, it is important that, in addition to explaining these strategies, the teacher be explicit about why they are important and when students can use them when reading on their own.

Second, this chapter discusses strategies for providing direct instruction in specific target words either before or after reading. The focus will be on strategies that provide students with active experiences, repeated exposures, and opportunities to relate the target words to existing concepts and experiences.

VOCABULARY STRATEGIES THAT TRANSFER TO INDEPENDENT READING

Metacognitive Context Instruction

Blachowicz and Zabroske (1990) worked with middle school remedial reading teachers to develop an effective set of strategies to enhance students' use of context clues while they are reading. The focus of their work was to help students develop a conscious, deliberate strategy—under their personal control—for inferring the meanings of unfamiliar words.

Why and when. Teachers talk aloud with their students about certain words in a reading assignment to explain why and when context clues are useful. The teachers verbalize the processes and decisions about using (and, in some situations, trying not to use) context clues to determine, at least in part, word meanings.

What. Teachers and students locate different types of context clues in everyday text and make a list for the classroom.

How. Teachers encourage students to use the following routine when trying to use context to determine a word meaning:

1. Look—before, at, after the word
2. Reason—to connect what they know with what the author tells them
3. Predict—a possible meaning
4. Resolve or redo—decide if they know enough, should try again, or consult an expert or reference

Instruction begins with teacher demonstration and progresses to guided practice. At this stage students, with teacher support, talk aloud as they locate context clues and use the clues, along with prior knowledge, to predict word meanings.

In their developmental work Blachowicz and her colleagues worked with students for 3 months, focusing on the why, what, and how of context use through weekly lessons dealing with two words from regular classroom reading materials. Beginning in the fourth month of school, student teams led the weekly context lessons. Students on a team chose two words from their reading assignment that they thought would be unfamiliar to most students. They modeled the use of context with one word and led the class in a discussion of the second word.

Contextual Analysis

As discussed above, students do make use of contextual analysis when reading, thus expanding their reading vocabulary. Sometimes, of course, distinct context clues for unfamiliar words are not provided in naturally occurring text. However, even when context clues are available students do not always avail themselves of the clues.[14] For example, Carnine, Kameenui, and Coyle (1984) found that sixth-grade students were able to determine the meanings of unfamiliar words through the use of context clues only about 40 percent of the time. Students appeared to have the greatest difficulty when contextual information was separated from unfamiliar words (for example, Farmers usually plow around hills instead of up and down. This method is called *contour* plowing.), and when they had to make an inference to determine a word's meaning (The class was having an end-of-the-year party. It was a very *raucous* affair.). They were much better at using more transparent context clues, such as synonyms stated in the form of an appositive.

Fortunately, students can be taught to improve their skill in using context clues to determine approximate word meanings. A modification of an instructional technique developed by Carnine, Kameenui, and Coyle (1984) is presented below.

What, Why, and *When.* First, the teacher explains to students *what* they will be working on and *why* this is important. They will be learning how to look for meaning clues for unfamiliar words that will help them better understand what they are reading. Contextual analysis is a convenient skill to use when reading because if students are able to generate an approximate meaning for an unfamiliar word, they will not be forced to stop and use the dictionary. Although using the dictionary can be useful, they are not always available, and stopping to consult them can interfere with one's train of thought.

How. Next, the teacher demonstrates contextual analysis examples from everyday reading, i.e., the material the students are currently using. The teacher reads aloud a paragraph containing an unfamiliar word (for example, "I don't know what *raucous* means.") and talks about other words in the same sentence or in nearby sentences that provide clues to the word's meaning (*end-of-the-year* and *party* seem like clue words for *raucous*). The teacher then puts this information together to come up with an approximate meaning for the word. ("Well, a party at the end of the year would probably be pretty noisy. Kids would be excited about school ending and summer vacation starting. I think *raucous* must mean noisy.") After several demonstrations, the teacher and students can work as a group to locate clue words and derive approximate meanings for unfamiliar words in the students' everyday texts.

For independent application, students can complete an assignment such as this. While reading on their own, they can stop to write down clue words and approximate meanings for unfamiliar words. These can be words that have been targeted by the teacher or words students have noticed on their own. Later they can bring their ideas, potential clues, and recollections about their thought processes to the reading discussion. The teacher should explain that this skill should be used whenever they are having difficulty comprehending a paragraph because of an unfamiliar word.

Although it is not important for students to label context clues, it is useful for teachers to know about the following types of context clues (target words and clue words are in italics):

1. Direct definition: We have more *pollution* today than in the past. Pollution is *waste that has been added to natural resources.*
2. Restatement: The farmers planted *shelterbelts,* or *rows of trees,* by their fields to break the wind.
3. Synonym: The students had a *raucous* end-of-the-year party. The party was so *noisy* that the principal stopped in to see what was happening.
4. Comparison: A *dust storm* is like a *blizzard.*
5. Contrast: Dan is a *diligent* student whereas Paul is *lazy.*
6. Inference based on text information or prior knowledge or experience: Jason was *furious.* As soon as he finished putting the puzzle together, his *baby brother pushed it from the table onto the floor.*
7. Example: Everyone in the family was *slight.* Michelle, for instance, *weighed only 70 pounds but was 12 years old.*

Discussions about what the author did to provide a context clue for a particular word (for example, gave a direct definition, made a comparison) may teach students to look for these types of context clues when they are reading independently.

Another approach to using context clues is the vocabulary overview guide,[15] which will be discussed following the next section on using the dictionary.

Using the Dictionary

Helping students learn to use the dictionary to locate the meaning of an unfamiliar word is obviously an important activity. After learning how to locate a word in the dictionary (or glossary), the next step is learning how to select the most appropriate definition for the word. Words seldom have only one meaning, yet students have the tendency to write down the first dictionary definition provided.

It is inadvisable to ask students to look up the meanings of unfamiliar words presented in isolation prior to reading. Instead, target words should be presented in everyday context. If necessary, a dictionary should be consulted during or after reading. In this way, students will have a context for each word they locate in the dictionary. They should be encouraged to read through all of the definitions provided for a word before selecting the one that seems to be most appropriate to the text usage. In fact, there is some evidence that the most common problem middle school readers face is "jumping" at the first available definition without trying to match definition to context. Group discussion in which students are asked to explain their reasons for selecting one particular definition over others should follow dictionary work.

Another activity, which may be particularly beneficial for low-achieving readers, begins by having students keep a list of unfamiliar words they come across during reading. These words might come from either assigned or independent reading material. Group meetings with the teacher can focus on unfamiliar words from common reading assignments, and students can meet individually with the teacher to discuss unfamiliar words from independent reading material. After relocating the words in the reading material in which they occurred, the teacher and students use contextual analysis plus the dictionary to determine meanings for the unfamiliar words.

The Vocabulary Overview Guide

Carr (1985) has developed a useful metacognitive vocabulary strategy that helps students locate unfamiliar words as they are reading on their own, to define these words, and to relate them to their personal experience.

What, *Why*, and *How*. First the teacher explains to students that they will be learning how to locate and define unfamiliar words as they are reading and to relate these words to their own experience. This will help them better understand a particular selection they are reading and develop their general vocabulary. The teacher then models the procedure as he reads a particular selection and writes unfamiliar words and their page numbers on the board or a piece of paper. The teacher uses context clues first and then the dictionary to determine and write down the meanings of the unfamiliar words.

Next, the teacher shows students how to complete the vocabulary overview guide. The title of the reading selection is listed at the top of a sheet of paper. Category labels, reflecting the topics of unfamiliar words, are listed under the title of the reading selection. The unfamiliar words may describe or be associated with these category titles. For example, a section from a social studies book entitled "Egypt—A Developing Nation" might contain unfamiliar terms such as *hydroelectric power* and *irrigation* that are associated with the category title, "the Aswan Dam." Similarly, *mosque* and *artisan* would be associated with the category title "Cairo." The unfamiliar words are listed under the appropriate category titles. Next, definitions or synonyms, as determined from context or the dictionary, are written under the unfamiliar words. Finally, personal clues that connect the unfamiliar words to personal experiences are written in boxes below the unfamiliar words. For example, for the unfamiliar word *mosque* a student might write the personal clue, "like Greek Orthodox church downtown." An example of a vocabulary overview guide is presented in Figure 12.1.

Why and *When.* In addition to helping students use this procedure, the teacher can explain that whenever they are reading on their own and they encounter an unknown word, they can use context clues to generate an approximate word meaning. They can look the word up in the dictionary if they feel the need for a more precise definition. Teachers can encourage students to prepare a vocabulary guide while or after completing a reading assignment.

Using Structural Analysis

Knowing the meanings of common prefixes, suffixes, and roots can be useful when trying to determine the meanings of unfamiliar words containing these elements. For example, if students know that *trans* means *across*, then they will probably understand that a trip was made across the Atlantic Ocean when they read the sentence, The pilgrims made a transatlantic voyage. Common prefixes, suffixes, and roots are listed in Figure 12.2.

FIGURE 12.1. Example of a Vocabulary Overview Guide

ASWAN DAM

- Hydroelectric Power
  - Niagara Falls
  - electricity from fast-running water
- Irrigation
  - ditches by rice fields
  - bringing water to dry farmland

CAIRO

- Mosque
  - Greek church downtown
  - Moslem church
- Artisan
  - man who carves wooden ducks
  - skilled craftsman

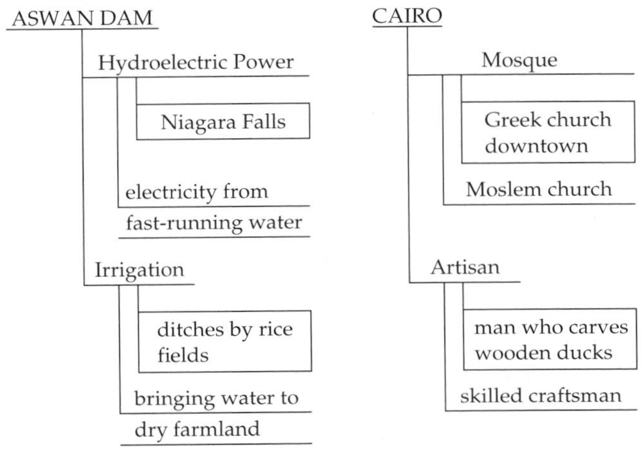

Prefixes	Examples
anti (against, opposing)	antifreeze, antisocial
bi (two, twice)	bicycle, biweekly
circum (around)	circumnavigate, circumvent
co, con, com, col (with, together; to the same degree)	cooperate, conversation, coauthor
counter (contrary, opposing; complementary)	counterproductive, counterpart
de (do the opposite of, remove, reduce, get off)	deemphasis, dethrone, devalue, detrain
dis (deprive of, opposite, not)	disable, disunion, disagreeable
in, im, il, ir (not, in)	illogical, imperil
inter (between, reciprocal)	international, interrelation
intra (within)	intramural, intravenous
mis (bad, badly; lack of)	misjudge, mistrust
non (not)	nonconformity, noncommercial
post (after, behind)	postwar, postlude
pre (before, in front of)	prehistoric, premolar
pro (before, in front of; favoring)	proclaim, pro-America
re (again, back)	retell, recall
retro (backward)	retroactive, retrospective
semi (half, to some extent)	semiannual, semiconscious
sub (under, secondary, less than completely)	subsoil, subtropic, substandard
super (more than, over, above)	superhuman, superior
trans (across, change)	transatlantic, transfer
un (not, do the opposite of, remove from)	unskilled, unfold, unhand

Suffixes	Examples
able, ible (able to)	capable, forcible
al (pertaining to)	fictional
ance (action or process, quality or state)	performance, despondence
ation (action or process)	discoloration
ative (of, tending to)	authoritative, talkative
dom (realm, state of being)	kingdom, freedom
er, or, ist (performer of)	farmer, pianist
ful (full of, having qualities of, quantity)	eventful, peaceful, roomful
hood (state of being, instance of a quality)	boyhood, falsehood
ic (of, containing, characterized by)	panoramic, alcoholic, allergic
ish (being, characteristic of, somewhat)	Spanish, boyish, purplish
ism (act of, condition of)	criticism, barbarianism
less (not having, unable to act)	childless, helpless
ly (like, every, in a specified manner)	fatherly, hourly, slowly
ment (action or process, condition)	development, amazement
ness (state of, quality of)	goodness
ous (having)	poisonous
ship (quality, profession)	friendship, authorship
tion, sion, ion (the act of)	decision, motion
ty, ry, ity (condition of)	safety, purity
ward (in the direction of, in spatial or temporal direction)	leftward, upward

FIGURE 12.2. Common Prefixes, Suffixes, and Roots

Roots	Examples	
audio (hear)	audiometer, audiovisual	**285**
auto (self)	automobile, automatic	CHAPTER *12* *Vocabulary* *Instruction*
bene (good)	beneficial, benefit	
bio (life)	biology, biography	
chrono (time)	chronological, chronic	
cosmo (world)	cosmopolitan, cosmos	
fac, fact, fic (make, do)	facilitate, factory	
geo (earth)	geology, geography	
gram, graph (written or drawn)	telegram, telegraph	
logo (speech)	logic, catalog	
logy (science of)	biology, geology	
mal (bad, inadequate)	malpractice, malformed	
micro (small)	microcomputer, microcosm	
mis, mit (send)	submit, admit	
mov, mot (move)	move, motion	
phobia (fear)	claustrophobia, hydrophobia	
poly (many)	polygamous, polyunsaturated	
port (carry)	portage, transportation	
scope (instrument for seeing)	telescope, microscope	
scrib, scrip (write)	prescription, scribble	
spect, spic (look, see)	spectacles, inspect	
ven, vent (come)	convention, event	
vid, vis (see)	visible, video	

FIGURE 12.2. Common Prefixes, Suffixes, and Roots *(cont.)*

In general, isolated discussions and drills on lists of prefixes, suffixes, and roots will not be very effective; they are likely to be even less effective with low-achieving readers. The most appropriate time to discuss their meaning is when students come across an example in their reading. The teacher can record the word containing the element on a chalkboard, along with several other examples. If possible, these examples should consist of words already known by the students. The teacher can ask the students for their ideas about the possible meaning of the element being studied. Since most affixes and roots have more than one meaning, all examples introduced at one time should demonstrate the same meaning. However, to forestall later over generalization on the part of students, the teacher can stress that the meaning for the affix or root, as used in the examples, is just one of several meanings that the element may have.

For reinforcement, the students may be provided with sentences containing examples of the affix or root just studied. The students' task is to use a combination of context clues and structural analysis knowledge to generate meanings for the various unfamiliar words. To check their meanings, students can locate the words in the dictionary. Variations of this type of practice activity are common in commercially available materials. An example is provided in Figure 12.3.

DIRECTIONS: Write meanings for the following underlined words. To do this use context clues plus your knowledge of the meaning of *circum*. If necessary, also use the dictionary.

1. The small sailing vessel set out to <u>circumnavigate</u> the globe.

_____

2. A barbed wire fence <u>circumscribed</u> the farm. _____

3. John <u>circumvented</u> the problem of taking Mary out to eat after the movie by going

   with her to his parents' house for dinner before the movie.

_____

4. Mr. Jones instructed his class to calculate the <u>circumference</u> of the circle.

_____

5. The <u>circumspect</u> mother fox stood on guard as her babies played in the sun.

_____

FIGURE 12.3. Prefix Practice Activity

Interpreting Ambiguous Words: Secondary Meanings and Homographs

Most words in the English language have multiple meanings, a primary meaning and one or more secondary meanings. Children are not very likely to know the secondary meanings of familiar words they encounter in reading materials.[16] This may lead to confusion and impair comprehension. Therefore, it is important for the teacher to help students with secondary meanings. First, they need to help students realize that primary meanings may not always fit the context. In other words, students need to develop a set for other meanings. Second, teachers need to help students attend to and determine the secondary meanings of particular words they come across in their reading. By focusing on secondary meanings, teachers will help students learn to deal with them. That is, students will become less confused when confronted with familiar words whose primary meanings do not make sense.

As a follow-up to discussing secondary meanings of words encountered in assigned reading, the teacher can ask students to keep a list of unfamiliar secondary meanings they encounter in their independent reading. These lists can be shared at later meetings. As an additional follow-up activity, the teacher can provide a practice activity consisting of a pair of sentences containing underlined words that have both a primary and a secondary meaning. The students' task is to use the sentence context to generate the appropriate meaning for each underlined word. Responses can be checked by locating the words in the dictionary and should also be shared in a group discussion. An example of a practice activity focusing on primary and secondary meanings is presented in Figure 12.4.

Homographs are words that are spelled alike but do not sound the same and have different meanings, such as de*sert* (leave) and *de*sert (dry land). As with secondary meanings, homographs may cause students problems if they do not expect them. Again, it is important that the teacher discuss homographs when they occur in assigned reading. Students should be encouraged to use context to determine the appropriate meaning and pronunciation for a particular

FIGURE 12.4. Practice Activity Focusing on Primary and Secondary Meanings
DIRECTIONS: Write meanings for the following underlined words

1. a. The old shed in the backyard <u>lists</u> to one side._____

   _____

   b. Did you make a <u>list</u> of the things we need to buy at the grocery? _____

2. a. Tom didn't know how to get out of the <u>scrape</u> he was in; he had a date with Mary

   and with Sue for Saturday night. _____

   b. Timmy <u>scraped</u> his knee when he fell off his bike. _____

   _____

3. a. Eating all of Aunt Matilda's cookies before I got home was a <u>base</u> thing to do.

   _____

   _____

   b. Peggy hit the ball and ran to first <u>base</u>. _____

   _____

4. a. At the <u>face</u> of the building are four beautiful marble columns._____

   b. Billy has a lot of freckles on his <u>face</u>. _____

   _____

5. a. You can get the answer <u>key</u> from me when you have completed all of the math

   problems. _____

   b. Grandma used an old skeleton <u>key</u> to open the door to the attic._____

   _____

homograph. As a follow-up to a discussion of homographs, students should be encouraged to keep and share a list of homographs that they find in their independent reading. For practice, students can be asked to generate the appropriate meaning for each member of a homograph pair in a set of sentences. An example is provided below.

1. I hope he did not *contract* the disease. _____
2. Ms. Smith pointed out that making the morning coffee was not in her *contract.* _____

Another practice activity would be for students to generate sentences using both members of a homograph pair. These sentences could be shared in the students' reading group. Two examples are provided below.

1. He made a *bow* to the girl with a *bow* in her hair.
2. She had a *tear* in her eye because of the *tear* in her dress.

A list of common homographs is provided in Figure 12.5.

LEARNING SPECIFIC WORDS

So far, we have discussed strategies that help students handle unfamiliar vocabulary when they encounter them. We turn now to the learning and teaching of specific words. As mentioned earlier, direct instruction in unfamiliar words enhances students' comprehension of specific reading material and contributes to their vocabulary growth.

Using Context and Relating Unfamiliar Words to Personal Experience

Gipe (1978, 1979) has developed an effective approach to vocabulary instruction that primarily uses contextual analysis and definitions but also incorporates two important aspects of vocabulary learning—receiving repeated exposures to unfamiliar words and relating words to personal experiences. A modification of this procedure is presented in the following section.

Prior to reading a particular assignment, unfamiliar words are presented one at a time on the board. The teacher reads aloud two sentences containing

FIGURE 12.5. Common Homographs

aged	converse	lead	relay
arch	convert	live	sewer
brass	desert	minute	shower
bow	digest	object	sow
bowed	do	perfect	subject
close	does	permit	tear
collect	dove	present	transfer
compact	entrance	primer	use
conduct	excuse	project	wind
console	incense	read	wound
content	intimate	record	
contract	invalid	refuse	

each word that provide good context clues to the word's meaning. The teacher asks students to write down the word and what they think it means. Approximate meanings generated by the students are discussed. In a third sentence the word is presented along with a definition. Then, students are asked to answer a question in which they relate the word to their own experience.

For example, for the word *clumsy,* the teacher writes the word on the board and reads, "The clumsy child stumbled and knocked the glass off the table. Someone who is clumsy may trip frequently and bump into things." The teacher directs students to write the word *clumsy* on a sheet of paper and to also write what they think it means. Possible meanings are discussed. Then, the teacher reads a sentence containing a definition for the word *clumsy.* "*Clumsy* means moving in an awkward manner." The students are then directed to answer the following question, "What might a clumsy shopper do at the grocery store?" Students share answers to this question.

Sentences and a question for the word *surplus* might include the following: "We had a surplus of food after the party was over. Our surplus showed us that we had bought too much food for the party. *Surplus* means having more of something than is needed. Do you or your family have a surplus of anything?" By participating in this sequence of activities, students receive several meaningful exposures to each unfamiliar word prior to reading. This will aid their retention of each word as well as its meaning.

Using the Keyword Method

Another effective technique for learning meanings of unfamiliar words is the key word method.[17] This method involves using mnemonics and imagery to learn the meanings of unfamiliar words.

Mnemonic techniques, strategies for transforming to-be-learned material into a form that makes the material easier to learn and remember, are known to facilitate memory. In addition, images or pictures seem to be particularly effective devices for coding information mnemonically.[18]

The keyword method involves presenting a vocabulary word along with a key word, that is, a familiar word that is phonetically similar to part or all of the vocabulary word. For example, *syrup* could be presented as a key word for *surplus, purse* for *persuade,* and *angel* for *angler.*

A picture is then presented that relates the key word to the meaning of the vocabulary word. For example, a cupboard full of syrup could be presented to illustrate the meaning of persuade, and an angel fishing could illustrate the meaning of angler. To clarify each picture, two characters in the picture are speaking. One character's comments contain the key word and the other's the vocabulary word. At the bottom of the picture, the vocabulary word is presented, followed by the key word in parentheses and a definition of the vocabulary word. An example of a keyword illustration is presented in Figure 12.6.

The teacher reads the characters' comments and the vocabulary word, key word, and definition at the bottom of the page. After discussing what is happening in the picture, the teacher explains or has the students explain how they will remember the meaning of the vocabulary word by thinking of the key word and picture.

SUPRLUS (SYRUP) having some left over,
having more than was needed

SOURCE: From J.R. Levin et al. (1982), Mnemonic versus nonmnemonic vocabulary-learning strategies for children, *American Educational Research Journal, 19*, 127. Copyright 1982, *American Educational Research Journal*, Washington, DC.

FIGURE 12.6. Example of a Keyword Illustration

In research using the keyword technique with children, actual pictures have been provided. Although pictures may be less practical for the classroom, it is important that the teacher help students develop an appropriate keyword illustration in the form of a mental image. The keyword procedure is not as effective when the students are expected to generate keyword images on their own.[19] For example, even if no picture such as the one in Figure 12.6 were available to help students learn the meaning of surplus, the teacher should help students come up with this or a similar image. The teacher could tell students to imagine a boy pouring a great amount of syrup on his pancakes because there are five more bottles of syrup in the cupboard. Next, the teacher could tell students that the boy was not worried about using too much syrup because he knows there is a surplus of syrup in the cupboard. Then the teacher could write the words *syrup* and *surplus* on the board and provide students with a definition for the word *surplus.*

Because it is a somewhat lengthy procedure, the keyword method is not an appropriate technique for introducing a large number of words before students read assigned material. Instead, the keyword method might be reserved for particularly important, difficult words. No one is quite sure why this approach works, since it appears so counterintuitive; after all, semantic associations, not phonetic associations, should lead to increased conceptual learning. Nonetheless, the data on the keyword approach consistently support its use in vocabulary acquisition.

Semantic Mapping

Completely at odds with the keyword approach is semantic mapping. Its basic premise is that people learn by relating the new to the known; that is, by relating new concepts to existing concepts and knowledge. In several recent studies it has been found that vocabulary instruction that helps students relate unfamiliar words and their meanings to known concepts has been more effective than conventional approaches that focus on learning definitions or using context to determine meanings of unfamiliar words.[20]

Semantic mapping[21] has consistently been found to be effective.[22] It involves linking a vocabulary word to as many related words as possible. It is a useful way to focus on a particularly important word that students have come across in a reading assignment.

Assume, for example, that students have just read a section in their social studies book about dry farming on the Great Plains. The teacher might develop a semantic map for the concept *dry farming* on the board while students make copies on individual sheets of paper.

First, the teacher writes *dry farming* in the middle of the board. As the students free-associate with this word, the teacher lists their ideas on the board. Then, different categories of information pertaining to the word and the free associations are developed by the class. One category might be definition, and the students would provide a definition for *dry farming*. A second category might be reasons for dry farming, and students would list the reasons. A third category might be types of crops grown through dry farming, and students would list crops such as wheat and oats. A fourth category might be places where dry farming is used, and students would list states such as Montana, Colorado, and Wyoming. An example of a semantic map for the concept *dry farming* is presented in Figure 12.7.

Another approach to semantic mapping involves taking a familiar concept pertaining to a pending reading selection and having students generate ideas

FIGURE 12.7. Semantic Map

definition	reasons for using
1/2 land planted	not much rainfall
1/2 land fallow	soil dry

Dry Farming

where used	types of crops
Montana	wheat
Wyoming	oats
Colorado	

performers   animals

acrobats   lions
 trapeze artists   tigers
 lion *trainer*   elephants
tightrope walker   monkeys

Circus

clowns   clown tricks

WHITEFACE   *TINY* CAR TRICK
AUGUST   SAW-A-CLOWN-IN-*HALF*
ACROBAT
MIDGET
 TALL (ON *STILTS*)

NOTE: Words included in the map before reading, based on students' background knowledge, are in regular type. New words added after reading are in capitals. Vocabulary words that were selected by the basal authors of this story about the circus as words in need of attention are indicated by asterisks.

FIGURE 12.8. Pre-Post Semantic Map

related to the concept. After reading, new concepts gleaned from the material can be added to the map.[23]

For example, if students are going to read a story or a book about the circus, the teacher and students can generate a semantic map for the word *circus* before reading. After reading, new words can be added to the map. An example of such a semantic map is presented in Figure 12.8. Words included in the map before reading, based on students' background knowledge, are in regular type. New words added after reading are in capital letters. In the example, vocabulary words selected by the basal authors for this particular story are indicated by asterisks.

Semantic Feature Analysis

Semantic feature analysis[24] is another technique that helps students learn the meanings of unfamiliar words by relating them to known words. The technique involves looking at the similarities and differences of related concepts. Like semantic mapping, semantic feature analysis has been found to be an effective technique for developing students' vocabulary.[25]

Semantic feature analysis involves the teacher's taking a category such as *fruit* and listing in the left-hand column a few members of the category, such as *apple*, *peach*, and *plum*. Features germane to the category, such as *smooth, skin, seeds,* and *pit*, are listed in a row across the top of the grid. The teacher and students use a system of pluses and minuses to determine which members of the category under investigation have the particular features listed. If one of the category members is a newly introduced vocabulary word, students will be able to see how this new word is similar to, yet different from, other words already known.

Category—Types of Boats

Category Members	Manpower	Tips Easily	Fast	Expensive	Use on Rivers	Use on Lakes
Canoe	+	+	−	−	+	+
Sailboat	−	?	−	?	−	+
Rowboat	+	−	−	−	−	+
Powerboat	−	−	+	+	?	+

FIGURE 12.9. Example of a Semantic Feature Analysis Grid

For example, if the new vocabulary word is *canoe,* the teacher introduces the category *boats.* The teacher lists *canoe* at the top of the column of category members and asks students to add other types of boats to the grid. Next, students are asked to add boat features to the grid. They complete the grid by using pluses and minuses to match boats and features. An example of a semantic feature analysis grid is provided in Figure 12.9. A plus means *yes* (this category member has this feature), a minus means *no,* and a question mark means *maybe.*

After completing the grid, the teacher and students discuss the category members and features. Questions such as What two category members are most alike? and What two category members are most different? can be asked to stimulate discussion. Students may also think of other category members or features to add to the grid.

DEVELOPING STUDENTS' INTEREST IN WORDS

This chapter concludes with a number of suggestions for developing students' interest in words. It is important that teachers be enthusiastic about new words and their meanings and to instill this enthusiasm in their students. One of the best ways to build students' enthusiasm for words is to engage them in vocabulary games and other entertaining vocabulary-related activities. It is hoped that through such activities students will develop their vocabulary knowledge and become more attentive to new words they encounter.

Sharing New Words Heard Outside of School

Students often enjoy what is actually a sophisticated version of show and tell in which they share with the class new words they have learned outside of school. The teacher can simply set aside 10 minutes once or twice a week for students to present and define new words they have encountered. Students should be prepared to tell how they came across a particular word and to explain the context in which the word was used. For example, students might pick up new words at the dinner table, on TV, from the newspaper or a book they are reading, or from a list of unfamiliar words they have been keeping as part of their reading in school. Students' attention to unfamiliar words usually increases if they know they have the opportunity to share them in school. As an additional

This student is sharing his new vocabulary word with the rest of the class. *(Peter Vadnaie)*

motivator, students can keep personal lists of new words on charts displayed in their classroom. Every time someone brings in a new word to share, it can be added to her list.

Illustrating New Words

Students often enjoy using pictures to illustrate new words they have learned. One possible activity involves cartoons. Students can make cartoons to go with new words, or they can simply add new captions to existing cartoons. For example, in a "Peanuts" cartoon in which Charlie Brown asks Snoopy if he wants to go downtown with him, the vocabulary word *accompany* might replace *go*. Similarly, students can write captions for magazine pictures that illustrate vocabulary words. The captions should contain the new vocabulary words. For example, to illustrate the word *adorned* a student might find a picture of a person wearing a bizarre object and write a caption beneath the picture using the word *adorned*.

Completing Crossword Puzzles

Many students enjoy crossword puzzles, which may or may not be made up of new vocabulary words. However, even if crossword puzzles are not made up of new vocabulary words, they are useful for general vocabulary development and for developing students' interest in words.

Students often enjoy making simple crossword puzzles for others to complete. An example of a simple crossword puzzle is provided in Figure 12.10. In this example, in only one instance do the letters in a column spell an actual

DIRECTIONS: Use the words below to answer the questions and to fill in the cross-word puzzle.

learned	electric	pilot
immortal	trade	quarrel

1. What do you do if you give a friend a baseball card and get one from them?
2. What would you be if you never died?
3. What type of clock has to be plugged in?
4. What does the teacher hope you have done after you've read your science book?
5. What is someone who flies a plane called?
6. What is a fight with words called?

*

1. t r a d e
2. i m m o r t a l
3. e l e c t r i c
4. l e a r n e d
5. p i l o t
6. q u a r r e l

Read the word spelled downward under the star. It spells the name of a famous person you will read about. Write the name on the line.

Amelia

FIGURE 12.10. Simple Crossword Puzzle

word. If students were making their own crossword puzzles, they may want to create words for rows but not columns to keep their task simple.

Playing Vocabulary Games

A number of commercial games are available, such as "Scrabble" and "Spill-and-Spell," that are valuable for promoting general vocabulary growth as well as for developing students' interest in words. A rule for such games might be that students give a definition for any word they have constructed, or at least an example of its use, to demonstrate they know what the word means.

"Concentration" is another vocabulary game that is easy to prepare. For example, the teacher or students can make pairs from vocabulary words and synonyms or antonyms for these words. Or, new vocabulary words can be matched with definitions.

Vocabulary games are a good way to develop students' interest in words. *(James Silliman)*

SUMMARY

This chapter discussed approaches to vocabulary development and problems with conventional vocabulary instruction. Suggestions for initial vocabulary instruction focusing on strategies students can use when reading on their own were provided. The primary purpose of these strategies is to help students obtain meanings for unfamiliar words while reading so their comprehension is not impaired. In addition, general vocabulary growth occurs as students attend to unfamiliar words.

Suggestions for vocabulary instruction in specific words were also provided. Three of the strategies presented involve relating new vocabulary words to already known words or to students' own experiences. A fourth strategy given involves using mnemonics and imagery to help students remember the meanings of new words. Finally, activities for developing students' interest in words and word meanings were discussed. Collecting words outside of school, illustrating vocabulary words, and playing vocabulary games were offered as ways to heighten students' awareness of and interest in words.

Suggested Activities

1. Locate appropriate materials and teach two or three students how to use context clues to determine word meanings. If students are not available, teach the technique to peers in your class.
2. Locate two or three important words in a student textbook and prepare keyword illustrations, dialogue, and definitions for these words.

3. Locate two or three important words in a student textbook and develop a semantic map for each of these words with a group of two or three students or with peers in your class.

Suggested Reading

BLACHOWICZ C. L., and ZABROSKE B. (1990). Context instruction: A metacognitive approach for at-risk readers. *Journal of Reading, 33:* 504–508.
   The authors discuss problems with typical context instruction for secondary students and present an effective approach for improving students' use of context clues while reading.

CARR, E. (1985). The vocabulary overview guide: A metacognitive strategy to improve vocabulary comprehension and retention. *Journal of Reading, 28:* 684–689.
   Carr presents a technique that helps students learn new words by relating them to their background knowledge.

LEVIN J. R. (1981). The mnemonic 80s: Keywords in the classroom. *Educational Psychologist, 16:* 65–82.
   Discusses the keyword technique.

SCHWARTZ R. (1988). Learning to learn vocabulary in content area textbooks. *Journal of Reading, 32:* 108–119.
   The author describes a mapping procedure, concept of definition instruction, which has been used successfully to guide students in their learning of new concepts in content area material.

Notes

1. See Anderson and Freebody (1981) and Sternberg and Powell (1983).
2. See Anderson and Freebody (1981).
3. See Nagy and Anderson (1984) and Nagy and Herman (1984).
4. See Beck, McKeown, and McCaslin (1983), Graves (1987),and Ornanson, Beck, McKeown, and Perfetti (1984).
5. See Freebody and Anderson (1983).
6. See Carnine, Karneenui, and Coyle (1984) and Rankin and Overholser (1969).
7. See Beck, Perfetti, and McKeown (1982), Jenkins, Stein, and Wysocki (1984), Kameenui, Carnine, and Freschi (1982), and Stahl (1983).
8. See Beck, McKeown, and McCaslin (1983), Jenkins, Pany, and Schreck (1978), and Omanson, Beck, McKeown, and Perfetti (1984).
9. See McNeil (1984).
10. See Beck, McKeown, McCaslin, and Burkes (1979), Durkin (1978–1979), Graves (1987), and Jenkins and Dixon (1983).
11. See Blachowicz (1985) and Eeds and Cockrum (1985).
12. See Beck, Perfetti, and McKeown (1982), Jenkins, Stein, and Wysocki (1984), McKeown, Beck, Omanson, and Perfetti (1983), and Mezynski (1983).
13. See Eeds and Cockrum (1985), Jenkins, Pany, and Schreck (1978), Johnson, Toms-Bronowski and Pittelman (1982), and Margosein, Pascarella, and Pflaum (1982).
14. See McKeown (1985).
15. See Carr (1985).
16. See Mason, Knisely, and Kendall (1979).
17. See Levin et al. (1984), Levin, McCormick, Miller, Berry, and Pressley (1982), and Pressley, Levin, and Miller (1981).
18. See Levin (1981).
19. See Levin (1981).

20. See Eeds and Cockrum (1985), Johnson, Toms-Bronowski, and Pittleman (1982), and Margosein, Pascarella, and Pflaum (1982).
21. See Johnson and Pearson (1984).
22. See Johnson, Toms-Bronowski, and Pittleman (1982) and Margosein, Pascarella, and Pflaum (1982).
23. See Johnson, Toms-Bronowski, and Pittleman (1982).
24. See Johnson and Pearson (1984).
25. See Johnson, Toms-Bronowski, and Pittleman (1982).

CHAPTER 13

VOCABULARY ASSESSMENT

OVERVIEW

As you read this chapter you may want to use these themes to guide your understanding and reflection.

- General vocabulary knowledge is difficult to assess and can probably best be achieved through the use of commercial standardized tests.
- A constructed answer format is preferable to a multiple choice format for vocabulary assessment because it more closely approximates what a reader must do when he encounters an unfamiliar word in text.
- For vocabulary assessment an unfamiliar word should be presented within the context of sentences because a word's meaning depends on its context.

This chapter on vocabulary assessment first discusses assessment of students' general vocabulary knowledge, then provides suggestions for assessing specific vocabulary strategies that students can use when they encounter unknown words in their reading. These strategies include using context, using the dictionary, structural analysis, and interpreting ambiguous words. The discussion then turns to strategies for assessing students' learning of specific words. These may be words discussed before or after students have read basal reader stories, trade books, content textbooks, or other material. These suggestions for assessment will closely parallel the suggestions for instruction provided in Chapter 12. The chapter concludes with a discussion about using the reading difficulties record sheet to record information about vocabulary.

The suggestions for vocabulary assessment presented in this chapter assume that vocabulary words are presented in context because the meaning of words depend on their context. Although examples are provided using both the constructed answer (for example, students are asked to provide definitions or give meanings for words) and multiple-choice formats, the constructed answer format is stressed because this approach more closely approximates reading. In independent reading, a student is not provided with several choices for a word's meaning when confronted with an unfamiliar word. Instead, the student will most likely generate an approximate meaning for a word and continue reading. The student may occasionally stop to look up an unknown word in the dictionary, but this is not something that readers do on a regular basis.

ASSESSMENT OF GENERAL VOCABULARY KNOWLEDGE

Assessment of general vocabulary knowledge is difficult because of the problems associated with developing an appropriate sample of words.[1] Random sampling of words from the dictionary does not take into account word frequency. Selecting words from a frequency list is more appropriate, yet determining the numbers of words to select from different frequency levels remains a problem. Using a commercial standardized test is recommended, as opposed to a teacher-made test, to obtain an indication of a student's reading vocabulary because general vocabulary knowledge is so difficult to assess.

Most achievement tests include some measure of reading vocabulary knowledge. General achievement tests that contain vocabulary subtests include the following: *Comprehensive Tests of Basic Skills, Iowa Test of Basic Skills, Metropolitan Achievement Tests,* and *SRA Achievement Series.* Reading tests that contain vocabulary subtests include the following: *Gates-MacGinitie Reading Tests* and *Nelson Denny Reading Test.* The *Diagnostic Reading Scale,* the *Durrell Analysis of Reading Difficulties,* the *Gates-McKillop-Horowitz Reading Diagnostic Tests,* and the *Stanford Diagnostic Reading Test* are diagnostic reading tests that include measures of auditory vocabulary. Finally, the *Peabody Picture Vocabulary Test* is an individually administered test of verbal knowledge.

Tests employ different approaches and have limitations that need to be acknowledged if used. For example, many of these tests present words in isolation. This represents an unnatural situation since words are almost always encountered in some context.

These tests also do not reflect children's incremental knowledge of vocabulary. They do not indicate the extent to which a child may be developing a more precise understanding of a particular vocabulary concept.[2] For example, children might select the right answer on one of these tests because they know that the item tested, *bungalow,* is a type of shelter, but they don't know how it is different from *shack* or *shed.* A high performer's score on this type of test may overestimate the child's knowledge of vocabulary, while a low performer's score may underestimate it. One also needs to exercise caution in using vocabulary test results with children from diverse backgrounds. Because many of these tests are based on word frequency counts that reflect the vocabulary of middle- and upper-class students, the scores of lower-class students may not accurately represent their real vocabulary knowledge.[3]

The tests mentioned above by no means provide a comprehensive list of all vocabulary tests that are currently available to assess general vocabulary knowledge. For more complete information on available tests as well as specific descriptions of other information concerning individual tests, teachers should consult the latest edition of *Buros Mental Measurements Yearbook* and the actual tests themselves.

Using Context

Contextual analysis to determine word meanings is a skill that becomes important at about the third-grade reading level. Generally, below this level there are not many words students encounter in their reading that have unfamiliar meanings.

To assess a student's ability to use context clues to determine word meanings, the teacher should use words that the student does not already know. These words can be determined by presenting students with a list of eight or ten less frequently encountered vocabulary words from their instructional selections. The students are asked to write down meanings for any words they know (Task 1). Initially, the words can be presented in sentences with minimal context clues to determine if students know particular words even without the benefit of good context clues. Next, the teacher can present the same eight or ten words in sentences containing good context clues and ask the students to generate meanings for the words (Task 2). When students complete these tasks independently, the sentences should not contain words that would cause decoding problems. Alternately, the teacher or an aide could be on hand to assist students with decoding problems. For each student the teacher should come up with a score indicating the number of words defined correctly from context (Task 2) out of the total number of words not originally known (Task 1). An example of a student's performance on such an informal context test is presented in Figure 13.1.

It is important to score responses on this type of test leniently, since different meanings, based on context, may be possible. The goal of this test is to assess a student's ability to use context to determine word meanings and, consequently, all reasonable responses should be accepted. Consider, for example, the following sentence: Mrs. Jones forbids Tommy to go near the river because it is dangerous. For the word *forbids,* a response such as *does not want* would be reasonable even if it is not as accurate as a response such as *will not allow.*

A single informal context test containing eight or ten items does not provide a teacher with sufficient information concerning a student's ability to use context clues to determine word meanings. As mentioned in Chapter 6, a more reliable technique is to take a number of samples over time of a student's performance on a skill or strategy. After initial assessment, a teacher must judge whether or not a student's use of context analysis to determine word meanings indicates that special attention to this skill is needed. One way to help form this judgment is to compare a low-achieving reader's performance with that of average reading peers. However, it is important for the teacher to bear in mind that different words and different context sentences or texts were used with the low-achieving readers, thus making direct comparisons with better readers impossible.

A more naturalistic variation of this assessment procedure involves having students locate challenging vocabulary words in their reading selections. The teacher should first determine which words students already know. This can be done by asking students to provide meanings for words in sentences with minimal context clues. Then, the teacher directs students to locate the same words in the selection and to use context to generate approximate meanings for the words. Students should be encouraged to read the entire paragraph containing a target vocabulary word because context clues often are provided in neighboring sentences as well as in the sentence where the word occurs. By the way, it can be instructive if some of the contexts are not particularly helpful. One of the lessons that all readers need to learn is that strategies don't work in *every* situation. An example of this type of test is presented in Figure 13.2.

NOTE: Parts 1 and 2 should be on separate sheets of paper

✔ = word meaning known in Part 1.
✔✔ = correct word meaning given in Part 2 for word not known in Part 1.

PART 1 DIRECTIONS: Write as many definitions or synonyms as you know for the following underlined words:

✔ a. She complained of an <u>ache</u>. _____ *pain* _____

✔ b. The building was <u>ancient</u>. _____ *old* _____

    c. The <u>crystal</u> was on the shelf. _____

    d. I will <u>dye</u> the shirt. *to not be alive*

    e. The man wanted to express his <u>gratitude</u>. _____

    f. There was a <u>musket</u> in the closet. *animal like a weasel*

    g. John will <u>navigate</u>. _____

    h. The man <u>seized</u> a child in the crowd. _____

PART 2 DIRECTIONS: Give a meaning for each underlined word:

✔ a. Susie has a stomach <u>ache</u> after eating so much candy.
     _____ *pain* _____

✔ b. Tom said the church was <u>ancient</u> because it was built in 1683.
     _____ *old* _____

✔✔ c. Mrs. Jones's good <u>crystal</u> bowl shattered when it fell off the
     shelf. _____ *glass* _____

✔✔ d. The children had a pleasant time <u>dyeing</u> Easter eggs.
     _____ *coloring* _____

    e. When you get a present from someone, you should show your
     <u>gratitude</u> by sending them a thank-you note.
     _____ *happy* _____

✔✔ f. The pioneer shot the wolf with his <u>musket</u>. _____ *gun* _____

✔✔ g. The man <u>navigated</u> his boat across the Atlantic Ocean.
     _____ *sailed* _____

    h. The bank robber <u>seized</u> someone in the bank to be his hostage.
     _____ *shot* _____

Total number not known in Part 1 ___ *6* ___

Number correct in Part 2 out of number not known in Part 1 *4/6*

FIGURE 13.1. Student's Performance on an Informal Context Test

PART 1 DIRECTIONS: Write as many definitions or synonyms as you know for the following underlined words:

    a. She complained of an <u>ache</u>. _____

    b. The building was <u>ancient</u>. _____

    c. The <u>crystal</u> was on the shelf. _____

    d. I will <u>dye</u> the shirt. _____

    e. The man wanted to express his <u>gratitude</u>. _____

    f. There was a <u>musket</u> in the closet. _____

    g. John will <u>navigate</u>. _____

    h. The man <u>seized</u> a child in the crowd. _____

PART 2 DIRECTIONS: Locate each word on the page in your basal reader that is listed. Read the paragraph that the word is in. Then give a meaning for each of the following words.

    a. ache: page 92 _____

    b. ancient: page 95 _____

    c. crystal: page 97 _____

    d. dye: page 97 _____

    e. gratitude: page 101 _____

    f. musket: page 102 _____

    g. navigate: page 105 _____

    h. seize: page 107 _____

FIGURE 13.2. Informal Context Test Using the Students' Basal Reader

A third approach to assessing students' use of context clues involves a multiple-choice format. First, students are asked to provide meanings for eight or ten vocabulary words presented in sentences with minimal context clues. Then, students are presented with a set of eight or ten sentences, each one containing an underlined vocabulary word followed by three or four synonyms or brief definitions. The students' task is to use the context of the sentence to select that definition or heading that best fits the underlined word. Again, it is important to use vocabulary words from a student's basal reader or from material on the student's instructional level. An example of this type of test format is as follows:

Mrs. Jones's good *crystal* bowl shattered when it fell off the shelf. (*plastic, glass, wood*)

The multiple-choice approach to assessing the use of context has one advantage: the test is easier for students to complete because they do not have to generate responses in the second part of the test. The biggest disadvantage of this approach is its inability to approximate a natural reading situation in which students must generate their own meanings for unfamiliar words.

Using the Dictionary

Like contextual analysis, using the dictionary to locate appropriate definitions for unfamiliar words is a strategy that becomes important once students are reading challenging material with a lot of novel vocabulary (usually third-grade level and above). At this point in the curriculum, it becomes important to assess students' ability to use the dictionary.

To assess students' ability to locate appropriate dictionary definitions for specific vocabulary words, it is essential that unknown, unstudied words be presented in context.

One approach simply involves underlining or highlighting five to ten challenging words in a text. Students should locate the underlined words in the dictionary and select the definitions that best fit in the sentences. Examples are provided in Figure 13.3.

Another approach involves students locating five to ten words in a textbook, finding each of the words in the dictionary, and using the context of the textbook passage to select the most appropriate dictionary definition. An advantage of this approach is that it approximates what readers would do in a normal reading situation if they were really stumped. In either case it is important to use sentences or passages that do not present serious decoding difficulties. Passages should be from books that the students can handle (i.e., at their instructional levels) and someone (teacher, aide, or peer) should be present to assist with reading definitions in the dictionary.

As with skill in using context clues, the teacher initially will have to use professional judgment about the instructional needs of low-achieving readers when it comes to dictionary use. After instruction and practice in locating words in the dictionary and selecting appropriate definitions, improvements should be seen in students' performance on the type of informal test shown in Figure 13.4 and in their disposition to consult dictionaries in everyday reading.

FIGURE 13.3. Informal Test on Using the Dictionary to Determine Words' Meaning

DIRECTIONS: Look up each underlined word in the dictionary. Read all of the definitions and then write on your paper the definition that best fits the underlined word as it is used in these sentences.

1. John held the school <u>record</u> for the 100-yard dash.

   definition: _____

2. Sally was not able to <u>figure</u> out the answer to the math problem.

   definition: _____

3. Tom likes to read the sports <u>column</u> in the newspaper.

   definition: _____

4. Jane did not have a <u>solution</u> to her problem.

   definition: _____

5. Tina bought a beautiful <u>violet</u> dress.

   definition: _____

DIRECTIONS: Read each sentence below and write down what you think is the meaning of each word (which has one line under it) and each prefix (which has two lines under it).

1. Mr. Wilson took the <u>subway</u> to work instead of the bus because it was a lot quicker.

   subway _____

   sub _____

2. Temperatures in the sixties in August are <u>subnormal</u> for Texas.

   subnormal _____

   sub _____

3. The wizard <u>transformed</u> the frog into a beautiful princess.

   transformed _____

   trans _____

4. Ms. Smith was a <u>supervisor</u> who had twenty people working under her.

   supervisor _____

   super _____

5. Mr. and Mrs. Pertes took a <u>transatlantic</u> voyage from New York to London.

   transatlantic _____

   trans _____

6. They ship oil to the United States from the Middle East in <u>supertankers</u>.

   supertankers _____

   super _____

FIGURE 13.4. Informal Test of Students' Knowledge of Prefixes, Suffixes, or Roots

Using Structural Analysis

Students' use of structural analysis as an aid in determining word meanings should be assessed once it appears in the school curriculum generally at about the third- or fourth-grade level. Generally, students' knowledge of prefixes, suffixes, and roots is best assessed in context because affixes and roots seldom have a single meaning. One needs to know the context in which an affix or root occurs to determine the appropriate meanings of the element assessed.

The most transparent and straightforward task is to ask students to provide meanings for particular words and for each constituent prefix, suffix, or root as it was used in a particular context. Three or four examples of a particular affix or root should be included in a single test. Therefore, only a few affixes or roots should be tested at one time. An example of an informal structural analysis test is presented in Figure 13.4. This type of activity is often found in commercially available instructional materials.

The examples in Figure 13.4 use sentences that provide helpful context clues. When interpreting students' performance on this type of test, the teacher has to keep in mind that the test provides a measure of students' knowledge of specific affix or root meanings *plus* their ability to use context clues to generate word meanings.

These students are using the dictionary to select the best meaning for an unfamiliar word. *(Peter Vadnai)*

Because it is unimportant for students to memorize meanings for various prefixes, suffixes, or roots, drill and practice on structural elements is not necessary. It is more important that a student understand words containing these elements in informal structural analysis tests and during everyday reading experiences.

Interpreting Ambiguous Words

Teachers may want to assess students' ability to interpret secondary meanings (e.g. a *run* on the bank) and homographs (*wait* versus *weight*) once students have received corresponding instruction, or if they appear to be a frequent source of confusion. Informal tests of students' ability to interpret ambiguous words should include both words previously studied and words never seen before. In the first case, a teacher would be assessing students' knowledge of secondary meanings or meanings for homographs they had already studied. In the second case, a teacher would be assessing students' ability to use their general knowledge to help them interpret new meanings and new homographs.

To illustrate the latter point, if students have received instruction in some secondary meanings, they should have developed a set to anticipate word usage beyond the most common meanings. They should be ready to use context to help them generate approximate secondary meanings.

As with prefixes, suffixes, and roots, words demonstrating secondary meanings and homographs should not be presented in isolation. Instead, examples should be presented in context even though this approach will confound the assessment of students' ability to interpret ambiguous words with their ability to use context clues. However, this is not a serious problem since ambiguous words seldom occur in isolation. Furthermore, it is only through context that ambiguous words become unambiguous.

One approach to assessing students' knowledge of secondary meanings and homographs involves a constructed answer format. The students are presented with a set of eight or ten sentences containing underlined words that are either homographs or words with secondary meanings. The students' task is to generate meanings for the underlined words. Examples are provided below. In the blanks, students should write what they think each underlined word means.

1. Several old houses by the river <u>list</u> to one side and look like they're going to fall over. _____

2. The cowboys chased the wild horses across the <u>plain</u>. _____

Another approach to assessing students' ability to interpret ambiguous words involves a multiple-choice format. Instead of generating responses, as in the above examples, students are asked to select from among three or four choices the most appropriate definitions or meanings for the underlined terms. Examples of this format are provided below.

1. Several old houses by the river <u>list</u> to one side and look like they're going to fall over. (*a series, leans*) _____

2. The cowboys chased the wild horses across the <u>plain</u>. (*flat stretch of land, not fancy*) _____

ASSESSING STUDENTS' LEARNING OF SPECIFIC WORDS

To assess students' ability to provide synonyms or definitions for specific vocabulary words that have been studied, it is best to use a multiple-choice format. This is because using a constructed response format, in which students are asked to generate meanings for isolated words, is a difficult and unnatural task. Students will seldom need to provide synonyms or definitions for words in isolation, except on vocabulary tests.

Because words do not normally appear in isolation, even multiple-choice tests should present vocabulary words in sentences. To separate word knowledge from the ability to use context clues, the test sentences should provide minimal context clues. An example is provided below.

Kristie was *furious* when she knew what had happened.

    a. happy   c. sad

    b. angry   d. disappointed

In this example, all of the responses would make sense in the context of the sentence. The student has to know the meaning of *furious* to come up with the correct synonym for the word. However, selecting the appropriate synonym in the above example is easier than defining the word in isolation because of all the information provided by the item; the sentence implies that *furious* is an emotional response.

DIRECTIONS: Use the words at the bottom of the page to fill in the blanks in the sentences below.

1. Mr. Wilson was _____ when he found out that rabbits had eaten all of the lettuce in his garden.

2. A yellow flashing light means to go through the intersection with

   _____.

3. The dog was _____ when it quit running.

4. He _____ a dime from his mother's purse.

5. I did not _____ that you were trying to tell me it was time to go home.

6. Jerry _____ his old car that quit running by the side of the road and started to walk into town.

7. A diamond is a _____ gem.

8. The cat was _____ the mouse.

abandoned	panting	furious	realize
filched	caution	precious	stalking

Figure 13.5. Informal Word Meanings Test

An alternative approach to assessing students' knowledge of specific words involves a fill-in-the-blank format. Students are given approximately ten sentences in which a missing vocabulary word is indicated by a blank. The ten missing vocabulary words could be listed at the bottom of the page. The students' task would be to write the vocabulary words in the appropriate blanks. To do this, the students would have to know the meanings of the missing words. An example of this type of test is presented in Figure 13.5. As Figure 13.5 shows, it is important for the sentences to provide contexts that are sufficiently rich to enable students to discriminate among choices in the list.

Progress can be determined by keeping individual records of the students' performance over time.

ASSESSING INTEREST IN UNFAMILIAR WORDS

In addition to assessing students' abilities in specific vocabulary skills, such as using context clues or finding appropriate definitions in the dictionary, it is important to keep records that document changes in students' interest in words. One way to do this is through individual progress charts indicating the number of unfamiliar words collected by students every week or two from their independent reading. These charts should show increases if students have been paying more attention to unfamiliar words during independent reading. This same technique can be used to track the number of unfamiliar words brought in by students from sources outside of school. Again, one- or two-week recording intervals could be used. Charts such as this should be shared with parents in addition to information from formal and informal tests of vocabulary.

COMPLETING THE READING DIFFICULTIES SUMMARY SHEET

In this chapter we have discussed a number of ways to assess students' ability to determine meanings for unfamiliar words they encounter in their reading as well as their knowledge of specific vocabulary words that have been studied. Again, evaluation of the data depends heavily upon the teacher for interpretation. The remainder of this chapter helps the teacher with the task of data interpretation by considering Billy Stone's performance in vocabulary.

Figure 13.6 shows that Billy is performing with 59 percent accuracy on tests assessing his ability to use context clues. The teacher believes that instruction in this area is needed.

Billy is performing with 70 percent accuracy on tests assessing his ability to use the dictionary to determine word meanings. Because he is performing reasonably well and doing better at this skill than at using context clues, the teacher believes dictionary instruction is not a high priority at this time.

The teacher has not assessed Billy's skill in structural analysis (knowledge of affixes or roots) and secondary meanings or homographs. The teacher does not feel these are important to assess at this time because Billy is only reading on a beginning third-grade level and has not been encountering many words with affixes and secondary meanings, or homographs.

In terms of learning specific words, Billy is performing with about 60 percent accuracy on vocabulary tests. The teacher believes that Billy needs to spend more time coming to terms with the meanings of new words. She has decided to emphasize semantic mapping (see Chapter 12) in order to help Billy learn how to relate words to other words similar in meaning and function in our language.

As was pointed out in earlier chapters, all of the recommendations made for Billy Stone will be considered in Chapter 16.

SUMMARY

In this chapter, we discussed the assessment of vocabulary skills that students can use to determine word meanings when reading independently. It also discussed assessment of students' learning of specific word meanings and the use of the Reading Difficulties Record Sheet to plan for vocabulary instruction to help individual students.

Suggested Activities

1. Prepare an appropriate informal context test (as described in the chapter and illustrated in Figure 13.1). Have a student complete the test if possible and then score the test. As an alternative, your instructor may be able to provide you with several informal context tests completed by one student. Your task would be to score these tests and complete section IV.B of Figure 13.6.

2. Locate appropriate material and have a student select the best dictionary definition for relatively unfamiliar words you located in the material. As an alternative, your instructor may be able to provide you with several infor-

IV. Vocabulary

   A. General knowledge (from formal test)

   B. Using context

      10/6   4/6 (Number of words defined correctly out of number not known)
      10/13 3/5
      10/20 4/6
      10/27 2/5

      Comments:
      11/2   13/22 correct. Performing with 59% accuracy. Could use instruction in using context clues (when time allows).

   C. Using the dictionary

      10/6   7/10 (number correct)
      10/13 8/10
      10/20 7/10
      10/27 6/10

      Comments:
      11/2   28/49 correct. Performing with 70% accuracy. Not as high a priority for instruction as using context to determine word meanings.

   D. Structural analysis

      Comments
      11/2   Not assessed at this time.

   E. Secondary meanings/homographs

      Comments
      11/2   Not assessed at this time.

   F. Learning of specific words

      10/6   5/10   (fill-in-the-blank format)
      10/13 7/10
      10/20 6/10
      10/27 6/10

      Comments
      11/2   24/40 correct. Performing with 60% accuracy. Would benefit from more time spent on unfamiliar vocabulary words. Try to do more with semantic mapping.

   G. Interest in unfamiliar words

      Comments:
      11/2   Has added only five new words to his progress chart since 10/1. Let him illustrate new words he locates since he likes to draw.

FIGURE 13.6. Reading Difficulties Record Sheet: Vocabulary

mal dictionary tests (such as the one described above) that were completed by one student. Your task would be to score those tests and complete section IV.C of Figure 13.6.

Suggested Reading

BECK, I., and MCKEOWN, M. (1991). Conditions of vocabulary acquisition. In R. Barr, M. Kamil, P. Mosenthal, and P. D. Pearson (Eds.), *Handbook of reading research*, Vol. II. (pp. 789-814). New York: Longman.
Beck and McKeown discuss effective approaches to vocabulary assessment as well as instruction.

Notes

1. See Anderson and Freebody (1981).
2. See Stallman (1991).
3. See Bruce, Rubin, Starr, and Liebling (1984).

PART THREE

Traditional Approaches to Assessment of Reading Difficulties

In the previous parts of this book an approach to supplemental reading instruction and assessment was taken that emphasizes the close relationship that should exist between instruction and assessment. The classroom teacher is in an excellent position to determine how a child is responding to a lesson through observation and other informal means of assessment. This close connection between instruction and assessment is not characteristic of many traditional remedial programs, which begin with testing as the primary form of assessment and then follow with instruction that is aimed at overcoming the difficulties identified by the tests. Progress in such a program is often evaluated by the use of another test. This test-teach-test pattern relies much more heavily on formal measures of reading than seems appropriate. Of course, traditional approaches to assessment are not all bad, nor are they likely to disappear anytime soon. The third part of this book, in order to provide some balance and a basis for making comparisons, will look closely at assessment principles as well as at the tests that have been so prominent in traditional remedial reading programs.

Assessment Principles
Applied to Reading

Overview

As you read this chapter use the following list of main ideas to guide your understanding and reflection.

- Tests and testing can easily assume an importance in the lives of unsuccessful readers that is undeserved and even harmful.
- Test scores gain meaning when they are placed in context in one of several ways: specifying the content of the test, comparing scores on one test with other scores, or by comparing test scores with everyday performance.
- Teachers have a responsibility to provide parents with information that helps them understand the nature and content of a test their child has taken, the purpose for giving the test, and the ways to interpret a particular score.
- Norms indicate how pupils *have done* on a test, not how they *should do.*
- The primary purpose for all assessment in reading is decisionmaking.
- To be useful in educational decisionmaking, tests must be reliable and valid.
- A test that is valid for one purpose may not be valid for another.
- A reading test must match a teacher's notions of what is important in the reading process to be valid for her purposes.
- Low-achieving readers may perform below their potential on reading tests because of poor test-taking abilities and because norm-referenced tests are geared to the average pupil.
- Reading tests may fail to reveal what children have gained from instruction because program objectives do not match well with what the tests measure.

Gloria Sanchez and Audrea Berg walked to the corner bus stop in front of Thomas Jefferson Elementary School in brooding silence. Not until they had boarded a crowded bus and worked their way to standing positions near the rear exit doors did either woman speak. Finally Audrea asked her companion with some hesitation, "Did Renaldo's teacher have good things to say in your conference, Gloria?"

"It was better than I expected, Audrea. How did your conference with Joey's teacher go?" Gloria responded.

And with this tentative beginning the conversation rapidly gained momentum. Both mothers had been dreading the first parent-teacher conference of the year and appreciated the chance to share their thoughts, questions, and concerns with each other. As the bus turned at the final intersection before entering the block where their row houses stood side-by-side, Gloria volunteered the information they had both been avoiding.

"Renaldo got a 63 on his reading test," she said.

Mrs. Berg turned to face her friend with a warm smile saying, "Why, that's not so bad, Gloria. Joey got a 70. I think they must both be doing well in reading."

"I'm not so sure," Mrs. Sanchez moaned. "Sixty-three sounds like a low score to me. It sure isn't as good as a 70."

Mrs. Berg suggested they continue their discussion over a cup of coffee. Between sips the two concerned mothers began to wonder out loud just what the scores they had been told really meant.

This conversation is probably not at all uncommon. Many parents, and indeed many teachers and administrators, are not sure about some basic measurement principles. What does a test score of 63 mean? What other information is needed in order to judge it as a good or a bad score? How should Renaldo's score affect his teacher's plan for helping him progress in reading? This chapter identifies and explores some fundamental issues that bear on these and related issues. For those readers who have had a course in educational measurement, this chapter will serve as a review. For others this chapter will only introduce topics that require further study.

The fact that reading in general and remedial reading in particular are closely linked in the minds of many people with tests and test interpretation presents a genuine dilemma. Although the heavy use of formal tests is not recommended, remedial programs are often driven by them. Tests are used to identify low-achieving readers, their needs and weaknesses, and the progress that results from their remedial instruction. Tests are even used to evaluate the overall effectiveness of remedial programs.

In view of all this, it seems prudent to deal with testing in this and the following chapter if only to put the topic in perspective. Consequently, this chapter lays the groundwork by (1) dealing with the nature of test interpretation, (2) reviewing some fundamental principles of educational measurement, and (3) giving an overview of the various types of reading tests. The following chapter will then provide an introduction to specific tests that are illustrative of those likely to be used in schools.

WHAT'S IN A SCORE?

For some reason Mrs. Sanchez believed that Renaldo's score of 63 was not very good. But why? In isolation the number 63 has virtually no meaning. It represents a quantity, but without some context, some frame of reference, it cannot be interpreted. Mrs. Sanchez was apparently making some assumption that caused her to believe that 63 was a poor score. She may have assumed the num-

Parents can easily see how well their children perform certain physical skills but need help from teachers in knowing how to interpret test scores. *(Peter Vadnai)*

ber represented a percent, for example. In this case, her previous experience with schools and teachers may have led her to assume that 95 to 100 percent earns an A or excellent, 85 to 94 percent earns a B or good, and so forth. Within this system a score of 63 would probably receive an F or fail.

There are some obvious difficulties with an absolute system of this sort, the most serious being that no allowance is made for the fallibility of the test or the test maker. Let us suppose that 63 did represent a percent. Was Mrs. Sanchez right to think the score was poor? Not unless or until she has several other pieces of information can she deduce that. She needs to know, for example, how much progress a score of 63 percent represents for Renaldo. It may be that over the past three weeks he has doubled or tripled his performance on whatever the test measures. A single score can take on a different meaning if viewed in this context.

She might also consider what the test includes. Suppose Renaldo got 63 percent of the items right on the vocabulary test. This score takes on one complexion if the words were simple, high-frequency words from a basal reader and quite another complexion if they were technical terms taken from a science book. Also the fact that Renaldo is in second grade rather than seventh grade makes a percentage score of 63 on a basal reader test less alarming.

Let us try a different assumption about the 63 being a percentage score and consider it as a raw score. Typically this would mean Renaldo got 63 items correct (though it might mean he got even more items than that right but had his score reduced by some factor intended to correct for guessing, such as the number of items answered incorrectly). Is a raw score of 63 poor, as Mrs. Sanchez seemed to think? Suppose the test only included 64 items? In that case, Renaldo got all but one item correct. One could not do much better. But even here the issues raised earlier apply. The content of the test might be such that a perfect score is expected (for example, circling the letters of the alphabet when they are called by the teacher is a task a second grader should perform with close to 100 percent accuracy). It would also be helpful to know how much progress a raw score of 63 represents for Renaldo on the content of this particular test.

Whether 63 is a percentage or a raw score, another kind of information is still required in order to more completely interpret Renaldo's performance. We typically want to know how other pupils did on the same test. Even though the meaning of a score can be established through self-comparisons and progress toward a criterion, comparisons with other pupils can also provide useful information. Criterion-referenced testing will be examined in a moment, but first consider comparisons among pupils.

COMPARISONS TO OTHER PUPILS

Let us return to the Sanchez-Berg conversation. Suppose Mrs. Berg also reported that other scores on the test ranged from a high of 78 to a low of 40. With this information, Mrs. Sanchez would realize that Renaldo is much closer to the top than to the bottom of the group. This would seem to be good performance, yet her response might still be sympathetic if she thought Renaldo should be at the top. In any case, knowledge of the range of scores gives useful information insofar as interpreting a score.

Another piece of information parents often need is knowledge concerning the average score. There are several measures of central tendency including the mode (score achieved most frequently by the students), the median (score that has half the group above and half below), and the mean (the arithmetic average). If Mrs. Berg said the average score was 55, Mrs. Sanchez would realize that Renaldo's score is some distance above the average. This information helps in interpreting an individual student's performance on a test.

Most parents are probably sufficiently informed to judge the merit of their child's score given the top and bottom score in the class, and the mean (average) score. Some will realize that to interpret more completely the meaning of a score, it is also critical to know the spread or variability of the test scores. To illustrate, if the scores of Renaldo's classmates are tightly grouped around the mean of 55, his score of 63 is more extraordinary than if they are spread evenly from top to bottom. The statistic needed to know how much spread exists in the scores is the *standard deviation*. Without going into unnecessary detail, suffice it to say that the standard deviation is an index of how much scores vary on the average from the mean. A standard deviation of ±5 would indicate greater spread around the mean than ± 2, for example. If Renaldo's score of 63 was achieved on a test where the mean score was 55 and the standard deviation ±2, he would be among the top 1 percent of pupils taking the test. A larger standard deviation would indicate that scores are scattered further from the mean and that Renaldo's score is not quite so exceptional. The normal curve diagram in Figure 14.1 shows what percentage of a population usually falls within one and two standard deviations of the mean.

If Renaldo's teacher had given Mrs. Sanchez a more complete picture of his test score, the conversation at the beginning of this chapter might have sounded something like this.

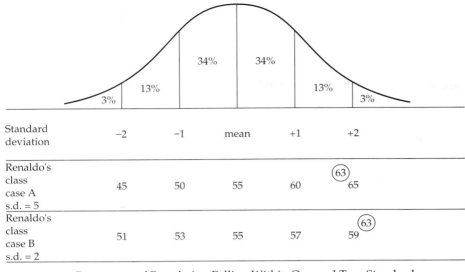

Standard deviation	−2	−1	mean	+1	+2
Renaldo's class case A s.d. = 5	45	50	55	60	⑥③ 65
Renaldo's class case B s.d. = 2	51	53	55	57	⑥③ 59

FIGURE 14.1. Percentage of Population Falling Within One and Two Standard Deviations of the Mean

"Renaldo's teacher told me he got a score of 63 in a published survey test the children at Thomas Jefferson always take in the fall of the year," Mrs. Sanchez reported. "The test has a vocabulary section and a paragraph comprehension section. Renaldo's class had an average score of 55. The standard deviation was ±5, and the range of scores was from 40 to 78. The teacher said the same test will be given again in the spring so we can see what progress Renaldo has made. Meanwhile she will use the test results to help her form reading groups."

With the above information, Mrs. Sanchez is in a much better position to understand and, therefore, support what the teacher is doing. The teacher has shown professional competence by providing adequate information to the parent concerning the type of test given, the purpose for giving the test, how the class did as a whole, how Renaldo did in particular, and what use will be made of the results in the future. There is a great deal more the teacher might have shared, information on test reliability and validity, for example, and how the class compared to national norms, but these facts are more important for the teacher and principal than for parents.

Now, to carry the scenario one step further, suppose that Audrea Berg listened to Gloria Sanchez's report with growing interest.

"That's fascinating," Audrea states. "Joey's class took the same test and his teacher gave me entirely different figures for her group. The class average was 61, the standard deviation was ±7, and the range was 45 to 91. Joey's class did better overall than Renaldo's, but I wonder which group is the most typical? Is Joey's class really high or is Renaldo's really low?" These are appropriate questions to ask if one really wants to make comparisons.

Whether appropriate or not, the American obsession with comparisons is a fact of life, and test publishers respond by supplying various types of norms. The following section looks more closely at norms and what they mean.

NORMS FOR COMPARING TEST PERFORMANCE

Test norms are nothing more than a summary of the scores achieved by a large group of pupils with known characteristics. They are in a real sense averages that permit comparisons. It is common for tests that are sold to a national market to have national norms, though state and local norms are often more useful and revealing depending on one's purposes. In any case, norms should not be confused with standards to be achieved. Norms indicate how pupils have done on a test, not how they should do. Four types of norms will be examined here: percentile rank, grade equivalents, standard scores, and stanines.

Percentile Rank Norms

How percentile rank norms work can be illustrated by looking at the score Renaldo achieved on his reading test. Renaldo's raw score of 63 on the test falls at the ninetieth percentile, meaning it is better than 90 percent of the second graders who took the test when it was being normed. Joey's score of 70 falls at the ninety-eighth percentile, meaning only 2 percent of the second graders taking the test did better when it was normed. By using the norms in the test manual, Renaldo's and Joey's teachers can translate the scores of all their students into percentile ranks, thereby enabling anyone who is interested to see how a score compares to those of other pupils. To answer Mrs. Berg's question about how the second-grade classrooms at Thomas Jefferson compare to typical schools, the teachers should consult the test manual for specific norms that permit school comparisons.

Percentile ranks are straightforward and relatively easy to understand, but they can still be misinterpreted. Most parents can understand that percentile ranks simply indicate what percentage of pupils in a particular group scored lower on a test than their child. Nevertheless, we should point out that national norms are sometimes inappropriate for judging a pupil's achievement because pupils included in the national pool come from a broad range of environments. Although this broad range is necessary for norms to be truly representative of all segments of the population, it may be more useful to know how pupils at Thomas Jefferson compare with other inner-city schools. In this case, special norms would be necessary.

Another limitation of percentile ranks is that units on percentile scales are not equal due to the preponderance of scores near the mean and the sparsity of scores at the extremes. (See Fig. 14.1.) As a result, percentile ranks are not very useful when it comes to assessing growth. Moving ten percentile points, from the sixtieth to the seventieth percentile, for example, represents a much smaller variation in raw score achievement than moving from the tenth to the twentieth percentile. Another concept that some have difficulty accepting is that a child who maintains his rank over time is making normal growth. A similar problem, which is also a reflection of human nature, is that most people believe that they (or their children) are better than average. (Garrison Keillor plays on this belief in describing the mythical town of Lake Wobegon as a place where "All the women are strong, all the men good-looking, and all the children are above average.") As a consequence, most people expect to be somewhere above the fiftieth percentile. Although half the population must fall below average on any variable, this fact seems easy to forget when scores are being translated using a table of norms.

Grade Equivalents

Another type of norm that is not as straightforward as percentile ranks is grade norms (sometimes called grade equivalents). Suppose Mrs. Sanchez told her friend Audrea that Renaldo scored at the third-grade level on the reading test. What does that mean? Should Renaldo be promoted to third grade immediately? Does this mean he should be reading a third-grade book even though he is in the second grade? To answer these questions, consider how a raw score of 63 gets translated into a grade equivalent of 3.6 (read third grade, sixth month).

Just as with percentile ranks, grade norms are determined by summarizing the test results achieved by the norming population. The scores of second-grade children are analyzed and some score, say 53, is found to be the mean. This raw score is then set equal to 2.0. The performance of third graders is examined and the average score found to be 60. This score is set equal to 3.0 and on it goes. The difference between a raw score of 53 and 60 is spread evenly (interpolated) across the interval 2.0 to 3.0 so that a raw score of 56 is equated to 2.5, 58 is equated to 2.7, and so forth.

Renaldo's score of 63 is somewhat higher than the average score of the third graders, so his grade equivalent equals 3.6. What can be said is that on this particular test Renaldo did slightly better than the average third grader. That is all it means.

Grade equivalents have been criticized by professional organizations such as the International Reading Association and American Educational Research Association because of their susceptibility to misinterpretation. There is no universal agreement regarding what constitutes second, third, or any other grade-level achievement in reading, so to report a pupil's test score according to grade level may *falsely* suggest that she should be placed in that grade for reading instruction. This mistaken notion ignores the fact that a given test inevitably ignores many other aspects of reading a typical third grader can perform. Furthermore, the grade-level equivalents reported for standardized tests do not match well with the difficulty levels of various reading material. Yet the temptation is strong to conclude that the reading level achieved on a given test is a good indication of which book(s) a child can or should read. It is probable that reading tests often overstate the level at which a child can read for daily instruction.

Finally, critics of reading instruction frequently build their case on the fact that a larger percentage of pupils read *below* grade level. Since the mean score is set equal to the grade in which pupils are enrolled, half the children *should* be below grade level. This is merely another example of the point made earlier that half of any group is below average—a simple fact of life that makes Keillor's Lake Wobegon statement humorous in a wry sort of way. These and other misunderstandings regarding the meaning of grade norms make them potentially harmful. Their use should be avoided altogether.

Standard Scores

A third type of norm is the standard score. This calculation involves translating raw scores into a regularized scale. One scale sets the mean equal to 50 and the standard deviation equal to 10. IQ scores are commonly reported as standard scores on a scale having 100 as the mean and 15 as the standard deviation. Other scales are also commonly used. In all cases the raw score is converted by subtracting the mean of the standard scale from the raw score and dividing by the standard deviation. Any basic educational measurement book will describe the steps involved.

The advantage of standard scores is that the results of several tests can be compared, even added and averaged. This is not acceptable with raw scores unless they have been converted to standard scores because differences in the variability of the several score distributions can easily distort the relative importance of each test. With some help parents can learn to interpret standard scores as evidenced by the general understanding that seems to exist for IQ and SAT scores. We recommend that the results of teacher-made tests be translated into standard scores for the sake of clarity and uniformity.

Stanines

A fourth type of norm that receives less attention than it deserves is the stanine, which is actually a variation on percentiles that breaks the full range of scores into nine groups as follows:

Stanine	Percentile Range	Group
9	96–100	Superior
8	89–96	Above average
7	77–89	Above average
6	60–77	Average
5	40–60	Average
4	23–40	Average
3	11–23	Below average
2	4–11	Below average
1	0–4	Far below average

Stanines are particularly useful in reporting a pupil's relative score because the false precision conveyed by a percentile rank is softened somewhat. Allowances for error due to measurement are made with stanines by grouping scores together that are probably not reliably different. Children near the upper or lower cutoff points for any given stanine are still treated inappropriately perhaps, but this limitation justifies the risk involved when the advantages of stanines over straight percentile ranks are considered. Stanines prevent us from making mountains out of mole hills by overinterpreting differences in raw scores. Renaldo's test score falls into the eighth stanine, whereas Joey's is in the ninth stanine. Mrs. Sanchez's intuitive feeling that 63 is significantly lower than 70 on the test is supported, but the difference between stanines 9 and 8 doesn't sound as great as 70 versus 63.

CRITERION-REFERENCED MEASURES

323

CHAPTER 14
Assessment
Principles Applied
to Reading

Earlier we suggested that performance on a reading test can be judged in a way that is not dependent upon comparisons among pupils. Knowing the letters of the alphabet was used as an example, an important bit of knowledge that all literate people must master sooner or later. In this case, accomplishing the learning objective is the critical issue, not whether a student masters a skill at the same time it is mastered by other pupils.

To illustrate, suppose that Joey scores at the ninety-eighth percentile on knowledge of the letters of the alphabet. He is clearly near the top of the group. Yet it is still possible that no one in the group knows the entire alphabet. Relative to his peers Joey is superior, but against the objective he is still inadequate. If the average reader only knows thirteen of the twenty-six letters, this becomes the fiftieth percentile. Joey may know twenty-one of twenty-six letters, making him well above average, but he still falls short of complete mastery (often called competence).

Over the past 15 to 20 years there has been a concern for accountability in education. The public mood has demanded that clear-cut objectives for instruction be established and pupil mastery of those objectives be monitored. In this atmosphere criterion-referenced testing (CRT) flourished. Some publishers and consulting firms even got into the business of performance contracting with school districts, an arrangement whereby the firms received payment for instruction they contracted to deliver, but only if a certain percentage of pupils mastered a set of targeted learning objectives as measured by criterion-referenced tests.[1] Although performance contracting seems to have gone the way of most educational panaceas, criterion-referenced tests and mastery of discrete skills are still very much in evidence today. Various skills management programs are available either as part of a basal reading program or as a separate system that is compatible with nearly any set of instructional materials. The next chapter will look closely at such a system. Here it is important to say that the actual items on a norm-referenced test are virtually indistinguishable from those on a CRT. How the items are packaged to form a test is somewhat different (that is, norm-referenced tests include items on a wide range of skills, whereas CRTs usually have many items on one specific skill), and how they are interpreted is markedly different.

Like most parents, Mrs. Sanchez and Mrs. Berg probably do not know the difference between norm-referenced and criterion-referenced tests. Consequently it becomes the teacher's job to clarify for parents what type of test was used and how to correctly interpret the score according to either norms or performance criteria. Any test that claims to be both norm-referenced and criterion-referenced is likely to have serious flaws since the underlying purpose of the two tests is markedly different. Norm-referenced tests must spread pupils over a wide range of scores and do so by including items that are intentionally difficult (no one should get a perfect score). Criterion-referenced tests have no such purpose and therefore include only items that pupils should be able to answer correctly if they have mastered the concept or skill being tested.

More will be said about CRTs later when different types of tests are described. Here the point should be made that interpretation of test results is an important and necessary task for the teacher. Interpretation is normally accomplished by referring to how others in a class, school, or norming group did on the same test, or by comparing performance to a performance criterion. A frame of reference makes interpretation possible and renders a score meaningful. Without interpretation, without some use of the results, the act of measuring reading performance is meaningless and unwarranted.

WHY GIVE TESTS ANYWAY?

It seems reasonable to assume that as Mrs. Sanchez and Mrs. Berg sat drinking coffee, their conversation might eventually have touched on why their sons took a reading test at all. Renaldo's teacher gave an answer of sorts when she indicated that fall and spring performance on the same test would be used as a measure of reading progress. But why is a measure of progress necessary? Although there could be a number of answers to that question, a central thread running throughout all of them relates to *instructional decisionmaking*. On the basis of measured progress the instructional program might be revised, Renaldo might be placed in a particular group, or the teacher might be encouraged to participate in an inservice program. Decisions will (must) be made about these and dozens of other matters that affect the instruction of Renaldo and Joey. To the extent that such decisions can be based on reliable, valid information, the decisions are likely to be defensible. To the extent that decisions are made on the basis of whim, folklore, or bias, they are likely to be indefensible.

Of course, reading performance can be measured in a number of ways. The most convenient and obvious way is to give a paper-and-pencil test. Another way is to have a pupil read orally from a graded textbook or a tradebook. Or teachers can simply observe how students respond to questions about the reading material. Or teachers could avail themselves of what is undoubtedly the most popular of current approaches to literacy assessment and begin to maintain a portfolio of key literacy activities for each student in their classrooms. Even flash cards can be used as a way of assessing one aspect of reading ability. Although these examples only scratch the surface, they serve to illustrate the vast number of ways in which teachers can assess a pupil's reading ability.

It might be useful at this point to distinguish between two terms used in the preceding paragraph. Thus far the terms *measure* and *assess* have been used to describe the act of gathering information about a pupil's performance. The two terms have similar though not identical meanings. Measurement involves "a comparison of something with a known standard . . . and often involves . . . assigning numbers to represent some property or characteristic."[2] For example, measurement is often done with a ruler or a scale (for example, a thermometer), the result being a number of some sort. In reading, performance is usually measured with a test. Assessment like measurement involves gathering data, but it is a broader term not so closely associated with quantification and the use of a known standard. Assessment includes testing as well as observation and interviewing conducted for the purpose of identifying strengths and weaknesses.[3]

This leads us to a crucial point about "measuring" reading performance. Even the slickest, most sophisticated-looking test is nothing more than a way of sampling reading behaviors. It may seem to be precise in the same way that measuring distance with a ruler is precise, but in reality paper-and-pencil tests are subject to the same limitations as are informal measures such as teacher observation. The danger is that test results are often used in a way that overestimates their accuracy and assigns them greater credibility than they deserve. Much as young children tend to believe anything they read in a book, adults seem prone to believe anything they get from a test. If tests can be demystified, their results will be used more wisely and more effectively.

SOME BASIC MEASUREMENT PRINCIPLES

The more confidence people have in the accuracy of the samples of reading behavior that are gathered, the more faith they can have in generalizations based on those samples. Earlier the concepts of reliability and validity were introduced but not discussed in any detail. It is now time for that discussion.

Test Reliability

The reliability of a test refers to the consistency of its results. In other words, a reliable test is one that is not subject to variation because of factors that are uncontrolled or unaccounted for. Whenever a test is given one hopes to get a true picture of how much a person knows or how well he can perform in some domain. Ideally the test will be 100 percent accurate, which means the results will not be subject to any error. In other words, the only test items Renaldo will get right are those he has the knowledge or skill to answer and the only ones he will get wrong are those he does not have the knowledge or skill to answer. The name given by measurement experts to this unsullied score is the true score (X_t). There is no direct way available to determine how a person's observed score (X_o) compares to his true score. If the test is subject to errors (X_e) that are unrelated to what the test is supposed to be measuring, the observed score could be quite different from the true score. The true score is found by subtracting measurement error from the observed score $(X_t = X_o - X_e)$. To have some idea of how much confidence one can have in the observed score, the notion of reliability is introduced. Using a procedure that will be described shortly, an estimate of measurement error is made. If reliability is high, measurement errors are minimal and the observed score is thought to be a close (good) estimate of the true score. If reliability is low, measurement errors are frequent and the observed score could be far from the true score. This seems simple enough if one knows how reliable the test is. But how is reliability determined?

Reliability coefficients look like correlation coefficients. A correlation coefficient shows what relationship exists between two sets of scores. A perfect relationship (that is, the same person had the highest rank score on each test, and so on down the line) is represented by a coefficient of ±1.0. (A perfect negative relationship is shown by a coefficient of −1.0. In this case the highest score on one test is paired with the lowest score on the other test, and so forth.) No relationship between scores yields a correlation coefficient of 0. Most reliability coefficients for standardized tests are in the range of +.6 to +.9, suggesting a positive, but imperfect, relationship between two sets of test scores.

Estimates of reliability are obtained by computing correlation coefficients based on the manipulation of test scores. Three approaches are often taken by the publisher or author. The test can be taken twice (with little or no time lapse between administrations to avoid the effects of additional learning). This is usually depicted as A_1 and A_2 (administration one and administration two) and is called *test-retest reliability*. The reason the test is taken twice is to see what agreement there is between the two set of scores. If agreement is high (that is, results are consistent) the observed scores are thought to be a close estimate of the true score. This means error due to measurement is minimal and greater confidence can be placed in scores obtained from the test.

A second approach involves using alternate forms of a test (assuming they exist) and is depicted as A and B (two forms). This is called *alternate forms reliability*.

The third approach to determining test reliability is to give the test only once but to treat half the items as test one and half the items as test two (often performance on odd-numbered items is compared to performance on even-numbered items). This approach is depicted as $\frac{1}{2}A$ and $\frac{1}{2}A$ and is called *split-half reliability*. Thus reliability can be calculated in three ways:

1. $A_1 - A_2$ (test-retest)
2. $A - B$ (alternate forms)
3. $\frac{1}{2}A - \frac{1}{2}A$ (split-half)

It should be clear that each approach has certain limitations insofar as estimating the amount of error is concerned. From a theoretical standpoint the test maker's goal is to eliminate measurement error. Any difference between the scores of two individuals on a test should reflect differences in the knowledge or skill being measured. If the test itself introduces variation in scores because of uncontrolled factors, this reduces the reliability of the results. In other words, such errors make it more difficult to determine how well the pupil knows what is being tested.

What can make a test unreliable? If guessing is not eliminated or at least minimized, it introduces a variable that affects reliability. If only a few behaviors are sampled, performance can be affected because the domain being tested is not covered systematically. If a test is so long it causes fatigue, reliability can be reduced. The discussion could go on indefinitely because dozens of factors can come into play.

Unless a test is fairly reliable it makes little sense to use it. If the results are subject to considerable measurement error, one cannot have much faith in their accuracy. If scores are not accurate, why use them? Any decision made using the results of an unreliable test could be made just as well by flipping a coin or drawing straws.

What level of reliability can be demanded of published standardized tests? Any test having reliability estimates below +.70 accounts for less of the variance (49 percent)[4] in scores than uncontrolled factors such as student motivation and guessing. It would seem a good rule of thumb to expect published tests to at least exceed this level. It should also be remembered that reliability coefficients are calculated in various ways. Split-half reliability coefficients are typically higher, as they should be considering the way they estimate errors (that is, one administration of the test only).

Having said all of the above, it should be pointed out that some reading tests do not report any kind of reliability coefficient. When this occurs one's suspicions should rise. These questions should be asked: Why has this fundamental step not been taken? Is another test available for which reliability estimates have been determined? Will it serve the user's needs just as well? Most reputable publishers and test authors take pains to develop a reliable test and readily share the appropriate information with the test user. In most cases reliability coefficients in the +.80 to +.95 range for the overall test will be found. Subtests typically have lower reliabilities than the total test because they have fewer items. This simply tells the users not to place much faith in the separate parts of the test but to use the total score for their decisionmaking.

Test Validity

Reliability is a necessary condition for using a test. However, test reliability alone is not sufficient. A test must also be valid, which means the test is capable of achieving certain aims. At a basic level, validity is concerned with whether a test measures what it claims to measure. This means, for example, that a test of intelligence should not measure some other ability such as reading. Many tests fail to meet this fundamental criterion—they measure something other than what they claim to measure. For example, a readiness test may measure the child's ability to follow directions more than it measures ability to discriminate among letters of the alphabet, or a spelling test may measure ability to recognize incorrect spellings more than it measures ability to write words correctly. These tests are not valid for their intended purposes.

Beyond this basic issue, the determination of a test's validity becomes increasingly complex. This is because a test that is perfectly suited to one aim—valid for one purpose—may be quite unsuited to another aim. No test publisher can be expected to anticipate the many uses to which a test may be put; consequently, the user must determine this aspect of validity. Too often the user incorrectly concludes that a published test must be valid or it would not be popular. It should be remembered, though, that the way some people use a test may be perfectly valid, and the way others use it quite invalid. A dramatic example of a mismatch between intention and use would involve using a typing test as a way of hiring teachers. Using this approach, better typists would get hired as teachers, although typing clearly is not a valid index of teaching ability. Yet a typing test would be quite appropriate for hiring secretaries (provided that is an important duty for secretaries to perform). Again, a test that is valid for one purpose is not necessarily valid for other purposes.

A classroom illustration: Suppose Mrs. James uses overall scores on the *Metropolitan Readiness Test* (Nurss & McGauvran, 1976) to group children for readiness instruction. This would seem to be a legitimate use of that test, at least according to the designers of the test. Suppose another teacher, Mrs. Mosberg, uses scores on the *Metropolitan* to give semester grades in reading. The test seems inappropriate for that purpose especially if Mrs. Mosberg's instructional program is only tangentially related to what is measured on the *Metropolitan.* To use the technical terminology of test designers, we would say that the *Metropolitan* does not possess high curricular validity in relation to the instructional program (i.e., curriculum) in Mrs. Mosberg's class. Put differently, we could say that the test does not match her curriculum.

Validity coefficients (numbers ranging from 0.00 to 1.00) are sometimes reported for published tests. When they are reported they often represent the extent to which the scores they yield agree with scores from some other measure of the same thing (this is concurrent or criterion validity). Group intelligence test scores are often correlated with the scores from an individually administered IQ test such as the Stanford-Binet, for example, with the intent of showing that a high degree of agreement exists between scores on both tests. To the extent that the Stanford-Binet is a true measure of intelligence, it can be a legitimate standard for establishing the validity of the group test.

Scores from reading tests are seldom compared with each other to demonstrate criterion validity. Those who develop reading tests often think their product is better than any other test available and, consequently, they are unlikely to recognize any other test as a standard of comparison. Instead, other ways of claiming validity are used. Content validity is claimed, for example, by describing how the content of the test matches up with a definition or conceptualization of reading. This is a highly subjective process of course, and particularly limited if the test user's definition of reading is different in part or in whole from that of the developers of the test. Even when the developers are quite explicit in stating their definition of reading, the user must still examine the test to see how the tasks the pupil performs relate to that definition. It is an easy matter to say in a definition that comprehension is fundamental, for example, and then to include on a test relatively few tasks that probe anything other than general knowledge (answering questions, for example).

Recently, assessment scholars have expanded the conventional notions of validity to include some corollary concepts. For example, García and Pearson (1991) have borrowed the term, *trustworthiness,* from qualitative evaluation to capture the importance of being able to trust both the depiction of a student's performance provided by administering the test and the decisions that we might make on the basis of performance on that test. So if a test revealed that a student had a low comprehension score but provided no plausible hypotheses about the underlying reasons for the score, it would rate low on trustworthiness.

A related concept, consequential validity, has also entered the national debate about tests and how we use them. Basically what this concept suggests is that educators are morally obligated to evaluate the consequences that tests have for individual students, different groups of students, or even entire schools or districts. Unlike other forms of validity that tend to be scaled on a low-to-high dimension the underlying scale for consequential validity seems to be negative-to-positive. So a test that places students (or perhaps an entire ethnic group) on an instructional track in which they are systematically denied access to higher order literacy activities could be said to have negative consequential validity. Conversely, a test that redirects instruction so that students receive needed comprehension instruction could be said to possess positive consequential validity.

A new variation on the notion of content validity is authenticity. Authenticity is analogous to curricular validity in the sense that with both concepts, a test is compared to some external standard of appropriateness. In the case of curricular validity, the external standard is the instruction offered in the school curriculum and the key question is, Does this test reflect what is taught in the curriculum? With authenticity, the external standards are various types of literacy tasks that people engage in across a variety of literacy environments. Authenticity would surely allow us to include some school-based literacy tasks, such as reading and responding to stories, getting information needed to solve a problem or complete a task, critically reviewing an essay or a story, and writing to communicate to different audiences. However, it would require us to exclude most of the purely didactic tasks and techniques to *prepare* students for authentic literacy tasks, such as workbook pages on letter-sounds, recognition of topic sentences for decontextualized paragraphs, isolated vocabulary matching activities, and grammar and punctuation exercises. The acid test of authenticity is whether the assessment promotes authentic uses of literacy; the key question is, Does this test reflect the ways in which we can expect students to use literacy for communication and learning purposes?

Clearly validity is a complex construct, with many variations and related concepts. But the common element in all validity analyses is relevance. When all is said and done, the basic validity question is, Does the test measure what it claims to measure?

An Example of Test Reliability and Validity

To illustrate how reliability and validity work, let us leave the field of reading for an area most adults have experienced first-hand, the behind-the-wheel driver's test. Certainly the citizens of a state are anxious to know that unsafe drivers are kept off the roads. Consequently, the behind-the-wheel test must be structured in such a way as to provide reliable and valid results. Under normal circumstances, the more behavior samples gathered, the greater the reliability. In the case of the driver's test, it is hoped that incompetent drivers would fail every time they took the behind-the-wheel test because the tasks performed measure most of the important behaviors involved in safe driving. Obviously, the less time the examiner spends with the driver, the fewer the behaviors that can be sampled. Thus a 5-minute ride around the block offers fewer opportunities to observe faulty performance than a 30-minute drive that includes highway driving, driving in heavy traffic, left- as well as right-hand turns, parallel parking, emergency stops, and so forth. Likewise a behind-the-wheel test that lasted several days could sample, for example, driving at night and driving in rain. Even then, driving in snow could be observed only if the test took place in the winter. One could question the reliability of a driver's test that did not sample enough of these diverse behaviors to be sure the domain of safe driving had been adequately covered. In short, the reliability of any test is dependent on sampling sufficient behaviors to be confident of the results.

The reliability of a test can also be affected by factors related to its administration and scoring. In a driver's test it would be extremely important for the examiner to know what behaviors constitute a proper left turn. Something as simple as when and how to signal the turn must be specified so that points can be awarded in a reliable fashion. If the examiner is not guided by explicit standards and deducts points in a haphazard manner depending on her mood or personal feelings toward the driver, this introduces an uncontrolled factor that lowers the reliability (and ultimately the safety of everyone on the road). If a signal must be given at least 200 feet from an intersection, but some drivers get by with a signal at only 150 feet, inconsistent scoring affects the results. Likewise, if one examiner scores left-hand turns one way and another examiner scores them another way, the reliability of the test is reduced.

In the case of a reading test that is reliable, the results should not be affected by who gives or scores the test. An error should be an error regardless of who makes it or who records it. Most standardized tests are fairly consistent because of the format used to elicit responses. Scoring masks, which permit the scorer to see the answers but not the child's name, are used to check a child's answers, and so forth. Of course, reliability may be gained at some cost since a standardized test eliminates some of the interaction between examinee and examiner that may provide unexpected insights into how a child approaches a reading task.

The person who knows the most about a driver's ability is his teacher—the person who sits alongside the learner watching progress and providing instruction when problems occur. Unless the examiner spends as much time with the driver under the same variety of conditions as the teacher, the "snapshot" taken during the test is not as reliable (or as valid) as the assessment the instructor has made over weeks and months. Teachers have much the same opportunity to observe over time. The day-to-day interaction of teaching and learning has built-in reliability that a brief test cannot achieve. Yet often the results of a reading test are believed even when they conflict with teachers' knowledge of students' ability.

Using the behind-the-wheel driver's test, it can also be seen how validity works by noting that actual driving performance is required. This is evidence of face validity. A paper-and-pencil test might be useful in determining a driver's knowledge of the laws that affect driving, but knowing the law is not the same as driving in a manner that conforms to the law. Only by observing a driver perform the act of driving can face validity be guaranteed. Is the behind-the-wheel test a valid test of driving ability in *all* respects? Not necessarily. Validity could be lowered if the driving sample is observed on the deserted street of the local fairgrounds during the off season rather than in normal city traffic, for example. Additionally, suppose the test were conducted in an automobile having an automatic transmission but the driver will use a car with a standard shift transmission once she passes the exam. Is this test a valid measure? Does it assure citizens that the driver is competent? Certainly not, because validity is lacking. The test of driving ability must sample behaviors that are critical to the domain supposedly being tested.

Our driving test example allows us to demonstrate several types of validity but does not address another type of validity that is extremely important to the assessment of reading ability, that of content validity. Driving ability is concrete in the sense that it can be observed in action, but reading is a mental operation not open to direct observation. What is happening in the reader's head must be inferred from what can be observed—oral reading, for example, or question answering. Yet oral reading is not an infallible way of measuring reading ability. Neither is question answering. Therefore, content validity is always problematic on a reading test. To obtain it the test author must make a clear statement about what conceptualization of reading undergirds the test. Then the tasks given in the test must be shown to relate directly to that conceptualization.

If content validity is approached in this way, users can decide if they accept the test author's underlying conceptualization and if the tasks performed by the examinee are appropriate. For example, a test that ignores comprehension and focuses all attention on vocabulary and word identification would not merit the label reading test. Such a test would have to be described more accurately so that users would recognize its scope and limitations. Unfortunately, this basic requisite is met by very few published reading tests. In most cases the user must decide what a test really measures and whether that information is of any value. The fact that some publisher prints and markets the test does not make it a valid measure of reading.

When selecting a reading test, the teacher must first make a conscious effort to clarify what purpose is to be served by the test. Once this is done, various tests can be examined against that purpose. *Tests must never dictate what the teacher will measure; the teacher must decide what is important to measure.* Just because something is included in a test does not make it important or worthwhile. This approach places a great deal of responsibility on the teacher, and while that may seem awesome, that is how it should be if teachers are to function as professional decisionmakers.

But the teacher is not alone in finding and appraising tests. Help is available in a number of places and forms. Those sources of information on reading tests are discussed next.

SOURCES OF INFORMATION ON TESTS

Suppose you have decided to go to a movie this weekend and there are several choices available at nearby theaters. How would you normally decide which movie to see? Your approach is probably not much different from others. The first step is to ask friends if they have seen any of the films playing at the nearby theaters. If a friend whose tastes you respect endorses a particular film, chances are good that you might choose it. A similar sequence of events is often followed when selecting a book for recreational reading.

Other sources of information on movies and books are the published reviews that appear in magazines, newspapers, and on television. The reviewer is normally an expert who has seen the movie or read the book recently and whose review tells enough about the film or book to give you a sense of its content and quality. Although you must still decide whether to invest your own money in a ticket, without reviews you would have precious little information on how to make a decision.

A movie and book review schema have been invoked so that test reviews may be discussed in this context. Although you are capable of evaluating a test by yourself, test reviews are readily available to assist your decisionmaking process. Test reviews appear in a number of sources, the most common being professional journals and the *Mental Measurements Yearbook*.

The Mental Measurements Yearbook

In 1938 O. K. Buros produced the first *Mental Measurements Yearbook* (*MMY*). Nine additional editions have appeared since then, the latest in 1985. The *MMY* is most noteworthy for its collection of high-quality reviews of tests. Because of his own high standards and the caliber of people he asked to review for the *MMY*, Buros assembled penetrating, well-documented opinions about hundreds of tests. Reviewers were instructed by Buros to prepare their reviews with these objectives in mind:

1. To provide test users with carefully prepared appraisals of tests for their guidance in selecting and using tests.
2. To stimulate progress toward higher professional standards of test construction by censuring poor work and by suggesting improvements.
3. To impel test authors and publishers to present more detailed information on the construction, validity, reliability, norms, uses, and possible misuses of their test.

O. K. Buros actually hoped to make it unprofitable financially and professionally for poor tests to be published. It is a judgment call as to how successful he has been in meeting that goal. Plenty of poor tests are published, purchased, and used even today but the situation might be even worse if the *MMY* had not been available. Since his death in 1978, the work of Buros's Institute of Mental Measurements has shifted to the University of Nebraska at Lincoln.

The *MMY* makes it possible for any test user to see what several experts have to say about a test. Reviews are relatively brief (600 to 1200 words in length), but are typically hard-hitting and frank in their appraisal. Just as you can disregard the advice of a friend or the reviewer for a local newspaper regarding a movie, you can ignore the advice of experts, but you do so having been alerted to their concerns.

The *MMY* includes reviews written especially for the *Yearbook* as well as reviews first published elsewhere. It is a reference any reading teacher should know first-hand and any school district should have available.

Reading Tests and Reviews

Because a test that was reviewed in a previous edition of the *MMY* was seldom reviewed in a subsequent edition (unless revision of the test had occurred), Buros saw a need to gather all reading test reviews from across all editions together into a single volume. This resulted in the publication of *Reading Tests and Reviews* in 1968.[5] An update of the 1968 publication was published in 1975. Undoubtedly, another update will appear shortly.

Reviews in Professional Journals

Many professional journals publish test reviews on a regular basis. Others review tests periodically. You can consult the following journals for reviews of reading tests: *The Reading Teacher, Journal of Reading, Reading Research and Instruction, Journal of Learning Disabilities,* and *Journal of School Psychology.*

Reviews in Professional Books

Some textbooks include reviews of reading tests. Among those with fairly extensive reviews are Spache (1981), Harris and Sipay (1985), and Bond, Tinker, and Wasson (1984). Of course, Chapter 13 of this textbook also consists of test reviews.

Publications of the IRA

Two collections of test reviews are published by the International Reading Association (IRA). They are *Reading Tests for Secondary Grades* (Blanton, Farr, and Tuinman, 1972) and *Diagnostic and Criterion-Referenced Reading Tests: Reviews and Evaluation* (Schell, 1981).

In addition, several IRA publications include useful essays on important issues related to tests, measurement, and evaluation in reading. These include *Reading: What Can Be Measured?* by Farr and Carey (1986); *Reading Tests and Teachers: A Practical Guide* by Schreiner (1979); *Assessment Problems in Reading* by MacGinitie (1973); *Informal Reading Inventories* by Johnson, Kress, and Pikulski (1987); *Measuring Reading Performance* by Blanton, Farr, and Tuinman (1974); *Approaches to the Informal Evaluation of Reading* by Pikulski and Shanahan (1982a); and *Reading Comprehension Assessment* by Johnston (1983).

Standards for Evaluating Tests

The first step in learning to evaluate reading tests is to take a course in educational tests and measurement. Any such course should help a user develop a set of personal standards for evaluating tests. In all likelihood the user will also be introduced to a publication of the American Psychological Association (APA) titled *Standards for Educational and Psychological Testing* (1985). This joint publication of APA, the American Educational Research Association (AERA), and the National Council on Measurement in Education (NCME) serves to assist the test user by establishing criteria that an acceptable test must meet. The coordinator of research and evaluation in any school system should have a copy of this publication.

The following standards provide a basic set of guidelines for evaluating reading tests that can be adapted to your own purposes.

I. General Features
   A. Title
   B. Date of publication
   C. Author
   D. Level and forms
   E. Purpose as described by author
   F. Time for administration
   G. Scoring
   H. Cost
II. Technical Features
   A. Are the directions for administration clear?
   B. If norm-referenced, are the norms adequate to my purpose(s)?

In addition to consulting published reviews on a
test, a teacher should also make a personal evaluation of a test with her own instructional goals
and program in mind. *(James Silliman)*

    C. What evidence of overall test reliability is provided? subtest reliability?
    D. What evidence of test validity is provided?
       1. Is an explicit statement made concerning the definition of reading
         undergirding the test?
       2. Does the test appear to measure what I regard to be important for
         success in learning to read?
    E. Does the test provide information that will be useful in planning read-
      ing instruction?
III. General Considerations
    A. Does the test provide needed information beyond what I have avail-
      able from other sources?
    B. Does the test match my program objectives?
    C. Is the test appropriate for my students in terms of difficulty and
      length?
    D. Have I taken the test myself in order to understand its content as an
      examinee?
IV. Recommendations
    A. On balance, is use of this test justified?
    B. Which students should take this test? For what purposes?

TYPES OF PUBLISHED READING TESTS

335

*CHAPTER 14
Assessment
Principles Applied
to Reading*

It makes a good deal of sense to group published reading tests according to their similarities. For example, tests that are appropriate for a particular grade level or ones that have a common format should be grouped together. What has emerged over time is the practice of grouping tests according to the reading functions they attempt to measure.[6] Thus tests of general silent reading ability are grouped together under the heading *Survey Tests;* tests that measure the application of reading skills to meet a need for information are called *Study Skills Tests;* tests that identify specific strengths and weaknesses in learning to read are called *Diagnostic Tests;* and so forth.

Universal agreement on how to group tests is by no means evident in the literature. Reasonable people can disagree on how tests should be categorized and into which category a particular test fits. This should not come as any surprise since one's beliefs about the reading process have a direct bearing on how tests will be viewed. The following seven-category organizational scheme offered by Lapp and Flood (1978) appears to be functional: (1) readiness, (2) survey, (3) diagnostic, (4) oral reading, (5) study skills, (6) special and content area, and (7) miscellaneous reading tests. (The *MMY* employs the same categories with two exceptions: speed is a separate category and survey tests are simply called reading tests.) This text is concerned primarily with categories 2, 3, and 4 (survey, diagnostic, and oral reading tests). Skills management systems as an example of criterion-referenced tests will also be examined. Many basal reader programs now include tests that are based on the skills management scheme. The following section will describe each type of test and give examples. In Chapter 15 detailed reviews are given for a sample of tests in each category described here in order to illustrate each type.

Survey Reading Tests

A survey reading test is one designed to measure a student's general reading performance. Survey tests are administered on a group basis, are norm-referenced, and have as a primary purpose the ranking of students from high to low in reading achievement. Consequently items are included in the test that are expected to be easy for everyone as well as items that are expected to be hard for everyone. This provides both a floor and a ceiling for the test, enabling even poor readers to demonstrate some ability and superior ones to experience some difficulty. According to testing theory this contributes to the validity of the test by sampling the entire domain under scrutiny. In practical terms this means the test will include a large number of items the average student will get wrong. This does not reflect poorly on the child, since to rank students along a continuum it is necessary to ask everyone to perform tasks that some will not be able to do.

It is necessary to highlight the difficulty level of survey tests in order to demonstrate their limitations to the user and help guide day-to-day instruction. (As you will see later, a diagnostic test does not artificially spread children from high to low. Diagnostic tests are akin to criterion-referenced tests in that they help identify where a student could profit from further instruction, such as knowledge of prefixes.) Survey tests do not represent in any systematic way the various subskills thought by the test author to constitute the reading process and in this sense do not guide daily instruction. They do determine how well the child can perform in a general reading situation.

Typically only two scores are obtained with a reading survey test: comprehension and vocabulary. As with any test, the teacher will want to note exactly how a particular survey test goes about determining the child's score (or level of achievement) in these two broad areas. For example, the comprehension score often is based on only one means of assessment (typically through multiple-choice questions) using very brief passages. The topic of one of these passages may not be familiar or interesting to a particular student and consequently may distort accurate determination of comprehension. Likewise, vocabulary measurement is fraught with many difficulties.

In short, teachers must be cautious in concluding that any test, particularly a survey test that is designed to rank children from high to low for the sake of comparison, is a totally satisfactory indicator of reading ability. With these cautions in mind, consider now how survey reading tests *can* help teachers. Survey tests are useful in identifying the child's reading level, and consequently are of some value in matching the child with appropriate instructional materials. They can also help teachers decide how children might be grouped for daily instruction. In other words, the distribution of scores from a test such as the *Gates-MacGinitie* (MacGinitie and MacGinitie, 1989) can be used with other information to form tentative reading groups and to help select reading materials that are at an appropriate level of difficulty for each group. (Remember that a grade equivalent from the test does not translate neatly or directly to a comparable basal reader grade level or textbook readability score. The matching of child and book is far more complex than this and has been addressed elsewhere in this book (pp. 116–119). In other words, the children who are reading in the range 3.0–3.5 according to the *Gates-MacGinitie* cannot automatically be assigned to the third-grade book in the Houghton-Mifflin reading program.) Survey tests can also help teachers gain some sense of growth in general reading ability for a group of children over the course of an entire school year.

The *Gates-MacGinitie* Reading Test is reviewed in the next chapter. Other survey tests include: *California Achievement Test: Reading* (1978), and the *Iowa Silent Reading Test* (Farr, 1973).

Diagnostic Reading Tests

A diagnostic reading test is designed to provide a teacher with a profile of a student's relative strengths and weaknesses (see Figure 14.2). Rather than having one or two general scores that represent the child's overall reading performance (as from a survey test), diagnostic tests break reading into various subskills such as knowledge of phonics, structural analysis, literal comprehension, inferential comprehension, and reading rate, and they obtain scores for each of these areas. The rationale underlying a diagnostic test is that instruction can be planned to help students improve in areas where performance is low. Often referred to as

Name _John Kohler_ School _____

Grade _3 rd_ Teacher _____ Date_____

$(1.40 \times 3.1) + 1 = 5.3$

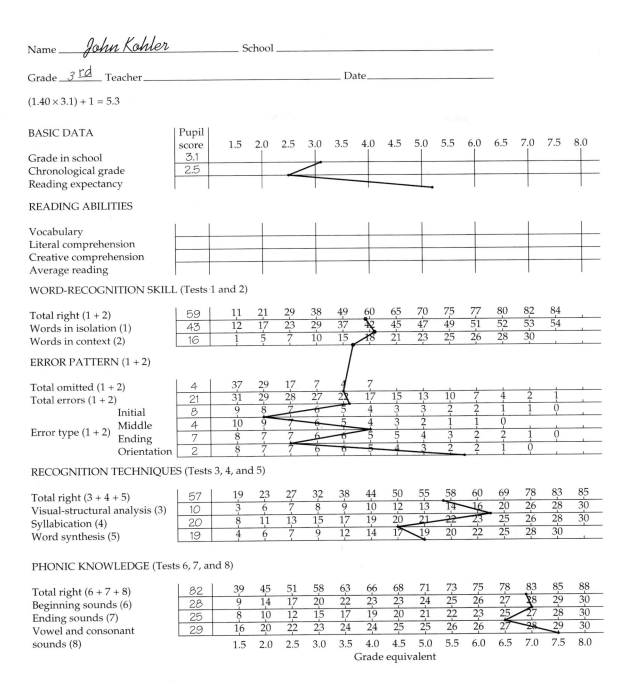

BASIC DATA	Pupil score	1.5	2.0	2.5	3.0	3.5	4.0	4.5	5.0	5.5	6.0	6.5	7.0	7.5	8.0
Grade in school	3.1														
Chronological grade	2.5														
Reading expectancy															

READING ABILITIES

Vocabulary															
Literal comprehension															
Creative comprehension															
Average reading															

WORD-RECOGNITION SKILL (Tests 1 and 2)

Total right (1 + 2)	59	11	21	29	38	49	60	65	70	75	77	80	82	84	
Words in isolation (1)	43	12	17	23	29	37	42	45	47	49	51	52	53	54	
Words in context (2)	16	1	5	7	10	15	18	21	23	25	26	28	30		

ERROR PATTERN (1 + 2)

Total omitted (1 + 2)	4	37	29	17	7	4	7								
Total errors (1 + 2)	21	31	29	28	27	22	17	15	13	10	7	4	2	1	
Error type (1 + 2) Initial	8	9	8	7	6	5	4	3	3	2	2	1	1	0	
Middle	4	10	9	7	6	5	4	3	2	1	1	0			
Ending	7	8	7	7	6	6	5	5	4	3	2	2	1	0	
Orientation	2	8	7	7	6	6	5	4	3	2	2	1	0		

RECOGNITION TECHNIQUES (Tests 3, 4, and 5)

Total right (3 + 4 + 5)	57	19	23	27	32	38	44	50	55	58	60	69	78	83	85
Visual-structural analysis (3)	10	3	6	7	8	9	10	12	13	14	16	20	26	28	30
Syllabication (4)	20	8	11	13	15	17	19	20	21	22	23	25	26	28	30
Word synthesis (5)	19	4	6	7	9	12	14	17	19	20	22	25	28	30	

PHONIC KNOWLEDGE (Tests 6, 7, and 8)

Total right (6 + 7 + 8)	82	39	45	51	58	63	66	68	71	73	75	78	83	85	88
Beginning sounds (6)	28	9	14	17	20	22	23	23	24	25	26	27	28	29	30
Ending sounds (7)	25	8	10	12	15	17	19	20	21	22	23	25	27	28	30
Vowel and consonant sounds (8)	29	16	20	22	23	24	24	25	25	26	26	27	28	29	30
		1.5	2.0	2.5	3.0	3.5	4.0	4.5	5.0	5.5	6.0	6.5	7.0	7.5	8.0

Grade equivalent

FIGURE 14.2. Graphic Profile

diagnostic-prescriptive instruction, this approach springs from the belief that progress in reading is usually blocked by specific weaknesses that can be remediated once they have been identified (diagnosed).[7] For example, a teacher who sees that John scores at or near the expected level of achievement on all but one of the various subtests would focus instruction on the low area. Thus diagnostic tests are important for identifying specific areas needing attention.

To have confidence in a diagnostic reading test, a teacher must address several concerns. First, there is the question of whether the test actually measures the ability it claims to measure. A diagnostic reading test may purport to assess sight vocabulary, for example, but unless there is a way for the examiner to control how long a word is exposed, word analysis can occur. This is simply an illustration of test validity, of course. Beyond this obvious concern is a second more subtle question the teacher must resolve that also relates to test validity: Are the skills tested those that the teacher feels constitute the act of reading? Do the subtests reflect in some direct way the skills, abilities, knowledge, and attitudes that are crucial to reading?

Often subtests are included in diagnostic tests simply because tradition dictates it; at other times they are included because they seem to differentiate between successful and less successful readers. In either case, it is entirely possible that the subtest measures nothing of consequence or that it measures something that does not lend itself to instruction.

As various diagnostic reading tests are described in the next chapter the teacher should consider whether the subtests match his notions about what is important in learning to read, and how the skills are measured. Unless a test fits well with a teacher's conception of reading, it is unlikely to help him identify a student's strengths and weaknesses, or plan appropriate instruction.

Group Diagnostic Reading Tests

Some diagnostic tests are designed to be given in a group setting. The obvious advantage of this type of test is that much less of the teacher's time is needed to gather and score responses. If the test is well constructed, a group diagnostic test can provide the detailed information needed to plan appropriate remedial work. The strengths and weaknesses of each child are easily identified when a profile of results is developed. The only real disadvantage of a group test is that nonverbal clues easily monitored in an individual setting are difficult to observe in a group setting.

One widely used group diagnostic reading test is the *Stanford Diagnostic Reading Test* (Karlsen, Madden, & Gardiner, 1981). It is reviewed in the next chapter. Other examples of group diagnostic tests include the *Doren Diagnostic Reading Test of Word Recognition* (Doren, 1973) and the *McCullough Word Analysis Test* (McCullough, 1963).

Individual Diagnostic Reading Test

Because an individual diagnostic reading test is administered to pupils one at a time, and most tests of this type take a minimum of 30 minutes to administer (and some take as long as 90 minutes), it is difficult for a busy teacher to give such tests. Of course, the face-to-face interaction involved in individual diagnostic testing permits the teacher to gather vital nonverbal clues and thereby develop a more complete picture of how a student reacts in a reading situation.

Individual diagnostic reading tests are of two basic types: the full battery and oral reading test (IRI). The major distinction between these two types, which will become more apparent as descriptions of specific instruments are presented in Chapter 15, is that the full battery includes numerous subtests of specific skills in isolation whereas the IRI is a set of graded paragraphs to be read aloud. The following individually administered diagnostic test batteries are reviewed in Chapter 15.

Durrell Analysis of Reading Difficulty 3rd Edition (Durrell & Catterson, 1980)

The Woodcock Reading Mastery Tests (Woodcock, 1973)

Botel Reading Inventory (Botel, 1978)

Diagnostic Reading Scales (Spache, 1981b)

Oral Reading Tests: Informal Reading Inventories

Oral reading tests, often called informal reading inventory (IRI), consist of a collection of brief passages written at various difficulty levels. Pupils typically begin the IRI at a level expected to be easy for them and read aloud while the teacher notes breaks in fluency that fit into common error categories such as omissions, mispronunciations, substitutions, and so forth. Silent reading as well as listening can also be tested with an IRI. Comprehension is usually checked by asking the pupils questions on the content of the passages read.

An IRI is commonly used for the purpose of determining (1) what level of material pupils can read successfully on a daily basis for instruction (often called the instructional level), (2) what level of material is too difficult (frustration level), and (3) what level is easy (independent or recreational level). Judgments concerning what level of material fits each of these categories for a particular child are normally based on percentages of word recognition and comprehension accuracy. Criteria described by Betts (1946) continue to be used by many teachers, though Powell (1971), Pikulski (1974), Spache (1981b), and others have questioned their validity. Betts suggests that 95 percent word recognition accuracy and 75 percent comprehension accuracy represent the child's instruction level.

In the broadest sense of the term, this determination of reading levels is a type of diagnosis. That is, information that might be useful in planning appropriate daily instruction is gathered. In a more narrow use of the term *diagnostic* (that is, to determine a pupil's strengths and weaknesses in specific skill areas), the IRI enables the skilled teacher to gather information of a highly detailed nature that must be interpreted in order to be useful. Goodman, Watson, and Burke (1987) describe a system for analyzing each oral reading miscue according to its graphophonic, syntactic, and semantic acceptability, for example. Other systems for examining oral reading miscues also exist.[8] In every case, the intent is the same: The examiner seeks to understand the strategies employed by children while they read as reflected in their oral reading behavior.

Several of the tests listed previously include a subtest that has many of the characteristics of an IRI. The *Durrell* and the *Spache,* for example, include several sets of graded paragraphs along with a system for recording oral reading errors and a means for checking comprehension. In a full diagnostic battery the graded passages approach is just one of many subtests.

In Chapter 15 the *Qualitative Reading Inventory* by Leslie and Caldwell (1990) and *Analytical Reading Inventory*, fourth edition by Woods and Moe (1989) are reviewed. Other commercial IRIs include the following:

Burns, Paul C., and Roe, Betty D. (1985). *Informal Reading Inventory* (2nd ed.). Boston: Houghton-Mifflin.

Ekwall, Eldon E. (1979). *Ekwall Reading Inventory*. Boston: Allyn and Bacon.

Fry, Edward (1981). *Reading Diagnosis: Informal Reading Inventories*. Providence, RI: Jamestown Publishers.

Gilmore, John V., and Gilmore, Eunice, C. (1968). *Gilmore Oral Reading Test*. Orlando, FL: Harcourt Brace Jovanovich.

Gray, William S. (1967). *Gray Oral Reading Test*. New York: Bobbs-Merrill.

Johns, Jerry (1981). *Basic Reading Inventory*. Dubuque, IA: Kendall/Hunt.

McCracken, Robert (1966). *Standard Reading Inventory*. Klamath Falls, OR: Klamath Printing Co.

Rinksy, Lee Ann, and DeFossard, Esta (1980). *The Contemporary Classroom Reading Inventory*. Scottsdale, AZ: Gorsuch Scarisbrick.

Silvaroli, Nicholas (1982). *Classroom Reading Inventory* (4th ed.). Dubuque, IA: Wm. C. Brown.

Spache, George (1981). *Diagnostic Reading Scales*. Monterey, CA: California Test Bureau/McGraw-Hill.

Sucher, Floyd, and Allred, Ruel A. (1973). *Reading Placement Inventory*. Oklahoma City, OK: Economy.

Skills Management Systems

It is hard to explore the topic of diagnostic reading tests and ignore the existence of a group of devices commonly called skills management systems. They began to emerge in the late sixties and early seventies largely in response to growing public demands for accountability in education. To be accountable, it was necessary for schools to specify what they expected students to learn and to have a way of measuring who had learned it and who had not. Literacy, a major concern of the public, was immediately tackled by those who advocated a systems approach. Today skills management systems are an integral part of nearly all basal reading programs. Additionally, systems that are not keyed to any particular set of instructional materials are also available.

The following is a partial list of skills management systems for reading:

Criterion Reading: Individualized Learning Management System. New York: Random House, 1970–1971.

Fountain Valley Reading Skills Tests. Richard L. Zweig Associates, Inc. Huntington Beach, CA: 1971–1975.

Analysis of Skills: Reading. Scholastic Testing Service, Inc. Bensenville, IL: 1974–1976.

Individual Pupil Monitoring System—Reading. Boston: Houghton-Mifflin, 1974.

Mastery: An Evaluation Tool: Reading. Chicago: Science Research Associates Inc., 1974–1976.

Objectives-Referenced Bank of Items and Tests: Reading and Communication Skills. New York: CTB/McGraw-Hill, 1980.

Prescriptive Reading Inventory. New York: CTB/McGraw-Hill, 1972–1977.

PRI/IS. New York: CTB/McGraw-Hill, 1980.

Reading: IOX Objectives-Based Tests. Instructional Objectives Exchange. Los Angeles: 1973–1976.

SPIRE Individual Reading Evaluation. New Dimensions in Education, Inc. Plainview, NY: 1970–1973.

Wisconsin Design for Reading Skill Development. Learning Multi-Systems, Inc. University of Wisconsin, Madison, WI: 1970–1972.

Although it would be inaccurate to contend that all skills management systems are identical, there are enough common features among them to enable one to generalize a bit. Most of them include a list of instructional objectives that relate to teaching children to read. Typically the objectives are stated in behavioral terms and related to specific skills believed to be important to success in reading. They also include a series of tests that are designed to measure student achievement on each skill. The concept of skill mastery is often applied to student performance with some cutoff score being used to distinguish between those who have mastered a skill and those who have not. Finally, most skills management systems include a record-keeping system that permits the teacher to keep track of which skills a particular student has mastered (or, stated another way, which tests the child has passed). Chapter 15 will look at one particular system in greater detail to give a better idea of how all such systems work.

SPECIAL PROBLEMS IN TESTING UNSUCCESSFUL READERS

Earlier in this chapter we stated that tests often play an inordinately important role in the lives of low-achieving readers and in the conduct of remedial programs. In fact, a stated purpose for this chapter was to give teachers the information needed to develop an appreciation for the limits of tests. Before closing, this chapter must also take a look at the special problems encountered in testing low-achieving readers.

Lack of Test-Taking Skills

Many pupils identified as low-achieving readers are very poor test takers. One reaction to that statement might be, "Of course, that's because they usually lack the knowledge or skills being tested." Lack of skills and knowledge does not usually account for the entire discrepancy between the test scores of good and poor readers. Often low-achieving readers perform worse than they should on tests because whatever knowledge or skill they do have is obscured by a lack of "test-wiseness." Here is a simple example to illustrate this point. Pupils who know how to take a timed test realize that it is self-defeating to spend an inordinate amount of time on an especially difficult question. They learn to make a guess at a correct answer and to go on to other, easier questions. If time permits, once all the relatively easy questions have been answered, the pupil can return to the more difficult questions, study them, and change the earlier guess if that seems appropriate. In contrast, poor test takers often dawdle over a difficult question hoping to figure it out before continuing. By doing so they never reach many of the easier questions and consequently they end up with a lower score than they might have achieved.

Another case in point involves eliminating unlikely alternatives in a multiple-choice question. Good test takers increase their chances of getting an item right even when they are not sure of the correct answer by eliminating the choices they know are incorrect and guessing among the remaining alternatives. If two of four alternative choices can be eliminated, the pupil then has a 50–50 chance of guessing the right answer. According to testing theory the pupil is getting credit for knowing something about the topic being tested. In the same situation poor test takers realize they do not know which answer is correct and often fail to respond at all. Especially under directions not to guess, poor test takers are inclined to adopt a conservative strategy resulting in no response even when they can positively eliminate one or several of the choices but are not sure which of the remaining choices is correct.

Low-achieving readers can be helped by learning how to take tests more effectively. Contrary to what some may think, this is not cheating; it is merely helping pupils to demonstrate what they know. Although much has been done to help adults improve their test-taking abilities,[9] there is little research suggesting ways that teachers can maximize the performance of children on tests.[10] Test training is advocated for all pupils, but particularly for low-achieving readers who are constantly being tested and then manipulated according to the results of those tests. Merely changing such pupils' attitudes toward test taking can be a big step in the right direction. Too often their past failure in testing discourages them from even trying on new tests.

Norm-Referenced Tests Geared to the Average Pupil

Another problem in testing low-achieving readers is the fact that general screening tests (for example, achievement batteries and survey reading tests) are developed with the average pupil in mind. In other words, pupils at the extremes (high or low) are not measured as accurately by tests that are designed for a particular grade level. The reason for this is fairly straightforward—the bulk of the items on such tests are geared to the level being tested. Although a few easy and a few hard items are included to provide a ceiling and a floor, not enough of either is included to provide a reliable spread among pupils at the extremes. The result for low-achieving pupils is failure to measure what they do know. Since the test contains only a few items at their knowledge and skill level, their achievement may be grossly underestimated.

In what may seem to be a contradiction, it should also be said that the performance of low-achieving readers may be overestimated by norm-referenced tests that use grade equivalents. Even a score of zero typically has a grade level designation. As the difficulty level of the test goes higher, the grade equivalent of a score of zero goes higher as well. This absurdity only underscores the inappropriateness of giving pupils a test that is too difficult for them. Almost no useful information is gained by giving a reader operating at a primer level a survey test designed for fourth graders. What a teacher can do is use an easier form of the test in what is called out-of-level testing to see what knowledge and skills the pupil has. The norms are not applicable in this case, of course, but are probably unnecessary anyway since you already know the pupil is extremely low by comparison to her peers.

Failure to Match Program Objectives

The effectiveness of special instruction is typically measured in a surprising way. Based on the mistaken belief that daily work is not adequate evidence of growth and progress, decisionmakers often insist that general achievement tests such as the *Gates-MacGinitie* be used to document gains on a pre- and post-test basis due to targeted instruction in special programs. In fact, the funding of these programs is often tied to a mandate for an independent measure of growth. The difficulty with this approach is that remedial instruction is almost always focused on a pupil's special needs. If the effectiveness of remediation is in question, measures are needed that relate directly to the remedial instruction. The issue of test validity is basic here. The *Gates-MacGinitie* or other survey test is a general measure that relates only in an indirect way to remedial instruction. Even diagnostic tests are ill-suited to a pre- and post-test design. Few are available in alternate forms and most lack the subtest reliability that would be required to use them for evaluation purposes.

The very best evidence available to document the effects of instruction is the daily work the teacher keeps for each child. Worksheets, anecdotal records, written assignments, teacher-made progress tests, checklists, and the like provide a more useful cumulative record of what the pupil has learned. It is, in fact, exactly this logic of privileging assessments that arises as a natural part of instruction that underlies the current popularity of portfolios. Reading teachers should not passively accept standardized testing as a legitimate measure of the effectiveness of their programs. If a test score is required by some authority, supply it but also supply the supplementary information you have accumulated for the program. The issues of reliability and validity apply to informal measures just as much as they do to formal measures, but the very nature of evidence gathered over time from daily instruction contributes to their reliability and validity.

Gains Realized During Remediation

It is natural to be interested in how much progress a pupil has made during special remedial programs. Two problems associated with interpreting gains measured with tests should be identified. The first has to do with regression toward the mean and the second concerns using normal growth as a basis for comparison. It is important that you understand these concepts so that you can evaluate reports about the latest innovation critically and so that you will not make the mistake of claiming gains for your pupils when the gains cannot be attributed to your instruction.

The phenomenon of regression toward the mean simply means that the chances of an extremely high or low performance being repeated or exceeded are small. Stated another way, chances are good that a person who did very poorly on something will not do as poorly next time. Applied to the measurement of reading this means the pupil who was lowest on a test will probably not be as low next time by virtue of chance alone. The student's score will probably be closer to the mean (average).

In selecting pupils for a remedial program those who score extremely low on a test are often chosen. If no instruction were provided these same pupils would probably do better on the next test because of regression toward the mean (some would do worse, but far more would do better). In a carefully controlled experiment the researcher is obliged to control for regression toward the mean by randomly assigning half the subjects in a remedial program to a control group (one not receiving the remedial instruction). Regression should operate in both groups thus making it possible to identify gains due to the treatment alone. A teacher will not have the luxury of creating a control group since all readers deserve the best we can offer in instruction. However, an understanding of the regression phenomenon should help keep some perspective regarding any gains the pupils achieve.

Gain scores are typically figured by subtracting a pre-test score from a post-test score. As indicated earlier, such calculations are often done with grade equivalents because there is apparent meaning in a gain of 2.3 (2 years, 3 months). There are several cautions concerning gain scores. First, it is normal for pupils to gain something during the course of a year because they have lived that long. To claim that all gains are due to instruction ignores that fact. Second, not all pupils should gain the same amount in a year's time. Brighter students will gain more than a year, slower students less than a year. Third, grade equivalents are like percentiles in that pupils are not spread evenly from top to bottom but form a bell-shaped curve. A gain from an extremely low score is not as difficult to achieve because there are fewer pupils at that level. The same gain in raw score points results in a greater grade equivalent gain at the lower or upper levels than it does near the middle. Finally, gains in reading do not usually occur in a steady fashion, but tend to occur in spurts and plateaus. Norms smooth out the uneven aspects of growth across an interval of grade equivalents thus masking the true nature of progress pupils normally make. A full year spurt in only 3 months can seem extraordinary when compared to normal growth, yet little or no additional growth may occur in the next 6 to 9 months.

Spache (1981b) reviews several methods for judging the significance of gain scores and recommends the use of residual gains as suggested by Rankin and Tracy (1965). The technical aspects of teaching teachers to correct gain scores for initial status, intelligence, and so forth are not as important as sensitizing them to the dangers of using simple gain scores as an index of growth. In the final analysis the use of standardized test scores as the primary way of evaluating individual pupil growth or program effectiveness is not desirable.

SUMMARY

This chapter has focused on measurement principles as they apply to working with unsuccessful readers. Despite beliefs that published tests have serious limitations for day-to-day decisionmaking in an instructional setting, it is important to know how to select and interpret tests.

The concepts of reliability and validity were discussed and sources of information on published tests were described. Special problems encountered in the use of tests with low-achieving readers were also examined.

Suggested Activities

1. Examine a norm-referenced reading test and a criterion-referenced reading test. Compare the types of tasks the examinee is asked to perform on each type of test. Determine how a score of 50 percent correct on each test would be interpreted. Explain why the scores on a criterion-referenced test are normally higher (in the sense that fewer items will be missed on the average).

2. Examine the administrator's manual for a variety of standardized reading tests. Determine whether reliability coefficients are reported or not and list the tests from high to low on the basis of the coefficients. Decide which of the reliability coefficients are based on split-half procedures and which are based on alternate forms or test-retest procedures. Do a similar analysis on the reported validity of these tests. Using reliability and validity as the only criteria, decide which of the tests would be best to use.

3. Plan a series of lessons that are designed to help children become better takers of standardized tests. Concentrate on one type of test (true-false, multiple-choice, or matching). You may wish to consult the references identified in this chapter or elsewhere on helping children become test-wise.

Suggested Reading

AHMANN, J. STANLEY, and GLOCK, MARVIN D. (1981). *Evaluating student progress: Principles of tests and measurements* (6th ed.). Boston: Allyn and Bacon.

This is a college textbook for the basic course in tests and measurements. As such it addresses fundamental issues including the role of student evaluation in education, describes the characteristics of satisfactory measuring instruments (including test validity, reliability, and means for reporting students' relative test performance), and discusses teacher-built tests including methods by which tests of this sort can be evaluated. Standardized tests and the means for evaluating them are also discussed.

EBEL, ROBERT L., and FRISBIE, DAVID A. (1986). *Essentials of educational measurement* (4th ed.). Englewood Cliffs, NJ: Prentice-Hall.

This is a comprehensive college textbook on educational measurement principles. Both theoretical and practical issues related to measuring student achievement and progress are included. The topics of grading and reporting student achievement are presented in a separate chapter.

FARR, ROGER, and CAREY, ROBERT F. (1986). *Reading: What can be measured?* (2nd ed.). Newark, DE: International Reading Association.

This book reviews the professional literature concerned with measuring reading performance. It discusses the limitations of reading tests and provides guidelines for their evaluation.

MEHRENS, WILLIAM A., and LEHMANN, IRVIN, J. (1984). *Measurement and evaluation in education and psychology* (3rd ed.). New York: Holt, Rinehart and Winston.

This book provides an introduction to and overview of the basic principles involved in the construction, selection, evaluation, interpretation, and use of tests. It discusses the nature of norm- and criterion-referenced tests and how they can be used most effectively by a classroom teacher to plan and evaluate instruction. It contains an entire chapter devoted to interest, personality, and attitude inventories.

PIKULASKI, JOHN J., and SHANAHAN, TIMOTHY (Eds.) (1982). *Approaches to the informal evaluation of reading.* Newark, DE: International Reading Association.

This book summarizes alternative approaches that classroom teachers can take to formal, standardized tests of reading achievement on the premise that such approaches are especially helpful in planning and adjusting daily instruction.

Notes

1. See Hogan (1974).
2. See Harris and Hodges (1981).
3. See Harris and Hodges (1981).
4. Called the coefficient of determination and determined by squaring the correlation coefficient.
5. See Buros (1969).
6. See Harris and Sipay (1985).
7. See Cheek and Cheek (1980).
8. See Harris and Sipay (1985), Cunningham (1978).
9. See Sherman and Wildman (1982).
10. See Prell and Prell (1986).

CHAPTER 15

Diagnostic Reading Tests
OVERVIEW

As you read this chapter use the following list of main ideas to guide your understanding and reflection.

- Survey reading tests can be administered to groups of children, are norm referenced, and have as a main purpose the ranking of children from high to low. The *Gates-MacGinitie Reading Tests* are reviewed here as an example.
- Diagnostic reading tests are either group or individual tests and have as a main purpose the identification of strengths and weaknesses. Reviewed here as an example of group tests is the *Stanford Diagnostic Reading Test*. Individual tests reviewed are the *Durrell*, the *Woodcock*, the *Botel*, and the *Diagnostic Reading Scales*.
- Informal reading inventories are commonly used to determine what level of reading material a child can read on a daily basis but can also provide a skilled teacher with diagnostic information. The *Analytical Reading Inventory* and the *Qualitative Reading Inventory* are reviewed here as illustrative examples.
- Skills management systems are criterion-referenced tests designed to measure how well children perform on (or have mastered) some specific type of task. The *Prescriptive Reading Inventory* is reviewed in this chapter as an example.

One fact that becomes immediately evident to anyone who is involved in the teaching of reading is that literally dozens of tests are available to measure reading ability. Whether one riffles through the specimen test file in a curriculum lab at the nearest university, consults the test collection in the resources center of a local school system, or leafs through the *Eleventh Mental Measurements Yearbook* (Kramer & Conoley, 1992) or *Tests in Print III* (Mitchell, 1983), it is clear that reading is a favored area among writers and publishers of tests.

Lapp and Flood (1978) list a total of 260 reading and reading-related tests published in the United States. Piled one on top of another these tests alone would make a stack taller than a member of a college basketball team. Include the materials that accompany most tests (for example, administrator's manual, technical reports of test development, scoring masks, and so on) and the pile would dwarf all the members of a basketball team standing one on top of the other. Such statements are virtually meaningless, of course, but they serve to dramatize the fact that the testing of reading is hardly a neglected matter.

The various types of published reading tests were discussed in Chapter 14. The general purpose and nature of survey tests, diagnostic tests (group and individual), oral reading tests, and skills management systems (criterion-referenced tests) were described. It is the goal in this chapter to present selected examples of tests in each of the above categories as a way of introducing the teacher to the types and variety of instruments they will encounter in the marketplace. The tests chosen to be reviewed here are not necessarily the best nor the worst, the newest nor the most unusual. They simply serve as examples that will give a sense of what is available and enable the teacher to build a scaffolding or framework in which to fit other reading tests as they are encountered.

The following tests are reviewed in this chapter:

1. Survey reading test
   a. *Gates-MacGinitie Reading Tests*
2. Diagnostic reading tests
   a. Group administered
      (1) *Stanford Diagnostic Reading Test*
   b. Individually administered
      (1) *Durrell Analysis of Reading Difficulty*
      (2) *The Woodcock Reading Mastery Tests*
      (3) *Botel Reading Inventory*
      (4) *Diagnostic Reading Scales*
3. Informal Reading Inventory (IRI)
   a. *Analytical Reading Inventory*
4. Skills management system
   a. *Prescriptive Reading Inventory*

The reviews presented in this chapter are based on the application of standards for evaluating standardized tests described in Chapter 14. As a reminder those standards include the following key points:

Reliability: What evidence of overall test reliability is provided? Subtest reliability?

Validity: Is an explicit statement made concerning the definition of reading undergirding the test? Does the test appear to measure what is regarded as important for success in learning to read?

Other Technical Features: Are the directions clear and complete? If norm-referenced, are the norms adequate to the teacher's purpose?

Overall: On balance, is use of this test justified? Which students should take this test?

Keeping these standards in mind as you read the reviews that follow will give you a better sense of the purposes and organization underlying the comments. Other standards described in Chapter 14 can only be applied in a specific situation where an instructional program and a group of children can be used as a frame of reference. Additionally, when you work with students from diverse linguistic, cultural, or economic backgrounds, you need to remember that their reading skill may be underestimated by commercial tests because of overt bias or simple cultural mismatches. The section on assessment in Chapter 3 presents those issues in greater detail.

A SAMPLE SURVEY READING TEST:
THE GATES-MACGINITIE

First, it will be helpful to gain an overview of the *Gates-MacGinitie Reading Tests* (MacGinitie & MacGinite, 1989) and then to look more carefully at one level to see how it works. Keep in mind that the primary purpose here is to establish a base of understanding that permits the users to compare and contrast diagnostic tests with survey tests, not to look in detail at survey tests.

The *Gates-MacGinitie* is available in nine different tests appropriate for various grade levels ranging from prereading to tenth through twelfth grades. Vocabulary and comprehension are assessed by every level of the test (except prereading and readiness). Two forms of the test are available at every level (except prereading and readiness). The levels and areas measured are shown in Table 15.1. Each of the tests was developed from a large pool of items that had been tried out with a nationwide sample well in excess of 1000 students at each level. Analysis was also undertaken to identify and eliminate items that showed biased results on the basis of gender or race. Only effective items were retained for inclusion in the final forms of the tests. During the development stage, data were also gathered to be used in establishing appropriate time limits for the tests.

Once a final test form was ready, it was administered to samples of students representing communities throughout the nation that included a range of sizes, geographic locations, average educational level, and average family income. Test norms were then developed showing the average performance of students at a particular grade level. Reliability was determined through a test-retest method using alternate forms. Vocabulary and comprehension scores are generally in the .85 to .90 range for all levels. Extensive data describing

TABLE 15.1. Gates-MacGinitie Reading Tests

Test	Number of Forms	Grade Levels	Skill Areas
Readiness			
Primary A	2	2	Vocabulary, Comprehension
Primary B	2	3	Vocabulary, Comprehension
Primary C	2	3	Vocabulary, Comprehension
Survey D	3	4–6	Vocabulary and Comprehension
Survey E	3	7–9	Vocabulary and Comprehension
Survey F	2	10–12	Vocabulary and Comprehension

intercorrelations among subtests and between test scores and course grades are reported in the technical report. Technical information useful in judging differences between test scores is provided.

In short, the *Gates-MacGinitie Tests* are technically sound. Care has been taken to employ effective items, norms have been carefully developed, and attention is given in the test manual to proper interpretation of the results. Furthermore, different tests are available for relatively narrow ranges of grades making it possible to match students with tasks that are appropriate for their particular level of achievement.

Because they are survey tests, the *Gates-MacGinitie Tests* are global in nature—measuring pupil performance in broad areas. Based on what the tests include, it can be inferred that reading is viewed by the test authors as a process involving comprehension and is heavily dependent upon knowledge of vocabulary. As will be seen later, some diagnostic tests omit comprehension from what is measured. Word recognition is omitted from this test. Yet it is doubtful that the test authors actually believe word recognition is unimportant. It simply is not part of this test. The purpose of a survey test do not require that it tap all aspects of the reading process. For example, most tests ignore attitudes toward reading, interests, study skills, and a variety of other factors often thought to be important to reading. When a test is intended for diagnosis, however, it can ill afford to omit key areas. It must be a thorough measure of critical areas because instruction will be geared to the test results. A survey test such as *Gates-MacGinitie* cannot be used in the same way.

To illustrate, we will look at Level 3 of the *Gates-MacGinitie* to gain a fuller appreciation for what one test in the package actually measures. Level 3 is intended for Grade 3.

The first test is Vocabulary. It includes a total of forty-five items presenting words that grow progressively less common and more difficult. Each item consists of a phrase having an underlined word followed by four other words. The pupil chooses the word whose meaning is closest to the underlined word. Twenty minutes are allowed to complete this test.

The second test, Comprehension, contains forty-eight passages followed by two, three, or four multiple-choice questions. The length and complexity of the passages increase gradually. Some of the passages are expository in nature. Topics range from seasons in Africa to the harvest mouse. The pupil is permitted 35 minutes to work on this test.

Norms provided for the tests include grade equivalents, percentile scores, and standard scores. A separate technical manual provides detailed information on reliability and estimates of the standard error of measurement for each test.

Other forms of the *Gates-MacGinitie* are similar though not identical to Level 3. It is common practice in many schools throughout the United States to administer the *Gates-MacGinitie* or another survey reading test such as the *California Diagnostic Reading Tests* (1989) or the *Iowa Silent Reading Tests* (Farr, 1973) in the fall or spring of the year (or both) to obtain a measure of pupil progress in reading. All general achievement batteries such as the *SRA* (Naslund, Thorpe, & LeFever, 1978), *Metropolitan* (Prescott, Balow, Hogan, & Farr, 1978), *California Achievement Test* (1977), and *Iowa* (Hieronymus et al. 1982) also include a survey test of reading. What do the results of such tests tell a classroom teacher, particularly one who is concerned about students who need a lot of help? As was indicated in Chapter 14, survey tests are useful primarily as devices for ranking children from high to low on a global measure of reading ability. Almost no information that identified specific needs is provided. For this a teacher will need to use diagnostic tests and informal techniques. Survey tests can reveal which children are reading at a level far below their peers or far below their level of expectancy (a level typically determined with the use of an ability measure such as an IQ test). Further diagnosis is required in order to plan appropriate instruction; a survey test is useful only for initial screening in this process.

GROUP DIAGNOSTIC READING TESTS

Some diagnostic reading tests are designed to be given in a group setting. The obvious advantage of group tests is that much less of the teacher's time is needed to gather and score responses. If the test is well-constructed, a group diagnostic test can provide the detailed information needed to plan appropriate remedial work. The strengths and weaknesses of each child are easily identified when a profile of results is developed. The only real disadvantage of a group test is that nonverbal clues easily monitored in an individual setting are difficult to observe in a group setting.

One of the most widely used group diagnostic reading tests is the *Stanford Diagnostic Reading Test.*

Stanford Diagnostic Reading Test

The *Stanford Diagnostic Reading Test* (Karlsen, Madden, & Gardner, 1981) is available in two forms at four different levels. Level One (red level) is intended for use at the end of first grade, in second grade, and with low-achieving students in third grade and above. Subtests include auditory discrimination, basic phonic skills, auditory vocabulary, word recognition, and comprehension.

Level Two (green level) of the *SDRT* is designed for use in third and fourth grades and with low-achieving students in fifth grade and above. Five subtests are included to measure performance in auditory discrimination, phonetic analysis, structural analysis, auditory vocabulary, and comprehension.

Level Three (brown level) is intended for fifth through eighth grades and with low-achieving secondary school students. Subtests include phonetic analysis, structural analysis, auditory vocabulary, comprehension, and reading rate.

Level Four (blue level) of the *SDRT* is designed for use with students in ninth through twelfth grades and in community colleges. Seven subtests include phonetic analysis, structural analysis, word meaning, word parts, comprehension, reading rate, and scanning and skimming.

It is notable that decoding is assessed throughout the various levels of the *SDRT*. Phonetic analysis is one of the subtests even in the brown and blue levels. Likewise structural analysis with special attention to blending is a subtest in all but the first level test. That the upper-level tests designed for high school and even college students measures knowledge of consonant sounds, for example, or ability to blend sounds is surprising. A student who can do even one item on the comprehension subtest at these levels must know enough about sounds and symbols to make it superfluous to diagnose knowledge of consonant sounds and blending. It is highly unlikely that a high school student who is experiencing reading difficulty will profit much from instruction on vowel sounds, for example. Though less unusual, the measurement of auditory discrimination in a test designed for children in third grade and above is somewhat unnecessary.

In general, the *SDRT* is somewhat mechanistic in its approach to reading. Too much is made of a skills hierarchy that builds sequentially on phonics-based decoding. Despite this limitation, the *SDRT* is well-designed, thoroughly researched, and highly professional. As standardized tests go, this is one of the better group diagnostic tests.

The *SDRT* is a group test having answer sheets for either machine or hand scoring. A comprehensive manual for the test administrator provides a detailed description of the structure and content of the test. With the help of the manual, teachers should be able to determine in a fairly straightforward manner whether the conceptualization of reading underlying this test is consistent with their own. The test manual also includes a detailed listing of test objectives, a classification of each test item according to objective, and a cutoff score for judging student mastery of a particular skill. Of special note are the thorough and practical sections of the manual devoted to understanding, interpreting and using the test results. Those who misuse the SDRT have little justification for claiming that the manual didn't give a comprehensive explanation. This is a unique strength of the *SDRT*.

Reliability and standard error of measurement information are reported both for subtests and the total test. All coefficients are in the acceptable range. Two types of validity are discussed in the test manual: content validity and criterion-related validity. The former is properly identified as a matter left to those who use the test because it is only they who can determine whether the abilities assessed by the test reflect the instruction that has been provided. This determination is facilitated by a detailed listing in the manual of objectives and skill domains measured by the subtests as well as item clusters and item objectives.

Criterion-referenced validity is reported with reference to an external instrument only, the Reading Tests of the *Stanford Achievement Tests.* Correlation coefficients are in the .70 to .95 range, thus indicating a high level of agreement between the two tests. However, a comparison between the *SDRT* and another diagnostic reading test would seem more appropriate and more meaningful as an indicator of validity, in our opinion. The test authors recommend that users of the test should determine validity by examining the test contents against the objectives of the instructional program.

The *SDRT* provides the usual norm-referenced scores including percentile ranks, stanines, grade equivalents, and scaled scores for comparing performance across the various forms of the test. Significantly, the test manual discusses the nature and limitations of the various types of derived scores in terms a user of the test can easily understand. Appropriate cautions are provided to assist those who use derived scores to understand what they mean.

The *SDRT* also provides a criterion-referenced feature called "Progress Indicators." Test items that assess a particular skill are gathered together so that pupil performance on those items can be compared to a cutoff score. The test manual suggests that these scores are useful for diagnosing strengths and weaknesses in specific areas. Scores falling above the cutoff score are taken as an indication of competence. Scores falling below the cutoff score indicate competence that has not yet been achieved. There are reservations about the small number of items used to make this determination of competence. A teacher must understand the importance of supplementing any test score with additional evidence, of course, but one who does can use the *SDRT* as a means for guiding instructional plans. The *SDRT* "Progress Indicators" are subject to the same limitations that characterize all criterion-referenced tests (discussed in the previous chapter). In particular, test users will need to compare their own instructional objectives to the objectives of the test, a caution that *SDRT* authors make in the manual.

The *SDRT* is praiseworthy as a group test when used for initial screening. The authors' assumptions about the reading process, though traditional, are laid out clearly in the manual. The content of the test springs directly from the authors' conceptualization of reading that is clearly and explicitly stated in the test manual. Teachers who want to use this instrument will find it relatively easy to see how supplementary information can be gathered to give a more complete view of a child's reading abilities.

INDIVIDUAL DIAGNOSTIC READING TESTS

Because an individual diagnostic reading test is administered to one child at a time and because most tests of this type take a minimum of 30 minutes to administer (and some take as long as 90 minutes), a teacher who has many responsibilities can take only a limited amount of time to give such tests. Of course, the close face-to-face interaction involved in individual diagnostic testing permits the teacher to pay close attention to how a student responds. All manner of information can be gathered through nonverbal clues that permit the teacher to gather a more complete picture of how a student reacts in a reading situation.

Individual diagnostic reading tests are of two basic types: the full battery and the informal reading inventory (IRI). The major distinction between these two types, which will be more apparent as descriptions of specific instruments are presented here, relates primarily to the fact that the full battery includes numerous subtests of specific skills in isolation whereas the IRI is a set of graded paragraphs to be read aloud. The following full diagnostic batteries are described below:

Durrell Analysis of Reading Difficulty

The Woodcock Reading Mastery Tests

Botel Reading Inventory

Diagnostic Reading Scales

The Durrell Analysis of Reading Difficulty

The *Durrell* (1980) is a recently revised diagnostic test administered individually in 30 to 90 minutes, depending on which subtests are used. The primary purposes of the test are to: (1) "estimate the general level of reading achievement" and (2) "discover weaknesses and faulty reading habits that may be corrected in a remedial program."[1] The test consists of four sets of graded paragraphs to be used for assessing oral reading, silent reading, and listening comprehension; word cards and a tachistoscope for assessing word recognition and word analysis; subtests for listening vocabulary, sounds in isolation, visual memory of words, and sounds in words; a prereading phonics abilities inventory (with eight subtests); and a spelling test. The Individual Record Booklet provides a general checklist of instructional needs, a form to record general history data, a profile chart for summarizing the results of testing, and specific checklists for difficulties in oral reading, silent reading, listening comprehension, spelling, visual memory, and handwriting. The battery is intended for those whose reading ability is below seventh grade.

The *Durrell* is described as an instrument that should be given only by those who have been trained by someone having experience in the analysis and correction of reading difficulties. This careful delineation of who should use the *Durrell* is particularly important. As will be shown in this review, considerable professional judgment is required in properly administering, scoring, and interpreting the *Durrell*. Certain features of the *Durrell* make it *appear* to be more precise than an analysis of it implies. Because of its *apparent* objectivity and thoroughness, unsuspecting users of the *Durrell* can be led to expect more than the test delivers.

Even though it is a diagnostic test, norms are used throughout the *Durrell* to provide a basis for interpreting a pupil's score. This is somewhat odd because the significance of a pupil's performance on a diagnostic test is normally thought to lie in her unique pattern of strengths and weaknesses. Comparisons to other students are not particularly important or necessary in this sort of analysis. In any case, new norms were established for this revised form by working with university faculty from graduate reading programs in six communities across the United States. It is not clear in the test manual whether pupils in the norming group all attend schools in university towns, but the description of procedures used leaves one with that impression. If this is the case, this would be a serious limitation, since university communities are often atypical in many respects. A statement in the manual indicates that factors such as "language backgrounds, socioeconomic status, ethnic characteristics, and curriculum emphasis were taken into consideration" in selecting the norming group. Exactly what this means is not explained.

A minimum of forty children in each grade (1 through 6) at six different locations participated in the standardization of the *Durrell*. Thus norms for most parts of the test are based on the performance of over 1200 individuals.

Although the parts of the *Durrell* can be given in any order, the manual suggests that the Oral Reading and Word Recognition and Word Analysis tests be given first in order to decide which other tests are appropriate. These tests, therefore, will be examined first.

The individual administration of a diagnostic reading test offers the examiner an excellent opportunity to observe how the child tackles each task and to gain a sense of the child's confidence and attitude toward reading. *(Peter Vadnai)*

Oral Reading

The Oral Reading test is given to determine a child's instructional level. This test consists of eight paragraphs ranging from a short 21-word narrative about "My Cat" to a 129-word expository essay on "The History of Golf." The child reads each passage aloud while the teacher makes a written record of errors in four categories (omissions, mispronunciations, words supplied, and insertions). Errors self-corrected by the child are counted as one-half error per word. Repetitions, disregard of punctuation, awkward phrasing, improper intonation, and hesitations (up to 5 seconds) are all recorded, but *not* counted as errors. Instructions in the manual do not indicate why a self-correction is regarded as half an error or why other breaks in oral reading fluency are recorded but not counted as errors. A caution is provided that counting word errors must be "tempered by the examiner's judgment." The implications of this statement are not clarified but left to the examiner for interpretation. Here, then, is the first example of the need for considerable professional judgment, referred to earlier. Why are all errors recorded but certain errors counted and others not? What is the rationale for counting insertions as errors, for example, regardless of their nature and not counting disregard of punctuation as errors? Why is a self-correction half an error? An approach that does not count self-corrections as errors is preferable. Even a system that counts all errors equally would be acceptable. But in the *Durrell,* errors count as errors, half-errors, and no errors without justification. This is difficult to accept.

In addition to recording oral reading errors, the examiner also notes the length of time it takes a pupil to read each passage aloud. When seven or more errors are made on a single passage *or* the time required for reading a passage exceeds the time norms, the oral reading test is stopped. Using the table of norms for the last passage read successfully, a grade equivalent is determined using the elapsed time. Three levels of performances are given for each grade (that is, high second grade, medium second grade, and low second grade).

A procedure that assigns grade equivalents on the basis of elapsed reading time is questionable when hesitations of up to 5 seconds occur before the examiner supplies a word the pupil cannot read. The examiner is also instructed to correct mispronunciations that may affect comprehension. Time is racing by while these steps are taken, yet a difference of only 2 to 5 seconds in reading time can reduce the pupil's reading level by a full grade. The norms for rate of reading were based on a much smaller sample than the other norms (only 200 pupils) raising further doubts concerning the reliability of the procedure for turning time scores into grade equivalents.

One other observation seems appropriate. The manual suggests that "recurring errors that reflect minor differences in dialect" be ignored. The thought is admirable, but the execution is likely to be haphazard. Why focus on recurring errors? Is not any variation due to dialect one that should be ignored, whether it happens once or a dozen times? Furthermore, why are only minor differences ignored? Does this imply that major differences should not be ignored? What distinguishes a minor from a major difference? Without answers to these questions, it is difficult to apply the instructions given.

These attempts to modernize the *Durrell* according to recent research on miscue analysis are half-hearted and largely unsuccessful. Oral reading errors must be codified and analyzed according to a carefully designed scheme in order to be useful to the diagnostician. Here an outdated scoring system has been loosened and compromised in an attempt to pass inspection, but in the process it has thrown an enormous burden on the examiner. The norms provided for interpreting pupil performance on the oral reading passages cannot possibly be of any use since they were established on the basis of data collected under very loose conditions.

Comprehension is checked in the oral reading test with questions that probe recall of specific facts. More than three questions out of seven or eight (depending on the level) answered incorrectly indicates poor comprehension. As long as comprehension is above that level, it is not a factor in determining the pupil's instructional level. If comprehension falls into the poor range before reading speed exceeds the norms, an adjustment downward in the instructional level "may be appropriate." The manual indicates that this will seldom happen since pupils will be able to answer most of the comprehension questions. Despite the assurances, more specific instructions seem necessary.

A checklist of oral reading difficulties requires the examiner to decide whether phrasing is adequate, whether volume is too loud or too soft, whether the child loses his place easily, and so forth. No discussion in the manual is offered to help the instructor arrive at a judgment concerning what constitutes "poor enunciation of difficult words" or "poor posture," for example. Without this assistance the use of such a checklist is highly subjective and therefore meaningless. In fact, one would quarrel with several items on the list as true indicators of reading difficulty: "Guesses at unknown words from context," "Ignores word errors and reads on," and "Habitual addition of words," are three examples of behaviors on the checklist of difficulties that are often associated with success in reading, not difficulty.

Word Recognition and Word Analysis

This subtest involves the use of lists of words in isolation and a handheld tachistoscope made of cardboard. A shutter device enables the teacher to control to some extent the length of time a word is exposed to the pupil. Directions in the test manual indicate each word should be "flashed" for .5 of a second to "permit only one eye fixation." Words recognized at flash are taken as sight words or, more properly, words recognized without analysis. Spache (1981) correctly observes that .5 of a second is adequate for several fixations thus defeating the idea that no analysis occurs during the flash portion of this test. In any case, the identification of words in isolation is useful to the diagnostician in only a limited sense anyway since the words missed on this subtest might very well be recognized in context, a much more meaningful measure of reading ability.

The pupil progresses through the lists until seven successive errors are made. When a word is missed at flash, the shutter is reopened and the pupil is asked to study and pronounce it again. The second exposure is untimed and taken as a measure of word analysis. The child's attempts at pronouncing a word are written phonetically in the individual record book by the teacher for both flash and untimed exposure tasks. Norms are provided to permit conversion of scores into grade levels for flash and analysis alike. A checklist is provided to facilitate easy identification of behaviors that are noted during completion of this subtest (for example, "Will not try difficult words").

Silent Reading

Silent reading is assessed in the *Durrell* with a second set of graded paragraphs that are intended to be equal in difficulty to the oral reading paragraphs. No evidence to support the equivalence of the paragraphs is provided in the test manual, but similarity is apparent in the length of the passages, length of sentences, writing style employed, and topics presented. The purposes of the silent reading test are to determine the pupil's independent reading level and compare performance in silent reading with performance in oral reading. Performance in silent reading is assessed with a measure of time and unaided recall.

Upon completion of a passage the child is asked to tell "everything you can remember of that story." The upper-grade selections are actually essays, not stories, but this technicality is unimportant. A breakdown of the text of each passage into idea units is provided in the teacher's record booklet. As the child recalls an idea from the passage, a check is made giving credit for that recollection. Recent developments in discourse analysis[2] make the *Durrell* scoring procedure seem crude and arbitrary by comparison, but the idea of assessing comprehension through free recall rather than question asking is noteworthy. Recent research on the validity of free recall suggests that it, too, has limitations as a measure of comprehension.[3] However, relatively few tests approach comprehension in any way other than through direct questioning. The *Durrell* procedure provides for follow-up questions to probe further recall once free recall has been exhausted. Scores are turned into grade equivalents using norms developed on the same group of 200 children in second through sixth grades that were used to develop norms for the oral reading test.

It is difficult to accept several assumptions made by the test authors with respect to the silent reading test. No rationale is given for using a different comprehension measure for silent reading (free recall) than for oral reading (question answering). This becomes a problem when performance on the two tests is then compared. Differences in performance on the two tests would be extremely difficult to interpret even if comprehension were assessed in the same manner on each test. When the assessment procedure changes, the problem of interpretation is exacerbated. It is also difficult to follow the logic of calling performance on the oral reading test the instructional level and performance on the silent reading tests the independent reading level. The only explanation given in the test manual is that unaided recall is a higher order task than question answering, which is not convincing.

The *Durrell* does not seem to conform to the traditional standards for determining reading levels (as exemplified by Betts) nor any other explicitly stated standards in determining instructional and independent levels. Although the value of comparing oral and silent reading performance is questionable, the *Durrell* explicitly states this as a goal of the test but then fails to indicate how such a comparison should be undertaken, why such as a comparison is desirable, or which differences and similarities between the two are worth noting. The manual includes no discussion of this matter and the *Individual Record Booklet* asks the examiner only to indicate whether silent reading was the same, better, or worse than oral reading in speed, recall, and "security." How such differences, once observed, are to be interpreted by the teacher is not clear. From one perspective, better performance in silent reading would be normal in all three categories.

Imagery

The *Durrell* also ventures into assessing an aspect of comprehension that is experiencing a rebirth in recent years—imagery. Though Spache (1981) is critical of this aspect of the *Durrell,* the optional questions that invite reader description of what "you see in your mind" are potentially revealing. Research reported by Paivio (1971) suggests that poor readers are characterized by impoverished mental imagery as they read. No other diagnostic reading test attempts to examine this ability. The fact that prior to reading no instructions are given to the child about forming mental images while reading may be an important limitation in generalizing the imagery results obtained on the *Durrell.* It is also odd that after going to some lengths to measure imagery the only recording of the results is to indicate whether the "flow" is "rich" or "poor." No direction is given in the test manual concerning how to decide what is "poor flow" or how to remediate problems in this domain. This seems to be another example of major responsibility being thrown on the examiner without adequate direction or explanation.

Listening Comprehension

A third set of passages is provided in the *Durrell* for assessing listening comprehension as an estimate of reading capacity. After hearing the examiner read a passage aloud, the student responds to seven or eight factual (detail) questions. The student's listening level is the level where not more than two questions are missed. The listening score is apparently used to determine whether performance is substantially different from potential (though this language is not used in the examiner's manual). Though listening is often used as a way of establishing the child's capacity or reading expectancy, the looseness with which the *Durrell* handles this topic is disappointing. No rationale is offered nor is any system given for judging how much discrepancy between silent reading and listening is significant. What seems especially strange is that the examiner is discouraged from establishing an upper level with the listening test. "There is little point in trying to establish an upper level since the purpose of this test is to learn whether or not reading difficulty rests upon lack of comprehension."[4] This explanation seems unsatisfactory since the stated purpose of the test is to estimate reading capacity. How can capacity be estimated unless the top is determined?

The *Durrell* provides a fourth set of supplementary passages that can be used for retesting in any of the areas previously mentioned (oral reading, silent reading, or listening), or to examine other abilities of interest to the teacher.

In their review of the *Durrell,* Schell and Jennings (1981) comment on the lack of information about the readability level of the four sets of graded passages. They complain that special importance is attached to the norms because no effort is made to show how the passages have been standardized. We have less concern about the actual grade level of each passage than about the relative difficulty of one passage in comparison to the next and equivalence from test to test (that is, oral reading, silent reading, and so on). Nevertheless, we agree with Schell and Jennings that the test authors are obligated to pay more attention than they have to the readability of the passages.

A new test added to this latest version of the *Durrell* makes further use of the same words included in the Word Recognition and Word Analysis Test (though the order of the words has been scrambled). Called Listening Vocabulary, this new test presents five lists of fifteen words each drawn from certain ideational clusters in *Roget's International Thesaurus.* The words on any one list fit into each of three categories. For example, one list includes words that relate to the categories of time, size, and color. When a word (for example, *red, large, year*) is called by the examiner, the child's task is to decide into which category it fits. The words grow gradually more difficult in each list. Testing is stopped in one list and moved to the next list when the child has missed or omitted three words in a row. A score is obtained by totaling the correct responses to all lists and consulting the table of grade norms.

The stated purpose of the Listening Vocabulary Test is to provide a second index of reading capacity and to permit a comparison of listening vocabulary and listening comprehension in recognizing the same words. It is difficult to accept the assumption that knowing the meaning of isolated words spoken aloud (at least well enough to classify them into one of three categories) is a particularly valid estimate of reading capacity. The test manual reports that performance on the Listening Vocabulary Test correlates at only a .38 level with scores on the *Metropolitan Reading Test* among primary-grade children. This suggests that the Listening Vocabulary Test is not a particularly good predictor of actual reading achievement. With upper-grade children a somewhat higher (.58), though not remarkable, correlation was found. These relationships are quite similar to those typically found between general intelligence and reading ability. The claim made in the test manual that Listening Vocabulary is a more direct measure of reading capacity than the usual measures of intelligence seems overdrawn. If a general measure of intelligence is already available for a pupil, it seems advisable to simply omit this test. The very low relationship found between Listening Comprehension and Listening Vocabulary (.22 at the primary level and .57 at the intermediate level) suggests that little agreement exists between the two indexes of reading capacity provided by the *Durrell.* Of the two, Listening Comprehension is preferred since it at least involves pupil response to connected discourse.

Other Subtests

The remaining subtests of the *Durrell* are ones a teacher would use selectively. Some are intended for the nonreader or the child who is reading on a first-grade level. Other subtests are for second-grade level and below, third-grade level and below, and so forth. Although no set sequence is mandated for administering the various subtests, the oral and silent reading passages, the listening task, and the word recognition lists are typically given to all pupils first. Based on performance in those areas a determination is made concerning which additional tests to give. Thus the child who struggles with even the easiest passage during oral and silent reading and recognizes few words in isolation might normally be tested for hearing sounds in words, for example. On the other hand, a child who reads the third- or fourth-grade passage successfully might be tested for visual memory of words and spelling.

The various subtests have titles that are fairly descriptive of their content. In most subtests the assumption is made that a matching task is easiest, an identification task is somewhat more difficult, and a naming or producing task is more difficult. Thus the child who can name letters when they are shown can surely find a letter when it is named and match letters when they are shown. Conversely, when the child cannot match letters she probably cannot name letters. Consequently the *Durrell* is built on certain assumptions about what skills are important to success in reading. While the assumptions about which skill precedes another skill are made fairly explicit in the test manual, no discussion is given concerning what conceptualization of reading the test supports. One can infer that phonics knowledge is believed to be important and that use of context and structural analysis are believed to be unimportant by looking at the subtests provided. The subtests include the following:

Sounds in Isolation

    Letters

    Blends and Digraphs

    Phonograms

    Affixes (Initial)

    Affixes (Final)

Spelling

Phonic Spelling of Words (Nonsense Words)

Visual Memory of Words

Identifying Sounds in Words

Prereading Phonics Abilities Inventories

    Syntax Matching

    Identifying Letter Names in Spoken Words

    Identifying Phonemes in Spoken Words

    Naming Letters (Lowercase)

    Writing Letters from Dictation

    Naming Letters (Uppercase)

    Identifying Letters Named

In conclusion, the revised *Durrell* is disappointing. As a comprehensive test of reading it is insufficient. Important and basic aspects of reading are ignored. Oral reading errors are scored in a haphazard manner. Far too much emphasis is placed on the use of norms. Furthermore, the heavy dependence on time in judging a pupil's performance is inappropriate and misleading. Assumptions about skills hierarchies are made that are not acceptable. Information is gathered that the manual fails to justify or explain, and insufficient discussion is provided concerning how to interpret the results of the various tests. Some unique features of the *Durrell* are interesting and potentially revealing. The system for scoring comprehension with retellings and the attention given to imagery are examples of features that are intriguing. However, even in these areas problems exist. On balance, use of *Durrell* should be avoided.

The Woodcock Reading Mastery Tests

Another individually administered diagnostic test, the *Woodcock* (1973), is published by American Guidance Service (AGS). A new version was published in 1987. Like several other AGS tests, the *Woodcock* is in the form of a sturdy, hard-covered, ring-type binder that serves as an easel when placed on a table between the student and the teacher. Stimulus materials are presented to the student by flipping a page from the teacher's side across the top of the easel to the child's side. Directions are visible on the teacher's side of the easel, thus facilitating smooth administration of the test while permitting good eye contact with the child.

The *Woodcock* includes two forms and is intended for kindergarten through twelfth grade. Five subtests each yield a separate score as well as contribute to a total score. The subtests are Letter Identification, Word Identification, Word Attack, Word Comprehension, and Passage Comprehension. All student responses are made orally and are recorded by the teacher on a separate answer sheet.

The test is described as being appropriate for measuring individual reading growth, detecting reading problems, grouping students for instruction, evaluating curriculum and programs, and accountability. The test author estimates that an entire form of the test can be administered in 20 to 30 minutes, although Tuinman[5] indicates that 30 to 50 minutes is a more realistic time estimate. No special training in administering the *Woodcock* is necessary according to the manual accompanying the test. In fact, even paraprofessionals (volunteers and teachers' aides, for example) are identified as appropriate examiners. This assertion is questionable since the value of any individually administered diagnostic test derives partly from the observations that only a skilled professional can make during the examination. Woodcock is probably correct in his assumption that, with experience, a competent paraprofessional can follow the directions sufficiently well to produce a reliable score, however.

The subtest on Letter Identification involves a straightforward task that requires the student to say the name of a letter as the examiner points to it. Forty-five letters are included in both capital and lowercase forms as well as in a variety of type faces (including cursive, gothic, roman, and italic). The value of spreading scores across a scale that ranges from first to fourth grade is a mystery. Letter identification is essentially a readiness factor that has no importance once the child is reading. Why an entire subtest of a diagnostic instrument attends to this relatively narrow matter is unclear.

The second subtest, Word Identification, presents the examinee with a list of 150 words in isolation to be read aloud without assistance. The words are presented in order of difficulty and, for the preprimer through third grade levels, are drawn from seven basal reading programs. Above that level they are drawn from the Thorndike-Lorge list. Provision is made for starting each student at a point in the list appropriate to his expected level of achievement. It is odd that the test manual indicates, "There is no assumption that the subject . . . has ever seen the word before." This subtest is primarily a test of sight vocabulary. The way the words were selected suggests that high frequency words are involved. Since the next subtest purports to measure word attack, the author's assertion regarding the examinee's familiarity with the words seems incongruous.

The subtest on Word Attack consists of fifty nonsense words students must pronounce presumably by applying their knowledge of phonics and structural analysis. Again, items are arranged in order of difficulty; however, all examinees begin with item number one and proceed until five successive errors indicate a ceiling has been reached. The nonsense words have been created to test knowledge of "most consonant and vowel sounds, common prefixes and suffixes, and frequently appearing irregular spellings." Nonsense words are used, of course, to eliminate the possibility that words will be identified at sight. Yet the test manual states, "In several cases, including the sample item, the words are, in fact, real but most likely unknown to the subject."[6] Why the author states an important assumption and then violates it is unknown and bothersome.

Word Comprehension, often called vocabulary, is a measure of the examinee's knowledge of word meaning. The *Woodcock Test* employs an analogy format (such as *snow-cold* = *sun* – _____) to obtain a vocabulary score. A total of seventy analogies ranging from simple to complex is provided. Though one might argue that ability to manipulate concepts is a deeper and therefore better measure of word meaning than merely matching synonyms, for example, it seems evident that analogies require far *more* than knowledge of words. Problem solving and reasoning are needed in solving analogies and, therefore, analogies are not used in any other reading test. This subtest seems to be seriously flawed as a reading measure.

The final subtest of the *Woodcock,* Passage Comprehension, is described as a modified cloze procedure task. A total of eighty-five items, each requiring the student to supply a word that fits into a blank, comprise the subtest. Picture clues are given with the first twenty-two items. Initially only one phrase or sentence is used. In later more difficult items, up to three or four sentences are used. Dwyer comments on the ineffectiveness of this subtest in getting at higher level comprehension abilities and states: "There is no evidence of attempts to measure higher level reading skills such as inference, evaluation of logic, or analysis; instead, the use of abstruse materials seems to be relied on for difficulty."[7] Tuinman cautions that even students who decode poorly can do many of the items on this subtest correctly by responding exclusively to the picture clues.[8]

The author of the *Woodcock* test offers no explanation for the overall scheme used in creating this test. No attempt is made, for example, to specify how each subtest addresses a critical or important aspect of the reading process. No conceptualization of reading is offered as a point of reference for the subtests. Several of the subtests are traditionally a part of diagnostic reading tests (for example, word comprehension), but at least one (letter identification) is not. Several test reviewers have questioned the inclusion of the letter identification test.[9] It seems inappropriate to make a score from this subtest equal to the other subtests in arriving at an overall score on the *Woodcock.* Other aspects of the *Woodcock* that reviewers have justifiably questioned include: (1) the claim that the test is both norm-referenced and criterion-referenced (mastery of a skill at a particular grade level is, in part, a function of the instructional program used) and (2) the procedures used to establish test validity (important assumptions about the statistical procedure used are not met).

The conclusion drawn from this information is that the *Woodcock* test has very little value as a diagnostic instrument but might be used as a general screening device if the limitations cited here and in Buros (1978) are kept in mind.

Botel Reading Inventory

The *Botel Reading Inventory* (1981) has been included with other individual diagnostic reading tests even though parts of the *Botel* can be given in a group setting. This seems appropriate because *parts* of the *Botel* must be given individually, thus disqualifying it as a group test.

The *Botel Reading Inventory* (Form A and B) consists of four subtests: (1) Decoding, (2) Spelling, (3) Word Recognition, and (4) Word Opposites. The primary purpose of the *Botel* is to assist teachers in estimating the placement of pupils in textbooks. Given this purpose, the *Botel* might be regarded as a survey test. The test manual indicates that the *Botel* is also useful for "determining which common syllable/spelling patterns the student can decode and encode." With this information "it is then possible to plan appropriate instructional programs to advance the students' competence in those patterns not yet mastered."[10] Therefore, it is concluded that the test is diagnostic in nature although comprehension is addressed only from the standpoint of placement.

Interestingly enough, and quite in contrast with most diagnostic reading tests, the *Botel* contains absolutely no running text (connected discourse) to be read by pupils but confines itself instead to lists of words read or heard. This represents the most extreme example of breaking the act of reading into component parts. In effect, here is a test of reading that does not require the pupil to read in the normal sense of the word. This is a significant point that must be considered in evaluating the *Botel*.

The decoding competency section of the *Botel* includes twelve subtests of ten items each that are organized into seven levels. Each level appears to build on previous levels in a skills hierarchy that moves from simple to more complex. Thus Level One (Parts 1 through 3) is labeled "Awareness of Sounds and Letter Correspondences" and consists of subtests on Letter Naming, Beginning Consonant Sound/Letter Patterns. Subtests in Level One may be given in a group setting. The remaining tests (Parts 4 through 12) are given individually. Level Two (Parts 4 through 5) is labeled "Decoding Simple, Highly Regular Syllables" and includes subtests on CVC pattern words and CVCe pattern words. Subsequent levels (Parts 6 through 12) step through progressively longer and less regular words with subtests on various consonant-vowel patterns. Level Six (Part 11) focuses on different parts of speech (for example, muscle-muscular) and Level Seven (Part 12) uses nonsense words.

In Part 1 (Letter Naming) the student's task is to draw a line under one of six letters in a row when the teacher says its name. Part 2 is identical except that initial consonants are marked when a word that begins with a particular letter is given. Part 3 uses the same approach except that a word that rhymes with two stimulus words given aloud is underlined. Parts 4 through 12 require the student to read words aloud to the examiner.

The mastery level is set at 80 percent correct for all subtests in the Decoding section. This is a change from the 1970 edition, in which 100 percent success was expected. Like the 1970 edition, the 1981 version indicates that instruction should focus on the skills where test performance falls below the mastery level.

There are several problems with the Decoding subtests. First, the subtests seem too short to have satisfactory reliability. Given what is known about error in measurement, it is hazardous to draw conclusions about a student's knowledge of consonants, for example, using only ten items. Coupled with the concern for the inadequate sample of behaviors gathered by the *Botel* is dissatisfaction with the assumption made here about the hierarchical nature of reading. Certainly no empirical evidence exists to support the need to master consonant sounds before learning vowel sounds. We question the logic of such an assertion, yet a faithful follower of this test is directed to embrace such an approach.

The second subtest of the *Botel*, Spelling Placement, is a traditional spelling test. That is, the teacher says a word aloud, uses it in a sentence, then repeats the word. Subjects write the word on their paper. The *Botel* includes five graded lists of twenty words each for this subtest; one list for first and second grade, and a separate list each for third through sixth grade. The first level at which a student's score falls below 80 percent accuracy is identified as the instructional level. Systematic instruction at this level is recommended by the *Botel*. No explanation is given concerning why a spelling subtest is included in a reading test, nor is any discussion offered as to how the results of this subtest should be used diagnostically for planning specific spelling lessons by the teacher.

The subtest on word recognition is administered individually and consists of eight lists of words with twenty words per list. Each list corresponds to a reading level—preprimer through fourth grade. Words were chosen for the preprimer through third-grade lists from common words found in five major basal readers. The fourth-grade words were drawn from the Thorndike-Lorge list. The student's task on this subtest is to read each word aloud beginning with a level where "he is likely to have 100 percent correct." The teacher records three types of errors: (1) mispronunciation, (2) substitutions, and (3) refusals (no response). Once performance falls below 70 percent accuracy on two successive levels, the testing is stopped. The instructional reading level is determined by identifying the highest list read with 70 percent accuracy or above. The reading level of subjects who pass the hardest word list (fourth grade) is determined by performance on a different subtest, the Word Opposites Test.

It is important to note that Goodman (1969) and others have demonstrated that the identification of words in isolation is more difficult than in context. Whatever limitation this places on the *Botel* is widely shared among diagnostic tests since nearly all have a subtest identical or similar to the *Botel* (using words in isolation). More significant is the approach taken in the *Botel* to scoring errors. The examiner is encouraged to make a written record of the child's incorrect responses presumably for the purpose of making a qualitative examination of errors. Yet no assistance is given in differentiating between a mispronunciation and a substitution. Without the benefit of context the examiner would be hard pressed to know when an error qualifies as a substitution and when it is a mispronunciation. The *Botel* also suggests that variations associated with regional and dialectal differences be accepted, but no examples are given to help the teacher understand what this means or how it can be accomplished. The *Botel's* directions with respect to hesitations (no response) are vague. Hesitations (up to 6 seconds) are not errors, but "more than several such responses at any level are indicative of insecurity and should be considered when establishing the pupil's reading level." This raises the following questions: Exactly how many hesitations qualify as "more than several?" What constitutes "consideration" of the errors? Should the reading level be reduced a full step, two steps, or more?

The Word Opposites subtest can be given in a group setting. It presents pupils with an isolated word and three alternative choices. The task is to pick the word that "means the opposite or nearly the opposite." The example given is

1. no   ok   *yes*   not

Then lists beginning at Grade one and ranging up to senior high level in difficulty are included. Words for this subtest were selected in the same manner as words for the Word Recognition Test.

Performance on the Word Opposites subtest is compared to an 80 percent accuracy standard. Once the pupil's performance falls below this standard on two successive lists (grade levels), testing is stopped and the instructional reading level determined to be the level at which better than 80 percent accuracy was achieved.

The test manual does not caution teachers to be sure that the meaning of *opposite* is known by the pupil. With only one example given prior to testing, the possibility exists that some students will fail to realize what is expected on this subtest. This same format is often used in workbooks and tests for identification of synonyms.

The presentation of words in isolation in the *Botel* is an artificial and unrealistic task insofar as normal reading is concerned; shades of meaning for many words are often unclear until they are used in context. For example, the word *colorless* is given with these alternatives: *jovial, glamorous, ignorant, drastic.* Which means the opposite of *colorless?* The keyed answer is *glamorous.* But consider these uses of the alternative responses.

The atmosphere at the carnival was *jovial.*

The brightest yellow paint was a *drastic* change in the appearance of the room.

Is *glamorous* the best opposite of colorless? None of these choices seem particularly good to us, but *jovial* and *drastic* can be as appropriate as *glamorous* in some contexts.

The Word Opposites subtest is normally given as a reading test, that is, students work through the items on their own reading the words silently. Used in this way, the test is intended to provide an estimate of comprehension. Unless one has a terribly narrow view of how reading comprehension occurs, this subtest seems to raise more questions about pupil performance than it gives answers.

Used as a listening test (teachers read to pupils while they follow along marking their own answers), the Word Opposites subtest is described as a measure of "reading potential." Given a "wide difference" (not quantified beyond this in the manual) between the silent reading and listening scores (presumably) on two forms of the *Botel,* the vague claim is made that the test indicates "a remedial program could be started to bring performance more in line." No rationale is offered for this claim. No research supporting the use of listening comprehension as a measure of reading potential is cited, nor are any clues given as to what such a remedial program would include.

A point has been made in each test review presented in this chapter to examine what conceptualization of reading a particular test seems to reflect. Test authors have an obligation to make an explicit statement about what they think is important in the reading process and to discuss how their test addresses those elements. (This is referred to as "content validity.") Relatively few test authors meet this fundamental expectation in an explicit manner. Most test authors come at the task in a roundabout way. The *Botel* is a good example of the latter approach.

One can infer that Dr. Botel believes two aspects of the reading act are important and measurable: word recognition and comprehension. Word recognition evidently occurs in Botel's view by learning to recognize particular spelling patterns. Furthermore, an optimal sequence exists for mastering those patterns if the nature of the test format and instructions for interpretation are any indication of the author's beliefs. Decoding evidently leads to comprehension in a linear fashion beginning with letter naming and progressing through various consonant and vowel combinations. Comprehension occurs if the meanings of words recognized are known by the reader.

This seems a gross oversimplification of the reading process. Furthermore, the subtests of the *Botel* in many cases do not measure what the labels indicate. The Word Recognition subtests based on words that follow certain spelling patterns, for example, tell only whether the pupil is familiar with particular words, not whether a student can generalize about sound-symbol relationships in certain combinations of letters. In other words, the word *hope* in Part 5 of the Decoding subtest might be a sight word for a child, but the *Botel* includes it in a list of words that represent the CVCe pattern. Does the child who reads it know the "final silent e rule" or is this a word she recognizes at sight? It is also questionable whether ten items sufficiently sample each "skill domain" to provide a reliable measure. And, finally, Botel's argument that mastery of one decoding "skill must precede instruction on the next skill" is unconvincing.

The Word Recognition and Decoding sections of the *Botel* are narrow and insufficient, in our estimation, but the assessment of comprehension is grossly inadequate. Knowledge of word meanings is identified by the *Botel* as "the most important factor" in determining reading comprehension. From this premise the shaky conclusion is drawn that a single measure of word meanings using a word opposites task is appropriate for assessing comprehension. To compound this problem, isolated words are used to get at the pupil's knowledge of words. Although it is true that no claims are made in the test manual concerning the diagnostic value of the *Botel* in the area of comprehension, even accurate placement of a pupil in appropriate reading material requires a more sensitive measure of comprehension than this.

Validity is claimed for the *Botel* in several ways. Criterion-related validity (meaning the test correlates positively with some respected measure) is established by comparing scores on two subtests of the *Botel* (Word Recognition and Word Opposites) with actual placement in the Ginn basal readers. Although a fairly good sample of pupils was involved in this effort (over 600), several limitations seem evident. What is true for the Ginn program as it is used in one school district is not an especially accurate criterion for judging correct matching of pupils and materials.[11]

A second study based on the IRI scores of only thirty fourth-grade students produced correlation coefficients in the .77 to .94 range; however, such a small sample makes these results difficult to interpret.

High reliability is claimed for the *Botel* for both alternate forms and for internal consistency. There is no reason to doubt that results of the two forms would agree; the word lists come from common pools. However, the reported internal consistency appears to be oddly conceived. Scores for the Word Recognition and Word Opposites subtests were compared. The high correlations (.88 to .95) are cited as evidence of high reliability, but present a probability that both subtests are simply measuring the same abilities. How this demonstrates reliability is difficult to fathom. It seems to suggest that one can get at whatever the *Botel* measures regardless of which subtest one uses. This, in turn, casts considerable doubt on the accuracy of the labels assigned to the subtests and fails to address reliability altogether.

One last concern in the area of validity and reliability seems relevant. Nowhere are the Spelling and Decoding subtests compared with the results of other tests or placement results. This omission is especially troublesome given the general concern for the narrowness of the Decoding subtests. Since it is the Decoding subtests of the *Botel* that are described as having diagnostic value, this omission is a serious limitation. On balance, we cannot recommend the *Botel* for use by a classroom teacher.

Diagnostic Reading Scales

The *Diagnostic Reading Scales* (Spache 1981a) were revised in 1981. The full test battery includes a graded word list (divided into three levels), two sets of graded reading passages (eleven in each set), and twelve separate word analysis and phonics tests intended for supplementary use. The *Scales* are administered individually to the student, who makes all responses orally. The entire test can be given in about 60 minutes. A prudent caution in the *Examiner's Manual* indicates that the professional judgment involved in using and interpreting this test (and the caution should include any diagnostic test) requires supervised training in a clinical setting. In response to feedback from those who have used the *Scales*, the 1981 version includes a 90-minute cassette tape designed for inservice training in correct administration of the test. Special emphasis is given in the tape, as well as in the *Examiner's Manual*, to testing a student who speaks a nonstandard English dialect. This addition makes the *Scales* unique among diagnostic tests and enhances its value significantly.

The *Scales* are designed for use with students who are functioning at first-through seventh-grade levels. Stated purposes for the tests include the evaluation of oral and silent reading abilities and auditory comprehension. Although the manual indicates that the *Scales* are intended to help in the identification of a student's functional reading levels (that is, instructional, independent, and potential), an explicit disclaimer is made to distinguish between these levels as defined by Spache and the levels obtained from an IRI (in the manner of Betts). The criteria were established for determining the reading levels through actual tryouts with children. Thus success with the 2.2 level paragraph, for example, is judged by comparing the student's oral reading error rate with that of other students on that same material, not by applying a general word recognition accuracy level (for example 95 percent) regardless of the passage read.

The first subtest of the *Scales* requires the student to read aloud from a word list until five consecutive words are missed. The words came from the Durrell Word list and are grouped by difficulty on the basis of trials with about 100 students at each level of the *Scales*. The word lists are used, in part, as a pretest to determine which level should be used when entering the reading selection subtest. The manual also indicates that sight-word vocabulary and decoding strategies on words in isolation can be studied with the Word Recognition Lists. A word analysis checklist near the end of the *Examiner's Manual* is provided to help the teacher summarize observations about techniques the student uses on words in isolation and in context. Discussion in the *Examiner's Manual* indicates that performance on lists of isolated words is predictive of the child's instructional level. The test author, George Spache, is careful to point out that reading words in isolation requires different skills than reading words in context (except, he notes, for beginning readers). Information on how well the child reads words in context is obtained from the next subtest. Spache suggests that different instructional needs are revealed if a student is more successful with words in isolation or words in context. Errors detected under these two conditions should not be combined for analysis according to the *Manual,* a proper caution in our view.

A table is provided in the *Examiner's Manual* that enables the teacher to determine at which level to enter the reading selections for oral reading. This decision is made by using the number of isolated words read correctly in the first subtest.

The second subtest, Reading Selections, consists of eleven graded paragraphs ranging from grade levels 1.4 to 7.5 in difficulty. Two forms or sets of selections are provided to permit retesting on new material. Both narrative and expository material are included. As the pupil reads a selection aloud the teacher notes errors in the following categories: omission, addition, substitution, repetition, and reversal. Hesitations are not counted as errors and no provision is made for aiding the child. After a 5-second pause, the child is encouraged to try a word, then skip it and go on if no response is given. Errors corrected spontaneously by the child are not counted. Multiple errors on the same word or phrase are counted as only one error.

The number of errors noted during oral reading of a passage is important in determining the child's instructional level. Each passage indicates the maximum number of errors permitted. Once that number has been exceeded, the previous level (where the maximum was not exceeded) is taken as the child's instructional level *if comprehension is adequate.*

Comprehension is assessed by means of questions the child answers orally when asked by the teacher. Seven questions are asked at levels 1.4–2.2, eight questions at level 2.4 and above. All questions are of a recall nature but involve language manipulations (transformations) that prevent mere rote answers. Field testing was conducted during development of the *Scales* to eliminate questions that were clearly not passage-dependent. The test author maintains that what may appear to be general knowledge to an adult may be unknown to a child, thus making a question passage-dependent for the child. Performance criteria for judging the child's comprehension are based on a 60 percent standard. Thus passages with seven questions require four correct responses and passages with eight questions require five correct responses for minimally acceptable performance. Several reviewers have questioned the use of a 60 percent criterion in earlier versions of the *Scales* for correct placement of students.[12] The 1981 *Examiner's Manual* states that more stringent standards yield underestimates of reading ability as determined by tryouts of the test with children using other oral reading tests, teacher judgment, and mental age as the external criterion.

The child's instructional level is found by determining the level at which oral reading accuracy *and* comprehension meet the minimum levels indicated. Thus a child who makes only ten errors on the 5.5 passage (below the maximum of thirteen allowed) but misses four of eight comprehension questions has failed one of the criteria. The instructional level in this case would be 4.5, the previous level where both criteria were met. The converse is also true: A child could answer seven of eight questions correctly but not advance to the next level because of excessive oral errors. The test manual suggests that in this case the teacher should decide if the reading errors are significant ones and if sufficient understanding is evidenced to override the oral error performance. By going on to the next passage a teacher can usually get further information to assist in judging which is the student's instructional level.

It should be noted that no attempt is made in the *Scales* to undertake qualitative analysis of oral reading miscues. Except for the practice of eliminating errors that are self-corrected and disregarding dialect differences, the *Scales* take a quantitative approach to oral reading errors in determining instructional level. The *Examiner's Manual* is careful to explain that some types of errors are more significant than others, but that the difficulty level of the material being read is a factor in the kinds of errors made at different levels. Furthermore, to be reliable, miscue analysis must be based on a significant number of errors— probably fifty at the minimum. Because the passages in the *Scales* are short, they will not generate a sufficient number of miscues to make detailed analysis meaningful. Suggestions are given in the *Examiner's Manual* for looking at the graphic, phonic, syntactic, and semantic content of errors in an informal, though unsystematic way, for possible insights into the child's reading strategies. These insights can be recorded in the Word Analysis Checklist provided in the *Examiner's Record Book.*

After determining the child's instructional reading level via oral reading, the *Scales* direct the examiner to have the student silently read the selection one level above the orally read selection that was failed. While the pupil reads, the teacher takes note of the time required to complete the selection. The teacher then asks the comprehension questions and records in the record book whether or not they are answered correctly. When the child's performance drops below 60 percent correct the silent reading test is terminated. The highest level at which the child reads with minimum accuracy is taken as the independent reading level.

Finally, the potential reading level is determined by having the teacher read to the pupil beginning one level above the last level read silently. Again the comprehension questions are asked following the completion of each selection. The 60 percent criterion is applied here in exactly the same manner as in determining the independent level.

The *Examiner's Manual* defines the instructional, independent, and potential levels and describes the use of each level in a classroom. The instructional level indicates the level of materials to be used for daily instruction. The independent level indicates the level of materials to be used for practice reading in both groups oral reading and individual silent reading. It should be pointed out that because the terms are used in an unconventional way by Spache, for most children the independent level will be higher than the instructional level, a relationship that is normally reversed. Since the *Manual* is clear concerning just how the terms are being used, no problem arises with this difference as long as teachers are alert to the way the terms are defined. In any case, the independent level as determined by the *Scales* is not comparable to the independent level as it is usually designated by conventional informal reading inventories.[13] The potential level represents the level to which a child's reading performance can be raised with appropriate instruction. This notion is given considerable elaboration in the *Examiner's Manual* along with factors that must be considered in judging a child's potential.

The first two subtests in the *Scales*, the Word Recognition Lists and the Graded Reading Selections, are normally given to all students according to the sequence described above. Depending on what is learned from these tests, the teacher may decide to give some, all, or none of the remaining subtests. The Word Analysis and Phonics subtests have been sequenced according to their approximate difficulty for primary students but can be given in any order. These subtests are not recommended by the *Manual* for students reading above the fourth grade level for the very good reason that the skills tested are not directly related to reading comprehension.

Few tests are as direct and clear as this one in identifying assumptions made about the definition of reading being employed by the author. Additionally, Spache indicates that the supplementary subtests are not reliable enough to justify detailed interpretation of the scores. Appropriate cautions are also given about not judging pupil performance on the various subtests without allowing for the de-emphasis on phonics, for example, will not do as well on these subtests. The development of local standards is recommended for the Word Analysis and Phonics Tests.

The 1981 version of the *Scales* has expanded the number of supplementary word analysis tests from eight to twelve. Subtests now include the following:

1. Initial Consonants
2. Final Consonants
3. Consonant Digraphs
4. Consonant Blends
5. Initial Consonant Substitution
6. Initial Consonant Sounds Recognized Auditorially
7. Auditory Discrimination
8. Short and Long Vowel Sounds
9. Vowels with R
10. Vowel Diphthongs and Digraphs
11. Common Syllables or Phonograms
12. Blending

It is significant that nonsense words and real words beyond the sight word vocabulary of third graders are used in these subtests. This has been done to reduce the chances that children's performance will reflect their ability to recognize a word at sight rather than by applying their knowledge of the ability being tested. Thus, obvious care has been taken to make each subtest a valid measure of the ability indicated. For example, Test 6, Initial Consonant Sounds Recognized Auditorially, requires the child to listen to a word pronounced by the teacher and tell with which letter the word begins. Twenty-three items are included in this subtest. Three of the supplementary subtests have only nine or ten items (Initial Consonant Substitution, Vowels with *r*, and Blending). All others have fifteen or more items. The increased length of the supplementary tests is a positive feature of the 1981 revision of the *Scales*.

A review of the 1975 edition of the *Scales* by Schreiner is critical of the clarity of the test manual.[14] The 1981 version is markedly improved in this regard.

A question and answer format is followed that is particularly clear and useful. Most questions raised were anticipated, and full yet succinct answers were provided. Proper cautions in using, interpreting, and supplementing the *Scales* are given in the *Manual*.

Reliability and validity data for the *Scales* are reported in a *Technical Report* (no date) available from the publisher. Evidence is reported to demonstrate that the 1981 revision corrects the tendency of earlier versions to overestimate students' reading ability. Some of this evidence relates to analysis of the reading passages using current readability formulas. Other evidence relates to the results of testing conducted by the publisher with students in first to eighth grades. Scores obtained with the *Scales* were compared to pupil performance on various standardized tests (for example, *Gates-MacGinitie Reading Tests, Iowa Test of Basic Skill,* etc.), the level of classroom reader assigned, and a teacher estimate of the child's reading level. High intercorrelations (at or above .80) were found among these variables.

Reliability was determined by retesting students after a period of two to eight weeks with the alternate set of reading selections. A correlation coefficient of .89 was found, thus suggesting a fair amount of consistency for test results obtained with the *Scales*. The Word Analysis and Phonics Tests yielded correlation coefficients on a test-retest basis in the .60 and above range for first and second grade with only one significant deviation (i.e., Initial Consonant Sounds Recognized Auditorially). These findings lend importance to the caution raised earlier about not placing confidence in the scores of individual subtests (a caution the *Examiner's Manual* is careful to make). On balance, the validity and reliability of the *Scales* seems well-documented.

The *Examiner's Manual* specifies a general theory of reading diagnosis underlying the *Scales* and explains how each subtest relates to the reading process. One can make inferences about what view of reading the author holds. Both bottom-up and top-down processes are acknowledged in the discussion, but the tests themselves appear to focus more on textual factors. However, the test is not an embodiment of one reading theory. A rationale is given for the content of each subtest. An extensive section of the *Manual* is devoted to interpretation of the results. The *Diagnostic Reading Scales* would be useful to a classroom teacher.

COMMERCIAL IRIs

Summaries by Jongsma and Jongsma (1981) and Harris and Niles (1982) compared and contrasted over a dozen commercial IRIs. While marked differences were found to exist among the inventories examined, there was also a commonality that distinguished IRIs from other instruments.

Analytical Reading Inventory

The Woods and Moe (1989) *Analytical Reading Inventory* is typical of most IRIs in the following respects: (1) lists of high-frequency words in isolation are provided for testing word identification and for determining which passages should be used as a starting point (2) graded passages from the primer level through ninth grade are provided in three separate forms (the 1989 edition also includes expository passages in a Science Form and a Social Studies Form with passages for Grades 1–9) (3) comprehension is assessed through retelling and with the use of questions that are given to probe understanding at both a factual and inferential level (4) forms are provided for recording and summarizing a student's performance and (5) criteria are stated for judging the student's level of performance on each passage (independent, instructional, and frustration levels).

The development of the *ARI* is described in fair detail in the test booklet. Topics of interest to children were selected and an attempt was made to make each form of the inventory comparable. The difficult level of each passage was examined via readability procedures, the number of different words was controlled as were average sentence length, and the longest sentence for each level was controlled. Comprehension questions of six types were developed according to a taxonomy and care was taken to make each question passage-dependent. The inventory was field-tested with children and revised on the basis of difficulties encountered. Not all IRIs are developed with attention to the above details nor is the process of development always described in the test booklet.

The *ARI* manual includes very little assistance for the teacher beyond how to administer the inventory and record the results. Roughly four pages of text are devoted to interpreting the results and providing appropriate follow-up instruction.

Seven types of oral reading miscues are noted in the *ARI*. They are omissions, insertions, substitutions, aided words, repetitions, reversals, and hesitations. Self-corrections are not counted as errors. A simplified "Qualitative Analysis Summary Sheet" focuses attention on whether a meaning change is

In an IRI testing situation the teacher makes notes concerning each deviation from the test as a child reads aloud. *(Peter Vadnai)*

involved in each miscue. The *ARI* does not give miscue analysis the full discussion it deserves, but this edition is an improvement in that regard over previous editions.

One other aspect of the *ARI* deserving special mention is the fact that the topic of each passage is briefly described for the examiner. The manual cautions that cuing prior to reading should be minimized but that some sort of introduction is appropriate if the student would otherwise be confused about the topic. The effect of introducing a passage when giving an IRI is unknown. According to Harris and Niles (1982), only three of twelve IRIs they examined included introductory statements. It is entirely possible that some students perform better when an advanced organizer is employed. The looseness of the *ARI* instructions on this matter are troublesome. How does the examiner decide who is confused and who is not? How much background should be built? We are inclined to avoid any kind of introductory remarks when giving an IRI. Interestingly, unlike some IRIs, *ARI* does not provide a title for each passage. This, too, is a variable that may affect IRI performance in an unknown way. Some IRIs (*Silvaroli,* for example) give both a title and a brief introduction to the passage (some also provide an illustration).

Qualitative Reading Inventory

While the *ARI* is similar in content and purpose to most IRIs, one new IRI stands above all others in its attention to controlling and accounting for factors that may be important in understanding how a reader is attempting to process written text. Authored by Leslie and Caldwell (1990), the *Qualitative Reading Inventory (QRI)* represents a standard to which other reading tests (formal and informal) might aspire. Published as a spiral bound, 8 1/2" x 11" booklet, the *QRI* provides sufficient information about the rationale undergirding the instrument, steps taken in its development (including pilot testing and revisions based on the findings of this piloting), administration and scoring of the *QRI,* and interpreting the results to enable an experienced diagnostician to pick up and use the package immediately with complete confidence.

Inexperienced reading teachers could be introduced effectively to reading assessment by an expert diagnostician through the use of the *QRI* in either a preservice or inservice program. The manual is almost textbook-like in content and serves as a model with respect to clarity, comprehensiveness, and authenticity. Significant questions about the reading process are embedded in the discussion and relevant research is cited to explain why certain procedures were adopted in developing the *QRI*. Claims regarding validity and reliability are carefully documented and fully explained in the test manual.

The *QRI* is like all commercial IRIs in some fundamental ways. For example, lists of words and graded paragraphs are provided along with questions that can be asked to check comprehension, criteria are given for judging the student's level of performance, and forms are provided so that oral reading miscues can be noted by the teacher. Close examination of the *QRI* reveals that a number of significant features have been added to make this IRI modern and consistent with what is known about factors that are important to reading performance. These features include the following:

1. Narrative and expository passages are provided at each readability level.
2. Two types of narrative passages are provided: goal-based and nongoal-based.
3. All passages are self-contained units.
4. Prior knowledge is assessed for each passage with a word association task.
5. Comprehension is assessed through both unaided recall and questions.
6. Comprehension questions include ones calling for explicit understanding and ones calling for implicit understanding.
7. The word lists contain words taken from the passages at each reading level.
8. The word lists contain phonetically regular and irregular words.
9. Provision is made for assessing whether words are recognized at sight (i.e., automaticity of response is assessed) or through analysis.
10. Reading miscues are analyzed qualitatively (including contextual acceptability, graphic similarity, and self-corrections).

Some of these features are unique to the *QRI*, other features are found in a few but not all IRIs. The attention given to assessing prior knowledge is a particularly attractive feature, in our view. The test manual provides a useful and convincing discussion concerning why it is important to assess familiarity with a topic as part of a diagnosis. One minor disappointment is that the passage dependency of comprehension questions in the *QRI* is not discussed by the authors as a factor in testing nor is it explored in the validation section of the manual. The authors might have acknowledged that familiarity with a topic enables some students to answer questions without reading the passages. Steps can be taken in the development of an IRI to assure that questions are passage dependent (can only be answered if the passage has been read), but the results often lead to questions that give an undue focus on minute detail. On balance, the free association method of accounting for prior knowledge used in the *QRI* is preferable even though it is less exact.

The *QRI* is an exceptionally good informal reading test that classroom teachers will be able to use in a number of ways. One chapter of the test manual describes how results can be used for placement decisions, to plan supportive and remedial instruction, and to determine reader strengths and weaknesses. Only modest and well-founded claims are made by the authors for the *QRI* and several case studies are offered to help teachers see how they might make similar use of the results.

SKILLS MANAGEMENT SYSTEMS: PRESCRIPTIVE READING INVENTORY

A general description of skills management systems was provided on pages 323–324 of the previous chapter. An in-depth look at one such system follows.

The *Prescriptive Reading Inventory* (1977) was first published in 1972 and has been updated and refined periodically since that time. The *PRI* is described by the publisher as a "criterion-referenced testing system that measures mastery of reading objectives commonly taught in kindergarten through grade 6.5."

We have made it a point in our test reviews to discuss the implicit or explicit conceptualization of reading that the authors of a test use to develop their instrument. The *PRI*, like many other tests, is not explicit in specifying an underlying definition of reading. Unlike most other tests, the claim is made that the *PRI* is "constructed upon a set of behaviorally stated objectives most widely found in the national curriculum." On further examination it becomes clear that what this means is that five of the "most widely used basal reading programs" were taken to represent the "national curriculum." The test objectives were developed by identifying the reading behaviors implicit in the instructional programs of the five basals, pooling those objectives, grouping them according to similarities, and organizing them on a continuum from early decoding skills to critical thinking.

This procedure initially resulted in the identification of 1248 behavioral objectives. The publisher carefully explains that these objectives merely represent common instructional methods and do not imply a definition of reading. The disagreement is, of course, that what gets tested becomes what is important. In this approach, reading becomes the sum of the parts after being broken into specific skills the pupil will be asked to master. It is true that the *PRI* suggests repeatedly that teachers should decide how well the test objectives match their instruction and adjust their use of the tests accordingly. Despite these cautions, however, the *PRI* by its very nature invites the teacher to regard reading as a set of separate behaviors that must be mastered in a particular sequence to achieve literacy. Furthermore, the *PRI* is presented as a device that is appropriate for determining who has attained mastery and who has not for the purpose of individualizing subsequent instruction.

The PRI consists of six levels as follows:

Level I	Grades K.0–1.0
Level II	Grades K.5–2.0
Level A/Red	Grades 1.5–2.5
Level B/Green	Grades 2.0–3.5
Level C/Blue	Grades 3.0–4.5
Level D/Orange	Grades 4.0–6.5

The tests can be administered in a group setting and are available in either hand- or machine-scorable versions.

The Level B test consists of 153 items that purport to measure the pupil's mastery of the objectives assigned to Grades 2.0–3.5 by the test authors. The *Interpretive Handbook* provided with the test indicates that forty objectives are addressed by the Level B test. To illustrate, these objectives are included: "The student will identify a correct possessive form, as used in a phrase, from among the given singular, plural, singular possessive, and plural possessive forms of the same word," and "The student will define words in isolation by matching certain words with their definitions."

With respect to the objective on possessives, six items are included in the test. Two items require the child to choose the correct form of a possessive to go into a blank in a sentence. For example

The _____ ball is round.

children	childrens
childrens'	children's

Four items are based on a simple line drawing and two short sentences related to that drawing. For example, one drawing shows two kittens playing with a ball. The first sentence says, "I have two kittens." The child's task is to choose one of three words that best fits the blank in the second sentence.

They are _____ kittens.

my   your   their

The second objective is measured by four items that give the child an isolated word and four definitions. The child selects the answer that tells what the word means. For example

follow   a young man

go in front

come or go after

make someone hurry

These examples give some feel for the type of items included in the *PRI*.

There are several problems with the test content. The first has to do with some items not measuring the objectives they purport to measure. In a review of the *PRI*, Farr suggests that enough problems exist in this realm to cause him to rate the *PRI* relatively low on the criterion.[15] He gives an example from the Level A test (the same problem appears in Level B) in which the child is told to find the word that has the same vowel sound as the underlined word. Here knowledge of terminology is being measured, not knowledge of sound-symbol associations.

A second problem with the *PRI* relates to a lack of reliability. The examples given above clearly illustrate that relatively few items measure any one objective. Consequently, few behaviors are sampled and little confidence can be placed in the results. This is particularly troublesome when judgments are being made about whether a child has mastered a skill. By missing more than one item the child fails an objective. Conversely, by guessing correctly on only a few items a child can pass an objective.

The *PRI* tests are quite lengthy and, although untimed, take as much time as three hours to administer on a single level. As a result these tests would probably be given at the beginning of the year only. A second set of tests, the *PRI Interim Tests*, are available for monitoring student progress throughout the school year. The *Interim Tests* are keyed to the same skill objectives as the *PRI*, of course, and provide additional information about mastery of a particular skill.

The *PRI* is subject to the same limitations that plague nearly all skills management systems. The first of these concerns the important concept of mastery that underlies criterion-referenced testing. Once a person has mastered something, it would seem that further growth in that skill or ability is unnecessary (even impossible). Yet it is obvious that the reading act requires the application of skills mastered in materials that grow progressively more difficult. Thus a comprehension skill (if such a thing exists) apparently mastered when reading easy material may not generalize to harder material. Ability to draw conclusions while reading a simple narrative, for example, does not lend itself to absolute mastery. The same skill may not be performed successfully in a

Michener novel where the ideas and language are much more complex. Mastery is a notion that might apply to knowing the multiplication tables or even the letters of the alphabet but does not apply to the thinking and problem solving skills basic to reading with understanding.

Even more basic than the above, however, is the lack of evidence that one must master the skills identified in the *PRI* (or other SMS) in order to read successfully. The fact that good readers do better on certain test items does not establish the content validity of that skill. It does not follow that readers will perform better by learning the skill or knowledge measured by those test items.

Nearly all criterion-referenced tests have built into them certain assumptions regarding an optimal sequence for skill acquisition. In most cases this sequence is hierarchical in nature—that is, the skills tested build one upon another with one apparently serving as a prerequisite for the next. No evidence exists to indicate that these assumptions are applicable to reading. Yet teachers who use and believe skills management systems are led to accept the structure built into them.

There are serious reservations about any skills management system and we urge that teachers not use them if they have a choice in the matter.

As noted in Chapter 12, most basal reader programs now include a skills management system. The free standing system reviewed here is more representative of all such systems than one tied to a particular instructional program.

SUMMARY

This chapter provided detailed information about several types of reading tests—a survey test, two group and four individually administered diagnostic tests, an informal reading inventory, and a skills management system. The primary purpose was to examine these tests as examples of commercially prepared tests that can be purchased for use in the classroom and clinic. The contents of each test were described and cautions and concerns that need to be considered in their administration and interpretation were raised. Daily instruction can be planned and evaluated more effectively with the use of informal measures than with formal tests such as the ones reviewed in this chapter. However, the informed teacher needs to be aware of formal tests and how to use them wisely. In certain situations, commercial tests are useful, but only if they are understood as samples of reading behavior gathered under controlled conditions.

Suggested Activities

1. Borrow a standardized reading test from your professor or curriculum lab. Reading through the administrator's manual for the test noting the following:

   How to give the test

   How to score the test

   How to interpret the results of the test

   Validity and reliability of the test

   Take the test yourself. Watch for tasks that are ambiguous or confusing. Ask yourself how well performance on the items in this test match with your own perception of what is important in reading.

2. Locate a review of the test you examined in activity 1 (above) in the Mental Measurements Yearbook or other collection of test reviews. Read the review and compare the reviewers' comments to your own observations.

3. Administer the test examined in activities 1 and 2 (above) to a child, score the results, and develop a plan for incorporating the findings into the child's daily instruction. If possible, administer another reading test to the same child, score, interpret, and compare the results. Determine whether the implications for instruction from the two tests are consistent. Discuss your conclusions with the child's classroom teacher.

Suggested Reading

JOHNSON, MARJORIE SEDDON, KRESS, ROY A., and PIKULSKI, JOHN J. (1987). *Informal reading inventories* (2nd ed.). Newark, DE: International Reading Association.

This book describes the nature of and purposes for using informal reading inventories (IRIs). It provides guidance on the administration, recording, and scoring of IRIs, and for interpreting the results in a diagnostic manner. It includes instructions for constructing IRIs and gives three case examples.

JOHNSTON, PETER H. (1984). Assessment in reading. In P. David Pearson (Ed.), *Handbook of reading research* (pp. 147–182). New York: Longman.

This chapter reviews and summarizes investigations concerned with the assessment of reading and argues that the heavy reliance on product measures evident in the literature is largely inconsistent with the current emphasis on process in reading instruction and reading research.

KRAMER, J.J., & CONOLEY, J.C. (1992). *Eleventh mental measurements yearbook.* Lincoln, NB: The University of Nebraska Press.

This yearbook updates and extends the eight previous editions of this standard reference previously edited by founder Oscar K. Buros on educational tests and testing. It provides comprehensive information on standardized tests of all types including oral reading, reading readiness, special fields of reading, reading speed, study skills, and miscellaneous reading tests. Basic information is provided about each test (title, copyright date, cost, author, publisher, and so forth) followed by a test references section listing all known references on the construction, validity, use, and limitations of the test. Several reviews written by experts are then provided for each test.

SCHELL, LEO M. (ED.) (1981). *Diagnostic and criterion-referenced reading tests: Review and evaluation.* Newark, DE: International Reading Association.

Provides critical reviews of twelve of the most commonly used reading tests.

SCHREINER, ROBERT (ED.) (1979). *Reading tests and teachers: A practical guide.* Newark, DE: International Reading Association.

Testing is described in this booklet as only one part of the total classroom evaluation process. The appropriate way to select tests, how to develop valid and reliable tests, and how to use test results in planning instruction are also discussed.

Notes

1. See Durrell and Catterson (1980).
2. See Fredrickson (1975) Grimes (1975).
3. See Smith (1979).
4. See Durrell and Catterson (1980).
5. See Buros (1978).

6. See Woodcock (1973), p. 21.
7. See Buros (1978), p. 1304.
8. See Buros (1978).
9. See Dwyer (1978) Tuinman (1978) Houck and Harris (1976).
10. See *Botel Reading Inventory Administration Manual* (Botel, 1978), p. 6.
11. See Spache (1981).
12. See Stafford (1974) Schreiner (1978).
13. See Mosenthal (1981).
14. See Buros (1978).
15. See Buros (1978).

PART FOUR

Providing Supplemental Reading Instruction

The final part of this book brings together the elements that have been introduced and discussed in all of the previous parts. Specific suggestions are made for integrating the various elements into a cohesive and coherent program of supplemental instruction for students who need additional help. Instruction and assessment are described as regular classroom activities and as activities that can occur outside the regular classroom. The role of the special education or reading teacher in providing supplemental help within or outside of the classroom is also discussed.

HELPING LOW-ACHIEVING READERS IN AND OUTSIDE OF THE REGULAR CLASSROOM

OVERVIEW

As you read this chapter you may wish to use the following list of main ideas to guide your understanding and reflection.

- Classroom teachers and specialized teachers—special education, Chapter 1, or special reading teachers—should work together to provide supplemental reading instruction for low-achieving readers.
- Supplemental instruction for low-achieving readers should focus on the acceleration of students' learning as opposed to a traditional approach to remediation that has focused on repetition of low-level activities and a slow pace.
- Low-achieving readers with the same need can be grouped together for focused instruction.

The basic premise of this book is that students experiencing difficulty with reading should receive special, additional instruction in reading within the regular classroom. This instruction should be provided or directed by the classroom teacher with assistance from special teachers such as reading specialists, Chapter 1 teachers, and special education learning disability teachers.

Recent analyses of remediation in reading provided through compensatory (Chapter 1 of the Education and Consolidation Improvement Act [ECIA] of 1981) and special education funding (Education for All Handicapped Children Act [EHA] of 1975) have been discouraging.[1] Students receiving Chapter 1 or special education services for reading have not been found to receive more reading instruction than average and above average reading peers. In fact, these low-achieving readers often receive less reading instruction than their peers. This is, to a large part, due to time spent traveling and preparing to travel to and from the regular classroom.

Additionally, the quality of reading instruction received by students in Chapter 1 and special education programs does not appear to be better, and perhaps may be worse, than what these students would have received in the regular classroom.[2] Remediation for low-achieving readers has been found primarily to involve the individual completion of skill sheets and to focus on decoding words in isolation. Low-achieving readers typically spend less time reading connected text than do better-reading peers and spend little time engaged in higher order academic skills. *Individualization* often consists of the teacher or an aide monitoring children's work on individual skill sheets with little instructional explanation being offered about strategies for better reading.

Remediation in reading provided through Chapter 1 and special education services has met with limited success.[3] From the few well-designed Chapter 1 evaluations that have been done, Slavin (1987) reports about a three percentile annual gain for students in Chapter 1 programs. Glass (1986) suggests that the effects of achievement for special education programs are limited. Furthermore, children who begin receiving Chapter 1 or special education services seldom return to regular education with no further need for remediation.[4]

Due to the problems with a pullout approach to remediation and a lack of success reported for Chapter 1 and special education learning disabilities programs, many authorities in the field have argued that special interventions for low-achieving readers should focus on accelerated learning and be provided primarily within the regular classroom.[5] In the next section we will discuss how a classroom teacher might provide supplemental reading instruction for low-achieving readers in his classroom. We will also discuss what a specialist (i.e., reading specialist, Chapter 1 teacher, learning disabilities teacher) might do to work with the classroom teacher to assist low-achieving readers.

The ideas presented in this chapter are only suggestions. Obviously, there are many ways in which the assessment procedures and instructional strategies presented can be implemented. Some of the ideas presented here may not work for some teachers. There are many differences from situation to situation that cannot be addressed in our illustrations. For example, some schools will have more assistance from reading specialists or reading tutors, such as through Chapter 1 funding, than in the school described here. In that case reading specialists or tutors could provide more of the supplemental instruction and assessment and classroom teachers less. Some schools will have minimal assistance from reading specialists. Where minimal assistance is available, teachers will still be able to provide supplemental reading instruction and assessment in their classrooms but at a slower pace. Our hope, however, is that the following suggestions will make it easier for teachers to visualize how additional specialized reading instruction for low-achieving readers might be provided within their classrooms and buildings.

HELPING LOW-ACHIEVING READERS IN THE REGULAR CLASSROOM

385

CHAPTER 16
*Helping Low-
Achieving Readers
In and Outside of the
Regular Classroom*

Chapter 6 recommended that a classroom teacher ideally have no more than six or eight low-achieving readers so that maximum attention can be directed toward providing these below-average readers with supplemental instruction in reading. By *low-achieving readers* we mean students who are reading below grade level and whose reading difficulties are interfering with their success in school. By *supplemental reading instruction* we mean reading instruction that is in addition to instruction provided by the regular program and that helps low-achieving readers learn essential word recognition, comprehension, and vocabulary strategies they need in order to become skilled readers. These are strategies applied to actual reading that they have not learned through the regular program or through experience with reading as have most of their better reading peers.

If a teacher has more than eight low-achieving readers, the assessment and instruction procedures outlined in Part Two should still be followed. Oral reading analysis can be conducted as students are reading aloud individually or in groups for the purpose of assessment.

Supplemental instruction can be provided to subgroups of low-achieving readers experiencing the same problem, such as inability to attack one-syllable words or lack of skill in comprehension monitoring. Record keeping will be more difficult for a classroom teacher with more than eight low-achieving readers but needs to be done to whatever extent possible.

The following sections present situations reflecting how one intermediate grade teacher and one primary teacher at Pinewood Elementary School organize for reading instruction so they are able to provide special reading instruction for low-achieving readers in their classrooms along with assistance from a Chapter 1 teacher.

Using Flexible Groups to Provide Supplemental Instruction

Mr. Davis teaches fifth grade. He has six low-achieving readers in his homeroom from across the fifth grade who are reading on a second- or third-grade level. He also has twenty-two students who are average or above average readers.

Mr. Davis is Billy Stone's teacher. Chapters 9, 11, and 13 considered word recognition, comprehension, and vocabulary difficulties experienced by Billy, based on data collected from actual reading tasks. Billy's reading difficulties are summarized in Figure 16.1 along with the diagnosed reading difficulties for the five other low-achieving readers in Mr. Davis' class. These lists of difficulties will change throughout the year as instruction is provided and additional assessment data are collected. However, Mr. Davis believes he has sufficient data to begin instruction in clear areas of need.

The students below are fifth-grade students reading on a beginning third-grade level. Their remedial needs in terms of instruction in word recognition, comprehension, and vocabulary are listed below.

Billy Stone

> Word Recognition
>> Using a general word recognition strategy
>> Knowing CVCe pattern
>> Knowing sounds for *i, ea*
>> Analyzing one-syllable and two- or more syllable words
>> Self-correcting nonsemantic errors
> Comprehension
>> Comprehension monitoring
>> Using fix-up strategies
>> Reading and answering questions based on expository text
>> Answering inference questions
>> Reading for main ideas of paragraphs
> Vocabulary
>> Using context clues
>> Learning specific words

Marcia Alexander

> Word Recognition
>> Using a general word recognition strategy
>> Analyzing two- or more syllable words
> Comprehension
>> Comprehension monitoring
>> Using fix-up strategies
>> Reading and answering questions based on narrative and expository text
>> Answering fact and inference questions
>> Reading for main ideas of paragraphs

Mike Hopson

> Word Recognition
>> Using a general word recognition strategy
>> Knowing the CVCe pattern
>> Knowing sounds for *ow, ou*
>> Analyzing two- or more syllable words
> Comprehension
>> Using fix-up strategies
>> Understanding and answering questions based on expository text
>> Answering inference questions
>> Reading for main ideas of paragraphs
> Vocabulary
>> Using the dictionary

FIGURE 16.1. Instructional Needs of Low-Achieving Readers in a Fifth-Grade Classroom

Amanda Winger

387

CHAPTER 16
*Helping Low-
Achieving Readers
In and Outside of the
Regular Classroom*

Word Recognition
Analyzing two- or more syllable words
Self-correcting nonsemantic errors
Comprehension
Comprehension monitoring
Using fix-up strategies
Understanding and answering questions based on narrative and expository text
Answering fact and inference questions
Understanding anaphoric relationships
Reading for main ideas of paragraphs
Vocabulary
Using context clues to determine meanings for unfamiliar words
Using the dictionary

Terry Phillipson

Word Recognition
Recognizing *ever/very, was/saw*
Using a general word recognition strategy
Knowing the CVCe pattern
Knowing sounds for *ea, oo, ou, ow*
Analyzing one-syllable and two- or more syllable words
Self-correcting nonsemantic errors
Comprehension
Comprehension monitoring
Using fix-up strategies
Understanding and answering questions based on expository text
Answering inference questions
Reading for main ideas of paragraphs
Vocabulary
Using context clues to determine meanings of unfamiliar words
Learning specific words

Wayne Woods

Word Recognition
Knowing the CVCe pattern
Analyzing two- or more syllable words
Self-correcting nonsemantic errors
Comprehension
Comprehension monitoring
Using fix-up strategies
Understanding and answering questions based on expository text
Reading for main ideas of paragraphs
Vocabulary
Using context clues to determine meanings for unfamiliar words
Learning specific words

FIGURE 16.1. Instructional Needs of Low-Achieving Readers in a Fifth-Grade
Classroom (*Cont.*)

Let us consider how Mr. Davis uses the information in Figure 16.1 to plan for special instruction in reading for these low-achieving readers. Mr. Davis realizes that he cannot attend to all of the areas in need of instruction at one time. He will have to make decisions about where he and Ms. Schmidt, a Chapter 1 teacher, should begin instruction. Mr. Davis and Ms. Schmidt consider the reading difficulties of all six low-achieving readers and look for what they believe are the most crucial skills that need to be learned at this time by the greatest number of students. The instructional needs of the six low-achieving readers in Mr. Davis' class are summarized in Figure 16.2.

Mr. Davis plans to provide special instruction in word recognition once a week and in comprehension or vocabulary once a week. In addition, Ms. Schmidt will come to Mr. Davis' room once a week to provide instruction in either word recognition, comprehension, or vocabulary for students who need extra help.

In the area of word recognition (refer back to Chapter 8), Mr. Davis decides to provide instruction to all six readers once a week in a general word recognition strategy with special emphasis on the analysis of multisyllabic (2+ syllable) words. Four of the six readers in this group, including Billy Stone, need to learn a general word recognition strategy and all six need help in analyzing multisyllabic words. In Mr. Davis' judgment, after the students have received sufficient instruction in the general word recognition strategy and in the analysis of multisyllabic words, as evidenced by their performance during oral reading

FIGURE 16.2. Summary of Six Low-Achieving Readers' Special Reading Needs (listed in Figure 16.1)

Word Recognition

Using a general word recognition strategy: four students
Knowing the CVCe pattern: three students
Knowing sounds for *ea*: two students
Knowing sounds for *ow*: two students
Knowing sounds for *ou*: two students
Knowing sounds for *i*: one student
Knowing sounds for *oo*: one student
Analyzing one-syllable words: two students
Analyzing two- or more syllable words: six students
Self-correcting nonsemantic errors: four students

Comprehension

Comprehension monitoring: five students
Using fix-up strategies: six students
Understanding and answering questions based on narrative text: two students
Understanding and answering questions based on expository text: six students
Answering inference questions: six students
Answering fact questions: two students
Understanding anaphoric relationships: one student
Reading for main ideas of paragraphs: six students

Vocabulary

Using context clues to determine meanings for unfamiliar words: four students
Using the dictionary: two students
Learning specific words: four students

analysis sessions, he will provide symbol-sound correspondence instruction once a week to students based on need (for example, four students, including Billy, need help with the CVCe pattern; two, again including Billy, with sounds for *ea*, and so forth). For the four students, including Billy, needing help with correcting nonsemantic errors, Mr. Davis will use the oral reading for meaning procedure. He plans to conduct this with one student while the other students are silently reading novels for literature groups. He will conduct oral reading for meaning with two students once or twice a week for approximately a month and then with the other two students for a month.

389

CHAPTER 16
*Helping Low-
Achieving Readers
In and Outside of the
Regular Classroom*

In the area of comprehension (refer back to Chapter 10), Mr. Davis decides to provide instruction once a week for all six students in the comprehension rating procedure. Five of the six students, including Billy, need help with comprehension monitoring, and all six need help with fix-up strategies. Ms. Schmidt will provide instruction once a week for all six students in the reciprocal teaching procedure, which is designed to help students better understand expository text, because all six students have difficulty with expository text. Later, Ms. Schmidt will provide instruction in the question-answer relationship procedure for five of the six students, including Billy, who are having difficulty with inference questions. Either Mr. Davis or Ms. Schmidt at a later point will instruct all six students in reading for main ideas of paragraphs. However, Mr. Davis and Ms. Schmidt have decided it will be more beneficial to focus initially on general comprehension-fostering strategies such as the comprehension rating, reciprocal teaching, and question-answer relationship procedures than to focus on the specific skill of reading for main ideas.

In the area of vocabulary (refer back to Chapter 12), Mr. Davis plans to focus on helping students use context clues to determine meanings of unfamiliar words when the students are reading. Four of the six students, including Billy, need help in this strategy. Mr. Davis will provide special instruction in using context clues to determine word meanings if he feels that the emphasis he has placed on this strategy has been insufficient with the vocabulary words in the stories the students are reading for regular reading class.

Not all, but many of the needs of the low-achieving readers in Mr. Davis' reading class will be met by the plan presented above. Actually, at some time during the school year, all of Billy Stone's reading needs, at least as far as those listed in Figure 16.1 are concerned, will be addressed by Mr. Davis' plan for supplemental reading instruction.

After collecting information on students' reading abilities during the first month of school, Mr. Davis usually provides instruction in a word recognition skill once a week and a comprehension or vocabulary skill once a week during a 20-minute period set aside for supplemental instruction in reading. A student who does not need instruction in a specific skill can engage in independent reading or other reading-related activities.

Sometimes Mr. Davis spends the time set aside for special help for his low-achieving readers on assessment activities. For instance, he may spend 10 minutes introducing an assessment activity, such as the comprehension rating task or a written activity on using context to determine word meanings, which his six low-achieving readers can complete independently while he spends 10 minutes questioning some of these students individually about their comprehension monitoring skills.

Once a week for about 20 minutes Mr. Davis conducts oral reading analysis with these six students. He spends 10 minutes listening to the students read their latest story orally and then spends 10 minutes completing oral reading analysis sheets for each student. To find the free time needed to complete the sheets, Mr. Davis has the students work in groups of three to prepare comprehension questions that they will later present to their peers.

Mr. Davis may also have the students compose answers to questions on instructional level material at some other time during the week. After Mr. Davis has discussed the answers to written comprehension questions with his low-achieving readers he takes a few minutes to record students' comprehension scores on the reading difficulties record sheets. While he does this the students work together on a skill they have recently received instruction in, such as using context to determine word meanings, based on their latest story. Independent reading also provides Mr. Davis with an opportunity to meet with individual students, collect important data on their progress, and record it on reading difficulties record sheets.

As has already been pointed out, in addition to the special help these six readers receive, Ms. Schmidt comes to Mr. Davis' room to assist Mr. Davis with both initial assessment at the beginning of the school year and ongoing assessment during the year. She also provides additional special instruction for subsets of the six low-achieving readers based on diagnosed needs.

Mr. Davis has devised a plan that allows him, with assistance from Ms. Schmidt, to provide his low-achieving readers with supplemental instruction in reading. This instruction is in addition to the regular reading program. It focuses on essential word recognition, comprehension, and vocabulary strategies that his low-achieving readers have not learned to use when actually reading. Many of these strategies, such as a general word recognition strategy or comprehension monitoring, have been learned by better readers with minimal explicit instruction. However, explicit instruction, based on diagnosed need, in the strategies presented in Chapters 8, 10, and 12 is needed to help low-achieving readers overcome their reading difficulties.

Organization in a Second-Grade Classroom

This section will describe a plan for supplemental reading instruction in a primary classroom. Mrs. Parker teaches second grade. She has eight students in her homeroom who are reading on a first-grade level at the beginning of the school year. She has eighteen other students in her class who are average or above average readers.

During the first month of school, Mrs. Parker spends 15 minutes per day administering informal assessments (e.g., IRIs, informal phonics inventories, surveys of reading habits and dispositions) to her low-achieving readers. At this time the rest of the students in the class are engaged in independent reading. Ms. Schmidt also comes to Mrs. Parker's classroom to help with this initial assessment.

Mrs. Parker teaches reading for 90 minutes per day. Twice a week she spends 30 minutes providing special instruction to subsets of her eight low-achieving readers based on similar diagnosed needs.

391

CHAPTER 16
Helping Low-
Achieving Readers
In and Outside of the
Regular Classroom

Whenever students are not working directly with the teacher in reading they are engaged in independent activities. All students in the classroom spend 15 or 20 minutes per day in independent reading, 20 to 30 minutes per day in other independent activities such as listening to stories on tape, playing reading games, browsing in the media center, doing artwork and writing related to independent reading, and retelling favorite stories with puppets and flannel-board figures.

Once or twice a week for about 20 minutes Mrs. Parker conducts oral reading analysis with eight students. As the students are reading from a book at their instructional level, Mrs. Parker takes notes about the accuracy and quality of their oral reading. Like Mr. Davis, she finds time to complete the oral reading analysis sheets by giving the students a cooperative assignment; in her case she asks them to reread material with partners.

Once a week Mrs. Parker obtains informal data about the comprehension of these eight readers. Usually she asks them to compose answers to comprehension questions as an independent activity. Often, an aide is available to help them with this task. Mrs. Parker also spends a few minutes once a week recording notes and scores from this informal work. Since Mrs. Parker recognizes their difficulty with expository text, she breaks down the notes and scores into narrative and expository categories. She also makes notes about progress on more factual recall and more inferential tasks. By examining patterns over time, she is able to track progress.

During the 30 minutes set aside twice a week for special reading instruction, Mrs. Parker works with one or more of the low-achieving readers at any one time. She may work with six of her low-achieving readers who need help with segmenting and blending one-syllable words while the other two low-achieving readers work on an independent activity. Or, she may spend 20 minutes helping all eight of her low-achieving readers with comprehension monitoring skills and 10 minutes conducting oral reading for meaning with one student.

On some days during the 30 minutes set aside for special help for low-achieving readers, Mrs. Parker conducts additional assessment. Some of this assessment, such as assessing students' basic sight word knowledge or questioning them about comprehension monitoring or their use of a general word recognition strategy, has to be done individually. But, for a great deal of the assessment that needs to be done, such as assessing students' comprehension rating skills, their ability to answer different types of questions, or their understanding of anaphoric relationships, a written assessment activity can be introduced to a group of students and completed as an independent activity.

Twice a week for 30 minutes after lunch, rotating among the eight low-achieving readers, Mrs. Parker completes the reading difficulties record sheets and makes decisions about the most appropriate instruction for subsets of the group based on similar diagnosed needs. While she is doing this, an aide or parent/senior citizen volunteer reads aloud to her students and supervises the class as they engage in independent reading.

In addition to the 30 minutes twice a week that Mrs. Parker sets aside for supplemental reading instruction for her low-achieving readers, Ms. Schmidt comes to the classroom twice a week for 30 minutes. She assists Mrs. Parker with initial and ongoing assessment and provides additional instruction to subsets of the eight low-achieving readers in Mrs. Parker's class based on similar diagnosed needs.

Alternatives to Ability Grouping for Reading Instruction

Ability grouping for reading instruction at the elementary school level has been the predominant practice in American schools.[6] In recent years, however, this practice has been questioned.[7] A number of studies have found that students in low-ability and higher-ability groups are treated differently, with more attention to lower-level tasks in low-ability groups; that low-ability group members tend to spend less time reading and less time on task during reading instruction; and that students in low-ability groups have lower self-concepts and lower social status than students in higher ability groups.[8]

In general, research on the effects of ability-grouped versus heterogeneous classes for reading instruction has not found ability grouping to lead to higher reading achievement than heterogeneous classes.[9] Barr and Dreeban (1991), however, point out that research is limited since there have been so few classes using a heterogeneous approach for reading instruction to compare to ability-grouped classes. More research in this area is needed.

The examples for supplemental instruction we have just provided from a fifth and second grade classroom are based on notions of short-term, flexible grouping based on diagnosed need. Nevertheless, the existing research suggests that alternatives to ability grouping should be considered for at least some of the regular, developmental reading instruction that is provided in elementary classrooms. Experiences with the reading of literature, in which children are not ability-grouped, is one possibility. Cooperative learning activities, discussed in Chapter 5, are an excellent way for children of different abilities to work together. Cooperative learning groups work particularly well when students are learning how to read difficult content area textbooks.

Helping Exceptional Students with Reading

The focus of this book is on initial and ongoing supplemental instruction and assessment for students experiencing reading difficulties. A number of the students at any grade level who are experiencing difficulty in reading will be exceptional students, students who have qualified for special education services. Students designated as learning-disabled, in particular, have often been found to have reading difficulties.[10]

In general, the strategies for instruction and assessment in word recognition, comprehension, and vocabulary that were presented in Part Two of this book should be used with exceptional students who are experiencing difficulty with reading as well as with other low-achieving readers who are not receiving special education assistance. Special education teachers trained in working with various types of exceptional students will need to use their judgment and guide classroom teachers regarding the choice of appropriate instructional strategies and assessment techniques for exceptional students. For the most part, the instructional strategies and assessment techniques presented in Part

Two of this book apply equally as well to students classified as learning-disabled as well as low-achieving readers.

393

CHAPTER *16*
*Helping Low-
Achieving Readers
In and Outside of the
Regular Classroom*

Teachers may find that the instructional strategies and assessment techniques presented have to be modified to some extent for use with certain exceptional students. Again, special education teachers should provide guidance to classroom teachers in terms of needed modifications. Texts on teaching exceptional children, such as those by Bauer and Shea (1989) and Bryan and Bryan (1986), are good sources of information on teaching techniques that have been found to be effective with certain types of exceptional students.

Students classified as exceptional will be receiving individualized help from special education teachers. Depending on what has been determined to be most beneficial for particular students, they may receive reading instruction in the regular classroom or from a special education teacher. If the regular classroom teacher is providing instruction, the special education teacher should operate in a manner similar to the Chapter 1 teacher described in the previous section. That is, the special education teacher should work with the teacher to plan the most beneficial supplemental reading program possible for an exceptional student who is having difficulty in reading. As part of this program, the special education teacher should come to the classroom to provide the exceptional student with individualized reading instruction.

If reading instruction comes primarily from special education teachers, they should follow the suggestions for instruction and assessment presented in Part Two to the extent that these suggestions are appropriate for individual students.

SPECIAL READING INSTRUCTION OUTSIDE OF THE REGULAR CLASSROOM

Previous chapters of this book have demonstrated the conviction that supplemental reading instruction for low-achieving readers is an activity that can and should occur in the regular classroom. This book was written primarily for the classroom teacher and has taken the position throughout that within the daily instructional program there are numerous opportunities to assess reading progress and to adjust immediately to the needs of students experiencing difficulty. We believe that potential problems can be prevented if and when classroom teachers feel empowered to address them.

Despite the belief that this supplemental instruction is an ongoing responsibility of the classroom teacher, it would be irresponsible of us to suggest that all reading problems can or will be handled in this fashion. Special reading instruction has been provided by special education and reading teachers for decades, and there are no signs that this approach is about to be abandoned. (However, fewer remedial programs, especially federally funded ones such as Chapter 1, will exist in the future, thus making regular classroom assistance even more important than it has been.) The intent of this comment should be clear: Special supplemental reading programs should not be abandoned. Reading clinics (the name often used to identify special remedial programs provided outside the regular classroom) often offer the best means for helping some children. Indeed, the techniques for instruction and assessment provided in this book are appropriate for reading teachers outside of as well as within the regular classroom. However, a main theme of this text is that supplemental reading instruction can and should be an ongoing activity of the regular teacher. Consequently a more complete discussion of clinical reading programs has been left for other textbooks written especially for the specialist in reading.

EFFECTIVE SUPPLEMENTAL READING INSTRUCTION

Suppose for a moment that you are the parent of a child who is having difficulty with reading. What type of instruction would you like to see available in your child's school? In other words, what does an effective supplemental reading instruction look like?

Speaking for ourselves, we would like to see an emphasis on the preventive maintenance principle advocated by one of the U.S. auto manufacturers. Preventive maintenance means routine care of important items and systematic inspection of areas where undetected problems could become serious if allowed to continue. With your automobile this means changing the oil, oil filter, air filter, spark plugs, and the like on a regular basis and checking wheel bearings, brake linings, transmission fluid, and so forth according to a schedule. With this approach one does not wait until a transmission begins to slip to have it inspected. By the time a transmission slips it may be too late to merely add transmission fluid; expensive repairs may be necessary.

In a school reading program, the regular classroom serves as a preventive care center. Problems in reading are avoided to whatever extent possible by systematically monitoring the child's progress. Through largely informal means, the skillful teacher determines that progress is being made in important areas. Numerous opportunities are provided for reviewing and practicing new concepts and skills. When evidence of confusion or misunderstanding is found, instruction is provided immediately to overcome the problem. Some authorities call in-class attention to problems of this type *corrective instruction,* others use the term *remediation.* The label is less important than the idea that problems are dealt with routinely by the classroom teacher at the time they are discovered. Furthermore, the teacher is constantly watching for evidence that supplemental instruction is needed and regards this as a normal occurrence.

Before describing our vision of effective reading instruction, there are several additional points that should be made about the regular classroom as a preventive care center. Returning to one of our on-going themes, the teacher's conceptualization of reading is critical when seeking evidence of growth and, conversely, problems, in reading. As pointed out earlier, a skillful classroom teacher regards temporary difficulties in reading as normal. Here it should be emphasized that what the teacher regards as an error and what the teacher considers to be evidence of a difficulty are critical. It is one thing to believe that occasional difficulties are normal and quite another thing to believe that some traditional errors are not really errors at all but simply reflect the imprecise, constructive nature of the reading act. This perspective has been discussed fully at various places in this text so further elaboration seems unnecessary. It should be obvious that what the teacher regards as a reading problem is dependent on one's conceptualization of reading, which in turn has immediate implications for how supplemental reading instruction for low-achieving readers is approached.

395

CHAPTER *16*
Helping Low-
Achieving Readers
In and Outside of the
Regular Classroom

The teacher who takes a strictly quantitative approach to oral reading miscues, for example, might identify a particular child's miscue level as evidence of the need for supplemental instruction and subsequent instruction might focus on accuracy in word pronunciation. The result might be better oral reading (more accurate) but less comprehension. Given the teacher's view of reading, the supplemental instruction has seemingly been effective. Given our view, it probably was not.

Another aspect of the classroom as a preventive care center concerns the philosophy that early identification and treatment of reading difficulties are desirable. If correction can be handled by the classroom teacher, early identification and treatment can be accomplished without labeling the problem and putting the child into the remedial category. This is exactly the course of action we would advocate. Conversely, if early identification and treatment involves referral to a specialist, we have serious reservations because once attention has been called to a difficulty, it can take on a life of its own. A self-fulfilling prophecy can occur. On the other hand, given time, room to work through the problem, and support from a skillful teacher, the child's problem will often resolve itself. A teacher who regards the classroom as a preventive care center will be cautious in referring children for special help that might cause them to believe they have a genuine problem.

Related to the above point is the belief that in a preventive care center the progress of a child should not be compared to that of other children. The teacher accepts individual rates of progress and uneven growth as normal. Materials are matched to the child's reading level and emphasis is placed on individual progress.

Effective supplemental reading instruction does not conform to one pattern—different teachers have success with different approaches. But in our experience the best programs are characterized by the following principles:

1. Pupils are selected for specialized instruction on the basis of their potential to benefit from such help. Stated another way, low rank in reading achievement is not the sole basis for selection.
2. Pupil progress is documented in a number of ways and shared with the child. Day to day student gains are emphasized. Comparisons with other learners are avoided in favor of self-comparisons.
3. Instructional approaches and materials are built on the child's personal interests and are adjusted to the child's reading level.
4. Supplemental instruction for students experiencing difficulty in reading is approached in a way that is different from what has been used before with the learner. The novelty inherent in a change of methods is used to full advantage by giving the child a fresh start in new materials and with new techniques.
5. The learner is introduced to this extra instruction in a way that guarantees success. Tasks are pitched at a level and in such a manner as to break the cycle of failure all low-achieving readers experience daily. The language experience approach is an example of a method that can be employed to assure success.

6. Instruction is based on the individual strengths and needs of the learner. Lock-step programs that ignore the child's uniqueness are avoided.
7. Instruction is related to actual reading as much as possible with minimal drill on isolated skills. Predictable books of high interest are used to ensure success and keep motivation high.
8. The learner is encouraged to select appealing materials from among those the teacher believes are written at a level the child can handle easily.
9. Information about (a) the nature of the instruction being provided, (b) progress being made, and (c) how regular classroom instruction can be adjusted to accommodate the child's needs are communicated regularly by the special education or special reading teacher to the classroom teacher.

SUMMARY

This chapter provided examples of how classroom teachers might implement reading programs of supplemental reading instruction in their classrooms for their low-achieving readers. It explained how special education or special reading teachers might work with classroom teachers to help low-achieving readers improve their reading.

Regardless of which type of teacher is working with low-achieving readers, the instructional strategies and assessment techniques that were presented in Part Two of this book are sound procedures to follow. Generally, the instructional strategies recommended are word recognition, comprehension, and vocabulary strategies that low-achieving readers are taught to use as they are reading actual text. These strategies may enhance student's comprehension as they are reading, may help them monitor their ongoing comprehension, or may help them overcome a difficulty they are having in word recognition, comprehension, or vocabulary.

In general, the assessment techniques recommended involve the frequent sampling or measuring of student performance in aspects of word recognition, comprehension, and vocabulary based on students' regarding of connected text. Through such assessment the teacher can best determine what a low-achieving reader is having difficulty with when the student is actually reading.

Classroom teachers must attempt to help low-achieving readers in their classrooms overcome their reading difficulties because in many instances, low-achieving readers will receive most of their reading instruction from their classroom teachers. Reading specialists and special education teachers should work with classroom teachers, to the extent that such assistance is available, to help low-achieving readers overcome their reading difficulties. Finally, teachers and parents should consider the possibility of low-achieving readers receiving one-on-one tutoring if such assistance is economically and logistically feasible and if it seems that individuals will likely benefit from an individual tutoring program.

Most low-achieving readers can make significant improvements in reading if they are given the appropriate instruction. This book was written to provide teachers with suggestions for instruction and assessment that involve low-achieving readers in actual reading and will be most beneficial in helping them make significant improvements in reading.

Suggested Activities

397

CHAPTER 16
*Helping Low-
Achieving Readers
In and Outside of the
Regular Classroom*

1. Look at data provided by your instructor on a group of low-achieving readers, such as the data presented in Figure 16.1. Based on these data, decide what you would do and when in terms of providing additional instruction in word recognition, comprehension, and vocabulary. Your instructor will need to inform you about the grade level of the students and the number of other readers in the classroom.
2. If you are currently teaching, prepare a schedule for reading instruction that makes provisions for supplemental reading instruction for low-achieving readers. Base your schedule on your current teaching situation.

Suggested Reading

JOHNSTON, P., and ALLINGTON, R. (1991). Remediation. In R. Barr, M. Kamil, P. Mosenthal, and P. D. Pearson (Eds.), *Handbook of reading research*, Vol. II, 984–1012. New York: Longman.

The authors provide a brilliant discussion of the problems with remedial reading instruction as provided through Chapter 1 and special education services. They argue for the need to eliminate these traditional approaches to remedial reading by providing early intervention programs and by increasing classroom teacher expertise in instructing children with reading difficulties.

LIPSON, MARJORIE Y., and WIXSON, KAREN K. (1986). Reading disability research: An interactionist perspective. *Review of Educational Research, 56*, 111–136.

This article addresses the issue of what "causes" reading disabilities. The authors argue that current views are the result of a "search for pathology" that focuses exclusively on the learner for the causes of reading difficulty. They present an alternative view that takes into account the "interactive" nature of reading, a view that emphasizes other variables such as the materials being read, the purposes for reading, and the context in which the reading is taking place.

Notes

1. See Allington and McGill-Franzen (1989), Haynes and Jenkins (1986), Johnston and Allington (1991), Ysseldyke, Thurlow, Mecklenburg, and Graden (1984).
2. See Allington and McGill-Franzen (1989).
3. See Johnston and Allington (1991), Carter (1984), Glass (1986).
4. See Gartner and Lipsky (1987), McGill-Franzen (1987).
5. See Johnston and Allington (1991), Gartner and Lipsky (1987).
6. See Barr and Dreeban (1991).
7. See Allington (1983), Anderson, Hiebert, Scott, and Wilkinson (1985), Barr and Dreeben (1991).
8. See Allington (1983), Barr and Dreeban (1991), Hiebert (1983).
9. See Barr and Dreeban (1991), Eldridge and Butterfield (1986), Kamil and Rauscher (1990).
10. See Gaskins (1982).

Appendices

Appendix A: Multicultural Literature

Prepared by Kathryn Meyer Reimer

AFRICAN AMERICAN

Primary

Aagard, J. (1989). *The calypso alphabet.* New York: Holt.

Aardema, B. (1975). *Why mosquitos buzz in people's ears.* New York: Dial.

Adoff, A. (1973). *Black is brown is tan.* New York: Harper & Row.

Adoff, A. (1988). *Flamboyan.* San Diego, CA: Harcourt, Brace, Jovanovich.

Adoff, A. (1991). *In for winter, out for spring.* San Diego, CA: Harcourt, Brace, Jovanovich.

Aliki. (1965). *A weed is a flower: The life of George Washington Carver.* New York: Simon & Schuster.

Bang, M. (1983). *Ten, nine, eight.* New York: Greenwillow.

Bryan, A. (1986). *Beat the story drum, pum-pum.* New York: Atheneum.

Bryan, A. (1989). *Turtle knows your name.* New York: Atheneum.

Caines, J. (1982). *Just us women.* New York: Harper & Row.

Clifton, L. (1974). *Some of the days of Everett Anderson.* New York: Holt.

Clifton, L. (1983). *Everett Anderson's goodbye.* New York: Holt.

Daly, N. (1985). *Not so fast Songololo.* Middlesex, England: Puffin Books.

Feelings, M. (1981). *Mojo means one.* New York: Dial.

Flourney, V. (1985). *The patchwork quilt.* New York: Dial.

Greenfield, E. (1974). *She come bringing me that little baby girl.* New York: Lippincott.

Greenfield, E. (1974). *Sister.* New York: Crowell.

Greenfield, E. (1975). *Me and Neesie.* New York: Harper & Row.

Greenfield, E. (1978). *Honey, I love.* New York: Harper & Row.

Greenfield, E. (1988). *Grandpa's face.* New York: Philomel.

Grifalconi, A. (1986). *The village of round and square houses.* Boston: Little, Brown.

Grifalconi, A. (1989). *Osa's pride.* Boston: Little, Brown.

Hale, S. J. (1990). *Mary had a little lamb.* New York: Scholastic.

Haley, G. (1970). *A story, a story.* New York: Atheneum.

Havill, J. (1986). *Jamaica's find.* New York: Scholastic.

Howard, E. (1988). *The train to Lulu's.* New York: Bradbury.

Howard, E. (1991). *Aunt Flossie's hats (and crab cakes later).* New York: Clarion.

Hudson, C., and Ford, B. (1990). *Bright eyes, brown skin.* Orange, NJ: Just Us Books.

Johnson, A. (1989). *Tell me a story mama.* New York: Orchard.

Johnson, A. (1990). *Do like Kyla.* New York: Orchard.

Johnson, A. (1990). *When I am old with you.* New York: Orchard.

Jones, R. (1991). *Matthew and Tilly.* New York: Dutton.

Langstaff, J. (1987). *What a morning! The Christmas story in black spirituals.* New York: Macmillan.

Keats, E. J. (1964). *Whistle for Willie.* New York: Viking.

Keats, E. J. (1967). *Peter's chair.* New York: Harper.

Lewin, H. (1981). *Jafta.* Minneapolis, MN: Carolrhoda.

Mathis, S. (1971). *Sidewalk story.* New York: Puffin.

McKissack, P. (1986). *Flossie and the fox.* New York: Dial.

McKissack, P. (1988). *Mirandy and brother wind.* New York: Knopf.

McKissack, P. (1989). *Nettie Jo's friends.* New York: Knopf.

Mollel, T. (1991). *The orphan boy.* New York: Clarion.

Monjo, F. N. (1970). *The drinking gourd.* New York: Harper.

Ringgold, F. (1991). *Tar beach.* New York: Crown.

San Souci, R. (1989). *The talking eggs.* New York: Dial.

Schroeder, A. (1989). *Ragtime Tumpie.* Boston: Joy Street.

Shelby, A. (1990). *We keep a store.* New York: Orchard.

Steptoe, J. (1969). *Stevie.* New York: Harper.

Steptoe, J. (1980). *My daddy is a monster . . . sometimes.* New York: Lippincott.

Steptoe, J. (1987). *Mufaro's beautiful daughters.* New York: Lothrop, Lee, & Shepard.

Steptoe, J. (1988). *Baby says.* New York: Lothrop, Lee, & Shepard.

Wahl, J. (1991). *Tailypo!* New York: Holt.

Walters, M. P. (1986). *Justin and the best biscuits in the world.* New York: Lothrop, Lee, & Shepard.

Yarbrough, C. (1979). *Cornrows.* New York: Coward-McCann.

Yarbrough, C. (1989). *Shimmershine queen.* New York: Putnam.

Intermediate

Adler, D. (1989). *Jackie Robinson.* New York: Holiday House.

Adoff, A. (1968). *I am the darker brother.* New York: Macmillan.

Adoff, A. (1970). *Malcolm X.* New York: Crowell.

Cameron, A. (1981). *The stories Julian tells.* New York: Pantheon Books.

Clifton, L. (1979). *The lucky stone.* New York: Dell.

Giovanni, N. (1985). *Spin a soft black song.* New York: Farrar, Straus, & Giroux.

Greenfield, E. (1973). *Rosa Parks.* New York: Crowell.

Greenfield, E. (1977). *Mary McLeod Bethune.* New York: Crowell.

Greenfield, E. (1988). *Under the Sunday tree.* New York: Harper & Row.

Greenfield, E. (1989). *Nathaniel talking.* New York: Black Butterfly.

Guy, R. (1973). *The friends.* New York: Bantam.

Hamilton, V. (1967). *Zeely.* New York: Macmillan.

Hamilton, V. (1968). *The house of Dies Drear.* New York: Macmillan.

Hamilton, V. (1971). *The planet of Junior Brown.* New York: Macmillan.

Hamilton, V. (1974). *M. C. Higgins, the great.* New York: Macmillan.

Hamilton, V. (1983). *Willie Bea and the time the martians landed.* New York: Greenwillow.

Hamilton, V. (1985). *The people could fly.* New York: Knopf.

Hamilton, V. (1988). *Anthony Burns: The defeat and triumph of a fugitive slave.* New York: Knopf.

Hamilton, V. (1988). *In the beginning: Creation stories from around the world.* San Diego, CA: Harcourt, Brace, Jovanovich.

Hamilton, V. (1990). *Cousins.* New York: Philomel.

Hansen, J. (1986). *Yellow bird and me.* New York: Clarion.

Harris, J. C. (1987). *Jump again! More adventures of Brer Rabbit* (adapted by Parks, B. and Malcolm, J.). San Diego: Harcourt, Brace, Jovanovich.

Hooks, W. H. (1990). *The ballad of Belle Dorcas.* New York: Knopf.

Hopkins, L. B. (1969). *Don't you turn back: Poems by Langston Hughes.* New York: Knopf.

Lester, J. (1968). *To be a slave.* New York: Dell.

Lester, J. (1982). *This strange new feeling.* New York: Dial.

Lester, J. (1987). *The tales of Uncle Remus: The adventures of Brer Rabbit.* New York: Dial.

Lester, J. (1989). *More tales of Uncle Remus: The further adventures of Brer Rabbit.* New York: Dial.

Lester, J. (1969). *Black folktales.* New York: Grove Press.

Lyons, M. (1990). *Sorrows kitchen: The life and folklore of Zora Neale Hurston.* New York: Scribner's.

Mathis, S. (1975). *Hundred penny box.* New York: Viking.

McKissack, P. (1989). *The long hard journey: The story of the pullman porter.* New York: Walker.

Meltzer, M. (1984). *Black Americans: A history in their own words.* New York: Crowell.

Meltzer, M. (1987). *Mary McLeod Bethune.* New York: Viking Penguin.

Myers, W. D. (1975). *Fast Sam, Cool Clyde, and Stuff.* New York: Puffin.

Myers, W. D. (1984). *Motown and Didi.* New York: Viking.

Myers, W. D. (1988). *Me, Mop and the Moondance Kid.* New York: Delacorte.

Myers, W. D. (1988). *Scorpions.* New York: Harper & Row.

Myers, W. D. (1990). *The mouse rap.* New York: Harper.

O'Dell, S. (1989). *My name is not Angelica.* New York: Dell.

Price, L. (1990). *Aida.* San Diego, CA: Harcourt, Brace, Jovanovich.

Taylor, M. (1976). *Roll of thunder, hear my cry.* New York: Dial.

Taylor, M. (1981). *Let the circle be unbroken.* New York: Dial.

Taylor, M. (1987). *The friendship.* New York: Dial.

Taylor, M. (1987). *The gold cadillac.* New York: Dial.

Taylor, M. (1990). *The road to Memphis.* New York: Dial.

Taylor, M. (1991). *Mississippi bridge.* New York: Dial.

Walter, M. P. (1986). *Justin and the best biscuits in the world.* New York: Knopf.

Winter, J. (1988). *Follow the drinking gourd.* New York: Knopf.

ASIAN AMERICAN

Primary

Bang, M. (1985). *The paper crane.* New York: Greenwillow.

Demi. (1980). *Liang and the magic paintbrush.* New York: Holt.

Friedman, I. (1984). *How my parents learned to eat.* Boston: Houghton Mifflin.

Lee, J. M. (1987). *Ba-nam.* New York: Holt.

Louie, A. (1982). *Yeh-shen: A Cinderella story from China.* New York: Philomel.

Stanley, F. (1991). *The last princess.* New York: Macmillan.

Surat, M. (1983). *Angel child, dragon child.* New York: Scholastic.

Waters, K. (1990). *Lion dancer.* New York: Scholastic.

Xiong, B. (1989). *Nine-in-one grr! grr!* San Francisco, CA: Children's Book Press.

Yashima, T. (1958). *Umbrella.* New York: Viking.

Young, E. (1989). *Lon Po Po.* New York: Putnam.

Intermediate

Ashabranner, B. (1987). *Into a strange land.* New York: Putnam.
Buck, P. S. (1947). *The big wave.* New York: Crowell.
Coerr, E. (1977). *Sadako and the thousand paper cranes.* New York: Dell.
Hamanaka, S. (1990). *The journey.* New York: Orchard.
Lord, B. B. (1984). *The year of the boar and Jackie Robinson.* New York: Harper & Row.
Meltzer, M. (1980). *Chinese Americans.* New York: Crowell.
Morimoto, J. (1987). *My Hiroshima.* New York: Viking.
Uchida, Y. (1971). *Journey to Topaz.* Berkeley: Creative Arts.
Vuong, L. (1982). *The brocaded slipper and other Vietnamese tales.* New York: Lippincott.
Yee, P. (1989). *Tales from Gold Mountain.* New York: Macmillan.
Yep, L. (1975). *Dragonwings.* New York: Harper & Row.
Yep, L. (1977). *Child of the owl.* New York: Harper & Row.
Yep, L. (1989). *The rainbow people.* New York: Harper & Row.

NATIVE AMERICAN

Primary

Ata, T. (1989). *Baby rattlesnake.* San Francisco, CA: Children's Book Press.
Baker, O. (1981). *Where the buffaloes begin.* New York: Warne.
Baylor, B. (1975). *The desert is theirs.* New York: Scribner's.
Baylor, B. (1976). *Hawk, I'm your brother.* New York: Scribner's.
Bierhorst, J. (1984). *Spirit child: A story of the nativity.* New York: Morrow.
Carter, F. (1976). *The education of Little Tree.* Albuquerque, NM: University of New Mexico Press.
De Paola, T. (1983). *The legend of Bluebonnet.* New York: Putnam.
Esbensen, B. J. (1989). *Ladder to the sky.* Boston: Little, Brown.
Goble, P. (1978). *The girl who loved wild horses.*
Lattimore, D. (1987). *The flame of peace: A tale of the Aztecs.* New York: Harper & Row.
McDermott, G. (1974). *Arrow to the sun.* New York: Viking.
Miles, M. (1971). *Annie and the old one.* Boston: Little, Brown.
Miller, M. (1987). *My grandmother's cookie jar.* Los Angeles: Price/Stern/Sloan.
Steptoe, J. (1984). *The story of Jumping Mouse.* New York: Morrow.
Wheeler, B. (1986). *Where did you get your moccasins?* Winnipeg, MAN: Pemmican.
Yolen, J. (1990). *Sky dogs.* San Diego, CA: Harcourt, Brace, Jovanovich.

Intermediate

Ashabranner, B. (1986). *Children of the Maya: A Guatamalan Indian odyssey.* New York: Dodd, Mead.
Baylor, B. (1976). *And it is still the way: Legends told by Arizona Indian children.* New York: Scribner's.
Freedman, R. (1987). *Indian chiefs.* New York: Holiday House.
Freedman, R. (1988). *Buffalo hunt.* New York: Holiday House.
George, J. (1972). *Julie of the wolves.* New York: Harper.
Highwater, J. (1977). *Anpao: An American Indian odyssey.* New York: Lippincott.
Hoyt-Goldsmith, D. (1991). *Pueblo storyteller.* New York: Holiday House.
Jenness, A. (1989). *In two worlds: A Yup'ik Eskimo family.* Boston: Houghton Mifflin.

Keegan, M. (1991). *Pueblo boy.* New York: Dutton.
Norman, H. (1989). *How Glooskap outwits the Ice Giants and other tales of the Maritime Indians.* Boston: Little, Brown.
O'Dell, S. (1970). *Sing down the moon.* Boston: Houghton Mifflin.
Sneve, V. D. H. (1972). *High Elk's treasure.* New York: Holiday House.
Sneve, V. D. H. (1972). *Jimmy Yellow Hawk.* New York: Holiday House.
Sneve, V. D. H. (1989). *Dancing teepees.* New York: Holiday House.
Speare, E. G. (1983). *Sign of the beaver.* Boston: Houghton Mifflin.
Tobias, T. (1970). *Maria Tallchief.* New York: Crowell.
Yue, C. and Yue, D. (1986). *The pueblo.* Boston: Houghton Mifflin.
Yue, D. and Yue, C. (1984). *The tipi: A center of Native American life.* New York: Knopf.

HISPANIC AMERICAN

Primary

Baylor, B. (1963). *Amigo.* New York: Macmillan.
Belpre, P. (1960). *Perez and Martina.* New York: Warne.
Belpre, P. (1965). *Dance of the animals.* New York: Warne.
Belpre, P. (1969). *Santiago.* New York: Warne.
Belpre, P. (1973). *Once in Puerto Rico.* New York: Warne.
Brown, T. (1986). *Hello amigos!* New York: Holt.
Delacre, L. (1989). *Arroz Con Leche.* New York: Scholastic.
Delacre, L. (1990). *Las Navidads.* New York: Scholastic.
De Paola, T. (1980). *The lady of Guadalupe.* New York: Holiday.
Dorros, A. (1991). *Tonight is carnaval.* New York: Dutton.
Martel, C. (1976). *Yagua days.* New York: Dial.
Rohmer, H. (1989). *Uncle Nacho's hat.* Emeryville, CA: Children's Book Press.

Intermediate

Cameron, A. (1988). *The most beautiful place in the world.* New York: Knopf.
Maestas, J. G. and Anaya, R. A. (1980). *Cuentos! Tales from the Hispanic Southwest.*
Meltzer, M. (1982). *Hispanic Americans.* New York: Crowell.
Mohr, N. (1977). *In Nueva York.* New York: Dell.
Mohr, N. (1979). *Felita.* New York: Dial.
Mohr, N. (1986). *Going home.* New York: Dial.
Soto, G. (1990). *Baseball in April and other stories.* San Diego, CA: Harcourt, Brace, Jovanovich.
Soto, G. (1991). *Taking sides.* San Diego: Harcourt, Brace, Jovanovich.
Thomas, P. (1978). *Stories from El Barrio.* New York: Knopf.

MIDDLE EASTERN

Primary

Heide, F., and Gilliland, J. (1990). *The day of Ahmed's secret.* New York: Lothrop, Lee, and Shepard.
Pitkanen, M. (1991). *The children on Egypt.* Minneapolis, MN: Carolrhoda.

Intermediate

Staples, S. (1989). *Shabanu, daughter of the wind.* New York: Knopf.

CARRIBEAN

Primary

Lessac, F. (1989). *Carribean canvas.* New York: Lippincott.
Lessac, F. (1984). *My little island.* New York: Harper.
Pomerantz, C. (1989). *The chalk doll.* New York: Lippincott.

APPALACHIAN

Primary

Rylant, C. (1982). *When I was young in the mountains.* New York: Dutton.
Rylant, C. (1991). *Appalachia: The voices of sleeping birds.* New York: Harcourt, Brace, Jovanovich.

Intermediate

Paterson, K. (1985). *Come sing, Jimmy Jo.* New York: Avon.

Appendix B: Books for Low-Achieving Readers (ages 6-12)

RL = Reading Level (grade)
IL = Interest Level (age)

Adler, David. *Cam Jansen and the Mystery of the Stolen Corn Popper.* 1986. RL:3 IL:7-10. One of several.

Adler, David. *The Carsick Zebra and Other Animal Riddles.* 1983. RL:2-3 IL:5-11.

Bauer, Marion Dane. *On My Honor.* 1986. RL:4 IL:9-12.

Blume, Judy. *Freckle Juice.* 1971. RL:3 IL:8-10.

Boynton, Sandra. *Chloe and Maude.* 1983. RL:2 IL:5-9.

Brenner, Barbara. *Wagon Wheels.* 1978. RL:2 IL:5-9. Easy reader.

Bulla, Clyde. *Daniel's Duck.* 1979. RL:2 IL:6-9. Historical fiction. Easy reader.

Bulla,Clyde. *The Chalk Box Kid.* 1987. RL:3 IL:7-10. Realistic fiction.

Cameron, Ann. *The Most Beautiful Place in the World.* 1989. RL:3 IL:8-10.

Catling, Patrick. *The Chocolate Touch.* 1952. RL:3-4 IL:7-11.

Christian, Mary Blount. *Penrod's Pants.* 1986 RL:1 IL:6-9.

Dalgliesh, Alice. *The Courage of Sarah Noble.* 1954. RL:3 IL:6-10. Historical fiction.

Davis, Deborah. *The Secret of the Seal.* 1989. RL:3 IL:8-10.

Donnelly, Judy. *The Titanic Lost and Found.* 1987. RL:3 IL:7-11. One in the Step into Reading Series, Step 3. (Random House).

Erickson, Russell. *Warton and Marton.* 1976. RL:3-4 IL:6-10. One of several.

Estes, Eleanor. *The Hundred Dresses.* 1944. RL:4 IL:8-10.

Fleischman, Sid. *The Whipping Boy.* 1986. RL:4 IL:9-12.

Franklin Watts First Library. A series of science books on many topics. RL:3-4 IL:5-12.

Gardiner, John. *Stone Fox.* 1980. RL:3-4 IL:9-11.

Giff, Patricia. *Fish Face.* 1984. RL:2 IL:6-9. One of several in Kids of the Polk Street School series.

Greenwald, Sheila. *Rosie Cole's Great American Guilt Club.* 1985. RL:3 IL:8-10

Harrison, David. *Wake Up Sun.* 1986. RL:1 IL:4-8. A Step into Reading, Step 1 book (Random House). Others in this series also recommended.

Heide, Florence Parry. *Tales of the Perfect Child.* 1985. RL:3 IL:7-10.

Hill, Kirpatrick. *Toughboy and Sister.* 1990 RL:3 IL:7-11.

Hurwitz, Johanna. *Class Clown.* 1987. RL:3 IL:8-10.

Hurwitz, Johanna. *Much Ado About Aldo.* 1978. RL:3 IL:8-10.

Jukes, Mavis. *No One Is Going to Nashville.* 1983. RL:3 IL:8-10.

Keller, Charles. *Alexander the Grape: Fruit and Vegetable Jokes.* 1982. RL:3-4 IL:6-12.

Kessler, Leonard. *Old Turtle's Riddle and Joke Book*. 1986. RL:2 IL:5-10.

Kline, Suzy. *Orp*. 1989. RL:4 IL:9-11.

Let's-Read-and-Find-Out. Harper and Row (paper) Crowell (hard cover). A series of science books on many topics. RL:3-4 IL:5-12.

Levy, Elizabeth. *Frankenstein Moved in on the Fourth Floor*. 1979. RL:3 IL:7-11. One of several mysteries by Levy.

Levy, Elizabeth. *Something Queer Is Going On*. 1973. RL:2 IL:7-11. One of several mysteries in series.

Lobel, Arnold. *Frog and Toad Are Friends*. 1970. RL:1-2 IL:4-9. Easy reader. One of several about Frog and Toad. Other easy readers by Lobel also recommended.

MacLachlan, Patricia. *Sarah, Plain and Tall*. 1985. RL:4 IL:7-12. Historical fiction.

McDaniel, Becky. *Katy Couldn't*. 1985. RL:1 IL:4-7. Others in Rookie Reader Series also recommended.

McKissack, Patricia. *Who Is Coming?* 1986. RL:1 IL:4-8. Rookie Reader Series.

Marshall, Edward. *Four on the Shore*. 1985. RL:1 IL:6-9.

Marshall, Edward. *Fox All Week*. 1989. RL:1 IL:6-9. One of several.

Monjo, F. F. *Drinking Gourd*. 1970. RL:2 IL:6-11. An I Can Read History Book.

Monjo, F. F. *Indian Summer*. 1968. RL:2 IL:6-11. An I Can Read History Book.

Naylor, Phyllis Reynolds. *Shiloh*. 1991. RL:4 IL:7-12

New True Books. Children's Press. A series of informational books on many science and social studies topics. RL:2-3 IL:5-12.

Parish, Peggy. *Amelia Bedelia and the Baby*. 1981. RL:2 IL:4-9. An easy reader. One of several.

Parsons, Alexandra. *Amazing Cats—Eyewitness Juniors*. 1990. RL:3 IL: 6-10. One in a series.

Peterson, John. *The Littles*. 1967. RL:3 IL:5-10. One of several.

Robinson, Nancy. *Just Plain Cat*. 1981. RL:3 IL:6-10.

Schwartz, Alvin. *All of Our Noses Are Here and Other Noodle Tales*. 1985. RL:1 IL:6-9.

Schwartz, Alvin. *In a Dark, Dark Room and Other Scary Stories*. 1984. RL:2 IL:5-9. An easy reader.

Schwartz, Alvin. *Ten Copycats in a Boat and Other Riddles*. 1980. RL:2 IL:5-10.

Schwartz, Alvin. *There Is a Carrot in My Ear and Other Noodle Tales*. 1982. RL:1 IL:6-9.

Scieszka, Jon. *Knights of the Kitchen Table*. 1991. RL:3 IL:6-10.

Sharmat, Marjorie. *Nate the Great Stalks Stupidweed*. 1986. RL:2 IL:4-10. One of several. Mystery.

Shreve, Susan. *The Flunking of Joshua T. Bates*. 1984. RL:3 IL:8-10.

Simon, Seymor. *Animal Fact/Animal Fable*. 1979. RL:3 IL:5-12.

Simon, Seymor. *Einstein Anderson, Science Sleuth*. 1980. RL:3-4 IL:9-12. One of several. Science mysteries.

Steptoe, John. *Stevie*. 1969. RL:2 IL:6-9.

Sobol, Donald. *Encyclopedia Brown and the Case of the Midnight Visitor*. 1977. RL:3-4 IL:7-12. One of several. Mystery.

Take a trip to. Franklin Watts, Publisher. A series of books on other countries. RL:3 IL:5-12.

Thomas, Jane Resh. *The Comeback Dog*. 1981. RL:4 IL:7-12.

Voight, Cynthia. *Stories about Rosie*. 1986. RL:3L:5-10.

Walsh, Jill Patton. *The Green Book*. 1982. RL:4 IL:9-12. Easy science fiction.

Yolan, Jane. *Commander Toad and the Big Black Hole*. 1983. RL:2 IL:6-10. Easy reader. One of several.

Appendix C: READING DIFFICULTIES RECORD SHEET

WORD RECOGNITION ASSESSMENT

Student Information

Name: Travis

Age: 9

Grade: 3

Note: Travis has been in the main third grade reading group. He has, however, been struggling, and both his second and third grade teachers have considered moving him to the lower group (Scott-Foresman's Focus Program). His mother, who is a teacher at this school, has resisted this move, and she asked me to get information on how to help him at home and to help her decide if he should move to the lower group next year.

I. Reading Level
   A. Results of the Spache Diagnostic Reading Scales test
      Instructional Level   3.5
      Independent Level   4.5
      Potential Level   5.5
   B. Ongoing assessment of Instructional Level
      To find passages for him to read to me, I used a former reading basal. I found two passages in the 3-1 book and two passages in the 3-2 book that he could read with between 92.6 percent and 95.3 percent accuracy. However, I did also try him on several passages that I could not use because his accuracy level was too low. This suggests to me that his reading level is third grade, but probably not as high as a typical child at the end of third grade, which is the time of year at which I am testing him.

II. Word Recognition
   A. Basic Sight Words
      Over the four passages, 26 percent of Travis' errors were on basic sight words. All of these errors were automatic, which suggests that he is

simply reading them too fast and not paying enough attention to them nor to the context of the passage. Travis does not seem to have a specific problem with any particular sight word, although four out of the fifteen errors (27%) involved mixing up "a" and "the."

B. General Word Recognition Strategy

Travis successfully decoded 64 percent of the words he stopped to try to decode across the four passages. He does not omit words that he does not recognize but stops and tries to decode them. On 4/26, 4SD/10NSD; on 4/28, 8SD/2NSD; on 5/11, 14SD/4NSD; on 5/14, 11SD/5NSD. Total: 37SD/21NSD. 37/21+37 = 64 percent. Out of total errors, 58 percent were automatic (4/26/90-7/17, 4/28/90-12/17, 5/11/90-6/10, 5/14/90-8/13, Total: 33/57 = 58 percent).

C. Phonic Analysis

1. Spache Phonics Subtests

   Travis scored at or above average for his grade level on all of the subtests except for

   Long and Short Vowels: 11/16 when the average is 12.4
   Vowels with R: 5/10 when the average is 7.6
   Vowel Diphthongs and Digraphs: 22/30 when the average is 24.6

2. Consistent errors in symbol-sound correspondence knowledge or ability to analyze 1 and 2+ syllable words. Travis seems to know the basic symbol-sound correspondences. When he makes an error of this type it usually involves a vowel combination. Five of his errors did involve an *r* in combination with a vowel. Other than this, however, he did not show a pattern indicating a consistent problem with a specific vowel combination. Most of Travis's phonics errors involve word analysis problems. Of the times he deliberately but unsuccessfully tried to decode a word, 76 percent of the time he made a word analysis error. Word analysis errors made up 53 percent of his total number of errors. Thirty percent of the time the error was on a one syllable word, and 70 percent of the time the error was on a two syllable word.

D. Structural Analysis

Seven of Travis's fifty-seven errors, or 12 percent, involved prefixes or suffixes. Three involved omitting something and three involved adding something. Four involved suffixes and three involved prefixes. Since the errors followed no clear pattern, and were not a large proportion of his errors, it would seem that Travis does not have a specific problem with prefixes or suffixes. Attention to his more basic word analysis problem should help in this area as well.

E. Contextual Analysis

Of Travis' total number of errors, 36 percent of them were semantically appropriate. Of his semantically inappropriate substitutions, Travis self-corrected his errors an average of 48 percent of the time. On the first passage (4/26/90), nonsemantic errors were only 27 percent self-corrected. So after that session, I did a little on-the-spot teaching about listening for errors that didn't make sense and going back and fixing them. After each of the subsequent sessions, I went back and pointed out times that he did do this. I also read sentences to him the way he had read them to me for times that he didn't self-correct. He was easily able to spot his errors and correct them then. It was good to see that during each later session he self-corrected more and more of his semantically inappropriate substitutions (4/28/90—46 percent; 5/11/90—50 percent). On the last session (5/14/90) he was correcting 67 percent of his errors.

F. Fluency

Travis is a fairly smooth oral reader, and he can read with a nice rhythm and good expression when he is not stopping to sound out words or self-correct errors. The more he stops to sound out or self-correct words, of course, the less smooth his reading becomes. It would be nice if by paying more attention to some of those basic sight words, he could avoid some of the unnecessary automatic errors that cause him to stop and self-correct.

On two occasions I timed his silent reading as he continued reading the passages we were working on. His silent reading rates were 92 and 108 words per minute. With the average reading rates for third graders being 109–130 wpm, Travis's silent reading rate is on the slow end of average.

III. Suggestions for Further Instruction

A. I would continue the work I began in encouraging Travis to listen to himself read and correct anything that does not sound right or doesn't make sense. He seemed to respond to having his successes and errors pointed out to him, and so it would be helpful for him to read into a tape recorder and keep a chart of how many times he was able to self-correct these kinds of errors.

B. Travis is also making quite a few automatic errors, half of which are basic sight words. Since the sight word problem does not seem to involve specific words that need to be taught, and since they are all automatic, he is probably just going too quickly over these little words. This could also be corrected by Travis reading into a tape recorder and keeping a chart of the number of errors he makes on these little words. This is not his biggest problem, but it is an area that could be improved by calling it to his attention and with a little bit of effort on his part.

C. Travis seems to have a specific problem with r-controlled vowels and could use a little direct instruction on them. I would model and then have him practice sounding out a group of them in isolation at first. Then I would pay particular attention to words with r-controlled vowels that we meet in actual text. A chart could also be kept by the teacher of the percentage of these words that he is getting correct.

D. The area that Travis will need the most help and long term instruction in will be his word analysis problem. He usually starts the word correctly, but gets mixed up in the middle. He needs to be taught to go through a word carefully, small piece by small piece. He needs to pay careful attention to prefixes, suffixes, blends and vowel combinations—particularly ones with r. To do this, the teacher will need to use everyday text and begin by doing modeling first and then letting Travis practice with assistance from the teacher. After several of the sessions, we looked back at some one syllable and two or more syllable words that Travis had missed. Some Travis could get with an extra look, and some we worked on together. This is the kind of work Travis will need more of.

FINAL NOTE

Since Travis does not have comprehension problems (I briefly checked his comprehension of the passages, and he did well on the comprehension portions of the Spache), his word recognition problems are not of a severe nature, and his reading level does not seem too far below grade level, I would not recommend moving Travis down to a lower group. I will definitely share my findings and suggestions with his teachers and his mother, and I am confident that his mother will continue to help Travis throughout the summer.

KEY		ORAL READING ANALYSIS SHEET	

1. Substitution is written above actual word
   sc = self-corrected   sd = successfully decoded*
   tp = teacher pronunciation
		Story:	The First Balloon Flight in North America

2. + = successfully used, − = unsuccessfully used, 0 = didn't try, blank = automatic but wrong			
3. + = self-corrected, − = not self-corrected, 0 = semantic substitution		Child:	Travis
4. Substitution did not involve correct analysis - one syllable		Date:	4/26/90
5. Substitution did not involve correct analysis - multisyllabic		Teacher:	K. LaBoone
6. Apparent difficulty, i.e. sound/symbol correspondence, basic sight words, inflectional ending, affixes			

	1 Error	2 General Word Recognition Strategy	3 Non-Semantic Substitutions	4 1 Syllable Word	5 2+ Syllable Word	6 Apparent Difficulty
1.	Paragraph Philadelphia	−	−		X	
2.	events imaginative	−	−		X	
3.	Tob Toby	−	0		X	omitted y ending
	canyon sc cannon	+	+			
4.	Roger hard g Roger	−	0			soft g
5.	Wells Wallace	−	0		X	
6.	this his		0			BSW - his (this)
7.	woke awoke		0		X	left off prefix "a"
8.	fallen failed	−	0			ai
	other sc another	+	0			
9.	stroll soar	−	−	X		
	ticks sc tickets	+	+			

* Column 7, as seen on pages 202, 204, 207–209, has been incorporated into columns 1 and 2 on pages 411–418. For example, on page 414 "already" was a word Travis hesitated on but then successfully decoded.

KEY	ORAL READING ANALYSIS SHEET

1. Substitution is written above actual word
  sc = self-corrected   sd = successfully decoded
  tp = teacher pronunciation
	Story: The First Balloon Flight in North America

2. + = successfully used, – = unsuccessfully used, 0 = didn't try, blank = automatic but wrong	
3. + = self-corrected, – = not self-corrected, 0 = semantic substitution	**Child:** Travis
4. Substitution did not involve correct analysis - one syllable	**Date:** 4/26/90
5. Substitution did not involve correct analysis - multisyllabic	**Teacher:** K. LaBoone
6. Apparent difficulty, i.e. sound/symbol correspondence, basic sight words, inflectional ending, affixes	

	1 Error	2 General Word Recognition Strategy	3 Non-Semantic Substitutions	4 1 Syllable Word	5 2+ Syllable Word	6 Apparent Difficulty
10.	site seats		0	X		ea omitted "s" ending
11.	the his		0	X		BSW - his (the)
12.	sent spent		–	X		S P
13.	along long		–	X		added prefix "a"
14.	horses hours		–	X		ou
15.	Beyon Bowen	–	0		X	ow
16.	gobbled cobbled	–	–			initial "c" (said "g")
17.	strolling	–	–		X	oar
	asked sc answered	+	+			

Number of words __230__   Number of errors __17__   Word recognition accuracy __93%__
Number of times nonsemantic substitutions self-corrected/total number
of nonsemantic substitutions __3/11 = 27%__
Number of semantic substitutions __10__
Number of "didn't try" errors __0__
Number of errors involving analysis __13__
Number of times words deliberately and successfully decoded (column 2) __4__
Number of times words deliberately and unsuccessfully decoded (column 2) __10__
Number of times word automatic but wrong (column 2) __7__

KEY		ORAL READING ANALYSIS SHEET	
1. Substitution is written above actual word sc = self-corrected sd = successfully decoded tp = teacher pronunciation		Story: The Sack of Diamonds	
2. + = successfully used, − = unsuccessfully used, 0 = didn't try, blank = automatic but wrong			
3. + = self-corrected, − = not self-corrected, 0 = semantic substitution		Child: Travis	
4. Substitution did not involve correct analysis - one syllable		Date: 4/26/90	
5. Substitution did not involve correct analysis - multisyllabic		Teacher: K. LaBoone	
6. Apparent difficulty, i.e. sound/symbol correspondence, basic sight words, inflectional ending, affixes			

	1 Error	2 General Word Recognition Strategy	3 Non- Semantic Substitutions	4 1 Syllable Word	5 2+ Syllable Word	6 Apparent Difficulty
	tall sc tale	+	+			
1.	along alone		−		X	Ō
	expart sc except	+	+			
2.	hard breath her breath hundredth	−	−		X	
3.	enjoiced rejoice		−		X	-re +ed
4.	where there		−			BSW there (where)
5.	suppers surprise	−	−		X	ur pr
	apsposed sc	+	+			
6.	who oh		0	X		BSW - oh (who)
	are sc hare	+	+			
7.	the a		0	X		BSW - a (the)
	viewible sc	+	+			
	her sd	+				

<table>
<tr><td colspan="2">KEY</td><td colspan="2">ORAL READING ANALYSIS SHEET</td></tr>
</table>

KEY	

1. Substitution is written above actual word
   sc = self-corrected   sd = successfully decoded
   tp = teacher pronunciation
	ORAL READING ANALYSIS SHEET
	
	Story: The Sack of Diamonds

2. + = successfully used, − = unsuccessfully used, 0 = didn't try, blank = automatic but wrong	
3. + = self-corrected, − = not self-corrected, 0 = semantic substitution	Child: Travis
4. Substitution did not involve correct analysis - one syllable	Date: 4/26/90
5. Substitution did not involve correct analysis - multisyllabic	Teacher: K. LaBoone
6. Apparent difficulty, i.e. sound/symbol correspondence, basic sight words, inflectional ending, affixes	

	1 Error	2 General Word Recognition Strategy	3 Non- Semantic Substitutions	4 1 Syllable Word	5 2+ Syllable Word	6 Apparent Difficulty
8.	sky nights		0	X		
9.	*were*	0				
10.	every very		−			BSW - very (every)
11.	was is		0	X		BSW - is (was)
	already sd	+				
12.	coat cloak		0	X		cl
13.	*a*	0				
14.	years year		0 +	X		+ ending "s"
15.	where here		−			BSW - here (where)
16.	these sc this		0 +			BSW - this (these)
	treeshur treasure sc	+	+			
17.	*and* (covered)	0				

Number of words ___302___   Number of errors ___17___   Word recognition accuracy ___94%___
Number of times nonsemantic substitutions self-corrected/total number
of nonsemantic substitutions _____6/13 = 46%_____
Number of semantic substitutions ___7___
Number of "didn't try" errors ___3___
Number of errors involving analysis ___10___
Number of times words deliberately and successfully decoded (column 2) ___8___
Number of times words deliberately and unsuccessfully decoded (column 2) ___2___
Number of times word automatic but wrong (column 2) ___12___

KEY	ORAL READING ANALYSIS SHEET
1. Substitution is written above actual word sc = self-corrected sd = successfully decoded tp = teacher pronunciation	Story: Bats in the Dark
2. + = successfully used, − = unsuccessfully used, 0 = didn't try, blank = automatic but wrong	
3. + = self-corrected, − = not self-corrected, 0 = semantic substitution	Child: Travis
4. Substitution did not involve correct analysis - one syllable	Date: 4/26/90
5. Substitution did not involve correct analysis - multisyllabic	Teacher: K. LaBoone
6. Apparent difficulty, i.e. sound/symbol correspondence, basic sight words, inflectional ending, affixes	

	1 Error	2 General Word Recognition Strategy	3 Non- Semantic Substitutions	4 1 Syllable Word	5 2+ Syllable Word	6 Apparent Difficulty
	furm sc fur	+	+			
1.	early leathery	−	−		X	
	stretched sd	+				
2.	babies Bat					
	Mom sc Mother	+	0			
	the sc that	+	0			
	males sc mammals	+	+			
3.	turn truly	−	0		X	tru (tur)
4.	then they		−	X		BSW - they (then)
	flutter sd	+				
5.	roasting roosting	−	−			∞
	the sc they	+	+			
	for sc to	+	0			

KEY	ORAL READING ANALYSIS SHEET
1. Substitution is written above actual word sc = self-corrected sd = successfully decoded tp = teacher pronunciation	Story: Bats in the Dark
2. + = successfully used, – = unsuccessfully used, 0 = didn't try, blank = automatic but wrong	
3. + = self-corrected, – = not self-corrected, 0 = semantic substitution	Child: Travis
4. Substitution did not involve correct analysis - one syllable	Date: 4/26/90
5. Substitution did not involve correct analysis - multisyllabic	Teacher: K. LaBoone
6. Apparent difficulty, i.e. sound/symbol correspondence, basic sight words, inflectional ending, affixes	

		1 Error	2 General Word Recognition Strategy	3 Non- Semantic Substitutions	4 1 Syllable Word	5 2+ Syllable Word	6 Apparent Difficulty
		daybreak sd	+				
		kid sc kind	+	+			
		insect sd	+				
		most moths	+	+			
		deepest sd	+				
6.		thing tight		–	X		igh
		darting sd	+				
7.		that at		0	X		BSW - at (that)
8.		fly high		0	X		
9.		speeding speed		0	X		+ ing
10.		complĕt complete	–	–			ē

Number of words __214__   Number of errors __10__   Word recognition accuracy __95.3%__
Number of times nonsemantic substitutions self-corrected/total number
of nonsemantic substitutions __5/10 - 50%__
Number of semantic substitutions __7__
Number of "didn't try" errors __0__
Number of errors involving analysis __7__
Number of times words deliberately and successfully decoded (column 2) __14__
Number of times words deliberately and unsuccessfully decoded (column 2) __4__
Number of times word automatic but wrong (column 2) __6__

418

KEY	ORAL READING ANALYSIS SHEET
1. Substitution is written above actual word sc = self-corrected sd = successfully decoded tp = teacher pronunciation	Story: Gillespie and the Guards
2. + = successfully used, – = unsuccessfully used, 0 = didn't try, blank = automatic but wrong	
3. + = self-corrected, – = not self-corrected, 0 = semantic substitution	Child: Travis
4. Substitution did not involve correct analysis - one syllable	Date: 5/14/90
5. Substitution did not involve correct analysis - multisyllabic	Teacher: K. LaBoone
6. Apparent difficulty, i.e. sound/symbol correspondence, basic sight words, inflectional ending, affixes	

		1 Error	2 General Word Recognition Strategy	3 Non-Semantic Substitutions	4 1 Syllable Word	5 2+ Syllable Word	6 Apparent Difficulty
1.		county country	–	0		X	
2.		boys brothers		0		X	
		father sd	+				
		they sc from	+	+			
		the sc a	+	0			
3.		the a		0	X		BSW - a (the)
		instead sc inside	+	+			
4.		darkness darkest	–	0		X	
		bandage sd	+				
		very sc every	+	+			
5.		the a		0	X		BSW - a (the)
6.		then when		0			BSW - When (then)
7.		enjoy join	–	–	X		BSW - the (a)

		KEY		ORAL READING ANALYSIS SHEET	

<table>
<tr><td colspan="4">KEY</td><td colspan="2">ORAL READING ANALYSIS SHEET</td></tr>
</table>

KEY

1. Substitution is written above actual word
   sc = self-corrected   sd = successfully decoded
   tp = teacher pronunciation

2. + = successfully used, − = unsuccessfully used,
   0 = didn't try, blank = automatic but wrong

3. + = self-corrected, − = not self-corrected, 0 = semantic
   substitution

4. Substitution did not involve correct analysis - one syllable

5. Substitution did not involve correct analysis - multisyllabic

6. Apparent difficulty, i.e. sound/symbol correspondence, basic
   sight words, inflectional ending, affixes

ORAL READING ANALYSIS SHEET

Story: Gillespie and the Guards

Child: Travis

Date: 5/14/90

Teacher: K. LaBoone

	Error	1 General Word Recognition Strategy	2 General Word Recognition Strategy	3 Non-Semantic Substitutions	4 1 Syllable Word	5 2+ Syllable Word	6 Apparent Difficulty
8.	a / the			0	X		BSW - the (a)
	pondered sc / proud		+	+			
9.	surrounded / announced		−	−		X	
	float sc / fool		+	+			
10.	gem / gleaming			−		X	
	shining sc / shimmering		+	0			
	that sc / what		+	+			
	flocking sd		+				
11.	places / palace			0		X	
12.	described / disguised		−	0		X	
13.	place / palace			0		X	

Number of words __214__   Number of errors __13__   Word recognition accuracy __94%__
Number of times nonsemantic substitutions self-corrected/total number
of nonsemantic substitutions __6/9 = 67%__
Number of semantic substitutions __12__
Number of "didn't try" errors __0__
Number of errors involving analysis __12__
Number of times words deliberately and successfully decoded (column 2) __11__
Number of times words deliberately and unsuccessfully decoded (column 2) __5__
Number of times word automatic but wrong (column 2) __8__

Word Recognition Checklist of Abilities

	Level of Success		
	Low	Medium	High
Avoiding automatic errors			
Avoiding errors with basic sight words			
Successfully analyzing words			
Successfully applying symbol-sound correspondences			
Attempting hard words (# of "didn't try" errors)			
Pausing and successfully decoding (SD vs. NSD)			
Self-correcting (especially errors that don't make sense, nonsemantic substitutions)			
Reading with fluency			

Comments/instructional focus and data:

Appendix D: READING DIFFICULTIES RECORD SHEET

COMPREHENSION ASSESSMENT

Name: Tami
Age: 9
Grade: 3

A. Comprehension Monitoring
  1. Knowing when do/don't understand

Date	Pages/Level	Overall Rating	Comprehension
5/17	"Saturday Surprise" p. 34-28 (3^1)	3	38% (written)
5/17	"Space Shuttles" p. 5-15 (3)	3	29% (oral)
5/21	"Oceans" p. 5-19 (3)	3	50% (written)
5/21	"Benjy" p. 7-13 (3^1)	2	43% (oral)

Comments: Tami's comprehension ratings indicate that she is not confident of her ability to comprehend what she reads. This assessment is fairly accurate, as her scores show. Her comprehension is poor. Material was determined to be at an appropriate level in terms of Tami's decoding ability.

  2. Locating Sources of Comprehension Difficulty
  Comments: Tami did not know how to look back in the text for answers. When asked to look for clues in a particular spot, she could not find any clues, even when broad hints were given.

  3. Fix-up Strategies
  Comments: Tami has little idea of how to fix up poor comprehension. When asked, she says "I don't know" or "I forgot." She appears not to expect that what she reads will necessarily make sense to her.

  4. General Comments
  Tami needs to learn that reading should make sense, and to think about understanding as she reads. She needs to begin to use fix-up strategies when she is not comprehending.

B. General Comprehension

Date	Pages	Story	% Accuracy Narrative	% Accuracy Expository	% Accuracy Literal	% Accuracy Inferential	Background Knowledge	Type of Incorrect Responses*
5/17	34-38	"Saturday Surprise"	38%		33%	40%	M	4x no response (E) 1x wrong answer (D)
5/17	5-15	"Space Shuttles"		29%	67%	0%	L	
5/21	5-19	"Oceans"		50%	100%	0%	L	3x no response (E) 1x wrong answer (D)
5/21	7-13	"Benji"	43%	——	50%	40%	M	
		Averages for all passages	41%	40%	63%	20%		

Comments: Tami does best answering literal questions. She has a great deal of trouble with inferential questions and needs strategies to help her in that area. She has difficulty with both narrative and expository passages. Her most frequent type of incorrect response was no response at all. She needs help learning to take risks when she thinks she doesn't know an answer.

* See page 268.

C. Drawing Inferences

Date	Pages	Story	% Accuracy Text-based	% Accuracy Prior Knowledge-based
5/17	34-38	"Saturday Surprise"	29%	100%
5/17	5-15	"Space Shuttles"	34%	0%
5/21	5-19	"Oceans"	57%	0%
5/21	7-13	"Benjy"	50%	0%
Average for all passages			43%	25%

Comments: Tami did not seem to be able to use context or other clues for test-based inference questions, or to use prior knowledge to answer inference questions when the answers were not in the text, with any consistency. She needs strategies for both.

Additional Recommendations:

Tami appears to be a very good reader; orally, she reads beautifully, and a listener would never guess that she had a problem with comprehension. However, she is unable to understand much of what she reads and is unaware of what to do about it. She has been kept at grade level until recently, when it became obvious that comprehension skills were a problem for her.

Tami seems to have below average background knowledge, and that affects her ability to comprehend. Taking the time to discuss unfamiliar reading material with her would help build her background knowledge and demonstrate to her how to draw on that knowledge. Hanson and Pearson's approach would be one way to help her realize the need to use what she knows to interpret what she reads.

She needs to be taught to be aware of her own understanding as she reads—to focus her attention on getting the meaning. Comprehension-monitoring strategies such as comprehension rating, summarizing, and the self-monitoring checklist would be helpful.

Tami also needs assistance in discovering the cause of her difficulty with comprehension and instruction on fix-up strategies that she can use to correct those difficulties. She also needs help in answering inference questions. The inference-awareness procedure and the QAR procedure would be useful in this regard.

The reading materials Tami has been using are too difficult for her, even though she is able to read them well. She should be given materials at a much lower reading level so that she can experience some success with comprehension skills and learn what it means to read with understanding.

"Saturday Surprise"
(Written questions)

Type*	Response**		
L	E		1. What does Uncle Charlie do every Saturday? (Takes Peggy places.)
I (TB)	E	X	2. When he took her to "a bench in the sky," where was he taking her? (NR)

I (TB)	E	X	3. Where were they when they went "to the moon?" (NR)
L	D	X	4. What was the bad news Peggy's mother had for her this Saturday? (Peggy had one shoe on and one shoe off.)
I (TB)			5. Where had they been planning to go this time? (Around the city in a boat.)
L	E	X	6. What does Peggy's mother do on Saturdays? (NR)
I (TB)	E	X	7. What did Uncle Charlie find for Peggy to do, since he can't go with her this Saturday? (NR)
I (PK)			8. How do you think Peggy felt about these plans? (Bad; she didn't like it.)

*   L = literal
   I = inferential
 TB = text-based inferential
 PK = prior knowledge-based inferential
** A = all parts of question not answered
  B = response doesn't fit question
  C = response too general or vague
  D = response incorrect (not due to A, B, and C above)
  E = no response

"Space Shuttles"
(Oral answers)

Type

L		1. What is the name of the space shuttle described? (Columbia)
I (TB)	X	2. What can the space shuttle do that planes and rockets can't do? (Didn't know)
L	X	3. Where is the fuel carried? (Didn't know)
I (TB)	X	4. Why are the rocket boosters needed? (Didn't know)
L	X	5. What happens to the fuel tanks when they are empty? (They fall off.)
I (TB)	X	6. Why are the small thrusters used? (I forgot.)
I (PK)	X	7. What does "orbiting the earth" mean? (Didn't know)

"Oceans"
(Written questions)

Type	Response	
L		1. Does the world have more land, or water, in it? (Water)
L		2. What do we call the largest bodies of water on earth? (Oceans)
L		3. Where do the waters of the Atlantic and Pacific Oceans meet? (Arctic)

I   E   4. Where does the color of the ocean come from?
(TB)   E   (two answers)
           X   a. (NR)
           X   b. (NR)

L   5. Pieces of ice floating in the cold ocean water are called (Icebergs).

I (TB)   D   X   6. Where do icebergs come from? (Mountains)

I (PK)   E   X   7. How do you think the author knows so much about oceans? (NR)

"Benjy and the Barking Bird"
(Oral answers)
<u>Type</u>

L   1. Who was coming for a visit? (Aunt Sarah)

L   X   2. Who was Tilly? (Dog)

I (TB)   X   3. What could Tilly do better than Benjy? (Don't remember)

I (TB)   4. How did Benjy feel about Tilly's barking? (Unhappy; birds shouldn't bark.)

I(TB)   X   5. Why did Benjy want to put Tilly's cage in the trash can? (He didn't like it.)

I (TB)   6. How did Benjy feel when Tilly escaped? (Happy)

I (PK)   X   7. Do you think Benjy will be in trouble? (No; nobody would mind.)

Comprehension Checklist of Abilities

	Level of Success		
	Low	Medium	High
Monitoring comprehension			
Applying fix-up strategies			
Reading questions correctly			
Avoiding vague/general answers			
Answering factual questions			
Informational			
Narrative			
Answering text-based inferential questions			
Informational			
Narrative			
Answering prior knowledge-based inferential questions			
Informational			
Narrative			
Answering questions in general			
Oral			
Written			
Looking back in text to answer questions			
Orally summarizing			
Informational			
Narrative			
Summarizing in writing			
Informational			
Narrative			
Studying informational text			
Responding in a literature journal (on fiction or nonfiction)			
Participating in a literature discussion (on fiction or nonfiction)			

Comments/instructional focus and data:

References and Further Reading

Ackerly, S. S., & Benton, A. L. (1947). Report of a case of bilateral frontal lobe defect. *Proceedings, Association for Research on Nervous and Mental Disease, 27,* 479–504.

Adams, A., Carnine, D., & Gersten, R. (1982). Instructional strategies for studying content area texts in the intermediate grades. *Reading Research Quarterly, 18,* 27–55.

Adams, M. J. (1990). *Beginning to read: Thinking and learning about print. A summary.* Prepared by S. Stahl, J. Osborne, & F. Lehr. Urbana, IL: Center for the Study of Reading.

Alexander, J. E., & Filler, R. C. (1976). *Attitudes and reading.* Newark, DE: International Reading Association.

Allington, R. L. (1980a). Poor readers don't get to read much in reading groups. *Language Arts, 57,* 872–876.

Allington, R. L. (1980b). Teacher interruption behaviors during primary-grade oral reading. *Journal of Educational Psychology, 72,* 371–377.

Allington, R. L. (1983). The reading instruction provided readers of differing reading ability. *The Elementary School Journal, 83,* 548–559.

Allington, R. L., & McGill-Franzen, A. (1989). School response to reading failure: Instruction for Chapter 1 and special education students in grades two, four and eight. *The Elementary School Journal, 89,* 529–542.

Ames, R., & Ames, C. (Eds.). (1984). *Research on motivation in education: Vol. 1. Student motivation.* New York: Academic Press.

Anderson, L. M. (1989). Learners and learning. In M. C. Reynolds (Ed.), *Knowledge base for the beginning teacher.* New York: Pergamon.

Anderson, R. (1977). The notion of schemata and the educational enterprise. In R. C. Anderson, R. J. Spiro, & W. E. Montague (Eds.), *Schooling and the acquisition of knowledge.* Hillsdale, NJ: Lawrence Erlbaum.

Anderson, R. C., Armbruster, B. B., & Kantor, R. N. (1980). *How clearly written are children's textbooks? Or, of bladderworts and alfa.* (ERIC Document Reproduction Service No. ED 192 275)

Anderson, R. C., & Biddle, W. B. (1975). On asking people questions about what they are reading. In G. Bower (Ed.), *The psychology of learning and motivation* (Vol. 9, pp. 90–129). New York: Academic Press.

Anderson, R. C., & Freebody, P. (1981). Vocabulary knowledge. In J. Guthrie (Ed.), *Comprehension and teaching: Research reviews* (pp. 77–117). Newark, DE: International Reading Association.

Anderson, R. C., Hiebert, E. H., Scott, J. A., & Wilkinson, I. A. (1985). *Becoming a nation of readers. The report of the Commission on Reading.* Washington, DC: National Institute of Education.

Anderson, R. C., Mason, J., & Shirey, L. (1984). The reading group: An experimental investigation of a labyrinth. *Reading Research Quarterly, 20,* 6–38.

Anderson, R. C., & Nagy, W. E. (1991). Word meanings. In R. Barr, M. Kamil, P. Mosenthal, and P. D. Pearson (Eds.), *Handbook of reading research,* (Vol. 2). New York: Longman.

Anderson, R. C., & Pearson, P. D. (1984). A schema-theoretic view of basic processes in reading comprehension. In P. D. Pearson (Ed.), *Handbook of reading research* (pp. 255–292). New York: Longman.

Anderson, R. C., Reynolds, R. E., Schallert, D. L., & Goetz, E. T. (1977). Frameworks for comprehending discourse. *American Educational Research Journal, 14*, 367–382.

Anderson, R. C., Spiro, R. J., & Anderson, M. C. (1978). Schemata as scaffolding for the representation of information in connected discourse. *American Educational Research Journal, 15*, 433–440.

Anderson, R., Wilson, P., & Fielding, L. (1988). Growth in reading and how children spend their time outside of school. *Reading Research Quarterly, 23*, 285–303.

Anderson, T. H. (1980). Study strategies and adjunct aids. In R. J. Spiro, B. C. Bruce, & W. F. Brewer (Eds.), *Theoretical issues in reading comprehension* (pp. 483–502). Hillsdale, NJ: Lawrence Erlbaum.

Andre, M. E. D. A., & Anderson, T. H. (1978–1979). The development and evaluation of a self-questioning study technique. *Reading Research Quarterly, 14*, 605–623.

Annett, M. (1972). Handedness, cerebral dominance and the growth of intelligence. In D. Bakker & D. Laty (Eds.), *Specific reading disability*. Rotterdam: Rotterdam University Press.

Anyon, J. (1980). Social class and the hidden curriculum of work. *Journal of Education, 162*, 67–92.

Anyon, J. (1981). Elementary schooling and the distinctions of social class. *Interchange, 12*, 118–132.

Applebee, A. N., Langer, J. A., & Mullis, I. V. S. (1987). *The nation's report card: Learning to be literate in America: Reading*. Princeton: Educational Testing Service.

Arlin, M., & Roth, G. (1978). Pupils' use of time while reading comics and books. *American Educational Research Journal, 15*, 201–216.

Arlin, M., Scott, M., & Webster, J. (1978–1979). The effects of pictures on rate of learning of sight words. *Reading Research Quarterly, 14*, 645–660.

Askov, E. N. (1973). *Primary pupil reading attitude inventory*. Dubuque, IA: Kendall/Hunt.

Au, K. H. (1979). Using the experience-text-relationship method with minority children. *The Reading Teacher, 32*, 677–679.

Au, K. H. (1981a). Comprehension-oriented reading lessons. *Educational Perspectives, 20*, 13–15.

Au, K. H. (1981b). Participation structures in a reading lesson with Hawaiian children: Analysis of a culturally appropriate instruction event. *Anthropology and Education Quarterly, 11*, 91–115.

Au, K. H., & Mason, J. (1981). Social organization factors in learning to read: The balance of rights hypothesis. *Reading Research Quarterly, 17*, 115–152.

Auerbach, E. R. (1989). Toward a social-contextual approach to family literacy. *Harvard Educational Review, 59*, 165–181.

August, D., & Garcia, E. E. (1988). *Language minority education in the United States*. Springfield, IL: Charles C. Thomas.

Bailey, M. H. (1967). The utility of phonics generalizations in grades one through six. *The Reading Teacher, 20*, 413–418.

Baker, L., & Brown, A. L. (1984). Metacognitive skills and reading. In P. D. Pearson (Ed.), *Handbook of reading research* (pp. 353–394). New York: Longman.

Balow, B. (1965). The long term effect of remedial reading. *The Reading Teacher, 18*, 581–586.

Balow, B. (1971). Perceptual-motor activities in the treatment of severe reading disability. *The Reading Teacher, 24*, 513–525.

Balow, I. H. (1963). Lateral dominance characteristics and reading achievement in the first grade. *Journal of Psychology, 55*, 323–328.

Balow, I. H., & Balow, B. (1964). Lateral dominance and reading achievement. *American Educational Research Journal, 1*, 139–143.

Bandura, A. (1977). Self-efficacy: Toward a unifying theory of behavioral change. *Psychological Review, 84*, 191–215.

Bandura, A., & Schunk, D. H. (1981). Cultivating competence, self-efficacy, & intrinsic interest through proximal self-motivation. *Journal of Personality & Social Psychology, 41*, 586–598.

Baratz, J. C., & Shuy, R. W. (1969). *Teaching black children to read.* Washington, DC: Center for Applied Linguistics.

Barbe, W. B., & Abbott, J. L. (1975). *Personalized reading instruction: New techniques that increase reading skill and comprehension.* West Nyack, NY: Parker.

Barnitz, J. G. (1980). Syntactic effect of the reading comprehension of pronoun-referent structures by children in grades two, four and six. *Reading Research Quarterly, 15,* 268–289.

Barnitz, J. G. (1985). *Reading development of nonnative speakers of English.* Orlando, FL: Harcourt Brace Jovanovich.

Barr, R., & Dreeban, R. (1991). Grouping students for reading instruction. In R. Barr, M. Kamil, P. Mosenthal, & P. D. Pearson (Eds.), *Handbook of reading research,* (Vol. II, pp. 85–910). New York: Longman.

Barrett, J. (1970). *Animals should definitely not wear clothing.* New York: Atheneum.

Bartlett, B. J. (1978). *Top-level structure as an organizational strategy for recall of classroom text.* Unpublished doctoral dissertation, Arizona State University.

Bateman, B. (1964). Learning disabilities: Yesterday, today, and tomorrow. *Exceptional Children, 31,* 167–177.

Bateman, B. (1968). The efficacy of an auditory and a visual method of first grade reading instruction with auditory and visual learners. In H. K. Smith (Ed.), *Perception and reading.* Newark, DE: International Reading Association.

Bauer, A., & Shea, T. (1989). *Teaching exceptional students in your classroom.* Boston: Allyn & Bacon.

Baumann, J. F., & Schmitt, M. B. (1986). The what, why, how, and when of comprehension instruction. *The Reading Teacher, 39,* 640–647.

Baumann, J. F., & Stevenson, J. A. (1982). Understanding standardized reading achievement test scores. *The Reading Teacher, 35,* 648–655.

Beck, I., & McKeown, M. (1991). Conditions of vocabulary acquisition. In R. Barr, M. Kamil, P. Mosenthal, & P. D. Pearson (Eds.), *Handbook of reading research,* (Vol. II, pp. 789–814). New York: Longman.

Beck, I. L., McKeown, M. G., & McCaslin, E. S. (1983). Vocabulary development: All contexts are not created equal. *Elementary School Journal, 83,* 177–181.

Beck, I., McKeown, M., McCaslin, E., & Burkes, A. (1979). *Instructional dimensions that may affect reading comprehension: Examples from two commercial reading programs* (LRDC Publication 1979/20). Pittsburgh, PA: University of Pittsburgh, Learning Research and Development Center.

Beck, I. L., Perfetti, C. A., & McKeown, M. G. (1982). The effects of long-term vocabulary instruction on lexical access and reading comprehension. *Journal of Educational Psychology, 74,* 506–521.

Becker, W. C., & Carnine, D. W. (1976). *Direct instruction—A behavior theory model for comprehensive educational intervention with the disadvantaged.* Paper presented at the 8th Symposium on Behavior Modification, Caracas, Venezuela, February, 1976.

Becker, W. C., Engelmann, S., & Carnine, D. W. (in press). The direct instruction model. In R. Rhine (Ed.), *Encouraging change in America's school: A decade of experimentation.* New York: Academic Press.

Beebe, M. J. (1980). The effect of different types of substitution miscues on reading. *Reading Research Quarterly, 15,* 324–336.

Belmont, L., & Birch, H. G. (1965). Lateral dominance, lateral awareness, and reading disability. *Child Development, 36,* 57–71.

Berkowitz, S. (1986). Effects of instruction in text-organization on sixth-grade students' memory for expository reading. *Reading Research Quarterly, 21,* 161–178.

Betts, E. A. (1946). *Foundations of reading instruction.* New York: American Book Company.

Biemiller, A. (1979). Changes in the use of graphic and contextual information as a function of passage difficulty and reading achievement level. *Journal of Reading Behavior, 11,* 307–318.

Bishop, R. S. (1987). Extending multicultural understanding through children's books. In B. Cullinan (Ed.), *Children's literature in the reading program* (pp. 60–67). Newark, DE: International Reading Association.

Blachowicz, C. (1985). Vocabulary development and reading: From research to instruction. *The Reading Teacher, 38,* 876–881.

Blachowicz, C., & Zabroske, B. (1990). Context instruction: A metacognitive approach for at-risk readers. *Journal of Reading, 33,* 504–508.

Blanton, W. E., Farr, R., & Tuinman, J. J. (Eds.). (1972). *Reading tests for secondary grades: A review and evaluation.* Newark, DE: International Reading Association.

Blanton, W., Farr, R., & Tuinman, J. (1974). *Measuring reading performance.* Newark, DE: International Reading Association.

Boehnlein, M. M., & Hagar, B. H. (Eds.). (1985). *Children, parents, and reading.* Newark, DE: International Reading Association.

Bond, G. L., & Dykstra, R. (1967). The cooperative research program in first grade reading instruction. *Reading Research Quarterly, 2,* 5–142.

Bond, G. L., Tinker, M. A., & Wasson, B. B. (1984). *Reading difficulties: Their diagnosis and correction* (5th ed.). Englewood Cliffs, NJ: Prentice Hall.

Bormuth, J. R., Manning, J. C., Carr, J. W., & Pearson, P. D. (1970). Children's comprehension of between- and within-sentence syntactic structures. *Journal of Educational Psychology, 61,* 349–357.

Botel, M. (1978). *Botel Reading Inventory.* Chicago: Follett.

Bransford, J. D., Stein, B. S., Vye, N. J., Franks, J. J., Auble, P. M., Mezynski, K. J., & Perfetti, C. A. (1982). Differences in approaches to learning: An overview. *Journal of Experimental Psychology: General, 111,* 390–398.

Bridge, C. A., & Tierney, R. J. (1981). The inferential operations of children across text with narrative and expository tendencies. *Journal of Reading Behavior, 13,* 201–214.

Bridge, C. A., Winograd, P. N., and Haley, D. (1983). Using predictable materials vs. preprimers to teach beginning sight words. *The Reading Teacher, 36,* 884–891.

Bristow, P. S. (1985). Are poor readers passive readers? Some evidence, possible explanations, and potential solutions. *The Reading Teacher, 39,* 318–325.

Bristow, P. S., Pikulski, J. J., & Pelosi, P. L. (1983). A comparison of five estimates of reading instructional level. *The Reading Teacher, 37,* 273–279.

Brogan, P., & Fox, L. K. (1961). *Helping children read: A practical approach to individualized reading.* New York: Holt, Rinehart and Winston.

Brophy, J. (1981). Teacher praise: A functional analysis. *Review of Educational Research, 51,* 5–32.

Brophy, J. (1987a). On motivating students. In D. C. Berliner & B. U. Rosenshine (Eds.), *Talks to teachers* (pp. 201–245). New York: Random House.

Brophy, J. (1987b). Synthesis of research on strategies for motivating students to learn. *Educational Leadership, 45,* 40–47.

Brown, A. L., & Day, J. D. (1983). Macrorules for summarizing texts: The development of expertise. *Journal of Verbal Learning and Verbal Behavior, 22,* 1–14.

Brozo, W. G., Schmelze, R. V., and Spires, H. A. (1983). The beneficial effect of chunking on good readers' comprehension of expository prose. *Journal of Reading, 26,* 442–449.

Bruce, B. C., Rubin, A. D., Starr, K. S., & Liebling, C. (1984). Sociocultural differences in oral vocabulary and reading material. In W. S. Hall, W. Nagy, & R. Linn (Eds.),

Spoken words: Effects of situation and social group on oral word usage and frequency (pp. 466–480). Hillsdale, NJ: Lawrence Erlbaum.

Bryan, T., & Bryan, J. (1986). *Understanding learning disabilities* (3rd ed.). Palo Alto, NY: Mayfield.

Bryant, N. D. (1972). Silent reading diagnostic tests. In O. K. Buros (Ed.), *Seventh mental measurements yearbook* (pp. 1122–1124). Highland Park, NJ: Gryphon Press.

Burke, S. M., Pflaum, S. W., & Krafle, J. D. (1982). The influence of Black English on diagnosis of reading in learning disabled and normal readers. *Journal of Learning Disabilities, 15*(1), 19–22.

Burmeister, L. E. (1968). Usefulness of phonics generalizations. *The Reading Teacher, 21,* 349–356.

Burns, P., Roe, B., & Ross, E. (1983). *Teaching reading in today's elementary schools.* Boston: Houghton-Mifflin.

Buros, O. K. (n.d.) Suggestions to MMY reviewers. Mimeographed.

Buros, O. K. (1969). *Reading tests and reviews.* Highland Park, NJ: Gryphon Press.

Buros, O. K. (1972). *Seventh mental measurements yearbook.* Highland Park, NJ: Gryphon Press.

Buros, O. K. (1975). *Reading tests and reviews II.* Highland Park, NJ: Gryphon Press.

Buros, O. K. (1978). *Eighth mental measurements yearbook.* Highland Park, NJ: Gryphon Press.

Butkowsky, I. S., & Willows, D. M. (1980). Cognitive motivational characteristics of children varying in reading ability: Evidence for learned helplessness in poor readers. *Journal of Educational Psychology, 72,* 408–422.

Butler, R., & Nisan, M. (1986). Effects of no feedback, task-related comments, and grades on intrinsic motivation and performance. *Journal of Educational Psychology, 78,* 210–216.

Byers, P., & Byers, H. (1972). Nonverbal communication and the education of children. In C. B. Cazden, V. P. John, & D. Hymes (Eds.), *Functions of language in the classroom* (pp. 3–31). New York: Teachers College Press.

Byers, R. K., & Lord, E. E. (1943). Late effects of lead poisoning on mental development. *American Journal of Diseases of Children, 66,* 471–493.

Calfee, R. C., Lindamood, P., & Lindamood, C. (1973). Acoustic-phonetic skills and reading: Kindergarten through twelfth grade. *Journal of Educational Psychology, 64,* 293–298.

California Achievement Tests (1977). Monterey, CA: CTB/McGraw-Hill.

California Diagnostic Reading Tests. (1989). Monterey, CA: CTB/McGraw-Hill.

Capobianco, R. J. (1966). Ocular-manual laterality and reading in adolescent mental retardates. *American Journal of Mental Deficiency, 70,* 781–785.

Capobianco, R. J. (1967). Ocular-manual laterality and reading in achievement in children with special learning disabilities. *American Educational Research Journal, 2,* 133–137.

Carden, M. (1936). *The Carden method, Manual I.* Glen Rock, NJ: MacCarden.

Carnine, D. W., Kameenui, E. J., & Coyle, G. (1984). Utilization of contextual information in determining the meaning of unfamiliar words. *Reading Research Quarterly, 19,* 188–204.

Carnine, D., & Silbert, J. (1979). *Direct reading instruction.* Columbus, OH: Charles E. Merrill.

Carr, E. (1985). The vocabulary overview guide: A metacognitive strategy to improve vocabulary comprehension and retention. *Journal of Reading, 28,* 684–689.

Carr, E., Dewitz, P., & Patberg, J. (1989). Using cloze for inference training with expository text. *The Reading Teacher, 42,* 380–385.

Carr, E. M., Dewitz, P., & Patberg, J. P. (1983). The effect of inference training on children's comprehension of expository text. *Journal of Reading Behavior, 15,* 1–18.

Carter, L. (1984). The sustaining effects study of compensatory and elementary education. *Educational Researcher, 12,* 4–13.

Carver, R., & Hoffman, J. (1981). The effect of practice through repeated reading on gain in reading ability using a computer-based instructional system. *Reading Research Quarterly, 16,* 374–390.

Chall, J. S. (1983). *Learning to read: The great debate* (2nd ed.). New York: McGraw-Hill.

Chall, J. S., Roswell, F. G., & Blumenthal, S. H. (1963). Auditory blending ability: A factor in success in beginning reading. *The Reading Teacher, 17,* 113–118.

Cheek, M. C., & Cheek, E. H., Jr. (1980). *Diagnostic-prescriptive reading instruction.* Dubuque, IA: William C. Brown.

Cheyney, A. B. (1984). *Teaching reading skills through the newspaper.* Newark, DE: International Reading Association.

Chomsky, C. (1978). When you still can't read in third grade: After decoding what? In S. J. Samuels (Ed.), *What research has to say about reading instruction* (pp. 13–30). Newark, DE: International Reading Association.

Clay, M. M. (1985). *The early detection of reading difficulties.* Portsmouth, NH: Heinemann Educational Books.

Cleary, D. M. (1978). *Thinking Thursdays: Language arts in the reading lab.* Newark, DE: International Reading Association.

Clements, S. (1966). *Minimal brain dysfunction in children: Terminology and identification.* National Institute of Neurological Diseases, Monograph No. 3, Public Health Publications No. 1415. Washington, DC: Government Printing Office.

Clymer, T. (1963). The utility of phonics generalizations in the primary grades. *The Reading Teacher, 16,* 255–257.

Cohen, P. A., Kulik, J. A., & Kulik, C. C. (1982). Educational outcomes of tutoring: A meta-analysis of findings. *American Educational Research Journal, 19,* 237–248.

Cohen, R. R. (1966). *Remedial training of first grade children with visual perceptual retardation.* Unpublished doctoral dissertation, University of California at Los Angeles.

Collins, A., Brown, J. S., & Larkin, K. (1980). Inference in text understanding. In R. J. Spiro, B. C. Bruce, & W. F. Brewer (Eds.), *Theoretical issues in reading comprehension.* Hillsdale, NJ: Lawrence Erlbaum.

Collins, A. M., & Quillian, M. R. (1969). Retrieval time from semantic memory. *Journal of Verbal Learning and Verbal Behavior, 8,* 240–247.

Collins, J. (1982). Discourse style, classroom interaction and differential treatment. *Journal of Reading Behavior, 14,* 429–437.

Comer, J. P. (1988). Educating poor minority children. *Scientific American, 259*(5), 42–48.

Comer, J. P., Schraft, C. M., & Sparrow, S. S. (1980). *A social skills curriculum for inner city children.* New Haven, CT: Yale Child Study Center.

Committee for Economic Development (1987). *Children in need: Investment strategies for the educationally disadvantaged.* New York: Author.

Cooper, J. D., Cooper, L. D., Roser, N., Harris, L. A., Smith, C. B. (1972). *Decision making for the diagnostic teacher* (pp. 14–16). New York: Holt, Rinehart and Winston.

Covington, M. V. (1983). Motivated cognitions. In S. G. Paris, G. M. Olson, & H. W. Stevenson (Eds.), *Learning and motivation in the classroom.* Hillsdale, NJ: Lawrence Erlbaum.

Covington, M. (1984). The self-worth theory of achievement motivation: Findings & implications. *The Elementary School Journal, 85,* 5–20.

Criscuolo, N. P. (1981). Creative homework with the newspaper. *Reading Teacher, 34,* 921–922.

Cruickshank, W. M. (1966). *The teacher of brain-injured children: A discussion of bases for competency.* Syracuse, NY: Syracuse University Press.

Cudd, E. T., & Roberts, L. (1989). Using writing to enhance content area learning in the primary grades. *The Reading Teacher, 42,* 392–404.

Cullen, A. (1978). *Blackboard, blackboard on the wall, who is the fairest one of all?* Harlin Quist, Inc.

Cummins, J. (1979). Linguistic interdependence and the educational development of bilingual children. *Review of Educational Research, 49,* 222–251.

Cunningham, P. (1979). Match informal evaluation to your teaching practices. *The Reading Teacher, 31,* 51–56.

Cunningham, P., Hall, D., & Defee, M. (1991). Non-ability grouped, multi-level instruction: A year in a first-grade classroom. *The Reading Teacher, 44,* 566–571.

Cziko, G. A. (1992). The evaluation of bilingual education: From necessity and probability to possibility. *Educational Researcher, 21,* 10–16.

D'Angelo, K. (1982). Correction behavior: Implications for reading instruction. *The Reading Teacher, 35,* 395–399.

Daniels, S. (1971). *How 2 gerbils . . . and I taught them how to read.* Philadelphia: Westminster Press.

Davey, B. (1988). The nature of response errors for good and poor readers when permitted to reinspect text during question-answering. *American Educational Research Journal, 25,* 399–414.

Davey, B. (1989). Assessing comprehension: Selected interactions of task and reader. *The Reading Teacher, 42,* 694–697.

Davey, B., & McBride, S. (1986). Effect of question-generation training on reading comprehension. *Journal of Educational Psychology, 78,* 256–262.

Davey, B., & Porter, S. M. (1982). Comprehension-rating: A procedure to assist poor comprehenders. *Journal of Reading, 26,* 197–202.

Davidson, N., & O'Leary, P. W. (1990). How cooperative learning can enhance mastery teaching. *Educational Leadership, 67,* 30–33.

Davis, F. B. (1944). Fundamental factors in comprehension in reading. *Psychometrika, 9,* 185–197.

Davis, F. B. (1968). Research in comprehension in reading. *Reading Research Quarterly, 3,* 499–545.

Davis, W. E., & McCaul, E. J. (1990). *At-risk children and youth: A crisis in our schools and society.* Orono, ME: University of Maine, College of Education, Institute for the Study of At-Risk Students.

Dechant, E. (1968). *Diagnosis and remediation of reading disability.* West Nyack, NY: Parker.

Deci, E. L., & Ryan, R. M. (1985). *Intrinsic motivation and self-determination in human behaviors.* New York: Plenum.

Delacato, C. H. (1966). *Neurological organization and reading.* Springfield, IL: Charles C. Thomas.

Delpit, L. D. (1988). The silenced dialogue: Power and pedagogy in educating other people's children. *Harvard Educational Review, 58*(3), 280–298.

Deno, S. (1985). Curriculum-based measurement: The emerging alternative. *Exceptional Children, 52,* 219–232.

Deno, S. L., Marston, D., & Tindal, G. (1986). Direct and frequent curriculum-based measurement: An alternative for educational decision making. *Special Services in the Schools, 2,* 5–27.

Deno, S., Mirken, P., & Chiang, B. (1982). Identifying valid measures of reading. *Exceptional Children, 49,* 36–45.

Dewitz, P., Carr, T., & Patberg, J. (1987). Effects of inference training on comprehension and comprehension monitoring. *Reading Research Quarterly, 22,* 99–121.

DiBennedetto, B., Richardson, E., & Kochnower, J. (1983). Vowel generalization in normal and learning disabled readers. *Journal of Educational Psychology, 75,* 576–582.

Diener, C. I., & Dweck, C. S. (1980). An analysis of learned helplessness: The processing of success. *Journal of Personality & Social Psychology, 39,* 940–952.

Doctorow, M., Wittrock, M. C., & Marks, C. (1978). Generative processes in reading comprehension. *Journal of Educational Psychology, 70,* 109–118.

Dolch, E. W. (1942). *The basic sight word test.* Champaign, IL: Garard.

Dole, J. A., Duffy, G. G., Roehler, L. R., & Pearson, P. D. (1991). Moving from the old to the new: Research on reading comprehension instruction. *Review of Educational Research, 61,* 239–264.

Dole, J., & Pearson, P. D. (in press). Explicit comprehension instruction: A review of research and a new conceptualization of instruction. *Elementary School Journal.*

Doren, M. (1973). *Doren Diagnostic Reading Test of Word Recognition Skills.* Circle Pines, MN: American Guidance Service.

Dorr-Bremme, D. W., & Herman, J. L. (1986). *Assessing student achievement: A profile of classroom practices.* Los Angeles: University of California, Center for the Study of Evaluation.

Dowhower, S. (1987). Effects of repeated reading on second-grade transitional readers' fluency and comprehension. *Reading Research Quarterly, 42,* 502–507.

Dowhower, S. (1989). Repeated reading: Research into practice. *The Reading Teacher, 42,* 502–507.

Dreeben, R., & Gamoran, A. (1986). Race, instruction, and learning. *American Sociological Review, 51,* 660–669.

Duffy, G. G., & Roehler, L. R. (1986). *Improving classroom reading instruction.* New York: Random House.

Duffy, G., & Roehler, L. (1987). Improving reading through the use of responsive elaboration. *The Reading Teacher, 40,* 514–521.

Duffy, G., Roehler, L., & Herrman, B. (1988). Modeling mental processes helps poor readers become strategic readers. *The Reading Teacher, 41,* 762–767.

Duffy, G., Roehler, L., Sivan, E., Rackliffe, G., Book, C., Meloth, M., Vavrus, L., Wessellman, R., Putnam, J., & Bassiri, D. (1987). The effects of explaining the reasoning associated with using reading strategies. *Reading Research Quarterly, 22,* 347–367.

Durkin, D. (1966). *Children who read early.* New York: Columbia University Press.

Durkin, D. (1978–1979). What classroom observations reveal about comprehension instruction. *Reading Research Quarterly, 14,* 481–533.

Durkin, D. (1981a). Reading comprehension in five basal readers series. *Reading Research Quarterly, 16,* 515–544.

Durkin, D. (1981b). *Strategies for identifying words* (2nd ed.). Boston: Allyn and Bacon.

Durkin, D. (1984a). Do basal manuals teach reading comprehension? In R. C. Anderson, J. Osborn, & R. J. Tierney (Eds.), *Learning to read in American schools: Basal readers and content texts* (pp. 29–38). Hillsdale, NJ: Lawrence Erlbaum.

Durkin, D. (1984b). Is there a match between what elementary teachers do and what basal reader manuals recommend? *The Reading Teacher, 37,* 734–745.

Durkin, D. (1984c). *The decoding ability of elementary school students* (Reading Education Report No. 49). Urbana: University of Illinois, Center for the Study of Reading.

Durkin, D. (1987). A classroom-observation study of reading instruction in kindergarten. *Early Childhood Research Quarterly, 2,* 275–300.

Durrell, D., & Catterson, J. H. (1980). *Analysis of reading difficulty* (3rd ed.). New York: The Psychological Corporation.

Dweck, C. S. (1986). Motivational processes affecting learning. *American Psychologist, 41,* 1040–1048.

Dweck, C. S., & Elliott, E. S. (1983). Achievement motivation. In E. M. Hetherington (Ed.), *Handbook of child psychology* (Vol. 4, pp. 643–691). New York: Wiley.

Dwyer, C. A. (1978). Woodcock reading mastery tests. In O. K. Buros (Ed.), *Eighth mental measurements yearbook* (pp. 1303–1305). Highland Park, NJ: Gryphon Press.

Edelsky, C., & Harman, S. (1988). One more critique of reading tests—With two differences. *English Education, 20*(3), 157–171.

Educational Horizons. (Winter 1988). *66*(2), Bloomington, IN: Pi Lambda Theta.

Edwards, P. A. (1989). Supporting mothers attempting to provide scaffolding for bookreading. In J. B. Allen & J. Mason (Eds.), *Risk makers, risk takers, risk breakers: Reducing the risks for young learners* (pp. 222–250). Portsmouth, NH: Heinemann Educational Books.

Edwards, P. A., & García, G. E. (in press). The implications of Vygotskian Theory for the development of home-school programs: A focus on storybook reading. In V. John-Steiner, C. Panofsky, & L. Smith (Eds.), *Interactionist approaches to language and literacy.* Cambridge, MA: Cambridge University Press.

Edwards, P. A., & García, G. E. (1991). Parental involvement in mainstream schools: An issue of equity. In M. Foster & S. Goldberg (Eds.), *Readings on equal education* (Vol. 11). New York: AMS Press.

Eeds, M. (1985). Bookwords: Using a beginning word list of high frequency words from children's literature K-3. *The Reading Teacher, 38,* 418–423.

Eeds, M., & Cockrum, W. A. (1985). Teaching word meanings by expanding schemata vs. dictionary work vs. reading in context. *Journal of Reading, 28,* 492–497.

Ehri, L. C., Deffner, N. D., & Wilce, L. S. (1984). Pictorial mnemonics for phonics. *Journal of Educational Psychology, 76,* 880–893.

Ehri, L. C., & Roberts, R. T. (1979). Do beginners learn printed words better in context or in isolation? *Child Development, 50,* 675–685.

Ehri, L. C., & Wilce, L. S. (1980). Do beginners learn to read function words better in sentences or in lists? *Reading Research Quarterly, 15,* 451–476.

Ehri, L. C., & Wilce, L. S. (1983). Development of word identification speed in skilled and less skilled beginning readers. *Journal of Educational Psychology, 75,* 3–18.

Ehri, L. C., & Wilce, L. S. (1987). Does learning to spell help beginners learn to read words? *Reading Research Quarterly, 22,* 47–65.

Ekwall, E. E. (1979). *Ekwall Reading Inventory.* Boston: Allyn and Bacon.

Ekwall, E., & Shanker, J. (1983). *Diagnosis and remediation of the disabled reader* (2nd ed.). Boston: Allyn & Bacon.

Eldredge, J. L., & Butterfield, D. (1986). Alternatives to traditional reading instruction. *The Reading Teacher, 40,* 32–37.

Emans, R. (1967). The usefulness of phonics generalizations above the primary grades. *The Reading Teacher, 20,* 419–425.

Epstein, J. L. (1988, Winter). How do we improve programs for parent involvement? *Educational Horizons,* pp. 58–59.

Epstein, J. L. (1991). Paths to partnership: What we can learn from federal, state, district, and school initiatives. *Phi Delta Kappan, 72,* 344–349.

Erickson, F., & Mohatt, G. (1982). Cultural organization of participation structures in two classrooms of Indian students. In G. Spindler (Ed.), *Doing the ethnography of schooling: Educational anthropology in action* (pp. 132–174). New York: Holt, Rinehart and Winston.

Ervin, J. (1982). *How to have a successful parents and reading program: A practical guide.* Boston: Allyn & Bacon.

Estes, T. H. (1971). A scale to measure attitudes toward reading. *Journal of Reading, 15,* 135–138.

Farr, R. (1969). *Reading: What can be measured?* Newark, DE: International Reading Association.

Farr, R. C. (1973). *Iowa Silent Reading Test.* New York: Psychological Corporation.

Farr, R. (1978). Prescriptive reading inventory. In O. K. Buros (Ed.), Eighth mental measurements yearbook (pp. 1274–1277). Highland Park, NJ: Gryphon Press.

Farr, R., & Anastasiow, N. (1969). *Review of reading readiness tests.* Newark, DE: International Reading Association.

Farr, R., & Carey, R. F. (1986). *Reading: What can be measured?* (2nd ed.). Newark, DE: International Reading Association.

Fernald, G. M. (1939). *Remedial techniques in basic school subjects.* New York: McGraw-Hill.

First Teachers: A family literacy handbook for parents, policy-makers, and literacy providers. (1989). Washington, DC: Barbara Bush Foundation for Family Literacy.

Fisher, C. W., Fibly, N. N., Marliave, R., Cohen, L. S., Dishaw, M. M., Moore, J. E., & Berliner, D. C. (1978). *Teaching behaviors, academic learning time, and student achievement: Final report of phase III-B, beginning teacher evaluation study.* San Francisco: Far West Educational Laboratory for Educational Research and Development.

Flood, J., & Lapp, D. (1989). Reporting reading progress: A comparison portfolio for parents. *The Reading Teacher, 42,* 508–514.

Flood, J., & Lapp, D. (1990). Reading comprehension instruction for at-risk students: Research-based practices that can make a difference. *Journal of Reading, 33,* 490–498.

Fox, B., & Routh, D. K. (1975). Analyzing spoken language into words, syllables, and phonemes: A developmental study. *Journal of Psycholinguistic Research, 4,* 331–342.

Frase, L. T., & Schwartz, B. J. (1975). The effect of question production and answering on prose recall. *Journal of Educational Psychology, 67,* 621–635.

Fredericks, A. D. (1982). Developing positive reading attitudes. *The Reading Teacher, 36,* 38–40.

Fredericks, A. D., & Rasinski, T. V. (1990). Working with parents: Whole language and parents: Natural partners. *The Reading Teacher, 43,* 692–694.

Fredericks, A. D., & Taylor, D. (1985). *Parent programs in reading: Guidelines for success.* Newark, DE: International Reading Association.

Fredrickson, C. H. (1975). Representing logical and semantic structure of knowledge acquired from discourse. *Cognitive Psychology, 7*(3), 371–458.

Freebody, P., & Anderson, R. C. (1983). Effects on text comprehension of differing proportions and locations of difficult vocabulary. *Journal of Reading Behavior, 15,* 19–40.

Frostig, M., & Home, D. (1964). *The Frostig program for the development of visual perception.* Chicago: Follett.

Fry, E. (1981). *Reading diagnosis: Informal reading inventories.* Providence, RI: Jamestown Publishers.

Fuchs, L., Deno, S. L., & Mirkin, P. K. (1984). The effects of frequent curriculum-based measurement and evaluation on pedagogy, student achievement, and student awareness of learning. *American Educational Research Journal, 21,* 449–460.

Fuchs, L., Fuchs, D., & Deno, S. (1982). Reliability and validity of curriculum-based informal reading inventories. *Reading Research Quarterly, 18,* 6–26.

Fuchs, L., Fuchs, D., & Maxwell, L. (1988). The validity of informal reading comprehension measures. *Remedial and Special Education, 9,* 20–28.

Gaetz, T. M. (1991). *The effects of a self-monitoring checklist on elementary students' post reading question-answering performance.* Unpublished doctoral dissertation, University of Minnesota.

Gaffney, J., & Anderson, R. C. (1991). Two-tiered scaffolding: Congruent processes of teaching and learning. In E. Hiebert (Ed.) *Literacy for a diverse society: Perspectives, practices, and policies.* New York: Teachers College.

Gambrell, L. B., & Bales, R. J. (1986). Mental imagery and the comprehension-monitoring performance of fourth- and fifth-grade poor readers. *Reading Research Quarterly, 21,* 454–464.,

García, G. E. (1991). Factors influencing the English reading test performance of Spanish-speaking Hispanic children. *Reading Research Quarterly. 26,* 371–392.

García, G. E., & Pearson, P. D. (1990). *Modifying reading instruction to maximize its effectiveness for all students* (Tech. Rep. No. 489). Urbana: University of Illinois, Center for the Study of Reading.

García, G. E., & Pearson, P. D. (1991). *Literacy assessment in a diverse society* (Tech. Rep. No. 525). Urbana: University of Illinois, Center for the Study of Reading.

García, G. E., Pearson, P. D., & Jiménez, R. T. (1990). *The at-risk dilemma: A synthesis of reading research* (Study 2.2.3.3b). Urbana: University of Illinois, Reading Research and Education Center.

García, G. E., Stephens, D. L., Koenke, K. R., Pearson, P. D., Harris, V. J., & Jiménez, R. T. (1989). *A study of classroom practices related to the reading of low-achieving students: Phase one* (Study 2.2.3.5). Urbana: University of Illinois, Reading Research and Education Center.

Garner, R. (1980). Monitoring of understanding: An investigation of good and poor readers' awareness of induced miscomprehension of text. *Journal of Reading Behavior, 12*, 55–64.

Garner, R., Hare, V. C., Alexander, P., Haynes, J., & Winograd, P. (1984). Inducing use of a text lookback strategy among unsuccessful readers. *American Educational Research Journal, 21*, 789–798.

Garner, R., & Reis, R. (1981). Monitoring and resolving comprehension obstacles: An investigation of spontaneous text lookbacks among upper grade good and poor comprehenders. *Reading Research Quarterly, 16*, 569–582.

Garner, R., Wagoner, S., & Smith, T. (1983). Externalizing question-answering strategies of good and poor comprehenders. *Reading Research Quarterly, 18*, 439–447.

Garner, A., & Lipsky, D. (1987). Beyond special education: Toward a quality system for all students. *Harvard Educational Review, 57*, 367–395.

Gaskins, I. W. (1982). Let's end the reading disabilities/learning disabilities debate. *Journal of Learning Disabilities, 15*, 81–83.

Gelb, I. J. (1966). *A study of writing.* Chicago: University of Chicago Press.

Gersten, R., & Carnine, D. (1986). Direct instruction in reading comprehension. *Educational Leadership, 43*, 70–78.

Gillingham, A., & Stillman, B. (1966). *Remedial teaching for children with specific disability in reading, spelling and penmanship.* Cambridge, MA: Educator's Publishing Service.

Gilmore, J. V., and Gilmore, E. C. (1968). *Gilmore Oral Reading Test.* Orlando, FL: Harcourt Brace Jovanovich.

Gipe, J. (1978–1979). Investigating techniques for teaching word meanings. *Reading Research Quarterly, 14*, 624–644.

Gitelman, H. F. (1983). Newspaper power. *The Reading Teacher, 36*, 831.

Glass, G. (1986). The effectiveness of special education. *Policy Studies Review, 2*, 65–78.

Glass, G. V., & Robbins, M. P. (1967). A critique of experiments on the role of neurological organization in reading performance. *Reading Research Quarterly, 3*, 5–52.

Glasser, W. (1986). *Control theory in the classroom.* New York: Harper and Row.

Golinkoff, R. (1975–1976). A comparison of reading comprehension processes in good and poor comprehenders. *Reading Research Quarterly, 11*, 623–659.

Goodman, K. S. (1969). Analysis of oral reading miscues: Applied psycholinguistics. *Reading Research Quarterly, 5*, 9–30.

Goodman, K. (1976). Reading: A psycholinguistic guessing game. In H. Singer & R. Rugdell (Eds.), *Theoretical models and processes of reading* (2nd ed.). Newark, DE: International Reading Association.

Goodman, K. S., & Burke, C. (1982). Dialect barriers to reading comprehension: Revisited. (Reprinted in F. Gollasch (Ed.), *Language and literacy: The selected writings of Kenneth S. Goodman: Vol. II. Reading, language, and the classroom teacher.* London: Routledge & Kegan Paul.)

Goodman, Y. M., & Burke, C. L. (1972). *Reading miscue inventory manual: Procedures for diagnosis and evaluation.* New York: Macmillan.

Goodman, Y. M., Watson, D. J., & Burke, C. L. (1987). *Reading miscue inventory: Alternative procedures.* New York: Richard C. Owen.

Gordon, C. J. (1980). *The effects of instruction in metacomprehension and inferencing on children's comprehension abilities.* Unpublished doctoral dissertation, University of Minnesota.

Gordon, C. J. (1985). Modeling inference awareness across the curriculum. *Journal of Reading, 28,* 444–447.

Graham, S. (1984). Teacher feelings and student thoughts: An attributional approach to affect in the classroom. *The Elementary School Journal, 85,* 91–104.

Graves, M. (1987). The roles of vocabulary instruction in fostering vocabulary development. In M. G. McKeown & M. E. Curtis (Eds.), *The nature of vocabulary acquisition.* Hillsdale, NJ: Lawrence Erlbaum.

Gray, W. S. (1967). *Gray Oral Reading Test.* New York: Bobbs-Merrill.

Greedwood, C., Delquaddri, J., & Hall, R. (1981). *Code for instructional structure and student academic responses: CISSAR.* Kansas City, KS: University of Kansas, Juniper Gardens Children's Project, Bureau of Child Research.

Grimes, J. E. (1975). *The thread of discourse.* The Hague, Netherlands: Mouton.

Grinnell, P. C. (1989). *How can I prepare my young child for reading?* Newark, DE: International Reading Association.

Groden, G. (1969). Lateral preference in normal children. *Perceptual and Motor Skills, 28,* 213–214.

Haddock, M. (1976). The effects of an auditory and auditory-visual method of blending instruction on the ability of prereaders to decode synthetic words. *Journal of Educational Psychology, 68,* 825–831.

Hagen, J. (1979). *Semantically oriented approaches to prereading vocabulary instruction.* Unpublished doctoral dissertation, University of Wisconsin.

Hall, M. (1981). *Teaching reading as a language experience.* Columbus, OH: Charles E. Merrill.

Hanf, M. B. (1971). Mapping: A technique for translating reading into thinking. *Journal of Reading, 14,* 225–230, 270.

Hansen, J. (1981). The effects of inference training and practice on young children's comprehension. *Reading Research Quarterly, 16,* 391–417.

Hansen, J., & Pearson, P. D. (1982). *An instructional study: Improving the inferential comprehension of fourth grade good and poor readers.* Urbana: University of Illinois, Center for the Study of Reading.

Hansen, J., & Pearson, P. D. (1983). An instructional study: Improving the inferential comprehension of fourth grade good and poor readers. *Journal of Educational Psychology, 75,* 821–829.

Harris, A. J. (Ed.). (1970a). *Casebook on reading disability.* New York: David McKay.

Harris, A. J. (1970b). *How to increase reading ability* (5th ed.). New York: David McKay.

Harris, A. J., & Sipay, E. R. (1980). *How to increase reading ability: A guide to developmental and remedial methods* (7th ed.). New York: Longman.

Harris, A. J., & Sipay, E. R. (1985). *How to increase reading ability: A guide to developmental and remedial methods* (8th ed.). New York: Longman.

Harris, L. A., & Niles, J. A. (1982). An analysis of published informal reading inventories. *Reading Horizons, 22,* 159–174.

Harris, L. A., & Smith, C. B. (1986). *Reading instruction: Diagnostic teaching in the classroom* (4th ed.). New York: Macmillan.

Harris, T. L., & Hodges, R. E. (Eds.). (1981). *A dictionary of reading and related terms.* Newark, DE: International Reading Association.

Hartlage, L. C. (1976). Vision deficits and reading impairment. In G. Leisman (Ed.), *Basic visual processes and learning disability* (pp. 151–162). Springfield, IL: Charles E. Thomas.

Hayes, D., & Tierney, R. (1982). Developing readers' knowledge through analogy. *Reading Research Quarterly, 17,* 256–258.

Haynes, M., & Jenkins, J. (1986). Reading instruction in special education resource rooms. *American Educational Research Journal, 23,* 161–190.

Heath, S. B. (1983). *Ways with words: Language, life, and work in communities and classrooms.* Cambridge, MA: Cambridge University Press.

Heathington, B. S., & Alexander, J. E. (1984). Do classroom teachers emphasize attitudes toward reading? *The Reading Teacher, 37,* 484–488.

Hegge, T., Kirk, S. A., & Kirk, W. (1965). *Remedial reading drills.* Ann Arbor, MI: George Wahr.

Helfeldt, J. P., and Lalik, R. (1976). Reciprocal student-teacher questioning. *The Reading Teacher, 30,* 283–287.

Helfgott, J. (1976). Phonemic segmentation and blending skills of kindergarten children: Implications for beginning reading acquisition. *Contemporary Educational Psychology, 1,* 157–169.

Henderson, A. T. (1988). Parents are a school's best friend. *Phi Delta Kappan, 70,* 148–153.

Herber, H. H. (1970). *Teaching reading in content areas.* Englewood Cliffs, NJ: Prentice-Hall.

Hiebert, E. (1983). An examination of ability grouping for reading instruction. *Reading Research Quarterly, 18,* 231–255.

Hiebert, E., Colt, J., Catto, S., & Gury, E. (1992). Reading and writing of first-grade students in a restructured Chapter 1 program. *American Educational Research Journal, 29,* 545–572.

Hiebert, H. (1991). Research directions: The development of word-level strategies in authentic literacy tasks. *Language Arts, 68,* 234–240.

Hieronymus, J. D., Hoover, K. R., Oberley, N. K., Frisbie, D. A., Dunbar, S. B., Lewis, J. C., & Lindquist, E. F. (1990). *Iowa Test of Basic Skills* (Form J). Chicago: Riverside.

Hillerich, R. (n. d.). *50 ways to raise book worms, or using independent reading.* Boston: Houghton Mifflin.

Hogan, T. P. (1974). Reading tests and performance contracting. In W. Blanton, R. Farr, & J. Tuinman (Eds.), *Measuring reading performance* (pp. 51–65). Newark, DE: International Reading Association.

Holmes, B. C. (1983). The effect of prior knowledge on the question answering of good and poor readers. *Journal of Reading Behavior, 15,* 1–18.

Houck, C., & Harris, L. A. (1976). Woodcock reading mastery tests, *Journal of School Psychology, 14,* 77–79.

Hull, C. L. (1952). *A behavior system.* New Haven: Yale University.

Hymes, D. (1972). Introduction. In C. B. Cazden, V. P. John, & D. Hymes (Eds.), *Functions of language in the classroom* (pp. xi–ivii). New York: Teachers College Press.

Idol, L. (1987). Group story mapping: A comprehension strategy for both skilled and unskilled readers. *Journal of Learning Disabilities, 20,* 196–205.

Irwin, J. (1980). The effects of explicitness and clause order on the comprehension of reversible causal relationships. *Reading Research Quarterly, 15,* 477–488.

Jacobowitz, T. (1988). Using theory to modify practice: An illustration with JP3R. *Journal of Reading, 32,* 126–131.

Jacobs, J. E., & Paris, S. G. (1987). "Children's Metacognition About Reading." Issues in Definition, Measurement, and Instruction. *Educational Psychologist, 22,* 255–278.

Jacobs, J. N. (1968). Visual perceptual training program. *Educational Leadership Research Supplement.*

Jenkins, J., Stein, M., & Wysocki, K. (1984). Learning vocabulary through reading. *American Educational Research Journal, 21,* 767–788.

Jenkins, J. L., & Dixon, R. (1983). Vocabulary learning. *Contemporary Education Psychology, 8,* 237–260.

Jenkins, J. R., Pany D., & Schreck, J. (1978). *Vocabulary and reading comprehension: Instructional effects* (Tech. Rep. No. 100). Urbana: University of Illinois, Center for the Study of Reading.

Johns, Jerry (1981). *Basic reading inventory.* Dubuque, IA: Kendall/Hunt.

Johnson, D., Toms-Bronowski, S., & Pittleman, S. (1982). *An investigation of the effectiveness of semantic mapping and semantic feature analysis with intermediate grade level children* (Program Report No. 83–3). Madison, WI: Wisconsin Center for Education Research.

Johnson, D. D. (1976). *Johnson basic sight vocabulary test manual.* Lexington, MA: Ginn.

Johnson, D. D., & Pearson, P. (1975). Skills management systems: A critique. *The Reading Teacher, 28,* 757–764.

Johnson, D. D., & Pearson, P. D. (1978). *Teaching reading vocabulary.* New York: Holt, Rinehart and Winston.

Johnson, D. D., & Pearson, P. D. (1984). *Teaching reading vocabulary* (2nd ed.). New York: Holt, Rinehart & Winston.

Johnson, D. W., & Johnson, R. T. (1984). Cooperative small-group learning. *Curriculum Report, 14,* 1–6.

Johnson, D. W., & Johnson, R. T. (1990). Cooperative learning and achievement. In S. Sharan (Ed.), *Cooperative learning: Theory and research.* New York: Praeger.

Johnson, D. W., Johnson, R. T., Holubec, E., & Roy, P. (1984). *Circles of learning: Cooperation in the classroom.* Alexandria, VA: Association for Supervision and Curriculum Development.

Johnson, M. S., & Kress, R. A. (1965). *Informal reading inventories.* Newark, DE: International Reading Association.

Johnson, M. S., Kress, R. A., & Pikulski, J. J. (1987). *Informal reading inventories.* Newark, DE: International Reading Association.

Johnston, P. (1981). *Background knowledge, reading comprehension and test bias.* Unpublished doctoral dissertation, University of Illinois.

Johnston, P. H. (1983). *Reading comprehension assessment: A cognitive basis.* Newark, DE: International Reading Association.

Johnston, P. H. (1984a). Prior knowledge and reading comprehension test bias. *Reading Research Quarterly, 19,* 219–239.

Johnston, P. H. (1984b). Assessment in reading. In P. D. Pearson (Ed.), *Handbook of reading research.* New York: Longman.

Johnston, P. (1985). Understanding reading failure: A case study approach. *Harvard Educational Review, 55,* 153–177.

Johnston, P., & Allington, R. (1991). Remediation. In R. Barr, M. L. Kamil, P. Mosenthal, & P. D. Pearson (Eds.), *Handbook of reading research,* (Vol. 2, pp. 984–1012). White Plains, NY: Longman.

Johnston, P., & Pearson, P. D. (1982). *Prior knowledge, connectivity, and the assessment of reading comprehension.* Urbana: University of Illinois, Center for the Study of Reading.

Johnston, P. H., & Winograd, P. N. (1985). Passive failure in reading. *Journal of Reading Behavior, 17,* 279–301.

Jongsma, K. S., & Jongsma, E. A. (1981). Test review: Commercial informal reading inventories. *The Reading Teacher, 34,* 697–705.

Jordan, C., Tharp, R. G., & Vogt, L. (1985). Translating culture: From ethnographic information to educational program. *Anthropology and Education Quarterly, 16,* 105–123.

Journal of Reading. (1981). Misuse of grade equivalents, *25,* 112.

Juel, C. (1980). Comparison of word identification strategies with varying context, word type, and reading skill. *Reading Research Quarterly, 15,* 358–376.

Juel, C. (1983). The development and use of mediated word identification. *Reading Research Quarterly, 18,* 306–327.

Juel, C. (1988). Learning to read and write: A longitudinal study of fifty-four children from first through fourth grade. *Journal of Educational Psychology, 80,* 437–447.

Juel, C. (1991). Beginning reading. In R. Barr, M. Kamil, P. Mosenthal, & P. D. Pearson (Eds.), *Handbook of reading research* (Vol. 2). New York: Longman.

Juel, C., & Holmes, B. (1981). Oral and silent reading of sentences. *Reading Research Quarterly, 16*, 545–568.

Juel, C., & Roper-Schneider, D. (1985). The influence of basal readers on first grade reading. *Reading Research Quarterly, 20*, 134–152.

Kameenui, E. J., Carnine, D. W., & Freschi, R. (1982). Effects of text instruction and instructional procedures for teaching word meanings on comprehension and recall. *Reading Research Quarterly, 17*, 367–388.

Kamil, M., & Rauscher, W. C. (1990). Effects of grouping and difficulty of materials on reading achievement. In J. Zutell & S. McCormick (Eds.), *Literary theory and research: Analyses from multiple paradigms.* Chicago: National Reading Conference.

Karlsen, B., Madden, R., & Gardner, E. (1981). *Stanford Diagnostic Reading Test.* Cleveland: Psychological Corporation.

Karweit, N. (1989). Effective preschool programs for students at risk. In R. E. Slavin, N. L. Karweit, & N. A. Madden (Eds.), *Effective programs for students at risk* (pp. 239–252). Boston: Allyn & Bacon.

Kennedy, L. D., & Halinski, R. S. (1975). Measuring attitudes: An extra dimension. *Journal of Reading, 18*, 518–522.

Kephart, N. (1960). *The slow learner in the classroom.* Columbus, OH: Charles E. Merrill.

Kershner, J. R. (1983). Laterality and learning disabilities: Cerebral dominance as a cognitive process. *Topics in Learning and Learning Disabilities, 3*, 66–74.

Kibby, M. W. (1979). Passage readability affects the oral reading strategies of disabled readers. *Reading Teacher, 32*, 390–396.

Kirk, S. A., Kliebhan, J. M., & Lerner, J. W. (1978). *Teaching reading to slow and disabled learners.* Boston: Houghton-Mifflin.

Kirschenbaum, H., Simon, S., & Napier, R. W. (1971). *Wad-Ja-Get? The grading game in American education.* New York: Hart.

Klare, G. (1984). Readability. In P. D. Pearson (Ed.), *Handbook of reading research.* (pp. 681–644). New York: Longman.

Klausmeier, H., & Ripple, R. (1971). *Learning and human abilities* (3rd ed.). New York: Harper and Row.

Koskinen, P., & Blum, I. (1986). Paired repeated reading: A classroom strategy for developing fluent reading. *The Reading Teacher, 40*, 70–75.

Kramer, J. J., & Conoley, J. C. (1992). *Eleventh mental measurements yearbook.* Lincoln, NB: Buros Institute of Mental Measurements.

Kraus, R. (1974). *Herman the helper.* New York: Prentice Hall.

Kress, R. A. (1972). Silent reading diagnostic tests. In O. K. Buros (Ed.), *Seventh mental measurements yearbook* (pp. 1124–1125). Highland Park, NJ: Gryphon Press.

Kuhn, T. S. (1962). *The structure of scientific revolutions.* Chicago: University of Chicago Press.

Kurth, R., & Kurth, L., (1987). *The use of time in informal reading instruction in elementary schools.* Paper presented at the annual meeting of the American Educational Research Association, Washington, D.C.

Labbo, L. D., & Teale, W. H. (1990). Cross-age reading: A strategy for helping poor readers. *The Reading Teacher, 44*, 362–369.

LaBerge, D., & Samuels, S. J. (1974). Toward a theory of automatic information processing in reading. *Cognitive Psychology, 6*, 294–323.

Labov, W. (1982). Objectivity and commitment in linguistic science: The case of the Black English trial in Ann Arbor. *Language in Society, 11*, 165–201.

Lambert, W. E. (1978). Cognitive and socio-cultural consequences of bilingualism. *The Canadian Modern Language Review, 34*, 537–547.

Lambert, W. E., & Tucker, G. R. (1972). *Bilingual education of children.* Rowley, MA: Newbury House.

Langer, J. (1980). Relation between levels of prior knowledge and the organization of recall. In M. L. Kamil & A. J. Moe (Eds.), *Perspectives on reading and instruction.* Washington, DC: National Reading Conference.

Langer, J. A. (1981). From theory to practice: A prereading plan. *Journal of Reading, 25,* 152–156.

Langer, J. A. (1984). Examining background knowledge and text comprehension. *Reading Research Quarterly, 19,* 468–481.

Language Arts. (January 1989.) 66A(1), Urbana, IL: National Council of Teachers of English.

Lapp, D., & Flood, J. (1978). *Teaching reading to every child.* New York: Macmillan.

Lauritzen, (1982). A modification of repeated readings for group instruction. *The Reading Teacher, 35,* 456–459.

Lawson, L. J. (1968). Ophthalmological factors in learning disabilities. In H. R. Myklebust (Ed.), *Progress in learning disabilities* (Vol. I, pp. 147–181). New York: Grune and Stratton.

"Legislative update—Changes in the Law"(1988). *Forum* (Vol. XI, No. 5). Wheaton, MD: The National Clearinghouse for Bilingual Education.

Leinhardt, G., Zigmond, N., & Cooley, W. W. (1981). Reading instruction and its effects. *American Educational Research Journal, 18,* 343–361.

Lepper, M. R. (1983). Extrinsic reward and intrinsic motivation: Implications for the classroom. In J. M. Levine & M. C. Wang (Eds.), *Teachers & student perception: Implications for learning* (pp. 281–317). Hillsdale, NJ: Lawrence Erlbaum.

Lepper, M. R., & Hodell, M. (1989). Intrinsic motivation in the classroom. In C. Ames & R. Ames (Eds.), *Research on Motivation in Education:* Vol. 3. Goals & cognitions (pp. 73–106). New York: Academic Press.

Lesgold, A. M. (1974). Variability in children's comprehension of syntactic structures. *Journal of Educational Psychology, 66,* 333–338.

Lesgold, A. M., & Perfetti, C. A. (1978). Interactive processes in reading comprehension. *Discourse Processes, 1,* 323–336.

Leslie, L. (1980). The use of graphic and contextual information by average and below-average readers. *Journal of Reading Behavior, 12,* 139–150.

Leslie, L., & Caldwell, J. (1990). *Qualitative reading inventory.* Glenview, IL: Scott, Foresman.

Leslie, L., & Osol, P. (1978). Changes in oral reading strategies as a function of quantities of measures. *Journal of Reading Behavior, 10,* 442–444.

Leu, D. J. (1982). Oral reading error analysis: A critical review of research and application. *Reading Research Quarterly, 17,* 420–437.

Levin, H. M. (1987). *Towards accelerated schools.* Unpublished manuscript, Stanford University.

Levin, H. M. (1988). *Structuring schools for greater effectiveness with educationally disadvantaged or at-risk students.* Unpublished paper prepared for the Commission on Public School Administration and Leadership of the Association of California School Administrators, Stanford University.

Levin, J. R. (1981). The mnemonic '80s: Keywords in the classroom. *Educational Psychologist, 16,* 65–82.

Levin, J. R., Johnson, D. D., Pittleman, S., Levin, K., Shriberg, L., Toms-Bronowski, S., & Hayes, B. (1984). A comparison of semantic- and mnemonic-based vocabulary-learning strategies. *Reading Psychology, 5,* 1–15.

Levin, J. R., McCormick, C. B., Miller, G. E., Berry, J. K., & Pressley, M. (1982). Mnemonic versus nonmnemonic vocabulary-learning strategies for children. *American Educational Research Journal, 19,* 121–136.

Lewkowicz, N. K. (1980). Phonemic awareness training: What to teach and how to teach it. *Journal of Educational Psychology, 72,* 686–700.

Liberman, I. Y. (1970). Segmentation of the spoken word and reading acquisition. *Bulletin of the Orton Society, 23,* 65–77.

Lindsay, P., & Norman, D. (1972). *Human information processing.* New York: Academic Press.

Logan, J. W., & García, J. (1983). An examination of ethnic content in nine current basal series. *Reading Horizons, 23,* 165–169.

MacGinitie, W. H. (Ed.). (1973). *Assessment problems in reading.* Newark, DE: International Reading Association.

MacGinitie, W. H., & MacGinitie, R. K. (1989). *Gates-MacGinitie Reading Tests* (3rd ed). Chicago: Riverside.

MacMillan, D. L. (1973). *Behavior modification in education.* New York: Macmillan.

Madden, L. (1988). Improve reading attitudes of poor readers through cooperative reading teams. *The Reading Teacher, 42,* 194–199.

Madden, N. A., & Slavin, R. E. (1987). *Effective pull-out programs for students at risk.* Paper presented at the annual convention of the American Educational Research Association, Washington, DC.

Maehr, M. L. (1989). Thoughts about motivation. In C. Ames & R. Ames (Eds.), *Research on motivation in education: Vol. 3. Goals & cognitions* (pp. 299–315). New York: Academic Press.

Manis, F. R. (1985). Acquisition of word identification skills in normal and disabled readers. *Journal of Educational Psychology, 77,* 79–80.

Manzo, A. V. (1969). The request procedure. *Journal of Reading, 13,* 123–126.

Margosein, C. M., Pascarella, E. T., & Pflaum, S. W. (1982). The effects of instruction using semantic mapping on vocabulary and comprehension. *Journal of Early Adolescence, 2,* 185–194.

Marsh, G., & Desberg, P. (1978). Mnemonics for phonics. *Contemporary Educational Psychology, 3,* 57–61.

Marshall, N., & Glock, M. D. (1978–1979). Comprehension of connected discourse: A study into the relationships between the structure of text and information recalled. *Reading Research Quarterly, 14,* 20–56.

Marston, D., & Magnusson, D. (1985). Implementing curriculum-based measurement in special and regular education settings. *Exceptional Children, 52,* 266–276.

Marston, D., & Magnusson, D. (1988). Curriculum-based measurement: District level implementation. In J. García, J. Zins, & M. Curtis (Eds.), *Alternative educational delivery systems: Enhancing instructional options for all students.* Washington, DC: National Association of School Psychologists.

Martin, B. (1967). *Brown bear, brown bear, what do you see?* New York: Holt, Rinehart and Winston.

Marzano, R. J., Greenlaw, J., Tish, G., & Vodehnal, S. (1978). The graded word list is not a shortcut to an IRI. *The Reading Teacher, 31,* 647–651.

Maslow, A. (1970). *Motivation and personality.* New York: Harper and Row.

Mason, J. M. (1976). Overgeneralization in learning to read. *Journal of Reading Behavior, 8,* 173–182.

Mason, J. M. (1983). An examination of reading instruction in third and fourth grade. *The Reading Teacher, 36,* 906–913.

Mason, J., & Au, K. (1990). *Reading instruction for today* (2nd ed.). Glenview, IL: Scott, Foresman.

Mason, J. M., & Kendall, J. R. (1979). Facilitating reading comprehension through text structure manipulation. *The Alberta Journal of Educational Research, 25,* 68–76.

Mason, J. M., Kniseley, G., & Kendall, J. (1979). Effects of polysemous words on sentence comprehension. *Reading Research Quarterly, 15,* 49–65.

Mathewson, G. C. (1976). The function of attitude in the reading process. In H. Singer & R. Ruddell (Eds.), *Theoretical models and processes of reading* (2nd ed.) (pp. 655–673). Newark, DE: International Reading Association.

Mathewson, G. C. (1985). Toward a comprehensive model of affect in the reading process. In H. Singer & R. Ruddell (Eds.). *Theoretical models and processes of reading* (3rd ed.) (pp. 841–857). Newark, DE: International Reading Association.

Mazurkiewicz, (1976). *Teaching about phonics.* New York: St. Martin's.

McAllister, E. (1990). *Peer teaching and collaborative learning in the language arts.* Indiana University, ERIC Clearinghouse on Reading and Communications Skills. (ERIC Document Reproduction Service No. ED 325 818).

McBeath, P. M. (1966). *The effectiveness of three reading preparedness programs for perceptually handicapped kindergarteners.* Unpublished doctoral dissertation, Stanford University.

McCormick, C. E., & Mason, J. (1989). Fostering reading for Head Start children with little books. In J. B. Allen & J. Mason (Eds.), *Risk makers, risk takers, risk breakers: Reducing risks for young learners* (pp. 154–177). Portsmouth, NH: Heinemann Educational Books.

McCracken, R. (1966). *Standard Reading Inventory.* Klamath Falls, OR: Klamath Printing.

McCullough, C. (1963). *McCullough Word Analysis Test.* Lexington, MA: Personnel.

McDermott, R. P. (1977). The ethnography of speaking and reading. In R. W. Shuy (Ed.), *Linguistic theory: What can it say about reading* (pp. 153–185). Newark, DE: International Reading Association.

McGill-Franzen, A. (1987). Failure to learn to read: Formulating a policy problem. *Reading Research Quarterly, 22,* 475–490.

McKenna, M. C. (1983). Informal reading inventories: A review of the issues. *The Reading Teacher, 36,* 670–679.

McKeown, M. (1985). The acquisition of word meaning from context by children of high and low ability. *Reading Research Quarterly, 20,* 482–496.

McKeown, M. G., Beck, I. L., Omanson, R. C., & Perfetti, C. A. (1983). The effects of long-term vocabulary instruction on reading comprehension: A replication. *Journal of Reading Behavior, 15,* 3–18.

McNeil, J. D. (1984). *Reading comprehension: New directions for classroom practice.* Glenview, IL: Scott, Foresman.

McNinch, G. H. (1981). A method for teaching sight words to disabled readers. *The Reading Teacher, 35,* 269–272.

Melmed, P. J. (1973). Black English phonology. The question of reading interference. In J. L. Laffey & R. Shuy (Eds.), *Language differences: Do they interfere?* (pp. 70–85). Newark, DE: International Reading Association.

Mezynski, K. (1983). Issues concerning acquisition of knowledge: Effects of vocabulary training on reading comprehension. *Review of Educational Research, 53,* 253–279.

Michaels, S. (1981). "Sharing time": Children's narrative styles and differential access to literacy. *Language in Society, 10,* 423–442.

Miller, S. D., & Smith, D. E. (1985). Differences in literal and inferential comprehension after reading orally and silently. *Journal of Educational Psychology, 77,* 341–348.

Mills, H., O'Keefe, T., & Stephens, D. (1992). *Looking closely: Exploring the role of phonics in one whole language classroom.* Urbana, IL: National Council of Teachers of English.

Minsky, M. (1975). A framework for representing knowledge. In P. H. Winston (Ed.), *The psychology of computer vision.* New York: McGraw-Hill.

Mitchell, J. V., Jr. (1983). *Tests in print III.* Lincoln, NB: Buros Institute of Mental Measurements.

Mitchell, J. V., Jr. (Ed.). (1985). *Ninth mental measurements yearbook.* Lincoln: University of Nebraska Press.

Moe, A. J. (1973). Word lists for beginning readers. *Reading Improvement, 10,* 11–15.

Moll, L. C. (1990, February). *Literacy research in community and classrooms: A sociocultural approach.* Paper presented at the conference on "Multi-disciplinary Perspectives on

Research Methodology in Language Arts," National Conference on Research in English, Chicago, IL.

Moll, L. (1991). Social and instructional issues in literacy instruction for "disadvantaged" students. In M. S. Knapp & P. M. Shields (Eds.), *Better schooling for the children of poverty: Alternatives to conventional wisdom* (p. 61–84). Berkeley, CA: McCutchan Publishing Corporation.

Monda-Amaya, L. E., & Pearson, P. D. (in press) Toward a responsible pedagogy for teaching and learning literacy. In C. Warger & M. Pugach (Eds.), *How new curriculum trends will affect special education.* New York: Teachers College.

Monson, D. L., & McClenathan, D. K. (Eds.). (1979). *Developing active readers: Ideas for parents, teachers, and librarians.* Newark, DE: International Reading Association.

Mosenthal, P. (1976–1977). Psycholinguistic properties of aural and visual comprehension as determined by children's abilities to comprehend syllogisms. *Reading Research Quarterly, 12,* 55–92.

Mosenthal, P. (1981). Diagnostic reading scales. In L. M. Schell (Ed.), *Diagnostic and criterion-referenced reading tests: Review and evaluation* (pp. 23–29). Newark, DE: International Reading Association.

Mullis, I. V. S., & Jenkins, L. B. (1990). *The reading report card, 1971–88: Trends from the nation's report card.* Princeton, NJ: National Assessment of Educational Progress, Educational Testing Service.

Nagy, W. E., & Anderson, R. C. (1984). The number of words in printed school English. *Reading Research Quarterly, 19,* 304–330.

Nagy, W. E., & Herman, P. A. (1984). *Limitations of vocabulary instruction* (Tech. Rep. No. 326). Urbana: University of Illinois, Center for the Study of Reading.

Nagy, W. E., Herman, P. A., & Anderson, R. C. (1985). Learning words from context. *Reading Research Quarterly, 20,* 233–253.

Nardine, F. E., & Morris, R. D. (1991). Parent involvement in the states: How firm is the commitment? *Phi Delta Kappan, 72,* 363–366.

Naslund, R. A., Thorpe, L. P., & Lefever, D. W. (1978). *SRA Achievement Series.* Chicago: Science Research Associates.

Natalicio, D. S. (1979). Reading and the bilingual child. In L. B. Resnick and P. A. Weaver (Eds.), *Theory and practice of early reading* (Vol. 3, pp. 131–149). Hillsdale, NJ: Lawrence Erlbaum.

National Center for Educational Statistics. (1988). *Education indicators.* Washington, DC: US Department of Education, Office of Educational Research and Improvement.

National Education Association. (1990). *Federal education funding: The cost of excellence.* Washington, DC: Author.

Nemko, B. (1984). Context versus isolation: Another look at beginning readers. *Reading Research Quarterly, 19,* 461–467.

Nolte, R. Y., & Singer, H. (1985). Active comprehension: Teaching a process of reading comprehension and its effect on reading achievement. *The Reading Teacher, 39,* 24–31.

Nurss, J. R., & McGauvran, M E. (1976). *Metropolitan Readiness Test.* New York: Psychological Corporation.

O'Donnell, P. (1970). A re-evaluation of research on lateral expression. *Journal of Learning Disabilities, 3,* 344–350.

Omanson, R. C., Beck, I. L., McKeown, M. G., & Perfetti, C. A. (1984). Comprehension of texts with unfamiliar versus recently taught words: An assessment of alternative models. *Journal of Educational Psychology, 76,* 1253–1268.

Oritz, R. K. (1983). Generating interest in reading. *Journal of Reading, 27,* 113–119.

Orton, J. L. (1966). The Orton-Gillingham approach. In J. Money (Ed.), *The disabled reader* (pp. 119–146). Baltimore: The Johns Hopkins University Press.

Orton, S. T. (1937). *Reading, writing and speech problems in children.* New York: W. W. Norton.

O'Shea, L. J., & Sindelar, P. T. (1983). The effects of segmenting written discourse on the reading comprehension of low- and high-performance readers. *Reading Research Quarterly, 18,* 458–465.

O'Shea, L., Sindelar, P., & O'Shea, D. (1985). The effects of repeated readings and attentional cues on reading fluency and comprehension. *Journal of Reading Behavior, 17,* 129–142.

Otto, W., & Chester, R. (1972). Sight words for beginning readers. *Journal of Educational Research, 65,* 435–443.

Owings, R. A., Peterson, G. A., Bransford, J. D., Morris, C. D., & Stein, B. S. (1980). Spontaneous monitoring and regulation of learning: A comparison of successful and less successful fifth graders. *Journal of Educational Psychology, 72,* 250–256.

Page, E. B. (1958). Teacher comments and student performance: A seventy-four classroom experiment in school motivation. *Journal of Educational Psychology, 49,* 173–181.

Paivio, A. (1971). *Imagery and verbal processes.* New York: Holt, Rinehart and Winston.

Palincsar, A. S., & Brown, A. L. (1984). Reciprocal teaching of comprehension-fostering and comprehension-monitoring activities. *Cognition and Instruction, 1,* 117–175.

Palincsar, A. S., & Brown, A. L. (1986). Interactive teaching to promote independent learning from text. *The Reading Teacher, 39,* 771–777.

Palincsar, A. S., & Brown, A. L. (1989). Guided, cooperative learning and individual knowledge acquisition. In L. B. Resnick (Ed.), *Knowing, learning, and instruction* (pp. 393–451). Hillsdale, NJ: Lawrence Erlbaum.

Palincsar, A. S., & Ransom, K. (1988). From the mystery spot to the thoughtful spot: The instruction of metacognitive strategies. *The Reading Teacher, 41,* 784–789.

Pallas, A. M., Natriello, G., & McDill, E. L. (1988). *Who falls behind: Defining the "at-risk" population: Current dimensions and future trends.* Paper presented at the Annual Meeting of the American Educational Research Association, New Orleans, LA.

Pallas, A. M., Natriello, G., & McDill, E. L., (1989). The changing nature of the disadvantaged population: Current dimensions and future trends. *Educational Researcher, 18*(5), 16–22.

Paratore, J. R., & Indrisano, R. (1987). Intervention assessment of reading comprehension. *The Reading Teacher, 40,* 778–783.

Parent Booklet Series. (1989). Various titles. Newark, DE: International Reading Assocation.

Paris, S. G., Cross, D. R., & Lipson, M. Y. (1984). Informed strategies for learning: A program to improve children's reading awareness and comprehension. *Journal of Educational Psychology, 76,* 1239–1252.

Paris, S. G., & Jacobs, J. E. (1984). The benefits of informed instruction for children's reading awareness and comprehension skills. *Child Development, 55,* 2083–2093.

Paris, S. G., Lipson, M., and Wixson, K. K. (1983). Becoming a strategic reader. *Contemporary Educational Psychology, 8,* 293–316.

Paris, S. G., & Myers, M. (1981). Comprehension monitoring, memory, and study strategies of good and poor readers. *Journal of Reading Behavior, 8,* 5–22.

Pearson, P. D., & Fielding, L. (1991). Comprehension instruction. In R. Barr, M. Kamil, P. Mosenthal, & P. D. Pearson (Eds.), *Handbook of reading research,* (Vol. 2). New York: Longman.

Pearson, P. D., & Gallagher, M. C. (1983). The instruction of reading comprehension. *Contemporary Educational Psychology, 8,* 317–344.

Pearson, P. D., Hansen, J., & Gordon, C. (1979). The effect of background knowledge on young children's comprehension of explicit and implicit information. *Journal of Reading Behavior, 11,* 201–209.

Pearson, P. D., & Johnson, D. D. (1978). *Teaching reading comprehension.* New York: Holt, Rinehart and Winston.

Pearson, P. D., & Spiro, R. (1980). Toward a theory of comprehension instruction. *Topics in Language Disorders, 1,* 71–88.

Peresich, M. L., Meadows, J. D., & Sinatra, R. (1990). Content area cognitive mapping for reading and writing proficiency. *Journal of Reading, 33,* 424–432.

Perfetti, C. A. (1985). *Reading ability.* New York: Oxford University Press.

Pflaum, S. W., & Bryan, T. H. (1980). Oral reading in the learning disabled. *Journal of Educational Research, 73,* 247–251.

Pflaum, S. W., & Pascarella, E. T. (1980). Interactive effects of prior reading achievement and training in context on the reading of learning-disabled children. *Reading Research Quarterly, 16,* 138–158.

Pflaum, S. W., Walberg, H., Karegianes, M. L., & Rasher, S. P. (1980). Reading instruction: A quantitative analysis. *Educational Researcher, 9,* 12–18.

Phi Delta Kappan. (January 1991). 72(5). Bloomington, IN: Phi Delta Kappa.

Phillips, S. (1972). Participant structures and communicative competence: Warm Springs children in community and classroom. In C. Cazden, D. Hymes, & V. John (Eds.), *Foundations of language in the classroom.* New York: Teachers College Press.

Phillips, S. U. (1983). *The invisible culture: Communication in classroom and community on the Warm Springs Indian Reservation* (p. 209–240). White Plains, NY: Longman.

Piaget, J. (1952). *The origins of intelligence in children* (2nd ed.). New York: International Universities Press.

Pikulski, J. J. (1974). A critical review: Informal reading inventories. *The Reading Teacher, 28,* 141–153.

Pikulski, J. J., & Shanahan, T. (Eds.). (1982a). *Approaches to the informal evaluation of reading.* Newark, DE: International Reading Association.

Pikulski, J. J., & Shanahan, T. (1982b). Informal reading inventories: A critical analysis. In J. J. Pikulski & T. Shananhan (Eds.), *Approaches to the informal evaluation of reading.* Newark, DE: International Reading Association.

Pinnell, G., DeFord, D., & Lyons, C. (1988). *Reading recovery: Early intervention for at-risk first graders.* Arlington, VA: Educational Research Service.

Pinnell, G., Fried, M., & Estice, R. (1990). Reading recovery: Learning how to make a difference. *The Reading Teacher, 43,* 282–295.

Potter, M., & Wamre, H. (1990). Curriculum-based measurement and developmental reading models: Opportunities for cross-validation. *Exceptional Children, 57,* 16–25.

Powell, W. R. (1971). The validity of the instructional reading level. In R. E. Leibert (Ed.), *Diagnostic viewpoints in reading.* Newark, DE: International Reading Association.

Powell, W. R. (1979). Reappraising the criteria for interpreting informal reading inventories. In D. DeBoer (Ed.), *Reading diagnosis and evaluation.* Newark, DE: International Reading Association.

Powell, W. R., & Dunkeld, C. G. (1971). Validity of the IRI reading levels. *Elementary English, 48,* 637–642.

Prell, J. M., & Prell, P. A. (1986). Improving test scores—Teaching test-wiseness. *Research Bulletin,* No. 5. Bloomington, IN: Phi Delta Kappa.

Prescott, G. A., Balow, I H., Hogan, T. P., & Farr, R. C. (1978). *Metropolitan Achievement Test* (6th ed.). San Antonio, TX: Psychological Corporation.

Pressley, M. (1976). Mental imagery helps eight-year-olds remember what they read. *Journal of Educational Psychology, 68,* 355–359.

Pressley, M. (1977). Imagery and children's learning. *Review of Educational Research, 47,* 585–622.

Pressley, M., Levin, J. R., & Miller, G. E. (1981). How does the keyword method affect vocabulary comprehension and usage? *Reading Research Quarterly, 16,* 213–226.

Quandt, I., & Selznick, R. (1984). *Self-concept and reading.* Newark, DE: International Reading Association.

Raffi (1989). *Five little ducks.* New York: Crown Publishers.

Raffi (1989). *Tingalayo.* New York: Crown Publishers.

Rankin, E. F., & Overholser, B. M. (1969). Reaction of intermediate grade children to contextual clues. *Journal of Reading Behavior, 1,* 50–73.

Rankin, E. F., & Tracy, R. J. (1965). Residual gain as a measure of individual differences in reading improvement. *Journal of Reading, 8,* 224–333.

Raphael, T. E. (1986). Teaching question-answer relationships revisited. *The Reading Teacher, 39,* 516–522.

Raphael, T. E., & Pearson, P. D. (1985). Increasing students' awareness of sources of information for answering questions. *American Educational Research Journal, 22,* 217–236.

Raphael, T. E., Winograd, P., & Pearson, P. D. (1980). Strategies children use when answering questions. In M. Kamil & A. Moe (Eds.), *Perspectives on reading research and instruction* (pp. 56–63). Washington, DC: National Reading Conference.

Raphael, T. E., & Wonnacutt, C. A. (1985). Metacognitive training in question-answering strategies: Implementation in a fourth grade developmental reading program. *Reading Research Quarterly, 20,* 282–297.

Rash, J., Johnson, T. D., & Gleadow, N. (1984). Acquisition and retention of written words by kindergarten children under varying learning conditions. *Reading Research Quarterly, 19,* 452–460.

Rasinski, T. (1989). Fluency for everyone: Incorporating fluency instruction in the classroom. *The Reading Teacher, 42,* 690–693.

The Reading Teacher. (monthly column). Newark, DE: International Reading Association.

Reder, L. M. (1980). The role of elaboration in the comprehension and retention of prose: A critical review. *Review of Educational Research, 50,* 5–33.

Reed, A. (1988). *Comics to classics: A parent's guide to books for teens and preteens.* Newark, DE: International Reading Association.

Richardson, J. S., & Morgan, R. F. (1990). *Reading to learn in the content areas.* Belmont, CA: Wadsworth.

Richek, M. (1976–1977). Reading comprehension of anaphoric forms in varying linguistic contexts. *Reading Research Quarterly, 12,* 145–165.

Richek, M. A., List, L., & Lerner, J. (1983). *Reading problems: Diagnosis and remediation.* Englewood Cliffs, NJ: Prentice-Hall.

Ringness, T. A. (1975). The affective domain in education. Boston: Little, Brown.

Rinksy, L. A., & DeFossard, E. (1980). *The contemporary classroom reading inventory.* Scottsdale, AZ: Gorsuch Scarisbrick.

Robbins, M. P. (1966). The Delacato interpretation of neurological organization. *Reading Research Quarterly, 1,* 57–58.

Robinson, F. P. (1941). *Diagnostic and remedial techniques for effective study.* New York: Harper & Brothers.

Robinson, H. (1972). Visual and auditory modalities related to methods for beginning reading. *Reading Research Quarterly, 8,* 7–39.

Roehler, L. R., & Duffy, G. G. (1984). Direct explanation of comprehension processes. In G. Duffy, L. Roehler, & J. Mason (Eds.), *Comprehension instruction: Perspectives and suggestions* (pp. 265–280). White Plains, NY: Longman.

Rollock, B. (1984). *The Black experience in children's books.* NY: New York Public Library.

Rosado, M. V. (1982). Reluctant readers respond to the newspaper. *Journal of Reading, 26,* 173.

Rosen, C. L. (1965). Visual deficiencies and reading. *Journal of Reading, 9,* 57–61.

Rosenblatt, L. M. (1978). *The reader, the text, the poem: The transactional theory of the literary work.* Carbondale, IL: Southern Illinois University Press.

Rosenblatt, L. M. (1983). *Literature as exploration* (4th ed.) New York: Modern Language Assoc. (originally published 1938).

Rosenshine, B., & Stevens, R. (1984). Classroom instruction in reading. In P. D. Pearson (Ed.), *Handbook of reading research*. White Plains, NY: Longman.

Rosenthal, R., & Jacobson, L. (1968). *Pygmalion in the classroom*. New York: Holt, Rinehart and Winston.

Roser, N. L. (1989). *Helping your child become a reader*. Newark, DE: International Reading Association.

Roser, N., & Frith, M. (Eds.). (1983). *Children's choices: Teaching with books children like*. Newark, DE: International Reading Association.

Rosso, B. R., & Emans, R. (1981). Children's use of phonics generalizations. *The Reading Teacher, 34,* 653–658.

Rotter, J. (1966). Generalized expectations for internal versus external control of reinforcement. *Psychological Monographs, 80,* 1–28.

Rowan, B., & Guthrie, L. F. (1989). The quality of Chapter I instruction: Results from a study of twenty-four schools. In R. E. Slavin, N. L. Karweit, & N. A. Madden (Eds.), *Effective programs for students at risk* (pp. 195–219). Boston: Allyn & Bacon.

Rowell, E. H. (1976). Do elementary students read better orally or silently? *The Reading Teacher, 29,* 367–370.

Rumelhart, D. E. (1979). Some problems with the notion of literal meanings. In A. Ortony (Ed.), *Metaphor and thought*. New York: Cambridge University Press.

Rumelhart, D. E. (1980). Schemata: The building blocks of cognition. In R. J. Spiro, B. C. Bruce, & W. F. Brewer (Eds.), *Theoretical issues in reading comprehension*. Hillsdale, NJ: Lawrence Erlbaum.

Rumelhart, D. E., & Ortony, A. (1977). The representation of knowledge in memory. In R. C. Anderson, R. J. Spiro, & W. F. Montague (Eds.), *Schooling and the acquisition of knowledge*. Hillsdale, NJ: Lawrence Erlbaum.

Rupley, W. H. (1979). ERIC/RCS: Using newspapers to teach reading. *The Reading Teacher, 33,* 346–349.

Ryan, E. B. (1981). Identifying and remediating failures in reading comprehension: Toward an instructional approach for poor comprehenders. In T. G. Waller & G. E. MacKinnon (Eds.), *Advances in reading research* (Vol. 2, pp. 223–261). New York: Academic Press.

Ryder, R. J., Graves, B. B., & Graves, M. F. (1989). *Easy reading: Book series and periodicals for less able readers* (2nd ed.). Newark, DE: International Reading Association.

Sadoski, M. (1985). The natural use of imagery in story comprehension and recall: Replication and extension. *Reading Research Quarterly, 20,* 658–667.

Salvia, J., & Ysseldyke, J. E. (1981). *Assessment in special and remedial education* (2nd ed.). Boston: Houghton-Mifflin.

Samuels, S. J. (1979). The method of repeated readings. *The Reading Teacher, 32,* 403–408.

Sarason, I. G. (1980). *Test anxiety: theory, research, & applications*. Hillsdale, NJ: Lawrence Erlbaum.

Sartain, H. W. (1970). *Reading attitude inventory*. Bloomington, IN: Indiana University, ERIC Clearinghouse on Reading and Communication Skills. (ERIC Document Reproduction Service No. ED 045 291)

Savignon, S. J. (1983). *Communicative competence: Theory and classroom practice*. Reading, MA: Addison-Wesley.

Saville-Troike, M. (1984). What really matters in second-language learning for academic achievement? *TESOL Quarterly, 18*(2), 199–219.

Schank, R. C. (1972). Conceptual dependency: A theory of natural language understanding. *Cognitive Psychology, 3,* 552–631.

Schell, L. M. (Ed.). (1981). *Diagnostic and criterion-referenced reading tests: Review and evaluation*. Newark, DE: International Reading Association.

Schell, L. M., & Jennings, R. E. (1981). Test review: Durrell analysis of reading difficulty (3rd ed.). *The Reading Teacher, 35,* 204–210.

Schoolfield, L., & Timberlake, J. B. (1968). *The phonovisual method book.* Washington, DC: Phonovisual Products.

Schreiner, R. L. (1978). Diagnostic reading scales (rev. ed.). In O. K. Buros (Ed.), *Eighth mental measurements yearbook* (pp. 1242–1243). Highland Park, NJ: Gryphon Press.

Schreiner, R. L. (Ed.). (1979). *Reading tests and teachers: A practical guide.* Newark, DE: International Reading Association.

Schunk, D. H. (1989). Self-efficacy and cognitive skill learning. In C. Ames & R. Ames (Eds.), *Research on motivation in education: Vol. 3. Goals & Cognitions* (pp. 13–44).

Schwartz, R. (1988). Learning to learn vocabulary in content area textbooks. *Journal of Reading, 32,* 108–119.

Sherman, T. M., & Wildman, T. M. (1982). *Proven strategies for successful test taking.* Columbus, OH: Charles E. Merrill.

Shoben, E. J. (1980). Theories of semantic memory: Approach to knowledge and sentence comprehension. In R. J. Spiro, B. C. Bruce, & W. F. Brewer (Eds.), *Theoretical issues in reading comprehension.* Hillsdale, NJ: Lawrence Erlbaum.

Silvaroli, N. (1982). *Classroom reading inventory* (4th ed.). Dubuque, IA: William. C. Brown.

Simons, H. D. (1979). Black dialect, reading interference, and classroom interaction. In L. B. Resnick & P. A. Weaver (Eds.), *Theory and practice of early reading* (Vol. 3, pp. 111–129). Hillsdale, NJ: Lawrence Erlbaum.

Simons, H., & Johnson, K. (1974). Black English syntax and reading interference. *Research in the Teaching of English, 8,* 339–358.

Singer, H. (1978a). Active comprehension: From answering to asking questions. *The Reading Teacher, 31,* 901–908.

Singer, H. (1978b). Gates-McKillop reading diagnostic tests. In O. K. Buros (Ed.), *Eighth mental measurements yearbook* (pp. 1252–1254). Highland Park, NJ: Gryphon Press.

Singer, H., & Donlan, D. (1982). Active comprehension: Problem solving schema with question generation for comprehension of complex short stories. *Reading Research Quarterly, 17,* 166–186.

Singer, H., Samuels, S. J., & Spiroff, J. (1974). Effects of pictures and contextual conditions on learning responses to printed words. *Reading Research Quarterly, 5,* 427–451.

Skinner, B. F. (1953). *Science and human behavior.* New York: Macmillan.

Slavin, R. (1987). Making Chapter 1 make a difference. *Phi Delta Kappan, 69,* 110–119.

Slavin, R. E. (1990). *Cooperative learning: Theory, research and practice.* Englewood Cliffs, NJ: Prentice Hall.

Slavin, R. E. (1991). Synthesis of research on cooperative learning. *Educational Leadership, 48,* 71–82.

Sledd, S. (1969). Bi-dialectalism: The linguistics of white supremacy. *English Journal, 58,* 176–184.

Smith, D. D. (1979). The improvement of childrens' oral reading through the use of teacher modeling. *Journal of Learning Disabilities, 12,* 39–42.

Smith, E. B., Goodman, K. S., & Meredith, R. (1970). *Language and thinking in the elementary school.* New York: Holt, Rinehart and Winston.

Smith, F. (1971). *Understanding reading: A psycholinguistic analysis of learning to read.* New York: Holt, Rinehart and Winston.

Smith, F. (1975). *Comprehension and learning.* New York: Holt, Rinehart and Winston.

Smitherman, G. (1986). *Talkin and testifyin: The language of Black America.* Detroit: Wayne State University.

Spache, G. (1976). *Investigating the issues of reading disabilities.* Boston: Allyn & Bacon.

Spache, G. (1981a). *Diagnostic reading scales.* Monterey, CA: California Test Bureau/ McGraw-Hill.

Spache, G. (1981b). *Diagnosing and correcting reading disabilities* (2nd ed.). Boston: Allyn and Bacon.

Spiegel, D. L. (1981). *Reading for pleasure: Guidelines.* Newark, DE: International Reading Association.

Spring, C., Blunden, D., & Gatheral, M. (1981). Effect on reading comprehension of training to automaticity in word-readings. *Perceptual and motor skills, 53,* 779–786.

Stafford, J. (1974). The diagnostic reading scales. *Reading World, 14,* 5–8.

Stahl, S. (1983). Differential word knowledge and reading comprehension. *Journal of Reading Behavior, 15,* 33–50.

Stallman, A. (1991). *Learning vocabulary from context: Effects of focusing attention on individual words during reading.* Unpublished doctoral dissertation, University of Illinois.

Stallman, A. C., & Pearson, P. D. (1990). Formal measures of early literacy. In L. M. Morrow & J. K. Smith (Eds.), *Assessment for instruction in early literacy* (pp. 7–44). Englewood Cliffs, NJ: Prentice Hall.

Standards for educational and psychological testing (1974). Washington, D. C.: American Psychological Association.

Standards for educational and psychological testing (1985). Washington, D. C.: American Psychological Association.

Stanovich, K. E. (1980). Toward an interactive-compensatory model of individual differences in the development of reading fluency. *Reading Research Quarterly, 16,* 32–71.

Stanovich, K. (1986). Matthew effects in reading: Some consequences of individual differences in the acquisition of literacy. *Reading Research Quarterly, 21,* 360–406.

Stanovich, K. E., Cunningham, A. E., & Feeman, D. J. (1984a). Intelligence, cognitive skills, and early reading progress. *Reading Research Quarterly, 19,* 278–303.

Stanovich, K. E., Cunningham, A. E., & Feeman, D. J. (1984b). Relation between early reading acquisition and word decoding with and without decoding. *Journal of Educational Psychology, 76,* 667–668.

Stanovich, K. E., Cunningham, A. E., & West, R. F. (1981). A longitudinal study of the development of automatic recognition skills in first graders. *Journal of Reading Behavior, 13,* 57–74.

Stauffer, R. G. (1969). *Directing reading maturity as a cognitive process.* New York: Harper and Row.

Stauffer, R. G. (1970). *The language experience approach to reading instruction.* New York: Harper and Row.

Sternberg, R., & Powell, J. (1983). Comprehending verbal comprehension. *American Psychologist, 38,* 878–893.

Stevens, K. C. (1981). Chunking material as an aid to reading comprehension. *Journal of Reading, 25,* 126–129.

Stevens, K. C. (1982). Can we improve reading by teaching background information. *Journal of Reading, 25,* 326–329.

Stevens, R. J., Madden, N. A., Slavin, R. E., & Farnish, A. M. (1987). Cooperative integrated reading and composition: Two field experiments. *Reading Research Quarterly, 22,* 433–454.

Stipek, D. J. (1988). *Motivation to learn: From theory to practice.* Englewood Cliffs, NJ: Prentice Hall.

Stoll, D. R. (Ed.). (1989). *Magazines for children.* Newark, DE: International Reading Association.

Sucher, F., & Allred, R. A. (1973). *Reading placement inventory.* Oklahoma City, OK: Economy.

Suchoff, I. B. (1981). Research in the relationship between reading and vision—What does it mean? *Journal of Learning Disabilities, 14,* 573–576.

Sulzby, E., & Teale, W. (1991). Emergent literacy. In R. Barr, M. Kamil, P. Mosenthal, & P. D. Pearson (Eds.), *Handbook of reading research,* (Vol. 2). New York: Longman.

Taylor, B. M. (1982). Text structure and children's comprehension and memory for expository material. *Journal of Educational Psychology, 74*, 323–340.

Taylor, B. M. (1984). The search for a meaningful approach to assessing comprehension of expository text. In J. Niles & L. Harris (Eds.), *Changing perspectives on research in reading, language processing and instruction* (pp. 257–263). Rochester, NY: National Reading Conference.

Taylor, B. M. (1985a). Improving middle-grade students' reading and writing of expository text. *Journal of Educational Research, 79*, 119–125.

Taylor, B. M. (1985b). *Teaching middle grade students to read for main ideas.* Paper presented at the annual meeting of the National Reading Conference, San Diego, CA.

Taylor, B. M. (1985c). Toward an understanding of factors contributing to children's difficulty summarizing textbook material. In I. J. Niles & R. Lalik (Eds.), *Issues in literacy: A research perspective* (pp. 124–131). Rochester, NY: National Reading Conference.

Taylor, B. M. (1986). Teaching middle grade students to summarize content textbook material. In J. Baumann (Ed.), *Teaching main idea comprehension.* Newark, DE: International Reading Association.

Taylor, B. M., & Beach, R. W. (1984). The effects of text structure instruction on middle grade students' comprehension and production of expository texts. *Reading Research Quarterly, 19*, 134–146.

Taylor, B. M., & Berkowitz, S. B. (1980). Facilitating children's comprehension of content area material. In M. Kamil and A. Moe (Eds.), *Perspectives on reading research and instruction* (pp. 64–68). Washington, DC: National Reading Conference.

Taylor, B. M., & Frye, B. J. (1988). Pretesting: Minimizing time spent on skill work for intermediate readers. *The Reading Teacher, 42*, 100–105.

Taylor, B. M., & Frye, B. J. (1990). *A district's plunge into a literature-based reading and language arts program in grades 1–6.* Unpublished manuscript, University of Minnesota.

Taylor, B. M., Frye, B. J., & Gaetz, T. (1990). Reducing the number of reading skill activities in the elementary classroom. *Journal of Reading Behavior, 22*, 167–180.

Taylor, B. M., Frye, B. J., & Maruyama, G. (1990). Silent reading and its effects on reading growth. *American Educational Research Journal, 27*, 351–362.

Taylor, B. M., Short, R., Frye, B. J., & Shearer, B. (1992). Classroom teachers prevent reading failure among low-achieving first grade students. *The Reading Teacher, 45*, 592–597.

Taylor, B. M., Olson, V., Prenn, M., Rybczynski, M., & Zakaluk, B. (1985). A comparison of students' ability to read for main ideas in social studies and to complete main idea worksheets. *Reading World, 24*, 10–15.

Taylor, B. M., & Nosbush, L. (1983). Oral reading for meaning: A technique for improving word identification. *The Reading Teacher, 37*, 234–237.

Taylor, B. M., & Pearson, P. D. (1988). *Classroom phonemic segmentation and blending test.* Unpublished manuscript, University of Minnesota.

Teale, W. H., & Sulzby, E. (1986). Emergent literacy as a perspective for examining how young children become writers and readers. In W. H. Teale & E. Sulzby (Eds.), *Emergent literacy: Writing and reading* (pp. vii–xxv). Norwood, NJ: Ablex.

Tharp, R. G. (1982). The effective instruction of comprehension: Results and description of the Kamehameha Early Education Program. *Reading Research Quarterly, 17*, 503–527.

Thomas, S. (1982). A comparison of different approaches to vocabulary instruction. Unpublished doctoral dissertation, University of Wisconsin.

Thorndike, R. L. (1973). *Reading comprehension education in fifteen countries.* New York: Wiley.

Tierney, R. J., & Cunningham, J. W. (1984). Research on teaching reading comprehension. In P. D. Pearson (Ed.), *Handbook of reading research* (pp. 609–655). White Plains, NY: Longman.

Tindal, G., Marston, D., & Deno, S. L. (1983). *The reliability of direct and repeated measure* (Research Report No. 109). Minneapolis, University of Minnesota, Institute for Research on Learning Disabilities.

Trachtenburg, P., & Ferruggia, A. (1989). Big books for little voices. Reaching high-risk beginning readers. *The Reading Teacher, 42,* 284–289.

Trelease, J. (1989). *The new read-aloud handbook.* Newark, DE: International Reading Association.

Troike, R. C. (1969). Receptive competence, productive competence, and performance. In J. E. Alatis (Ed.), *Monograph series on language and linguistics, 22,* 63–73.

Troike, R. C. (1984). SCALP: Social and cultural aspects of language proficiency. In C. Rivera (Ed.), *Language proficiency and academic achievement* (pp. 44–54). Avon, England: Multi-lingual Matters, Ltd.

Tuinman, J. J. (1978). Woodcock reading mastery tests. In O. K. Buros (Ed.), *Eighth mental measurements yearbook* (pp. 1306–1308). Highland Park, NJ: Gryphon Press.

Vacca, N. D., & Padak, R. T. (1990). Who's at risk in reading? *Journal of Reading, 33,* 486–488.

Valencia, S. (1990). A portfolio approach to classroom reading assessment: The whys, whats, and hows. *The Reading Teacher, 43,* 338–340.

Valencia, S., & Pearson, P. D. (1987). Reading assessment: Time for a change. *The Reading Teacher, 40,* 727–732.

van Dijk, T. A., & Kintsch, W. (1983). *Strategies of discourse comprehension.* New York: Academic Press.

Van Allen, R. (1976). *Language experiences in communication.* Boston: Houghton-Mifflin.

Veatch, J. (1959). *Individualizing your reading program.* New York: G. P. Putnam.

Veatch, J., Swicki, F., Elliott, G., Flake, E., Blakey, J. (1979). *Key words to reading: The language experience approach begins.* Columbus, OH: Charles E. Merrill.

Venezky, R. L., & Johnson, D. (1973). Development of two letter-sound patterns in grade one through three. *Journal of Educational Psychology, 64,* 109–115.

Vygotsky, L. S. (1962). *Thought and language.* Cambridge, MA: MIT Press.

Vygotsky, L. S. (1978). *Mind in Society: The development of higher psychological processes.* Cambridge, MA: Harvard University Press.

Wagner, G., & Hosier, M. (1970). *Reading games.* New York: Macmillan.

Wagoner, S. A. (1983). Comprehension monitoring: What it is and what we know about it. *Reading Research Quarterly, 17,* 328–346.

Wang, M. C. & Palincsar, A. S. (1989). Teaching students to assume an active role in their learning. In M. C. Reynolds (Ed.) *Knowledge base for the beginning teacher.* New York: Pergamon.

Wehlage, G., & Rutter, R. (1986). Dropping out: How much do schools contribute to the problem? *Teachers College Record, 87*(3), 374–392.

Weiner, B. (1974). *Achievement motivation as conceptualized by an attribution theory* (pp. 3–48). Morristown, NJ: General Learning Press.

Weiner, B. (1979). A theory of motivation for some classroom experience. *Journal of Educational Psychology, 71,* 3–25.

Weiner, B. (1984). Principles for a theory of student motivation and their application within an attributional framework. In R. Ames & C. Ames (Eds.), *Research on Motivation in Education: Vol. 1. Student Motivation* (pp. 15–38). New York: Academic Press.

Weiner, B. (1985). An attributional theory of achievement motivation and emotion. *Psychological Review, 92,* 548–573.

Weintraub, S. (1972). *Auditory perception and deafness.* Newark, DE: International Reading Association.

Weintraub, S., & Cowan, R. J. (1982). *Vision/visual perception: An annotated bibliography.* Newark, DE: International Reading Association.

White, R. W. (1959). Motivation reconsidered: The concept of competence. *Psychological Review, 66,* 297–333.

Wigfield, A., & Asher, S. R. (1984). Social and motivational influences on reading. In P. D. Pearson (Ed.), *Handbook of reading research.* White Plains, NY: Longman.

Williams, J. P. (1979). The ABD's of reading: A program for the learning-disabled. In L. B. Resnick & P. A. Weaver (Eds.), *Theory and practice of early reading* (Vol. 3, pp. 227–259). Hillsdale, NJ: Lawrence Erlbaum.

Williams, J. P. (1980). Teaching decoding with an emphasis on phoneme analysis and phoneme blending. *Journal of Educational Psychology, 72,* 1–15.

Williams, J. P. (1985). The case for explicit decoding instruction. In J. Osborn, T. Wilson, & R. C. Anderson (Eds.), *Reading Education: Foundations for a literate America* (pp. 205–213). Lexington, MA: Lexington Books.

Williamson, L. E., & Young, F. (1974). The IRI and RMI diagnostic concepts should be synthesized. *Journal of Reading Behavior, 6,* 183–194.

Willows, D. M., & Ryan, E. B. (1981). Differential utilization of syntactic and semantic information by skilled and less skilled readers in the intermediate grades. *Journal of Educational Psychology, 73,* 607–615.

Wilson, M. M. (1979). The processing strategies of average and below average readers answering factual and inferential questions on three equivalent passages. *Journal of Reading Behavior, 11,* 235–245.

Windsor, P., & Pearson, P. D. (1992). Children at risk: Their phonemic awareness and development in holistic instruction (Tehcnical Report No. 556). Urbana, IL: Center for the Study of Reading, University of Illinois.

Winograd, P. N. (1984). Strategic difficulties in summarizing texts. *Reading Research Quarterly, 19,* 404–425.

Wircenski, J. L., Sarkees, M. D., & West, L. L. (1990). *Instructional alternatives: Rescue strategies for at-risk students.* (Curriculum Report, Vol. 19, No. 4). Reston, VA: National Association of Secondary School Principals.

Wixson, K. (1979). Miscue analysis: A critical review. *Journal of Reading Behavior, 11,* 163-175.

Wong, J., & Au, K. (1985). The concept-text-application approach: Helping elementary students comprehend expository text. *The Reading Teacher, 38,* 612–618.

Woodcock, R. W. (1973). *Woodcock reading mastery test.* Circle Pines, MN: American Guidance Service.

Woods, M. L., & Moe, A. J. (1981). *Analytical reading inventory.* Columbus, OH: Charles E. Merrill.

Woods, M. L., & Moe, A. J. (1989). *Analytical reading inventory.* Columbus, OH: Charles E. Merrill.

Wright, G. (1979). The comic book—A forgotten medium in the classroom. *The Reading Teacher, 33,* 158–161.

Yacorzynsky, G., & Tucker, B. (1960). What price intelligence? *American Psychologist, 15,* 201–203.

Ysseldyke, J., & Algozzine, R. (1983). Where to begin in diagnosing reading problems. *Topics in Learning and Learning Disorders, 2,* 60–68.

Ysseldyke, J., Thurlow, M., Mecklenburg, C., & Graden, J. (1984). Opportunity to learn for regular and special education students during reading instruction. *Remedial and Special Education, 5,* 29–37.

Zakaluk, B., Samuels, S. J., & Taylor, B. (1986). A simple technique for estimating prior knowledge: Word association. *Journal of Reading, 30,* 56–60.

Zigmond, N., & Silverman, R. C. (1984). Informal assessment for program planning and evaluation in special education. *Educational Psychologist, 19,* 163–171.

Index